THE ARRL
OPERATING MANUAL
For Radio Amateurs

9th Edition

Editor

Mark J. Wilson, K1RO

Editorial Assistant

Maty Weinberg, KB1EIB

Cover Design

Sue Fagan, KB1OKW
Bob Inderbitzen, NQ1R

Production and Proofreading

Michelle Bloom, WB1ENT
Jodi Morin, KA1JPA
David Pingree, N1NAS
Kathy Ford

Published by:

ARRL *The national association for* AMATEUR RADIO

225 Main Street • Newington, CT 06111-1494 USA

www.arrl.org

Contents

Foreword

About the ARRL

The Amateur's Code

1   **Amateur Radio — All About Operating**
Ward Silver, NØAX

2   **VHF/UHF — FM, Repeaters, Digital Voice and Data**
Gary Pearce, KN4AQ

3   **VHF/UHF — Beyond Repeaters**
Michael Owen, W9IP

4   **Emergency Communications**
Rick Palm, K1CE

5   **Traffic Handling — Getting the Message Through**
Maria Evans, KT5Y

6   **DXing — Contacting Those Faraway Places**
Ward Silver, NØAX

7   **Contesting — Competitive Wireless**
Ward Silver, NØAX

8   **HF Digital Communications**
Steve Ford, WB8IMY

9   **Image Communications**
Art Towslee, WA8RMC, Dennis Bodson, W4PWF and Steven L. Karty, N5SK

10   **Amateur Satellites**
Steve Ford, WB8IMY

11   **Legally, Safely, Appropriately — The FCC Rules and You**
Dan Henderson, N1ND

12   **Operating Awards**
Steve Ford, WB8IMY

13   **References**

Your Amateur Radio license is in hand. After reading through *QST* Product Reviews and peppering the local hams with questions, you've assembled some equipment. An antenna hangs above your house or sits on your car. Now what?

Get on the air, of course!

Amateur Radio is a lifelong pursuit for many hams because of the endless variety of on-air operating activities to try. Running out of things to talk about with the usual gang? Expand your horizons: Try your hand at DXing and learn more about ham radio in other countries. Do you like to help others in your community? Get involved in emergency communications chapter. Want to do more than talk? Check out image communications or the digital modes. Do you like a little competition? Learn how to enter a contest.

The 9th edition of the *ARRL Operating Manual* is the latest in a long series of books that have helped hams — new and old — explore the pursuits that fall under the umbrella of Amateur Radio. Other books focus on the technical aspects, but this one is all about things to do with your gear. Whether you're looking for basic operating information or want to gain a deeper understanding of a specific topic, the material assembled here by our expert authors and editors will guide your way.

Your station is meant to be used. Get on the air and try something new!

David Sumner, K1ZZ
Chief Executive Officer
Newington, Connecticut
October 2007

Please Note: For this fourth printing of the *ARRL Operating Manual*, Mike Corey, W5MPC, ARRL Emergency Preparedness and Response Manager, has made a number of important updates to Chapter 4, "Emergency Communications." These revisions reflect the evolving relationships between radio amateurs and the agencies we serve.

The seed for Amateur Radio was planted in the 1890s, when Guglielmo Marconi began his experiments in wireless telegraphy. Soon he was joined by dozens, then hundreds, of others who were enthusiastic about sending and receiving messages through the air—some with a commercial interest, but others solely out of a love for this new communications medium. The United States government began licensing Amateur Radio operators in 1912.

By 1914, there were thousands of Amateur Radio operators—hams—in the United States. Hiram Percy Maxim, a leading Hartford, Connecticut inventor and industrialist, saw the need for an organization to band together this fledgling group of radio experimenters. In May 1914 he founded the American Radio Relay League (ARRL) to meet that need.

Today ARRL, with more than 150,000 members, is the largest organization of radio amateurs in the United States. The ARRL is a not-for-profit organization that:

- promotes interest in Amateur Radio communications and experimentation
- represents US radio amateurs in legislative matters, and
- maintains fraternalism and a high standard of conduct among Amateur Radio operators.

At ARRL headquarters in the Hartford suburb of Newington, the staff helps serve the needs of members. ARRL is also International Secretariat for the International Amateur Radio Union, which is made up of similar societies in 150 countries around the world.

ARRL publishes the monthly journal *QST*, as well as newsletters and many publications covering all aspects of Amateur Radio. Its headquarters station, W1AW, transmits bulletins of interest to radio amateurs and Morse code practice sessions. The ARRL also coordinates an extensive field organization, which includes volunteers who provide technical information and other support services for radio amateurs as well as communications for public-service activities. In addition, ARRL represents US amateurs with the Federal Communications Commission and other government agencies in the US and abroad.

Membership in ARRL means much more than receiving *QST* each month. In addition to the services already described, ARRL offers membership services on a personal level, such as the ARRL Volunteer Examiner Coordinator Program and a QSL bureau.

Full ARRL membership (available only to licensed radio amateurs) gives you a voice in how the affairs of the organization are governed. ARRL policy is set by a Board of Directors (one from each of 15 Divisions) elected by the membership. The day-to-day operation of ARRL HQ is managed by a Chief Executive Officer.

No matter what aspect of Amateur Radio attracts you, ARRL membership is relevant and important. There would be no Amateur Radio as we know it today were it not for the ARRL. We would be happy to welcome you as a member! (An Amateur Radio license is not required for Associate Membership.) For more information about ARRL and answers to any questions you may have about Amateur Radio, write or call:

ARRL—the national association for Amateur Radio

225 Main Street
Newington CT 06111-1494
Voice: 860-594-0200
Fax: 860-594-0259
E-mail: **hq@arrl.org**
Internet: **www.arrl.org/**

Prospective new amateurs call (toll-free):
800-32-NEW HAM (800-326-3942)
You can also contact us via e-mail at **newham@arrl.org**
or check out ARRLWeb at **http://www.arrl.org/**

Guide to ARRL Member Services

ARRL, 225 Main Street ◆ Newington, Connecticut 06111-1494, USA

**Tel: 860-594-0200, Mon-Fri 8 AM
to 5 PM ET (except holidays)
FAX:** 860-594-0303
e-mail: hqinfo@arrl.org
ARRLWeb: www.arrl.org

**VISITING ARRL
HEADQUARTERS AND W1AW**
Tours Mon-Fri at 9, 10, 11 AM; 1, 2, 3 PM
W1AW guest operating 10 AM to noon,
and 1 to 3:45 PM (bring your license).

**JOIN or RENEW
or ORDER Publications**
tel. **Toll Free 1-888-277-5289** (US)
International callers
tel. +1 (860) 594-0355

**INTERESTED IN
BECOMING A HAM?**
www.hello-radio.org
e-mail: newham@arrl.org
tel. 1-800-326-3942

News Center
ARRLWeb: www.arrl.org
ARRL Letter:
www.arrl.org/arrlletter

Public Relations/Advocacy
**Government Relations and
Spectrum Protection:**
www.arrl.org/regulatory-advocacy
e-mail: govrelations@arrl.org
Public and Media Relations:
www.arrl.org/media-and-public-relations

Membership Benefits
Membership Benefits (all):
www.arrl.org/membership
Awards: www.arrl.org/awards
Contests: www.arrl.org/contests
FCC License Renewal / Modification:
www.arrl.org/fcc-license-info-and-forms
QSL Service: www.arrl.org/qsl-bureau
Regulatory Information
www.arrl.org/national
Technical Information Service
www.arrl.org/technology
e-mail: tis@arrl.org
tel. 860-594-0214

Contributions, Grants and Scholarships
ARRL Development Office:
www.arrl.org/donate-to-arrl
e-mail: mhobart@arrl.org
tel. 860-594-0397

■ ARRL Diamond Club/Diamond Terrace
■ Spectrum Defense Fund
■ Education & Technology Fund
■ Planned Giving/Legacy Circle
■ Maxim Society

ARRL Foundation Grants and Scholarships:
www.arrl.org/the-arrl-foundation

Public Service
Public Service Programs:
www.arrl.org/public-service
Amateur Radio Emergency Service® (ARES®):
www.arrl.org/ares
ARRL Field Organization:
www.arrl.org/field-organization

Clubs, Exams, Licensing and Teachers
Find an Affiliated Club: www.arrl.org/find-a-club
Mentor Program:
www.arrl.org/mentoring-online-courses
Find a Licensing Class:
www.arrl.org/find-a-class
Support to Instructors:
www.arrl.org/volunteer-instructors-mentors
Find an Exam Session:
www.arrl.org/finding-an-exam-session
Volunteer Examiner Coordinator (VEC):
www.arrl.org/volunteer-examiners

Publications & Education
QST — Official Journal of ARRL:
www.arrl.org/qst
e-mail: qst@arrl.org
QEX — Forum for Communications Experimenters:
www.arrl.org/qex
e-mail: qex@arrl.org
NCJ — *National Contest Journal*:
www.arrl.org/ncj
e-mail: ncj@arrl.org
Books, Software and Operating Resources:
tel. 1-888-277-5289 (toll-free in the US);
www.arrl.org/shop
Advertising:
www.arrl.org/business-opportunities-sales
e-mail: ads@arrl.org
Continuing Education / Online Courses:
www.arrl.org/online-courses

The Radio Amateur is:

CONSIDERATE…never knowingly operates in such a way as to lessen the pleasure of others.

LOYAL…offers loyalty, encouragement and support to other amateurs, local clubs, and the American Radio Relay League, through which Amateur Radio in the United States is represented nationally and internationally.

PROGRESSIVE…with knowledge abreast of science, a well-built and efficient station and operation above reproach.

FRIENDLY…slow and patient operating when requested; friendly advice and counsel to the beginner; kindly assistance, cooperation and consideration for the interests of others. These are the hallmarks of the amateur spirit.

BALANCED…radio is an avocation, never interfering with duties owed to family, job, school or community.

PATRIOTIC…station and skill always ready for service to country and community.

—The original Amateur's Code was written by Paul M. Segal, W9EEA, in 1928.

chapter 1

Amateur Radio — All About Operating

Amateur Radio is all about operating — all the technology and procedures in the world are no substitute for hams getting on the air and making contact. That's what this book is about — how hams send their signals and why. Hams have found dozens of ways to have fun and engage in useful activities on the air. You'll find many of those described here — both to provide guidance in participating and for your general interest in unfamiliar forms of Amateur Radio.

You may have taken an interest in ham radio because of a specific need or activity — public service, emergency communications, interest in electronics or even radio controlled models! Right away, you'll find yourself immersed in Amateur Radio, learning the ropes of your preferred activity. As you operate and become more skilled, a curious thing will happen. You'll discover that there is considerable magic behind the front panel of your radio, out there between the antennas, and in the minds of your compatriot hams! Your Amateur Radio license is the gateway to exploring as much of that magic as you wish.

Amateur Radio provides opportunities to learn about and experiment with technology. It's also a way to learn electronic communication skills. It's a means to overcome the limitations of physical handicaps and enter an open arena of communications. It's fun and a great way to make friends. It's an opportunity to participate in public service activities. And it's an opportunity to serve your community and make your neighborhood a better place to live.

With all the communications technology available in the modern world, is there still a useful role for Amateur Radio? Certainly, there is! Part of the magic of everyday Amateur Radio arises from the "who's out there?" nature of all those hams sharing the bands. Whether you communicate with a regular circle of friends or spend your time tuning the bands in search of a new call sign, an unexpected surprise may be no farther away than your next CQ ("calling any station"). When disaster strikes and normal communications are knocked out for a time, hams step in and harness that magic for the public's benefit.

This *ARRL Operating Manual* covers the most popular activities in ham radio. No matter if you're completely new to Amateur Radio or an experienced ham looking for information on a new way to communicate, this book can help you decide what to operate, where to operate and how to operate. Think of your participation in Amateur Radio as a never-ending journey — there's always something new to explore, always something new to do!

WHY AMATEUR RADIO EXISTS

Amateur Radio owes its existence to international and national regulations. These regulations reflect the value of Amateur Radio as perceived by national and international leaders, giving it a place on the airwaves as a peer to commercial and military services. In the United States, the fundamental purpose of the Amateur Radio Service is expressed in the following principles outlined in Federal Communications Commission rule §97.1:

(a) Recognition and enhancement of the value of the amateur service to the public as a voluntary noncommercial communication service, particularly with respect to providing emergency communications.

(b) Continuation and extension of the amateur's proven ability to contribute to the advancement of the radio art.

(c) Encouragement and improvement of the amateur service through rules which provide for advancing skills

Steve, K4CMR and Jordan operate the Get On the Air station with the W4ZA club. Visiting a local Field Day site is a great way to learn about ham radio. (*WA4VUO photo*)

Who Reads the *Operating Manual*?

The *Operating Manual* has something for just about every ham, no matter what their level of skill or how long they've been licensed. While it can't possibly cover all of the different activities heard on the ham bands, it can provide an introduction and guide to many of those activities.

In each section, we'll introduce you to the basic terminology and ideas behind that particular aspect of ham radio. You'll learn why hams operate that way and why it is of interest.

Following the introduction, we'll explain how to actually "do " that kind of ham radio. There might be specific equipment or technical know-how that is required. You might need to learn some new terms or concepts. Most types of operating have guidelines or conventions that you'll be expected to follow. When you finish reading a chapter, you'll have the basic ideas under your belt.

The goal of the *Operating Manual* is both to educate you on some of the many ways in which hams make use of our spectrum allocations and to provide you with the necessary information to get started yourself. Remember that no one is expected to know everything about ham radio! Treat this book as your personal launching pad to enjoying a broad range of what ham radio has to offer.

Beginning Hams

If you are just getting started in ham radio, you'll find the *Operating Manual* to be a feast of information about ham radio. You may have read about these activities and even engaged in a couple, but here is the mainstream of the service! Start by skimming the book from cover to cover. Then go back to the parts you found most interesting and read those chapters in detail. Try a few of the activities on the air, using the book as a confidence-boosting guide. If you enjoyed them, keep it up! If not, try something else — ham radio is supposed to be en-

joyable and fun, not a job. Sooner or later, you'll find your "home" in ham radio. Keep the *Operating Manual* handy on your radio shack bookshelf as a reference and guide to on-the-air events and activities.

Intermediate Hams

Once you've been active for a while, you'll find yourself becoming comfortable with your favorite activities. You can use the *Operating Manual* to help you sharpen your skills as it describes the fine points of the service. By using the information here, you can avoid some of the common pitfalls and keep your enjoyment high as you learn.

You will probably find yourself branching out within ham radio, as well. For example, your main interest may be DXing, but you might be asked to provide some public service by working on a parade route communications team. Perhaps you've been working on earning awards, but have an opportunity to join a club multioperator contest team. It's time to grab your copy of the *Operating Manual* and do some reading about these unfamiliar activities! The information won't make you an instant expert, but it will help you get started as quickly as possible.

Experienced Hams

Once upon a time, reading *QST* every month was enough to keep a ham in touch with just about every significant type of operating in ham radio. No longer! Ham radio has grown to cover so many different activities that it's no longer possible for a single person to be an expert in every single one. New activities and types of operating are springing up all the time. New technology transforms old activities, as well. So even if you are the proverbial "jack of all trades," you'll find these chapters an introduction to something you haven't yet tried or a refresher on a familiar activity.

---

in both the communications and technical phases of the art.

(d) Expansion of the existing reservoir within the amateur radio service of trained operators, technicians, and electronics experts.

(e) Continuation and extension of the amateur's unique ability to enhance international goodwill.

These principles are quite broad, giving amateurs a lot of room to pursue their individual vision. As a result, Amateur Radio is continually changing and evolving — technologically and procedurally. At the same time, it carries these principles forward as traditions as old as radio itself. Amateur Radio, by definition, is the sum of the efforts of all amateurs.

Amateur Radio is a Service

If you have read the Public Service column and articles in *QST* and feature stories on the ARRL Web (**www.arrl.org**) you've seen the exploits of hams from all walks of life who have selflessly donated their time by providing emergency communication. Many, many more hams provide this service

than are given recognition by the media, but that's all part of being a ham — the intrinsic reward is the satisfaction of doing a job well. Just ask the hams that served in the aftermath of hurricane Katrina in 2005 and that fill in after smaller disasters every day.

You may or may not be called at some time to provide this service to your community. But by being prepared, honing your on-the-air operating skills to their sharpest, maximizing your equipment to obtain the best from it, and being prepared to pitch in should the need arise, you will be ready. In so doing, you will derive untold hours of satisfaction from the exciting hobby we know as Amateur Radio.

THE DIVERSITY OF HAMS

With a desire to serve her community in disasters and other emergencies, a Washington woman signs up for classes in first aid and techniques to support the local fire department. After receiving some training in use of handheld radios, a newspaper notice of Amateur Radio classes catches her eye.

Severe weather often threatens lives and property in the Midwest. Hams like Rick, KI5GT, work with NOAA's SKYWARN program to report and track storms.

After she passes her Technician exam she joins the local club and ARES team. Soon, her enthusiasm convinces her husband to become licensed and join the fun. During a subsequent weather-related emergency, they provide valuable service to their fellow citizens.

A boy asks his father how radios and computers work. They talk a bit and then begin to experiment. The talks and experiments lead to further study and the topics broaden. The boy's interest in technology continues to grow. He studies for and passes his first Amateur Radio license examination, and shortly after that he upgrades. He enjoys communicating, but the technology is what really attracts his interest. What does his future hold? No doubt he'll have a career in some field of electronics.

The young woman, every inch a competitor, shouted with joy as she read the results of the recent on-the-air competition.

On the air since before WWII, Bill, W4EHF, has been building equipment throughout his ham career and recently upgraded to Amateur Extra at the age of 93. (*K4MHM photo*)

Mother-daughter team KBØSQQ and KBØYHM operate 15 meter phone during the 2007 Field Day operation of the Boeing-Wichita club, KCØAHN. (*Charles Rasico photo*)

Not only had she beaten everyone else in her entry category in the contest, but she had also set a world record. She felt great! Elsewhere, a mechanic is working on a vehicle, but not to repair it for a customer. It's a special kind of mobile amateur station called a *rover*. The weekend of a major VHF+ contest is approaching quickly and he needs to have the new antenna mounts done in time to add to his team's score. They plan on operating from a plateau straddling a mountain pass. Will the vehicle be ready in time?

After work at his job in a large information technology department, the computer professional decides to work on his latest project — setting up a high-speed packet radio system for his club's digital Amateur Radio message-forwarding system. This is brand-new technology, so he's working with sketchy information, using his experience with networks and software to offer clues as to what he changes he should make. By mid-evening, he's able to connect his system with another high-speed node and pass several messages over the UHF radio link.

The middle-aged man turned in his chair when the computer beeped an alert. Yes! The station he had wanted to contact had been spotted on the air. That station was set up on an island in the Indian Ocean by a couple of hams, a husband-and-wife team who spend their vacations operating Amateur Radio from exotic locations. Yes, they have an antenna atop the apartment building where they live, but there's a big difference between operating from home and operating from an exotic location that great numbers of hams want to contact.

The young girl, having come home from school, went into her bedroom and turned on her radio. No music came from the radio. Instead, she picked up the microphone and called another Amateur Radio station. A familiar voice answered her call, "Hi, honey, how are you today? Over." She replied, "I'm fine, grandpa. Let me tell you what happened today..."

You might think you know these folks. It's possible, since they are real. But the descriptions fit many persons. All kinds of people enjoy communicating over the air. Kings and diplomats, homemakers and waiters, engineers and scientists, teachers and students, doctors and bookkeepers find fun, challenge and fulfillment in Amateur Radio. Day or night, hams are communicating with each other, helping others, doing technical experiments or just simply having fun by meeting new people.

THE WIDE VARIETY OF HAM ACTIVITIES

Hams are involved in all sorts of fun, challenging and fulfilling activities. That means not just from home, but on the move — in a car, or on a bike or hiking in the mountains. You might be on the sea or in the air — even in Earth orbit, where spacefaring hams have enjoyed using their radios from aboard the Space Shuttle and International Space Station.

The chapter titles of this book provide only partial insight into the scope of activities in which Amateur

Radio operators are engaged. So what sorts of things do hams do?

Near, Far, Wherever You Are

Some enjoy communicating locally or training for emergency communications ("emcomm") using small, inexpensive, low-powered VHF/UHF radios that operate on fixed channels using FM voice. Repeaters extend their limited range by amplifying and retransmitting their signals. Depending on where the repeater is located, you can talk with other hams 50 or even 100 miles away. Distances up to 30 miles are common.

Others are enchanted with using the ionosphere to bounce HF signals to and from faraway places thousands of miles away. The object of their quest is distant stations (DX). They try to contact as many distinct political and geographic areas as they can. The quest is complete when the contact is confirmed with a *QSL* card — a colorful and interesting postcard confirming contact with another station — in the mail or via a contact confirmation service such as the ARRL's *Logbook of the World* (**www.arrl.org/lotw**).

Hybrids of the VHF/UHF repeaters and the Internet have been developed by hams to extend the range of communications of those low-power radios to HF distances. The Internet Radio Linking Project (IRLP, **www.irlp.net**), Echolink (**www. echolink.org**), Yaesu's WIRES-II (**www.vxstd.com**) and D-STAR (**www.icomamerica.com/amateur/dstar**) systems combine radio and digitized voice to connect portable and mobile hams around the world.

DX (ham shorthand for long distance) holds a special fascination for many hams. It can be correctly defined in different ways. To most amateurs, DX is the lure of seeing how far away you can establish a QSO — the greater the distance, the better. DX is a personal achievement, bettering some previous "best distance worked," involving a set of self-imposed rules.

DX can also be competitive on a large scale, as "DXers" try to break through the pileups of people calling a rare DX station. DXers often aim for one of the DX-oriented awards such as ARRL's DX Century Club. DXing can be a full-time goal for some hams and a just-for-fun challenge for others. Regardless of whether you turn into a serious DXer or just have a little fun searching for entities you have yet to work, DXing is one of the most fascinating aspects of Amateur Radio.

Some enjoy the thrill and adventure of travel to and operating from the "other side of the pileup" from distant and exotic places. Hams often operate on a vacation trip to a warm island in the Caribbean to escape the freezing winter weather, or on a business trip to Europe or Asia. Others take special trips called *DXpeditions* to the ends of the Earth — Antarctica, desert islands and mountain kingdoms. There they make contacts at high rates for a few days as DXers around the world try to get their call signs "in the log."

Out of This World!

Hams are not limited to communication on the Earth. Many enjoy talking with astronauts and cosmonauts in orbit. Hams have been communicating with the Space Shuttle since Owen Garriott, W5LFL, took his 2 meter handheld radio to orbit on mission STS-9 in 1983. W5LFL contacted 250 hams from space, even King Hussein of Jordan (call sign JY1)! Today, nearly all

David, AJ5W and Harry, KC5TRB, prepare a balloon for launch with an Automatic Position Reporting System (APRS) tracker as part of the payload, a science experiment to measure ozone levels.

Bruce, KØYW, traveled to the home of Alex, KH6YY, on Oahu to make earth-moon-earth (EME) or "moonbounce" contacts on the 23 cm microwave band.

You don't have to use big antennas to contact amateur satellites. This group from Boulder Hill Elementary in Montgomery, Illinois made contacts through amateur satellite AO-51 during the 2007 School Club Roundup using this handheld antenna and radio.

residents of the International Space Station (ISS) are hams and regularly make contact with hams on the ground. The ISS ham radio station even has its own call sign, NA1SS. In 2006, Bill McArthur contacted all 50 states and 100 countries, achieving the first WAS and DXCC from space.

Hams also communicate with each other through satellites that hams themselves have designed and built. On such amateur organization is AMSAT (**www.amsat.org**). It is fully funded by amateurs and builds professional quality "birds." Some hams even bounce their signals to each other off the Moon. Others reflect their transmissions off of the active aurora or a short-lived meteor trail. Hams have been pioneers in many modes of communication, paving the way for many different commercial uses.

Competitions

The thrill of competition calls some hams to enter contests for a weekend of intense activity. It's a way to test station capability and operator skills. For the busy ham, it's a great way to cram a lot of contacts into a short period of time. For others, a contest involves operating away from home — perhaps with friends at a "super station" or on the road as a mobile or rover.

Contesting is to Amateur Radio what the Olympic Games are to worldwide amateur athletic competition: a showcase to display talent and learned skills, as well as a stimulus for further achievement through competition. Increased operating skills and greater station effectiveness may be the end result of Amateur Radio contesting, but the most common experience is *fun*.

The contest operator is also likely to have one of the better signals on the band — not necessarily by using the most elaborate or expensive station equipment, but by knowing how to get the most out of whatever resources are available. Competitive operation encourages continuous improvement in station and operator efficiency. Nearly every contest has competitors vying to see which one can work the most stations (depending on the rules of the particular contest) in a given time frame. In some contests, the top-scoring stations have consistently worked 100 or more stations per hour for the entire 48-hour contest period. Other contests are *sprints* — they run for just a few hours.

The ARRL contest program is so diverse that one contest or another appeals to almost every type of ham — the beginning contester and the old hand, the newest Technician and the most experienced Amateur Extra veteran, the "Topband" (160 meter) buff and the microwave enthusiast. Contest announcements appear in *QST* a few months before the contest, in *QST's* Contest Corral column, or on the ARRL Web at **www.arrl.**

New licensee Dan, KC2RKB, exercises his skills, engaged in "search and pounce" while operating ARRL Field Day with his Dad Walter, WS2Z.

Scott, KP2/NE1RD, combined vacation with ham radio. He traveled to the US Virgin Islands during the 2006 ARRL DX Phone Contest and used a portable station to have a great time working stations in the contest.

org/contest. There is at least one contest for every interest. A summary of the contest results appear in *QST* while detailed scores and analysis are posted on the ARRL Web.

Competition takes many forms. Hams who love to collect awards compete against themselves. Are they able to make contact with all the states? All the counties? All the prefectures of Japan or the provinces of Spain? The ARRL offers the awards listed in **Table 1-1**. Most other national amateur societies, private clubs and contest groups sponsor awards and certificates for various operating accomplishments. Many of the awards are very handsome paper certificates or intricately designed plaques very much in demand by awards chasers.

Some hams take to foot or vehicle with direction-finding equipment to see who's the best at finding a hidden transmitter. Their competitions may be local or international, such as the Amateur Radio Direction-Finding contests (**www.ardf-r2.org**).

Working Cooperatively

Those involved in *public service*, including *emergency communications* ("emcomm"), and *traffic handling* have to work together cooperatively to get the job done. Over many years of training and practice, hams have developed on-the-air procedures and organizations to communicate efficiently and effectively. By studying them and practicing with your local groups, you will become a valued member of an important volunteer service. Public service communications make Amateur Radio a valuable public resource, one that has been recognized by Congress and a whole host of federal, state and local agencies that serve the public.

Traffic handling involves passing messages to others over the amateur bands. Messages can be informal or constructed according

---

Table 1-1
ARRL Operating Awards
(www.arrl.org/awards/)

Award	Qualification
Worked All States (WAS)	QSLs from all 50 US states
Worked All Continents (WAC)	QSLs from all six continents
DX Century Club (DXCC)	QSLs from at least 100 foreign entities
VHF/UHF Century Club (VUCC)	QSLs from many grid locators
A-1 Operator Club	Recommendation by two A-1 operators
Code Proficiency	One minute of perfect copy from W1AW qualifying run
ARRL Membership	ARRL membership for 25, 40, 50, 60 or 70 years

to the rules of the *radiogram*, the ham radio equivalent of the telegram. Hams handle *third-party traffic* (messages for non-hams) in both routine situations and in times of disaster.

Nets are regular gatherings of hams who share a mutual interest and who use the net (short for "network") to further that interest. Their most common purpose is to pass traffic or participate in one of the many other ham activities, from awards chasing and DXing to just plain old talking among longtime friends. In an emergency or following a disaster, however, the net transforms into a powerful on-the-air coordination and information-sharing machine!

County and state hunting nets are very popular since they provide a frequency to work that 49th and 50th state for the ARRL WAS (Worked All States) award or rare county. Service nets are used by mobile and marine stations to request assistance, pass messages, or let their status be known.

There are nets dedicated to beginner or slow-speed CW operation. These can help a newcomer sharpen operating skills. To find the frequencies and meeting times of nets in your area, use the online net search facility via the ARRL Net Directory page at **www.arrl.org/FandES/field/nets**.

Rag Chewing

"Chewing the rag" refers to getting on the air and spending minutes (or hours!) in interesting conversation on virtually any and every topic imaginable. Without a doubt, the most popular operating activity is rag chewing. The rag chew may be something as simple as a brief chat on a 2-meter or 440-MHz FM repeater as you drive across town. It also may be a group of friends who have been meeting on 15-meter SSB every Saturday afternoon for 20 years. The essential element is the same — hams talking to each other on any subject that interests them.

PSK31, Packet and Other Digital Modes

Many years ago, RTTY (Baudot radioteletype) was the only digital mode. As computers became popular, then almost

Giorgio, IZ4AKS, enjoys working RTTY (radio-teletype) and is shown here operating from 1A4A at the Knights of Malta enclave in the heart of Rome.

essential in the ham shack, the number of digital modes available to hams has expanded quickly.

The first computer-based modes were the various flavors of AMTOR (Amateur Teleprinting Over Radio) and packet radio or just "packet" for short. Packet requires either a full computer or a terminal (display and keyboard or terminal emulation software on a computer) at each end, in addition to a packet radio controller and the radios themselves. The Automatic Position Reporting System (APRS), an offshoot of packet, is a popular application.

First conceived as a way for sailing hams to exchange messages while at sea, the Winlink 2000 amateur email system (**www.winlink.org**) has become a staple of public service and message handling. The Winlink 2000 system operates on both HF (via the PACTOR family of protocols) and VHF/UHF frequencies (via packet radio), using Amateur Radio to collect and deliver email.

PSK31 is a digital mode that has become very popular on the HF bands. It is a narrow-band, real-time digital mode that exploits the ubiquitous sound card. The software is even available free of charge over the Web.

The development and improvement of digital modes is one of the most active areas of experimentation by amateurs.

GETTING ON THE AIR

Let's say you've done your homework. You've studied hard and you passed your license exam. Congratulations! Like many newcomers to Amateur Radio, you probably have a Technician license, giving you full privileges on the VHF and UHF amateur bands and limited privileges on some of the HF bands. (A colorful free frequency privileges chart can be downloaded from **www.arrl.org/FandES/field/regulations/bands.html**.) Getting on the air for you may be as simple as finding a new (or used) VHF hand-held radio, charging the batteries and then talking with your new ham friends through a local FM repeater.

This is exactly how many hams begin their amateur operation — reliable, fun communication with a small group of friends in their own and nearby communities. With your Technician license in hand, you also can talk or send Morse code (CW) through the amateur satellites or to space shuttle astronauts. Or, with some additional equipment and some easy-to-find software, you can explore the VHF digital modes such as APRS. In addition, you can use SSB voice or CW to contact other stations on the VHF and UHF bands. These modes require transceivers and antennas that are different from those used for FM.

Effective in February 2007, the FCC dropped all Morse code requirements for amateur licensing and awarded Technician licensees the same privileges on the HF bands as Novice licensees. That means you can use CW on portions of the 80, 40, and 15 meters bands. On 10 meters, you can try CW, SSB, RTTY and other digital modes! When the 10 Meter Contest rolls around in December, there's every reason for you to jump in and join the fun, too!

It's hard to resist the lure of the HF bands, where many of today's most experienced hams got their start in ham radio. You'll hear hams on the repeater or at your radio club talking enthusiastically about their adventures on those lower-frequency bands. Someone may regale you with tales of how

Getting Started in Ham Radio

Okay, so you're interested in Amateur Radio (you probably wouldn't be reading this book if you weren't!). We hope we've piqued your interest about some of the neat things hams do. So, how do you get the information you need about specific aspects of our fascinating hobby? How do you go about getting your first license? And how do you go about setting up a station so you can actually start communicating with other hams?

First, let us introduce you to an organization dedicated specifically to Amateur Radio. It is the ARRL — the national association for Amateur Radio — and whose home page is located at www.arrl.org. The ARRL is the only not-for-profit organization set up to serve the more than 600,000 Amateur Radio operators (hams) in the United States, and you should become a member.

The ARRL produces an entire line of publications dedicated to the radio amateur, including the book you are now reading. These materials provide great ways to keep informed of news and technical developments. Moreover, through your ARRL membership you will be supporting ongoing efforts in the national and international arenas that will help ensure that ham frequencies remain ham frequencies in spite of pressures from commercial interests.

Just about anything you may need to know — whether it be from the technical or operating sides of the hobby — can be found in ARRL materials. The basic beginner's publication is *The ARRL Ham Radio License Manual*, which is used as a textbook by many instructors at local radio clubs.

The world-renowned ARRL journal, *QST*, published since 1915, is also an excellent source of technical, operating, regulatory and feature articles on all aspects of Amateur Radio. Since it is published each month, *QST* is a timely source of information all hams can use, and a significant benefit of ARRL membership. Contact the ARRL for membership information at 1-888-277-5289, or visit online at www.arrl.org/join.

ARRL on the Internet

The ARRL also maintains an excellent Web site at www.arrl.org. The Internet-connected ham can find late-breaking Amateur Radio news, as well as columns, feature articles and information on virtually anything related to ham radio. A search engine helps visitors to zero in on specific pages, and a US call sign server is available to all. The ARRL's Technical Information Service has dozens of informative pages and articles open to all on topics of interest to hams.

ARRL members may register to access special Web site features and services. One of the most popular is the *QST* "Product Review." Members can also search the on-line archive of *QST* "Product Review" columns from the past 20+ years. Product reviews provide no-nonsense technical and operating reviews of equipment to help guide your purchasing decisions. Members can also search the indexes of *QST* and *QEX*, ARRL's technical experimenter's magazine.

In addition, ARRL members can use the Web site to keep abreast of DXCC news, check HF propagation from the US to significant DX locations around the world, or sign up to receive free ARRL e-mail products. These include weekly editions of *The ARRL Letter* as well as W1AW/ARRL bulletins, ARRL Division and Section news, and newsletters full of contesting, emcomm and club topics. You can also sign up to receive announcements of new ARRL products, ARRL membership expiration notification, and amateur license expiration notification.

On-the-Air Bulletins

Up-to-the-minute information on everything of immediate interest to amateurs — from Federal Communications Commission policy-making decisions to propagation predictions, to news of DXpeditions — is also transmitted in W1AW bulletins. W1AW is the Amateur Radio station maintained at ARRL HQ in Newington, Connecticut. Bulletins are transmitted at regularly scheduled intervals on CW (Morse code), phone (voice) and several digital (teletype) modes on various frequencies. In addition there are Morse-code practice broadcasts. A schedule of W1AW transmissions appears regularly in *QST* and may also be obtained from ARRL HQ or www.arrl.org.

Local Clubs

When you seek answers to your questions about ham radio, don't overlook another great source of information — the experience of your fellow hams. There is nothing hams like to do better than share the vast wealth of experience they have in the hobby. Being human, most hams like to brag a little about their on-the-air exploits. A general question on a particular area of operation to a ham who has experience in that area is likely to bring you all kinds of data. A dedicated DXer will talk for hours on techniques for working a rare DX station. Similarly, a traffic handler will be only too happy to give you hints on efficient net procedures.

For the new ham (or potential ham), the problem may not be in asking the proper questions, but in finding another amateur of whom to ask the questions. That's where Amateur Radio clubs play an important role.

As a potential ham or a new ham, you might not know of an amateur in your immediate area. A good choice would be to try to find the time and meeting place for a nearby Amateur Radio club. What better source of information for the not-yet-licensed and the newly licensed than a whole club full of experienced hams? If you are not yet licensed, your local Amateur Radio club is also the place to find information, guidelines and courses that will prepare you for the FCC exams.

To find clubs in your area, check out the ARRL's online club search —www.arrl.org/FandES/field/club/clubsearch.phtml. There is also a toll-free telephone number for prospective hams: 800-32NEW-HAM (800-326-3942), or you can send e-mail to newham@arrl.org.

she has made friends many thousands of miles away, across oceans and continents. She might talk about the magic of that time when a ham in Calcutta answered her CQ on 20 meters, recalling that the Indian ham was as interested as she is in jazz and programming computers.

To earn the right to transmit on *all* the HF bands, you'll need to pass the General license exam. At the summit is the Amateur Extra license, which allows access to every part of every ham band. The General license provides you with the opportunity to try every bit of ham radio there is — you'll never regret making the effort to upgrade!

IN THE SHACK — YOUR EQUIPMENT

The first step in selecting your new station should be to make up a list to answer a few questions. Will you be operating HF or only VHF? How much room do you have — in other words, how big can your "shack" or operating position be? Do you have room outside for long antennas, such as HF dipoles, or high antennas such as HF verticals and VHF/UHF arrays? How much do you plan to spend, including rig, accessories, furniture, coax feed line and wire?

Some of these questions may not apply to your situation, and you may need to answer other questions not discussed here. The result of making your personal list, however, is to give you an idea of what you want, as well as your limitations.

The next step is to do some research. Take your time deciding what gear to get. Many sources of information on ham gear are available to you.

1) *Hands-on experience.* Try to use many different pieces of gear before you decide. This applies to VHF/UHF as well as HF gear. Ask a nearby ham friend or one or more of your fellow radio club members if you can use their station. Try your club's station. Note what you like and what features you don't care for in each of the stations you tried.

2) *Radio club members.* Ask members of your local radio club about their personal preferences in gear and antennas. Be prepared for a great volume of input. Every amateur has an opinion on the best equipment and antennas. Years of experimentation usually go into finding just the right station equipment to meet a particular amateur's needs. Listen and take note of each ham's choices and reasons for selecting a particular kind of gear. There's a lot of experience, time, effort and money behind each of those choices.

3) *Advertisements. QST* is chock-full of ads for all the newest up-to-date equipment, as well as some premium used gear. Read the ads, and don't be afraid to contact the manufacturers of the gear for further information. Their Web sites often have comparison charts and operating manuals you can download for free. Compare specifications and prices to get the best deal. If there is a dealer close to you, pay a visit and let them demonstrate some of the gear to you.

4) *Product Reviews. QST* also contains detailed Product Reviews, written by ARRL staff, that include reliable measurements made in the ARRL Laboratory. These definitive reviews pull no punches in describing the good and the less-desirable features of the equipment being evaluated.

5) *Web sites and Internet interest groups.* A number of Web sites are devoted to equipment reviews and discussion. They range from general-interest sites that let members review all kinds of ham gear, to discussion groups or sites devoted to one manufacturer or even a specific model. Try using your favorite Internet search engine to look for information on models that interest you.

After you've made your choice (most hams will trade station equipment often during their ham careers so don't worry about this being your final choice), consider the sources where you might find the right deal on a new or used transceiver. Remember to include shipping and handling in the cost, and inquire about warranty service. If you are inexperienced, try to enlist a seasoned amateur to help you before buying used equipment from any source. Several possible sources of equipment are:

1) *Local amateurs.* Many hams will have spare used gear and may be willing to part with this gear at a reasonable price. Be sure you know what a particular rig is going for on the open market before settling on a final price. If you are new to the hobby and you buy a rig from a local club member, you may be able to talk him or her into "Elmering" you (helping you) with the rig's installation and operation. Local clubs are the safest source of used equipment.

2) *Hamfests/flea markets.* Many radio clubs run small conventions called hamfests. Usually one of the big attractions of these events is a flea market where hams buy and sell used radios, antennas and accessories. Much used gear, usually in passable shape, can be found at reasonable prices. Local distributors and manufacturers of new ham gear and materials sometimes show up at these events, as well.

3) *Local ham radio or electronics dealers.* If you are lucky enough to live near a ham radio dealer or an electronics distributor that handles a line or two of ham gear, so much the better. The dealer can usually answer any questions you may have, will usually have a demonstration unit and will be pleased to assist you in purchasing your new gear.

4) *Internet.* The Internet has become one of the most popular forums for buying and selling Amateur Radio equipment. You'll find ham gear auctioned on eBay (**www.ebay.com**). You will also find used equipment for sale in the "classified ad" sections of ham Web sites such as eHam (**www.eham.net**), QRZ (**www.qrz.com**) and QTH (**swap.qth.com**).

If you are experienced with tools and basic electronic construction, you may even consider building some simple gear from a kit or from an article in a magazine or book. There's a lot of satisfaction to be had in telling the operator on the other end of your QSO, "The rig here is home brew." *The ARRL Handbook* has extensive coverage of construction and basic-to-advanced electronics theory information.

How Much Power?

In the ham radio community, there are both *QRO* (power output up to the full legal limit of 1500 W) and *QRP* (5 W output — or less) enthusiasts. Most hams run 100 to 150 W, the power level of typical transceivers. There are times when it is necessary to run the full legal power limit to establish and maintain solid communications or to compete effectively in a DX contest on certain bands. Most often, the 100-W level is more than enough to provide excellent contacts.

Some hams find the low initial cost of low power (QRP) HF equipment very attractive, especially since some are available in kit form. Beginning operators who are still developing the skills of making contacts often find QRP frustrating, however. By all means, try QRP any time, but it's recommended that you first get some experience at the 100-W level so that you know what to expect on the HF bands.

On VHF the situation is slightly different. Unless you are trying to work several hundred miles in an opening or operate a weak-signal mode, 5 to 10 W is enough power when coupled with a good antenna for excellent local communications.

VHF/UHF Gear

If you're interested mainly in voice and maybe packet radio communication with local amateurs, all you need is a VHF/UHF FM transceiver. FM transceivers are available for hand-held and mobile use. A mobile rig can also be used at home if you have a 12-V battery or suitable power supply. More capable fixed-station "base" transceivers are intended for use at home.

Fig 1-1 illustrates the choices available for a VHF or UHF station and how portable, mobile and home (fixed) rigs and antennas can be used to create a station that suits your needs from wherever you operate.

1) *Hand-held transceivers.* Hand-held transceivers put out from under a watt to 5 W or more. If the hand-held you're considering is capable of high-power operation, you'll want to be able to switch to low power when possible to conserve the battery. Most hand-helds offer a HIGH/LOW power switch. Good used hand-held transceivers sell from under $100. New transceivers start at about $125. If you use your hand-held rig while inside the car, you'll probably be disappointed with the performance of the attached "rubber duck" antenna. A mobile antenna outside the metal shell of the car will work much better.

2) *Mobile transceivers* have power outputs ranging from 10 to 50 W and are used with *mag-mount* or permanently attached mobile antennas mounted on the vehicle. In populated areas with many repeaters, any more than 10 W is probably unnecessary. Mobile transceivers are available used from under $100. New transceivers start at about $150 for a 50 W unit.

3) *Fixed-station transceivers.* A mobile rig connected to a power supply or 12-V automotive battery makes a good fixed station radio. It also can be disconnected and moved into the

car for mobile operation. Powering the rig from a battery has the added advantage of allowing emergency operation when the local power lines go down in a storm. A growing number of *all-band* fixed-station radios operate on the HF bands, as well as VHF and UHF. If you plan on operating HF from home, these would be a good choice. Home stations on VHF/UHF should always use external antennas if more than a few watts of power will be used.

4) *VHF packet radio.* Most VHF packet radio operation, including APRS, takes place on the 2-meter and 440-MHz bands. A mobile transceiver makes a good packet-radio station rig, too. You'll need a computer or terminal, plus a terminal node controller (TNC). Used TNCs are available, but new ones are only slightly more expensive. Newer units may offer "mailbox" features, where other hams can leave messages for you when you aren't home.

Remember that higher power levels can create an RF safety hazard. At the higher power levels of mobile and base transceivers, use external antennas and place mobile antennas away from the passenger compartment. For the higher-powered handheld transceivers, use a detachable speaker-mike and belt clip to keep the antenna away from your eyes and head. This important topic is discussed in the Safety chapter of *The ARRL Handbook.*

HF Equipment

It is a bit more challenging to put together an HF station than a VHF station. HF equipment generally covers more bands and modes and has greater requirements for frequency stability than an FM-only radio. Thus, HF gear is generally more expensive, and the antennas at HF are bigger than the flexible rubber antennas used on hand-held transceivers or the VHF ground-plane antenna mounted on the roof of your car or house.

There are so many different possible HF station configurations that it may be hard to choose the very best station to start out with. Most hams face other constraints — such as having a limited budget to spend for ham gear, or having restrictions on the size and location of antennas. Some hams have a difficult time installing any sort of antenna outdoors and they must resort to indoor or perhaps easily hidden "stealth" wire antennas.

1) *Transceivers.* HF transceivers (a transmitter plus a receiver) have been common since the late 1960s. Like all older gear, older transceivers are likely to have maintenance problems. Mobile use subjects a radio to a great deal of vibration and wide ranges of temperature. A rig showing signs of having been used for mobiling may not be a good choice for your first station.

Avoid antique vacuum-tube equipment for your first station. Years of aging and the higher temperatures can take their toll on electronic components. Tubes are expensive

Building your own equipment has always been popular with hams. This low power QRP transceiver, called "The HiMite," can be built from a kit and is designed for CW operation on 15 meters.

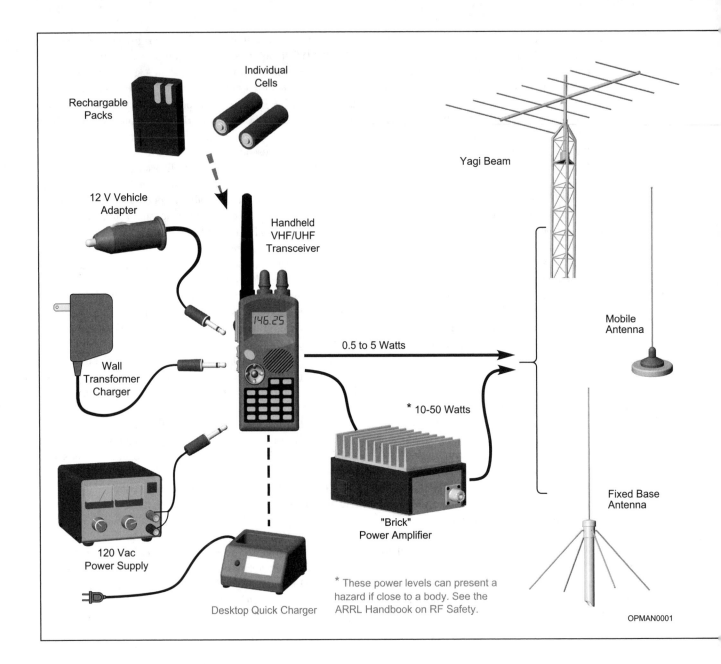

Rechargable
Packs

Individual
Cells

12 V Vehicle
Adapter

Handheld
VHF/UHF
Transceiver

Yagi Beam

146.25

0.5 to 5 Watts

Mobile
Antenna

Wall
Transformer
Charger

* 10-50 Watts

"Brick"
Power Amplifier

Fixed Base
Antenna

120 Vac
Power Supply

Desktop Quick Charger

* These power levels can present a
hazard if close to a body. See the
ARRL Handbook on RF Safety.

OPMAN0001

and those for old amateur gear can be hard to find. Unless you're very familiar with tube-type equipment or have a passion for vintage equipment, look for newer gear.

Transceivers manufactured in the 1970s were partly solid state. The transmitters usually had three tubes: two in the power amplifier and another serving as the driver stage. Some transceivers from this era had built-in ac power supplies. Mechanical parts, such as those used in the tuning assembly, may be impossible to obtain. Make sure everything works properly before you buy. Transceivers from this era probably won't operate on the 30, 17 and 12-meter bands, and some don't cover 160 meters either.

Transceivers manufactured after about 1980 featured fully solid-state designs. Tuning mechanisms had fewer mechanical parts to wear, and all-band operation became common. Many feature general-coverage receivers that tune continuously from below 100 kHz to 30 MHz. With the general-coverage

receiver you can listen to time and frequency-standard stations such as WWV and WWVH and enjoy a variety of shortwave broadcasting.

Equipment manufactured in the past ten years is the most desirable. These radios are fully solid-state, microprocessor-controlled, and have data and control interfaces for digital modes and station accessories. Later models also incorporate *digital signal processing* (DSP) features that provide advanced filtering and noise reduction. The improved performance and reliability are well worth the relatively small premium in price over older equipment now approaching collectible status.

2) *Homemade equipment*. Although most hams will not want to design or build their first stations, if you have a background in electronics, you might want to "homebrew" some of the accessory items, such as tuners, meters, audio processing equipment and interfaces.. Kits are available from a variety of sources, and many proven circuits appear in *The ARRL Handbook*.

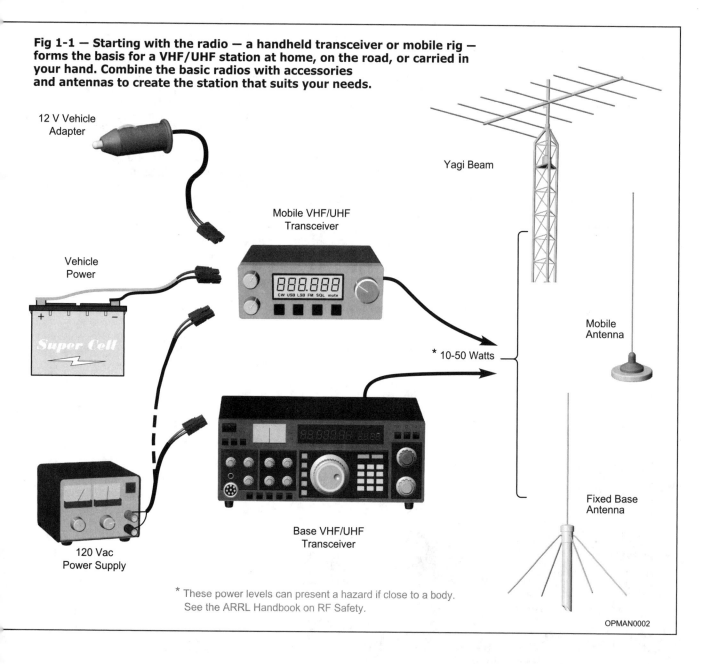

Fig 1-1 — Starting with the radio — a handheld transceiver or mobile rig — forms the basis for a VHF/UHF station at home, on the road, or carried in your hand. Combine the basic radios with accessories and antennas to create the station that suits your needs.

12 V Vehicle Adapter

Vehicle Power

Super Cell

120 Vac Power Supply

Mobile VHF/UHF Transceiver

888.888

CW USB LSB FM SQL mute

Base VHF/UHF Transceiver

Yagi Beam

* 10-50 Watts

Mobile Antenna

Fixed Base Antenna

* These power levels can present a hazard if close to a body. See the ARRL Handbook on RF Safety.

OPMAN0002

Accessories

A few accessories found in almost all stations either help set up and test equipment or help operate it.

SWR Indicator

This device is handy for testing an antenna and feed line when the antenna is first erected, and later to make sure the antenna is still in good shape. If an antenna tuner is used with a multiband antenna system, such as a 135-foot dipole or a G5RV antenna, an SWR (standing-wave ratio) indicator is essential for ensuring the tuner is adjusted for a reasonable SWR. All modern HF transceivers include an SWR indicator. External SWR meters can cost as little as $30. If you plan to operate both VHF and HF you will probably have to buy one for HF and a second for VHF/UHF.

Antenna Tuner

Although many transceivers include an internal anten-

na tuner, there are a number of reasons to have a separate tuner. They generally tune a wider range of impedances, are available with higher power handling ability, can be dedicated to specific antennas, and so forth. There are many antenna tuners available on the market, costing between $75 and $1500. (The more expensive models handle higher power and/or use microprocessor circuits for automatic adjustment.) The basic circuits are pretty simple, though, and many first-time homebrew projects are antenna tuners. (*The ARRL Handbook* and *ARRL Antenna Book* contain plans for building them.) By carefully shopping at hamfest flea markets you can often assemble your own for less than $50 in parts.

Keys, Keyers and Paddles

If you're interested in CW, you will need some means of sending code. You should start with a straight key until you feel you have the proper rhythm. The next step is to buy an electronic keyer and paddles, or use your computer to send code.

Real Radios Glow In the Dark

In many hobbies and avocations there are groups that specialize in traditional techniques and technology — wooden boats, steam power, bow and arrow hunting. While the majority of practitioners no longer utilize them, these venerable methods still perform their functions well and with unique qualities appreciated by their users. Amateur Radio's steam power is the vacuum tube and AM voice.

The vacuum tube, once king in electronics, is relegated to a few niche applications still not overrun by semiconductors. High-power amplifiers is where you'll find tubes still holding sway. There is also a certain romance to the tube rig. Unlike the quietly efficient chip-laden, microprocessor-controlled modern radio, a "steam radio" takes time to warm up, it has a characteristic aroma, and, with the lights low in the shack, the glow of filaments creates silhouettes of ventilation screens. When turned off, there is a delay as the pilot lamps and tubes cool, filaments (heaters to some) dropping from white-orange through cherry red to tungsten gray.

Audiophiles swear by the warm sound of their tube amplifiers with transformer-coupled outputs, and so do aficionados of antique radios. You'll find them tuning the bands like everyone else, answering CQs and holding nets. You might notice a different quality to their signals and, if you ask, they'll be glad to tell you about their old friends on the operating desk. As you browse the tables at the next hamfest, ask a few questions about that antique radio and see if the seller's face doesn't light up like a brand-new 811 final tube!

Hams have always taken pride in the quality and fidelity of their modulation. For some, the sound of an AM signal (the full, double-sideband-and-carrier AM) just can't be equaled by a SSB radio's steep filter skirts and sideband suppression. Because an AM transmitter does not remove frequencies below 300 Hz in order to eliminate the unwanted sideband and carrier remnants, the modulation can reproduce the warm basses of the voice.

A properly adjusted AM transmitter can sound very good indeed, including the high frequency sibilants and fricatives that make speech crisp and understandable. Accordingly, there is a group of hams that enjoy using AM, even though it is not as efficient in its use of spectrum as are its modern cousins. You can often find AM-ers around 3885 or 14,286 kc (the old abbreviation for kHz), sometimes using antique rigs for a doubly-interesting contact.

If you'd like to know more about ancient rigs, affectionately known as "boatanchors", and AM signals browse the references on AC6V's "Antique Ham Radios" and "AM" Web pages (www.ac6v.com) or the ARRL AM page at www.arrl.org/tis/info/am.html. If you'd like to listen to some vintage AM equipment or just give the 'AM' button on your newer rig a try, watch for on-the-air events such as the Classic Exchange or the Bruce Kelley Memorial 1929 QSO Party in *QST's* "Contest Corral".

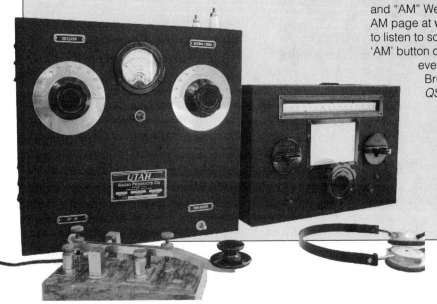

This Utah Junior transmitter and National FBXA receiver owned by W9AC date from the late 1930s and still make an appearance on the air from time to time.

Most modern transceivers have keyers built in, so all you need is a paddle. Paddles may be standard or *iambic* — able to send alternating dots and dashes. The iambic type requires less hand motion but takes a bit longer to master. Keyers cost from $20 to $250, and good paddles can cost $50 and up. Code-transmitting programs are available for most computers.

Computers

Computers have become a very valuable part of the ham shack. It is common to use a computer to send and receive Morse code, fax, slow-scan TV or digital modes. The same computer can be used for logging and record keeping, as well as connecting to the Internet. Many radios and accessories have computer control interfaces, mostly RS-232 although USB is becoming more popular.

Most ham computers are *Windows*-compatible, although the *Linux* and Macintosh communities are well-represented. Some hams still use *MS-DOS* applications, but most computers manufactured to run *Windows XP* and later versions cannot run *MS-DOS* programs. If you plan on using your computer to control amateur equipment, be sure it has at least one COM (serial) port or purchase USB-to-serial converters.

When considering a computer for the shack remember that a computer uses various oscillators inside that can generate annoying spurious signals in your receiver. These signals may interfere with on-air signals you are trying to hear. Some computers can be very sensitive to the presence of radio-frequency energy (RF), such as that generated by your nearby transceiver. For help with this topic see *The ARRL RFI Book*, which contains an entire chapter on solving computer problems in the shack.

Test Meter

An inexpensive digital multimeter capable of measuring voltage, current and resistance is very helpful around the shack. High accuracy is not needed for most projects. A $15 to $30 unit will pay for itself the first time you need to check the integrity of a coax connector you've just installed.

STATION SETUP AT HOME

How you set up a home station is determined by how much space you have, and how much equipment you have to squeeze into it. The table should be about 30 inches high and 30 inches deep. An old desk makes a good operating table. Stacking radios on top of one another prevents ventilation and may cause them to overheat. Build shelves for your equipment — office supply and home improvement stores often have inexpensive desktop shelves that work well for radios. It's also easier to change cables and move equipment around when you use shelves. Make sure you can get behind the gear to plug or unplug cables.

Assuming you use a computer, its monitor should be centered in front of your keyboard at a comfortable viewing height. Avoid neck and eye strain — don't place the monitor too far above or to the sides of the keyboard. Place the radios to one side of the keyboard. Check that you can see the frequency display and reach the operating controls of your radios easily. Continuously reaching across a computer keyboard to tune or operate a radio will cause strain on your back, shoulder and arms.

To prevent fatigue when operating on CW, place your key or paddle far enough from the edge of the table so your entire arm is supported. If you're not using a headset with a boom microphone, the microphone can be mounted on a stand placed on the table or on an extension that reaches in from the back or side.

The best way to test the arrangement of your station is to sit in the operating chair and operate. Don't be afraid to rearrange your equipment if the layout turns out to be uncomfortable. This is also a good reason not to make your first layout too permanent! Adjust the height and angle of all equipment until it's easy to see and use. If some knobs are too low, try placing spacers or blocks under the front feet of the rig. Too high? Try placing the spacers under the rear legs.

AC and RF Grounding

Be sure to have an ac safety ground at your station and connected to all equipment. It's a good idea to not even plug in equipment until its case is grounded. Electrical codes require all recent construction to have grounded (3-wire) ac outlets.

Place a grounding strap or *bus* at the back of the equipment and ground all equipment to it with short leads. Then connect the ground bus to the earth ground as directly as possible using copper strap, heavy wire, or metal braid such as shield from coaxial cable or strips of flashing copper. Connect the ground bus to your ac safety ground.

An earth ground for RF, such as an outside ground rod, is highly desirable to avoid RF feedback and interference to your station equipment. A cold-water pipe may also be used if it is metallic and extends into the ground around your home. The path from the ground bus to the earth should be as short and direct as possible.

If you live on a higher floor and a direct connection to an earth ground is not available, use a ground bus and be sure all equipment is connected to it. This keeps all equipment at the same RF potential, giving RF current no reason to flow between the various pieces and cause problems.

Safety should be a prime consideration. Use a master switch and make sure other people in the house know where it is and how to use it. Consider running your shack through a *GFI* (ground fault interrupt) outlet. Unfortunately not all ham gear, especially older units, will operate with these devices. By detecting unbalanced line currents and shutting off the voltage when unbalance occurs, however, they could save your life!

ANTENNAS

Antennas are important. The best (and biggest) transmitter in the world will not do any good if the signal is not radiated into the air. A good rule of thumb to follow is "always erect as much antenna as possible." The better your antennas, the better your radiated signal will be and the better you'll hear other stations. A good antenna system will make up for inadequacies or shortcomings in station equipment.

If you are thinking of a tower, talk to a few local hams before starting construction (or applying for a building permit). Local rules and ordinances may have a large impact on your plans. Many homes are also subject to *restrictive covenants* or other restrictions on external antennas. Be sure you know what you're allowed to do before digging a hole for a tower base, and get whatever building permits are required!

First VHF/UHF Antennas

One of the nice things about VHF and UHF operation is that the simplest antennas, if mounted high enough and clear of surrounding objects, will often do an excellent job. Ground planes, J-poles and simple beams can either be purchased at a reasonable cost or constructed in a home workshop. For ex-

Antenna Safety

Whatever antennas you select, install them safely. Don't endanger your life or someone else's for your hobby!
- Keep the antenna and its support well clear of any power lines, including the ac power service to your home.
- Make sure if the antenna or its support falls, it can't contact power lines.
- Install the antenna where it can't be easily contacted by people.

There is a thorough discussion on antenna safety in *The ARRL Handbook* and *The ARRL Antenna Book*.

ample, if you want to test a 2-element quad for 144 MHz, just take the design from the *ARRL Antenna Book*, build it from scrap wood and heavy gauge copper or aluminum wire, and run a few tests. The unit you built may not stay up for a long time in bad weather, but it will be fine for determining if this is the sort of antenna you want to put up permanently.

A simple ground-plane antenna is shown in **Fig 1-2**. It can be mounted by taping the feed line and bottom connector to a pole so that the antenna extends above the top of the pole. It can also be suspended by a length of fishing line or synthetic twine by lengthening the vertical element and bending the extra length into a loop. One end of the line is fastened to the loop and the other end is supported by a tree branch or rafter.

A Simple HF Antenna

The most popular — and a very effective — first HF antenna is the half-wavelength dipole. It consists of a half wavelength of wire divided in the center by an insulator. The insulator is where a feed line from your station is connected to each half of the wire. This construction is illustrated in **Fig 1-3**.

The dipole is very easy to erect and has a low SWR (standing wave ratio). SWR is the measure of how well an antenna is tuned to the desired frequency and of the match between its feed point impedance and the feed line's characteristic impedance.

A dipole can be fed with 50 Ω coaxial cable and used on one band. A single-band dipole fed with low-loss feed line, such as window or open-wire line, can also be used on other bands. In fact with an antenna tuner, a balun, and a random-length center-fed dipole you can actually operate on any HF band.

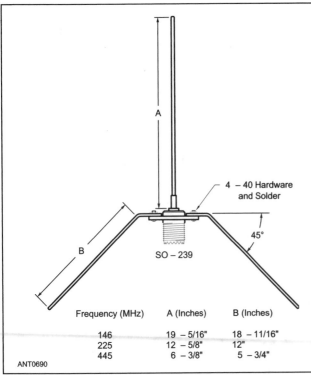

Frequency (MHz)	A (Inches)	B (Inches)
146	19 – 5/16"	18 – 11/16"
225	12 – 5/8"	12"
445	6 – 3/8"	5 – 3/4"

ANT0690

Fig 1-2 — A simple ground-plane antenna for VHF. The elements are made from ³/₃₂ or ¹/₁₆-inch brass welding rod or #10 or #12 bare copper wire.

Where to Put the Dipole?

The antenna should be as high and as far away from surrounding trees and structures as possible. Never put an antenna near power lines!

A dipole requires one support at each of its ends (perhaps trees, poles or even house or garage eaves), so survey your potential antenna site with this in mind. If you find space is so limited that you can't put up a straight-line dipole, don't give up! The dipole can also be held up by a single support in the middle with the ends secured closer to the ground — this is called an *inverted V*.

You can also slope or bend the dipole and it will still make plenty of contacts. You can put up an antenna under almost any circumstances, but you may need to use your imagination. Antennas want to work!

Dipole Antenna Parts

If this is the first time you have tried to put up a dipole by yourself the following parts list will give you some guidance.

1) *Antenna wire.* #12 or #14 hard-drawn Copperweld (copper-clad steel) is preferred, so the antenna won't stretch. Stranded or solid copper wire will also work but if used for a long antenna, the wire will probably have to be trimmed once it's been under tension for a while. Wire of this gauge is strong enough to support itself as well as the weight of the feed line connected at its center. Always buy plenty of wire. It never goes to waste!

2) *Insulators.* You need one center and two end antenna insulators for a simple dipole.

3) *Clamp.* Large enough to fit over two diameters of your coaxial cable to provide mechanical support.

4) *Coaxial Cable or "Coax".* Feed line made of a center conductor surrounded by an insulating dielectric. This in turn is surrounded by a braid called the shield and an outer insulating jacket. Use RG-58, RG-8X, RG-8, RG-213 or an equivalent. Look for coax with a heavy braid shield. Stick with brands sold by reputable ham radio dealers and avoid surplus or used cable for this first antenna.

A good alternative to coax is balanced open-wire or window line. Open-wire line is constructed using two parallel pieces of wire connected and spaced with plastic rods. Window line has a plastic jacket similar to TV 300-Ω wire with pieces of the center plastic removed to form "windows," lightening the line and reducing its losses. If you are sure you want to build a single-band dipole, stay with coax feed line, otherwise consider the tuner, balun and open-wire configuration.

5) *Connector.* Connects coaxial feed line to your rig. The standard connector on HF equipment is the SO-239 or "UHF" connector. You'll need a matching PL-259 connector for the coax. If your radio needs a different type of connector, check your radio's instruction manual for installation information. You also need connectors for the coax lines between your antenna tuner, SWR meter and your rig. If you are using an external antenna tuner or SWR meter, to connect them together you will need to make short coax *jumpers* that have a PL-259 on each end.

6) *Electrical tape and coax sealant.* This is needed to waterproof the connection between the coax feed line and the antenna. Otherwise water can get into the coax, eventually

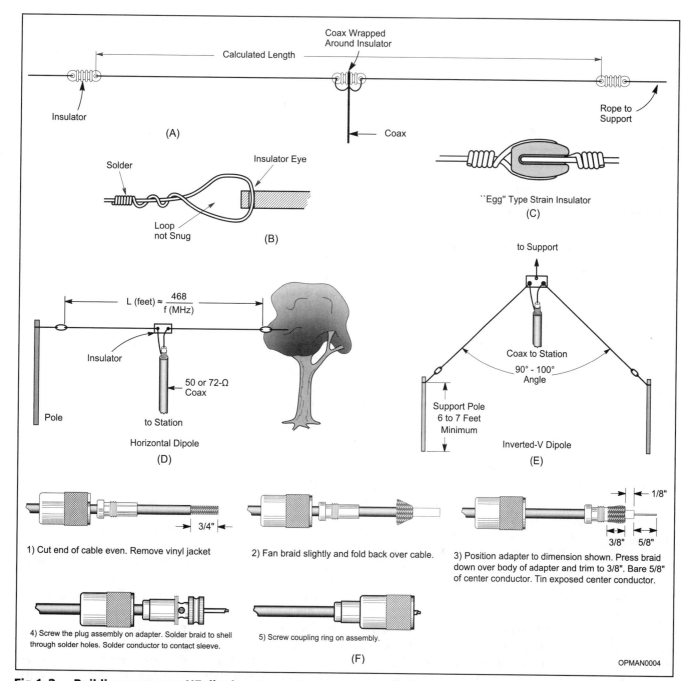

Fig 1-3 — Building your own HF dipole antenna is a popular project.

In the figure:

- (A) Calculated Length; Coax Wrapped Around Insulator; Insulator; Coax; Rope to Support
- (B) Solder; Insulator Eye; Loop not Snug
- (C) "Egg" Type Strain Insulator
- (D) Horizontal Dipole; $L\ (feet) \approx \dfrac{468}{f\ (MHz)}$; Insulator; 50 or 72-$\Omega$ Coax; to Station; Pole
- (E) Inverted-V Dipole; to Support; Coax to Station; 90° - 100° Angle; Support Pole 6 to 7 Feet Minimum
- (F) 1) Cut end of cable even. Remove vinyl jacket — 3/4"; 2) Fan braid slightly and fold back over cable. 3) Position adapter to dimension shown. Press braid down over body of adapter and trim to 3/8". Bare 5/8" of center conductor. Tin exposed center conductor. — 1/8", 3/8", 5/8"; 4) Screw the plug assembly on adapter. Solder braid to shell through solder holes. Solder conductor to contact sleeve. 5) Screw coupling ring on assembly.

OPMAN0004

ruining the feed line.

7) *Supporting rope or cord.* You need enough to tie the ends of the antenna to a supporting structure and also reach the ground when the antenna is lowered. That's about twice the height of the support plus the distance from the support to the end of the antenna. Use UV-resistant cord or rope to avoid degradation from exposure.

8) *SWR meter or antenna analyzer.* If your radio doesn't have an SWR meter built-in, you'll need to purchase a separate unit. The SWR meter is required for antenna adjustment and then for antenna tuner adjustment when operating. SWR meters are readily available and inexpensive, making them easier to buy than to build. An antenna analyzer is a self-contained device that connects to the antenna feed line and transmits a very low power signal to display the antenna SWR over a range of frequencies.

Gather all the parts you'll need for your chosen antenna. Almost everything is available from your local electronics store or from suppliers advertising in *QST*. When this is done, the fun of actually putting together your antenna can begin.

Putting It Together

Assembly is quite simple. Your dipole consists of two lengths of wire, each approximately ¼ wavelength long at your chosen (or lowest) operating frequency. These two wires are connected in the center, at an insulator, to the feed line. In our antenna the feed line, which brings the signals to and from your radio, is coaxial cable. Calculate the length of the half-wave

Table 1-2
Antenna Lengths in Feet

	½ wavelength	¼ wavelength
80 m	126' 6"	63' 3"
40 m	65' 8"	32' 10"
15 m	22' 2"	11' 11"
10 m	16' 7"	8' 3"

Remember to add about 1 foot to each end of the dipole for tuning adjustment.

dipole by using this simple formula:

antenna length in feet = 468/frequency in MHz

(The information in **Table 1-2** has approximate lengths already calculated.) Now measure the antenna wire, keeping it as straight as possible. To the length in the table, add an additional 8 inches on each end of the wire (that's 16 inches per antenna half) to allow for the mechanical loop through the insulator.

Carefully assemble your antenna, paying special attention to waterproofing the coax connections at the center insulator. Don't solder the antenna ends until later, when tuning is completed. Just twist them for now. Route the coax to your station, leaving a drip loop wherever the cable goes through a wall or window. Cut the coax to a length that will leave some excess for strain relief so your rig won't be pulled around during strong winds! Install the connectors according to the diagrams in Fig 1-3. If you use an external SWR meter, connect it between the end of the antenna feed line and the transmitter.

One trick used by old-timers is the addition of a 10,000-Ω resistor, soldered directly across the center insulator of the dipole. An ohmmeter in the shack when connected from one side of the feed line to the other should measure this value of 10,000 Ω. If it measures an open circuit, it means the feed line is disconnected or broken. A short circuit means the feed line or the connector is shorted. The high-value resistor has no effect on the antenna or SWR. Left in place it acts as a handy check on the antenna and feed line.

Raise the antenna into place and test it! Turn on your radio and reduce power to 10 W output or less. Follow the instructions in the radio's operating manual to measure SWR at several frequencies across the band for which the dipole was designed. Be sure to listen first and find a clear frequency so you don't unintentionally interfere with other hams using the band.

If the minimum SWR occurs at or near the desired operating frequency and the SWR is lower than 2:1 or so, your antenna is correctly tuned. Lower it, solder the ends of the antenna that are twisted around the insulators and hoist it back into place. Go operate!

If the *resonant frequency* at the minimum SWR is too low, the antenna is too long and it will need to be shortened. Lower it and remove six inches from each side of the dipole, then test SWR again. Keep notes! Assuming the resonant frequency increased when the antenna was shortened, keep shortening and testing until the resonant frequency is approximately correct. If the resonant frequency was too high, you can splice the antenna and add some length on each end. As the last step, when you are sure the length of the dipole is correct, solder the wire wrapped around the end insulators. When you complete the antenna, take a final set of SWR readings and keep them in a notebook for future reference, should you need to troubleshoot the antenna or feed line.

If you plan on building a number of antennas, a better way to tune the antenna that does not involve transmitting an unmodulated signal is to use an antenna *noise bridge* or an *antenna analyzer*. These instruments use extremely low power signals to measure SWR and are much more portable than a transmitter and SWR meter.

When all systems are go, get on the air and operate. As you settle into that first QSO with your new antenna, enjoy those feelings of pride, accomplishment and fun that will naturally follow. After all, that's what Amateur Radio is all about!

Problems and Cures

Many hams act as though the world will end if they put up an antenna and measure an SWR greater than 1.5:1. For most purposes an SWR of up to 3:1 is perfectly acceptable at HF with good quality feed lines 100 feet or less in length.

A high SWR that does not change when you change the antenna length by a foot or more (HF only) probably means something more serious is wrong with your simple, one-band dipole. Check to see if your coax is open or shorted. Make sure your antenna isn't touching anything and that all your connections are sound.

On bands such as 80 meters, the antenna likely won't have a low SWR over the whole band. In this case, tune the antenna for the highest frequency part of the band on which you wish to operate (the shortest antenna length). When you want to use the lower part of the band, lower the antenna and temporarily attach short lengths of wire at the end insulators, using heavy alligator clips or split-nut wire clamps.

MOBILE STATIONS

Mobile operation — from cars, RVs, boats and even bicycles — has experienced a renaissance in the past few years. The reason? Excellent, compact equipment and antennas! Hams have operated VHF and UHF from their vehicles for a long time, but with the advent of "all-band" radios that operate on everything from 160 meters through 70 cm, the mobile station no longer has to take a back seat to home operating.

This section introduces the most common mobile installation — for VHF/UHF FM operation. Then we'll extend the conversation to HF operating. Both types of installations have many aspects in common. While the vehicle is assumed to be a car, much of the information applies directly to other types of conveyance. Hamming while in motion places some extra requirements on the operator, too. If mobile operation sounds attractive to you, follow up with some of the resources listed at the end of the section.

Mobile Safety

Modern vehicles feature dozens of electronic gadgets and features for their owners, more than ever. A lot of work goes into making sure they are safe to use in a vehicle, especially on the road. When installing your mobile station, be sure to make safety your top priority.

Electrical Safety

Let's start with electrical safety. A vehicle moves and

vibrates continuously while in motion. Your radio will also experience wide swings in temperature nearly every day. Any connection that's not secure is going to work its way loose in short order. If it's a radio signal connection — such as a cable or antenna — you'll experience erratic signals and possibly damage the radio.

Loose power connections can be much more dangerous. A vehicle's electrical system (and that includes any vehicle with batteries of any size) packs a lot of energy. An accidental short circuit will rapidly heat wire to the point where connectors oxidize and insulation melts. A vehicle fire is an expensive proposition! Make sure that all wiring is secure, protected against chafing or pinching by metal surfaces, and properly fused.

A common source of electrical problems is using wire or circuits that aren't adequately rated for the power requirements of the radio. Your radio's manual will specify the correct gauge wire to use. Follow that recommendation! At the very least, your radio may not operate properly if the resistance in the power wiring causes voltage at the radio to drop below the specified minimum. Overloaded wiring and connectors will also get quite hot and could start a fire.

Expect the worst to happen and protect yourself against it with proper fusing as shown in **Fig 1-4**. Follow the recommendations of the manufacturer of your vehicle for installing a radio or other device. *Never* connect power leads directly to the vehicle's power system without proper fusing!

To minimize noise and voltage drops in the power wiring, connect the fused power leads directly to the battery, if possible. It may be more convenient to connect the negative lead to the vehicle battery ground strap where it is attached to the body or engine block. Fuses in *both* the positive and negative power leads will protect your radio's power wiring in case a positive wire comes in contact with the radio body or positive lead.

Mechanical Safety

It's important to mount or constrain your radio so that it can not become a hazard to you or your passengers. Even in normal driving, a radio sliding around on a seat, underfoot, or on a dashboard can be a distraction at the minimum and an injury hazard at worst. Some states do not allow drivers to have any equipment mounted on the dashboard. Check your local regulations about requirements for mounting radios, then follow them. Your radio's user manual may also have some suggestions and recommendations.

In most cars, there is a place on the console where a radio might be installed. If so, and it will look acceptable to you, that's a good place to mount the radio. You'll be able to see the radio's front panel and the radio can look professionally installed. It will generally be secure, even in an accident.

If there's no convenient location for the whole rig, consider a radio with a detachable front panel and mount the radio under a seat or in the trunk. You'll probably need a *separation cable* or *separation kit* so that the microphone and *control head* (the panel with the operating controls and display) can be mounted

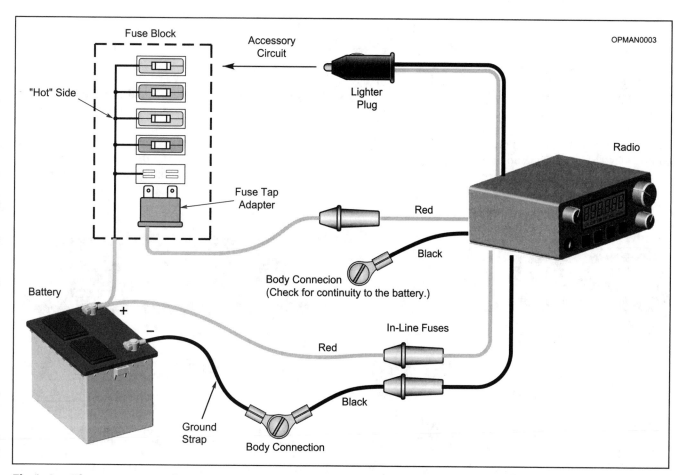

Fig 1-4 — There are several ways to power your mobile station. See text for discussion.

up front and convenient where you are while the body of the radio is elsewhere. Wherever you mount the radio, be sure it can't come loose in a crash and become an injury-causing projectile.

Cables can also get tangled in control wiring, springs, levers and all the other gadgetry in a car. Be very sure that the microphone, antenna, power and any other accessory cables are secure or that they can't wrap themselves around something or jam a pedal.

Driving Safety

You've heard about driving and talking on mobile phones and the hazards of inattention. Maybe you've observed it first hand because it's very common! Operating a mobile ham radio doesn't seem to be such a distraction because of the "push-to-talk" nature of ham communications. You're either talking or listening — never simultaneously as in a telephone conversation.

Nevertheless, don't hesitate to terminate a contact whenever you think you might need extra concentration on the road. You'll often hear a ham say, "I have to drive here" or "Time for both hands on the wheel" and sign off. That's a good idea. Don't compromise your safety or that of other drivers for a contact. If the contact is that important, pull over and devote your full attention to it.

Another driving distraction is having the radio controls placed where you have to take your eyes off the road to use them. **Fig 1-5** shows one example of placing a radio's detachable front panel in a location convenient to the driver. Stuffing a radio between a seat and the console is a good example of how *not* to mount a radio. You'll have to turn your head and look down to turn knobs or press buttons if your microphone doesn't have duplicate controls. Be sure the

Fig 1-5 — When planning your mobile installation, the radio needs to be somewhere convenient. Transceivers with detachable control heads or faceplates are a great choice for modern cars. It's easier to find a home for a compact control head, and the main body of the radio can go under a seat or in the trunk.

radio or control head is mounted where you can pay attention to your number one job — driving!

VHF/UHF Mobile

The most common mobile installation for VHF and UHF mobile is a dual-band radio such as the one shown in **Fig 1-6**. They come with all the necessary mounting hardware, microphone, and power cabling for a proper installation. Many have a detachable front panel that can serve as a control head as described above. All have adequate power output. Choosing one is largely a question of picking the secondary features that you want — automatic CTCSS tone detection, number of memories, scanning, receiving outside the amateur bands and so forth.

The antenna for VHF and UHF mobile should be a vertically-oriented "whip" solidly mounted on a flat metal surface of the vehicle such as the roof or trunk. Removable antennas with a magnetic mount (*mag mounts*) are very popular and work well — if your vehicle has steel exterior surfaces, which not all vehicles do. If your vehicle has plastic or aluminum body surfaces, consult the vehicle dealer about mounting antennas on the vehicle. You may wish to use a mount-on-glass antenna that does not require a ground plane to function.

Running the antenna cable into the interior of the car can be a challenge. Mag mount antennas are usually temporary, so the cable may be run through a door seal. If so, make sure the cable is not pinched hard enough to be deformed. Another problem is water getting in around the cable and you may have to experiment to find a spot where a cable will not give water a way in.

Trunk and hood mounts require a hole in the engine firewall or between the trunk and rear seat to run the cable. You may have to run the cable before installing the coax connector in order to fit through the existing holes.

Fig 1-6 — Modern VHF/UHF FM radios are compact, yet they pack plenty of power for solid repeater and simplex contacts. Single-band radios like the Yaesu FT-1802 (left) are often the most economical, but dualbanders (2 meters/70 cm) like the Alinco DR-635 (right) offer more flexibility.

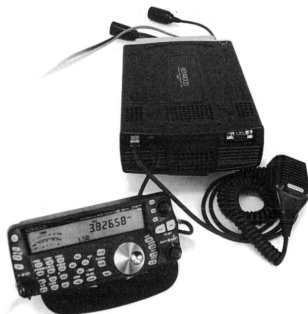

Fig 1-7 — Here are two of the many choices available if you're looking for something more than VHF/UHF FM in your car. ICOM's IC-7000 (left) operates on all bands from 160 to 2 meters, plus 70 cm. Kenwood's TS-480SAT includes 160 to 6 meters. Both radios include all modes — SSB, CW, AM, FM and digital. These radios can also be used as the transceiver in a home station.

Engine firewalls often have spare holes plugged with a grommet or the cable can be squeezed in along side an existing wire bundle. In the trunk, look under the trunk liner and around the rear decking for ways into the passenger compartment. Regardless of which way you run the cable, be sure it won't be chafed or cut by the edges of brackets or other protruding metal.

HF Mobile

While you'll occasionally see a full-blown HF transceiver mounted in a larger car, truck or RV, the most common HF mobile rig is one of the "all-band" radios. Some of the available radios are shown in **Fig 1-7**. These rigs typically put out 100 W on all HF bands through 6 meters and sometimes include 2 meters and 70 cm. (222 MHz is not covered because this is not an amateur band in most places outside of the US.) With a single radio, you can cover all of the most-used amateur spectrum!

All-band radios are a little larger than most VHF/UHF FM mobile radios and also draw considerably more current at full power. This makes them a little more difficult to mount in the passenger compartment. Most can be operated with the front panel mounted as a control head. At least two antenna cables are required for these radios — one is dedicated to HF or HF and 6 meters. VHF and UHF may be combined into a single connection or they may be separate. All of the same cautions apply to installing HF radios as for VHF and UHF gear.

HF antennas bring their own special needs to the vehicle environment. A quarter-wave whip for 2 meters is less than 20 inches long, but the same antenna on 10 meters, the highest HF band, is approximately 8 feet long. On lower-frequency bands, the length of a full-size antenna rapidly becomes impractical for mobile operation. Most HF mobile antennas are coiled up, or *loaded*, to get the full electrical length crammed into a mobile-sized package. While this enables the antennas to be used while in motion, it also cuts their efficiency dramatically.

The ground connection to the vehicle is also critical on HF

because the entire vehicle usually serves as the ground for the antenna. With the antenna efficiency already compromised, it becomes more important to avoid unnecessary ground losses. Many hams get good results using the "Hamstick" style mobile whips shown in **Fig 1-8**. You can see that multiple magnets are used, not only because the antennas are larger and require

Fig 1-8 — Many HF mobile stations use the single-band "Hamstick" style whip antennas. A hefty, multiple-magnet mount is required both to hold the large antenna on the car at driving speeds and to provide enough coupling to the car's metal surfaces.

additional holding power, but because the extra surface area of the magnets makes a better electrical connection to the vehicle surface. Whip style antennas can also be used with bumper or trailer-hitch mounts with good results. The key is to keep the base of the antenna, where current is the highest, in the clear and as high on the vehicle as possible.

Another type of HF mobile antenna that has become increasing popular is the "screwdriver" antenna. So-named because the initial designs used an electric screwdriver motor to adjust the antenna length, the antenna is a fixed-length whip tuned by moving sliding contacts along a coil at its base. Fixed mobile antennas, such as the Hamsticks, are relatively narrow-banded and must be retuned or changed in order to operate on greatly different frequencies within one band — for example 40 meter phone and 40 meter CW. The screwdriver type of antenna is tuned by the motor and can be used over a wide frequency range.

Operating SSB or CW on HF, the VHF/UHF operator will be surprised at how noisy the bands sound compared to the higher bands and noise suppression of FM. At HF, there is a lot more atmospheric noise. Noise is also generated in abundance by nearby motors, electrical lines, and even the vehicle's own ignition and accessory systems. The noise blankers found in the mobile radios can take out the worst of noise, but the HF operator typically just develops an "ear" for copying through it. The resources listed at the end of this section list numerous techniques for identifying and reducing or eliminating "mobile noise."

Keeping any kind of log while in motion is awkward at best and unsafe at worst, unless you train yourself to take notes without looking away from the road. A better idea is to just pull over and write the information in the log. Some operators use a digital voice recorder if they want to keep moving but still log the stations they work. The information is transcribed later.

Mobile Accessories

As in the home shack, there are a number of useful accessories that can make radio easier on the road. One of the most useful is the communications speaker, shown in **Fig 1-9**. The

Fig 1-9 — A separate communications speaker, such as the MFJ-383 shown here, can dramatically improve received audio quality and understandability in the mobile environment.

speaker in mobile radios is not very effective if the radio is installed under a seat, in the trunk or in a console. The external speaker can be mounted where sound is directed at the driver. (Most states do not allow the use of headphones while driving; check your local motor vehicle laws before doing so.) The frequency response of these speakers is tailored to the mobile environment, as well.

Antenna tuners are another common addition to the mobile HF station, allowing a fixed antenna to be used over a wider range. Auto-tuners are particularly popular, especially among boaters who use a single length of wire as their antenna for all bands. Several manufacturers offer tuners intended for use with mobile stations.

Even CW can be used on the road! Most operators prefer using a paddle due to the inconvenience of trying to use a straight key in a car. Paddles can be mounted on leg clips that hold them steady. Shops that sell aviation accessories often have lapboards or kneeboards that are quite suitable for mobiling, since pilots share many of the same concerns with hams.

Mobiling Activities

What can you do on the air while you're also on the road? Quite a bit! For starters, you can ragchew on any band just as well in motion as from home. In fact, the contacts tend to be longer because there are no interrupting phone calls or chores. Hilltopping on VHF and UHF is a popular practice, particularly during VHF+ contests.

If you like the idea of being the sought-after station, you may enjoy participating in the County Hunters program. Yes, people have actually made contact with all of the 3077 counties in the United States! A lot of those contacts are made with mobile stations, some of which have made a special trip to activity a lightly populated county or even two, transmitting from astride a county line. Your state QSO party probably encourages mobile operating, too, and out-of-state stations will be anxiously looking for you to increase their scores.

Mobile Resources

Browse the Web sites listed below for more information about mobile activities.

ARRL Mobile Information Page (**www.arrl.org/tis/info/HF-Mobile.html**); AC6V, Operating Modes (**www.ac6v.com/opmodes.htm**); KØBG, Web Site for Mobile Operators (**www.k0bg.com**); DX Zone's Mobile Page (**www.dxzone.com/catalog/Operating_Modes/Mobile**); Mobile Amateur Radio Awards Club, MARAC (**www.marac.org**); County Hunters (**www.countyhunter.com**); and ARRL Contest Corral (**www.arrl.org/contests**).

You can also find more technical information in *The ARRL Handbook* and *The ARRL Antenna Book*, as well as *Amateur Radio on the Move* and *Your Mobile Companion*, all available from your favorite ham radio dealer or the ARRL Web store.

EXPERIENCE? GET ON THE AIR!

Actual on-the-air operating experience is the best teacher. In this section, we will try to give you enough of the basics to be able to make (and enjoy!) your first QSO. Learn by doing and by listening to others. Don't be afraid to ask questions of someone who might be able to help. After all, we're in this hobby together, and assistance is only as far away as the closest ham.

How do you develop good operating habits? This *ARRL Operating Manual* is an excellent place to start. An entire chapter is devoted to each major Amateur Radio activity, from working DX to space communications. Each chapter has been written by a ham with considerable experience in that area. Experience, even through the words of others, is a powerful teacher. Take a look at the table of contents; you'll be amazed at the diversity and amount of good solid reference material you have at your fingertips.

LISTEN, LISTEN, LISTEN...!

The most efficient way to learn to do something is with a coach or *Elmer*. An Elmer is someone who helps a newcomer become an established, competent ham. Since there are established ways of doing things in the Amateur Radio Service because of rules or good practice, you'll learn most effectively by just plain, old-fashioned listening. All you need is a receiver and your ears.

Tune around the amateur frequency bands, and just listen, listen, listen. Listen to as many QSOs as you can. Learn how the operators conduct themselves, see what works for other operators and what doesn't, and incorporate those good operating practices into your own operating habits. You'll be surprised how much operator savvy you can pick up just by listening.

ON-THE-AIR EXPERIENCE FOR NEWCOMERS

When you're ready, fire up the rig to make your first QSO. Go for it! Nothing can compare with actual on-the-air experience. Remember, everyone on the air today had to make their first QSO at some time or other. They had the same tentativeness

Your First Contact

Are your palms sweaty, hands shaking and is there a queasy herd of butterflies (wearing spikes, perhaps) performing maneuvers in your stomach? Chances are you're facing your first Amateur Radio QSO. If so, take heart! Although some may deny it, the vast majority of hams felt the same way before firing up the rig for their first contact.

Although nervousness is natural, there are some preparations that can make things go a little more smoothly. Practicing QSOs face-to-face with a friend, or perhaps with a member of the local Amateur Radio club, is a good way to ease the jitters.

Some find it useful to write down in advance information you will use during the QSO. You might even go so far as to write a script for what you expect. After a couple of contacts, however, you'll find that you need little prompting.

The ideal security blanket to have with you as you make your first few QSOs is your Elmer or another experienced ham. You'll find that after your initial nervousness wears off you will do just fine by yourself. And you will have honored a ham friend by allowing him or her the privilege of sharing your first on-the-air contacts.

you might have now, but they made it just fine. So will you.

It's the nature of the ham to be friendly, especially toward other members of this wonderful fraternity we all joined when we passed that examination. Trust the operator at the other end of your first QSO to understand your feelings and be as helpful as possible. After all, he or she was once in your situation!

THE BANDS

Operating on the VHF/UHF bands is relatively straightforward for most modes of operation commonly employed there. Operating on the HF bands is a quite a bit more variable, because the propagation depends on a number of factors that are quite literally in outer space. The main influence on the Earth's ionosphere is the Sun, but the magnetic field of the Earth gets into the act very much as well in determining how HF signals are propagated from one place to another.

The sidebar "Picking a Band" gives you a generalized idea of what to expect on both the HF and the VHF/UHF bands, and **Fig 1-10** shows the Amateur Radio frequency allocations in the US. Never forget, however, that part of the excitement and mystery of the HF bands lies in their unpredictability from day-to-day, or even from hour-to-hour. As this edition is being written, at the minimum of the solar cycle, the higher HF bands (15, 12 and 10 meters) are quiet most of the time. When sunspots start appearing once again, those bands will fill with signals from around the world!

Table 1-3 shows the Considerate Operator's Frequency Guide, and **Table 1-4** shows the North American VHF/UHF/EHF Calling Frequencies. Try these frequencies first when looking for activity on a quiet band.

Propagation Beacons

By providing a steady signal on certain frequencies, HF beacons provide a valuable means of checking current propagation conditions — how well signals are traveling at the time you want to transmit.

The Northern California DX Foundation, in cooperation with the International Amateur Radio Union (IARU), has established a widespread, multi-band beacon network. This network operates on 14.100, 18.110, 21.150, 24.930 and 28.200 MHz. These beacons transmit at a sequence of power levels from 100 W down to 0.1 W in a repeating sequence. A full description with the most up-to-date status is on the NCDXF Web page: **www.ncdxf.org/beacon.htm**.

OPERATING — WHAT, WHERE AND HOW

You have read a little about the basics of ham radio and have some ideas about selecting a rig and station equipment and erecting a decent antenna system. Now it's time to learn a little more about how to go about playing the ham radio game.

To communicate effectively with other hams, we all need to use accepted operating procedures. The next part of this chapter briefly describes the major modes of ham radio communication and a few of the procedures and conventions that hams use on the air. Other chapters discuss the operating procedures for many specialized modes of communication in greater detail. But first we are going to look at operating HF voice and CW (Morse code).

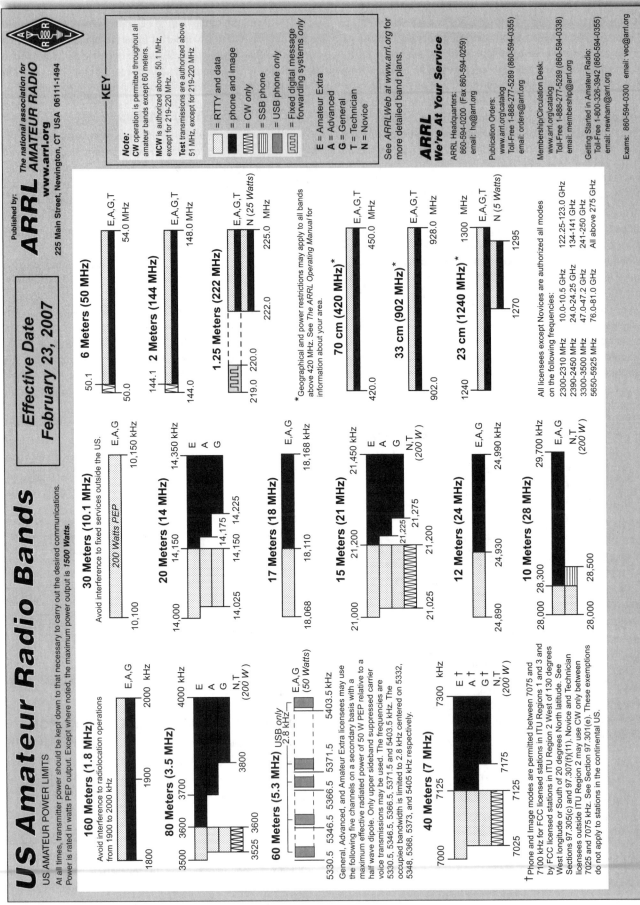

Fig 1-10 — Frequency Allocation Chart for US amateurs.

Table 1-3
The Considerate Operator's Frequency Guide

The following frequencies are generally recognized for certain modes or activities (all frequencies are in MHz) during normal conditions. These are not regulations and occasionally a high level of activity, such as during a period of emergency response, DXpedition or contest, may result in stations operating outside these frequency ranges.

Nothing in the rules recognizes a net's, group's or any individual's special privilege to any specific frequency. Section 97.101(b) of the Rules states that "Each station licensee and each control operator must cooperate in selecting transmitting channels and in making the most effective use of the amateur service frequencies. No frequency will be assigned for the exclusive use of any station." No one "owns" a frequency.

It's good practice — and plain old common sense — for any operator, regardless of mode, to check to see if the frequency is in use prior to engaging operation. If you are there first, other operators should make an effort to protect you from interference to the extent possible, given that 100% interference-free operation is an unrealistic expectation in today's congested bands.

Frequencies	Modes/Activities	Frequencies	Modes/Activities
1.800-2.000	CW	18.100-18.105	RTTY/Data
1.800-1.810	Digital Modes	18.105-18.110	Automatically controlled data stations
1.810	CW QRP calling frequency	18.110	IBP/NCDXF beacons
1.843-2.000	SSB, SSTV and other wideband modes		
1.910	SSB QRP	21.060	QRP CW calling frequency
1.995-2.000	Experimental	21.070-21.110	RTTY/Data
1.999-2.000	Beacons	21.090-21.100	Automatically controlled data stations
		21.150	IBP/NCDXF beacons
		21.340	SSTV
3.500-3.510	CW DX window	21.385	QRP SSB calling frequency
3.560	QRP CW calling frequency		
3.570-3.600	RTTY/Data	24.920-24.925	RTTY/Data
3.585-3.600	Automatically controlled data stations	24.925-24.930	Automatically controlled data stations
3.590	RTTY/Data DX	24.930	IBP/NCDXF beacons
3.790-3.800	DX window		
3.845	SSTV	28.060	QRP CW calling frequency
3.885	AM calling frequency	28.070-28.120	RTTY/Data
3.985	QRP SSB calling frequency	28.120-28.189	Automatically controlled data stations
		28.190-28.225	Beacons
7.030	QRP CW calling frequency	28.200	IBP/NCDXF beacons
7.040	RTTY/Data DX	28.385	QRP SSB calling frequency
7.070-7.125	RTTY/Data	28.680	SSTV
7.100-7.105	Automatically controlled data stations	29.000-29.200	AM
7.171	SSTV	29.300-29.510	Satellite downlinks
7.285	QRP SSB calling frequency	29.520-29.580	Repeater inputs
7.290	AM calling frequency	29.600	FM simplex
		29.620-29.680	Repeater outputs
10.130-10.140	RTTY/Data		
10.140-10.150	Automatically controlled data stations		

ARRL band plans for frequencies above 28.300 MHz are shown in *The ARRL Repeater Directory* and on **www.arrl.org**.

Frequencies	Modes/Activities
14.060	QRP CW calling frequency
14.070-14.095	RTTY/Data
14.095-14.0995	Automatically controlled data stations
14.100	IBP/NCDXF beacons
14.1005-14.112	Automatically controlled data stations
14.230	SSTV
14.285	QRP SSB calling frequency
14.286	AM calling frequency

Table 1-4
North American VHF/UHF/EHF Calling Frequencies

Band (MHz)	Calling Frequency	Band (MHz)	Calling Frequency
50	50.110 DX	432	432.010 EME
	50.125 SSB US, local		432.100 CW/SSB
	50.620 digital (packet)		446.000 National FM simplex frequency
	52.525 National FM simplex frequency	902	902.100
144	144.010 EME		903.100 East Coast
	144.100, 144.110 CW		906.500 National FM simplex frequency
	144.200 SSB		
	146.520 National FM simplex frequency	1296	1294.500 National FM simplex frequency
222	222.100 CW/SSB		1296.100 CW/SSB
	223.500 National FM simplex frequency	2304	2304.1 CW/SSB
		10000	10368.1 CW/SSB
			10280.0 WBFM

VHF/UHF Activity Nights
Some areas do not have enough VHF/UHF activity to support contacts at all times. This schedule is intended to help VHF/UHF operators make contact. This is only a starting point; check with others in your area to see if local hams have a different schedule.

Band (MHz)	Day	Local Time
50	Sunday	6 PM
144	Monday	7 PM
222	Tuesday	8 PM
432	Wednesday	9 PM
902	Friday	9 PM
1296	Thursday	10 PM

Picking a Band

By Jim Kearman, KR1S

160 and 80 Meters

Eighty meters, and its phone neighbor, 75 meters, are favorites for ragchewing. I frequently check out the upper frequencies of the CW subband. There I find both newcomers as well as old-timers trying to work the rust out of their fists. Around 3570 kHz you'll find the digital modes, including RTTY, PSK31 and packet. The QRP frequency is 3560 kHz. If you hear a weak signal calling CQ near 3560, crank down your power and give a call. Another favorite frequency is 3579.5 kHz. If you live in the eastern half of North America, listen for W1AW on 3581.5 (CW), 3597.5 (digital) or 3990 kHz (SSB). W1AW runs 1000 W to a modest antenna — an inverted V at 60 feet. If you can copy W1AW, you can probably work the East Coast, even with low power. AM operation is generally found between 3870 and 3890 kHz.

Even if you can't chase DX, you will find plenty to do on either band. Ionospheric absorption is greatest during the day, thus local contacts are common. At night, contacts over 200 miles away are more frequent, even with a poor antenna. Summer lightning storms make for noisy conditions in the summer, while winter is much quieter. You may also be troubled by electrical noise here. A horizontally polarized antenna, especially one as far from buildings as possible, will pick up less electrical noise.

Topband, as 160 meters is often called, is similar to 80 meters. QSOs here tend to be a bit more relaxed with less QRM. DX is frequent at the bottom of the band. Don't let the length of a half-wave dipole for 160 keep you off the band; a 25 or 50-foot "long wire" can give you surprisingly good results if a good ground system is available. One favorite trick is to connect together the center conductor and shield of the coax feed line of a 40 or 80-meter dipole and load the resulting antenna as a "T," working it against the station ground.

60 Meters

Unlike other HF amateur bands, 60 meters is *channelized*. This means that you have to operate on specific frequencies. The FCC granted General, Advanced and Amateur Extra licensees access to channels centered on 5332, 5348, 5368, 5373 and 5405 kHz. Amateurs may operate upper-sideband voice *only* at a maximum of 50 W effective radiated power (ERP) to a half-wavelength dipole antenna — no beams or other directional antennas allowed. As a result, 60 meters is strictly a low-power, voice-only band. Despite the limitations, it has intriguing potential. The propagation on 60 meters combines the best of 80 and 40 meters.

40 and 30 Meters

I must confess to being biased in favor of these bands, especially 40 meters. If I could only have a receiver that covered one band, it would be 40. Running 10 W from my East Coast apartment (indoor antenna) I can work European hams, ragchew up and down the coast, check into Saturday morning QRP nets, and listen to foreign broadcast stations besides. Yes, 40 is a little crowded. Look at the bright side: You won't be lonely. I think it's possible to work someone on 40 any time of the day or night.

From a modest station, daytime operation on 40 is easier than at night. The skip (distance you can work) during the day is shorter, but that helps reduce interference. Most other countries have SSB privileges down to 7050 kHz. During the day, they, and the broadcasters, won't bother you much. QRPers hang around and above 7030 kHz. Digital operators work around 7070 to 7125 kHz. Even when the foreign broadcasters are booming in, you usually can find someone to work there. Hams operating AM are typically around 7290 kHz. Forty is a good band for daytime mobile SSB operation, too. You'll find plenty of activity, and propagation conditions tend to be stable enough to allow you to ragchew as you roll along.

The 30-meter band has propagation similar to 40 meters. Skip distances tend to be a little longer on 30 meters, and it's not so crowded. At present, stations in the US are limited to 200 W output on this band. DX stations seem to like the low end of the band, from 10100 to 10115 kHz. Ragchewers often congregate above 10115. We share 30 meters with other services, so be sure you don't interfere with them. SSB isn't allowed on 30, but you can use CW and the digital modes.

20 Meters

As much as I like 40 and 30 meters, I have many fond memories of 20 meters as well. When I upgraded my license to General in 1963, I made a beeline to 20 meters. To this day, I can't stay away for long. A 20-meter dipole is only 33 feet long, and that doesn't have to be in a straight line. Many US hams have worked their first European or Australian contacts with a dipole and 100 W.

Many hams consider 20 meters the workhorse DX band. At the bottom of a solar cycle, 20 meters may be usable in a particular direction for only a few hours a day. Even then, 20 is usually open to somewhere in the world throughout the day and night. For example, from New England, 20 is open to some part of South America for 24 hours a day, whatever the level of sunspots might be. On the other hand, 20 meters can be open to the Far East for as much as 13 hours of the day (with very weak signals) when sunspot activity is low, while it can be open all day during periods of high solar activity.

There's plenty of room on the band. CW ragchewers hang out from 14025 to 14070 kHz, where you start hearing digital stations. The international QRP frequency is 14060 kHz. The sideband part of the band is sometimes pretty busy and then it may be difficult to make a contact with low power or a modest antenna. Look above 14250 for ragchewers. Impromptu discussion groups that sometimes spring up on 20 SSB make for interesting listening, even if you don't participate. If you like photographs, look around 14230 kHz for slow-scan TV. You'll need some extra equipment (as discussed in the Image Communications chapter of this book) to see the pictures.

17, 15 and 12 Meters

Except during years of high solar activity, you'll do most of your operating during daylight hours. Propagation is usually better during the winter months. Seventeen and 12 meters aren't as crowded as 15 meters. Fifteen, though, is not nearly as crowded as 20. On 15, the QRP calling frequency is 21060 kHz. Don't forget that CW can be found all the way up to 21200 kHz. No special frequencies are used for QRP operation on 17 and 12. SSB operation is much easier on 17 and 12 because of lower activity. Low activity doesn't mean no activity — when those bands are open, you'll find plenty of stations to work. You only need one at a time, after all. Digital operation is found from 21070 to 21110 kHz, and around 18100 and 24920 kHz.

Practical indoor, outdoor, mobile or portable antennas for these bands are simple to build and install. It's even possible to make indoor beam antennas for the range of 18 to 25 MHz.

10 Meters

The 10-meter band stretches from 28000 to 29700 kHz. During years of high solar activity, 10 to 25 W transceivers will fetch plenty of contacts. When the sun is quiet, there are still occasional openings of thousands of miles. Ten meters also benefits from sporadic-E propagation. You'll find most sporadic-E openings in the summer, but they can happen anytime. Sporadic-E openings happen suddenly and end just as quickly. You may not be able to ragchew very long, but you'll be amazed at how many stations you can work.

SSB activity is heaviest in the Novice/Technician subband from 28300 to 28500 kHz. The lower end of the band (tune up from the bottom edge) is a good place to look for CW activity, as is the QRP calling frequency at 28060 kHz. You can operate 1200-baud packet radio on 10 meters, whereas we're limited to 300 baud on the lower bands. Digital operation takes place from 28070 to 28120 kHz.

Higher in the band, above 29000 kHz, you'll find amateur FM stations and repeaters, and the amateur satellite subband. AM operation is also popular between 29000 and 29200 kHz.

Operating on 50 MHz and Above

The VHF/UHF/microwave bands offer advantages to the low-power operator. The biggest plus is the relatively smaller antennas used. A good-sized 2-meter beam will easily fit in a closet when not in use. Portable and mobile operation on these bands is also easy and fun.

6 Meters

Six meters is perhaps the most interesting amateur band. When solar activity is high, worldwide QSOs are common. When solar activity is low, however, opportunities for long-distance communication decrease. Sporadic-E propagation, which I mentioned earlier, is the most reliable DX mode during periods of low solar activity.

With small antennas, like 3-element beams, it's possible to work 1000 miles on sporadic E. Three-element 6-meter beams don't fit well inside houses or apartments, but you might be able to put one in an attic or crawl space. Even if you can only use a dipole, you'll be able to work locals, and snag some more-distant stations when the band opens.

Just about any mode found on the HF bands is used on 6 meters. CW and SSB operation take place on the lower part of the band. Higher up you'll find FM simplex and repeater stations. Another mode you'll sometimes find on 6 meters is radio control (RC) of model planes, boats and cars.

2 Meters

Simply stated, 2 meters is the most popular ham band in North America. From just about any point in the US, you can probably work someone on 2 meters, 24 hours a day. Most hams know about 2-meter FM, APRS and packet radio operation, but CW and SSB are used here too. There's even an amateur satellite subband on 2 meters.

CW and SSB operation is done mostly with horizontally polarized antennas. FM and packet operators use vertical polarization, while satellites can be worked with either. A popular 2-meter antenna called a *halo* is perfect for indoor or mobile use on CW or SSB. The omnidirectional *halo* has no gain, but you'll be able to work locals, and up to 100 miles during band openings.

FM and packet usually require only a simple vertical antenna. The *ARRL Repeater Directory* will tell you what repeaters are available in your area. This book lists repeaters the bands from 29 MHz to 1.2 GHz and above.

The 222 and 430-MHz Bands

Every mode used on 2 meters is found on 222 except satellite communication. The 430-MHz or 70-cm band is second only to 2 meters in VHF/UHF activity. Multiband hand-held and mobile FM transceivers are available at prices only slightly higher than single-band rigs. If you think you'd like to try these bands in addition to 2 meters, look into a multiband rig.

One mode you'll find on 70 cm that isn't allowed on the lower frequencies is fast scan amateur television (ATV). Assuming you already have a broadcast TV set, all you need is a receive converter, transmitter, antenna and camera. Inexpensive cameras designed for home-video use are fine for ATV. ATV repeaters may be found in larger metropolitan areas. They're listed in the *ARRL Repeater Directory*.

33 cm (902 MHz) and Up

As you go higher in frequency, the size of antennas gets smaller. This fact allows you to use very high-gain antennas that aren't very big. Commercial equipment is available for the bands through 10 GHz. You'll also find kits (the tuned circuits are etched onto the circuit boards).

Because antennas are so small, it's possible to have 20 to 30-dB gain antennas that fit in your car's trunk. In comparison, a big 20-meter beam might offer only 10 dB of gain. Operating from the field with battery-powered equipment is very popular, especially during VHF/UHF/microwave contests. Thanks to high-gain antennas, contacts over several hundred miles are possible with equipment running 1 or 2 W.

Phone Operating Procedures

These phone or voice operating procedures apply to operation on the HF bands as well as SSB on VHF/UHF. Procedures used on repeaters are different since the operation there is channelized — that is, anyone listening to the repeater will hear you as soon as you begin to transmit. Therefore there is no need to call CQ. Each repeater may use a slightly different procedure. There is a complete discussion of repeater operations in the FM chapter of this book.

Learning procedures is straightforward: Listen to what others are doing, and incorporate their good habits into your own operating style. Use common sense in your day-to-day phone QSOs, too:

(1) Listen before transmitting. Ask if the frequency is in use before making a call on any particular frequency.

(2) Give your call sign as needed, using the approved ITU (International Telecommunication Union) Phonetics. These phonetics are given in **Table 1-5**.

(3) Make sure your signal is clean and your audio undistorted. Do not turn your microphone gain up too high. If you have a speech processor, use it only when you are sure it is properly adjusted. Don't take the chance of transmitting spurious (out of band) signals.

(4) Only occupy the frequency as long as you need it. This gives as many operators as possible a chance to use the frequency spectrum.

(5) Give honest signal reports. **Table 1-6** lists what the various RST reports mean.

Whatever band, mode or type of operating you choose, there are three fundamental things to remember. The first is that courtesy costs very little and is often amply rewarded by bringing out the best in others. The second is that the aim of each radio contact should be 100% effective communication. The good operator is never satisfied with anything less. The third is that "private" conversations with another station are actually *public*. Keep in mind that many amateurs are uncomfortable discussing so-called controversial subjects such as sex, religion or politics over the air. Also, never unnecessarily give any information on the air that might be of assistance to the criminally inclined, such as when you are going to be out of town!

Using the proper procedure is very important. Voice operators say what they want to have understood, while CW operators have to spell it out or abbreviate. Since the speed of transmission on phone is generally between 150 and 200 words per minute, the matter of readability and understandability is critical to good communication. The good voice operator uses operating habits that are beyond reproach.

Correct phone operation is more challenging than it first may appear, even though it does not require the use of code or special abbreviations and prosigns. Most people have acquired imperfect habits of pronunciation, intonation and phraseology even before entering Amateur Radio! Remember that the other operator can't see you. Understanding you depends solely on your voice coming over the airwaves. It's easy to acquire bad

---

Table 1-5
The Phonetic Alphabet

When operating phone, a standard alphabet is often used to ensure understanding of call letters and other spelled-out information. Thus Larry, WR1B, would announce his call as Whiskey Romeo One Bravo if he felt the station on the other end could misunderstand his call. Phonetics are not routinely used when operating VHF-FM.

A — Alfa (**AL** FAH)
B — Bravo (**BRAH** VOH)
C — Charlie (**CHAR** LEE)
D — Delta (**DELL** TAH)
E — Echo (**ECK** OH)
F — Foxtrot (**FOX** TROT)
G — Golf (GOLF)
H — Hotel (HOH **TELL**)
I — India (**IN** DEE AH)
J — Juliet (**JEW** LEE ETT)
K — Kilo (**KEY** LOH)
L — Lima (**LEE** MA)
M — Mike (MIKE)
N — November (NO **VEM** BERR)
O — Oscar (**OSS** CAR)
P — Papa (PAH **PAH**)
Q — Quebec (KEY **BECK**)
R — Romeo (**ROW** ME OH)
S — Sierra (SEE **AIR** AH)
T — Tango (**TANG** OH)
U — Uniform (**YOU** NEE FORM)
V — Victor (**VIK** TORE)
W — Whiskey (**WISS** KEY)
X — X-Ray (**EX** RAY)
Y — Yankee (**YANG** KEY)
Z — Zulu (**ZOO** LOU)

The **boldfaced** syllables are emphasized.

Table 1-6
The RST System

Readability
1 — Unreadable
2 — Barely readable, occasional words distinguishable
3 — Readable with considerable difficulty
4 — Readable with practically no difficulty
5 — Perfectly readable

Signal Strength
1 — Faint signals, barely perceptible
2 — Very weak signals
3 — Weak signals
4 — Fair signals
5 — Fairly good signals
6 — Good signals
7 — Moderately strong signals
8 — Strong signals
9 — Extremely strong signals

Tone
1 — Sixty-cycle ac or less, very rough and broad
2 — Very rough ac, very harsh and broad
3 — Rough ac tone, rectified but not filtered
4 — Rough note, some trace of filtering
5 — Filtered rectified ac but strongly ripple-modulated
6 — Filtered tone, definite trace of ripple modulation
7 — Near pure tone, trace of ripple modulation
8 — Near perfect tone, slight trace of ripple modulation
9 — Perfect tone, no trace of ripple or modulation of any kind

If the signal has the characteristic steadiness of crystal control, add the letter X to the report. If there is a chirp, add the letter C. Similarly for a click, add K. (See FCC Regulations §97.307, Emissions Standards.) The above reporting system is used on both CW and voice; leave out the "tone" report on voice.

habits of speech, so be prepared to put in a bit of effort to speak clearly and not too quickly. This is particularly important when talking to a DX station that speaks a different language.

Avoid using CW abbreviations (including "HI" which is CW for laughter) and Q signals on phone, although QRZ (for "who is calling?") has become accepted. Otherwise, plain language should be used. Keep jargon to a minimum. Some hams use "we" instead of "I," "handle" instead of "name" and "Roger" instead of "that's correct." These expressions are not necessary and do not contribute to better operating. No doubt you will hear many more.

Initiating a Contact

There are three ways to initiate a voice contact: call CQ (a general call to any station), answer a CQ, or call at the end of the other person's QSO. If activity on a band seems low and you have a reasonable signal, a CQ call may be worthwhile.

Before calling CQ, it is important to find a frequency that appears unoccupied by any other station. This may not be easy, particularly in crowded band conditions. Listen carefully — perhaps a weak DX station is on frequency.

Always listen before transmitting. Make sure the frequency isn't being used *before* you call. If, after a reasonable time, the frequency seems clear, ask if the frequency is in use, followed by your call: "Is the frequency in use? This is N1OJS." If as far as you can determine no one responds, you are ready to make your call.

CQ calls should be kept short. Long calls are unnecessary. If no one answers, you can always call again. Think of each CQ as an advertisement for your station. A caller tuning across your signal should hear a friendly voice, clean audio, and plenty of time between your CQs for them to respond.

If you do transmit a long call, a potential contact may become impatient and tune elsewhere. You may also interfere with stations that were already on the frequency but whom you didn't hear in the initial check. If two or three calls produce no answer, there may be interference on the frequency. It's also possible that the band isn't open.

An example of a short CQ call would be: "CQ CQ Calling CQ. This is N1OJS, November-One-Oscar-Juliet-Sierra, November-One-Oscar-Juliet-Sierra, calling CQ and standing by."

When replying to a CQ, give both call signs clearly — yours and the CQing station. Use the standard phonetics to make sure the other station gets your call correctly. Phonetics are necessary when calling in a DX pileup and initially in most HF contacts but not usually used when calling into an FM repeater.

When you are calling a specific station, it is good practice to keep calls short and to say the call sign of the station called only once followed by your call repeated twice. VOX (voice operated switch) operation is helpful. If properly adjusted, it enables you to listen between phrases so that you know what is happening on the frequency. "N1OJS N1OJS, this is W2GD, Whiskey-Two-Golf-Delta, Over."

Once contact has been established, it is no longer necessary to use the phonetic alphabet or sign the other station's call. According to FCC regulations, you need only sign your call every 10 minutes, or at the conclusion of the contact. (The exception is handling international third-party traffic; you must sign both

---

Table 1-7
Q Signals
These Q signals are the ones used most often on the air. (Q abbreviations take the form of questions only when they are sent followed by a question mark.)

QRG	Will you tell me my exact frequency (or that of ___)? Your exact frequency (or that of ___) is ___ kHz.	QSL	Can you acknowledge receipt (of a message or transmission)? I am acknowledging receipt.
QRL	Are you busy? I am busy (or I am busy with ___). Please do not interfere.	QSN	Did you hear me (or) on ___ kHz? I did hear you (or ___) on ___ kHz.
QRM	Is my transmission being interfered with? Your transmission is being interfered with ___ (1. Nil; 2. Slightly; 3. Moderately; 4. Severely; 5. Extremely.)	QSO	Can you communicate with direct or by relay? I can communicate with ___ direct (or relay through).
QRN	Are you troubled by static? I am troubled by static ___. (1-5 as under QRM.)	QSP	Will you relay to ___? I will relay to.
QRO	Shall I increase power? Increase power. QRP Shall I decrease power? Decrease power. QRQ Shall I send faster? Send faster (___ WPM).	QST	General call preceding a message addressed to all amateurs and ARRL members. This is in effect "CQ ARRL."
QRS	Shall I send more slowly? Send more slowly (___ WPM).	QSX	Will you listen to ___ on ___ kHz? I am listening to ___ on ___ kHz.
QRT	Shall I stop sending? Stop sending.	QSY	Shall I change to transmission on another frequency? Change to transmission on another frequency (or on ___ kHz).
QRU	Have you anything for me? I have nothing for you.		
QRV	Are you ready? I am ready.	QTB	Do you agree with my counting of words? I do not agree with your counting of words. I will repeat the first letter or digit of each word or group.
QRX	When will you call me again? I will call you again at __ hours (on ___ kHz).		
QRZ	Who is calling me? You are being called by (on ___ kHz).	QTC	How many messages have you to send? I have ___ messages for you (or for ___).
QSB	Are my signals fading? Your signals are fading.	QTH	What is your location? My location is ___ .
QSK	Can you hear me between your signals and if so can I break in on your transmission? I can hear you between signals; break in on my transmission.	QTR	What is the correct time? The time is ___ .

calls in this instance.) A normal two-way conversation can thus be enjoyed, without the need for continual identification. The words "Over" or "Go Ahead" are used at the end of a transmission to show you are ready for a reply from the other station.

Signal reports on phone are two-digit numbers using the RS portion of the RST system (no tone report is required). The maximum signal report would be "59"; that is, readability 5, strength 9. On FM repeaters, RS reports are not appropriate. When a signal has fully captured the repeater, this is called "full quieting."

CW Operating

Using Morse code is a common bond among many HF operators who take pride in their code proficiency. It takes practice to master the art of sending good code on a hand key, bug (semi-automatic key) or electronic keyer. It takes practice to get that smooth rhythm, practice to get that smooth spacing between words and characters, and practice to learn the sound of whole words and phrases, rather than just individual letters.

CW (standing for *continuous wave*) is an effective mode of communication. CW transceivers are simpler than their phone counterparts, and a CW signal can usually get through very heavy QRM (interference) much more effectively than a phone signal.

To reduce transmission time and increase efficiency when using Morse code, hams use shortcuts and abbreviations during a CW QSO. Many were developed within the ham fraternity, while some are borrowed from old-time telegraph operators. *Q signals* are among the most useful of these abbreviations. A list of the most popular Q signals is in **Table 1-7**. You don't have to memorize all the Q-signals, just keep a copy handy to your operating table.

After using some of the Q signals and abbreviations a few times you will quickly learn the most common ones without needing any reference. With time, you'll find that as your CW proficiency rises, you will be able to communicate almost as quickly on CW as you can on the voice modes. A list of common CW abbreviations is in **Table 1-8**.

It may not seem that way to you now, but your CW sending and receiving speed will rise very quickly with on-the-air practice. For your first few QSOs, carefully choose to answer the calls from stations sending at a speed you can copy (perhaps another first timer on the band?). Courtesy on the ham bands dictates that an operator will slow his or her code speed to accommodate another operator. Don't be afraid to call someone who is sending just a bit faster than you can copy comfortably. That operator will generally slow down to meet your CW speed. If necessary, ask the other operator to "PSE QRS" to slow down a little. Helping each other is the name of the game in ham radio.

To increase your speed, you may wish to continue to copy the code practice sessions from W1AW, the ARRL HQ station. (West Coast stations can tune in the West Coast runs as described in *QST* and on the ARRL Web.) It might be a good idea to spend some time sending in step (on a code-practice oscillator — not on the air, of course) with a code training program; this approach will help develop your sending ability.

Correct CW Procedures

The best way to establish a contact, especially at first, is to

Many hams enjoy operating outdoors as part of a camping trip or other vacation. Tom, K7TPD, is shown here operating 40 meter CW on an outing with the Radio Society of Tucson K7RST.

listen until you hear someone calling CQ. CQ means, "I wish to contact any amateur station." Avoid the common operating pitfall of calling CQ endlessly; it clutters up the airwaves and keeps others from calling you. The typical CQ would sound like this: CQ CQ CQ DE K5RC K5RC K5RC repeated once or twice and followed by K. The letter K is a prosign inviting any station to go ahead. If there is no answer, pause for 10 seconds or so and repeat the call.

If you hear a CQ, wait until the ham finishes transmitting (by ending with the letter K), then call: K5RC DE W1HSR W1HSR AR. (AR is equivalent to *over*). In answer to your call, the called station will begin the reply by sending W1HSR DE K5RC R. That R (*roger*) means that he has received your call correctly. Suppose K5RC heard someone calling him, but didn't quite catch the call because of interference (QRM) or static (QRN). Then he might come back with QRZ? DE K5RC K (Who is calling me?).

The QSO

During the contact, it is necessary to identify your station only once every 10 minutes and at the end of the communication. Keep the contact on a friendly and cordial level, remembering that the conversation is not private and many others, including nonamateurs, may be listening. It may be helpful at the beginning to have a fully written-out script typical of the first couple of exchanges in front of you. A typical first transmission might sound like this: W1HSR DE K5RC R TNX CALL. UR 599 599 QTH NEVADA NAME TOM. HW? W1HSR DE K5RC KN. This is the basic exchange that begins most QSOs. Once these basics are exchanged the conversation can turn in almost any direction. Many people talk about their jobs, other hobbies, families, travel experiences, and so on.

Both on CW and phone, it is possible to be informal, friendly and conversational; this is what makes the Amateur Radio QSO enjoyable. During a CW contact, when you want the other station to take a turn, the recommended signal is KN (*go ahead, only*), meaning that you want *only* the contacted station to come back to you. If you don't mind some- one else breaking

Table 1-8
Some Abbreviations for CW Work
Although abbreviations help to cut down unnecessary transmission, make it a rule not to abbreviate unnecessarily when working an operator of unknown experience.

AA	All after	OC	Old chap
AB	All before	OM	Old man
ABT	About	OP-OPR	Operator
ADR	Address	OT	Old timer; old top
AGN	Again	PBL	Preamble
ANT	Antenna	PSE	Please
BCI	Broadcast interference	PWR	Power
BCL	Broadcast listener	PX	Press
BK	Break; break me; break in	R	Received as transmitted; are
BN	All between; been	RCD	Received
BUG	Semi-automatic key	RCVR (RX)	Receiver
B4	Before	REF	Refer to; referring to; reference
C	Yes (correct)	RFI	Radio frequency interference
CFM	Confirm; I confirm	RIG	Station equipment
CK	Check	RPT	Repeat; I repeat; report
CL	I am closing my station; call	RTTY	Radioteletype
CLD-CLG	Called; calling	RX	Receiver
CQ	Calling any station	SASE	Self-addressed, stamped envelope
CUD	Could	SED	Said
CUL	See you later	SIG	Signature; signal
CW	Continuous wave (i.e., radiotelegraph)	SINE	Operator's personal initials or nickname
DLD-DLVD	Delivered	SKED	Schedule
DR	Dear	SRI	Sorry
DX	Distance, foreign countries	SSB	Single sideband
ES	And, &	SVC	Service; prefix to service message
FB	Fine business, excellent	T	Zero (number)
FM	Frequency modulation	TFC	Traffic
GA	Go ahead (or resume sending)	TMW	Tomorrow
GB	Good-by	TNX-TKS	Thanks
GBA	Give better address	TT	That
GE	Good evening	TU	Thank you
GG	Going	TVI	Television interference
GM	Good morning	TX	Transmitter
GN	Good night	TXT	Text
GND	Ground	UR-URS	Your; you're; yours
GUD	Good	VFO	Variable-frequency oscillator
HI	The telegraphic laugh; high	VY	Very
HR	Here, hear	WA	Word after
HV	Have	WB	Word before
HW	How	WD-WDS	Word; words
LID	A poor operator	WKD-WKG	Worked; working
MA, MILS	Milliamperes	WL	Well; will
MSG	Message; prefix to radiogram	WUD	Would
N	No	WX	Weather
NCS	Net control station	XCVR	Transceiver
ND	Nothing doing	XMTR (TX)	Transmitter
NIL	Nothing; I have nothing for you	XTAL	Crystal
NM	No more	XYL (YF)	Wife
NR	Number	YL	Young lady
NW	Now; I resume transmission	73	Best regards
OB	Old boy	88	Love and kisses

in to join the contact, just K (*go ahead*) is sufficient.

Ending the QSO

When you decide to end the contact or the other ham expresses the desire to end it, don't keep talking. Briefly express your thanks for the contact: TNX QSO or TNX CHAT — and then sign off: 73 SK KA1JPA DE WB1ENT. If you are leaving the air, add CL (*closing*) to the end, right after your call sign.

These ending signals, which indicate to the casual listener the status of the contact, establish Amateur Radio as a cordial and fraternal hobby. At the same time they foster orderliness

and denote organization. These signals have no legal standing; FCC regulations say little about our internal procedures.

Conducting the Contact

Aside from signal strength, name, and location, it is customary to exchange power level and antenna. This information helps both stations assess conditions. Keep in mind that many hams will not know the characteristics of your *Loundenboomer 27A3* and your *Signal Squirter 4*. Therefore, you may be better off just saying that your rig runs 100 W output and the antenna is a trap dipole. Once these routine details are out of the way, you can proceed to discuss virtually anything appropriate and interesting.

DX Contacts

DX can be worked on any HF band as well as occasionally on 6 meters. When the 11-year solar sunspot cycle favors 10 meters, worldwide contacts on a daily basis are commonplace on this band. Ten meters is an outstanding DX band when conditions are right and you don't need to run a lot of transmitter power to take advantage of it! A particular advantage of 10 for DX work is that effective beam-type antennas tend to be small and light, making for relatively easy installation. For these reasons, 10 meters is a favorite of many DXers.

Keep in mind that while many overseas amateurs have an exceptional command of English, they may not be familiar with many of our colloquialisms. Because of the language differences, some DX stations are more comfortable with the barebones type contact and you should be sensitive to their preferences. In unsettled propagation conditions, it may be necessary to keep the whole contact short. The good operator takes these factors into account when expanding on a basic contact.

When the time comes to end the contact, end it. Thank the other operator (once) for the pleasure of the contact and say good-bye: "73, G4BUO this is N1OJS, Clear." This is all that is required. Unless the other amateur is a good friend, there is no need to start sending best wishes to everyone in the household including the family dog! Nor is this the time to start digging up extra comments on the contact that will require a "final final" from the other station (there may be other stations waiting to call in).

Also understand that during a band opening on 10 meters or on VHF, you should keep contacts brief so as many stations as possible can work the DX coming through during what may be a brief opportunity. Brevity is also expected when contacting a DXpedition operating from some exotic location for just a few days.

Bill, EI/N7OU, says that there's nothing better than working CW with a battery powered rig on the beach during his recent walking tour of Ireland! (*Paula Moore photo*)

In Pursuit of ... DX

"I'll never forget the thrill of my first DX contact. It was on 15 meters CW. I heard a G3 (a station in England) calling CQ, and no one answered right away so I decided to give it a try. Success! With a lump in my throat and sweat on my palms, I managed to complete my first DX QSO and become hopelessly hooked. DX is great!"

Many hams can tell a similar story. DX is Amateur Radio shorthand for *long distance*; furthermore, DX is universally understood by hams to be a station in a foreign country. Chasing DX is one of the most popular activities in our hobby. If you operate on the HF bands, you can get in on the fun!

You don't need a super kilowatt station and huge antennas. The beauty of DXing is that your operating skills can overcome deficiencies in your station equipment. Pick the right frequency band and the right time of day (or night) and the DX stations will be there — ready to talk to you.

Check the "How's DX?" column in *QST*. It contains tips on propagation and news of interest to DXers. And don't forget to subscribe or tune in to the weekly W1AW DX bulletin for the latest DX news. Good DX!

Additional Recommendations

Listen with care. It is very natural to answer the loudest station that calls, but sometimes you will have to dig deep into the noise and interference to hear the other station. Not all amateurs can run a kilowatt or a large, high antenna. DX stations are also typically weaker than closer stations.

Use VOX or push-to-talk (PTT). If you use VOX, don't defeat its purpose by saying "aaah" to keep the relay closed. If you use PTT, let go of the mike button every so often to make sure you are not "doubling" with the other station. Don't filibuster.

Talk at a constant level. Don't ride the mike gain. Try to maintain the same distance between your mouth and the microphone. Keep the mike gain down to eliminate background noise. Follow the manufacturer's instructions for use of the microphone. Some require close talking, while some need to be turned at an angle to the speaker's mouth.

Speech processing (often built into contemporary transceivers) is a mixed blessing. It can help you cut through the interference and static, but if too much is used, the audio quality suffers greatly. Tests should be made to determine the maximum level that can be used effectively, and this should be noted or marked on the control. Be ready to turn it down or off if it is not really required during a contact.

The speed of voice transmission (with perfect accuracy) depends almost entirely on the skill of the two operators concerned.

Fig 1-11 — The ARRL Log Book is adaptable to all types of operating.

DATE	FREQ.	MODE	POWER	TIME	STATION WORKED	REPORT SENT	REPORT REC'D	TIME OFF	COMMENTS (QTH / NAME / QSL VIA)	QSL S	QSL R
16 Nov	3.537	CW	100	1800	KA1E8V	589	479	1835	Manomet, MA John	✓	✓
	10.140	RTTY	100	2031	WB8IMY	599	579	2102	Wallingford, CT Steve		
	50.145	SSB	10	2316	N1OJS	56	55		FN33 short opening!	✓	
17 Nov	28.025	CW	500	1605	KC4AAA	469	559	1607	South Pole - big pileup	✓	
	28.380	SSB	"	1622	DJ6QT	59	59	1626	Walter - Running QRP + dipole		
	24.950	"	100	1712	9A1A	59	59		New one! F9YT	✓	✓
20 Nov	3.520	CW	1000	0316	ON4UN	599	569	0318	Belgium - John Excellent signal	✓	
	3.847	SSB	100	0336	KA0HJD	57	57	0357	Des Moines, IA Kristen		
	"	"	"	0336	W0SH	58	57	0357	Palm Bay, FL Gary collects old keys		
26 Nov	14.070	PSK	50	1316	KA1JPA	599	579	1328	CT Jodi New to PSK31	✓	
	18.148	SSB	100	1412	AB2E	55	55	1417	Darrell, looking for new states	✓	✓
	21.002	CW	1000	1516	EA8ZS	599	599	33	DX Contest		
	21.027			1518	S56A	599	599	15			

Speak at a rate that allows easy understanding as well as permitting the receiving operator to record the information, if necessary.

RECORDKEEPING

Although the FCC does not require that amateur stations document their operations except for certain specialized occurrences, you can still benefit by keeping an accurate log. The FCC requires that you record the type of antenna and gain of any antenna other than a dipole that you use on the 60 meter band. This can be recorded in your log or kept on file separately. The FCC will also assume that you were the control operator for all contacts made from your station unless your log (or some other record) indicates otherwise.

Your Station Log

A well-kept log will help you preserve your fondest ham radio memories for years. It will also serve as a bookkeeping system should you embark upon a quest for ham radio awards, or decide to expand your collection of QSL cards.

Many amateurs have decided to computerize their log keeping because of its flexibility and additional features. There are many excellent computer programs for Amateur Radio logging, including specialized programs for contests and other types of operation. For a selection of programs, check the ads in *QST* or try AC6V's directory Web site at **www.ac6v.com/logging.htm**.

For the purposes of illustration, this section will refer to *The ARRL Logbook*, on sale at your local radio bookstore or directly from ARRL HQ. Many hams still keep a log on paper and a logbook (see **Fig 1-11**) provides a good method for maintaining contact data at your fingertips.

The log entry should include:

1) The call sign of the station worked.

2) The date and time of the QSO. Always use UTC (Universal Coordinated Time, sometimes also called GMT or Zulu time) when entering the date and time. Use UTC whenever you need a time or date in your ham activities. The use of UTC helps all hams avoid confusion through conversion to local time. See the sidebar "UTC Explained" for details.

3) The frequency or frequency band on which the QSO took place.

4) The emission mode used to communicate.

5) Signal reports sent and received.

6) Any miscellaneous data, such as the other operator's name or QTH that you care to record.

The FCC has devised a rather elaborate system of emission designators, but for logging simplicity most hams use

Guest Operator

An FCC rules interpretation allows the person in physical control of an Amateur Radio station to use his or her own call sign when guest operating at another station. Of course, the guest operator is bound by the frequency privileges of his or her own operator's license, no matter what class of license the station licensee may hold. For example, Joan, KB6MOZ, a Technician, is visiting Stan, N6MP, an Amateur Extra licensee. Joan may use her own call sign at N6MP's station, but she must stay within the Technician subbands. If Joan wishes to operate using Amateur Extra privileges, she can sign N6MP but only if Stan acts as the control operator.

When a ham is operating from a club station, the club call is usually used. Again, the operator may never exceed the privileges of his or her own operator's license. The club station trustee and/or the club members may decide to allow individual amateurs to use their own call signs at the club station, but it is optional. In cases where it is desirable to retain the identity of the club station (W1AW at ARRL HQ, for example), the club may require amateurs to use the club call sign at all times.

In the rare instance where the guest operator at a club station holds a higher class of license than the club station trustee, the guest operator must use the club call sign and his/her own call sign. For example, Dave NN1N, who holds an Amateur Extra license visits the Norfolk Technician Radio Club station, KA4CVX. Because he wants to operate the club station outside the Tech subbands, Dave would sign KA4CVX/NN1N on CW and "KA4CVX, NN1N controlling" on phone. (Of course, this situation would prevail only if the club requires that their club call sign be used at all times.)

UTC Explained

Ever hear of Greenwich Mean Time? How about Coordinated Universal Time? Do you know if it is light or dark at 0400 hours? This is important in Amateur Radio, so if you answered no to any of these questions, read on!

Keeping track of time can be pretty confusing when you are talking to other hams around the world. Europe, for example, is anywhere from 4 to 11 hours ahead of us here in North America. There are literally *dozens* of time zones around the world! Mass confusion would occur if everyone used their own local time without some single common reference time.

24-hour Universal Time is used both in station logs and on QSL cards.

To solve the issue of standardizing clocks, the time at Greenwich, England on the Prime Meridian of longitude has been universally recognized as the standard time in all international affairs, including ham radio. This is Coordinated Universal Time (abbreviated UTC). (For many years it was called Greenwich Mean Time or GMT.) Longitude on the surface of the Earth is measured in degrees east or west of the Prime Meridian (zero degrees), that runs approximately through Greenwich, England and is halfway around the world from the International Date Line. Using UTC when communicating with other hams means that wherever you are, you and the station you contact will be able to reference a common date and time.

Twenty-four-hour time also avoids the equally confusing question about AM and PM. If you hear someone say that a contact was made at 0400 hours UTC, you will know immediately that this was 4 hours past midnight, UTC, since the new day always starts just after midnight. Likewise, a contact made at 1500 hours UTC was 15 hours past midnight, or 3 PM (15 − 12 = 3) UTC.

Maybe you have begun to figure it out: Each day starts at midnight, 0000 hours. Noon is 1200 hours, and the afternoon hours merely go on from there. You can think of it as adding 12 hours to the normal PM time (2 PM is 1400 hours, 9:30 PM is 2130 hours, and so on). However you learn it, be sure to use the time everyone else does — UTC — as in the chart below.

The photo shows a specially made clock, with an hour hand that goes around only once every day, instead of twice a day like a normal clock. Clocks with a digital readout that show time in a 24-hour format are quite popular as a station accessory.

UTC	EDT/AST	CDT/EST	MDT/CST	PDT/MST	PST
0000*	2000	1900	1800	1700	1600
0100	2100	2000	1900	1800	1700
0200	2200	2100	2000	1900	1800
0300	2300	2200	2100	2000	1900
0400	0000*	2300	2200	2100	2000
0500	0100	0000*	2300	2200	2100
0600	0200	0100	0000*	2300	2200
0700	0300	0200	0100	0000*	2300
0800	0400	0300	0200	0100	0000*
0900	0500	0400	0300	0200	0100
1000	0600	0500	0400	0300	0200
1100	0700	0600	0500	0400	0300
1200	0800	0700	0600	0500	0400
1300	0900	0800	0700	0600	0500
1400	1000	0900	0800	0700	0600
1500	1100	1000	0900	0800	0700
1600	1200	1100	1000	0900	0800
1700	1300	1200	1100	1000	0900
1800	1400	1300	1200	1100	1000
1900	1500	1400	1300	1200	1100
2000	1600	1500	1400	1300	1200
2100	1700	1600	1500	1400	1300
2200	1800	1700	1600	1500	1400
2300	1900	1800	1700	1600	1500
2400	2000	1900	1800	1700	1600

Time changes one hour with each change of 15 degrees in longitude. The five time zones in the US proper and Canada roughly follow these lines.

*0000 and 2400 are interchangeable. 2400 is associated with the date of the day ending, 0000 with the day just starting.

the following common abbreviations:

Abbreviation	Explanation
CW	telegraphy on pure continuous wave
MCW	tone-modulated telegraphy
SSB	single-sideband suppressed carrier
AM, DSB	double-sideband with full, reduced or suppressed carrier
FAX	facsimile
FM	frequency- or phase-modulated telephony
RTTY	radioteletype
PSK	PSK31 or similar mode
TV or SSTV	fast-scan television or slow-scan television

QSLing

The QSL card is the final courtesy of a QSO. It confirms specific details about your two-way contact with another ham. Whether you want the other station's QSL as a memento of an enjoyable QSO or for an operating award, it's wise to have your own QSL cards and know how to fill them out. That way, when you send your card to the other station, it will result in the desired outcome (a confirming card sent back to you). And you'll be ready to respond if the other operator wants a QSL from you. Some examples are shown in **Fig 1-12**.

Your QSL

Your QSL card makes a statement about you. It may also hang in ham radio shacks all over the world. So you will want to choose carefully the style of QSL that represents you and your station. There are many QSL vendors listed in the Ham Ads section of *QST* each month, and others can be found online with your favorite search engine. A nominal fee will bring you samples from which to choose or you may design and/or print your own style. The choice is up to you. See the accompanying sidebar for more information on QSLs.

Electronic QSLing

As of this writing in 2007, electronic QSLing — the paperless confirmation of contacts using computer systems — is catching on with more and more hams. As postage rates continue to rise, expect more QSLing to be done on-line. The ARRL's *Logbook of the World* system (**www.arrl.org/lotw**) currently stores more than 100 million contacts!

To use electronic QSLing systems, you'll need to store your log on your computer. The logging program then creates lists of your contacts and sends them to the QSLing system where they can be cross-referenced against other submitted contacts. The various QSLing systems all have their own security processes and not all of them are accepted by the many award sponsors, including the ARRL. Check to be sure your electronic contact confirmations will be accepted!

Other electronic systems accept QSO information from individual stations, then print and forward the paper QSLs at a price that is discounted from mailing separate cards. Look for QSLing practices to change dramatically during the time this edition is in print!

NOW GO MAKE SOME CONTACTS

That finishes our quick tour of operating procedures. Your knowledge will grow quickly with on-the-air experience. Enjoy

Fig 1-12 — QSL cards are a longstanding ham radio tradition. They're often personalized with artwork and information about station equipment, antennas or other interests.

the learning process. Ham radio is such a diverse activity that the learning process never stops — talk to most long-time hams, and they'll tell you there is always something new to learn!

QSLing — The Final Courtesy

QSL cards are a tradition in ham radio. Exchanging QSLs is fun, and they can serve as needed confirmations for many operating awards. Even though electronic QSLing systems are replacing the old-style printed cards, hams will probably continue to exchange them after an initial contact.

You'll probably want your own QSL cards, so look in *QST* or online for companies that sell them, or you may even want to make your own. Modern color printers and computer software make that easy. Your QSL should be attractive, yet straightforward. All necessary QSO information on one side of the card will make answering a QSL a relatively simple matter.

A good QSL card should be the standard 3.5 × 5.5-inch size (standard post card size) and should contain the following information, written in permanent blue or black ink that won't fade with time or in light:

1) *Your call.* If you were portable or mobile during the contact, this should be indicated on the card along with the actual location from which the contact was made.

2) *The geographical location of your station.* Again, portables/mobiles should indicate where they were during the contact. If your location counts specially for an award such as Islands On the Air, include that information. Show your county (or parish or borough, etc) and your four-character or six-character Maidenhead grid locator.

3) *The call of the station you worked.* This isn't as simple as it sounds. Errors are very common here. Make sure it is clear if the call contains the numeral 1 (one), capital I ("eye") or lower case l ("el").

4) *Date and time of the contact.* Use UTC for both and be sure to convert the time properly from local time, if that's how you keep your log. It is best to write out the date in words to avoid ambiguity. Use May 10, 1995 or 10 May 1995, rather than 5/10/95. Most DX stations will use 8-2-95 to mean February 8, 1995. The day is written before the month in many parts of the world.

5) *Frequency.* The band in wavelength (meters) or approximate frequency in kHz or MHz is required.

6) *Mode of operation.* Use accepted abbreviations, but be specific. CW, SSB, RTTY, PSK31 and AM are clear and acceptable. FCC emission designations

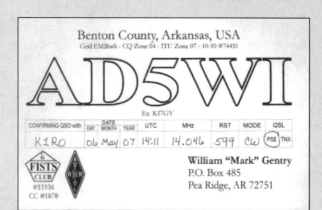

(J3E and so forth) are not always understood by DX stations.

7) *Signal report.* Use the RST system — 59, 569, and so on.

8) Leave no doubt the QSL is confirming a two-way contact by using language such as "confirming two-way QSO with" or "2 X" or "2-Way" before the other station's call.

Other items, such as your rig, antenna and so on, are optional but may hams like to include them.

If you make any errors filling out the QSL, destroy the card and start over. Do not make corrections or mark-overs on the card, as such cards are not acceptable for awards purposes.

For QSLing within the United States, you can find the other station's address from many online call sign servers. Some Web sites just publish information directly from the FCC's database, while others such as QRZ (www.qrz.com) allow users to customize and update information in their records. If you really need the other station's QSL card, perhaps for an operating award, it's a good idea to include a self-addressed, stamped envelope (SASE).

Now comes the problem of how to get your QSLs to the DX station. You can send QSL cards directly to the DX station or the DX station's QSL manager, making sure to include a self-addressed envelope and return postage.

Sending them directly can be expensive, so many amateurs use the ARRL's QSL Service. This is an outgoing service for ARRL members to send DX QSL cards to foreign countries at a minimum of cost and effort.

To receive QSL cards from DX (overseas) stations, the ARRL sponsors incoming QSL Bureaus, provided free for all amateurs throughout the United States and Canada. Each call area has its own bureau staffed totally by volunteers. To expedite the handling of your QSL cards (both incoming and outgoing), be sure to follow the bureau's requirements at all times.

See the DXing chapter for much more information about exchanging QSL cards with DX stations, either directly or through the QSL bureau.

Gary Pearce, KN4AQ

chapter 2

VHF/UHF — FM, Repeaters, Digital Voice and Data

For almost 40 years, FM has been a dominant mode of Amateur Radio operation. FM and repeaters fill the VHF and UHF bands, and most hams have at least one handheld or mobile FM radio. It wasn't always so, of course, and after decades of stability, change is creeping in again.

A BRIEF HISTORY

Until the late 1960s, the VHF and UHF Amateur Radio bands were mostly quiet, wide-open spaces. They were home to a relatively small number of highly skilled and dedicated operators who used high power CW and SSB with large antennas on tall towers to defy the phrase "line-of-sight" that is generally applied to communication on these frequencies. But this operation used just a small fraction of the 4-MHz-wide bands at 6 and 2 meters, and an even smaller fraction of the 30-MHz-wide 70-cm (420-450 MHz) band. A somewhat larger number of hams enjoyed low power, local operation with AM transceivers on 6 and 2 meters. But still, our spectrum was greatly underutilized, while public-safety and commercial VHF/UHF two-way operation, using FM and repeaters, was expanding rapidly.

The business band grew so rapidly in the early '60s that the FCC had to create new channels by cutting the existing channels in half. Almost overnight, a generation of tube-type, crystal-controlled FM equipment became obsolete and had to be replaced with radios that met the new channel requirements. Radios that had seen service in everything from police cars and taxicabs to cement trucks fell into the hands of hams for pennies on the original dollar. This equipment was designed to operate around 150 MHz and 450 MHz, just above the 2-meter and 70-cm ham bands. It was fairly easy to order new crystals and retune them to operate inside the ham bands. Hams who worked in the two-way radio industry led the way, retuning radios and building repeaters that extended coverage. Other hams quickly followed, attracted by the noise-free clarity of FM audio, the inexpensive equipment, and the chance to do something different. They began filling the fallow ground of our VHF and UHF bands.

That initial era didn't last long. The surplus commercial equipment was cheap, but it was physically large. All-tube radios

This classic mobile installation was shown in "Amateur FM and Repeaters" by Les Cobb, W6TEE, and Jay O'Brien, W6GDO, in October 1969 *QST*. The control head for the 2-meter FM transceiver is just to the right of the steering wheel, next to an HF mobile transceiver. In those days, the transceiver was usually a converted commercial tube-type monster mounted in the trunk. In the 1970s, solid-state amateur gear took over, with the entire radio fitting in the space needed for the old control heads. We've come full circle, with today's detachable faceplates and extension cables for mounting our mobile radios under the seat or in the trunk.

ran hot and consumed lots of power. And retuning the radios required skills and test equipment that the average ham didn't have. By the early 1970s, American and Japanese manufacturers recognized an untapped market and began building solid-state equipment specifically for the Amateur Radio FM market. The frequency-synthesizer, perfected in the mid-1970s, eliminated the need for crystals. The stage was set for this little boom to become the explosion that changed the face of Amateur Radio. Few hams today don't operate at least some VHF/UHF FM, and for many hams, FM *is* Amateur Radio. Manufacturers have added plenty of new features to equipment over the years, but the basic FM operating mode remained the same.

Going Digital

In the 1980s, ham radio experimenters added a new twist to FM: digital data. The personal computer was just catching on. One aspect of that — computer-to-computer communication — was in early development using telephone lines. Why not radio? VHF/UHF FM proved to be ideal for this use. Hams began modulating their FM radios with tones and adapted the telephone X.25 protocol to radio, calling it AX.25. They called the whole system *packet radio* (the data is sent in short bursts called packets), and both telephone-based and radio-based systems grew in parallel. Bulletin Boards (BBS) — central computers that allowed individuals to post and read files and text messages and send an early form of e-mail — were developed for both systems. The ham radio system was called PBBS for packet bulletin-board system. Both peaked in popularity in the mid-1990s. After that, the Internet's broader reach and ease-of-use ended the telephone-based bulletin-board system.

Packet radio survived. The ham radio PBBS system is a shell of what it was in the '90s, but one special interest, the *DX PacketCluster*, is hanging on. This is a special form of PBBS used by DXers for "spotting" DX stations (that's letting others know that a DX station is operating on a specific frequency… after you've worked them, of course). Another popular use for FM data is *APRS*, the *Automatic Packet Reporting System*, which is best known for sending GPS location information over the air so a ham's position can be pinpointed on a map. APRS is actually more than that — a tactical information system for quickly distributing text and data to a group of hams.

Going Even More Digital

At the start of the new century, anyone applying the term *digital* to Amateur Radio was almost certainly talking about text or files, but probably not real-time audio. That is changing. And anyone talking about worldwide ham radio communication was probably *not* talking about VHF/UHF FM. That is changing, too, and the changes are related.

Digitized audio has been popular since audio compact discs (CDs) were introduced in the 1980s. In the '90s, technology advanced enough to reduce the bandwidth needed for digital audio, especially voice, to be carried over the Internet and narrowband radio circuits. The first digital-voice public safety radio systems appeared, generically called APCO-25, and a variety of Internet voice systems for conferencing and telephone-like use were developed under the general heading VoIP (Voice over Internet Protocol).

When the first generation of APCO-25 radios got old enough to be replaced, hams took some of the surplus radios and put them on the ham bands, echoing the dawn of Amateur Radio FM in the '60s. Hams also adapted VoIP for use linking repeaters over the Internet with networks labeled IRLP, EchoLink, WIRES and eQSO. And the Japan Amateur Radio League (JARL) developed a true ham-radio standard called D-STAR, a networked VHF/UHF repeater system for digital voice (DV) and data that is beginning to make inroads around the world.

It will be decades, if ever, before DV supplants FM as the primary voice mode on VHF/UHF. But you will see it grow, and observe many similarities and a few differences in operation. VoIP is solidly entrenched in routine operation. Packet radio is hanging in there. Our VHF/UHF bands are busy places, indeed.

WHAT IS A REPEATER?

Let's take a few steps back and cover the basics. We'll start with FM voice repeaters, then move on to newer systems.

First, what exactly is a *repeater*? And why do we use one?

Without repeaters, the communication range between amateur VHF-FM mobile and handheld radios at ground level is limited — five to 15 miles for mobiles, and just a couple of miles for handhelds. The distance you can communicate is usually referred to as *line-of-sight* — you can talk about as far as you can see (if you cut down the trees). The higher the antenna, the greater the range, but for mobile and handheld use, higher antennas aren't practical.

To extend our range, we use repeaters. See **Fig 2-1**. A repeater is a specially designed receiver/transmitter combination. Repeater antennas are located on tall towers, buildings, or mountains, giving repeaters much greater range than radios with antennas near the ground. When you're in range of a repeater, you can talk to everyone else in range of that repeater.

When you operate through a repeater, its receiver picks up your signal on the *input* frequency, and the transmitter retransmits — or repeats — you on the *output* fre-

The most basic VHF FM hand-held transceivers can provide hours of enjoyment and utility in a variety of settings. They are the first step toward participation in the many activities described in this chapter.

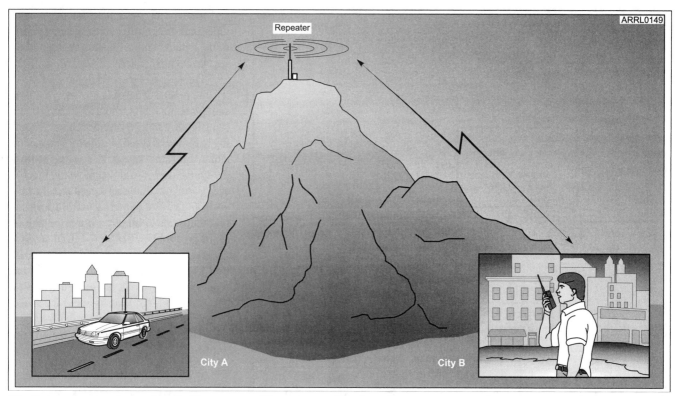

Fig 2-1 — A repeater extends the range of its users, allowing them to communicate over longer distances.

quency. The two frequencies a repeater uses are called a *repeater pair*, and the space between them is called the *offset*. Repeater pairs and offsets for each VHF/UHF band were standardized by the hams who developed repeaters in the 1970s, although there are some regional differences around the country.

Using a real-world example, one common 2-meter repeater pair is 146.34 and 146.94 MHz. In the shortcut language of FM, this would be called 34/94 (pronounced three-four, nine-four) or just simply 94 (nine-four). In this pair, 34 is the input frequency, and 94 is the output frequency. The offset for this and most 2-meter repeaters is 600 kHz, and nearly every radio manufactured for 2 meters since 1980 is pre-programmed for this offset. Given all the standards and the shortcut language, it's common to hear one ham tell another, "Meet me on the 94 repeater."

Repeater coverage depends on a variety of factors, but primary are antenna height, terrain and output power. Those three factors apply to the repeater, your station and the station you want to talk to. You have to factor all sides of this equation if you want to know how far you might be able to talk through a repeater. But it's not that complicated in practice.

Here's another real world example: level ground, a repeater antenna at 500 feet, and two mobiles running 50 W. Reliable coverage from such a system would extend about 30 miles from the repeater. "Fringe" coverage — distances where you can probably use the repeater but signals will be weak and may drop out — can extend another 20 miles or so. If one mobile is near the southern limit of the repeater's coverage area, and the other mobile is near the northern end, that could be almost 100 miles between them, *much* better than the five to 15 miles they could talk without a repeater.

Put that repeater on a mountaintop, and the coverage jumps to a radius of 100 miles or more — 200 miles between mobiles at opposite ends of the coverage area. Except that mountains usually come somewhat bunched together, and if you drive around the back side of the next mountain, it'll block your signal from the repeater.

Additional Features

Repeaters can have many features beyond just extending the range of mobile or handheld radios. One especially useful feature is called *autopatch* (automatic telephone patch). A telephone line and special control equipment at the repeater allow you to make local phone calls from your radio.

Now, autopatch is not exactly a replacement for a cellular phone. You can't use Amateur Radio — including autopatch — for your business. You can't receive calls, you can make only local calls, and your conversation is not private! Everybody else listening to the repeater hears your call. Still, autopatch is handy, within its limitations. Autopatch used to be a really big thing, until cell phones became cheap.

Other common repeater features include voice announcements of the time, club meetings and activities; a talking S-meter or voice recorder to let you know how well the repeater is hearing you; a NOAA weather receiver to rebroadcast storm alerts; and links to other repeaters via radio or the Internet, a topic we'll cover in more detail later.

Repeater Hardware

Check out **Fig 2-2**. Repeaters consist of the receiver and transmitter mentioned above, and a couple more special devices. One is a *controller* that routes the audio between the receiver

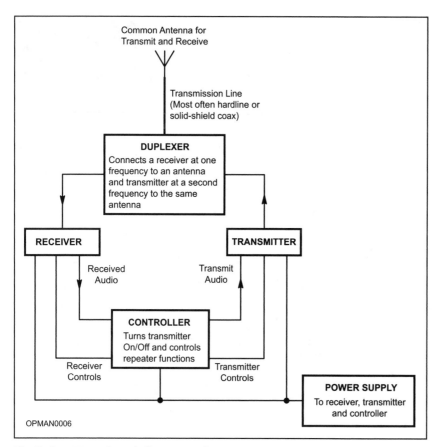

Fig 2-2 — Functional diagram of a repeater.

and transmitter, keys the transmitter, provides remote control for the repeater licensee or designated control operators, and all the special features listed above.

The second device is the *duplexer* that lets the repeater transmit and receive on the same antenna. Think about it — a high power transmitter and a sensitive receiver, operating in close proximity within the same band, using the same antenna! You might think the transmitter would just blow the receiver away. But the duplexer keeps the transmit energy out of the receiver with a series of tuned circuits. Without a duplexer, the receiver and transmitter would need separate antennas, and those antennas would need to be 100 or more feet apart on a tower. Some repeaters do just that, but most use duplexers. A 2-meter duplexer is about the size of a two-drawer filing cabinet.

Receiver, transmitter, controller, and duplexer: the basic components of most repeaters.

HOW DO YOU USE REPEATERS?

There are literally thousands of repeaters across the US (and the world). Each one

FM and Repeater-Speak

access code — one or more numbers or symbols that are keyed into the repeater with a telephone tone pad to activate a repeater function, such as an autopatch.

autopatch — a device that interfaces a repeater to the telephone system to permit repeater users to make telephone calls. Often just called the *patch*.

channel — the pair of frequencies (input and output) used by a repeater (example — the 94 machine would use the frequency pair 146.340 and 146.940).

channel step — the difference (in kHz) between FM channels. The common steps are 15 and 20 kHz for 2-meter repeaters, 20 kHz for 222 MHz repeaters, and 25 kHz for 440 MHz repeaters.

closed repeater — a repeater whose access is limited to a select group. (see open repeater).

control operator — the Amateur Radio operator who is designated to control the operation of the repeater, as required by FCC

regulations.

courtesy tone — an audible indication that a repeater user may go ahead and transmit.

coverage — the geographic area within which the repeater provides communications.

CTCSS — Continuous Tone Coded Squelch System. A system of subaudible tones which operate the squelch of a receiver when the corresponding subaudible tone is present on a transmitted signal.

crossband — communications to another frequency band by means of a link interfaced with the repeater.

DCS — Digital Coded Squelch. A newer version of CTCSS that uses a subaudible digital code instead of an analog tone to selectively open a receiver's squelch.

digipeater — digital repeater, a packet radio repeater.

duplex — a mode of communication in which you transmit on one frequency and receive on another frequency.

duplexer — a device that permits the use of one antenna for both

transmitting and receiving with minimal degradation to either incoming or outgoing signals.

frequency coordinator — an individual or group responsible for recommending channels for new repeaters with a minimum chance of interference to existing repeaters.

full duplex — a mode of communication in which you transmit and receive simultaneously.

full quieting — a received signal that contains no noise.

half duplex — a mode of communication in which you transmit at one time and receive at another time.

hand-held transceiver — a portable transceiver small enough to fit in the palm of your hand, clipped to your belt or even in a shirt pocket.

hang-time — the amount of time a basketball player remains airborne before dunking the ball. Or, the amount of time a repeater transmitter remains on the air after the user signal drops on the input. The courtesy tone beeps during the hang-time.

Repeater systems aren't designed for cosmetic appeal. This photo shows the repeater, controller and duplexer for a 2-meter repeater.

can have its own peculiarities and unique operating procedures, but there are some basics that apply to almost all of them. Any time you try to tell a ham how to operate a radio, you risk an argument. But then, that's what the *Operating Manual* is all about. So we'll take that risk, if you'll keep in mind that this is just a guide, and some people in some places might do it different!

Plain Old Talking

Mostly, you're here to get on the air and chat, right? So first you set your radio for the repeater you want to use. Don't know how to find a local repeater frequency? The *ARRL Repeater Directory* is great for that, and local hams can help, too. In most areas, somebody has posted a listing of local repeaters on a Web site. Just be aware that there are quite a few repeaters listed that are not actually on the air. Some may be down for maintenance, but many have been off for a long time. It's a problem nationwide. At the very least, you can just scan across the band for activity.

Once you've selected a repeater and dialed it up on your radio, the first thing you should do is... *listen* for a while.

First, listen to observe operating procedure. Don't assume everyone you hear is doing it right—you'll hear good procedure and bad. Over time you'll sort it out.

Second, and this applies every time you flip on the radio, listen for a while because repeaters are party lines. Lots of people use them on and off throughout the day, and the one you've selected may be busy with another conversation right

input frequency — the frequency of the repeater's receiver (and your transceiver's transmitter).

intermod — interference caused by spurious signals generated by intermodulation distortion in a receiver front end or transmitter power amplifier stage.

key up — to turn on a repeater by transmitting on its input frequency.

Li-Ion — Lithium-Ion battery. Longer life, smaller and lighter than Ni-Cd, Li-Ion batteries are becoming more popular for use with handheld radios.

LiTZ — Long Tone Zero (the *i* is added for pronunciation). An alert system that uses a DTMF tone pad-sent zero (0) keyed for at least three seconds to request emergency or urgent assistance.

machine — a repeater system (slang).

magnetic mount, mag-mount — an antenna with a magnetic base that permits quick installation and removal from a motor vehicle or other metal surface.

NiCd — a nickel-cadmium battery that may be recharged many times;

often used to power portable transceivers. Pronounced *NYE-cad*.

NiMH — nickel-metal-hydride battery; rechargeable, offers more capacity and lighter weight than an NiCd battery. Often used to power portable transceivers.

offset — the spacing between a repeater's input and output frequencies.

open repeater — a repeater whose access is not limited.

output frequency — the frequency of the repeater's transmitter (and your transceiver's receiver).

over — a word used to indicate the end of a voice transmission.

polarization — the plane an antenna system operates in; most repeaters are vertically polarized.

radio direction finding (RDF) — the art and science of locating a hidden transmitter.

Repeater Directory — an annual ARRL publication that lists repeaters in the US, Canada and other areas.

separation, split — the difference (in kHz) between a repeater's

transmitter and receiver frequencies. Also called *offset*. Repeaters that use unusual separations, such as 1 MHz on 2 meters, are sometimes said to have odd splits.

simplex — a mode of communication in which you transmit and receive on the same frequency.

squelch tail — the noise burst heard in a receiver that follows the end of an FM transmission.

time-out — to cause the repeater or a repeater function to turn off because you have transmitted for too long.

timer — a device that measures the length of each transmission and causes the repeater or a repeater function to turn off after a transmission has exceeded a certain length.

tone pad — an array of 12 or 16 numbered keys that generate the standard telephone dual-tone multifrequency (DTMF) dialing signals; resembles a standard telephone keypad.

Amateur Radio repeaters often share tower space with commercial, public-safety and broadcast systems. The ham repeater antenna is the four-loop array mounted off the left side of the tower.

line concept. Maybe somebody else wants to use the repeater when you're done. There's no hard rule. It depends on the time of day, and who else might want to use the repeater. Rush hours are prime time for mobiles, evening is also a busy time, while 2 AM is pretty empty. Some repeaters are busy all day, and some are rarely used. Learn the local procedures and rules set down by the repeater's sponsor.

For a long time, the conventional wisdom has been that repeaters are for mobiles, and base stations should stay off of them during drive-time. Ask the locals about that, too.

Three-Way Radio

Not all conversations are strictly two-way. Three, four or five or more hams can be part of a roundtable conversation (five or more will be pretty unwieldy). A freewheeling round-table is a lot of fun ... and it poses a problem: When the person transmitting now is done, who transmits next? Too often, the answer is everybody transmits next, and the result is a mess. The solution is simple. When you finish your transmission in the roundtable, specify who is to transmit next. "... Over to you, Rick. KN4AQ."

We Pause For Station Identification

The FCC rules say you must ID once every 10 minutes. Most repeater owners are big on clear identification when you use their repeaters, but you don't have to overdo it. Give your call sign when you first get on (this isn't required by the rules, but it's common practice), then once every 10 minutes, and again when you sign off. You don't have to give anyone else's call sign at any time, although sometimes it's a nice acknowledgment of the person you're talking to, like a handshake. (Actually, if you're handling third-party traffic through a foreign station, you do have to say that station's call sign when you sign off.)

Breaking In

Repeaters are shared resources — the party-line. There are many times and reasons that a conversation in progress might be interrupted. You might break in to join the group and add your comments on the subject at hand. Someone might break in on you to reach someone else who is listening to the repeater. You might have to report an emergency. How to break in is the subject of debate and disagreement. Here are some suggestions:

1) Pick a good time. If you have an emergency, a good time is *now*. That's why there's a pause between transmissions. Otherwise, listen a bit. Read the ebb and flow of the conversation. One of the fastest ways to establish a reputation as a jerk is to frequently butt your way onto the air without regard for the people already talking.

2) Give your call, and say what you want. When you've listened and decided it's okay to break in now, transmit quickly when one station stops, before the beep, and say something like this: "KN4AQ, can I make a short call?" or "KN4AQ, can I add my 2 cents?"

now. So listen first. (Does anyone remember what *party lines* are? Kids, ask your grandparents!)

If the repeater isn't busy, key your transmitter and say something like "This is KN4AQ, listening." (Use your own call, not mine, please). You could, I suppose, call CQ, the traditional method for generating a contact on HF. That never caught on with FM and repeaters, though, and someone will probably tell you not to do it. You certainly don't need a 30 second long CQ designed to attract the attention of hams tuning across the band. On a repeater, your audience is already there, waiting with squelched receivers. So if you want to start a trend or become notorious, say, "CQ, this is KN4AQ."

When you release your transmit button, most repeaters will stay on the air for a few seconds (called *hang time*), and many will send some kind of beep (a *courtesy tone*). Then, the repeater transmitter drops off the air. The beep is there to remind everyone to leave a pause between transmissions in case someone wants to break in. Even if there's no beep, leave a pause. Somebody may have just come across a traffic accident and needs the repeater to report it. If nobody leaves a pause between transmissions, they can't break in.

If somebody answers you, then have a good time! You can talk about anything you want — there are not many rules about the content of Amateur Radio conversation. You can't use ham radio to conduct your business, but you can talk about where you work and what you do. Prime time TV language has been peppered with some mild profanity. Let's discourage that. You're not having a private conversation — you may have lots of listeners, some of them children. Keep that in mind as you choose language and subject matter.

How long do you talk? I see you're catching on to the party-

3) What about saying "break?" The problem with the word "break" is that nobody knows exactly what it means, and everybody has to stop to find out. Some hams will tell you that "break" means "I just want to join in or make a call," and "break-break" means "I have very important traffic," and "break-break-break" means "I have a dire emergency." That's fine, but not everybody knows that. Plain English works better.

Maybe somebody's breaking in on you. What do you do? Easy — let them transmit, right now, unless you know absolutely and for sure that they do not have an emergency. Maybe somebody just says "break" or drops in their call, when what they really mean is "HELP!" So let them talk. Say "go ahead," and give your call sign. And if they're interrupting your perfectly good conversation for no reason but to hear themselves talk, well, bite your lip and be glad you know better.

The exception is when someone actually announces an emergency. Then CLEAR THE DECKS! DO NOT TRANSMIT except to turn the frequency over to them if they hesitate. The station that declared the emergency has the frequency, and unless they ask for your help, don't give it. Unless... always an unless... they obviously *don't* know how to handle the situation... and you *do*.

#$%~‡@&#+*!!

What was that I just heard? Foul language and nasty noises on the repeater? Jamming? Sounds like something straight out of CB! I'm *outraged*, and I'm gonna tell that sucker off! He can't get away with that on our repeater! Gimmie that microphone!

Cool down. It doesn't happen often, but it does happen. It's a big world out there, and there are some bad people in it. Some of them find a ham radio now and then, and discover the delight of offending an audience.

The key word is *audience*. Deliberate interference and bad language are designed to make you react. The person doing it wants to *hear* you get mad. They love it. And if they don't get it, they go away, usually quickly. So when you hear the rare nasty stuff on the repeater, please ignore it completely. Don't mention it at all on the air. Don't mention that you're not mentioning it. Sometimes a repeater control operator will decide that the best way to handle the situation is to turn off the repeater for a while, but the rest of us should be silent.

Making an Autopatch Call

An autopatch allows you to make local phone calls from your Amateur Radio transceiver, through that special control equipment and a telephone line connected to a repeater.

The autopatch may require an access code, much like a computer password, but sent in DTMF tones (Touch-Tones). Some repeaters have *open autopatch*, allowing anyone to use it. Their access code is often just a * (star). Other repeaters have *closed autopatch*. The patch codes are disclosed to members only, although usually members are encouraged to place calls for hams traveling through town.

The procedure for using an autopatch depends on the policy of the repeater's sponsor, and on the design and programming of the control system. You really need to get some local information from the club or repeater owner before proceeding. This is a basic guide to prepare you for what to expect:

First, make sure the repeater isn't busy. If you've just turned on your radio and don't want to wait a minute to see if the channel is active, you might ask "is this frequency in use? KN4AQ." If you have a clear channel, then here's what you do:

Identify yourself and your intentions: "KN4AQ autopatch." Then stop for a second, just in case the repeater wasn't really clear.

Key your transmitter again, then follow local procedure to dial the access code and the phone number. You may or may not hear the controller dial the call, but pretty soon you will hear the line ring.

The party you called says "hello," and you transmit and talk.

Most people on the telephone end get a little confused by autopatches until they've had some experience with them. When you are transmitting, they can't interrupt you, but they don't know that. You can reduce this problem by keeping your comments very short, and releasing your transmit button immediately after your last word.

Another common source of autopatch confusion is the Dead Phone Effect. When you transmit, some noise accompanies your voice on the phone line, even if you have a very good signal into the repeater. And when you stop transmitting, there's usually a little click or pop on the line, then it goes silent. The party on the line thinks the phone's gone dead. They will say "Hello? Hello? Are you still there?" or something like that. We enjoy it.

When you're done with the call, say good-bye, just like on a regular phone call, and let the party on the phone hang up. Then you hit the "kill code," which on many autopatches is the # button. And identify again, "KN4AQ, clear autopatch." Listen to make sure you successfully killed the patch (the repeater may talk to you, or beep, or just drop). Some repeater owners will ask for a bit more complex procedure, like identifying the person you were talking to.

Business calls on an Amateur Radio autopatch are a sensitive area. In September 1993, the FCC relaxed the rules on some business-type communication. You should get a copy of the rules and become familiar with all of them, but here we're specifically talking about §97.113, Prohibited Communications.

The FCC says you cannot use Amateur Radio for your business or employment, but now you can use Amateur Radio for personal communications that involve dealing with a business. The often-cited example is "using an autopatch to order a pizza" — in the past, this would have been illegal. Now, this kind of call is legal, but some repeater owners still prohibit all types of "business" traffic.

Join the Club

Repeaters and digital systems cost money for equipment, phone lines, power, rent and maintenance. If you use a repeater or digital system regularly, or just rely in it being there when you need it, join the club or donate to the group that maintains it. Money and expertise, or sometimes just muscle, are equally appreciated. Then do feel free to use any other open system now and then, knowing you've done your part.

DX!

Well, you probably won't be hearing Europe on 2-meter FM anytime soon (except via Internet linking), but VHF does have its own form of DX. Earlier we talked about a repeater that had about a 30-mile range. Usually. Sometimes, though, VHF/UHF "opens up," and stations can be heard for hundreds of miles. This weather-related phenomenon is a book-length subject. Just know that VHF/UHF band openings are a double-edged sword.

It's exciting to talk to someone 200 miles away, and it's okay, too. But keep in mind that repeaters were designed to cover local territory, not half the country. So when the band opens up, there is the potential for lots of interference as well as lots of fun. Repeaters on the same frequency, 120 miles apart, will suddenly seem too close together. You could very easily be keying up two or more of them at once, even from a handheld! To be responsible, get to know where your signal is going (the *ARRL Repeater Directory* will help). Use a directional antenna, minimum power and keep your conversation short.

Almost every repeater is ringed by co-channel neighbors — repeaters using the same frequency — between 100 and 200 miles away. You'll want to be sensitive to those neighbors as you decide how much power and antenna to use when talking on your local machine.

How much power is too much? Within the local coverage area of most repeaters, 5 W into a mobile antenna is all you need. Some mobile radios can do 50 W, and that's excessive until you reach the fringe. At home, with an antenna up on the roof, 50 W is *really* excessive for talking through a local repeater. When the band is open, even a 5 W mobile signal can travel to the neighboring co-channel repeater. At those times, patience and courtesy will help a lot.

SIMPLEX

You don't have to use a repeater to communicate on 2-meter FM! You can use simplex, which means your radio talking to my radio directly. We do have that five to 15 mile range — much more if we're using our home stations. So with that range, why not use simplex?

In the past, FM operators were advised to use simplex whenever they could, and reserve repeater use for those times when you were out of simplex range. Today there are plenty of repeaters, so that's not such an issue. Simplex offers its own challenges and rewards, so give it a try.

But don't just pick any old frequency your radio can generate to talk simplex! You may end up on the input of a repeater and interfere with people you can't hear. Use the Band Plan simplex channels shown in **Table 2-1**, beginning with 146.52 MHz, the national simplex channel.

WHAT BAND PLAN?

Yes, there is a plan organizing frequency use for 2 meters (and, for that matter, every Amateur Radio band). For the most part, band plans are voluntary. The FCC regulates only a few modes and band segments. Band plans for HF are international, and you'll find them on the ARRL Web site. The ARRL also has band plans for VHF/UHF, though these are subject to modification by state and regional frequency coordination groups. There's a lot more going on than FM and repeaters. The 2-meter

Table 2-1
Simplex Channels

Simplex channels in 15 kHz channel step areas*:	Simplex channels in 20 kHz channel step areas:
146.43	146.42
146.46	146.44
146.49	146.46
146.52 (National Simplex Channel)	146.48
145.55	146.50
146.58	146.52 (National Simplex Channel)
147.42	146.54
147.45	146.56
147.48	146.58
147.51	147.42
147.54	147.44
147.57	147.46
	147.48
	147.50
	147.52
	147.54
	147.56
	147.58

*This chart for the *15 kHz channel step areas* leaves out the "15 kHz" channels (for example, 146.445 between 146.43 and 146.46) for a good reason. You need physical separation of many miles between stations using 15 kHz channel steps to avoid interference. With repeaters, this physical separation is part of the coordination process. But simplex channel use is not coordinated, so to reduce interference, avoid using the "15 kHz" channels.

band has space for CW and SSB, beacons, packet, satellite operation and even EME (Earth-Moon-Earth) operation. See the sidebar, "Band Plans" for a look at how one regional group has made sense of 2 meters.

The complete 2-meter band plan is even more detailed than that list shows. The repeater input and output segments are divided into more than 100 individual channels for repeaters and simplex operation. This channelized operation is also voluntary, but FM and repeaters wouldn't work if hams followed the HF practice of operating on any empty frequency they wanted to use. We do not use channel numbers, though. We refer to each channel by frequency (146.94) or by a shortcut of the frequency as described earlier (just "nine-four").

The 2-meter band plan looks complex, perhaps even convoluted, doesn't it? That's because 2 meters grew in spurts, a little here, a little there. In the early 1960s, there was just a little AM and SSB activity clustered right above 145.0 MHz. FM and repeaters were barely getting started, around 146.94 MHz. The rest of the band was empty. FM began to grow, but it was constrained by FCC regulations that let Technician licensees use only 145.0 to 147.0 MHz. Satellites were launched, packet was invented, and rule changes moved Techs, repeaters and the legacy SSB/CW activity around the band. Everyone needed a slice of the pie, and the result is the band plan you see in the inset. When teaching a class, I say that 2 meters is carved up like a Halloween pumpkin.

To make things even more confusing, within the FM and repeater segments of 2 meters, there are two different channel steps: 15 kHz and 20 kHz. As shown in **Fig 2-3**, east of the Mississippi River, most states use 15 kHz steps for the repeater segment above 146 MHz, and 20 kHz steps below 146 MHz, for reasons discussed later. Many western states, along with Michigan and Alabama, use 20 kHz steps throughout the band. Look up your local plan in the *Repeater Directory*.

The 2-meter offset, though, is consistent nationwide at 600 kHz for almost every repeater. That offset is programmed in most radios sold today. Below 147.0 MHz, most repeater offsets are "negative" (the input frequency is the lower frequency), and above 147.0 MHz more offsets are "positive" (the input frequency is the higher frequency).

Channel Spacing

Why is channel spacing in some areas 15 kHz and others 20 kHz? The FM parameters we use today were originally designed for 30 kHz channels, and that's what we used in the early 1970s. But as FM and repeater use exploded, we were quickly running out of channels for new repeaters in the major metro areas. The easy choice was to cut the channel steps in half, to 15 kHz. The 30 kHz spacing was wasteful, but 15 kHz pinched a little too hard. Our FM signals really occupy about 16 kHz of spectrum, and our receivers are designed to separate signals pretty well at about 20 kHz. To make 15 kHz work, adjacent channel repeaters need to be some distance apart so their signal is weak in the territory of their adjacent channel neighbor. Most areas use about 50-mile separation. You may find circumstances in which you want to hear a repeater on one channel, but you get splatter from another repeater 15 kHz above or below it. You're probably about halfway between the two. Most of the time, though, the plan works well enough.

So what about 20 kHz? That came about with a rules change. Fearing that repeaters would overrun the entire 2-meter band, the FCC limited them to 146-148 MHz. The 15 kHz split took the pressure off for a little while, but soon all of those channels were used up, and the FCC opened the 144.5-145.5 MHz segment to repeaters (and gave the whole band to Technician licensees).

Repeater councils agreed that there were enough problems with the 15 kHz channel step arrangement that this new segment should use 20 kHz as the ideal channel spacing. After that, a group of states, beginning with Texas, saw logic in biting the bullet and going to 20 kHz across *both* repeater segments on 2 meters. They argued that even though that plan yielded fewer *total* channels, the flexibility gained by not having to separate adjacent-channel repeaters by 50 miles yielded more *usable* channels in metropolitan areas.

By this time most users were operating synthesized radios, so only the repeater owners had to buy crystals and retune duplexers. The plan was adopted in Texas and many other western states, and in Michigan and Alabama in the east. But the rest of the country decided not to follow. So we sit with two band plans to this day.

Band Plans

The term *band plan* refers to an agreement among concerned VHF and UHF operators and users about how each Amateur Radio band should be arranged. The goal of a band plan is to reduce interference between all the modes sharing each band. Aside from FM repeater and simplex activity, CW, SSB, AM, satellite, amateur television (ATV) and radio control operations also use these bands. (For example, a powerful FM signal at 144.080 MHz could spoil someone else's long-distance CW contact.) The VHF and UHF bands offer a wide variety of amateur activities, so hams have agreed to set aside space for each type.

When considering frequencies for use in conjunction with a proposed repeater, be certain both the input and output fall within subbands authorized for repeater use, and do not extend beyond the subband edges. FCC rules define frequencies available for repeater use.

Here is an example of the ARRL 2-meter band plan as modified for local use by SERA, the Southeastern Repeater Association, which is the recognized frequency coordinator in eight states. The band plan accommodates many different uses. Note that the band plan in your area may be different from this one. It's best to check with your local frequency coordinator if you have any questions.

Frequency (MHz)	Operation
144.000-144.050	EME CW
144.050-144.100	General CW Operation
144.100	CW National Calling Frequency
144.100-144.200	EME and Weak Signal SSB
144.200-144.300	General SSB Operation
144.200	SSB National Calling Frequency
144.275-144.300	Propagation Beacons
144.300-144.500	Multi-Mode Operation
144.390	APRS Nationwide
144.510-144.890	FM Repeater Inputs
144.910-145.090	FM Digital/Packet Simplex
145.110-145.490	FM Repeater Outputs
145.510-145.770	FM Digital/Packet Simplex
145.800-146.000	Satellite Sub-Band
146.010-146.505	FM Repeater Inputs
146.400-146.585	FM Voice Simplex and Alternate Repeater Inputs
146.520	FM National Calling Frequency
146.610-147.390	FM Repeater Outputs
147.405-147.585	FM Voice Simplex and Alternate Repeater Inputs
147.600-147.990	FM Repeater Inputs

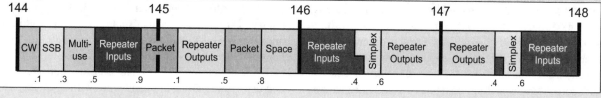

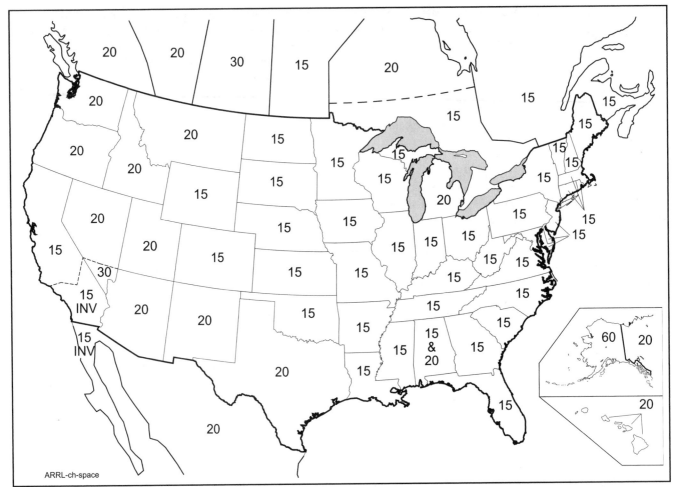

Fig 2-3 — This map shows 2-meter channel spacing in the US and southern Canada. Spacing is in kHz unless otherwise specified. Check with your regional frequency coordinator for more information.

The Name Game

Now, before describing the band plans for the other VHF/UHF bands, this is as good a place as any for a review of the irregular way we refer to our bands. "Six meters" and "2 meters" are usually referred to that way, by their approximate wavelength, and rarely by their frequency (50 and 144 MHz, respectively). The next two bands, "222" and "440," are most commonly referred to by frequency, and not by wavelength (1.25 meters and 70 centimeters, respectively). I'd wager that most hams don't even know that the 222 MHz band is also "one and a quarter meters." This inconsistent nomenclature is most likely just because it's easier to say "2 meters" and "440" — "70 centimeters" is a mouthful. And one more note: You'll hear most old-timers call the 222 MHz band just "220," the band's original lower limit before we lost the bottom 2 MHz in an FCC reallocation to business radio. We're still mad about that, and old habits die hard.

Now back to the band planning discussion.

The 440 MHz band is more regular, with all channel steps being 25 kHz (though some areas are in the process of dividing those in half — to 12.5 kHz — to make room for more repeaters). Everyone uses a 5 MHz offset, but in the early days, hams disagreed about which way to set the input and output frequencies, with some regions putting the repeater transmitter on the higher frequency (much of the northeast, and California), and

some regions putting it on the lower frequency (much of the south, midwest and west except for California). That difference persists today.

The band is huge, running from 420 to 450 MHz. FM and repeaters fill the top 10 MHz (that's why it's called "440"). CW and SSB take a small sliver at 432 MHz, and a satellite band takes a bit more. The bulk of the band is reserved for ATV (amateur television) that requires 6 MHz per channel.

Six meter FM also has regular channel steps — 20 kHz — but regional differences in offset, with some areas using 1 MHz and some using 500 kHz. Check your local listing. The 6-meter FM calling frequency is another aberration. At 52.525 MHz, it does not conform to the 20 kHz channel step plan.

The 222 MHz band is the most regular of all. That band was the last to be occupied by FM and repeaters, and it was planned after the other bands were hashed out or left in an "agree to disagree" state. It uses 20 kHz channel steps and a 1.6 MHz offset throughout the band, and throughout the country. The only areas of dispute are at the bottom of the band. When we lost the bottom 2 MHz in 1988, the band plan changed to accommodate CW and SSB operators on what had been repeater input channels. Not all of the repeaters that had been using that part of the band were willing or able to move to new frequencies.

HF Repeaters — Your DX Connection!

Imagine having a QSO with a station in Ecuador while you're on your way to work. Instead of a large HF rig under your dashboard, there is only a small transceiver that might easily be mistaken for a 2-meter FM unit at first glance. You're only running 10 or 20 W, yet the Ecuadorian station is giving you a 59 report. How is this possible?

Well, all the FM repeater action isn't confined to the VHF and UHF bands. There are a large handful of repeaters on 10-meters around the US and the world. "Wideband" FM is permitted only above 29.0 MHz, and there are four band-plan repeater channels (outputs are 29.62, 29.64, 29.66 and 29.68 MHz), plus the simplex channel 29.60 MHz. Repeaters on 10 meters use a 100 kHz offset, so the corresponding inputs are 29.52, 29.54, 29.56 and 29.58 MHz.

Repeater operation on 10 meters is a mixed blessing. Band openings have the potential for fun — you can key up a repeater thousands of miles away. That enjoyment is dampened by the interference generated when multiple repeaters are keyed up at the same time. The ARRL has a CTCSS plan to help reduce the problem, but not many repeater owners follow the plan, and too many leave their machines on "carrier access." Mostly what you'll hear on 10 meter FM are short, often frustrating contacts, ended by interference from other stations or repeaters. But there are enough "golden nugget" contacts to make the mode popular with a lot of hams.

Now, check out the frequency coverage of your shiny new 2-meter FM handheld. It covers the whole band, doesn't it? But if you use it any-old-where, you might interfere with someone — maybe an SSB operator, or a satellite station or a repeater input. Please stick to the band plan channels. If we all do that, we'll all get maximum use and enjoyment out of our bands.

FREQUENCY COORDINATION

The last step in band planning is frequency coordination. You've got all those repeaters, and all those channels, but who decides what repeater operates on what channel? That's the job of frequency coordinators. They range in size from individuals covering part of one state to large organizations covering multiple states. Someone wishing to put up a new repeater contacts their local frequency coordinator (listed in the *ARRL Repeater Directory*) to find out what frequency they can use that won't interfere with existing repeaters. That is, *if* there is an available frequency. In much of the country, all of the available 2-meter channels are occupied, and in the larger cities, all of the 440 band channels are occupied.

It is an ongoing struggle to find available channels for new repeaters, but it is being done. Use of tone squelch, described later, allows repeaters to be placed a little closer together. Old repeaters are sometimes taken off the air when the owner loses interest, and a new one can occupy the channel. And too many repeaters exist only "on paper" — in the *Repeater Directory*

and in the coordinator's database, but not actually on the air. When these repeaters are identified, they can be replaced by new systems.

Coordinators consider several parameters when they receive a request to coordinate a new repeater: distance to co-channel and adjacent-channel neighbors, antenna height, terrain and power. Repeaters can typically be located 75 to 125 miles apart on the same frequency, but particularly wide-coverage repeaters on mountaintops or tall towers need a little more separation. In areas that use 15 kHz channel steps, adjacent channel repeaters need about 50 miles between them. Repeaters on 20 kHz channel steps need less separation, and some areas require no geographic separation between repeaters on 20 kHz adjacent channels.

The new DV (digital voice) modes are creating a challenge for frequency coordinators. D-STAR in particular is growing quickly enough that coordinators are receiving requests for new repeater channels that they don't have. D-STAR provides an advantage in spectrum use. Its signal is narrower than analog FM, so more D-STAR repeaters would fit in a given amount of spectrum. That may help over time when channels can be realigned to place DV repeaters on adjacent channels. For now, most DV repeaters are just occupying conventional channels, and some analog repeater owners have converted to DV on their existing channels. A few DV repeaters are being experimentally squeezed in between analog repeaters, with some distance helping to prevent interference. APCO-25 digital repeaters now in use take up almost as much spectrum as analog FM. A new generation of P-25 radios will use about the same spectrum as D-STAR.

Frequency coordination is not *required* by the FCC, but the rules do says that if there is interference between repeaters, and one is not coordinated, the uncoordinated repeater "has primary responsibility to resolve the interference." FCC enforcement over the past decade has put some teeth into frequency coordination, and some uncoordinated repeaters have been taken off the air. The vast majority of repeaters are coordinated.

EMERGENCIES

Repeaters are excellent tools for emergency communication. That's why we leave a pause between transmissions — you never know when someone (you) will need the repeater in an emergency. Beyond local incidents, repeaters are in regular use by our Amateur Radio emergency organizations (ARES, RACES, SKYWARN and others) for training and during disasters.

ARRL Amateur Radio Emergency Service (ARES)

ARES is the Amateur Radio Emergency Service, sponsored by the ARRL. During any kind of emergency, ARES operators will be using repeaters for local coordination and passing traffic. During these operations, the active repeater will probably be closed to regular conversations. But unless a major disaster has hit the area, there will be other repeaters available for regular activity. Ask the net control station for the status of the repeater.

Radio Amateur Civil Emergency Service (RACES)

RACES is a parallel program under the control of Federal, state and local emergency managers. In many areas, hams have dual membership in RACES and ARES programs, and they are integrated and share the same leadership.

SKYWARN

We use repeaters to help the National Weather Service (NWS) in an operation called SKYWARN. Most areas of the country are covered by repeaters dedicated to SKYWARN during bad weather. When severe weather threatens your area, listen to your local SKYWARN repeater, and follow instructions from the net-control station. Weather spotter reports fill in what the NWS calls "ground truth" — the actual conditions on the ground that Doppler radar can't detect directly. Many NWS offices have Amateur Radio stations that are activated for direct reports during severe weather. SKYWARN is a program of the NWS, but in many areas the Amateur Radio component is run by the local ARES leadership.

Public Service Events

Hams across the country regularly help charitable organizations with communications during fundraising events like bike-a-thons, marathons, triathlons and walks. This activity can keep a repeater very busy, so it isn't compatible with other hams chatting on the same channel. During the event a repeater will again be closed to routine operation. If you need to make a call, ask the net control station and most likely you can use the repeater for a minute with no problem.

Nets

Repeaters are great places for nets, and there are lots of nets. A net, short for "network of stations," is an organized on-the-air activity. We've mentioned a few already, like SKYWARN and ARES, but there can be many other types: traffic nets, rag-chew nets, specialty topic nets, club information nets and more. When a net is active on a repeater, the repeater is closed to other activity. The net-control is in charge of the frequency, and all communication should be directed to that station first.

You might be a little nervous the first time you check into a net. Listen carefully to see how it works, and when the net control station calls for check-ins, tell them it's your first net. They'll take some extra time with you to help figure it out. Many new hams find that checking into a net is the *easiest* way to make their first contact.

GIVING DIRECTIONS

What's "giving directions" doing in a repeater operating guide? Just listen for a while, and you'll hear why. We give a lot of directions on repeaters, to locals in an unfamiliar part of town, and to traveling hams visiting the area. And, sad to say, too often we do it badly.

One person will give adequate directions, and someone else just has to break in to give his favorite shortcut. Or somebody gives a two-minute long string of street names and landmarks, non-stop. We literally fall all over each other trying to be too helpful!

If someone has given directions that will get the traveler to her destination, let it be. Make a correction only if the directions are dead wrong. If it's your turn to give the directions, keep them short and simple. And it might be helpful to find out where the mobile station is before telling him where to go!

LiTZ Operation and Wilderness Protocol

Mutual Assistance Procedures for VHF/UHF FM

One of the great features of Amateur Radio is it gives hams the ability to provide mutual assistance to one another. There are two common procedures currently in place for mutual assistance on VHF/UHF FM frequencies. The first is LiTZ, a DTMF (tone keypad) based all-call priority alerting system. The second is the Wilderness Protocol.

LiTZ (the *i* is added to make it easier to pronounce) is a simple method to indicate to others on an amateur VHF/UHF FM radio channel that you have an immediate need to communicate with someone, anyone, regarding a priority situation or condition.

LiTZ stands for Long Tone Zero. The LiTZ signal consists of transmitting DTMF zero for at least 3 seconds. After sending the LiTZ signal, the operator announces by voice the kind of assistance that is needed. For example:

(5-second-DTMF-zero) "This is KA7BCD."

"I'm on Interstate 5 between mileposts 154 and 155. There's a 3-car accident in the southbound lane. Traffic has been completely blocked. It looks like paramedics will be needed for victims. Please respond if you can contact authorities for help. This is KA7BCD."

If your situation does not involve safety of life or property, try giving a general voice call before using LiTZ. Use LiTZ only when your voice calls go un-answered or the people who respond can't help you.

When you see the notation LiTZ for a repeater in *The ARRL Repeater Directory*, that means it's highly likely that someone will receive and respond to LiTZ signals transmitted on the input frequency of the repeater. Please note, however, that if a CTCSS tone is needed to access that repeater you should transmit that CTCSS tone along with your LiTZ signal.

The type and nature of calls that justify the use of LiTZ may vary from repeater to repeater, just as other uses vary. Here are some general guidelines that may be suitable for most repeaters and simplex calling channels.

TIMERS

Almost all repeaters have something called *timers*. A timer is a clock in the controller that starts counting down when you begin to transmit through the repeater. Typically this clock starts from about three minutes, though some can be shorter. If you transmit continuously through the repeater past its timer length, the repeater will go off the air (we call it "timing out"). Repeater timers usually reset when you, the user, stop transmitting. If the repeater has a courtesy beep, the timer may reset when you hear the beep. So you have to keep your transmissions under the timer length, and always wait for the beep, to avoid being dumped by the repeater timer.

The three-minute timer is one way to comply with the FCC rules for stations being operated by remote control (most repeaters are remotely controlled). They are not designed as punitive measures for gabby hams... but come to think of it, given the party-line nature of repeaters, and the potential for

LiTZ Use Guidelines

Event/Situation	Waking Hours (0700-2200 LT)	Sleeping Hours (2200-0700 LT)
Calling CQ	no	no
Calling a buddy	no	no
Weekly Test of LiTZ	yes	no
Club Message	yes	no
Driving Directions	yes	no
Report Drunk Driver	yes	yes
Car Break Down	yes	yes
Safety Life or Prop	yes	yes

Wilderness Protocol

The Wilderness Protocol is a suggestion that those outside of repeater range should monitor standard simplex channels at specific times in case others have priority calls. The primary frequency is 146.52 MHz with 52.525, 223.5 446.0 and 1294.5 MHz serving as secondary frequencies.

This system was conceived to facilitate communications between hams that were hiking or backpacking in uninhabited areas, outside repeater range. However, the Wilderness Protocol should not be viewed as something just for hikers.

It can (and should) be used by everyone anywhere repeater coverage is unavailable. The protocol only becomes effective when many people use it.

The Wilderness Protocol recommends that those stations able to do so should monitor the primary (and secondary, if possible) frequency every three hours starting at 7 AM, local time, for 5 minutes (7:00-7:05 AM, 10:00-10:05 AM, . . . 10:00-10:05 PM, etc.).

Additionally, those stations that have sufficient power resources should monitor for 5 minutes starting at the top of every hour, or even continuously. Priority transmissions should begin with the LiTZ signal. CQ-like calls (to see who is out there) should not take place until four minutes after the hour.

that emergency traffic, it's a good idea to keep your brilliant monologues a bit shorter anyway. If you must ramble on, orator that you are, don't forget to let the timer reset, and check if somebody else needs the repeater, after a minute or two.

A common misconception is that timers keep repeater transmitters from overheating. Repeater transmitters are designed for continuous duty, and don't need the rest.

INTERFERENCE

Interference is an overused word in FM and repeaters. Hams call any sound they don't expect to hear "interference," but I'm particularly referring to the sound of hams talking on your repeater's co-channel neighbor 100 miles away during a band opening. Unless that's preventing you from communicating, and you were using the frequency first, that's not interference.

But given that the hallmark of FM is silence when a desired signal is not present, any extraneous noise is at least unpleasant.

Radio Direction Finding

Radio direction finding (RDF), also known as foxhunting, rabbit hunting and hidden-transmitter hunting, has become a very popular type of VHF/UHF FM radiosport.

Here's how the scene plays out — You and the ham club folks are sitting around the local diner on a seasonable Sunday evening. After coffee, someone suggests a rabbit hunt might be fun. Excitement begins to grow, all the old hands dash off for their special DF antennas and black boxes as someone is elected to be the rabbit. The rabbit then hides a transmitter in the woods, a park or other inconspicuous place. For this purpose the transmitter can simply be a small self-contained unit set to transmit a signal at appropriate intervals, or it might be you in your car with the PTT button in your hot little hand.

After an appropriate time interval, the others in the hunt (equipped with their direction-finding equipment), go out to try to be the first to find the hidden transmitter. It can take minutes, or it can last until the rabbit is asked to identify the awesome place he or she located to hide! Foxhunting is great entertainment (and just as often keenly challenging team competition) at hamfests and club outings.

RDF also has a serious side. The FCC uses highly sophisticated DF equipment to track illegal signals to their source. Repeater operators can, and do, make use of the skilled DF and foxhunting folks on occasion to track down repeater jammers and unlicensed intruders. DF skills can also be handy for tracking down stolen transceivers that suddenly pop up on the air, obviously being operated by people who are not familiar with normal Amateur Radio operating procedures.

Locating a hidden transmitter is an art form and, like any other art, takes a great deal of practice to perfect. Homebrew DF antennas and equipment are both inexpensive and relatively easy to construct. So, next time you have the opportunity to participate in a foxhunt, take advantage of it to hone your direction-finding skills for the real thing.

Specialized direction finding equipment makes it much easier to locate sources of interference. "Foxhunts" are good practice for the day that you need to hunt down a signal that's interfering with your repeater.

There are several sources, and a few solutions.

One source is the neighboring repeater. You may hear that repeater, or its users may key up your repeater, especially during a band opening.

Another common source of noise is "intermod," short for intermodulation. That happens when two or more signals that are off your listening frequency mix and create a new signal (a *mixing product*) that is on the channel you've tuned to. Mixing is a fundamental principle of radio, but in this case it's working against you, not for you. The source of the signals could be strong nearby transmitters, in or out of the ham band (pager transmitters are often involved, because they run high power, are on the air a lot, and are modulated with annoying *beeeep booop braaaap* tones).

The culprit doing the mixing is likely your receiver. Some receivers are better at rejecting mixing products than others, and *QST* product reviews give specs on that.

Finally, the explosion of computer and other consumer electronics has filled the spectrum with weak signals. They don't carry far, but they're all around you — in your house, your neighbor's house and nearby businesses.

Solutions? For intermod, an external filter in your antenna line will help by keeping the offending signal from reaching your receiver. There are two types, *bandpass* and *notch*. A bandpass filter lets in only the ham band, and keeps the pagers and police dispatchers out. Most ham FM radios are designed to let you listen to the business and public safety bands (including the NOAA weather transmitters at 162 MHz). A bandpass filter will take all that out. A notch filter will eliminate just a small slice of spectrum, usually the pager frequencies since they're a prime source. If that does the job, then you can listen to your repeater and still hear the cops chase the robbers, without the noise of intermod.

Consumer electronics must be filtered at the source, and you'll need to consult a specialized reference like *The ARRL RFI Book* for the details. Some of it can't be eliminated, and the section on coded squelch, next, might provide workable solution.

So we're back to that neighboring repeater. Frequency coordination pushed it as far away as practical. Some repeater owners feel they're entitled to a clear frequency — after all, they're coordinated. That's not possible any more, given the number of repeaters on the air. Ham repeaters, like their business and public-safety band neighbors, are increasingly turning to coded squelch to let everyone live together in peace.

CODED SQUELCH

Squelch is the circuit in FM radios that turns off the loud rush of noise that you would hear when there is no signal on the channel you're listening to. Most of the time, hams use *noise squelch*, also called *carrier squelch*, a squelch circuit that lets any signal at all come through. But there

Table 2-2
CTCSS Tone Frequencies
The purpose of CTCSS is to reduce cochannel interference during band openings. CTCSS-equipped repeaters and receivers respond only to signals transmitted with the required CTCSS tone. These receivers do not respond to signals on their inputs that lack the correct tone. The standard ANSI/EIA frequencies (in Hz) are as follows:

67.0	103.5	159.8	199.5
69.3	107.2	162.2	203.5
71.9	110.9	165.5	206.5
74.4	114.8	167.9	210.7
77.0	118.8	171.3	218.1
79.7	123.0	173.8	225.7
82.5	127.3	177.3	229.1
85.4	131.8	179.9	233.6
88.5	136.5	183.5	241.8
91.5	141.3	186.2	250.3
94.8	146.2	189.9	254.1
97.4	151.4	192.8	
100.0	156.7	196.6	

are ways to be more selective about what signal gets to your speaker or keys up your repeater. That's generically known as *coded squelch*, and more than half of the repeaters on the air require you to send coded squelch to be able to use the repeater. See **Fig 2-4**.

CTCSS

The most common form of coded squelch has the generic name *CTCSS* (Continuous Tone Coded Squelch System), but is better know by Motorola's trade name PL (Private Line), or just the nickname "tone." It adds a "subaudible" tone to your transmitted audio, one of 50 very specific frequencies between 67 and 254 Hz (see **Table 2-2**). Yes, humans can hear these frequencies quite well, so they're *sub*audible only because your receiver's audio circuit is supposed to filter them out. A receiver with CTCSS will remain silent to all traffic on a channel unless the transmitting station is sending the correct tone. Then the receiver sends the transmitted audio to its speaker.

In commercial radio service, this allows Jane's Taxi Company and Bob's Towing Service to use the same channel without having to listen to each other's traffic. In Amateur Radio, some repeaters require users to send the correct CTCSS tone to use the repeater. This may mean the repeater is *closed*, for use only by members, but more likely it is simply being used to avoid being keyed up by users of their co-channel neighbor 100 miles away. Most radios built since the early 1980s have a CTCSS encoder built in, and most radios built since the early '90s also have a CTCSS *decoder* built in.

If your local repeater sends a CTCSS tone, you can use your de-

Fig 2-4 — Setting squelch codes in a Kenwood TH-F6 Handheld. (A, left) shows the menu for setting a CTCSS code, while (B) shows setting a DCS code. With most radios, selecting DCS sets the radio in encode and decode mode, while CTCSS allows an encode-only mode, or encode-decode.

coder to monitor just that repeater, and avoid hearing the co-channel neighbor, intermod or the annoying fizzes of nearby consumer electronics.

DCS

A newer form of coded squelch is called *DCS* (Digital-Coded Squelch). DCS appeared in commercial service because CTCSS didn't provide enough tones to keep everyone out of each other's hair, so DCS adds another hundred or so code options. DCS started showing up in ham radios a few years ago. It's safe to say that few open repeaters (repeaters open to any and all users) use DCS, since many radios don't have it. It will be years, if ever, before DCS is in routine ham radio use, but there will certainly be specialized uses.

Don't confuse DCS with the new DV digital voice modes. DCS is added to ordinary analog FM voice — it doesn't make the voice signal digital in any way.

DTMF

DTMF (Dual Tone Multi Frequency) can also be used as a form of squelch, to turn a receiver on, though it's more often used to control various functions like autopatch and talking S-meters. Some repeaters that require CTCSS have a DTMF "override" that puts the repeater into carrier-squelch mode for a few minutes if you send the proper digits.

Tone Trouble

Coded squelch is useful in reducing the problems with unwanted signals, but it introduces some new problems. One is education. You have to teach your user community about the tone. Most hams get it pretty quickly these days, but there are a few who need a lot of hand-holding, or are just resistant to change. Repeater tone requirements are listed in the *ARRL Repeater Directory*, so they're not hard to find.

Travelers, though, have a big problem with tone. Say you're on the road away from home, scanning the band for activity. The radio stops on an active repeater, but you can't key it up because it requires CTCSS, and you don't know the tone frequency. You can look it up in the *Repeater Directory* — but that's not a good idea for a solo driver.

Newer radios have a "tone scan" feature that will hunt the tone, *if* the repeater is sending tone. Most repeaters that require tone also transmit their tone, but they don't have to. Some radios make it easy to scan for tone, and some bury the function several layers deep in menus — again not a safe activity for a solo driver. Some helpful repeaters announce their tone along with their voice ID. In some areas of the country, most of the repeaters use the same tone, so if you know one, you know them all.

The best idea is to plan your trip in advance, and look up the repeater frequencies and tones you'll encounter along the way. Then program them into your radio's memories. The ARRL's *TravelPlus* CD-ROM repeater database makes this easier. And most newer radios can be programmed by computer with special software and an interface cable. It still takes some time, but these tools make radio operation on the road a lot easier and more fun.

LINKED REPEATERS

Most repeaters are standalone devices, providing their individual pool of coverage and that's it. But a significant number of repeaters are linked — connected to one or more other repeaters. Those other repeaters can be on other bands at the same location, or they can be in other locations, or both. This lets users communicate between different bands and across wider geographic areas than they can on a single repeater.

There are many ways to link repeaters. Two-meter and 440 repeaters on the same tower can just be wired together, or they may even share the same controller. Repeaters within a hundred miles or so of each other can use a radio link — separate link transmitters and receivers at each repeater, with antennas pointed at each other. Repeaters farther apart can "daisy-chain" their links to cover even wider territory. There are a few linked repeater systems in the country that cover multiple states with dozens of repeaters, but most radio-linked repeater systems have more modest ambitions, covering just part of one or two states.

VoIP and the Internet, introduced earlier, have taken repeater linking to a new level, creating the ability to tie repeaters together around the world and in nearly unlimited number. **Fig 2-6** shows one example. We'll talk more about Internet linking shortly.

There are several ways linked repeaters can be operated, coming under the categories of *full-time* and *on demand*. Full-time linked repeaters operate just as the name implies — all the repeaters in a linked network are connected all the time. If you key up one of them, you're heard on all of them, and you can talk to anyone on any of the other repeaters on the network at any time. You don't have to do anything special to activate the network, since it's always there.

In an on-demand system, the linked repeaters remain iso-

Fig 2-5 — The hardware controller at the heart of the Yaesu WIRES-II system.

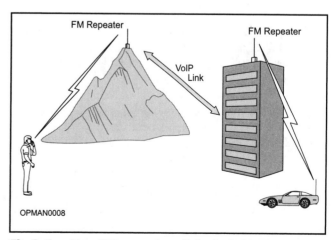

Fig 2-6 — Two FM repeaters linked via VoIP.

Is It Legal?

By Brennan Price, N4QX and
ARRL General Counsel Chris Imlay, W3KD

What Part 97 regulations govern VoIP-assisted Amateur Radio?

All of them or none of them, depending on whether you're asking about the "VoIP-assisted" or the "Amateur Radio" part of VoIP-assisted Amateur Radio.

Many callers to the ARRL's Regulatory Information Branch over the last few years have focused on the novelty of the Internet when asking questions about the legal uses of certain systems. Such focus is misdirected. Part 97 does not regulate systems; it regulates stations. The Commission doesn't care what a ham has feeding his or her station; it cares that the *station* — not the Internet, but the *station* — is properly operated. And all the rules that apply to any Amateur Radio station apply to one that retransmits audio fed to it by VoIP.

Fine, so the Commission doesn't care about the VoIP part. Are there any particular rules a ham considering such an operation should be aware of?

The obvious answer is *all of them*, but we'll focus on a few that are easy to overlook, particularly for stand-alone, single channel operations. The main points to remember:

- All stations must be controlled.
- Only certain types of stations may be automatically controlled.
- Simplex voice operations do not qualify for automatic control.
- Any station that is remotely controlled via radio must utilize an auxiliary station to execute said control, and auxiliary stations are restricted in frequency.

It's not as hard as it sounds. All you have to do is think about the type of station you're operating and how it's controlled. Let's look at a few examples.

Two automatically controlled repeaters are linked via VoIP. Is this legal?

Forget the VoIP linking, because that's the Internet. We're talking about two repeaters. Are repeaters legal? Yes. May repeaters be automatically controlled? Yes. There is no difference between this setup and two repeaters linked by another wired mechanism or by auxiliary stations. Assuming the two linked stations are repeaters, it is difficult to conceive of a situation where a VoIP link would not pass regulatory muster. The only caveat is that the VoIP software must prevent nonhams from accessing the repeaters from the Internet. The key here is to avoid any configuration that would (1) permit a nonham to key an amateur transmitter without the presence of a control operator, and (2) prevent the initiation by a nonham of a message via an Amateur Station without the presence of a control operator.

Is it permitted to enable *automatically controlled* simplex nodes?

No. Only certain types of Amateur Radio stations may be operated unattended, under *automatic control*. This means that there is no human control either at the station location or at a distance. These types of stations are space stations, repeaters, beacons, auxiliary stations and certain types of stations transmitting RTTY or data emissions.

Simplex VoIP nodes are neither repeaters, beacons nor auxiliary stations. Presumably, most are within 50 kilometers of the Earth's surface and are therefore not space stations. The VoIP technology implies a voice transmission, not RTTY or data. Therefore, none of the stations that qualify for automatic control describe a simplex VoIP node, and such a station must be locally or remotely controlled (as *any* Amateur Radio station is allowed to be).

Locally or remotely controlled—what does that mean?

A simplex VoIP node may be locally controlled by an operator who is present at the node. Such a node may also be *remotely controlled* at some other point, with the operator issuing commands via a wireline or radio control link. If a radio control link is used, it must utilize an auxiliary station. Auxiliary stations may operate only on frequencies in the 2-meter band or higher, with the exception of these specific segments: 144.0-144.5, 145.8-146.0, 219-220, 222.00-222.15, 431-433 and 435-438 MHz. It's this *remotely controlled* aspect that allows VoIP simplex nodes to operate legally — as long as they are on the right bands.

Let's consider some scenarios:

- A control operator is stationed and active at the VoIP node on any frequency. This is a locally controlled station, not at all unlike a typical operation on FM simplex. This is legal.
- A control operator communicates with and controls a simplex VoIP node with a handheld, transmitting and listening to the node on 223.52 MHz. This is wireless remote control. Such control must be executed by an auxiliary station and 223.52 MHz is an allowed frequency for such a station. This is legal.
- A control operator operates a simplex VoIP node at 147.42 MHz and is stationed at the node's transmitter. User stations access the node on the same frequency. This is legal. The VoIP node is being locally controlled, and any station may be locally controlled.
- A control operator operates a simplex VoIP node at 147.42 MHz. The control operator continually monitors the node's transmissions and can call a dedicated telephone line or use a dedicated Internet connection to turn the node on and off. User stations access the node on the same frequency. This is legal. The VoIP node is being remotely controlled via a wireline connection, and any station may be controlled in this manner.
- A control operator communicates with and controls a simplex VoIP node with a multiband handheld, transmitting to and continuously monitoring the node on 147.42 MHz. He or she sends power on/off commands with the same handheld, also on 147.42 MHz. This is wireless remote control. Such control must be executed by an auxiliary station, and 147.42 MHz is an allowed frequency for such a station. This is legal. The VoIP node is being remotely controlled via an auxiliary station of appropriate frequency, and any station may be controlled in this manner.
- Same configuration as either of the above two situations, except the control operator does not continuously monitor the VoIP node's transmissions. This operation is *not* legal. When a simplex VoIP node is enabled, it must be continually attended, either locally or remotely. A simplex VoIP node is no different than other FM simplex operations, and such operations may not be automatically controlled.

lated unless you take some action, usually by sending a code by DTMF digits, to connect them. Your DTMF sequence may activate all the repeaters on the network, or the system may let you address just one specific repeater, somewhat like dialing a telephone. When you're finished, another DTMF code drops the link, or a timer may handle that chore when the repeaters are no longer in use.

INTERNET LINKING

The Internet has expanded repeater linking exponentially, making worldwide communication through a local repeater commonplace. There are four Internet linking systems in common use. Two of them, IRLP and EchoLink, have reached critical mass in the US and are available almost everywhere.

Internet Radio Linking Project (IRLP)

IRLP is the most "radio" based linking system. User access is only via radio, using either simplex stations or repeaters, while linking is done using VoIP on the Internet. An IRLP system operator establishes a *node* by interfacing his radio equipment to a *Linux* based computer with an Internet connection, and then running IRLP software. Once that's set up, repeater users send DTMF tones to make connections, either directly to other individual repeater or simplex nodes (**Fig 2-7**), or to *reflectors* — servers that tie multiple nodes together as one big party line.

The direct connections work like on-demand linked repeaters. You dial in the node number you want to connect to (some systems have you add an access code first), and you are connected to the distant repeater (or simplex node, but repeaters greatly outnumber simplex nodes). Once connected, everyone on both ends can communicate. When you're finished, you usually take the link down with another DTMF sequence. Someone from a distant repeater can make a connection to you as well. Most nodes have a voice announcement that confirms the connection, and sometimes boasts a bit about the local system.

Reflectors work like a hybrid between on-demand and full-time linked repeaters. You can connect your local repeater to a reflector and leave it there all day, or you can connect for a

special purpose (like a net), and drop it when the event is over. Some reflectors are popular, busy places to connect and hear the world. Some are used for special events like weather nets, and some just wait quietly for a connection.

If you have an underutilized repeater in your area, connecting it to a busy IRLP reflector will bring it to life during much of the day.

At press time there were a little over 1000 IRLP nodes online and working worldwide. There were 22 reflectors operating, each of which has 10 independent "channels," so essentially 220 reflector paths available. You can fine more information at **www.irlp.net**.

EchoLink

EchoLink is the 800 pound gorilla of Internet linking, with more than 3600 users worldwide actively connected at press time, and tens of thousands more who could connect but are offline at the moment. EchoLink allows repeater connections like IRLP, and has Conference Servers, similar to IRLP reflectors that permit multiple connections. The big difference, and the reason EchoLink is so much bigger, is that it allows individuals to connect to the network from their computers. You can download EchoLink client software (for *Windows*), register yourself, and then connect to any repeater, individual or conference. Many of your connections won't go over the air at all, but proof of a ham license is required to register, so you'll be talking only to other hams.

The EchoLink conference servers all have more or less specific functions. Some are just regional gathering places (Tennessee, Tokyo, Eastern Utah), while some are topic or activity based (SKYWARN and National Hurricane Center Nets, Jamboree on the Air, Boring Technical Talk).

To use EchoLink with a computer, you need a sound card, a headset (or a microphone and speakers), and an Internet connection. EchoLink will work with a good dial-up connection, but broadband is better. The software presents you with a list of every "station" on the system (a bit overwhelming), and each Conference. You double-click on a station to connect, and push your spacebar to talk. Your initial setup will include getting audio levels set correctly, and, if you use a router with a firewall, you'll need to open some ports to allow the outbound EchoLink connection to pass through. Software and instructions are provided on the **www.echolink.org** Web site.

You can connect your EchoLink-enabled computer to your base station radio fairly easily through a sound card, and create an on-air node. If you do, pick your frequencies carefully. Don't pipe EchoLink to a local repeater without permission from the repeater owner. Watch your power output level — your base station isn't meant for continuous duty, but a busy EchoLink connection could have it transmitting a lot. And if you decide to create a full-time link from a computer to a repeater, consider using a dedicated UHF link frequency rather than just a base station on the repeater input. Same goes for IRLP connections.

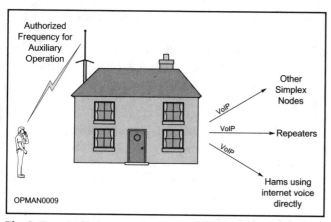

Fig 2-7 — A diagram of a VoIP simplex node. If a control operator is not physically present at the station location and the node is functioning with wireless remote control, the control link must follow the rules for *auxiliary* operation. See the sidebar, "Is It Legal?".

Other Systems

The two other Internet linking systems, WIRES-II and eQSO have not reached many US repeaters. WIRES-II sponsored by Yaesu, has a few US nodes, but many more in Japan. Like IRLP, it is an "all radio" system. **Fig 2-5** shows a WIRES-II hardware controller. eQSO is more popular in Europe and Asia, but in my brief survey, most of the nodes listed were off. Like EchoLink, it permits individual computer connections. It is the only system with provisions for non-hams ("SWL mode"). You can investigate them at **www.yaesu.com** and **www.eqso.net**.

Internet linking on both IRLP and EchoLink have become popular for emergency communications, with repeaters tied together for ARES and SKYWARN activity. The National Hurricane Center has been using both systems to take reports from hams as hurricanes approach landfall, and hams have been enthusiastic about participation. Of course, the Internet is infrastructure dependent, and both power and Internet access tend to disappear when storms reach their peak. Not surprisingly, stations along the coast also tend to disappear from the nets as Internet connections are lost. But in many cases Internet linking does provide another valuable tool in the emergency communications toolbox.

In the early days of Internet linking, some hams questioned whether or not it was really "ham radio." While some curmudgeons may still doubt it, the answer has come back a resounding "yes."

CROSSBAND REPEAT

Dual-band mobile radios — radios that cover two ham bands, usually 2 meters and 70 cm — are often designed to be mini-repeaters. Yes, you can run a little repeater right out of your car! This can be helpful if you want to operate a handheld radio, but need the oomph of a mobile radio to reach a distant repeater. For example, you're on the lower level of the mall with your handheld. You can't reach the local repeater from down there, but you can reach your car in the parking lot. With a crossband repeater in your car, you can relay your signal from the mall to the main repeater.

Crossband repeat operation in most mobile radios is very simple. See **Fig 2-8** for a typical example. When the crossband function is turned on, anything the radio hears on one band is retransmitted on the other. When the signal stops, the radio

goes into receive on both bands and waits for the next signal, on either band, to repeat. So down in the mall, you transmit on UHF. Your mobile hears you on its UHF receiver, and repeats you to the main repeater on 2 meters using its VHF transmitter. When you stop, it begins hearing the main repeater on VHF, flips itself around and repeats the main repeater back to you using its UHF transmitter. Simple as that is, it can take a while to wrap your mind around the concept.

There are some problems that limit the utility of crossband repeat. The biggest problem is *hang-time* on the main repeater — the time after somebody stops talking, but the repeater stays on the air, beeps, and then finally drops. On many repeaters that's several seconds, and when two hams are in conversation, the repeater *never* drops until they're done. Your crossband repeater can't tell the difference between a ham's transmission through the repeater and the hang time afterward. It's all just one long signal being received. So if you, down in the mall, are listening to two hams talk, you can't break in until they're done. As long as they're talking, your mobile never stops sending a signal to you, and never listens for you. (Something else to keep in mind here is that your mobile is now transmitting a lot, and it is not designed for continuous transmission. Keep it in low power.)

A repeater can be made "crossband repeat friendly" by having a very short hang-time, or by a specially designed CTCSS system. If the repeater sends tone only when a signal is on the input, and turns it off during the hang-time, your crossband repeater can use the tone to know when to transmit and when to shut off, allowing you to access the repeater between transmissions normally. Or, if you can hear the main repeater directly on your handheld but just can't get back to it, you can do one-way crossband repeat, from your handheld through the crossband mobile, but not from the repeater back to your handheld.

A few notes of caution: First, be very careful in configuring your crossband repeater. Choose frequencies wisely — your coordination group may have identified band segments for crossband repeat operation, so don't just plunk down anywhere you want. Do some research. And guard the "local" side of your crossband mobile with CTCSS or DCS. If you don't, and the squelch opens on your mobile, it will spew noise out to the main repeater. Crossband operation is particularly useful for emergency and public-service event work, but a noise-spewing, out-of-control crossband mobile can render a vital repeater useless.

Second, maintain control. The FCC rules require you to be in control of the transmitter, but are not specific about how you do that. If you can reach the car in a few minutes from inside the mall, that's probably good enough. But don't stop paying attention to it or leave the area.

Finally, you are required to ID *both* of your mobile's transmitters with your call sign. How do you ID the transmitter that's sending the main repeater signal back to you? None of the crossband repeaters on the market has an ID system built in. So it isn't easy.

Fig 2-8 — A Yaesu FT-8900 being prepared for crossband repeat. On the right side (the "local" side) of the display, note that the frequency is part of the area's band plan for crossband repeat. The UHF frequency is protected by encode and decode CTCSS, and the power level is set to low.

DIGITAL VOICE (DV) — THE NEW HORIZON

APCO-25 and D-STAR are digital voice systems making inroads into VHF/UHF Amateur Radio repeater operation. While both are digital, they are incompatible systems. Each has its own advantages and disadvantages.

APCO-25

Sometimes called just P-25, APCO-25 is a commercial system that's been in use in public-safety (police, fire, EMS) for almost 10 years. That means equipment is being "aged out" of commercial service and the old radios, often in very good condition, are cheap. Hams in a few areas of the country have begun putting P-25 repeaters on the air on the VHF and UHF ham bands. P-25 equipment was first marketed by Motorola under the brand Astro, and that's the brand you'll find most on eBay. But now P-25 is available from most commercial two-way radio manufacturers, including ICOM, Kenwood and Vertex Standard (maker of Yaesu equipment for Amateur Radio). None of them, though, make P-25 equipment specifically for Amateur Radio or puts P-25 capability into their ham radio lines.

Commercial P-25 equipment is not hard to modify for Amateur Radio. The right models can be reprogrammed for ham operation with software — no retuning required. And most models (and most repeaters) are dual-mode, analog and digital. So a repeater owner can convert an analog repeater to digital without leaving the analog users out in the cold. (Analog users will want to use CTCSS decode to avoid hearing the growl that P-25 makes in an analog receiver).

There are positives and negatives to operating a radio designed for commercial service. It'll probably be quite rugged, a plus if you're prone to dropping your handheld. And it may be more immune to intermod and other RF junk. To program it, though, you'll need to visit your local radio shop, or a local ham who's purchased the software and cables needed. You could buy them yourself, but they're expensive. You won't have the flexibility of adding and changing frequencies and memories that you do with true ham equipment. And there are no dual-band radios available. To those hams who prefer commercial equipment, this is a worthwhile tradeoff.

On the air, APCO-25 radios work much like conventional analog FM radios. The audio is a bit "metallic" or "robotic," but there is no noise or mobile flutter. The signal stays full-quieting until it drops off at the weak-signal threshold. P-25 radios send a bit of data at the beginning of a transmission that you can program to include your call sign. That will show up on the display of the receiving station. They can also send this data at the beginning of an analog transmission.

In public safety systems, P-25 radios are often part of linked systems. The linking is done by external equipment that has not found its way into Amateur Radio systems. Most P-25 repeaters are stand-alone, or part of limited networks like their analog cousins. There's no reason they can't be linked to analog repeaters, or use IRLP or EchoLink.

D-STAR

The all-amateur digital voice mode for VHF-UHF is called D-STAR. It was developed by the Japan Amateur Radio League (JARL), and it was designed from the ground up to be a networked system. The repeaters have an Ethernet port for connection to the Internet through a *Gateway* computer located at the repeater site, though the repeaters can be operated stand-alone with no Internet connection.

ICOM brought D-STAR to the US a few years ago as a 1200 MHz system, and in 2006 introduced a broader line of VHF, UHF and dual band mobiles, handhelds and repeaters. D-STAR handheld and mobile transceivers are all dual-mode, analog and digital, but the current ICOM repeaters are only digital. See **Fig 2-9**.

D-STAR shares P-25's slightly robotic sound, and its clarity and freedom from noise and picket-fencing. Both systems have a bit of "garble" as signals hover at the weak-signal threshold, but most of the time a signal is either perfectly clear, or it's gone. Some D-STAR repeater operators report slightly better range with D-STAR than with analog FM, though they'll admit that at the threshold when a D-STAR signal disappears, you might be able to pick some audio out of a very noisy analog signal.

The basic D-STAR operating experience is similar to analog — push to talk, release to listen. But the ICOM repeater controllers have a minimal design. There's no hang-time, no courtesy tone, and no provisions for the "extras" of other repeater controllers like voice ID, announcements, autopatch and talking S-meters. When you stop transmitting, usually you hear nothing. It's a little hard to tell if you've been heard until the station you're talking to returns and acknowledges your transmission. There is a short "hang-time" to the D-STAR repeater. It's not audible, but you can see it on your S-meter.

And there's more to see with D-STAR. Your radio displays

Fig 2-9 — ICOM launched D-STAR with a single radio for 1200 MHz, but quickly followed with a line of VHF/UHF mobiles, handhelds and repeaters. Here is a complete ICOM D-STAR repeater and controller, along with the ID-800 mobile and IC-91AD handheld. This equipment is getting ready for operation on the K4ITL repeater system in Raleigh, North Carolina.

the call sign of the station you're listening to, and sometimes the call sign of the repeater you're talking through. Users can program a short text message that is sent with each transmission and scrolls through listener's displays. In addition, D-STAR's voice signal always carries with it a 1200 bps data signal that can be used for text, small files — anything that fits in that low-speed connection. To use that data signal, you connect a computer with a special data cable. It can't be accessed from the radio directly. D-STAR fans are busy writing programs to take advantage of that signal.

D-STAR is designed to network using the Internet (for long hauls) or 10 GHz links (to route signals between local machines). Note that I'm being careful to *not* say that repeaters are linked, because D-STAR networking works differently from any other repeater linking described so far.

D-STAR digitized audio and data are routed using call signs. The first thing you do when you initialize your D-STAR radio is program your call sign via the front panel or using computer control software and the data cable. Next, you program the call sign of your local repeater, although the radios will pick up that call sign automatically the first time you use the repeater. Then, when you want to talk to someone, you program in their call sign, or a generic "CQ." See **Fig 2-10** for a sample D-STAR setup menu.

Finally, to talk to someone on a distant, networked repeater you have some options. You can enter the call sign of that repeater. You key up, and your voice appears on your local repeater and the distant one. Or, you can enter the call sign of a specific station, and the network will do all the routing for you. All the D-STAR networked repeaters talk to each other and pass along lists of who's keyed them up, and when.

Let's say you have a friend with a D-STAR capable handheld who travels for business. You don't know for sure if your friend is home today, or on the road somewhere. Turns out he *is* on the road, and when he landed at his destination, he made a transmission through the local D-STAR networked repeater. That repeater told your local repeater about it.

You want to call him. You program his call into a field on your radio, and then transmit. Your local repeater and Gateway route your audio to the distant repeater, and your friend hears you and responds. But note that before he responds, he must enter either your call sign, or the call sign of the repeater you're listening to, into his radio so the system will route his audio back to you. That's why I call it "networking" and not "linking." The repeaters are not linked together. Each individual transmission is routed based on the call signs embedded in that transmission.

Entering all those call signs can be a chore, again not one to try while driving. The ICOM radios have some capability to automatically store the routing of a call that was made to you, so you can respond more easily. And D-STAR "power users" have learned to use memories to store the call signs of individuals and repeaters they talk to and through regularly.

There is one thing D-STAR Gateways have not been programmed to do: link multiple repeaters together in one big roundtable. That's a limitation in the original software, and US hams are working on it. By the time you read this, it may be implemented.

Note that anyone can talk through a single D-STAR repeater, but to use a Gateway you must be registered with at least one Gateway somewhere on the network. That takes getting in touch with the local system operator, and may require supporting the club or repeater group.

There are a few more cute things D-STAR radios can do. One is *call sign squelch*. Since call signs of both the calling and receiving party are part of the data stream, you can set your radio to respond only to a signal addressed to you, by call sign. This flows through the network transparently. There are break-in modes designed to allow a third party to break into a conversation between hams who are using call sign squelch, and there's an emergency mode that will override the volume control setting on some radios to get everyone's attention.

An amazing amount of work and preparation went into D-STAR before it was introduced to America, and while it is a very usable system today, it is still a work in progress. Will D-STAR be *the* digital mode for the next generation? Will D-STAR, P-25 or any digital mode make significant inroads into our existing analog repeater infrastructure? Will your analog radio become obsolete anytime soon?

Only time will tell. There's no question that with an analog-only radio you will be missing out on the leading edge of new technology, at least when it arrives in your area. But nobody expects analog repeaters to disappear anytime soon.

Fig 2-10 — Part of the D-STAR menu on an IC-2820H mobile. This radio is configured to talk to anyone (CQCQCQ) through the KØMDG 2-meter digital repeater, making a local contact. The frequency (145.67) is becoming adopted in some areas as the D-STAR simplex channel. You wouldn't want to use 146.52 for digital simplex. Analog users on .52 would hear your signal as white-noise that they can't "squelch out."

VHF/UHF DIGITAL DATA MODES

Let's move on to the VHF/UHF data modes, and keep in mind that with the advent of digital voice, our language must now change. We can no longer assume that "digital" means just text or files in Amateur Radio. ICOM splits their D-STAR nomenclature into DV (Digital Voice) and DD (for 128 kbit/s Digital Data). We'll ignore for now the question of whether digitized voice is actually "data," but that question does bedevil our attempts to fit digital voice into the framework of Part 97.

We'll also note only in passing that RTTY was the first digital mode in use on VHF/UHF, as it was on HF. The pre-computer era saw a number of teletype repeaters around the country, with a handful of operators using big, mechanically complex teletype machines. Few if any are still in operation. It's a curiosity that personal computers gave new life to RTTY on HF, while also making packet radio possible, which killed off RTTY on VHF.

Over the years, packet radio in the VHF/UHF spectrum has been its own roller-coaster ride. In the 1980s, interest in personal computers, and an international network of packet radio bulletin boards (PBBS), made packet *the* new mode, though even at its peak, not every active ham had a packet station. Many who did operate packet, though, were wildly enthusiastic. The PBBS network with its automatic mail forwarding capability permitted hams to originate e-mail at their local 2-meter PBBS and have it delivered anywhere in the world where there was a PBBS. It could take a day for delivery cross-country, but remember, this was long before the Internet was widely available, and the general public had nothing like it. Our 1200 bit/s speed was state-of-the-art, or better. Some telephone modems were running just 300 bit/s in those days.

By the early 1990s, the PBBS network was so popular that it became overloaded with the amount of e-mail and bulletins it had to handle. In some areas, the spectrum became overloaded, too. But just as hams were beginning to experiment with higher speed packet (9600 bit/s and even 56 kbit/s), the Internet and its seemingly inexhaustible e-mail capabilities arrived and we all but abandoned the PBBS network.

But packet didn't die. Many PBBSs are still around, and packet radio is being used for other applications. Closing the '90s and continuing into the new century, local DX PacketClusters continue to operate in conjunction with Internet DX spotting. APRS (the Automatic Packet Reporting System), though, inherits most of the packet radio legacy of equipment, tower sites and interest. And Winlink 2000 on VHF/UHF is giving new life to packet for ARES and emergency applications. Given that, it's worth spending some time reviewing what packet is and how to put together and operate a packet station. The data side of D-STAR is truly an "infant" technology, but we'll take a look at its possibilities too, before we close this chapter.

WHAT IS PACKET?

It's hard to tell the short story, but I'll try. Packet is error-free digital communications (or at least it can be) from one computer to another. It can be live "keyboard to keyboard," like the various forms of instant message chat sessions on the Internet (and like RTTY, PSK31 some of the other "real-time" HF digital modes). But more often it is more like e-mail, with messages and small files passed through bulletin boards and mailboxes to be read later. Or it can be short bits of information like the weather at a home station, or the location of a mobile station.

To move these messages around, the output of a computer — text or files — is assembled into bundles or "packets" of data (usually about 100 or so characters). Each packet is transmitted as a rapidly shifting pair of audio tones that modulate an FM transmitter using AFSK (audio frequency shift keying, similar to RTTY on FM). The audio tones represent the zeros and ones of a serial binary data stream. The tones on the FM signal travel through the air, are received and demodulated, the packets are checked for integrity, then disassembled and the information is fed to a computer. If the information sent is text, it goes to a display for you to read. If the information is a file, it goes to your hard drive. Or it might place an icon on a map.

To be error-free, two packet stations (and no more than two) operate in a *connected* mode — that is, they examine each other's packets, and send an "acknowledgement" packet each time a good packet is received. If a packet is reported as bad, or isn't acknowledged at all, it's sent again. If the signal path fades, the computers keep trying for a while. Eventually they'll connect again and continue, or give up.

Packet stations can also operate *unconnected.* This mode is required if multiple stations are involved, as it would be overwhelming for several stations, perhaps dozens of stations, to try to acknowledge everyone else's packets. But operating unconnected means that the system will not be error free.

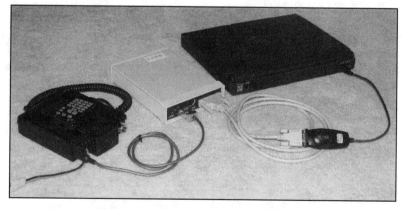

Here is one way to put together a packet station. A TNC, in this case a Kantronics KamPlus, is connected between the radio (an ICOM IC-207H) and a laptop computer. The radio connection is made through the dedicated data port, which leaves the microphone and speaker connections free for voice communication. The connection to the computer goes though a 25-pin to 9-pin modem cable, and a serial-to-USB adapter before plugging into the laptop's USB connection.

The Packet System

The other end of a packet connection can be a direct connection to another ham, just like voice simplex, but it's more likely to be a connection to a "node" — a PBBS, DX PacketCluster or an APRS node — or a "digipeater." There aren't many full-fledged repeaters dedicated to packet, partly because by the time packet got popular there wasn't much spectrum available for more repeaters, and partly because with digipeaters, we don't really need them.

Digipeaters are simplex devices that receive a packet, then re-send it more or less immediately after it's been received, all on one channel. A central PBBS might be ringed by digipeaters that help outlying users who can't reach the PBBS directly. Those digipeaters don't have to be on the same frequency as the PBBS. They can use a link radio, preferably on another band, to forward packets between you and the PBBS. It takes more hardware, but it eases congestion on a busy packet channel.

What Frequency?

PBBS activity on 2 meters started on 145.01 MHz, and much of it remains there. So if you're looking for local activity, that's a good place to start. Other popular packet channels are 145.03, .05, .07 and .09. In some areas, packet systems can be found on channels between 144.91 and 144.99 MHz, between 145.51 and 145.77 MHz, and on some FM voice simplex channels (which doesn't make voice operators happy).

DX PacketClusters will almost certainly *not* be on 145.01, so check with local DXers and packet operators. APRS is almost exclusively on 144.39 MHz, having moved from 145.79 MHz due to interference with satellite and space station activity. But speaking of space, the ISS and some satellites have packet capability.

There is no packet equivalent of the *ARRL Repeater Directory*. You'll have to search local resources to see what's on the air in your area.

ASSEMBLING A VHF PACKET STATION

All packet stations need a computer and a radio. Then they need a way to create and control the data packets and the audio tones that carry them. There are three ways to do this:

1) *A Terminal Node Controller (TNC)* — a separate box containing the hardware and firmware that does most of the work. The TNC includes a modem, and the computer mostly acts as a "dumb terminal" — just a keyboard and display.

2) *A standalone modem*, and TNC emulation software in the computer.

3) *A sound card* and computer control software, which puts all the work on the computer.

There are advantages and disadvantages to doing it each way.

TNC

The hardware device that handles the signal between the computer and the radio is called the TNC. For transmitting, a TNC assembles the computer's data into packets and encodes the tones that are fed to the radio's input. When receiving, the TNC gets the tones from the radio, decodes them, pulls the data out of the packets and sends it along to the computer for display.

Half of the TNC is the modem (*mo*dulator/*dem*odulator), the circuit that creates and decodes the tones that are transmitted over the air. The other half is the "intelligence" — the firmware that puts the packets together and takes them apart, and contains all the user commands. Most TNCs also include a mini-PBBS, usually called a mailbox, that lets you receive messages from other packet operators when your computer is off and your radio is unattended. Convenience, and that unattended mailbox operation, are the big advantages of a TNC. But it's the most expensive solution.

Modem

Packet modems are available that just create and decode the tones, and let you use your computer for the "intelligence." Packet modems are usually bundled with TNC-emulation software. Modems are cheaper than TNCs, but you have to have your computer up and running to use them.

Sound Card

Software is available that lets your computer do everything, and uses the sound card to create and decode the audio tones. The only external connections are the audio cables from the sound card to and from your radio, and a connection from the PC serial port to the radio's PTT. That's the cheapest solution — your cost is a few wires and connectors. But "sharing" your sound card with other programs means you'll pay a price in convenience, as you'll see, unless you've dedicated a computer to digital radio operation. Since many of us have an extra, older computer lying around collecting dust, that's not the extravagance it might seem to be.

Most of the software is written for the *Windows* operating system, but there are programs for *Macintosh* and *Linux* as well. Some programs are freeware, and some are shareware. A Web search for "Amateur Radio packet software" will yield a wealth of resources. Be careful, though. Packet radio's roots go well back into the DOS era, so not all of it will work with modern computers.

AGWPE (AGW Packet Engine) is one of those free *Windows* programs that's popular today. There's an excellent *AGWPE* tutorial on the Web at **www.soundcardpacket.info**. The *AGWPE* software is available for download at **www.elcom. gr/sv2agw/inst.htm**.

By the way, sound card software is also having a large impact on some other forms of VHF and HF digital communication. In fact, once you have your computer set up for a program such as *AGWPE*, you're ready to try other intriguing digital modes that use sound-card-based software, including some digital *voice* modes like *WinDRM*. You've already installed the necessary cables and interface hardware, so all you need to do is start a new program!

Radio Equipment

There is a lot of detail to consider in making the *data* side of packet radio software work, and we'll review some of that shortly. That detail seems to make some packet operators overlook the "radio" side of the equation. How much radio do you need? How much power? How much antenna? And do you want to operate 1200 bit/s, or move up to 9600 bit/s or faster?

If you're going to make your voice radio double as your

packet system, those questions may be moot. If that system is able to hit all the area voice repeaters, it'll probably hit the packet systems as well. Many newer radios are "9600-ready," and if yours is, you're set for that, too.

But using your voice radio for packet is a compromise, since packet operation can go on in the background while you are operating or monitoring voice repeaters. If you've got the means for a second radio and antenna, you can have a more effective station. But you shouldn't compromise on the radio or antenna. It has to work as well as, or better than, your voice radio. That's because a bunch of transmitters — nodes, digipeaters and other users — will be sharing the channel with you. TNCs are designed to wait until a channel is clear before transmitting, but if your neighbors can't hear you, they won't wait for you, so they might begin transmitting while you're on the air, clobbering you at the receiver you're trying to reach. The more stations that can hear each other in a geographic area, the better the system works. A signal in your geographic area that you can't hear is called a *hidden transmitter*. A puny signal that just barely reaches the desired node will be a hidden transmitter to a lot of other stations, and it will have trouble on a busy packet channel.

So get that packet antenna up in the air, and use a radio with 25 to 50 W. That may seem like violating the spirit (and rules) about running minimum power, but in this case you're doing everyone a favor.

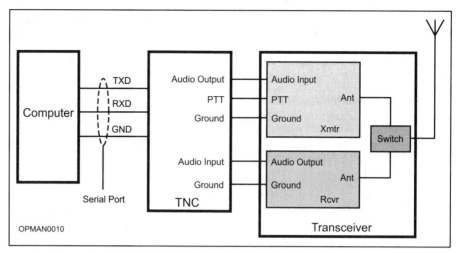

Fig 2-11 — The components and their interconnection in a typical packet radio station.

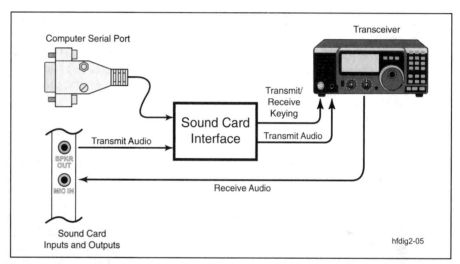

Fig 2-12 — A diagram of a typical setup for VHF digital communication using sound card software. The sound card interface handles the tasks of matching audio levels between the radio and the computer, and keying the radio. Commercial interfaces from a number of vendors can be found in the advertisements in *QST*.

Most radios made since the mid '80s will work fine for 1200 bit/s packet. More modern radios will have dedicated packet connections so you don't have to plug into the mic connector and come out of the speaker jack. Many radios made in since the late '90s have 9600 bit/s capability as well. That's a big improvement in speed, if there's a 9600 bit/s system in your area.

HARDWARE CONNECTIONS
TNC Connection

The TNC has at least two connectors: a computer port and a radio port (**Fig 2-11**). TNCs that can do 9600 bit/s may have a separate radio port for the higher speed connection.

The computer port connects to your computer's serial port. Here again you may see packet's 1980s roots — many TNCs still use a 25-pin RS-232 connector, while most computers have a 9-pin connecter, *if* they have a serial port at all! You can use a 25-pin to 9-pin adapter or cable, and if you don't have

a serial port, you can use a USB-to-serial adapter. Few TNCs come ready for USB.

The TNC's radio port requires four connections to the radio equipment: audio input, audio output, push-to-talk (PTT) and ground. Some radios have dedicated connectors for data. If your radio doesn't, you can use the microphone and speaker/headphone connections, but the data connector is better because the radio's volume control won't affect the level of the audio going to the TNC. You can turn the volume up to check on the received signal, then turn it down for operation (packet signals aren't very pleasant to listen to). And you won't have to unplug the TNC and plug in the mic to switch to voice operation.

The TNC will have level controls for output to the radio, and possibly for the input from the radio. Adjust those according to the TNC's manual.

Sound Card Connections and Levels

If you are using your sound card rather than a hardware

TNC, we need to spend some time discussing the connections to your sound card. Look at **Fig 2-12** for an illustration of a typical configuration. (This discussion focuses on *Windows* based computers, but similar connections and controls are available for Macintosh and *Linux* based computers.)

Connect the audio from your receiver to either the MIC INPUT or LINE INPUT on the computer. If you have a choice, use the LINE INPUT — it will match the signal level from your radio better. Laptops don't have a LINE INPUT, but the MIC INPUT software should have an adjustment to compensate.

For your transmit audio connection, you're looking for LINE OUTPUT, though laptops may just have a HEADPHONE OUTPUT. If you have hum, a line-coupling transformer of 1:1 ratio and 600 Ω impedance should help.

Don't use the digital input or output of your sound card. Even though you're operating a digital mode, you're making an analog audio connection between the computer and the radio.

Setting Sound Card Levels

Audio levels are set through two audio "control panels" on your computer. Your transmitter, fed by the LINE OUTPUT connection, is adjusted from the VOLUME CONTROL panel. Bring up this panel by double-clicking the speaker icon on the Taskbar. See **Fig 2-13** for a sample of the VOLUME CONTROL panel. Your PC can make a variety of sounds ("You've got mail,"), and you don't want *any* of them, except your TNC emulation software's tones, to go to your radio. Those sounds will be controlled by the WAVE control.

Check the MUTE box on all the other sources. Unfortunately, most of the internally generated computer sounds also pass through the WAVE control. All you can do to keep them from squirting out your packet radio is turn those programs off when you're running packet.

The receive audio from your radio, heading through your sound card and into your TNC emulation program, is selected and controlled by the RECORDING CONTROL panel (see **Fig 2-14**). This panel is opened from the VOLUME CONTROL panel by selecting OPTIONS, then PROPERTIES, then clicking on the RECORDING radio button, and clicking OK. Here you can select a single source (LINE IN or MICROPHONE for this operation) and adjust the volume.

Since you may be making these adjustments often, it'll be worth taking a minute to create shortcuts to these control panels

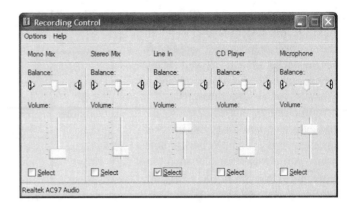

Fig 2-14 — The *Windows* Recording Control panel.

and keep them on your desktop or Quick Launch control bar. For the RECORDING CONTROL panel, right-click your desktop and select **New/Shortcut**. In the box labeled **Type the location of this item** enter:

%windir%\system32\sndvol32.exe /record

exactly as shown, including the "%" signs and the space between ".exe" and "/". That should create a shortcut to the RECORDING CONTROL panel. If not, use the BROWSE button to navigate to the **C:Windows/System32** folder and select the *sndvol32.exe* program, adding the **(space)/record** yourself. For a shortcut to the VOLUME CONTROL panel, follow the same procedure, but skip the **/record** part.

TNC COMMAND(S) AND CONTROL

If you buy a full, commercial TNC, you'll need a way to talk it — a program that lets you do actual packet operation. It will probably come with an operating program, which may be good enough, but there are several more advanced programs out there. The one I've used the most, *KaWin* for Kantronics TNCs, was last updated in 1997! Most of the programs out there are of that vintage, except the APRS programs, which are still being updated, and Winlink 2000, which is current.

Actually, TNCs can be operated by a simple terminal program (the program in *Windows XP* is called *HyperTerminal*), or, for that matter, a dumb terminal. TNCs have a long list of "command-line" type instructions for both set-up and operation. The details are in the instruction manuals. The control programs are just more elegant front-ends that feed the commands to the TNC.

You can leave most of the TNC's settings at their default, but whether you use an operating program or just *HyperTerminal*, you'll need to fill in some blanks and adjust some parameters. One blank is your call sign, called Mycall in the TNC's firmware. The TNC will be sending your call sign for identification and to make connections, so it has to know who you are (or is it who "it" is). A packet station's call sign often includes a Secondary Station Identification (SSID) that further identifies the station. The SSID is a dash, followed by a number from 1 to 15, for example

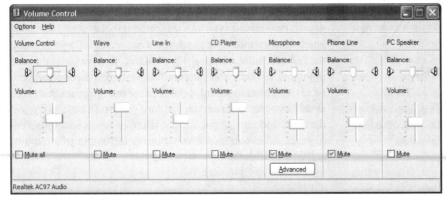

Fig 2-13 — The *Windows* Volume Control panel. Your sound card and software may show a somewhat different configuration.

KN4AQ-3. You need this because a single packet station may be available for live keyboarding using one SSID, a mailbox using another SSID, and as a digipeater using yet another SSID. Each is a separate setting in the TNC.

An important setting is Txdelay. That sets how long the TNC waits between "pushing" the PTT and sending data. We're talking about tenths of a second here. Some transmitters take two or three tenths of a second to get up to power, stabilize on frequency and send audio. Some can do it in well under a tenth of a second. In the world of packet, three-tenths of a second is a long time. About 200 to 300 milliseconds is typical for most 2-meter radios and 1200 bit/s. Shorter is a little better, so trim the time until things stop working, they add some back.

A TNC will keep a list of all the stations it's heard, noting whether it heard them directly or through a digipeater, and when they were heard (if you set the DAytime parameter). That's another reason to have a dedicated packet station. To see that list, you ask for the MHeard list. You can watch all the packet traffic on a channel scroll by your screen if the Monitor command turned ON, or just see packets sent to you with it OFF.

There are several old books that go into detail explaining TNC functions and setup. Some are out of print, but you can probably find them at hamfests. A good free, online resource is by Larry Kenny, WB9LOZ, at **www.choisser.com/packet**. It's telling that the Web site says "The author is no longer active in packet radio…; however he has left this material on the Internet for access by those who might find it helpful."

ON THE AIR

Once you've gotten your TNC connected and configured, it's time to make it play! If there's still a PBBS in your area, there's a pretty good chance it, or a node connected to it, is on 145.01 MHz. That was the original packet frequency on 2 meters. But you'll need to talk to local packet operators to see what frequencies are in use in your area.

To communicate with another station, a node or a PBBS, you *connect* to it. That puts you in the error-free mode mentioned earlier. Using your software, you enter the call sign (and SSID) of the station you want to connect to, and probably press the ENTER key. The TNC keys your radio and sends a connect request. If that station hears you, it responds quickly. Your TNC acknowledges the response, and the TNC's CONNECTED light comes on.

Now you're ready to communicate. If you've connected to an individual station, and the operator is present, you can have a real-time, keyboard-to-keyboard chat very much like the various instant-message programs on the Internet. If the operator is not present, you can enter his or her personal mailbox and leave a message (and retrieve a message left for you). TNCs respond to a limited number of commands from remote stations. You can tell it to send you its MHeard list — the list of all the stations it's heard recently.

If you've connected to a PBBS there won't be a live operator, but you've got a wider list of options to select from. You can list and read bulletins, and send and receive mail and bulletins. Some will have Internet connections so you can pass e-mail through the radio to the Internet. Talk to the sysop for more complete instructions.

At 1200 bit/s, packet operation will seem very slow com-pared to the Internet on a broadband connection. If signals are poor or the channel is busy, it can be excruciatingly slow, especially if you're trying to read a long message. Short messages can transfer quickly, though.

DX PACKETCLUSTER

DXers discovered the power of packet early in the game, and it's changed DXing for better or worse. In the good old days, DXers tuned the bands, hoping to come across a station in a needed country, or "entity" as they call them today. They knew about DXpeditions and rare country activations from bulletins in magazines, but that information was weeks or months old. Some areas had VHF voice repeaters dedicated to DX, so after someone worked a station, they announced it on the repeater. Then they chased away stations who came on to rag-chew.

Packet supercharged DX reporting, or spotting as it's called. DXers built PacketCluster systems — PBBS type packet nodes with specialized software — around the country, and linked them to cover wider regions (that's the "cluster" part). The PacketCluster is an easy way to report the call sign, country, frequency, time, strength and other useful parameters of the DX signal, and the location of the receiving station. That information quickly pops up on the display screen of all the other DXers in the region. You can configure the cluster to filter the spots you receive by band, country, mode and other ways so you only see spots of the stations you really need for an award or contest. PacketClusters also support quick, instant-message type notes between stations, and bulletins and e-mail like PBBSs.

PacketClusters operate in the connected mode — the cluster itself makes an individual connection to each station logged on — and you use your routine packet software. Spots are sent individually to you and everyone else logged in. That's quite a burst of traffic when a spot arrives. The Cluster does the filtering based on parameters you set, so it doesn't waste time sending you spots you don't want. There is specialized software available for picking off spot information while unconnected.

The downside of DX PacketClusters, according to some hams anyway, is that it makes DXing more like shooting fish in a barrel. It also makes things harder because "packet pile-ups" appear instantly. But the system is entrenched and it's not going away.

Although the Internet has largely usurped the DX Packet-Cluster function, RF systems remain on the air in many areas. You can search for a local system at **www.dxcluster.info**.

DX PacketClusters have their own unique set of commands for entering and retrieving spots. And many of them request or require specific TNC settings for users. Find your local sysop for that information.

AUTOMATIC PACKET REPORTING SYSTEM (APRS)

Just as packet systems in general were succumbing to competition from the Internet, APRS appeared, leading to a re-surgence of interest (and TNC sales). Some handheld and mobile radios include APRS capabilities or built-in TNC options.

When operating APRS, you, or a device at your station (GPS, weather monitor), send a bit of information to your TNC, which sends it to your radio for transmission on 144.39 MHz. An APRS digipeater relays your packets to all local stations, and

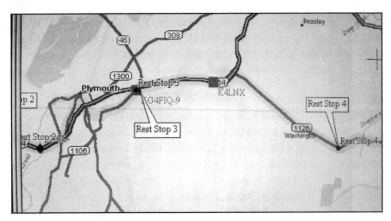

Fig 2-15 — APRS stations KG4FIQ-9 and K4LNX appear on a map during a public service event. The street-level mapping was accomplished by sending APRS data to Delorme's *Street Atlas* version 8 with the program *APRS-SA*.

to all surrounding digipeaters, which in turn relay your packet to all *their* local stations. That puts your data in the hands of stations for a hundred or so miles around. One of those stations also puts your information on the Internet, where it can be seen worldwide.

What information do you send? Many hams think of APRS first as a position reporting system, based on sending GPS location, speed and altitude data via packet to be displayed on a map. That concept is so infused with APRS that hams often think the acronym means automatic *position* reporting system. But as APRS developer Bob Bruninga, WB4APR, describes it on his own Web site, "The Automatic Packet Reporting System was designed to support rapid, reliable exchange of information for local, tactical real-time information, events or nets." All kinds of information can be exchanged across a region quickly using APRS. Bob lists text messages, weather info, traffic reports, EchoLink and IRLP node location and info and more, in addition to location data for fixed and mobile stations. "Think of APRS as a signaling channel to reveal ALL amateur radio resources and live activities that are in range of the operator at any instant in time," he writes.

On the receive end of things, you generally see some kind of map on your display, something like the one in **Fig 2-15**, showing the location of all the area APRS stations. For moving stations, the display can show the direction, speed and altitude as well. Other windows or boxes display the text notes, weather information and other data being sent. Maybe it's that map that makes people think P is for Position.

APRS Software and Hardware

To use APRS, you'll need some specialized software. Standard packet communication software won't do. A wide variety of software is available — more than we can fairly list here. Some of it includes maps (usually with limited detail), and some is designed to overlay APRS data on commercial mapping software, which gives it street-level detail. Like PBBS and DX PacketClusters, APRS has a list of special commands for telling your packets what to do. Your software handles most of those. For example, if you want to send a text message, you type the call sign of the recipient in a box, type the message in another box, and click SEND.

Unlike PBBS and DX PacketCluster systems, APRS uses only unconnected packets. That means that APRS data is not error-free. If you miss a packet due to interference or a signal fade, it's gone. Nobody's going to ask your TNC for an acknowledgement. But most APRS data is repeated routinely, so you'll get it next time. Text messages do have their own system for sending back an acknowledgement, but it's not guaranteed.

At home, the hardware you need is standard packet-system stuff — computer, TNC, radio, antenna. If you have an old TNC, or buy a used one, check to see if its firmware supports GPS data. You may need a firmware upgrade. In the US and Canada, all routine APRS traffic is on 144.39 MHz at 1200 bit/s. Special event traffic can be handled on other frequencies.

Mobile APRS is another story. You can run a full APRS station with a laptop computer and APRS software, or a slightly scaled-down version with a PDA and software, or you can have a transmit-only system that beacons your location, called a "tracker." Either way, you add a GPS to the mix.

For a full mobile station, you need a computer with two ports — one for the TNC and one for the GPS. Newer GPS receivers have USB connections, but most TNCs are built to connect to serial ports. If you have a newer laptop without a serial port, you can use a USB-to-serial adapter. The software will forward the GPS information to the TNC. The program will beacon your location as you move. How often it beacons is one of several parameters you'll need to set. Some programs get very detailed, allowing you to send a beacon when you've turned a corner, and send more beacons when you're moving at high speed, fewer when going slowly or stopped.

With a tracker, you have the GPS, the TNC and the radio, but no computer except to initially set things up. The GPS plugs into the TNC directly. There are some special, small TNCs on the market designed just to be trackers. The only receiving they do is to make sure they don't transmit when a channel is busy. With a tracker, you drive down the road, letting the world (including family and friends) know where you are. They don't need APRS to find you — there are several Web sites that will display your location. More on that in a minute.

"Path" Setting

As I mentioned earlier, digipeaters relay your packets to all the local stations, and also to all the surrounding digipeaters. Those digipeaters relay your packets again. So stations 100 or so miles away can see your location and information directly via RF. But your packets, and everyone else's, have to stop being relayed sometime, or 144.39 will be hopelessly overloaded, a problem that began to occur in the early 2000s.

To limit your relays, you load a parameter that sets how many relays your packet can have, and each digipeater reduces that number by 1 until it hits zero. Usually you want your information relayed only twice. The actual terminology you'll see in your software is "via WIDEn-N". This uses a parameter in the TNC called the "unproto path," which is a way to have *unconnected* packets relayed by digipeaters that otherwise would only be talking to stations that have connected to them. The

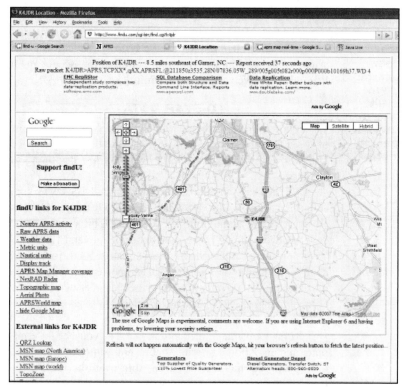

Fig 2-16 — Map and information for APRS station K4JDR in North Carolina as shown on www.findu.com. The data from K4JDR was received just 37 seconds before the inquiry was sent to the Web site.

"N" is the number of APRS digipeaters that should relay the packet, and the recommended number is 2 for fixed stations in metropolitan areas, and 3 for stations in very rural areas. That would look like "via WIDE2-2" for most stations.

To see a very elaborate explanation of this, and a recommendation for something called "proportional pathing" for trackers, do a Web search for the phrase "fix14439" (as in *fix 144.39 MHz* because it was broken).

APRS on the Internet

If you zoom out on an APRS map being fed by a radio that's been monitoring for a while (an hour or so), you'll see stations all across the region, maybe the whole country, not just within the range of two or three digipeaters. How did *they* get on the map?

The APRS network uses the Internet extensively for passing location information, messages and lots of other data. Somewhere near your local digipeater is one or more *IGate* stations that pick the signals off of local digipeaters and feed it to the APRS Internet System (APRS-IS). The IGate stations also send data back to the digipeater, and that's where those more distant station locations came from.

You can see the result of all this data on many Internet sites with just a browser. One of the most popular is **www.findu. com**. If you know a station is on APRS, enter this URL: **www. map.findu.com/***call sign**. (The * is a wildcard character that lets FindU display the station regardless of any SSID it may be using.) FindU will display the station location using Google-Maps, along with all the raw APRS data, weather charts from

weather reporting stations, and a list of all the other APRS stations nearby (which you can also see on maps, see **Fig 2-16**). If you run a tracker, big brother may be watching you, and seeing how fast you drive!

The Web site **www.aprs-is.net** has another view of the world, literally, of APRS. From the home page, select the *Live APRS-IS* link, then the *Java Live* link, then select maps and use instructions to zoom in to whatever location you choose to see all the APRS activity. If you don't zoom in enough, the screen will soon be filled with overlapping icons. The map in **Fig 2-17** was captured just as the USA map was beginning to draw, before it filled with stations.

This Internet connectivity allows you to send text messages from any APRS station to any APRS station, anywhere in the world covered by a digipeater and an IGate. And you can send a message to any e-mail address by addressing an APRS message to EMAIL, then putting the e-mail address as the first "word" of the message, and then the short text message. It would look like this:

EMAIL

then

kn4aq@arrl.net Hello, Gary. Are you going to the hamfest this weekend?

The APRS e-mail server will send you an acknowledgement, which you'll probably receive, but no guarantees.

PROPAGATION NETWORK (PROPNET)

"If the band is open and nobody is transmitting, can anybody hear it?"

That's the question at the top of the **www.propnet.org** Web site. Participating PropNET stations beacon signals using packet

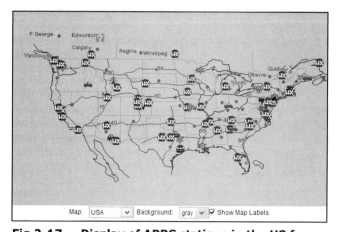

Fig 2-17 — Display of APRS stations in the US from www.aprs-is.net. This screenshot was taken just a second after accessing the Web site, just as the map was beginning to fill. A few seconds later, the map was covered with overlapping icons. You'll need to zoom in to a very local level to see anything when the map has filled in completely.

Fig 2-18 — This screenshot from the www.propnet. org Web site shows a real-time view of a band opening on 10-meters.

and PSK31 (with location information) on some HF and VHF bands, including 160, 30, 10, 6 and 2 meters. Receiving stations automatically forward the data to a PropNET server, and the results are available instantly on a series of maps on the Prop-NET Web site. See **Fig 2-18**. PropNET needs all the receiving stations it can get. Perhaps you'd like to help. In any case, it's interesting to see band-opening information real-time.

WINLINK AND VHF/UHF PACKET

Winlink 2000 is often thought of as a PACTOR based HF e-mail system for sailboats and RVers. But the developers of Winlink 2000, and its client programs *Airmail* and *Paclink MP* (which bridges e-mail with Winlink 2000), are eager for you to know that it is growing on VHF and UHF as well, primarily as a vehicle for ARES and served agency related emergency communications. On VHF/UHF, the Winlink 2000 system uses packet, D-STAR, or IEEE 802.11, but not PACTOR.

A VHF/UHF Winlink 2000 system can restore e-mail operation to an EOC that has lost its Internet connection or e-mail server, if there's a TELPAC Gateway within range. (VHF/UHF stations equipped to transfer *Paclink MP* messages to the Internet are called TELPAC [TELnet-to-PACket] Gateways.) If there is no VHF/UHF system in range, or if a widespread disaster has knocked the local TELPAC out, a Winlink HF system can handle the traffic. It won't be a 5 Megabit connection, to be sure, but it will get e-mail moving, with limited size attachments.

In practice, a Winlink 2000 equipped EOC, Red Cross office or any other emergency venue that has lost its Internet connection from a disaster or broken e-mail server, and that is equipped with a laptop computer with *Paclink*, a TNC, and a VHF radio and antenna, may continue their emergency e-mail operation using the Winlink 2000 radio e-mail domain. *Paclink MP*, running on the agency local area network (LAN), acts like any other e-mail server. However, on the outbound side, *Paclink MP* sends the data through an automatic hierarchical routing scheme — including Telnet, IEEE 802.11 links, D-STAR, packet, or HF PACTOR — via a TNC and radio, depending on the priority set for each of the five output levels available. For the level of priority set to packet, the TNC and radio will communicate to the Winlink 2000 network through the TELPAC Gateway, which forwards it for processing to one of the Winlink 2000 PMBOs. If the agency has an 802.11 based wireless network, a ham can provide the link from a mobile station parked outside.

As useful as this is, not enough hams know about it, and

it's sometimes been hard to "sell" it to emergency management officials. But ARES groups around the country are beginning to experiment with or implement the system, as documented in articles published in *QST*. For more information, see the main Winlink 2000 Web site at **www.winlink.org**.

D-STAR DATA

While D-STAR's digital voice capability is getting most of the attention, system operators say that the real power of D-STAR is in its data capability, which is just beginning to be tapped.

D-STAR has two very different data modes. The DV (voice) signal is part of a 4800 bit/s data stream. Of that, 2400 bit/s are used for the actual digitized voice, 1200 bit/s are used for "overhead" including forward error correction, and 1200 bit/s are going along for the ride as a data stream, called "low speed data," available to the user. D-STAR repeaters and Gateways pass the entire 4800 bit/s stream, so the data goes wherever the voice signal goes. You can send data while talking, just talk, or just send data — it's all the same signal.

To take advantage of this data stream, you need a computer and an optional interface cable, and some software. The low-speed data mode is not accessible from the radio front panel. Once again, a simple terminal program like *Windows HyperTerminal* will do, but dedicated D-STAR programs will work better. This data is not a complete protocol like AX.25 packet. It isn't even packet. If you enter some data, it just spits it out the transmitter. If you use *HyperTerminal* to send a data file, the file will spit out the transmitter, nonstop. D-STAR relies on the user software to build packets, determine error correction and such.

Only a few user-level programs have been developed so far (two keyboard-to-keyboard "chat" programs, and an APRS connection called D-PRS, are available at press time) but more are on the way from enthusiastic developers. This data stream is not compatible with any speed packet, but ICOM's mobiles have a separate data port that can run ordinary 1200 and 9600 bit/s packet with an external TNC in analog mode.

For more data power, think higher. Higher frequency, and higher speed. ICOM's 1200 MHz radio, the ID-1, supports 4800 bit/s DV with low-speed data like all the D-STAR radios, but it also can operate 128 kbps data through an Ethernet port on the back of the radio. ICOM calls this mode "DD." The 1200 MHz system uses a repeater for 4800 bit/s voice+data, and a separate data radio for 128 kbit/s data. The data radio shares its Internet connection with the radios in the field, and all you need to do is connect your computer to the ID-1's Ethernet port and fire up a browser. The radio appears as a network connection.

Of course 128 kbit/s is not considered "high speed" anymore. It's about double a good dial-up connection, but way below even the slowest DSL or cable connection. It is good enough for browsing sites that are not graphics-laden, but remember that all stations using the repeater are sharing that 128 kbit/s, so if several hams are pulling down data, they'll all experience a slowdown.

Emergency response agencies that are excited about having e-mail restored through ham radio will be ecstatic about having Internet browsing available. Much of the information they send and receive uses a browser interface. That capability hasn't been used in an actual emergency at press time, but it was tested at the Marine Corps Marathon in Washington, DC, in October 2006, and worked well. For years, hams staffing first-aid stations along the Marathon route have been using packet to send information on patients to a command center, where the data was transferred into a database. Using D-STAR, operators in the field could tap the database directly using a browser, entering and retrieving information.

They learned a few important lessons. First, the 1200 MHz data signal is fairly wideband compared to D-STAR or FM voice, so it needs a stronger signal to work over a given distance.

Second, you need to turn off all automatic software updates on a computer using D-STAR to reach the Internet. Myriad programs will unexpectedly launch their updates — anti-virus programs, media players, and *Windows* itself can bring the network to its knees trying to pull many huge upgrade files through the narrow pipe.

Despite the challenges, the system worked quite well and will become a permanent part of the event.

Are you digital yet? Right now, there's a pretty good chance that you are an "all-analog" ham. And analog isn't going away anytime soon. But more digital is on the way.

Michael Owen, W9IP

chapter 3

VHF/UHF — Beyond Repeaters

The radio spectrum between 30 and 3000 MHz is one of the greatest resources available to the radio amateur. The VHF and UHF amateur bands are a haven for ragchewers and experimenters alike; new modes of emission, new antennas and state-of-the-art equipment are all developed in this territory. Plenty of commercial equipment is available for the more popular bands, and building your own gear is very popular as well. Propagation conditions may change rapidly and seemingly unpredictably, but the keen observer can take advantage of subtle clues to make the most of the bands. Most North American hams are already well acquainted with 2-meter (144 MHz) or 70-cm (440-MHz) FM. For many, channelized repeater operation is their first exposure to VHF or UHF. However, FM is only part of the VHF/UHF story! A great variety of SSB and CW activity congregates on the low ends of all the bands, from 6 meters all the way to the end of the radio spectrum — and even to light beyond.

space. Thus established and widely known *calling frequencies* help stations find each other.

By knowing the best frequencies and times to be on the air, you will have little trouble making plenty of contacts, working DX, and otherwise enjoying the world above 50 MHz. **Fig 3-1** shows suggested plans for using CW and SSB on the VHF and UHF bands.

By far the two most popular bands are 6 and 2 meters, followed by 70 cm. The 125 cm (222 MHz) and 33 cm (902 MHz) bands are not available worldwide. For that reason, commercial equipment is more difficult to find for these bands, and thus they are less popular.

The next two higher UHF bands at 23 cm (1296 MHz) and 13 cm (2304 MHz) are attractive, in part due to more commercial equipment being offered to meet the demands of amateur satellite operators.

There is plenty of space on the VHF and higher bands for ragchewing, experimenting, working DX and many other activities unknown to the HF world. This means that whatever you like to do — chat with your friends across town, test amateur television or bounce signals off the moon — there is plenty of spectrum available. VHF/UHF is a great resource!

The key to enjoyable use of this resource is to know how everyone else is using it and to fol-

HOW ARE THE BANDS ORGANIZED?

One of the keys to using this immense resource properly is knowing how the bands are organized. Each of the VHF and UHF bands is many megahertz wide, huge in comparison to any HF band. Different activities take place in separate parts of each. Even in the low ends of each VHF and UHF band, where SSB and CW activities congregate, there is a lot of

Nothing screams VHF/UHF DX like a tower full of long, horizontally polarized Yagi antennas. This impressive setup belongs to Fred, N1DPM, and covers 6 meters through 10 GHz.

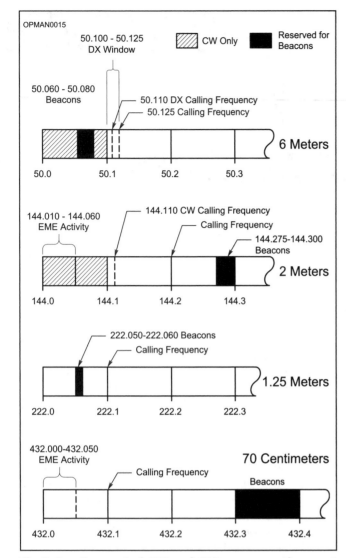

OPMAN0015

50.100 - 50.125
DX Window

CW Only

Reserved for Beacons

50.060 - 50.080
Beacons

50.110 DX Calling Frequency
50.125 Calling Frequency

6 Meters

50.0   50.1   50.2   50.3

144.010 - 144.060
EME Activity

144.110 CW Calling Frequency

Calling Frequency

144.275-144.300
Beacons

2 Meters

144.0   144.1   144.2   144.3

222.050-222.060 Beacons

Calling Frequency

1.25 Meters

222.0   222.1   222.2   222.3

432.000-432.050
EME Activity

70 Centimeters

Calling Frequency

Beacons

432.0   432.1   432.2   432.3   432.4

Fig 3-1 — Suggested CW and SSB usage on the most popular VHF and UHF bands. Activity on 144 MHz and higher centers around the calling frequencies.

Table 3-1
North American Calling Frequencies

Band (MHz)	Calling Frequency
50	50.090 general CW
	50.110 DX only
	50.125, general SSB
144	144.110 CW
	144.200 SSB
222	222.100 CW, SSB
432	432.100 CW, SSB
902	902.100 CW, SSB
	903.100 CW, SSB (East Coast)
1296	1296.100 CW, SSB
2304	2304.1 CW, SSB
10,000	10,368.1 CW, SSB

Table 3-2
Common Activity Nights

Band (MHz)	Day	Local Time
50	Sunday	6:00 PM
144	Monday	7:00 PM
222	Tuesday	8:00 PM
432	Wednesday	9:00 PM
902	Friday	9:00 PM
1296	Thursday	10:00 PM

quency to establish a contact, and then the two stations move up or down a few tens of kHz to chat. This way, everyone can share the calling frequency without having to listen to each other's QSOs. You can easily tell if the band is open by monitoring the call signs of the stations making contact on the calling frequency — you sure don't need to hear their whole QSO!

On 6 meters, a *DX window* has been established in order to reduce interference to DX stations. This window, which extends from 50.100 to 50.125 MHz, is intended for DX QSOs only. The DX calling frequency is 50.110 MHz. If you make a DX contact and expect to ragchew, you should move up a few kHz to clear the DX calling frequency. US and Canadian 6-meter operators should use the domestic calling frequency of 50.125 MHz for non-DX work. Because of increased crowding in the low end of the band in recent years, 50.200 MHz is becoming more popular as an alternative calling frequency. Once again, when contact is established, you should move off the calling frequency as quickly as possible.

ACTIVITY NIGHTS

Although it is possible to scare up a QSO on 50 or 144 MHz almost any evening (especially during the summer), in some areas of the country there is not always enough activity to make it easy to make a contact. Therefore, informal *activity nights* have been established so you will know when to expect some activity. Each band has its own night. **Table 3-2** shows the most common activity nights, but there is some variation in activity nights from place to place. Check with someone in your area to find out about local activity nights.

Activity nights are particularly important for 222 MHz and

low their lead. Basically, this means to listen first. Pay attention to the segments of the band already in use, and follow the operating practices that experienced operators are using. This way, you won't interfere with ongoing use of the band by others, and you'll fit in right away.

All of the bands between 50 and 1296 MHz have widely accepted calling frequencies (see **Table 3-1**). When there is little happening on the band, these are the frequencies operators will use to call CQ. For that reason, these are also the frequencies they are likely to monitor most of the time. Many VHF operators have gotten into a habit of tuning to one or more calling frequencies while doing something else around the shack. If someone wants a contact, you will already be on the right frequency to hear the call and make a contact.

The most important thing to remember about the calling frequencies is that they are not for ragchewing. After all, if a dozen other stations want to have a place to monitor for calls, it's really impolite to carry on a long-winded conversation on that frequency.

In most areas of the country, everyone uses the calling fre-

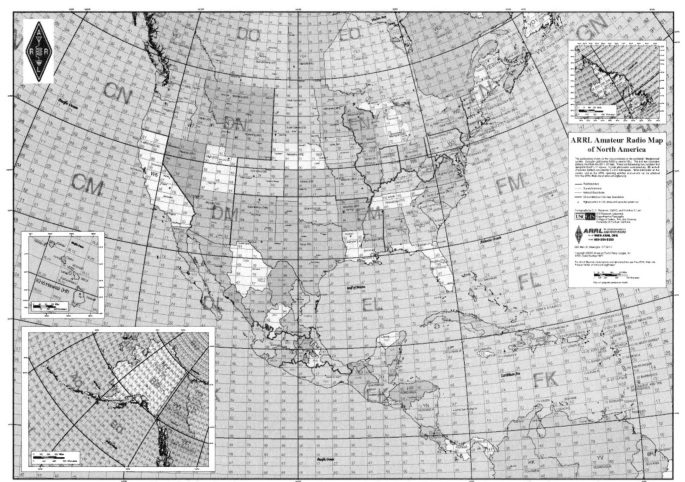

Fig 3-2 — ARRL Grid Locator Map. This colorful 27 × 39-inch map is available from the ARRL at www.arrl.org/catalog.

above, where there are relatively few active stations on the air on a regular basis. If you have just finished a new transverter or antenna for one of these bands, you will have a much better chance to try them out during the band's weekly activity night. That doesn't mean there is no activity on other nights, especially if the band is open. It may just take longer to get someone's attention during other times.

Local VHF/UHF nets often meet during activity nights. Nets provide a regular meeting time for hams on 6 and 2 meters primarily, although there are regional nets at least as high as 1296 MHz. Several regional VHF clubs sponsor nets in various parts of the country, especially in urban areas. For those whose location is far away from the net control's location, the nets may provide a means of determining if your station is operating up to snuff, or if propagation is enhanced. Furthermore, you can sometimes catch a rare state or grid locator checking into the net. For information on the meeting times and frequencies of the nets, inquire locally.

WHERE AM I?

One of the first things you are bound to notice on the low end of any VHF band is that most QSOs include an exchange of grid locators. For example, instead of trying to tell a distant station, "I'm in Canton, New York," I say instead "My grid is FN24." It may sound strange, but FN24 is easier to locate on a grid locator map than my small town.

So what are these grid locators? They are 1° latitude by 2° longitude sections of the Earth. A grid locator in the center of the US is about 68 by 104 miles, but grids change size and shape slightly, depending on their latitude.

Each locator has a unique two-letter/two-number identifier. The two letters identify one of 324 worldwide fields, which cover 10° latitude by 20° longitude each. There are 100 locators in each field, and these are identified by the two numbers. Exactly 32,400 grid locators cover the entire Earth. Two additional letters can be added for a more exact location, as in FN24kp. The extra two letters uniquely identifies a locale within a few miles.

There are several ways to find out your own grid square identifier. You can start by consulting **Table 3-3** and **Table 3-4**. By following the instructions shown in the tables, you will be able to locate your own grid. The hardest part is finding your location on a good map that has latitude and longitude on it; the rest is easy. Most high-quality road maps have this on the margins. Or, you could go a step further and purchase the topographic map of your immediate area from the US Geological Survey (**topomaps.usgs.gov**). Once you have your latitude and longitude, the rest is a snap!

The ARRL publishes a colorful, 27 × 39-inch grid- locator map (see **Fig 3-2**) of the continental United States and most populated areas of Canada. This map is available from ARRL

Table 3-3
How to Determine Your Grid Locator

1st and 2nd characters: Read directly from the map.

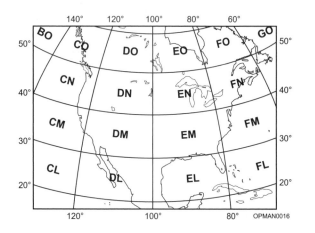

Degrees West Longitude	Third Character	Degrees West Longitude	Third Character	Degrees West Longitude	Third Character
60-61	9	88-89	5	114-115	2
62-63	8	90-91	4	116-117	1
64-65	7	92-93	3	118-119	0
66-67	6	94-95	2	120-121	9
68-69	5	96-97	1	122-123	8
70-71	4	98-99	0	124-125	7
72-73	3	100-101	9	126-127	6
74-75	2	102-103	8	128-129	5
76-77	1	104-105	7	130-131	4
78-79	0	106-107	6	132-133	3
80-81	9	108-109	5	134-135	2
82-83	8	110-111	4	136-137	1
84-85	7	112-113	3	138-139	0
86-87	6				

4th character: This number is the same as the 2nd single digit of your latitude. For example, if your latitude is 41° N, the 4th character is 1; for 29° N, it's 9, etc.

3rd character: Take the number of whole degrees west longitude, and consult the following chart.

This four-character (2-letter, 2-number) designator indicates your 2° by 1° grid locator for VUCC award purposes.

Wayne, N6NB, has been active on VHF+ for many years. Here he's seen at the operating position of his Rover station, used to activate multiple grids during VHF contests.

Doug, VE1PZ, at his station near Pictou, Nova Scotia. Doug runs an IC-706 and a 1200-W amplifier into a 9-element 6-meter Yagi on a tower that overlooks the Northumberland Strait.

online at **www.arrl.org/catalog**. If you are keeping track of grids for VUCC (the VHF/UHF Century Club award — see the **Operating Awards** chapter), you can mark each grid as you work it. The ARRL also publishes a *World Grid Locator Atlas*, available from the Web catalog as well.

For more grid locator information and resources, point your browser to **www.arrl.org/locate/gridinfo.html**.

PROPAGATION
Normal Conditions

What sort of range is considered normal in the world above 50 MHz? To a large extent, range on VHF is determined by location and the quality of the stations involved. After all, you can't expect the same performance from a 10-W rig and a small antenna on the roof as you might from a kilowatt and stacked beams at 100 feet.

On 2-meter SSB, a typical station probably consists of a low-powered multimode rig (SSB/CW/FM), followed by a 100-W amplifier, or one of the HF/VHF/UHF transceivers that includes SSB/CW at 50-100 W on this band. The antenna might be a single long Yagi at around 50 feet, fed with low-loss coax.

How far could this station cover on an average night using SSB? Location plays a big role, but it's probably safe to estimate that you could talk to a similarly equipped station about 200 miles away almost 100% of the time. Naturally, higher-power stations with tall antennas and low-noise receive preamps will have a greater range than this, up to a practical maximum of about 350-400 miles in the Midwest, less in the hilly West and East. It is almost always possible to extend your range significantly by switching from SSB to CW.

On 222 MHz, a similar station might expect to cover nearly the same distance, and perhaps 100 miles less on 432 MHz.

Table 3-4
More Precise Locator

To indicate location more precisely, the addition of 5th and 6th characters will define the *sub-grid*, measuring about 4 × 3 miles in the central US. Longitude-latitude coordinates on maps, such as US Department of the Interior Surveys, can be extrapolated to the nearest tenth of a minute, necessary for this level of locator precision. *This is not necessary in the VUCC awards program.*

5th character: If your number of degrees longitude is an *odd* number, see Fig A. If your number of degrees longitude is an *even* number, see Fig B.

Odd Longitude* (Fig A)

Minutes W. Longitude	5th Character
0-5	L
5-10	K
10-15	J
15-20	I
20-25	H
25-30	G
30-35	F
35-40	E
40-45	D
45-50	C
50-55	B
55-60	A

Even Longitude* (Fig B)

Minutes W. Longitude	5th Character
0-5	X
5-10	W
10-15	V
15-20	U
20-25	T
25-30	S
30-35	R
35-40	Q
40-45	P
45-50	O
50-55	N
55-60	M

6th character: Take the number of minutes of latitude (following the number of degrees) and consult the following chart.

Minutes N. Latitude	6th Character	Minutes N. Latitude	6th Character
0-2.5	A	30.0-32.5	M
2.5-5.0	B	32.5-35.0	N
5.0-7.5	C	35.0-37.5	O
7.5-10.0	D	37.5-40.0	P
10.0-12.5	E	40.0-42.5	Q
12.5-15.0	F	42.5-45.0	R
15.0-17.5	G	45.0-47.5	S
17.5-20.0	H	47.5-50.0	T
20.0-22.5	I	50.0-52.5	U
22.5-25.0	J	52.5-55.0	V
25.0-27.5	K	55.0-57.5	W
27.5-30.0	L	57.5-60.0	X

This assumes normal propagation conditions and a reasonably unobstructed horizon. This range is a lot greater than you would get for noise-free communication on FM, and it represents the sort of capability the typical station should seek. Increase the height of the antenna to 80 feet and the range might increase to 250 miles, probably more, depending on your location. That's not bad for reliable communication!

Band Openings and DX

The main thrill of the VHF and UHF bands for most of us is the occasional band opening, when signals from far away are received as if they are next door. DX of well over 1000 miles on 6 meters is commonplace during the summer, and the same distance at least once or twice a year on 144, 222 and 432 MHz in all but mountainous areas.

DX propagation on the VHF/UHF bands is strongly influenced by the seasons. Summer and fall are definitely the most active times in the spectrum above 50 MHz, although band openings occur at other times as well.

There are many different ways VHF and UHF signals can be propagated over long distances. These can be divided between conditions that exist in the troposphere (the weather-producing lowest 10 miles of the atmosphere) and the ionosphere (between 50 and 400 miles high). The two atmospheric regions are quite distinct and have little effect on each other.

Tropospheric Ducting — or Simply Ducting

Ducts are responsible for the most common form of DX-producing propagation on the bands above 144 MHz. Ducts are like natural waveguides that trap signals close to the Earth for hundreds of miles with little loss of signal strength. They come in several forms, depending on local and regional weather patterns. This is because ducts are caused by the weather. Ducts may cover only a few hundred miles, or they may include huge areas of the country at once.

Radiation Inversion (mostly summer). This common type of weak duct is caused by the Earth cooling off in the evening. The air just above the Earth's surface also cools, while the air a few hundred meters above remains warm. This creates an inversion that refracts VHF/UHF radio signals. If there is little or no wind, there may be a gradual improvement in the strength of signals out to a range of 100-200 miles (less in hilly areas) as evening passes into night. Radiation ducts mostly affect the bands above 144 MHz, and are seldom noticeable at 50 MHz.

Broad, regional ducts (late summer and early fall). These are the DXer's dream! In one of these openings, stations as far away as 1200 miles (and maybe more) are brought into range on VHF/UHF. The broad, regional type of ducting opening is caused by stagnation of a large, slow-moving high-pressure system. The stations that benefit the most are often on the south or western sides (the so-called back side) of the system. This sort of sluggish weather system may often be forecast just by looking at a weather map.

Wave-cyclone tropo (spring). These openings don't usually last long. They are brought about by an advancing cold front that interacts with the warm sector ahead of it. The resulting contrast in air temperatures may cause thunderstorms along the front. If conditions are just right, a band opening may result. These openings usually involve stations in the warm sector ahead of the cold front. You may feel that there's a pipeline between you and a DX station 1000 miles or more away. You may not be able to contact anybody else!

There are several other types of tropo openings, but space doesn't allow more than a brief discussion here. Coastal breezes sometimes cause long, narrow tropo openings along the East and Gulf Coasts. Rarely, cold fronts may cause brief openings as they slide under warmer air. US West Coast VHFers

Microwaves

The region above 1000 MHz is known as the microwave spectrum. Although European amateurs have made tremendous use of this rich resource, Americans lag behind somewhat. Commercial equipment from several European and US suppliers is becoming more widely available. The microwaves also provide great opportunities for building and experimenting, although entirely different construction techniques are required if amateurs are to build their own equipment. Nevertheless, the microwave bands are receiving a lot of attention from the experimentally minded among us. We can expect a considerable amount of progress as more amateurs try out the microwave bands.

The most popular microwave band in the USA is 10 GHz (3 cm). Using narrowband techniques (SSB/CW) and high-gain dish antennas, hams have made QSOs over 600 miles, but these are quite rare.

Most microwave activity is by prearranged schedules (at least in the US). This is partly because activity is so sparse and partly because antenna bandwidths are so narrow. With a 5° beamwidth, you would have to call CQ 72 times to cover a complete circle!

are always on the alert for the California-to-Hawaii duct that permits 2500-mile DX. For a very complete discussion of all the major forms of weather- related VHF propagation, see "The Weather That Brings VHF DX," by Emil Pocock, W3EP, in May 1983 *QST*.

The Scatter Modes

Long-distance communication on the VHF and lower UHF bands is possible using the ionosphere. Some modes are within the reach of modest stations, especially with advanced digital modes. Others require very large antennas and high power. They all have one thing in common: They take advantage of the scattering of radio waves whenever there are irregularities in the atmosphere. Very briefly, the main types are:

Tropospheric scatter. Scattering in the troposphere is actually the most common form of propagation. You use it all the time without even knowing it. Tropo scatter is what creates ordinary beyond-line-of-sight contacts every day. It is the result of scattering from blobs of air of wavelength size that have slightly different temperature or humidity characteristics than surrounding air. Maximum tropo-scatter distance is the same as your normal working distance. There is a maximum theoretical tropo-scatter distance at VHF/UHF using amateur techniques of about 500 miles, regardless of frequency.

Ionospheric forward scatter. Scattering from the D and lower reaches of the E layers propagate VHF signals from 500 to a maximum of about 1000 miles. Signals at 50 MHz are apt

to be very weak and fade in and out of the noise, even for the best equipped pairs of stations. Forward scatter contacts are much rarer at 144 MHz. SSB usually is not effective. The best times are at mid-day.

Meteor scatter. When meteors enter the Earth's atmosphere, they ionize a small trail through the E layer. This ionization typically lasts only a few seconds at 50 MHz, and for even shorter periods at higher frequencies. Before it dissipates, the ionization can scatter, or sometimes reflect, VHF radio waves. Meteor scatter signals may not last long, but they can be surprisingly strong, popping suddenly out of the noise and then slowly fading away. It is quite common on 6 meters, less so on 2 meters, and rare indeed on 222 and 432 MHz. No successful QSOs have been completed at higher frequencies. Operating techniques for this mode are discussed later.

Sporadic E (E_s or E-skip)

This type of propagation is the most spectacular DX-producer on the 50-MHz band, where it may occur almost every day from late May to early August. A less intense E_s season also occurs during December and January. Sporadic E is most common in mid-morning and again around sunset during the summer months, but it can occur any time, any date. E_s occurs on 2 meters several times a summer somewhere across the US.

E_s is the result of the formation of thin but unusually dense clouds of ionization in the E layer. These clouds appear to move about, intensify, and disappear rapidly and without warning. The causes of sporadic E are not fully understood.

Reflections from sporadic-E clouds make single-hop contacts of 500 to 1400 miles possible on 50 MHz and much more rarely on 144 MHz. Only two sporadic-E like contacts have been reported above 220 MHz. Multi-hop E_s contacts commonly provide several coast-to-coast openings on 6 meters

The promise of DX inspires VHF operators to travel, just as it does on HF. Clint, FS/W3ARS, headed to the Caribbean and made several hundred 6-meter QSOs with operators in the US and Canada, as well as South America. (*K3LP photo*)

Doug, N7CNH, operating an all-mode transceiver and halo antenna on 2 meters from Spencer Butte south of Eugene, Oregon. Doug had to carry the equipment as he hiked to the top.

each summer and even opportunities to work Europe and Japan! The longest sporadic-E contacts are in excess of 6000 miles, but these are rare.

Sporadic-E signals are usually quite strong, allowing even the most modest station to make long-distance contacts. Openings may last only 15 minutes or go on all day. So far, there has been no satisfactory way to predict when these elusive openings will make their appearance, but they are exciting when they do happen.

The NØDQS rover station runs grid expeditions in the midwest, operating from 6 meters through 24 GHz.

Aurora (Au)

The aurora borealis, or northern lights, is a beautiful spectacle which is seen occasionally by those who live in Canada, the northern part of the USA and northern Europe. Similar southern lights are sometimes visible in the southernmost parts of South America, Africa and Australia. The aurora is caused by the Earth intercepting a massive number of charged particles thrown from the Sun during a solar storm. These particles are funneled into the polar regions of the Earth by its magnetic field. As the charged particles interact with the upper atmosphere, the air glows, which we see as the aurora. These particles also create an irregular, moving curtain of ionization which can propagate signals for many hundreds of miles.

Like sporadic E, aurora is more evident on 6 meters than on 2 meters. Nevertheless, 2-meter Au is far more common than 2-meter sporadic E, at least above 40° N latitude. Au is also possible on 222 and 432 MHz, and many tremendous DX contacts have been made on these bands. Current record distances are over 1000 miles on 144, 222 and 432 MHz.

Aurora can be predicted to some extent from current reports of solar and geomagnetic activity, which can be found on most DX clusters, on Web sites sponsored by the National Oceanic and Atmospheric Administration, and on WWV broadcasts. At 18 minutes past each hour, WWV transmits a summary of the condition of the Earth's geomagnetic field. If the K index is 4 or above, you should watch for Au. Many VHFers have learned that a high K index is no guarantee of an aurora. Similarly, K indices of only 3 have occasionally produced spectacular radio auroras at middle latitudes. When in doubt, point the antenna north and listen!

Auroral DX signals are highly distorted. CW is the most practical mode, although SSB is sometimes used. Stations point their antennas generally northward and listen for the telltale hissing note that is characteristic of auroral signals. More about operating Au is presented later.

Auroral E (AuE)

Signals propagated by auroral-induced sporadic E sound very much like ordinary E-skip, but its causes and timing are quite different. Auroral E is induced by the same conditions that give rise to auroras, and like aurora, AuE is more common at northerly latitudes. Auroral E may accompany unusually strong auroras, but is more usually observed after midnight across the northern tier of states and Canada. Distances covered are similar to sporadic E.

Transequatorial Field-Aligned Irregularities (TE)

This unusual propagation mode creates paths of 2500 to 5000 miles on 50 MHz, and less commonly on 144 and 222 MHz. It involves some strict requirements. TE works only for stations equally distant from the geomagnetic equator. Common TE paths are from the Mediterranean to southern Africa, southern Japan to Australia, and the Caribbean and Venezuela to Argentina. The geomagnetic equator is displaced considerably to the south of the geographic equator in the Americas, so that only US stations from south Florida to southern California can normally make TE contacts into Argentina and Uruguay. TE-to E_s hook-ups on 50 MHz sometimes extend the possible coverage much further north.

TE appears almost exclusively in late afternoon and is more common around the March and September equinoxes, especially in years of high solar activity or when there is a geomagnetic storm. Signals have an unmistakable fluttery quality. TE is caused by two unusually dense regions of F-layer ionization that appear just north and south of the geomagnetic equator. Neither region is capable of propagating VHF signals over such long distances separately, but when linked together at the proper angles, some long north-south paths can result.

Earth-Moon-Earth (EME or Moonbounce)

This is the ultimate VHF/UHF DX medium! Moonbouncers use the Moon as a passive reflector for their signals, and QSO distance is limited only by the diameter of the Earth. Any two stations who can simultaneously see the Moon may be able to work each other via EME. QSOs between the USA and Europe or Japan are commonplace on VHF and UHF by using this mode. That's DX!

Previously the territory of only the biggest and most serious VHFers, moonbounce has now become more widely popular. Thanks to the efforts of pioneer moonbouncers such as Bob Sutherland, W6PO, and Al Katz, K2UYH, hundreds of stations are active, mainly on 144 and 432 MHz. This huge increase in activity especially by a handful of stations with gigantic antenna arrays, has encouraged many others to try making contacts via the moon.

Improvements in technology — low-noise amplifiers and

Cowles, K4EME, sets his sights on the moon with this antenna array.

better designs — have made it easier to get started. Also, several individuals have assembled gigantic antenna arrays, which make up for the inadequacy of smaller antennas. The result is that even modestly equipped VHF stations (150 W and one or two Yagis) are capable of making a few moonbounce contacts. Activity is constantly increasing. There is even an EME contest in which moonbouncers compete on an international scale.

Moonbounce requires larger antennas than most terrestrial VHF/UHF work. In addition, you must have a high-power transmitting amplifier and a low-noise receiving preamplifier to work more than the biggest guns. A modest EME station on 144 MHz consists of four long-boom Yagi antennas on an azimuth-elevation mount (for pointing at the Moon), a kilowatt amplifier and a low-noise preamplifier mounted at the antenna. On 432 MHz, the average antenna is eight long Yagis. You can make contacts with a smaller antenna, but they will be with only larger stations on the other end. Some UHFers have also built large parabolic dish antennas.

HOW DO I OPERATE ON VHF/UHF?
Normal Conditions

The most important rule to follow on VHF/UHF, like all other amateur bands, is to listen first. Even on the relatively uncrowded VHF bands, interference is common near the calling frequencies. The first thing to do when you switch on the radio is to tune around, listening for activity. Of course, the calling frequencies are the best place to start listening. If you listen for a few minutes, you'll probably hear someone make a call, even if the band isn't open. If you don't hear anyone, then it's time to make some noise yourself!

Stirring up activity on the lower VHF bands is usually just a matter of pointing the antenna and calling CQ. Because most VHF beams are rather narrow, you might have to call CQ in several directions before you find someone. Several short CQs are always more productive than one long-winded CQ. But don't make CQs too short; you have to give the other station time to turn the antenna toward you.

Give your rotator lots of exercise; don't point the antenna at the same place all the time. You never know if a new station or some DX might be available at some odd beam heading.

VHFers in out-of-the-way locations, far from major cities, monitor the bands in the hope of hearing you.

Band Openings

How about DX? What is the best way to work DX when the band is open? There's no simple answer. Each main type of band opening or propagation mode requires its own techniques. This is natural, because the strength and duration of openings vary considerably. For example, you wouldn't expect to operate the same way during a 10-second meteor-burst QSO as during a three-day tropo opening.

The following is a review of the different main types of propagation and descriptions of the ways that most VHFers take advantage of them.

Tropospheric Ducting

Tropospheric ducts, whatever their causes, affect the entire VHF through microwave range, although true ducting is rarely observed at 50 MHz. Ducts often persist for hours at a time, sometimes for several days, so there is usually no panic about making contacts. There is time to listen carefully and determine the extent of the opening and its likely evolution.

Ducts are most common in the Mississippi Valley during late summer and early fall, and they may expand over much of the country from the Rocky Mountains eastward. Sprawling high-pressure systems that slowly drift southeastward often

Who says portable operators have to rough it? John, N2PBY, and Al, NX2Q, show us a better way.

Jack, AB4CR, setting up portable antennas for his rover entry in the ARRL September VHF QSO Party.

portion of the 50 or 144 MHz bands. Schedules may enhance the chances of success, but in any case, patience and a willingness to deal with weak fluttery signals is required. Contacts are sometimes completed via meteor-scatter enhancement that by chance occurs at the same time.

Meteor Scatter

Meteor scatter is very widely used on 50 and 144 MHz, and it has been used on 222 and 432 as well. Operation with this exciting mode of DX comes under two main headings: prearranged schedules and random contacts. Either SSB or CW may be used, although SSB is more popular in North America. European-style high-speed CW meteor-scatter techniques, which use a computer to send and help receive Morse code sent at several hundred to several thousand characters per minute, has caught on in the US.

Meteor-Scatter Procedure

In a meteor-scatter QSO, neither station can hear the other except when a meteor trail exists to scatter or reflect their signals. The two stations take turns transmitting so that they can be sure of hearing the other if a meteor happens to fall. They agree beforehand on the sequence of transmission. One station agrees to transmit the 1st and 3rd 15 seconds of each minute, and the other station takes the 2nd and 4th. It is standard procedure for the western-most station to transmit during the 1st and 3rd.

It's important to have a format for transmissions so you know what the other station has heard. This format is used by most US stations for CW and SSB :

Transmitting	Means you have copied;
Call signs	nothing, or only partial calls
Call plus signal report (or grid or state)	full calls-both sets
ROGER plus signal report(or grid or state)	full calls, plus signal report (or grid or state)
ROGER	ROGER from other station

Remember, for a valid QSO to take place, you must exchange full call signs, some piece of information, and acknowledgment. Too many meteor QSOs have not been completed for lack of ROGERs. Don't quit too soon; be sure the other station has received your acknowledgment. Often, stations will add 73 when they want to indicate that they have heard the other station's ROGER.

Until a few years ago, it was universal practice to give a signal report which indicated the length of the meteor burst. S1 meant that you were just hearing pings, S2 meant 1-5 second bursts, and so on. Unfortunately, virtually everyone was sending S2, so there was no mystery at all, and no significant information was being exchanged.

Grid locators have become popular as the piece of information in meteor-scatter QSOs. More and more stations are sending their grid instead of S2. This is especially true on random meteor-scatter QSOs, where you might not know in advance where the station is located. Other stations prefer to give their state instead.

create strong ducts. The best conditions usually appear in the southwestern quadrant of massive highs.

Along the East Coast, ducting is more common along coastal paths of up to 1000 miles and sometimes longer. Stations in New England have worked as far as Cuba on 2 meters this way. The mountainous west rarely experiences long-distance ducting.

This void is partially made up by one of the most famous of all ducting paths, which creates paths from the West Coast to Hawaii. The famous trans-Pacific duct opens up several times a year in summer, supporting often incredibly strong signals over 2500 miles on 144 MHz through at least 5.6 GHz. Several world distance records have been made over this path. Other common over-water ducts appear across the Gulf of Mexico, mostly in early spring.

Ducts can be anticipated by studying weather maps and forecasts. Many VHFers also check television stations, especially in the UHF range, for early warnings of enhanced conditions. Check beacons on 144 MHz and higher, especially those you cannot ordinarily hear. Keep in mind that most forms of ducting intensify after sunset and peak just after sunrise. All of these techniques can enhance your chances of catching a ducting opening.

Ionospheric Forward Scatter

This mode is not used to its full potential, probably because forward scatter signals are often weak and easily overlooked. The best chances are for cooperating stations using CW in a quiet

Meteor Showers

Every day, the Earth is bombarded by billions of tiny grains of interplanetary debris, called meteors. They create short-lived trails of E-layer ionization which can be used as reflectors for VHF radio waves. On a normal morning, careful listeners can hear about 3-5 meteor pings (short bursts of meteor-reflected signal) per hour on 2 meters.

At several times during the year, the Earth passes through huge clouds of concentrated meteoric debris, and VHFers enjoy a meteor shower. During meteor showers, 2-meter operators may hear 50 or more pings and bursts per hour. Here are some data on the major meteor showers of the year. Other showers also occur, but they are very minor.

Major Meteor Showers

Shower	Date range	Peak date	Time above quarter max	Approximate visual rate	Speed km/s	Best Paths and Times (local)
Quadrantids	Jan 1-6	Jan 3/4	14 hours	40-150	41	NE-SW (1300-1500), SE-NW (0500-0700)
Eta Aquarids	Apr 21-May 12	May 4/5	3 days	10-40	65	NE-SW (0500-0700), E-W (0600-0900), SE-NW (0900-1100)
Arietids	May 29-Jun 19	Jun 7	?	60	37	N-S (0600-0700 and 1300-1400)
Perseids	Jul 23-Aug 20	Aug 12	4.6 days	50-100	59	NE-SW (0900-1100), SE-NW (0100-0300)
Orionids	Oct 2-Nov 7	Oct 22	2 days	10-70	66	NE-SW (0100-0300), N-S (0100-0200 & 0700-0900), NW-SE (0700-0800)
Geminids	Dec 4-16	Dec 13/14	2.6 days	50-80	34	N-S (2200-2400 and 0500-0700)

Most meteor-scatter work is done during major meteor showers, and many stations arrange schedules with stations in needed states or grid locators. In a sked, 15-second transmit-receive sequences are the norm for North America (Europeans use longer sequences). One station, almost always the western-most, will take the first and third 15-second periods of each minute and the other station takes second and fourth. This is a very simple procedure that ensures that only one station is transmitting when a meteor falls. See accompanying sidebar.

A specific frequency, far removed from local activity centers, is chosen when the sked is set up. It is important that both stations have accurate frequency readout and synchronized clocks, but with today's technology this is not the big problem that it once was. Schedules normally run for ½ hour or 1 hour, especially on 222 and 432 MHz where meteor-scatter QSOs are well earned!

The best way to get the feel for the meteor-scatter QSO format is to listen to a couple of skeds between experienced operators. Then, look in *QST* or ask around for the call sign of veteran meteor-scatter operators in the 800-1000 mile range from you (this is the easiest distance for meteor scatter). Call them on the telephone or catch them on one of the national VHF nets and arrange a sked. After you cut your teeth on easy skeds, you'll be ready for more difficult DX.

A lot of stations make plenty of meteor-scatter QSOs without the help of skeds. Especially during major meteor showers, VHFers congregate near the calling frequency of each band. There they wait for meteor bursts like hunters waiting for ducks. Energetic operators make repeated and brief CQs, hoping to catch an elusive meteor. When meteors blast in, the band comes alive with dozens of quick QSOs. For a brief time, normally five seconds to perhaps 30 seconds, 2 meters may sound like 20 meters! Then the band is quiet again. . . until the next meteor burst!

The quality of shower-related meteor-scatter DX depends on three factors. These three factors are well known or can be predicted. The most important is the radiant effect. The radiant is the spot in the sky from which the meteors appear to fall. If the radiant is below the horizon, or too high in the sky, you will hear very few meteors. The most productive spot for the radiant is at an elevation of about 45° and an azimuth of 90° from the path you're trying to work. The second important factor is the velocity of the meteors. Slow meteors cannot ionize sufficiently to propagate 144 or 222-MHz signals, no matter how many meteors there are. For 144 MHz, meteors slower than 50 km/s are usually inadequate (see accompanying sidebar detailing major meteor showers). Third, the shower will have a peak in the number of meteors that the Earth intercepts. However, because the peak of many meteor showers is more than a day in length, the exact time of the peak is not as important as most people think. Two interesting references are "Improving Meteor Scatter Communications," by Joe Reisert, W1JR, in June 1984 *Ham Radio*, and "VHF Meteor Scatter: an Astronomical Perspective," by M. R. Owen, W9IP, in June 1986 *QST*.

It takes a lot of persistence and a good station to be successful with random meteor scatter. This is mainly because you must overcome tremendous interference in addition to the fluctuations of meteor propagation. At least 100 W is necessary for much success in meteor scatter, and a full kilowatt will help a lot. One or two Yagis, stacked vertically, is a good antenna system. Antennas with too much gain have narrow beamwidths, and so often cannot pick up many usable meteor-scatter bursts.

In populated areas, it can be difficult to hear incoming meteor-scatter DX if many local stations are calling CQ. Therefore, many areas observe 15-second sequencing for random meteor-scatter QSOs, just as for skeds. Those who want to call CQ do so at the same time so everyone can listen for responses between transmissions. Sometimes a bit of peer pressure is necessary to keep everyone together, but it pays off in more QSOs for all. The same QSO format is used for scheduled and random meteor-scatter QSOs.

Meteor Scatter With WSJT

It may come as a surprise to learn that meteors are plunging into Earth's atmosphere around the clock, not just during annual meteor showers. Dust-grain meteors leave so-called *underdense meteor trails* that will reflect VHF radio signals, albeit briefly (seconds or fractions of seconds). Even in this narrow window of time, it is possible to communicate with bursts of digital data over distances of more than 1000 miles.

Joe Taylor, K1JT, set out to design a digital encoding scheme and software package to enable amateur QSOs using the brief *pings* (signal reflections) from underdense meteor trails. The result led to a computer program called *WSJT* (for "Weak Signal Communication, by K1JT") that implements a signal protocol called FSK441. The mode works so well that it has been rapidly embraced by the VHF fraternities in Europe and North America, and is now making inroads in Africa and the South Pacific as well.

If your station is capable of weak signal SSB work on the 6 meter or 2 meter bands — say, if you have 100 W or more to a modest Yagi up at least 40 feet — then with the help of *WSJT* you should be able to work similarly equipped stations in the 500-1100 mile range at nearly any time of the day or year. (On the minimum end of the scale, *WSJT* QSOs have been made with as little as 10 W.) With a higher antenna and more power, QSOs out to 1300 or 1400 miles become possible. QSOs have already been made with *WSJT* on 222 MHz as well, and contacts on 432 MHz might be possible near the peak of a major meteor shower.

What Do You Need?

WSJT requires an SSB transceiver, a computer running the *Windows* operating system, and a soundcard interfaced to the radio's "microphone in" and "speaker out" ports. *Linux* versions are also available. You will, of course, need a station capable of weak signal work on one or more VHF bands. The *WSJT* program is available for download free of charge at the Web site **physics.princeton.edu/pulsar/K1JT** and at the European mirror site **www.vhfdx.de/wsjt**.

You will need a sound card interface such as the ones discussed in the **HF Digital Communications** chapter. The DTR or RTS line of one of the computer's serial communication (COM) ports is used to key your transmitter's push-to-talk (PTT) line. Connections are also required between the transceiver audio output and computer sound card input, and vice versa. If your computer is already set up for packet radio, APRS or one of the sound-card-based HF digital modes, you already have everything you need to operate *WSJT*.

Timing is critical when it comes to *WSJT* meteor scatter because stations typically transmit for 30 seconds and then listen for 30 seconds. You will need a method of synchronizing your computer clock with UTC to an accuracy around one second or better. If you have an Internet connection and you are using *Windows XP*, look under Date and Time in the Control Panel. There you will find a function that will synchronize your PC. Otherwise, try a synchronizing utility program called *Dimen-*

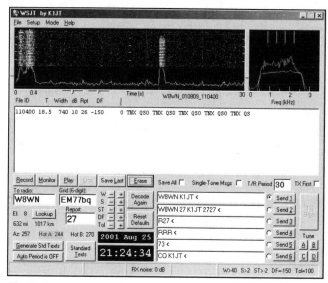

Fig 3-3 — *WSJT* software in action.

sion 4 that you can download from the Web at **www.thinkman. com/dimension4/**.

How Does It Work?

The encoding scheme used in *WSJT* was designed to make the best use of signals just a few decibels above the receiver noise, exhibiting rapid fading and Doppler shifts up to 100 Hz, and typically lasting from 20 to a few hundred milliseconds. One *WSJT* protocol uses a four-tone frequency shift keying at a rate of 441 baud. The adopted scheme was been given the technical name FSK441, although most people seem to be calling it simply "the *WSJT* mode."

An FSK441 transmission contains no dead spaces between tones or between characters; the typical short messages exchanged in meteor scatter QSOs are sent repeatedly and continuously, usually for 30 seconds at a time.

Fig 3-3 shows a screen-capture image of *WSJT* in operation. At the top of the form are two graphical areas. The larger one displays a "waterfall" spectrogram in which time runs left to right and audio frequency increases upward. The smaller graphical window at the right displays two spectral plots, also on a dB scale. The purple line graphs the spectrum of audio-frequency noise, averaged over the full 30 seconds; in the absence of any strong signal, it effectively illustrates the receiver's passband shape. The red line displays the spectrum of the strongest detected ping. Yellow tick marks at the top of this plot area (and also at the left, center, and right of the larger area) indicate the nominal frequencies of the four FSK441 tones.

The large text box in the middle of the *WSJT* screen displays decoded text from any pings detected in the receiving interval. One line of text appears for each validated ping.

Meteor scatter is not a communication mode well suited to ragchewing. QSOs can be completed much more easily if you adhere to a set of standard procedures. A standard message format and message sequence helps the process considerably. *WSJT* generates standard messages automatically, as illustrated in the text boxes at the lower right of Fig 3-3. The formats of the messages are designed for efficient transfer of the most essential information: the exchange of both call signs, a signal report or other information, and acknowledgments of same. Timed message sequences are necessary, and *WSJT* defaults to 30 second transmitting and receiving periods. Although other intervals can be selected, it helps to minimize QRM from nearby stations if everyone adheres to one standard. According to the procedures used by common consent in North America, the westernmost station transmits first in each minute.

At the start of a QSO, you should send the other station's call and your own call alternately. Then, as the QSO proceeds…

1. If you have received less than both calls from the other station, send both calls.

2. If you have received both calls, send both calls and a signal report.

3. If you have received both calls and a report, send R plus signal report.

4. If you have received R plus signal report, send RRR.

5. If you have received RRR — that is, a definite acknowledgment of all of your information — your QSO is officially complete. However, the other station may not know this, so it is conventional to send 73 (or some other conversational information) to signify that you are done.

Signal reports are conventionally sent as two-digit numbers chosen from nonoverlapping ranges. The first digit characterizes the lengths of pings being received, on a 1-5 scale, and the second estimates their strength on a 6-9 scale. The most common signal reports are "26" for weak pings and "27" for stronger ones, but under good conditions reports such as "38" and higher are sometimes used. Whatever signal report you decide to send to your QSO partner, it is important that you do not change it, even if stronger pings should come along later in the contact. You never know when pings will successfully convey fragments of your message to the other end of your path, and you want your received information to be consistent.

The 6- and 2-meter calling frequencies in common use for *WSJT* in North America are 50.270 and 144.140 MHz. Typical practice for calling CQ is to send something like CQ U5 K1JT or CQ D9 K1JT, indicating that you will listen for replies up 5 kHz or down 9 kHz from your transmitting frequency, and will respond on that frequency. However, the easiest way to initiate a QSO is to post an on-line invitation on a Web page known as Ping Jockey Central at **www.pingjockey.net/**. Someone at a suitable range from you will likely reply to such a posting, suggesting a specific frequency, and your QSO can begin. The ranges of frequencies now being used for *WSJT* in North America are 50.270-50.300 and 144.100-144.150 MHz.

More WSJT Modes

The latest version of *WSJT* also offers JT44 (**Fig 3-4**), a digital mode for moonbounce communication, and JT6M, a meteor-scatter mode designed primarily for 6-meter work. For complete details and more in-depth operating instructions, go to **physics.princeton.edu/pulsar/K1JT**.

Sporadic E

Sporadic-E signals are generally so loud and openings last long enough that no special operating techniques are necessary to enjoy this mode. On 6 meters, 10-W stations with simple antennas can easily make contacts out to 1000 miles or so. The band may open for hours on any summer day, with signals constantly shifting, disappearing and reappearing. A sporadic-E opening on 2 meters is much less common and typically lasts for less than an hour. Signals out to 1000 miles or so can be unbelievably strong, yet there is reason to be more alert. E-skip openings on 2 meters are rare and do not usually last long.

The main question for those hoping for sporadic E is when the band will open. Aside from knowing sporadic E is more common in summer mornings and early evenings than any other times, there is no satisfactory way to predict E-skip. It can appear any time.

Sporadic E affects lower frequencies first, so you can get some warning by listening to 10 meters. When E-skip shortens to 500 miles or so, it is almost certain that there is propagation somewhere on 6 meters. Some avid E-skip fans monitor TV channel 2 or 3 (if there is no local station) for signs of sporadic E.

Aurora and Auroral E

Aurora favors stations at high latitudes. It is a wonderful blessing for those who must suffer through long, cold winters because other forms of propagation are rare during the winter. Aurora can come at almost any time of the year. New England stations get Au on 2 meters about five to 10 times a year, whereas stations in Tennessee get it once a year if they're lucky. Central and Southern California rarely hear aurora.

The MUF of the aurora seems to rise quickly, so don't wait for the lower-frequency VHF bands to get exhausted before moving up in frequency. Check the higher bands right away.

You'll notice aurora by its characteristic hiss. Signals are distorted by reflection and scattering off the rapidly moving curtain of ionization. They sound like they are being transmitted by a leaking high-pressure steam vent rather than radio. SSB voice signals are so badly distorted that often you cannot understand them unless the speaker talks very slowly and clearly. The amount of distortion increases with frequency. Most 50-MHz Au contacts are made on SSB, where distortion

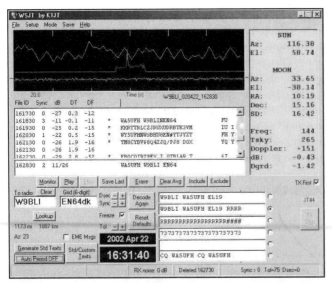

Fig 3-4 — The *WSJT* software suite running the JT44 moonbounce mode.

is the least. On 144, 222 and 432 MHz, CW is the only really useful means of communicating via Au.

If you suspect Au, tune to the CW calling frequency (144.110) or the SSB calling frequency (144.200) and listen with the antenna to the north. Maybe you'll hear some signals. Try swinging the antenna as much as 45° either side of due north to peak signals. In general, the longest-distance DX stations peak the farthest away from due north. Also, it is possible to work stations far south of you by using the aurora; in that case your antenna is often pointed north.

High power isn't necessary for aurora, but it helps. Ten-watt stations have made Au QSOs but it takes a lot of perseverance. Increasing your power to 100 W will greatly improve your chances of making Au QSOs. As with most short-lived DX openings, it pays to keep transmissions brief.

Aurora openings may last only a few minutes or they may last many hours, and the opening may return the next night, too. If WWV indicates a geomagnetic storm, begin listening on 2 meters in the late afternoon. Many spectacular Au openings begin before sunset and continue all evening. If you get the feeling that the Au has faded away, don't give up too soon. Aurora has a habit of dying and then returning several times, often around midnight. If you experience a terrific Au opening, look for an encore performance about 27 to 28 days later, because of the rotation of the Sun.

Dick, WB6DNX, sets up a demonstration of his 2304-MHz gear.

Auroral-E propagation is nearly a nightly occurrence in the auroral zone, but it may accompany auroras at lower latitudes. Do not be surprised to hear rough-sounding auroral signals on 6 meters slowly turn clear and strong! Auroral E is probably more common after local midnight after any evening when there has been an aurora. Auroral E propagation can last until nearly dawn. Six-meter contacts up to 2500 miles across northern latitudes (such as Maine to Yukon Territory) are not uncommon. Two-meter auroral E may also be commonplace in the arctic, but it is very rarely observed south of Canada.

PROPAGATION INDICATORS

Active VHFers keep a careful eye on various propagation indicators to tell if the VHF bands will be open. The kind of indicator you monitor is related to the expected propagation. For example, during the summer it pays to watch closely for sporadic E because openings may be very brief. If your area only gets one or two per year on 2 meters, you sure don't want to miss them!

Many forms of VHF/UHF propagation develop first at low frequency and then move upward to include the higher bands. Aurora is a good example. Usually it is heard first on 10 meters, then 6 meters, then 2 meters. Depending on your location and the intensity of the aurora, the time delay between hearing it on 6 meters and its appearance on 2 meters may be only a few minutes, to as much as an hour, later. Still, it shows up first at low frequency. The same is true of sporadic E; it will be noticed first on 10 meters, then 6, then 2.

Tropospheric propagation, particularly tropo ducting, acts in just the reverse manner. Inversions and ducts form at higher frequencies first. As the inversion layer grows in thickness, it refracts lower and lower frequencies. Even the most avid VHF operator may not notice this sequence because of lower activity levels on the higher bands. It may be true that ducting affects the higher bands before the lower ones, but it is more likely to be noticed first on 2 meters, where many more stations are normally on the air. Six-meter tropo openings are very rare because few inversion layers ever develop sufficient thickness to enhance such long-wavelength signals.

How can you monitor for band openings? The best way is to take advantage of commercial TV and FM broadcast stations, which serve admirably as propagation beacons. Television Channels 2 through 6 (54-88 MHz) are great for catching sporadic E. As the E opening develops, you will see one or more stations appear on each channel. First, you may see Channel 2 get cluttered with stations 1000 miles or more away, then the higher channels may follow. If you see strong DX stations on Channel 6, better get the 2-meter rig warmed up. Channel 7 is at 175 MHz, so you rarely see any sporadic E there or on any higher channels. If you do, however, it means that a major 2-meter opening is in progress!

The gap between TV Channel 6 and 7 is occupied partly by the FM broadcast band (88-108 MHz). Monitoring that spectrum will give you a similar feel for propagation conditions.

Several amateurs have built converters to monitor TV video carrier frequencies. A system like this can be used to keep track of meteor showers. It's a way of checking to tell if meteors are plentiful or not, even if there appears to be little activity on the amateur VHF bands. It also can alert you to aurora and sporadic E. A variety of systems for monitoring propagation have been discussed by Joe Reisert, W1JR, in the June 1984 issue of *Ham Radio*.

EME: EARTH-MOON-EARTH

EME, or moonbounce, is available any time the Moon is in a favorable position. Fortunately, the Moon's position may be easily calculated in advance, so you always know when this form of DX will be ready. It's not actually that simple, of course, because the Earth's geomagnetic field can play havoc with EME signals as they leave the Earth's atmosphere and as they return. Not only can absorption (path loss) vary, but the polarization of the radio waves can rotate, causing abnormally high path losses at some times. Still, most EME activity is predictable.

You will find many more signals off the Moon during times when the Moon is nearest the Earth (perigee), when it is overhead at relatively high northern latitudes (positive declination), and when the Moon is nearly at full phase. The one weekend per month which has the best combination of these three factors is informally designated the activity or skeds weekend, and most EMEers will be on the air then. This is particularly true for 432 EME; 144-MHz EME is active during the week and on non-skeds weekends as well. See accompanying sidebar on EME operating practices.

As with meteor-scatter, digital modes have appeared for EME as well. The *WSJT* software suite includes a mode known as JT44. This software has made moonbounce contacts possible using sound-card-equipped PCs, single Yagi antennas and about 150 W — a feat that seemed impossible just a few years earlier. It is possible that JT44, and digital modes that will likely appear in the future, will finally put EME communication within the grasp of amateurs with limited antenna space and equally limited bank accounts.

HILLTOPPING AND PORTABLE OPERATION

One of the nice things about the VHF/UHF bands is that antennas are relatively small, and station equipment can be packed up and easily transported. Portable operation, commonly called hilltopping or mountaintopping, is a favorite activity for many amateurs. This is especially true during VHF and UHF contests, where a station can be very popular by being located in a rare grid. If you are on a hilltop or mountaintop as well, you will have a very competitive signal. See accompanying sidebar for further information.

Hilltopping is fun and exciting because hills elevate your antenna far above surrounding terrain and therefore your VHF/UHF range is greatly extended. If you live in a low-lying area such as a valley, a drive up to the top of a nearby hill or mountain will have the same effect as buying a new tower and antenna, a high-power amplifier and a preamplifier, all in one!

The popularity of hilltopping has grown as equipment has become more portable. The box and brick (compact multimode VHF rig and solid-state 100 to 200-W amplifier) combination is ideally suited for mobile and portable operation. You need no other power source than a car battery, and even with a simple antenna your signals will be outstanding.

Many VHF/UHFers drive to the top of hills or mountains and set up their station. A hilltop park, rest area or farmer's field are equally good sites, so long as they are clear of trees and obstructions. You should watch out for high-power FM or TV broadcasters who may also be taking advantage of the hill's good location; their powerful signals may cause intermodulation problems in your receiver.

Antennas, on a couple of 10-foot mast sections, may be turned by hand as the operator sits in the passenger seat of the car. A few hours of operating like this can be wonderfully enjoyable and can net you a lot of good VHF/UHF DX. In fact, some VHF enthusiasts have very modest home stations but rather elaborate hilltopping stations. When they notice that band conditions are improving, they hop in the car and head for the hills. There, they have a really excellent site and can make many more QSOs.

In some places, there are no roads to the tops of hills or mountains where you might wish to operate. In this case, it is a simple (but sometimes strenuous) affair to hike to the top, carrying the car battery, rig and antenna. Many hilltoppers have had great fun by setting up on the top of a fire tower on a hilltop, relying on a battery for power.

Some VHF/UHFers, especially contesters, like to take the entire station, high power amplifiers and all, to hilltops for extended operation. They may stay there for several days, camping out and DXing. Probably the most outstanding example of this kind of operation is seen during VHF contests, from stations operating in the multioperator category. Dozens of operators and helpers bring equipment for 6 meters through

Longtime EME operator Philippe, F2TU, uses this huge dish antenna for moonbounce contacts on 432 MHz and higher bands.

microwaves to the highest mountaintops and contact everyone within range.

CONTESTS

The greatest amount of activity on the VHF/UHF bands occurs during contests. VHF/UHF contests are scheduled for some of the best propagation dates during the year. Not only are propagation conditions generally good, but activity is always very high. Many stations come out of the woodwork just for the contest, and many individuals and groups go hilltopping to rare states or grids.

A VHF/UHF contest is a challenging but friendly battle between you, your station, other contesters, propagation and Murphy's Law. Your score is determined by a combination of skill and luck. It is not always the biggest or loudest station that scores well. The ability to listen, switch bands quickly and to take advantage of rapidly changing propagation conditions is more important than brute strength.

There are quite a few contests for the world above 50 MHz. Some are for all the VHF and UHF bands, while others are for one band only. Some run for entire weekends and others for only a few hours. Despite their differences, all contests share a

Moonbounce Operating Practices

After traveling 400,000 km, bouncing off a poorly reflective Moon, and returning 400,000 km, EME signals are quite weak. A large antenna, high transmitter power, low-noise preamplifier and very careful listening are all essential for EME. Nevertheless, hundreds of amateurs have made EME contacts, and their numbers are growing.

The most popular band for EME is 144 MHz, followed by 432 MHz. Other bands with regular EME activity are 1296 and 2304/2320 MHz.

Moonbounce QSO procedure is different on 144 and 432 MHz. On 144 MHz, schedule transmissions are 2 minutes long, whereas on 432 they are 2½ minutes long. In addition, the meaning of signal reports is different on the two bands. The difference in procedure is somewhat confusing to newcomers. Most EMEers operate on only one band, so they grow accustomed to the procedure on that band pretty quickly.

Signal Report and Meaning

	144 MHz	432 MHz
T	Signal just detectable	Portions of calls copyable
M	Portions of calls copyable	Complete calls copied
O	Both calls fully copied	Good signal, easily copied
R	Both calls, and O signal report copied	Calls and report copied

What does this difference in reporting mean? Well, the biggest difference is that M reports aren't good enough for a valid QSO on 2 meters but they are good enough on 432. So long as everyone understands the system, then there is no confusion. On both bands, if signals are really good, then normal RST reports are exchanged.

The majority of EME QSOs are made without any prearranged schedules. Almost always, there is no rigid transmitting time-slot sequencing. Just as in CW QSOs on HF, you transmit when the other station turns it over to you. This is particularly true during EME contests, where time-slot transmissions slow down the exchange of information. Why take 10-15 minutes when two or three will do?

On the other hand, many QSOs on EME are made with the assistance of skeds. This is especially the case for newcomers and rare DX stations.

On 144 MHz, each station transmits for 2 minutes, then listens as the other station transmits. Which 2-minute sequence you transmit in is agreed to in advance. The

common terminology is even and odd. The even station transmits the 2nd, 4th, 6th, 8th. . . 2-minute segment of the hour, while the odd station transmits the 1st, 3rd, 5th. . . Therefore, 0030-0032 is an even slot, even if the sked begins on the half-hour. In most cases, the westernmost station takes the odd sequence. An operating chart, similar to many which have been published, will help you keep track.

During the schedule, at the point when you've copied portions of both calls, the last 30 seconds of your 2-minute sequence is reserved for signal reports; otherwise, call sets are transmitted for the full 2 minutes.

On 432 MHz, sequences are longer. Each transmitting slot is 2½ minutes. You either transmit first or second. Naturally, first means that you transmit for the first 2½ minutes of each 5 minutes.

144-MHz Procedure — 2-Min Sequence

Period	1½ minutes	30 seconds
1	Calls (W6XXX DE W1XXX)	
		Continue calls
2	W1XXX DE W6XXX	T T T T
3	W6XXX DE W1XXX	O O O O
4	RO RO RO RO	DE W1XXX K
5	R R R R R	DE W6XXX K
6	QRZ? EME	DE W1XXX K

432-MHz Procedure — 2½-Min Sequence

Period	2 minutes	30 seconds
1	VE7BBG DE K2UYH	Continue calls
2	K2UYH DE VE7BBG	Continue calls
3	VE7BBG DE K2UYH	T T T
4	K2UYH DE VE7BBG	M M M
5	RM RM RM RM	DE K2UYH K
6	R R R R R	DE VE7BBG SK

On 222 MHz, some stations use the 144-MHz procedure and some use the 432-MHz procedure. Which one is used is determined in advance. On 1296 and above, the 432 procedure is always used.

EME operation generally takes place in the lowest parts of the VHF bands: 144.000-144.070; 222.000-222.025; 432.000-432.070; 1296.000-1296.050. Terrestrial QSOs are strongly discouraged in these portions of the bands. Activity on 10 GHz EME, which requires only a few watts when used with dish antennas 10 feet or more in diameter, is becoming increasingly popular.

VHF Mountaintopping

By John F. Lindholm, W1XX

Mountaintopping and hilltopping (not quite so ambitious) have been popular activities as old as VHF operating itself. Few are blessed with a home operating location that facilitates a total command of the frequency. Consequently, ardent VHFers construct bigger and bigger arrays and amplifiers for the home station in order to produce that booming signal. Some, however, utilize the great equalizer to compete on an equal or superior footing with the big home stations-namely, a mountaintop location. Here, perched high above all the home stations, a small portable rig with a single Yagi antenna only a few feet off the ground suddenly sounds like a kilowatt feeding a killer antenna installed at home. Simple equipment performs amazingly well from a mountaintop QTH on VHF.

A mountaintop expedition can vary from a spur-of-the-moment Sunday afternoon picnic to a full-fledged weekend contest. Quick trips can also be conducted during band openings. Since a contest optimizes the opportunity to work a lot of stations on VHF, this sidebar is mostly a how-to for weekend contest operation conducted by one or two people. But this can be scaled down to a mountain-top stay of shorter duration.

The Times Are a Changin'

Old-timers will remember the drudgery of lugging boat anchors up rocky crevices. Dragging equipment and generators weighing hundreds of pounds up steep mountainsides was no picnic. Those who suffered sprained backs soon gave it up. The advent of solid-state equipment has made mountaintopping a far less strenuous activity. Even some of the highly competitive HF types have found new worlds to conquer above 50 MHz. The use of grid locators in the major VHF contests has tickled the innermost secret desire of every radio amateur — to be on the receiving end of a DX pileup. Now instead of going on safari to some distant DX land, you can head for the mountains — some nearby mountaintop located in a rare grid.

Choosing a Site

Choosing a mountaintop site involves considering how far you want to travel to get there, accessibility to the top of the mountain and its all-important grid locator. Ideally, your mountain is only a short driving distance away, towers into the cirrusphere, has a six-lane interstate to the top and rises within a grid that has never before been on the air!

Obviously, some of these considerations may have to be compromised. Your first step to finding VHF heaven involves extensive study of a road atlas. How far do you want to travel? Where are the mountains? How high are they? Can you drive to the top? Draw in the grid line boundaries so you can tell which square it is in. If you're not sure, ask some active VHFers which are the difficult grids to work. When you start zeroing in on a potential site, you may want to get a topographic survey map of the area to determine access roads and direction of drop-off from the summit.

Never operate from a mountaintop without first scoping it out in person. Access is most important. Thus far, I've operated from sites which I have reached by car, ferry, gondola, 4-wheel drive, motor home and hiking. Unless you are going with mini-radios and gel-cells, you want to get there without backpacking it. A passable road to the top is ideal. When checking out a 2-meter site, bring a compass and 2-meter FM hand-held. A call on 146.52-MHz simplex should tell you how good the location is. Are you blocked in any direction? Is it already RF-city with commercial installations — a potential source of interference? Will you be able to clear any trees with a lightweight mast? Then the prime requisite: Is there a picnic table permanently at the site? If not, plan on bringing an operating table and chair, even though they add considerable bulk and weight to transport.

Once you've selected an operating site, be sure you have secured the necessary permission to use the site. This may simply require verbal permission from some authority or the owner, or, it could involve a lengthy exchange of correspondence with a state environmental agency of forests and parks and the signing of a liability release. But be sure you have permission. The last thing you want is the local sheriff shining a flashlight in your eyes at 3 AM while you are enjoying a fantastic tropo opening on 2 meters. You'll find rangers on fire watch most helpful in pointing out how to obtain necessary permission.

Power Source

Unless you have the extreme luck to find a location that will permit you to just plug in, make plans for providing your own power. With a single-band operation from a car (with antenna mast mounted just outside the car window), the car battery will probably suffice. Run a set of heavy-duty jumper cables directly to the car battery. Even a solid-state brick amplifier can be run off the car battery without ill effects. Just in case, park the car facing downhill!

For a more serious effort involving several VHF and UHF bands, a generator is recommended. Unless you are running high-power amplifiers, a small generator is all you should need. Attractive generators in the 500 to 1000-W category that look more like American Tourister luggage are now available. Mine is a 650-W beauty that weighs in at 43 pounds, and runs for four hours on a half gallon of petrol. And quiet? You can hear the wings of a Monarch butterfly flutter at 50 paces. A 5-gallon gasoline can provides more than enough flammable juice for a contest weekend.

Equipment

A mountaintop location effectively places your antenna atop a natural tower of hundreds, or perhaps, thousands of feet. With this height advantage, compact, lightweight, low-powered radios that can be boosted up to the 50- to 100-W range with solid-state amplifiers will perform nicely.

---

basic similarity. In most North American contests, your score is determined by the number of contacts (or more precisely, the number of QSO points) you make, times some multiplier, which is most often grid locators. In most of the current major contests, you keep track of QSOs and multipliers by band. In other words, you can work the same station on each band for separate QSO and multiplier credit.

Listed below are the major VHF through microwave contests in North America. Other contests are popular in Europe and Asia, but these are not listed here because information about them is not usually available to most of us. All the listed contests are open to all licensed amateurs, regardless of their affiliation with any club or organization. Detailed rules for each contest are published in *QST*, *CQ* and the newsletters of the sponsoring

Low-powered portable transceivers are manufactured for just this purpose. The popular 10 and 25-W multimode rigs are also quite adequate. Many discontinued models can be obtained at a substantial savings through the Ham-Ads section of QST. Use of transverters operating with mobile-type HF radios should also be considered.

If you don't have any sizable trees to get over, you can use simple mast sections that fit together. I use 5-foot sections available at the popular shack of radios. They are easily transportable. Important too is the method of antenna rotation. If you can install the antenna mast right next to the operating position, do it. It will save all the hassle of installing motorized rotators. Nothing beats the Armstrong method for speed and simplicity. I use a cross-piece of aluminum tubing mounted with U-bolts to the mast at arm level (see Fig 3-5). This provides instantaneous antenna-peaking capability — a necessity on VHF/UHF. While home stations are twirling their antennas in every direction trying to peak a weak signal, I've already worked him!

Installing antennas for several bands on the same mast is recommended. They should be oriented in the same direction. Many contacts on UHF are the result of moving stations over from other bands. For example, in a contest if you move a multiplier to 432 MHz after first working on 2 meters, and both antennas are on the same mast, you will first want to peak the signal on 144 MHz. Then, when you move to 432 MHz where the antennas are probably a bit more sharp and propagation perhaps marginal, both antennas will be pointing at each other for maximum signal. This can make the difference in whether the contact is made.

If your mountaintop operation involves staying overnight, additional attention must be paid to having the proper survival equipment. The most luxurious way to go is a van or RV. Otherwise, a tent may be required. For the rugged outdoors type, this can be as appealing as the radio part. I find that cooking steaks over a campfire with a canopy of stars overhead (while a programmable keyer is calling CQ) is half the fun. But keep this aspect of the operation also simple as possible. Champagne and caviar can be held for another time. I've also found out the hard way that one can expect heavy winds on mountaintops. Large tents blow down easily in such weather.

Just because you're hilltopping in July or August, don't expect it will always be T-shirt and shorts weather. No matter what the season, expect to need a heavy jacket after dark. I always bring a heavy flannel shirt and ski jacket for night, and shorts in the daytime. And bring lightweight raingear, just in case. In the western mountains or during the winter anywhere, it can get cold and snow is always a possibility. And depending on the habitat, don't be surprised to be introduced to a critter or two, especially after dark!

Getting Started

Okay, you've read this far and are beginning to say to yourself: "Self, I think I'd like to try that." But there is a little voice of caution in you that says: "Don't go bonkers until you've sampled a little first." Good advice!

Start out by setting up on an easily accessible mountain for an afternoon during a contest period on a single band. For the first effort, I recommend 2 meters. With so many 10-W multimode rigs out there in radioland, 2 meters is your bread and butter band. Using a multi-element Yagi a few feet off the ground of a strategically located mountain or hill can whet your appetite. I first got hooked by operating from the side of a highway on Hogback Mountain, Vermont, with a 3-W portable 2-meter radio to a 30-W brick and 11-element Yagi. I was astounded by the results, with contacts hundreds of miles away. This launched my interest in acquiring more equipment for portable mountaintop use, each operation adding a new band or better antenna. The basic formula of keeping it lightweight and simple has prevailed, however.

Now what's keeping you from operating from atop that mountain?

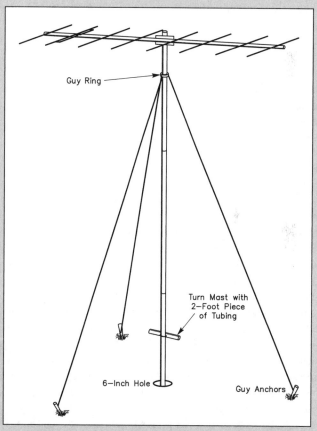

Guy Ring

Turn Mast with 2-Foot Piece of Tubing

6-Inch Hole

Guy Anchors

Fig 3-5 — A portable mast, assembled from interlocking sections of aluminum tubing or commercial mast, can raise one or two small Yagis to a height of 25 feet. The mast is rotated by hand.

organizations. For more information about contesting, see the **Contesting** chapter of this book.

1) *ARRL VHF Sweepstakes*: This one-weekend contest occurs in January. It is favored by clubs because it permits club members to pool their individual scores for the club's total. In addition, individuals and multioperator groups compete. Scores are determined by total QSO points per band multiplied by the number of grid squares worked per band. Activity is quite high during this midwinter contest, even though propagation conditions are often poor.

2) *ARRL June VHF QSO Party*: This contest is the highlight of the contest season for most VHFers. Scheduled for the second full weekend of June, the June Contest is often the most exciting of the major contests. Conditions on all the VHF bands

are usually good, with 6 meters leading the way. This contest covers all the VHF and UHF bands, and QSOs and multipliers are accumulated for each band. Score is determined by multiplying QSO points per band by grid locators per band. Single band and multiband awards are given to high-scoring individuals in each ARRL section. In addition, multioperator groups compete against each other, and the competition can be fierce!

3) *CQ Worldwide VHF Contest*: This contest is international in scope and is usually held over a July weekend on 6 and 2 meters. Score is the number of different grid locators worked per band times the number of QSO points per band. A multitude of awards are available.

4) *ARRL UHF Contest*: As its name suggests, this contest is restricted to the UHF bands (plus 222 MHz). It takes place over a full weekend in August. All UHF bands are permitted, and grids are the multiplier. Less equipment is involved for this contest than for contests which cover all VHF/UHF bands, so many groups go hilltopping for the UHF Contest.

5) *ARRL September VHF QSO Party*: The rules for this contest are identical to those for the June VHF QSO Party. This contest is also very popular, and many multioperator groups travel to rare states and grids for it. By the second weekend of September, most 6-meter sporadic E has disappeared, but tropo conditions are often extremely good. Therefore, the bands above 144 MHz are the scene of tremendous activity during the September contest. Some of the best tropo openings of recent decades have taken place during this contest, and they are made even better by the high level of activity.

6) *ARRL 10-GHz and Up Cumulative Contest*: Yes, there is a contest for those hardy souls who inhabit the microwave world of 10 GHz and higher. It takes place over two late summer weekends. Operators who change their locations during the contest may work the same stations over again. Scoring is the cumulative total of QSO points and distance of each contact in kilometers, for each band used. This is great fun, as nearly all participants head for their favorite hilltops and mountain-tops for maximum range.

7) *ARRL EME Contest*: This contest is devoted to moon-bounce. It takes place over several weekends, usually in the fall, with one weekend reserved for 2304 MHz and up and two weekends for 50-1296 MHz. The date of the contest is different each year because of the variable phase of the Moon. The dates are usually chosen by active moon- bouncers to coincide with the best combination of high lunar declination, perigee and the full phase of the Moon. This contest is international in scope. Score is the number of QSO points made via EME per band, multiplied by the number of US call districts and ARRL countries per band. You can enter using analog modes, digital modes, or a combination of both. Hundreds of EMEers participate in this challenging test of moonbounce capability.

Contests are lots of fun, whether you're actively competing or not. You don't have to be a full-time competitor to participate or to enjoy yourself! Most participants are not really competing in the contest, but they get on the air to pass out points, to have fun for awhile, and to listen for rare DX. Others try their hardest for the entire contest, keep track of their score and send their logs in for awards. Either way, the contest is a fun challenge.

If you don't plan on being a serious competitor, then you just need to know the exchange. The exchange is the minimum information that must be passed between each station to validly count the QSO in the contest. In all of the terrestrial VHF contests sponsored by the ARRL you need only send and receive calls and grids, with acknowledgments each way. Other contests require some different information, such as serial numbers or signal reports, so it pays to check the rules to make sure.

A serious contest effort requires dedication and effort, as well as a station that can withstand a real workout. Contests are a challenge to operators and equipment alike. A good contest score is the result of hard work, a good station and favorable propagation. A good score is something to be proud of, especially if there is lots of stiff competition. And with the popularity of VHF and UHF contests these days, competition is always stiff!

Serious contesting requires using a computer logging program. Several are available through vendors who advertise in *QST*, *NCJ* and other journals. Laptop computers are favored because they tend to produce less interference to the VHF bands and they are easier to take on portable operations. You can submit your log electronically via e-mail or on a disk. Check the current contest rules for exact requirements.

Many operators don't feel that their stations are competitive on all the VHF and UHF bands. This is no problem. You can contest on one, two, or as many bands as you like. Indeed, some contesters specialize. Most contest results recognize achievements on each band separately. This has the advantage of concentrating your efforts where your station is the strongest, allowing you to devote full time to just one band. You don't need to be high powered to compete as a single-band entry. Location makes a lot of difference, and hilltopping single-banders have had tremendous success, particularly if they go to a rare grid square.

Other operators like to try for all-band competition. In this case, it's a real advantage to be able to hop from one band to another. You can quickly check 6 meters for activity while also tuning 2 meters. Or, if you work a rare grid on one band, you can take advantage of the opportunity by asking the other station to

Joel, W5ZN, posts top VHF+ contest scores from this well-equipped shack in Arkansas. He's an avid DXer and grid chaser as well.

switch bands right then. Some contesters work one station on all possible bands within two minutes by band hopping! This is a speedy way to increase your grids and QSOs.

There are several other entry classes for the major VHF contests and variations on these classes in other events. (Check the rules for each contest, as entry classes vary somewhat.) Multioperator entries involve more than one operator. Many large multioperator efforts have operating positions for a dozen or more separate bands. Now that is an effort to put together! If your group is not ready for the big time, limited multioperator entries submit scores for four bands only.

In either case, successful multiop stations have learned to work cooperatively. The ability to operate simultaneously on several bands without mutual interference is important. Multiop efforts also have a foolproof system for passing messages from one operating position to another, especially referrals of a station from one band to another. If the operator of the 2-meter station in a multioperator entry works WØVD, for example, that operator may suggest immediately moving to 222 MHz and then 432 MHz. A message has to be sent to the operators at the 222 and 432 MHz positions to expect a call from WØVD at a particular frequency and time. Handwritten notes are simple and convenient if the operating positions are close together. Several logging programs have sophisticated features to pass messages among several computers that are networked together.

The rover class allows a station with one or two operators to move among two or more grid locators during the contest. Rovers may contact the same stations all over again from a different grid. Most rovers operate from a car, van or truck specially equipped for convenience and efficiency. Hilltops in rare grids are favored rover sites. Rovers must move the entire station, antennas and power supply to qualify. Special scoring rules apply to rovers.

Other popular entry classes appeal to single operators who contest with modest stations. The limited single operator does not limit the number of bands you may operate, but does place maximum power limits on each band. The single-operator QRP

class limits power output on all bands to a maximum of 10 W. Stations must run on a portable power source and may not be located at fixed or home locations.

SOURCES OF INFORMATION

Many VHF/UHF operators like to keep abreast of the latest happenings on the bands such as new DX records, band openings or new designs for equipment. There are many excellent sources for current information about VHF/UHF. In addition, they provide a way to share ideas and ask questions, and for newcomers to become familiar with operation above 50 MHz. Information sources include nets, newsletters, published columns, Web sites and e-mail lists (also known as e-mail "reflectors"). You can find links to a number of VHF/UHF resources at **www.arrl.org/qst/worldabove/**.

Nets

Several nets meet regularly on the HF and VHF bands so that VHF/UHFers can chat with each other. These are listed below. It's a good idea to listen first, before checking in the first time, so you'll know the format of the net. Some nets like to get urgent news, scheduling information and other hot topics out of the way early, and save questions and discussion until later. Others are more free-form. You can learn quite a bit just by tuning in to these nets for a few weeks. Regular participants in the nets are often very knowledgeable and experienced. The technical discussions which sometimes take place can be very informative.

1) *Nets on 75 meters.* The Central States VHF Society (**www.csvhfs.org**) sponsors a net on 3.818 MHz each Sunday evening (0230 UTC). It is open to all those interested in VHF and higher. The net provides a terrific source of technical information and is a good place to arrange for schedules and experimental tests.

A similar informal VHF net meets on Monday evenings (0200 UTC Tuesday, 0100 UTC during the summers) on 3.843 MHz. Both frequencies are also used for spontaneous nets, especially during contests, meteor showers and other unusual VHF propagation events.

2) *VHF Nets.* There are dozens of weekly nets that operate on 144 MHz around the country. Many 2-meter nets are sponsored by the Sidewinders on Two (SWOT) Amateur Radio Club. For current information on these nets, check the SWOT Web site at **www.swotrc.net**.

Other nets on 50 through 1296 MHz are sponsored by regional clubs, including the Northeast Weak Signal Society (New England), Mt Airy VHF Society (eastern Pennsylvania) and Western States Weak Signal Society (California). Other nets are run by local groups. Check locally for dates, times and frequencies.

3) *EME Nets.* International EME operators meet on 14.345 MHz each Sunday to arrange EME schedules and pass information. At 1600 UTC, the 432 MHz and higher EME crowd occupies the frequency. Starting at 1700 UTC, the more numerous 144-MHz EME operators gather. The 2-meter EME net often goes for more than an hour.

4) *International 6-Meter Liaison.* Avid 6-meter DX operators around the world monitor 28.885 MHz whenever there is a chance for intercontinental DX. There is no formal net, but

Portable operation is always popular in the VHF/UHF contests. Paul, W2TAU, tweaks his 10 GHz portable station during a January VHF Sweepstakes. (*K2QO photo*)

it is a place to exchange information (especially on current propagation conditions), arrange schedules, and pass other information related to 6-meter operating.

AWARDS

Several awards sponsored by ARRL help stir activity on the VHF and higher bands. (See the **Operating Awards** chapter.) Many of those originally designed for HF operators, including Worked All States (WAS), Worked All Continents (WAC) and DX Century Club (DXCC) are also coveted by operators on 6 meters and higher. The VHF/UHF Century Club (VUCC) is designed only for the world above 50 MHz.

WAS requires contacts with all 50 United States. Like other ARRL awards, QSL cards are required. The quest for this award has probably been responsible for much of the technical advancement of VHF/UHF operation during the past three decades. Moonbounce activity has benefited most directly because WAS on any band above 144 MHz requires EME capability. Even so, more than a dozen stations in the central part of the US have worked 48 states without resorting to moonbounce.

More than 1000 6-meter operators have earned WAS. During the peak of the most recent sunspot cycle, F_2 openings made transcontinental contacts common for many months. Amateurs in the continental US worked Alaska, Hawaii and tons of DX during that time. In quiet years, multi-hop E_s openings occur each summer to provide the slim chance of WAS on 6 meters.

Using portable moonbounce stations, several enterprising groups have mounted EME-DXpeditions to rare states. This has allowed quite a few hard working VHF/UHFers to complete WAS, even when there was no resident EME activity in some states. Hams have earned WAS on 2 meters, 222 MHz, 432 MHz and even 1296 MHz!

Many 6-meter operators have also worked all continents with the assistance of F_2 propagation. WAC is not impossible on the higher bands, as many 144 and 432 EME stations have accomplished this feat. WAC on the higher bands depends on EME activity from under-represented continents.

Several top-scoring stations in the annual EME contests have made QSOs on all continents during a single weekend. The rarest continent is probably South America, where only a small handful of EMEers are active. WAC is not possible on 222 or 902 MHz because these bands are not authorized for amateur use outside of ITU Region 2 (North and South America).

DXCC is also within the capability of the VHF crowd. Hundreds of DXCC awards have already been earned by 6-meter operators from around the world — unthinkable just 20 years ago. Even more astonishing are the 2-meter EME operators with DXCC certificates hanging on their walls! There is no technical reason why DXCC cannot be claimed on higher bands. It simply requires more EME activity from other countries.

VHF-UHF Century Club (VUCC)

The VUCC award is based on working and confirming a certain number of grids on the VHF/UHF bands. For 50 and 144 MHz, the number is 100. On 222 and 432 MHz, the number is 50, and on 902 and 1296 MHz the minimum number is

The dish at HB9Q is 15 meters in diameter and capable of making QSOs with low-power EME stations. (*HB9CRQ photo*)

25. 2.3-GHz operators need to work 10 grids, and five grids are required on the higher microwave bands. This is quite a challenge, and qualifying for the VUCC award is a real accomplishment!

VUCC endorsement stickers are available for those who work specified numbers of additional grids above the minimum required for the basic award. Some stations have exceeded 1000 grids on 6 meters, 500 on 2 meters, and 200 on 222 and 432 MHz. Impressive!

PROBLEMS

With the ever-increasing sharing of the VHF and UHF spectrum by commercial, industrial and private radio services, a certain amount of interference with amateur operation is almost inevitable. Amateurs are well acquainted with interference, and so we normally solve interference problems by ourselves.

Several main types of interference are common. The first is our old friend, television interference (TVI). Fundamental overload, particularly of TV Channels 2 and 3 from 6-meter transmitters, is still common. Some Channel 12 and 13 viewing is bothered by 222-MHz transmissions. Fortunately, as modern TV manufacturers have slowly improved the quality of their sets, the amount of TVI is beginning to decline.

A more common form of TVI is cable television interference (CATVI). It results from many cable systems distributing their signals, inside shielded cables, on frequencies which are allocated to amateurs. As long as the cable remains a closed system, in which all of their signal stays inside the cable and our signals stay out, then everything is usually okay. Despite the design intentions, cable systems are deteriorating because of age and have begun to leak. When a cable system leaks, your perfectly clean and proper VHF signal can get into the cable and cause enormous amounts of mischief. By the same token, the cable company's signals can leak out and interfere with legitimate amateur reception.

Other forms of radio frequency interference (RFI) is a common complaint of owners of unshielded or poorly designed electronic entertainment equipment. Amateur transmissions, especially high power, may be picked up and rectified, causing very annoying problems. RFI may include stereos, video-cassette recorders and telephones. The symptoms of RFI usually include muffled noises which coincide with keying or SSB voice peaks, or partial to total disruption of VCR pictures.

A few general principles may help in beginning your search for a solution to TVI/RFI problems:

1) With ordinary TVI, be sure your transmitter is clean, all coax connectors are tightened, and a good dc and RF ground is provided in your shack — before you look elsewhere for the cause of the problem. Then, find out if TVI affects all televisions or just one. If it's just one, then the problem is probably in the set and not your station.

2) With CATVI, remember that it is the cable company's responsibility to keep its system closed and in compliance with FCC rules. Unfortunately, the FCC's limits are loose enough that in some cases there will be interference-causing leakage from the system which is still within FCC limits. In that case, there is no easy solution to the problem. You may be pleasantly surprised by the cooperative attitude of some cable TV operators. (Cable company technicians often have worked overtime trying to solve CATVI complaints, but not everyone is so fortunate.)

3) In dealing with RFI, the main goal is to keep your RF out of the entertainment system. This is often solved rather simply by bypassing the speaker, microphone and power leads with disc ceramic capacitors. In other cases, particularly some telephones, you must also employ RF chokes. For further information on RFI and CATVI, consult *The ARRL RFI Book*, published by ARRL.

Several other types of interference plague VHF/UHF amateurs. These are the receive-only kinds of interference, which just affect your receiving capability. One form has already been mentioned: CATV leakage. For example, cable channel E is distributed on a frequency in the middle of the amateur 2-meter band. If the cable system leaks, you may experience very disruptive interference. Reducing leakage or perhaps eliminating the use of channel E may be satisfactory. This problem has vexed many stalwart VHFers already, and no end is in sight.

Scanner birdies may be a problem in your area. All scanners are superheterodyne-type receivers, which generate local oscillator signals, just as your receiving system does. Unfortunately, many scanners have inadequate shielding between the local oscillator and the scanner's antenna. The result is radiation of

Some amateurs are interested in making QSOs on higher and higher frequency bands. Frank, W6QI, used this station to work Gary, AD6FP, over a 343 km path on 47 GHz.

the oscillator's signal each time its channel is scanned — a very annoying chirp, swoosh or buzz sound every second or so. If the scanner's local oscillator frequency happens to fall near a frequency you're listening to, you'll hear the scanner instead. Amateurs can easily pick up 10-15 scanner birdies within 5 kHz of the 2-meter calling frequency. Very little can be done about this problem aside from installing tuned traps in everyone's scanners — an unattractive prospect to most scanner owners.

Many amateurs who operate 432 MHz have lived with radar interference for years. Radar interference is identified by a very rapid burst of noise which sounds vaguely like ignition noise, repeated on a regular basis. Although some radars are being phased out, many remain. Amateurs are secondary users of the 420-450 MHz band, so we must accept this interference. The only solution may be directional antennas which may null out the interference, not a very satisfying alternative in some cases. 432-MHz EMEers sometimes hear radar interference off the Moon!

NEW FRONTIERS

The VHF/UHF spectrum offers amateurs a real opportunity to contribute to their own knowledge as well as the advancement of science in general. We as amateurs are capable of several aspects of personal research which are not possible for the limited resources of most scientific research organizations. Although these organizations are able to conduct costly experiments, they are limited in the time available, geographic coverage and, sometimes, by the *It's impossible* syndrome. Hams, on the air 24 hours a day, scattered across the globe, don't know that some aspects of propagation are impossible, so they occasionally happen for us.

For example, professionals suggest that VHF meteor scatter is limited to frequencies below about 150 MHz, yet hams have made dozens of contacts at 222 and 432 MHz. A spirit of curiosity and a willingness to learn is all that is required to turn VHF/ UHF operating into an interesting scientific investigation.

Can amateurs make real contributions to understanding the limits of radio propagation? You bet! The following list includes just a few of the possibilities:

1) *Aurora on 902 or 1296*. Many aurora contacts have been made on 432 MHz; is aurora practical on 902 and 1296 MHz? Is aurora polarization sensitive?

2) *Unusual forms of F-layer ionospheric propagation —* FAI, TE and what else? Little is known about their characteristics, how they relate to overall geomagnetic activity and frequency. Amateurs can discover a lot here.

3) *Multiple-hop sporadic E on 50 MHz*. Single-hop propagation on this band is a daily occurrence during the summer. In recent years, multiple-hop openings have not been uncommon. Now that many European countries are beginning to allow 6-meter amateur operation, we can find out how many hops are actually possible! Several contacts over 6000 miles are well documented. Is there a limit to multiple-hop E_s?

4) *Meteor scatter*. Astronomers are very interested in the orbits of comets and their swarms of debris which give rise to meteor showers. It is often difficult for astronomers to observe meteors (because of clouds, moonlight and so on). Amateurs can make very substantial contributions to the study of meteors by keeping accurate records of meteor-scatter contacts.

5) *Polar-region propagation*. VHF radio propagation across the arctic regions is not well documented. Auroral E is probably a nightly occurrence in the auroral zone and has not been fully exploited. Some interesting paths at 50 and 144 MHz may yet be discovered.

6) *How effective is diversity reception* in different types of VHF/UHF reception? Stations with two or more antennas could investigate.

chapter 4

Emergency Communications

"During our nation's unprecedented Hurricane Katrina relief effort, Amateur Radio and the ARRL stepped up and delivered a vital public service. For 37 days, more than 200 Amateur Radio operators from 35 states and Canada deployed to the field through the American Red Cross processing center in Montgomery, Alabama.

"The storm surge damaged roads, buildings, vehicles and equipment, left people homeless, and knocked out power, sealing off almost all communications. But as Katrina subsided, another massive surge immediately took its place. I'm talking about the immense and sustained surge of recovery activity on the part of Amateur Radio to help assist the impacted people and relief agencies in the region.

"Amateurs of all genders, ages, types and backgrounds voluntarily deployed to Mississippi counties, communities and towns to set up stations at kitchens, shelters and emergency operations centers. Amateur Radio operators provided critical communications and passed hundreds of messages in and around the devastated region. Amateurs in the field selflessly served in many capacities, working long hours, living in terrible conditions, contending with heat, bugs, ants and in many cases much worse.

"While deployed the Amateur Radio operators supported many served agencies and hundreds of people in need. The Montgomery operation supplied amateurs to The Salvation Army, American Red Cross, church or religious organizations, emergency management agencies and emergency operations centers.

"During this event, my experiences affirmed that Amateur Radio operators are much more than hobbyists. I saw amateurs sacrifice, contribute and succeed in providing many weeks of critical communications and additional services to meet dynamic and unique needs. Amateurs created interoperable emergency communications systems where there were none and saved lives as a result. Moreover, they brought the love of a hobby, a variety of communications, contesting, training, and public service skills; and most of all applied the amateur "can-do spirit" to help people in need.

"It was a pleasure getting to meet hundreds of amateurs who worked to do the right thing for this relief effort. My appreciation and admiration extends to all Amateur Radio operators, at home or in the field, who served in this massive relief effort!" — *Greg Sarratt, W4OZK*

INTRODUCTION

Hams provide emergency communications because it is exciting, adventurous and serves the public. They work side-by-side with disaster relief agency officials from the Red Cross, Salvation Army, government emergency management and other entities, supplementing their communications of potentially life and property saving messages. "EmComm" is a longstanding function of Amateur Radio over decades, and is what hams are most famous for.

Why participate? The

Amateur Radio operators in New Mexico supported the activities of responding agencies when four wildfires broke out within a few miles of each other after a warm, dry winter. (*W5EJ photo*)

short answer is community service, to help save victims when a disaster such as a flood, hurricane, tornado, landslide, or even a terrorist attack, strikes your community. There is the thrill of working with disaster officials, aiding victims, and the deep camaraderie and team spirit that results from working with your fellow hams in what sometimes are desperate circumstances.

The entire arena of public safety and disaster management has seen quantum change since the cataclysmic events of the September 11, 2001, terrorist attacks, and especially Hurricane Katrina. Federal, state and local governments have poured financial resources into emergency management on a cosmic scale, and the public safety community has seen a surge the likes of which has not been seen before. More equipment, personnel, organization, plans, training, and programs have been developed and continue to be developed at all levels of government. Nongovernmental organizations (NGOs) have seen commensurate increases in activity as well. Major NGOs include the American Red Cross and Salvation Army.

There has never been a time when public safety planning and programming has seen a greater focus. And that has meant a major increase in the role of Amateur Radio in providing radio communications support for this surge of activity. Along with our enhanced role has also come the need to ratchet up our level of professionalism. This has been manifested by Amateur Radio emcomm operators taking new levels of training:

After Hurricane Katrina struck, Amateur Radio became a primary means of communication for those in Bay St. Louis, Mississippi.

ARRL EmComm Courses (two levels), American Red Cross training courses, and the Federal Emergency Management Agency (FEMA) courses on the National Incident Management System (NIMS) and the Incident Command System (ICS), two frameworks for governmental response that hams must be familiar with if they are to be part of any disaster response.

We'll close this introduction with the comments of then ARRL Vice President Kay Craigie, N3KN, in a report to the ARRL Board of Directors in January 2007: "Here in the USA, we see a post-Katrina emphasis on speeding up the deployment of sophisticated communications systems after disasters so that governmental and non-governmental organizations can get to work quickly. As the emergency telecomm world as a whole speeds up its reaction time, so we hams must be better organized, more capable, and as quick as possible on the scene after our

help is requested, if we are not to arrive after our window of usefulness has closed. Given ham radio's dependency on emergency communications as our reason to exist in this country, it would be suicidal to assume that what we have always been able to do, at the speed we have always been able to do it, will be just fine to maintain our relevance into the indefinite future."

PLANS

More than any other facet of Amateur Radio, emergency communication requires a plan — an orderly arrangement of time, personnel and activities that ensures that performance is smooth and objectives are met. Basically, a plan is a method of achieving a goal. Lack of an emergency communications plan could hamper urgent operations, defer crucial decisions or

Mike Hall, WB3FUP, was one of many who operated from the Stennis, Hancock County, Mississippi, Emergency Operations Center (EOC) after Hurricane Katrina. (*W4OZK photo*)

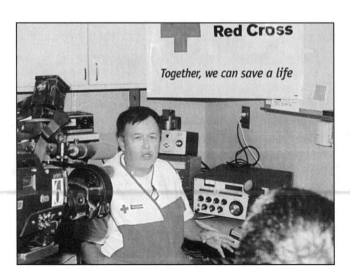

Red Cross and SATERN volunteer Ben Joplin, WB5VST, in Oklahoma City, is interviewed by local news media after getting word through to Louisiana officials that 15 people were stranded on a roof there. (*N7XYO photo*)

delay critical supplies. Be sure to analyze what emergencies are likely to occur in your area, develop guidelines for providing communications after a disaster, know the proper contact people and inform local authorities of your group's capabilities.

Start with a small plan, such as developing a community-awareness program for severe-weather emergencies. Next, test the plan a piece at a time, but redefine the plan if it is unsatisfactory. Testing with simulated-emergency drills teaches communicators what to do in a real emergency, without a great deal of risk. Finally, prepare a few contingency plans just in case the original plan fails.

One of the best ways to learn how to plan for emergencies is to join your local Amateur Radio Emergency Service (ARES) group (see the sidebar, "How to Get Started"), where members train and prepare constantly in an organized way. Before an emergency occurs, register with your ARRL Emergency Coordinator (EC). The EC will explain to civic and relief agencies in your community what the Amateur Service can offer in time of disaster. ARES and the EC are discussed later in this chapter.

Communications for city or rural emergencies each require a particular response and careful planning. Large cities usually have capable relief efforts handled by paid professionals, and there always seems to be some equipment and facilities that remain operable. Even though damage may be more concentrated outside a city, it can be remote from fire-fighting or public-works equipment and law-enforcement authorities. The rural public then, with few volunteers spread over a wide area, may be isolated, unable to call for help or incapable of reporting all of the damage.

It's futile to look back regretfully at past emergencies and wish you had been better prepared. Prepare yourself now for emergency communications by maintaining a dependable transmitter-receiver setup and an emergency-power source. Have a plan ready and learn proper procedures.

PROCEDURES

Aside from having plans, it is also necessary to have pro-cedures — the best methods or ways to do a job. Procedures become habits, independent of a plan, when everyone knows what happens next and can tell others what to do. Actually, the size of a disaster affects the size of the response, but not the procedures.

Procedures that should be widely known before disasters occur include how to coordinate or deploy people, equipment and supplies. There are procedures to use a repeater and an autopatch, to check into a net and to format or handle traffic. Because it takes time to learn activities that are not normally used every day, excessively detailed procedures will confuse people and should be avoided.

Specific Procedures

Your EC will have developed a procedure to activate the ARES group, but will need your help to make it work. A telephone alerting "tree" call-up, even if based on a current list of phone numbers, might fail if there are gaps in the calling sequence, members are not near a phone or there is no phone service.

Consider alternative procedures. Use alerting tones and frequent announcements on a well monitored repeater to round up many operators at once. An unused 2-meter simplex frequency can function for alerting; instead of turning radios off, your group would monitor this frequency for alerts without the need of any equipment modifications. Since this channel is normally quiet, any activity on it would probably be an alert announcement.

During an emergency, report to the EC so that up-to-the-minute data on operators will be available. Don't rely on one leader; everyone should keep an emergency reference list of relief-agency officials, police, sheriff and fire departments, ambulance service and National Traffic System (NTS) nets. Be ready to help, but stay off the air unless there is a specific job to be done that you can handle efficiently. Always listen before you transmit. Work and cooperate with the local civic and relief agencies as the EC suggests. During a major emergency, copy special W1AW bulletins for the latest developments.

Afterward, let your EC know about your activities, so that a timely report can be submitted to ARRL HQ. Amateur Radio has won glowing public tribute in emergencies. Help maintain this record.

"Experience is the worst teacher: it gives the test before presenting the lesson" (Vernon's Law). Train and drill now so you can be prepared for an emergency.

TRAINING

Since 9/11 and post-Katrina, training for public safety officials and ancillary personnel like Amateur Radio operators has mushroomed. Training and credentialing have become the norms for requirements of disaster responders. It is imperative that amateurs also take this additional training if they are to continue to serve major communications roles. New ARRL, Red Cross and FEMA training courses are musts for emcomm operators.

Amateur Radio operators need training in operating procedures and communication skills. In an emergency, radios don't communicate, but people do. Because radio amateurs with all sorts of varied interests participate, many of those who offer to

What is It Like?

In 2004, Florida was the scene of four calamitous hurricanes that ripped up lives and property. It was a wonder to monitor firsthand the Floridian radio amateurs fulfilling their public service mission by providing emergency communications for their neighbors and response agencies, in some cases directly in the path of harm's way.

As I huddled with my wife in the center of the living room of our wind-buffeted, boarded-up house in Flagler County during one storm, I listened with simultaneous horror and admiration as Assistant Emergency Coordinator (AEC) Merrill Musikar, KG4IDD, transmitted his mobile position out in the maelstrom on his way to delivering another radio to an emergency shelter full of terrified community members. That is dedication.

Merrill and his father, AEC Jay Musikar, AF2C, along with EC Art Cooper, AB4QQ, were providing communications support to the county's emergency operations center. With hams stationed at the EOC, other ARES operators out in the winds and rain used their mobile FM radios and handhelds to transmit messages involving damage reports, medical emergencies, needs for food, fuel, water and other supplies at shelters, and weather (SKYWARN) assessments back to emergency managers and planners.

It takes guts, a sense of community service and the spirit of adventure to go out and do that job. When it was all over, these hams received the accolades of a grateful community. — *Rick Palm, K1CE, from the* ARES E-Letter, *August 2005*

Stress Management

Emergency responders should understand and practice stress management. A little stress helps you to perform your job with more enthusiasm and focus, but too much stress can drive you to exhaustion or death.

Watch for these physiological symptoms:
- Increased pulse, respiration or blood pressure
- Trouble breathing, increase in allergies, skin conditions or asthma
- Nausea, upset stomach or diarrhea
- Muffled hearing
- Headaches
- Increased perspiration, chills, cold hands or feet or clammy skin
- Feeling weakness, numbness or tingling in part of body
- Feeling uncoordinated
- Lump in throat
- Chest pains

Cognitive reactions may next occur in acute stress situations; many of these signs are difficult to self-diagnose.
- Short term memory loss
- Disorientation or mental confusion
- Difficulty naming objects or calculating
- Poor judgment or difficulty making decisions
- Lack of concentration and attention span
- Loss of logic or objectivity to solve problems

Perhaps the best thing to do as you start a shift is to find someone that you trust and ask them to let you know if you are acting a bit off. If at some time they tell you they've noticed you're having difficulty, then perhaps it's time to ask for some relief. Another idea is to have some sort of stress management training for your group before a disaster occurs.

Not many ARES groups have a "navy," but in Ozaukee County (Wisconsin) they do! OZARES (Ozaukee County ARES) is attached to Emergency Management (EM) of the county, and EM has a 40-foot Rescue Boat that responds to emergencies on adjoining Lake Michigan during the boating season. On the dock at the right is Captain Jack Morrison (N9SFG). Most of his crew are also hams. During emergency runs in inclement weather, OZARES members staff the Emergency Communications Center (ECC) in the county's Justice Center and keep in constant contact with the boat via ham VHF, marine and 800 MHz public service band radios. The boat makes 50 to 60 emergency runs in a usual season. (WB9RQR photo)

help may not have experience in public service activities.

Proper disaster training replaces chaotic pleas with smooth, organized communications. Well-trained communicators respond during drills or actual emergencies with quick, effective and efficient communications. The ARRL recognizes the need for emergency preparedness and emergency communications training through sponsorship of the ARES and the Amateur Radio Emergency Communications Course that is a part of the ARRL Continuing Education Program (CEP).

Volunteers from all over the country assisted in pulling together information for these courses. These courses are intended for two audiences. Introduction to Emergency Communication (EC-001) is intended for those getting started in Amateur Radio emergency communication and general emcomm group members. Public Service and Emergency Communications Management for Radio Amateurs (EC-016) is intended for those in leadership positions such as Emergency Coordinators, District Emergency Coordinators and Section Emergency Coordinators.

All ARRL CEP courses are available on-line, through field instruction, or independent study. For further information, refer to **www.arrl.org/emergency-communications-training**.

Each on-line course has been developed in segments —

Additional Training for EmComm Operators Needed

In addition to the ARRL Emergency Communications Courses, field operators should also complete certain formal training courses:

- Red Cross combined course in Adult CPR/First Aid Basics
- Red Cross online Introduction to Disaster Services

For more information about Red Cross courses, see www.redcross.org/flash/course01_v01/.

- FEMA IS-100 (Introduction to Incident Command System)
- FEMA IS-200 (ICS for Single Resource and Initial Action Incidents)
- FEMA IS-700 (National Incident Management System)

For more information about FEMA courses, see training.fema.gov/IS/.

Except for the first two, all courses are free of charge, and CPR/First Aid may be free to members of the Red Cross. CPR/First Aid is the only course that requires periodic refreshers and the only course that must be taken in person rather than on the Internet.

Where FEMA courses exist in more than one current version — aimed at somewhat different audiences — any of the currently available versions will suffice.

learning units with objectives, informative text, student activities and quizzes. Courses are interactive and include direct communications with a Mentor/Instructor and other students. Mentors assist students by guiding them through the course. Students for each CEP course are required to pass a Final Assessment (exam) of 25 multiple choice questions each with a score of 80% or better. All students who successfully complete the course requirements and pass the assessments earn a certificate.

Additional training is available from your local ARES group. Contact them. Another training source is the National Weather Service and their SKYWARN program. SKYWARN is an organization composed primarily of radio amateurs trained by local emergency management to spot and report severe weather by Amateur Radio back to the emergency operations center. More on SKYWARN is found later in the chapter.

ON THE AIR TRAINING EXERCISES

Practical on-the-air activities, such as ARRL's Field Day and Simulated Emergency Test offer additional training opportunities on a nationwide basis for individuals and groups. Participation in such events reveals weak areas where discussions and more training are needed. Also, drills and tests can be designed specifically to check dependability of emergency equipment or to rate training in the local area.

Field Day

The ARRL Field Day (FD) gets more amateurs out of their cozy shacks and into tents on hilltops than any other event. You may not be operating from a tent after a disaster but the training you will get from FD is invaluable.

In the ARRL Field Day, a premium is placed on sharp operating skills, adapting equipment that can meet challenges of emergency preparedness and flexible logistics. Amateurs as-

semble portable stations capable of long-range communications at almost any place and under varying conditions. Alternatives to commercial power in the form of generators, car batteries, windmills or solar power are used to power equipment to make as many contacts as possible. FD is held on the fourth full weekend of June, but enthusiasts get the most out of their training by keeping preparedness programs alive during the rest of the year. See **www.arrl.org/contests/** for more information on this popular event.

Simulated Emergency Test

The ARRL Simulated Emergency Test (SET) builds emergency-communications character.

The purposes of SET are to:

- Help amateurs gain experience in communicating, using standard procedures under simulated emergency conditions, and to experiment with some new concepts.
- Determine strong points, capabilities and limitations in providing emergency communications to improve the response to a real emergency.
- Provide a demonstration, to served agencies and the public through the news media, of the value of Amateur Radio, particularly in time of need.

The goals of SET are to:

- Strengthen VHF-to-HF links at the local level, ensuring that ARES and NTS work in concert.
- Encourage greater use of digital modes for handling high-volume traffic and point-to-point welfare messages of the affected simulated-disaster area.
- Implement the Memoranda of Understanding between the ARRL, the users and cooperative agencies.
- Focus energies on ARES communications at the local level.

Public service events are excellent training for emergency communications. Amateurs in Michigan provided communications for an annual dog sled race using a variety of Amateur Radio modes and technologies. At left, an ATV station at the Start/Finish line was used to monitor teams' progress about 2 miles away. At right, Webster, W8QBX, collected and recorded times called in from various crossings, and Marv, KC8MLD, passed them to the Start/Finish line via digital modes. (*KC8JLH photos*)

• Increase use and recognition of tactical communication on behalf of served agencies; using less amateur-to-amateur formal radiogram traffic.

Help promote the SET on nets and repeaters with announcements or bulletins, or at club meetings and publicize it in club newsletters. SET is conducted on the first full weekend of October. However, some groups have their SETs any time during the period of September 1 through November 30, especially if an alternate date coincides more favorably with a planned communications activity and provides greater publicity. Specific SET guidelines are announced in *QST*.

Drills and Tests

A drill or test that includes interest and practical value makes a group glad to participate because it seems worthy of its efforts. Formulate training around a simulated disaster such as a tornado or a vehicle accident. Elaborate on the situation to develop a realistic scenario or have the drill in conjunction with a local event. Many ARES Section Emergency Coordinators (SECs) have developed training activities that are specifically designed for your state, section or local area. County Emergency Managers are often well practiced in setting up exercises that can help you sharpen your communications and general emergency reaction skills.

During a drill:

1) Announce the simulated emergency situation, activate the emergency net and dispatch mobiles and portables to served agencies.

2) Originate messages and requests for supplies on behalf of served agencies by using tactical communications. (Don't forget to label each message with a "this is a drill only" header, no matter what mode is used to transmit it.)

3) Use emergency-powered repeaters and employ digital modes. Use and test a simplex frequency.

4) As warranted by traffic loads, assign liaison stations to receive traffic on the local net and relay to your section net. Be sure there is a representative on each session of the section nets to receive traffic coming to your area.

After a drill:

1) Determine the results of the emergency communications.

2) Critique the drill.

3) Report your efforts, including any photos, clippings and other items of interest, to your SEC or ARRL HQ.

Public Event Communications

The local ARES group often finds itself providing radio communications support for town parades, bicycle tours, boat races, marathons and so forth. These events provide radio amateurs with excellent on-the air experience and training for when disasters come along. Take advantage of all of these opportunities to hone your skills, and those of your local ARES organization. See the *ARRL Special Events Communications Manual* for additional tips on operating public events.

Net Operator Training

Network discipline and message-handling procedures are fundamental emergency preparedness concepts. Training should involve as many different operators as possible in Net Control Station and liaison functions; don't have the same operator performing the same functions repeatedly or you will lose valuable training experience for the other members of the group. There should be plenty of work for everyone. Good liaison and cooperation at all levels requires versatile operators who can operate different modes. Even though phone operators may not feel comfortable on digital modes, and vice versa, encourage net operators to gain familiarity on all modes by giving them proper training. They can learn by logging for a regular operator in that mode.

If no local emergency or traffic net exists, you or your club should consider initiating a net on an available 2-meter repeater, and coordinate these efforts with the trustee(s) of the repeater you'll use. Encourage club members to participate in traffic-handling activities, either from their home stations or as a group activity from a message center.

Ask your ARRL Section Emergency Coordinator, county

Emergency Manager or Emergency Coordinator to conduct a seminar for your group on communicating with first responder personnel such as police, firefighters or emergency medical technicians. They use procedures that are different from those used in Amateur Radio. It is likely that your ARES and/or Radio Amateur Civil Emergency Service (RACES) group will need to communicate with them in real situations.

For more information on NTS and traffic handling, see the **Traffic Handling** chapter.

HANDLING MESSAGES

Message handling is the essence of emergency communications by radio amateurs. Following a disaster, the potential customers for Amateur Radio services include both official organizations communicating among themselves, and citizens who are without the conventional means to contact their friends and family. It is difficult for the service provider to place an exclusive priority on one or the other, particularly if the means exist to service both customers. Regardless of the method used, the customer being serviced, or who is providing the service, effective communications requires the successful completion of all three major communications phases of origination, transport, and delivery. Originating messages from within a disaster area requires a minimum of one Amateur Radio operator, is often the primary focus, and can usually be accomplished. Without the concurrent provision for the transport and delivery phases, however, originating messages is futile.

Traditional Amateur Radio networks consist of at least two Amateur Radio operators on a common mode and frequency, which satisfies all three communications phases. As the distance between the origination and destination locations increases, additional operators are required to relay the messages: the transport and delivery phases. Irrespective of the mode and frequency used, these are referred to as manual networks, and all function similarly. In the US, we best know this as the National Traffic System, which allows processing of messages by their assigned priority.

Semi-automatic networks require an Amateur Radio operator to originate a message, but use automatic systems to execute the transport and delivery phases. These systems provide higher speed and accuracy, require specific and detailed addresses, and require additional equipment at the origination point. The best known of these systems are NTS-Digital and Winlink 2000, both of which treat all messages as having the same priority. Semi-automatic networks are ill-suited for high priority warning communications, and should never be used to the exclusion of near real-time networks, such as voice. *The greatest value to the customer is provided when all available communications networks are used.*

Emergency Operations Center (EOC)

Amateur Radio emergency communications and message handling are frequently parts of the Incident Command System (ICS), and emergency operations center (EOC) functioning. See **Fig 4-1**. The ICS is a way to control initial and subsequent activities in emergency and disaster situations, and is the standard management model used by all levels of government for disaster response.

Consider an automobile accident where a citizen or an

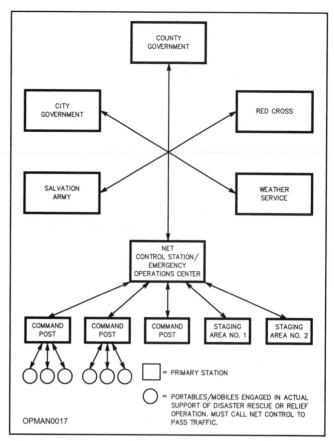

Fig 4-1 — The interaction between the EOC/NCS and the command post(s) in a local emergency.

amateur, first on the scene, becomes a temporary Incident Commander (IC) when he or she calls for or radios a message for help. A law-enforcement officer is dispatched to the accident scene in a squad car and, upon arriving, takes over the IC tasks. Relief efforts, like those in this simple example of an automobile accident, begin when someone takes charge, makes a decision and directs the efforts of others.

The EOC responds to the IC through message communications and subsequent dispatching of equipment and helpers, anticipating needs to supply support and assistance. It may send more equipment to a staging area to be stored where it can be available almost instantly or send more people to react quickly to changing situations. All of this depends on message handling; in many instances, by radio amateurs.

If the status of an accident changes (a car hits a utility pole, which later causes a fire), the IC sends a message to the EOC with an updated report then keeps control even after the support agencies arrive and take over their specific responsibilities: Injuries — medical; fires — fire department; disabled vehicles — law enforcement or tow truck; and utility poles — utility company. By being outside the perimeter of dangerous activities, the EOC can use the proper type of radio communications, concentrate on gathering data from other agencies and then provide the right response.

Whether there is a minor vehicle accident or a major disaster operation, the effectiveness of the amateur effort in an emergency depends mainly on handling information.

A Tour of a Modern County EOC

In Florida, Flagler county's new Emergency Operations Center is a marvel and necessity as the hub of a potential ground zero for natural and man-made disaster. It provides a platform for ARES members when trouble strikes.

Flagler county has been the fastest growing county in the country. Located on the upper east coast of Florida, between famous Daytona Beach and historic St. Augustine, it has 19 miles of coastline, and a rural western aspect of lakes, creeks, and farmland. The county is 485 square miles, with a population of 70,000 mostly along or near the coast.

It is also a ground zero for natural disaster, exposed to the ferocity of hurricanes, tornadoes and even tsunamis. As the county's population and consequent tax base increased, new infrastructure was needed, approved, and developed, including a new emergency operations center (EOC) for county emergency management. At a cost of $7.2 million, it is a technological and ergonomic marvel, a modern bunker of communications and other equipment, which serves as home to the county Emergency Management Division. Under the respected leadership of Troy Harper, and emergency management technician Bob Pickering, KB4RSY, a complement of experts in various emergency management functions converge at the EOC for drills and day-to-day monitoring and activity, as well as the real thing when it hits the fan here in severe weather alley.

Several communication services are in place at the new EOC, including ARES. It is imperative that radio amateurs appreciate their role at the EOC, and have a good working knowledge of all aspects of EOC functioning. Let's take a tour with this goal in mind.

Location, Location, Location

The EOC building is strategically sited away from the immediate coastline by five miles, but close to other government offices and facilities in the county seat of Bunnell. Built on a large open parcel, it is less likely to be hit by flying debris and fire. It is a storm-fortified structure, with few windows; it looks more like a prison. Indeed, it probably seems like a prison for the disaster functionaries when locked down during a major situation.

Upon entering the lobby, a large meeting room on the right serves as a training center. State of the art multimedia technology provide for effective presentations. Off the left of the lobby is the Media Room, where journalists and reporters receive status reports and feed their home bases. On the other side of a locked door, the Dispatch Center (911) has six dispatchers managed by the Sheriff's Office, for fire, rescue and police functions. A 24-hour warning point for public schools (each school also has a weather alert radio) is run from the Dispatch Center.

The EOC uses two primary communication systems for these functions: a new state-of-the-art analog/digital 800 MHz trunking system and a good, old-fashioned VHF FM system. This flexibility is essential as Fire/Rescue services are on the VHF system only, as is the Division of Forestry, another critical component in the mostly forested county. The Fire Flight Helicopter, which includes a med-evac function, has 800 MHz, VHF and UHF assets. The 800 MHz system includes six antenna towers, and simulcasts on the VHF channels.

Down the hall is the Broadcast Studio, where officials can voice public warnings and information over the standard commercial broadcasting frequencies on the AM and FM bands.

Communications Room

Next, is the Communications Room, which also serves as Pickering's office. Wall-to-wall radios include four dual-band mobile-style radios, an HF radio (Kenwood TS-520S), numerous handhelds on charge docks, GMRS radios, and CB-REACT radios. An EMWIN system for receiving and displaying technical weather information and radar images is up on a computer monitor. A 60-foot conduit for coax runs to a hardened antenna farm on the south side of the building. Antennas sit atop a 55-foot collapsible US Towers support, and a smaller section of Rohn 45.

The Break Room is just what its name suggests, and features an industrial, restaurant-scale kitchen for feeding "shut-ins" for an extended period of time. The Bunk Room offers comfortable bunks for downtime, sleeping 120. The physical plant is on city water, with no well, but has its own fuel farm for self-sufficiency over the potential long haul.

Hub

The hub of the EOC is the Operations Room, a large room with desks arranged in classroom style facing the front of the room where two larger desks host the command and control officials in charge. Each desk has a telephone system, and a laptop. The desks are dedicated to emergency support functions (ESFs), and certain principal geographic areas of the county such as Beverly Beach, Flagler Beach, Palm Coast, Marineland, and Bunnell.

Emergency Support Functions at the Flagler EOC

EOC functions are organized as follows:
ESF 1 – Transportation
ESF 2 – Communications and Technology
ESF 3 – Public Works
ESF 4 – Fire
ESF 5 – Information and Planning
ESF 6 – Mass Care
ESF 7 – Resource Support
ESF 8 – Health/Medical
ESF 9 – Search and Rescue
ESF 10 – HAZMAT
ESF 11 – Food/Water
ESF 12 – Energy and Utilities
ESF 13 – Military Support
ESF 14 – Public Information
ESF 15 – Volunteers and Donations
ESF 16 – Law Enforcement
ESF 17 – Animal Services
ESF 18 – Special Needs
ESF 19 – Business and Industry
ESF 20 – Damage Assessment

Other positions include desks for Utilities, Finance, Logistics and Planning. A position and desk are also present for the Florida Department of Transportation (FDOT) and the Florida Department of Law Enforcement (FDLE), both state agencies. Finally, a separate position/desk is located in the back of the room for the Public Information official, where he or she can see all of the activity.

Affixed to the walls of the Operations Room are huge LCD monitors displaying EMWIN, NOAA Weather Radar, CNN, and other information channels. Cameras record hub activity. The EOC uses E-Team software for computer management of operations. The entire physical plant can be powered by 35 kW generators, housed in bunkers on the south side of the building.

Communications with Tallahassee

The telephone is the first choice for EOC communications with the Florida State EOC at Tallahassee. If telephone service is not available, the staff turns to its ESATCOM satellite-based phone and EAS system, which will be replaced soon by the National Warning System (NAWAS), a comprehensive party line network of telephone circuits connecting state and Federal warning points throughout the United States, funded by FEMA. Although NAWAS is a national system, the day-to-day operation is under the control of individual states. Other satellite phone services are also available. AM radio is also a backup system.

Amateur Radio Supports the EOC

And, of course, Amateur Radio can also be used: In a major incident, ARES operators at the EOC check into the Northern Florida ARES Net on 3950 kHz, and communicate directly with their state counterparts and officials including well-known EOC technicians John Fleming, WD4FFX, and Kimo Montague, K4IMO, at the Tallahassee facility.

Flagler county has two major Amateur Radio organizations, the Flagler Emergency Communications Association (FECA), which is comprised of ARES, GMRS, SKYWARN and REACT operators and hardware assets; and the Flagler Palm Coast Amateur Radio Club (FPCARC), which is more of a general interest club with members supporting the EOC as needed, and the CERT program in specific neighborhoods. The FPCARC also has a repeater. Both entities are devoted to serving the public in times of need.

EOC Leadership

The Flagler amateur community has been fortunate to have leaders, especially Bob Pickering, at the EOC who have the foresight to include Amateur Radio in their emergency operations plans. It has been a symbiotic relationship: Amateur Radio supports the EOC and is included in planning, training, drills, and actual events, and in turn, interest in Amateur Radio is fulminated in the public, and more are licensed through local VE sessions sponsored by both Amateur Radio clubs.

The Radio Amateur Volunteer at the EOC

The ARES or other volunteer amateur operator at the EOC must not only know his or her Amateur Radio system and organization, but also know the rest of the systems and functions of the center if he/she is to fulfill his or her potential for utility to the emergency management officials. Make it a priority to fully understand and know the functions of all aspects of your EOC. Only then will you be able to make the fullest contribution possible.

THE INCIDENT COMMAND SYSTEM (ICS)

An incident is an occurrence, either caused by humans or natural phenomena, that requires response actions to prevent or minimize loss of life or damage to property and/or the environment. Examples of incidents include:

- Fire, both structural and wildland.
- Natural disasters, such as tornadoes, floods, ice storms or earthquakes.
- Human and animal disease outbreaks.
- Search and rescue missions.
- Hazardous materials incidents.
- Criminal acts and crime scene investigations.
- Terrorist incidents, including the use of weapons of mass destruction.
- National Special Security Events, such as Presidential visits or the Super Bowl.
- Other planned events, such as parades or demonstrations.

Given the magnitude of these types of events, it's not always possible for any one agency alone to handle the management and resource needs.

Partnerships are often required among local, State, Tribal, and Federal agencies. These partners must work together in a smooth, coordinated effort under the same management system.

The Incident Command System, or ICS, is a standardized, on-scene, all-hazard incident management concept. ICS allows its users to adopt an integrated organizational structure to match the complexities and demands of single or multiple incidents without being hindered by jurisdictional boundaries.

ICS has considerable internal flexibility. It can grow or shrink to meet different needs. This flexibility makes it a very cost effective and efficient management approach for both small and large situations. (The previous description is from FEMA Independent Study Course IS-100.)

The Incident Command System uses *clear text and common terms*. The ability to communicate within the ICS is absolutely critical. An essential method for ensuring the ability to communicate is by using common terminology and clear text. All communications are to be in plain English. That is, use clear text. Do not use radio codes, agency-specific codes, or jargon. ICS establishes common terminology allowing diverse incident management and support entities to work together.

The ICS command function may be carried out in two ways:

As a *Single Command* in which the Incident Commander will have complete responsibility for incident management. A Single Command may be simple, involving an Incident Commander and single resources, or it may be a complex organizational structure with an Incident Management Team.

As a *Unified Command* in which responding agencies and/or jurisdictions with responsibility for the incident share incident management.

Major ICS functions such as planning, logistics, operations, finance and working with the press are described in detail so the organization size can change to match the particular incident's requirements. The IC can consist of only a single individual for a small incident or it can expand to a Command Staff for a large incident.

ICS has a concise span of control. Since management works well with a small number of people, the ICS typically is designed so that throughout the system, no leader has more than about five people reporting to them.

In some areas the ICS evaluates and determines what resources will be needed to start recovery. Amateur communicators are typically within the Logistics Section, Service Branch and Communications Unit of an ICS (**Fig 4-2**).

National Incident Management System

On February 28, 2003, President Bush issued Homeland Security Presidential Directive-5. HSPD-5 directed the Secretary of Homeland Security to develop and administer a National Incident Management System (NIMS). NIMS provides a consistent nationwide template to enable all government, private-sector, and nongovernmental organizations to work together during domestic incidents. You can also find information about NIMS at **www.fema.gov/nims/**.

While most emergency situations are handled locally, when there's a major incident help may be needed from other jurisdictions, the state or the federal government. NIMS was developed so responders from different jurisdictions and disciplines can work together better to respond to natural disasters and emergencies, including acts of terrorism. NIMS benefits include a unified approach to incident man-age-ment; standard command and

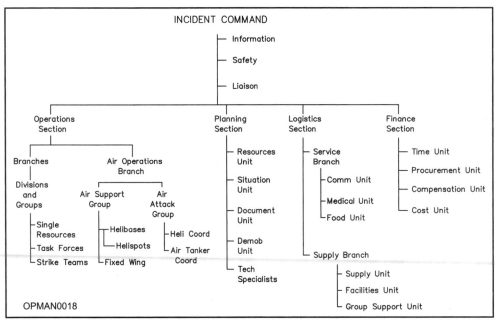

Fig 4-2 — The Incident Command System structure.

management structures; and emphasis on preparedness, mutual aid and resource management.

Tactical Traffic

Whether traffic is tactical, by formal message, packet radio or amateur television, success depends on knowing which to use, and how to use it.

Tactical traffic is first-response communications in an emergency situation involving a few operators in a small area. It may be urgent instructions or inquiries such as "send an ambulance" or "who has the medical supplies?" Tactical traffic, even though unformatted and seldom written, is particularly important in localized communications when working with government and law-enforcement agencies. Note, however, that logs should be kept by hams passing tactical traffic. A log may be relevant later for law enforcement or other legal actions, and can even serve to protect the Amateur Radio operator in some situations.

The 146.52 MHz FM calling frequency — or VHF and UHF repeaters and net frequencies (see **Fig 4-3**) — are typically used for tactical communications. This is a natural choice because FM mobile, portable and fixed-station equipment is so plentiful and popular. However, the 222 and 440 MHz UHF bands provide the best communications from steel or concrete structures, have less interference and are more secure for sensitive transmissions.

One way to make tactical net operation clear is to use tactical call signs — words that describe a function, location or agency. Their use prevents confusing listeners or agencies who are monitoring. When operators change shifts or locations, the set of tactical calls remains the same; that is, the tactical call remains with the position even if the operators switch. Amateurs may use tactical call signs like "Parade Headquarters," "Finish Line," "Red Cross," "Net Control" or "Weather Center" to promote efficiency and coordination in public service communication activities. However, amateurs must identify with their FCC-assigned call sign at the end of a transmission or series of transmissions and at intervals not to exceed 10 minutes.

Another tip is to use the 12-hour local-time system for time and dates when working with relief agencies, unless they understand the 24-hour or UTC systems.

Taking part in a tactical net as an ARES team member requires some discipline and following a few rules:

1) Report to the Net Control Station (NCS) as soon as you arrive at your assigned position.

2) Ask the NCS for permission before you use the frequency.

3) Use the frequency for traffic, not chit-chat.

4) Answer promptly when called by the NCS.

5) Use tactical call signs.

6) Follow the net protocol established by the NCS.

7) Always inform the NCS when you leave service, even for a short time.

In some relief activities, tactical nets become resource or command nets. A resource net is used for an event that goes beyond the boundaries of a single jurisdiction and when mutual aid is needed. A command net is used for communications between EOCs and ARES leaders. Yet with all the variety of nets, sometimes the act of simply putting the parties directly on the radio — instead of trying to interpret their words — is the best approach.

Formal Message Traffic

Formal message traffic is long-term communications that involve many people over a large area. It's generally cast in standard ARRL message format and handled on well estab-

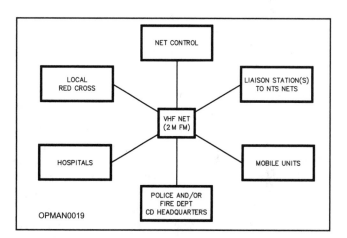

Fig 4-3 — Typical station deployment for local ARES net coverage in an emergency.

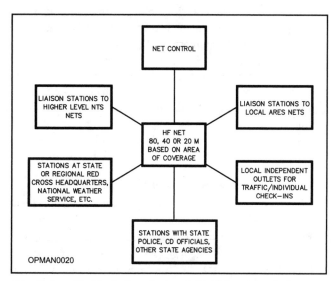

Fig 4-4 — Typical structure of an HF network for emergency communications.

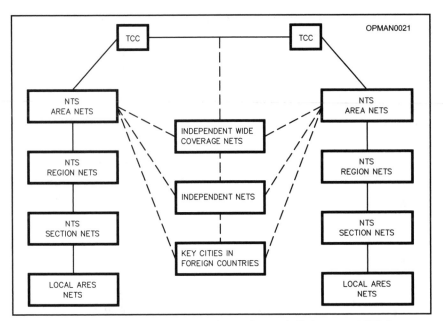

Fig 4-5 — Emergency communications through liaison to NTS for handling formal message traffic.

lished National Traffic System (NTS) nets, primarily on 75-meter SSB, 80-meter CW or 2-meter FM (see **Fig 4-4**). In addition, there is a regular liaison to the International Assistance and Traffic Net, IATN, now officially designated the NTS Atlantic Region Net (ARN). The net meets on 14.303 MHz daily at 1130 UTC (1100 during the summer), to provide international traffic outlets, as suggested in **Fig 4-5**.

Formal messages can be used for severe weather and disaster reports. These radiograms, already familiar to many agency officials and to the public, avoid message duplication while ensuring accuracy. Messages should be read to the originators before sending them, since the originators are responsible for their content. When accuracy is more important than speed, getting the message on paper before it is transmitted is an inherent advantage of formal traffic.

Packet Radio

Packet radio is a powerful tool for traffic handling, especially with detailed or lengthy text or messages that need to be more secure than those transmitted by voice. Prepare and edit messages off line as text files. These can then be sent error free in just seconds, an important timesaver for busy traffic channels. Public service agencies are impressed by fast and accurate printed messages. Packet radio stations can even be mobile or portable. Relaying might be supplemented by Winlink 2000 (**www.winlink.org**), a system equipped to handle messages among HF, the Internet and packet radio VHF stations.

Image Communications

Image communication offers live pictures of an area to allow, for example, damage assessment by authorities. Amateur television (ATV) in its public service role usually employs portable fast-scan television (FSTV), which displays full motion, has excellent detail, can be in color and has a simultaneous sound channel. Although a picture is worth a thousand words, an ATV system requires more equipment, operating skill and

preparation than using a simple hand-held radio.

Video cameras and 420-430 or 1240-1294 MHz radios can transmit public service images from a helicopter to a ground base station equipped with video monitors and a VCR for taping. Image communication works well on the ground, too. Video coverage of severe weather adds another dimension to your ability to serve the public.

Slow scan TV (SSTV) is also popular for damage assessment. Portable SSTV operations can use a digital still image camera, laptop computer and handheld or mobile transceiver. Signals may be relayed through a repeater to increase their range. More information on these modes may be found in the **Image Communications** chapter.

Automatic Packet Reporting System (APRS)

APRS is an Amateur Radio technology that incorporates Global Positioning System (GPS) receiver tracking, weather instrumentation stations, digital cartography mapping, radio direction finding equipment and comprehensive messaging in one package. APRS has been adopted by some SKYWARN and ARES organizations as frontline technology for severe weather operations. Such a system provides accurate, real-time weather telemetry that SKYWARN operators and National Weather Service meteorologists use to issue severe weather warnings and advisories.

A combination of APRS and Emergency Management Weather Information Network (EMWIN) can be used to transmit warnings to field spotters to help track a storm's movement as well as report tornadoes or hail. A mobile APRS with GPS capability can be an essential tool during and following a large scale disaster to pinpoint critical locations in an area void of landmarks, such as forest fires or search and rescue activities. New APRS-friendly radios put tactical messaging capability in the palm of your hand. See the **VHF/UHF — FM, Repeaters and Digital Voice and Data** chapter for more information on these modes.

Internet

The Internet provides a fluent, high speed conduit to communicate locally or over great distances. During nonemergency conditions, websites and e-mail are essential tools to help keep ECs in touch with many served agencies. Amateur Radio operators can contact their local organization or publicize emergency preparedness activities. Some Emergency Operation Centers have installed satellite-based Internet facilities with backup generator electricity.

AMATEUR RADIO GROUPS

The Amateur Radio Emergency Service

In 1935, the ARRL developed what is now called the Amateur Radio Emergency Service (ARES), an organization of radio amateurs who have voluntarily registered their capa-

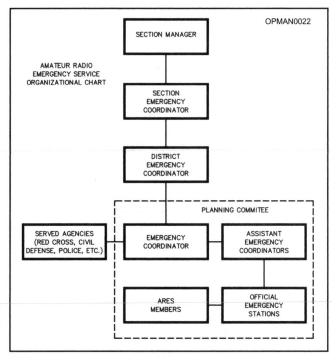

AMATEUR RADIO
EMERGENCY SERVICE
ORGANIZATIONAL CHART

Fig 4-6 — Section structure for ARES.

bilities and equipment for emergency communications (see **Fig 4-6**). They are groups of trained operators ready to serve the public when disaster strikes and regular communications fail. ARES often recruits members from existing clubs, and includes amateurs outside the club area, since emergencies do not recognize boundary lines.

Are you interested in public service activities, or preparing for emergency communications? Join ARES in your area and exchange ideas, ask questions and help with message centers, sports events or weather spotting. Any licensed amateur with a sincere desire to serve is eligible for ARES membership. The possession of emergency-powered equipment is a plus, but it is not a requirement. An ARES group needs to refresh its training with meetings, scheduled nets, drills or real emergencies. An effective ARES group is to our benefit, as well as to the benefit of the entire community. Information about ARES may be obtained from your ARRL Section Manager (contact information is available from **www.arrl.org** or a recent issue of *QST*).

The Amateur Radio Emergency Service has responded countless times to communications emergencies. ARES also introduces Amateur Radio to the ever-changing stream of agency officials. Experience has proven that radio amateurs react and work together more capably in time of emergency when practice has been conducted in an organized group. There is no substitute for experience gained — before the need arises.

Official Emergency Station (OES)

After you get some ARES training and practice, you might want to refine your skills in emergency communications. If you possess a full ARRL membership, there are several opportunities available. The first is the OES appointment, which requires regular participation in ARES including drills, emergency nets and, possibly, real emergency situations. An OES aims for high standards of activity, emergency-preparedness and operating skills.

Emergency Coordinator (EC)

Next, when you feel qualified enough to become a team leader of your local ARES group, consider the EC appointment, if that position is vacant in your area. An EC, usually responsible for a county, is the person who can plan, organize, maintain response-readiness and coordinate for emergency communications (see **Fig 4-7**).

Much of the work involves promoting a working relationship with local government and agencies. The busy EC can hold meetings, train members, keep records, encourage newcomers, determine equipment availability, lead others in drills or be first on the scene in an actual disaster. Some highly populated or emergency-prone areas may also need one or more Assistant Emergency Coordinators (AEC) to help the EC. The AEC is an appointment made by an EC. The AEC position can be held by a ham with any class of license; they need not be ARRL members.

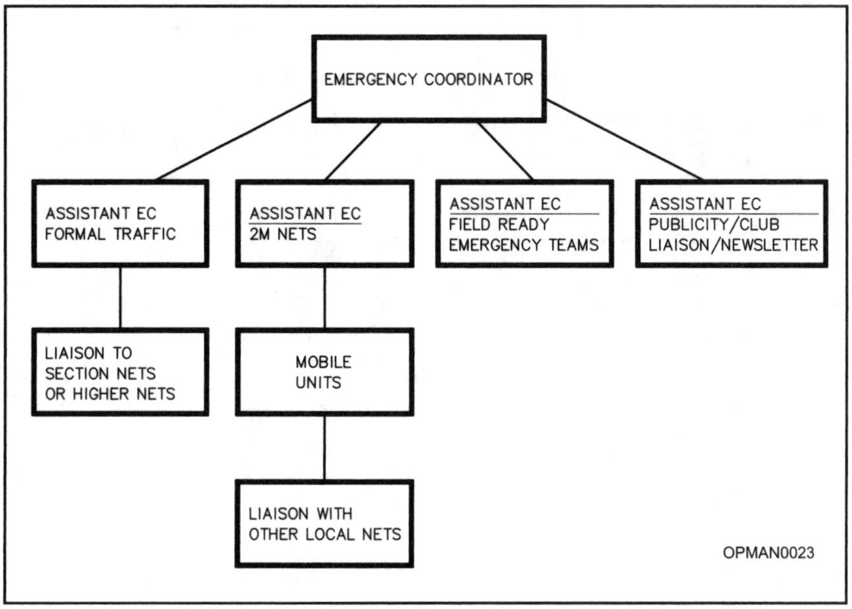

District Emergency Coordinator (DEC)

If there are many ARES groups in an area, a DEC may be appointed. Usually responsible for several counties, the DEC coordinates emergency plans between local ARES groups, encourages activity on ARES nets, directs the overall communication needs of a large area or can be a backup for an EC. As a model emergency communicator, the DEC trains clubs in tactical traffic, formal traffic, disaster communications and operating skills.

Fig 4-7 — Local ARES structure for a county, city or other area of coverage.

Local ARES volunteers are the heart and soul of emergency communications. Williamson County (TN) EC Bill Gerth, W4RK (left), operates at the Williamson Medical Center station with Allen Lovett, K4XXG, the Director of Medical Services for the county.

Section Emergency Coordinator (SEC)

Finally, there is one rare individual who can qualify as top leader of each ARRL Section emergency structure, the SEC. Only the Section Manager can appoint a candidate to become the SEC. The SEC does some fairly hefty work on a section-wide level: making policies and plans and establishing goals, selecting the DECs and ECs, promoting ARES membership and keeping tabs on emergency preparedness. During an actual emergency, the SEC follows activities from behind the scenes, making sure that plans work and section communications are effective.

ARRL Field Organization

The overall leader of the ARRL Field Organization in each section is the Section Manager, who is elected by the ARRL membership in that section. For further details on the Field Organization, visit these ARRL Web pages for more information: **www.arrl.org/FandES/field/org/** and **www.arrl.org/sections/**.

RADIO AMATEUR CIVIL EMERGENCY SERVICE

The Radio Amateur Civil Emergency Service (RACES) was set up in 1952 as a special phase of the Amateur Radio

---

ARES Personal Checklist

The following represents recommendations of equipment and supplies ARES members should consider having available for use during an emergency or public service activity.

Forms of Identification
✓ ARES Identification Card
✓ FCC Amateur Radio license
✓ driver's license

Radio Gear
✓ VHF transceiver
✓ microphone
✓ headphones
✓ power supply/extra batteries
✓ antennas with mounts
✓ spare fuses
✓ patch cords/adapters (coax and audio)
✓ SWR meter
✓ extra coax

Writing Gear
✓ pen/pencil/eraser
✓ clipboard
✓ message forms
✓ logbook
✓ note paper

Personal Gear (short duration)
✓ snacks
✓ liquid refreshments
✓ throat lozenges
✓ personal medicine
✓ aspirin
✓ extra pair of prescription glasses
✓ sweater/jacket

Personal Gear (72-hour duration)
✓ foul-weather gear
✓ three-day supply of drinking water
✓ cooler with three-day supply of food
✓ mess kit with cleaning supplies
✓ first-aid kit
✓ personal medicine
✓ aspirin
✓ throat lozenges
✓ sleeping bag
✓ toilet articles
✓ mechanical or battery powered alarm clock
✓ flashlight with batteries/lantern
✓ candles
✓ waterproof matches
✓ extra pair of prescription glasses

Tool Box (72-hour duration)
✓ screwdrivers
✓ pliers
✓ socket wrenches
✓ electrical tape
✓ 12/120-V soldering iron
✓ solder
✓ volt-ohm meter

Other (72-hour duration)
✓ HF transceiver
✓ hatchet/ax
✓ saw
✓ pick
✓ shovel
✓ siphon
✓ jumper cables
✓ generator, spare plugs and oil
✓ kerosene lights, camping lantern or candles
✓ ⅜-inch hemp rope
✓ highway flares
✓ extra gasoline and oil

Service conducted by volunteer licensed amateurs. It is currently designed to provide emergency communications to local or state governmental agencies during times when normal communications are down or overloaded.

RACES operation is authorized during periods of local, regional or national civil emergencies by the FCC upon request of a state or federal official. While RACES was originally based on potential use during wartime, it now encompasses all types of emergencies and natural disasters. RACES is sponsored by Federal Emergency Management Agency, but is usually administered by a state-level Office of Emergency Management.

Amateurs operating in a local RACES organization must be officially enrolled (registered). RACES operation is conducted by amateurs using their own primary station licenses, and by existing RACES stations. The FCC no longer issues new RACES (WC prefix) station call signs. Operator privileges in RACES are dependent upon, and identical to, those for the class of license held in the Amateur Radio Service. All of the authorized frequencies and emissions allocated to the Amateur Radio Service are also available to RACES on a shared basis.

When operating in a RACES capacity, RACES stations and amateurs registered in the local RACES organization may not communicate with amateurs not operating in a similar capacity. See FCC regulations for further information.

Although RACES and ARES are separate entities, the ARRL advocates dual membership and cooperative efforts between both groups whenever possible. The RACES regulations make it simple for an ARES group whose members are all enrolled in and certified by RACES to operate in an emergency with great flexibility. Using the same operators and the same frequencies, an ARES group also enrolled as RACES can "switch hats" from ARES to RACES or RACES to ARES to meet the requirements of the situation as it develops. For example, during a "non-declared emergency," ARES can operate under ARES, but when an emergency or disaster is officially declared by a state or federal authority, the operation can become RACES with no change in personnel or frequencies.

Where there currently is no RACES, it would be a simple matter for an ARES group to enroll in that capacity, after a presentation to the civil-preparedness authorities. For more information on RACES, contact your State Emergency Management, or FEMA.

THE NATIONAL TRAFFIC SYSTEM

In 1949 the ARRL created the National Traffic System to handle medium and long-haul formal message traffic through networks whose operations can be expedited to meet the needs of an emergency situation.

The main function of NTS in an emergency is to link various local activities and to allow traffic destined outside of a local area to be systematically relayed to the addressee. In a few rare cases, a message can be handled by taking it directly to a net in the state where the addressee lives for rapid delivery by an amateur there within toll-free calling distance. However, NTS is set up on the basis of being able to relay large amounts of traffic systematically, efficiently and according to an established flow pattern. This proven and dependable scheme is what makes NTS so vital to emergency communications. See the **Traffic Handling** chapter for more information on NTS.

Additional details on ARES and NTS can be found online in these ARRL resources: *Public Service Communications Manual*, (**www.arrl.org/public-service-communications-manual**); *NTS Manual* (**www.arrl.org/nts-manual**), and the *ARRL Net Search* (**www.arrl.org/net-directory-search**). Information on emergency and public service communications also appear regularly in *QST*.

GOVERNMENT AND NGO RELIEF AGENCIES

Government and non-governmental organizations (NGOs) as relief agencies provide effective emergency management to help communities in disasters. They often rely on normal communications channels, but even reliable communications systems may fail, be unavailable or become overloaded in an emergency. Furthermore, in disaster situations, agency-to-agency radio systems may be incompatible.

Fortunately, Amateur Radio communicators can serve and support in these situations. We can bridge communications gaps with mobile, portable and fixed stations. We also supply trained volunteers needed by the agencies for collection and exchange of critical emergency information.

As government and relief agencies become more dependent on volunteer programs, they quickly recognize the value of efforts of radio amateurs who serve the public interest. This public recognition is important support for the continued existence and justification of Amateur Radio.

By using Amateur Radio operators in the amateur frequency bands, the ARRL has been and continues to be in the forefront of supplying emergency communications, either directly to the general public or through various agencies. In fact, there are several organizations that have signed formal agreements with the ARRL: American Red Cross; National Weather Service; Department of Homeland Security — Citizen Corps, FEMA; Association of Public-Safety Communications Officials — International; National Communications System; National Association of Radio and Telecommunications Engineers; Salvation Army; Society of Broadcast Engineers; Quarter Century Wireless Association; and Radio Emergency Associated Communication Teams. Each of these agreements is available on the ARRL Web site at **www.arrl.org/served-agencies-and-partners**.

The American National Red Cross and the Salvation Army extend assistance to individuals and families in times of disaster. Red Cross chapters, for example, establish, coordinate and maintain continuity of communications during disaster-relief operations (both national and international). These agencies have long recognized that the Amateur Radio Service, because of its excellent geographical station coverage, can render valuable aid.

In June 2003, ARRL became an official affiliate program of Citizen Corps, an initiative within the Department of Homeland Security (DHS) to enhance public preparedness and safety. The new Statement of Affiliation (SoA) makes ARRL an affiliate under the four charter Citizen Corps programs — Neighborhood Watch, Volunteers in Police Service, Community Emergency Response Teams and Medical Reserve Corps. The League joins the National Safety Council, Points of Light Foundation, National Voluntary Organizations Active in Disaster, National Volunteer Fire Council, National

Fire Protection Association, Save A Life Foundation and The Jaycees as Citizen Corps affiliate programs. Today, Citizen Corps groups are at the community level and state levels to assist first responders.

The Statement of Affiliation calls on the Department of Homeland Security and ARRL to raise public awareness of Amateur Radio as a safety resource. DHS and ARRL will cooperate in providing training and accreditation for Amateur Radio emergency communications. They will work together to promote the formation of local Citizen Corps councils and assist them with education, training and volunteer service opportunities that support first responders, disaster relief organizations and community safety efforts.

ARRL has worked very closely with the Federal Emergency Management Agency (FEMA) beginning in 1984 when a Memorandum of Understanding was inked that helped ARRL volunteers coordinate their services with emergency management at all levels of government. FEMA's job was as a "last responder," as opposed to first responders (the local, county and state emergency management agencies).

The National Communication System (NCS) is a confederation of government agencies and departments established by a Presidential Memorandum to ensure that the critical telecommunication needs of the Federal Government can be met in an emergency. The ARRL Field Organization continues to participate in communications tests sponsored by NCS to study telecommunications readiness in any conceivable national emergency. Through this participation, radio amateurs have received recognition at the highest levels of government.

The Association of Public Safety Communications Officials — International (APCO) and amateurs share common bonds of communications in the public interest. APCO is made up of law-enforcement, fire and public-safety communications personnel. These officials have primary responsibility for the management, maintenance and operation of communications facilities in the public domain. They also establish international standards for public-safety communications, professionalism and continuity of communications through education, standard-ization and the exchange of information.

The National Weather Service (NWS) consists of a national headquarters in Washington, DC, six regional offices and over 200 local offices throughout the US. The ARRL Field Organization cooperates with NWS in establishing SKYWARN networks for weather spotting and communications. SKYWARN is a plan sponsored by NWS to report and track destructive storms or other severe weather conditions.

An increased awareness of radio amateur capabilities has also been fostered by ARRL's active participation as a member of the National Volunteer Organizations Active in Disaster (NVOAD). NVOAD coordinates the volunteer efforts of its member-agencies (the Red Cross and Salvation Army are among its members).

ARRL and radio amateurs continue to accelerate their presence with these agencies. This enhanced image and recognition of Amateur Radio attracts more "customers" for amateurs and our communications skills.

WORKING WITH SERVED AGENCIES

Amateur Radio affords public-safety agencies like those listed above and local police and fire officials, with an extremely valuable resource in times of emergency. Once initial acceptance by the authorities is achieved, an ongoing working relationship between amateurs and safety agencies is based on the efficiency of our performance. Officials tend to be very cautious and skeptical about those who are not members of the public-safety professions. At times, officials may have trouble separating problem solvers from problem makers, but they often accept communications help if it is offered in the proper spirit.

Here are several image-building rules for working with served agencies:

• *Maintain group unity.* Work within ARES, RACES or local club groups. Position your EC as the direct link with the agencies.

• *Be honest.* If your group cannot handle a request, say so and explain why. Safety personnel often risk their lives based on a fellow disaster-worker's promise to perform.

• *Equip conservatively.* Do not have more signs, decals and antennas than used by the average police or fire vehicle. Safety professionals are trained against overkill and use the minimum resources necessary to get the job done.

• *Look professional.* In the field, wear a simple jump suit or jacket with an ARES patch to give a professional image and to help officials identify radio operators.

• *Respect authority.* Only assume the level of authority and responsibility that has been given to you.

• *Publicize Amateur Radio.* If contacted by members of the press, restrict comments solely to the amateurs' role in the situation. Emergency status and names of victims should only come from a press information officer, or the government agency concerned.

Following the September 11, 2001, attack, the net control station at the Pentagon was photographed just before photos were banned from the area. The partially-hidden operator in the center is Chris Hanslets, KA8UNO. *(K9MX photo)*

The public service lifeline provided by Amateur Radio must be understood by public-safety agencies before the next disaster occurs. Have an amateur representative meet with public-safety officials in advance of major emergencies so each group will know the capabilities of the other. The representative should appear professional with a calm, businesslike manner and wear conservative attire. It is up to you to invite the local agencies to observe or cooperatively participate with your group.

SHIFTING NEEDS OF SERVED AGENCIES

Cross-Training in Agency Functions

More cross-training in served agency functions will add value to our contributions. Especially in the case of the American Red Cross, amateurs can increase their value to the agency by taking advantage of training courses offered for several disaster relief functions: damage assessment, shelter management, mass care and feeding, for examples.

Traditionally, amateurs have declined to perform functions unrelated to their primary radio communication interest and training. Indeed, ARRL literature has cautioned amateurs against providing unrelated services, encouraging them to concentrate on their role as radio communicators only. The caution was founded on a healthy concern that amateurs performing unrelated functions for which they were not trained would become liabilities rather than assets, and cause Amateur Radio to lose credibility. However, if we do not broaden our perspective on Amateur Radio's traditionally limited role, we minimize our utility and risk finding ourselves outside looking in when it comes to serving agencies engaged in future disaster relief. Proper training and certification in the various functions are the keys to a successful bid for greater utility and corresponding perpetuation of our public service tradition.

Integration with Other Systems

Integration of amateur systems with non-amateur systems will increase utility and value. APRS, an Amateur Radio developed technology, now incorporates computers, the Internet, weather stations and the GPS. As another example, Winlink 2000 developers have interfaced Internet e-mail and HF radio using PACTOR. Hybrid systems such as these may represent an opportunity to enhance our contributions to served agencies for the future. Emergency managers and NWS personnel all appreciate the value of APRS and similar systems in gathering information, and supporting communications from locations not serviced by their own.

Cross-Training with Other Radio Systems

More cross-training with other radio systems will make amateur operators more valuable in the EOC. A Collier County, Florida, emergency manager said at a Florida conference that he has a need for operators who are capable of operating *all* communication systems in the EOC. "When hams come in, they should be able to operate anything."

Thus, we may not only need to integrate amateur systems with other systems, but we may also want to promote programs to train our ARES volunteers to develop proficiency with new systems that do not directly integrate with Amateur Radio.

Over the last few years, Florida has seen members of Amateur Radio response teams carrying cell phones and pagers. During Hurricane Andrew, municipal agencies often tasked amateurs with operating government radios. In 1992, most municipal communication employed conventional two-way radio. Today, it's 800 MHz trunking. Do amateurs today know what a trunked radio system is and how it operates? Could our volunteers operate a satellite telephone terminal to relay messages? And move it from one location to another and aim it correctly at the satellite?

The Telecommunications Committee of the Florida Emergency Planners Association (FEPA) has been asked to extend training to ARES and RACES operators in new technologies adopted by county and state emergency management agencies, rendering our amateurs more valuable in the emergency operations center. When the dust settles in a disaster, we will be remembered for how useful we were to the overall response, not whether we were using our own equipment or someone else's.

Interagency Communication

We should continue to emphasize our role in providing interagency communications during multi-agency responses. The provision of interagency communication has always been a solid, traditional role for Amateur Radio, and it appears that the need will be perpetuated for the future. Despite the institution of new telecommunication technologies in the public safety sector, there is a continuing inability of responding agencies to communicate with one another at a disaster site. As emergency responses become more sophisticated and the proliferation of new disaster response agencies continues, the need for interagency communications at a disaster site will become even more profound.

A Unified Front

Amateurs need to present a unified front to the agencies they serve. Infighting and turf wars, especially between ARES and RACES, are as old as the program itself. Toss in the mix of clubs who claim monopolies over served agencies and emergency responses in their communities, and the result is confusion and disorganization as seen by the agency officials who don't have the time to deal with it.

An educational campaign with our volunteers and clubs should be undertaken to ensure that Amateur Radio presents an orderly, professional face to the agencies we serve.

Our Unique Capabilities

Amateurs should emphasize the unique "decentralization" characteristic of the amateur service. Radio amateurs are already geographically dispersed throughout the areas to be affected by disaster. We are found in just about every community across the country. We're already everywhere that relief agencies would like to be, but can't, because of the obvious limitations. We need to reaffirm this unique characteristic in selling ourselves to the served agency community.

Expand the Client base

Expanding our client base with new agencies to serve will maximize opportunities for Amateur Radio. If we lose the opportunity of serving some agencies as a result of our being displaced by new technology, we can hedge our bets for the future by expanding our client base; i.e. by drafting new and possibly nontraditional entities to serve. Looking for new clients to serve, some have been working with district schools in establishing an emergency communication network, with a permanent station at district HQ.

Other sectors for expanding our client base: public works departments, utility companies, transportation companies, hospitals, convalescent centers, senior citizen homes, and child care centers.

Summary

If we work to adapt to our served agency's new needs, and keep up our public service record established more than 85 years ago intact, we can continue to count on the valuable returns. Such support from our served agencies is priceless and we must do everything we can to safeguard it.

MAJOR DISASTERS AND CALAMITIES

On September 11, 2001, Amateur Radio operators mobilized within minutes of the first attack of the World Trade Center in New York City, then responded magnificently in the Washington, DC, area and in western Pennsylvania. On September 11, 2001, and in the times since, Amateur Radio operators have demonstrated their readiness, perhaps as never before.

While ARES and RACES training might not have readied them to fully comprehend the terrible events of that day, Amateur Radio operators were among the first to volunteer their stations, their skills and themselves. Providing emergency communications tops the list of reasons that validate Amateur Radio in the eyes of the Federal Communications Commission. Given the ubiquity of cellular phones these days, some may have predicted this particular mission would evaporate. When the terrorists struck in New York City and Washington, DC, on September 11, however, commercial telecommunications systems — wired and wireless — were severely compromised. In the immediate aftermath of the crisis, telephone lines were jammed, and cell systems were overwhelmed.

Amateur Radio played a role in helping to restore order. "Never have I felt more strongly about what a great privilege it is to be part of the extraordinary global community of Amateur Radio," declared ARRL President Jim Haynie, W5JBP, as amateurs sprang into action to do their part.

Nature relentlessly concocts severe weather and natural calamities that can cause human suffering on a large scale, and create needs which victims cannot alleviate without assistance. The Hurricane Katrina disaster of 2005 is a prime example.

Amateur Radio operators, specializing in communications, are involved in a variety of these situations. Here are several typical categories in which Amateur Radio operators play a role:

- Severe-weather spotting and reporting
- Supporting evacuation of people to safe areas
- Shelter operations
- Assisting government groups and agencies
- Victim rescue operations
- Medical help requests
- Critical supplies requests
- Health-and-Welfare traffic
- Property damage surveys and cleanup

There are several major disaster networks that come into play during large scale events: The SATERN Net (Salvation Army Team Emergency Radio Network) provides emergency communication support to the Salvation Army and populations at large, during disasters. They hold high profile nets on twenty meters during major incidents, and have a long history of excellence, discipline and service. SATERN members handle traffic in tornadoes, floods, hurricanes, fires, aircraft accidents, bombings, earthquakes, and more. See the SATERN Web site at **www.satern.org**.

The Maritime Mobile Service Net is composed of hams who serve and assist those in need of communications from foreign countries and on the high seas. According to its Web site **www.mmsn.org** the primary purpose of the net is for handling traffic from maritime mobiles, both pleasure and commercial,

This American Red Cross Emergency Communications Vehicle carries many different kinds of communications gear, including Amateur Radio. Increasingly, amateurs must be familiar with the various communications systems used by served agencies in addition to Amateur Radio. (*Elizabeth Leslie photos*)

At the Salvation Army Team Emergency Network (SATERN) communications center in New York City, Jim Wingate, WA2EIU (standing), and Michael Gomez, N2WGC, review field reports from canteen and feeding locations before forwarding them to the Salvation Army logistical officer. This operation supported the relief efforts after the September 11, 2001, terrorist attacks. (*SATERN photo*)

and overseas deployed service personnel. They also assist missionaries and persons working abroad. The Net meets every day from 12 PM until 9 PM Eastern Standard Time, and from 12 PM until 10 PM Eastern Daylight Time, on 14.300 MHz. They cover the entire Atlantic Ocean, Mediterranean Sea, the Caribbean Sea and the eastern Pacific Ocean.

The network is recognized by the United States Coast Guard and has an excellent working relationship. The MMSN has handled hundreds of incidents involving vessels in distress, medical emergencies in remote locations and passing health and welfare traffic in and out of areas affected by natural disasters.

Another major player is the Hurricane Watch Net, which is described below under the heading "Hurricanes."

Severe Weather Spotting and Reporting

Nasty weather hits somewhere every day. Long ago, amateurs exchanged simple information among themselves about the approach and progress of storms. Next, concerned hams phoned the weather offices to share a few reports they thought might be of particular interest to the public. National Weather Service forecasters were relying on spotters: police, sheriff, highway patrol, emergency government and trained individuals who reported weather information by telephone. But when severe weather strikes, professional spotters may be burdened with law-enforcement tasks, phone lines may become overloaded, special communication circuits might go out of service

or, worse yet, there can be a loss of electrical power. Because of these uncertainties, weather-center officials welcomed amateur operators and encouraged them to install their battery-powered radio equipment on site so forecasters could monitor the weather nets, request specific area observations and maintain communications in a serious emergency.

Those first, informal weather nets had great potential to access perhaps hundreds of observers in a wide area. Many Meteorologists-in-Charge eagerly began to instruct hams in the types of information needed during severe-weather emergencies, including radar interpreting. Eventually, Amateur Radio SKYWARN operations developed as an important part of community disaster preparedness programs. Accurate observations and rapid communications during extreme weather situations now proves to be fundamental to the NWS. Amateur Radio operators nationwide are a first-response group invaluable to the success of an early storm-warning effort. Weather spotting is popular because the procedures are easy to learn and reports can be given from the relative safety and convenience of a home or an auto.

Weather reports on a severe-weather net are limited to drastic weather data, unless specifically requested by the net-control operator. So, most amateurs monitor net operations and transmit only when they can help.

Weather forecasters, depending on their geographical location, need certain information.

During the summer or thunderstorm season report:
• Tornadoes, funnels or wall clouds.
• Hail.
• Damaging winds, usually 50 miles per hour or greater.
• Flash flooding.
• Heavy rains, rate of 2 inches per hour or more.

During the winter or snow season report:
• High winds.
• Heavy, drifting snow.
• Freezing precipitation.
• Sleet.
• New snow accumulation of 2 or more inches.

Here's a four-step method to describe the weather you spot:
1) *What*: Tornadoes, funnels, heavy rain and so on.
2) *Where*: Direction and distance from a known location; for example, 3 miles south of Newington.
3) *When*: Time of observation.
4) *How*: Storm's direction, speed of travel, size, intensity and destructiveness. Include uncertainty as needed. ("Funnel cloud, but too far away to be certain it is on the ground.")

Alerting the Weather Net

The Net Control Station, using a VHF repeater, directs and maintains control over traffic being passed on the Weather Net. The station also collates reports, relates pertinent material to the Weather Service and organizes liaison with other area repeaters. Priority Stations, those that are assigned tactical call signs, may call any other station without going through net control. The NCS might start the net upon hearing a National Oceanic and Atmospheric Administration (NOAA) radio alert, or upon request by NWS or the EC. The NCS should keep in mind that the general public or government officials might be listening to net operations with scanners.

Here are some guidelines an NCS might use to initiate and handle a severe-weather net on a repeater:

1) Activate alert tone on repeater.

2) Read weather-net activation format.

3) Appoint a backup NCS to copy and log all traffic — and to take over in the event the NCS goes off-the-air or needs relief.

4) Ask NWS for the current weather status.

5) Check in all available operators.

6) Assign operators to priority stations and liaisons.

7) Give severe-weather report outline and updates.

8) Be apprised of situations and assignments by EC.

9) Periodically read instructions on net procedures and types of severe weather to report.

10) Acknowledge and respond to all calls immediately.

11) Require that net stations request permission to leave the net.

12) During periods of inactivity and to keep the frequency open, make periodic announcements that a net is in progress.

13) Close the net after operations conclude.

At the Weather Service

The NCS position at the Weather Service, when practical, can be handled by the EC and other ARES personnel. Operators assigned there must have 2-meter hand-held radios with fully charged batteries. The station located at the NWS office may also be connected to other positions with an off-

Regional Coordination Function: The Major Disaster Emergency Coordinator Proposal

The Major Disaster Emergency Coordinator (MDEC) is proposed to be an appointed position that will be filled from applicants vetted by their Section Manager/Section Emergency Coordinator. The MDEC will be activated by ARRL Headquarters on an as-needed basis to be the head of the Disaster Field Team (DFT). The DFT will be composed of volunteers from the ARRL national ARES database and will be activated to fill the emergency communications needs that are beyond the capability of the affected Section or Sections. As soon as the DFT is no longer needed, it will be disbanded. The MDEC and the DFT will supplement and aid the Section. They are not intended to replace or assume the authority of the Section staff.

The MDEC is accountable for carrying out the duties of the position in accordance with ARRL policies established by the Board of Directors and shall act in the best interests of Amateur Radio. The MDEC will be activated by and is responsible to the person performing the function of ARRL Disaster Response Emergency Manager (DREM) in response to disasters or large scale exercises that will/have overwhelmed Section resources and require outside resources from the national database.

In discharging these responsibilities, the MDEC:

1) Will act as an ARRL representative, coordinator, manager to the served agency or multiserved agencies when requested. Will implement and maintain Emergency communications services and systems to support served agency requests.

2) Coordinates with the affected Section Manager(s) and Section Emergency Coordinator(s) to augment served agency needs, local nets and other emergency communications functions. Recruits, appoints, and supervises the DFT leadership to administer the Field Organization's principal areas of responsibility in the disaster zone. These areas are emergency communications, message traffic relay, technical activity / problem solving, volunteer monitoring, government relations, public relations in the general community, information services for amateurs, and cooperation with served agencies.

3) Maintains a close liaison with the Logistics Section of the unified Command.

4) Will be familiar with served agency practices, procedures and methods.

5) Appoints qualified operators from the national database to other volunteer positions in support of Field Organization objectives, and may authorize Disaster Field Team staff to make such appointments.

6) Is responsible for requesting and coordinating people and equipment resources for the disaster area.

7) Supervises the activities of the disaster field team staff, monitors the performance of the Field Organization volunteers, and provides guidance as necessary to ensure that appointees act in the best interests of Amateur Radio and in accordance with ARRL policies.

8) Maintains liaison with the ARRL DREM; makes periodic reports to the DREM regarding the status of disaster activities; receives from the DREM information and guidance pertaining to matters of mutual concern and interest. Writes, or supervises preparation of a daily status report that is submitted to the DREM via whatever means available. This report will be based on a daily log and input from served agencies and a daily net conducted with the base and all field stations.

9) Maintains up-to-date qualifications in ICS, NIMS, First Aid, and CPR. Completes all three levels of the ARRL Emergency Communications courses. Completes FEMA courses IS-100, IS-200, and IS-700. Completes other appropriate disaster training offered by the American Red Cross and other organizations.

10) Maintains a continuous state of readiness for deployment to a disaster zone on short notice under difficult conditions.

11) Keeps well informed concerning matters of ARRL policy so as to administer the disaster field team in accordance with current policy.

MDEC appointees must be members of the ARRL. MDEC appointments should be renewed on a regular basis. Two or three years is the suggested periodicity. The MDEC will be managed by and must meet the requirements set by the ARRL DREM. The MDEC must represent the highest standards of the ARRL, Amateur Radio and the served agencies.

At the American Red Cross radio room in Brooklyn, Daytime Shift Manager Mark Dieterich, N2PGD (standing), checks the volunteer shift schedule. Simone Lambert, KA1YVF, handles schedule management from the World Trade Center Disaster Relief Communications registration Web site. Both volunteered from Rhode Island.

the-air intercom system. This allows some traffic handling without loading up the repeater. Designate a supplementary radio channel in anticipation of an overload or loss of primary communications circuits.

If traffic is flowing faster than you can easily copy and relay, NWS personnel may request that a hand-held radio be placed at the severe-weather desk. This arrangement allows them to monitor incoming traffic directly. Nevertheless, all traffic should be written on report forms. If a disaster should occur during a severe-weather net, shift to disaster-relief operations.

Repeater Liaisons

Assign properly equipped and located stations to act as liaisons with other repeaters. Two stations should be appointed to each liaison assignment. One monitors the weather repeater at all times and switches to the assigned repeater just long enough to pass traffic. The second monitors the assigned repeater and switches to the weather repeater just long enough to pass traffic. If there aren't enough qualified liaison stations, one station can be given both assignments.

Weather Warnings

NWS policy is to issue warnings only when there is absolute certainty, for fear of the "cry wolf" syndrome (premature warnings cause the public to ignore later warnings). Public confidence increases with reliable weather warnings. When NWS calls a weather alert, it will contact the local EC by phone or voice-message pager, or the EC may call NWS to check on a weather situation.

Hurricanes

A hurricane is declared when a storm's winds reach 75

miles per hour or more. These strong winds may cause storm-surge waves along shores and flooding inland.

A Hurricane *Watch* means a hurricane may threaten coastal and inland areas. Storm landfall is a possibility, but it is not necessarily imminent. Listen for further advisories and be prepared to act promptly if a warning is issued.

A Hurricane *Warning* is issued when a hurricane is expected to strike within 24 hours. It may include an assessment of flood danger, small-craft or gale warnings, estimated storm effects and recommended emergency procedures.

Amateurs, in the 4th and 5th call areas in particular, can spot and report the approach of hurricanes well ahead of any news service. In fact, their information is sometimes edited and then broadcast on the local radio or TV to keep citizens informed.

The Hurricane Watch Net on 14.325 MHz, for example, serves either the Atlantic or Pacific during a watch or warning period and keeps in touch with the National Hurricane Center. Frequent, detailed information is issued on nets when storms pose a threat to the US mainland. In addition to hurricane spotting, local communicators may announce that residents have evacuated from low-lying flood areas and coastal shore. Other amateurs across the country can help by relaying information, keeping the net frequency clear and by listening.

Tornadoes

A tornado is an intensely destructive whirlwind formed from strongly rising air currents. With winds of up to 300 miles per hour, tornadoes appear as rotating, funnel-shaped clouds from gray to black in color. They extend toward the ground from the base of a thundercloud. Tornadoes may sound like the roaring of an airplane or locomotive. Even though they are short-lived over a small area, tornadoes are the most violent of all atmospheric phenomena. Tornadoes that don't touch the ground are called *funnels*.

A Tornado *Watch* is issued when a tornado may occur near your area. Carefully watch the sky.

A Tornado *Warning* means take shelter immediately, a tornado has actually been sighted or indicated by radar. Protect yourself from being blown away, struck by falling objects or injured by flying debris.

"Tornado alley" runs in the 5th, 9th and 10th US call areas. Amateurs in these areas often receive Tornado Spotter's Training and refresher courses presented by NWS personnel.

Amateur Radio's quick-response capability has reduced injuries and fatalities by giving early warnings to residents. Veteran operators know exactly how serious a tornado can be. They've seen tornadoes knock out telephone and electrical services just as quickly as they flip over trucks or destroy homes. Traffic lights and gas pumps won't work without electricity, creating problems for motorists and fuel shortages for electric generators.

After a tornado strikes, amateurs provide communications in cooperation with local government and relief agencies. Welfare messages are sent from shelters where survivors receive assistance. Teams of amateurs and officials also survey and report property damage.

Floods, Mud Slides and Tidal Waves

Floods occur when excessive rainfall causes rivers to overflow their banks, when heavy rains and warmer-than-usual temperatures melt excessive quantities of snow, or when dams break. Floods can be minor, moderate or major. Floods or volcanic eruptions may melt mountain snow, causing mud slides. A tidal wave or tsunami is actually a series of waves caused by a disturbance that may be associated with earthquakes, volcanoes or sometimes hurricanes.

Don't wait for the water level to rise or for officials to ask for help; sound the alarm and activate a weather net immediately. Besides handling weather data for NWS, enact the response plans necessary to relay tactical flood information to local officials. Assist their decision making by answering the following questions:

1) Which rivers and streams are affected and what are their conditions?

2) When will flooding probably begin, and where are the flood plain areas?

3) What are river-level or depth-gauge readings for comparison to flood levels?

Mobile operators may find roads flooded and bridges washed out. Flood-rescue operations then may be handled by marine police boats with an amateur aboard. If power and telephones are out, portable radio operators can help with relief operations to evacuate families to care facilities where a fixed station should be set up. The officials will need to know the number and location of evacuees. As the river recedes, the water level drops in some areas, but it may rise elsewhere to threaten residents. Liaisons to repeaters downstream can warn others, possibly through the federal Emergency Alert System, of impending flooding. Property-damage reports and welfare traffic will usually be followed by disaster relief and cleanup operations.

Winter Storms

A Winter Storm *Watch* indicates there is a threat of severe winter weather in a particular area. A Winter Storm *Warning* is issued when heavy snow (6 inches or more in a 12-hour period, 8 inches or more in a 24-hour period), freezing rain, sleet or a substantial layer of ice is expected to accumulate.

Freezing rain or freezing drizzle is forecast when expected rain is likely to freeze when it strikes the ground. Freezing rain or ice storms can bring down wires, causing telephone and power outages.

Sleet consists of small particles of ice, usually mixed with rain. If enough sleet accumulates on the ground, it will make roads slippery.

Blizzards are the most dangerous of all winter storms. They are a combination of cold air, heavy snow and strong winds. Blizzards can isolate communities. A Blizzard *Warning* is issued when there is considerable snow and winds of 35 miles per hour or more. A *Severe Blizzard Warning* means that a heavy snow is expected, with winds of at least 45 miles per hour and temperatures 10° F or lower.

Travelers advisories are issued when ice and snow are expected to hinder travel, but not seriously enough to require warnings. Blizzards and snowstorms can create vehicle-traffic problems by making roads impassable, stranding motorists or drastically delaying their progress.

In some areas, local snowmobile club members or 4-wheel-drive-vehicle enthusiasts cooperate with hams to coordinate and transport key medical personnel when snowdrifts render roads almost impassable. They may also assist search teams looking for motorists.

Brush and Forest Fires

A prolonged period of hot, dry weather parches shrubs, brush and trees. This dry vegetation, ignited by lightning, arson or even a helicopter crash, can start a forest fire. The fires quickly become worse when winds spread the burning material.

An amateur who spots a blaze that has the potential of growing into a forest fire can radio the Park Service and ask them to dispatch a district ranger and firefighting equipment. When fires are out of control, hams help with communications to evacuate people, report the fires' movement or radio requests for supplies and volunteers. ARES groups over a wide geographical area can set up portable repeaters, digital links or ATV stations.

Amateurs, in the 6th and 7th US call areas in particular, should get adequate safety training, including fire line safety and fire shelter deployment. Even then, travel to a fire operation only upon receiving clear dispatch instructions from a competent authority. If you don't have proper training, inform whoever is in charge of your lack of training to prevent being given an inappropriate or dangerous assignment.

Fire safety rules are of special importance in an emergency, but also should be observed every day to prevent disaster. Since most fires occur in the home, even an alert urban amateur can spot and report a building on fire. Fires are extinguished by taking away the fuel or air (smother it), or by cooling it with water and fire-extinguishing chemicals. A radio call to the fire department will bring the needed control. The Red Cross generally helps find shelter for the homeless after fires make large buildings, such as apartments, uninhabitable. So even in cities, communications for routing people during and after fires may be needed.

Earthquakes and Volcanic Eruptions

Earthquakes are caused when underground forces break and shift rock beneath the surface, causing the Earth's crust to shake or tremble. The actual movement of the earth is seldom

When an ice storm struck central Kentucky, local ARES volunteers helped with communications in the Emergency Operations Center for more than a week. (*Rob Neuzel photo*)

After wildfires struck San Diego County (CA), Ted, W6GMQ, and Fred, N6QKE, set up a portable station at a Red Cross shelter in a school soccer field. They provided the main communications link from the shelter while phones were out. (*N6QKE photo*)

a direct cause of death or injury, but can cause buildings and other structures to collapse and may knock out communications, telephone service and electrical power. Most casualties result from falling objects and debris, splintering glass and fires.

Earthquakes strike without warning, but everyone knows that the quake happened. Amateurs should first ensure that the immediate surroundings and loved ones are safe, and then begin monitoring the ARES frequencies. Amateurs are often the first to alert communities immediately after earthquakes and volcanic eruptions occur. Their warnings are definitely credited with lessening personal injuries in the area.

Amateurs may assist with rescue operations, getting medical help or critical supplies and helping with damage appraisals. There will be communications, usually on VHF or UHF, for Red Cross logistics and government agencies. After vital communications is handled, the rest of the world will be trying to get information through Health-and-Welfare traffic.

Shelter Operations

A shelter or relief center is a temporary place of protection where rescuers can bring disaster victims and where supplies can be dispensed. Many displaced people can stay at the homes of friends or relatives, but those searching for family members or in need are housed in shelters.

Whether a shelter is for a few stranded motorists during a snowstorm, or a whole community of homeless residents after a disaster, it is an ideal location to set up an Amateur Radio communication base station. An alternate station location would be an ARES mobile communications van, if available, near the shelter.

Once officials determine the locations for shelters, radio operators can be assigned to set up equipment at the sites. In fact, the amateur station operators could share a table with shelter registration workers. Make sure you obtain permission for access to the shelter to assist and do not upset the evacuees. Use of repeaters and autopatches allows Welfare phone calls for those inside the shelters to inform and reassure friends, families and relatives.

Health-and-Welfare Traffic

There can be a tremendous amount of radio traffic to handle during a disaster. This will free phone lines that remain in working order for emergency use by those people in peril.

Shortly after a major disaster, Emergency messages within the disaster area often have life-and-death urgency. Of course, they receive primary emphasis. Much of their local traffic will be on VHF or UHF. Next, Priority traffic, messages of an emergency-related nature but not of the utmost urgency, are handled. Then, Welfare traffic is originated by evacuees at shelters or by the injured at hospitals and relayed by Amateur Radio. It flows one way and results in timely advisories to those waiting outside the disaster area.

Incoming Health-and-Welfare traffic should be handled only after all emergency and priority traffic is cleared. Don't solicit traffic going to an emergency because it can severely overload an already busy system. Welfare inquiries can take time to discover hard-to-find answers. An advisory to the inquirer uses even more time. Meanwhile, some questions might have already been answered through restored circuits.

Shelter stations, acting as net control stations, can exchange information on the HF bands directly with destination areas as propagation permits. Or, they can handle formal traffic through a few outside operators on VHF who, in turn, can link to NTS stations. By having many NTS-trained amateurs, it's easy to adapt to whatever communications are required.

Property Damage Surveys

Damage caused by natural disasters can be sudden and extensive. Responsible officials near the disaster area, paralyzed without communications, will need help to contact appropriate officials outside to give damage reports. Such data will be used to initiate and coordinate disaster relief. Amateur Radio operators offer to help but often are unable to cross roadblocks established to limit access by sightseers and potential looters. Proper emergency responder identification will be required to gain access into these areas. In some instances, call-letter license plates on the front of the car or placards inside windshields may help. It's important for amateurs to keep complete and accurate logs for use by officials to survey damage, or to use as a guide for replacement operators.

Accidents and Hazards

The most difficult scenarios to prepare for are accidents and hazardous situations. They are unpredictable and can happen anywhere. Generally, an emergency *autopatch* is used only to report incidents that pose threats to life or personal safety, such as vehicle accidents, disabled vehicles or debris in traffic, injured persons, criminal activities and fires.

Using the keypad featured on most modern VHF hand-held and mobile radios, the operator activates a repeater autopatch by sending a particular code. The repeater connects to a telephone line and routes the incoming and outgoing audio accordingly. By dialing 9-1-1 (or another emergency number), the operator has direct access to law-enforcement agencies.

Vehicle Accidents

Vehicle-accident reports, by far the most common public service activity on repeaters, can involve anything from bikes, motorcycles and automobiles, to buses, trucks, trains and airplanes. Law-enforcement offices usually accept reports of such incidents anywhere in their county and will relay information to the proper agency when it pertains to adjacent areas.

Here's a typical autopatch procedure:

1) Give your call and say "emergency patch."

2) Drop your carrier momentarily.

3) Key in the access code.

4) Dial the emergency number (usually 911).

5) Wait for police or fire operator.

6) Answer the questions that the operator asks.

7) After operator acknowledges, dump the patch by keying in the dump code.

8) Give your call and say "patch clear."

9) Don't stay keydown! Talk in short sentences, releasing your push-to-talk switch after each one, so the operator can ask you questions.

When you report a vehicle accident, remain calm and get as much information as you can. This is one time you certainly have the right to break into a conversation on a repeater. Use plain language, say exactly what you mean, and be brief and to the point. Do not guess about injuries; if you don't know, say so. Some accidents may look worse than they really are; requesting an ambulance to be sent needlessly could divert it away from a bona-fide accident injury occurring at the same time elsewhere. And besides, police cruisers are generally only minutes away in an urban area.

Here's what you should report for a vehicle accident:

1) Highway number (eg, I-43, SR-94, US-45).

2) Direction of travel (North, South, East, West).

3) Address or street intersection, if on city streets, or closest exit on highway.

4) Traffic blocked, or if accident is out of traffic.

5) Apparent injuries, number and extent.

6) Vehicles on fire, smoking or a fuel spill.

Example: "This is WB8IMY, reporting a two-car accident, I-94 at Edgerton, northbound, blocking lane number two, property damage only."

The first activities handled by experts at a vehicle-accident scene are keyed to rescue, stabilize and transport the victims. Then they ensure security, develop a perimeter, handle vehicle traffic and control or prevent fires from gasoline spills. Finally, routine operations restore the area with towing, wrecking and salvage.

The ability to call the police or for an ambulance, without

Bill, KE5DHY, maintains communications with the State of Texas EOC during the annual Simulated Emergency Test.

depending on another amateur to monitor the frequency, saves precious minutes. Quick reaction and minimum delay is what makes an autopatch useful in emergencies. The autopatch, when used responsibly, is a valuable asset to the community.

Freeway Warning

Many public-safety agencies recommend that you do not stop on freeways or expressways to render assistance at an accident scene unless you are involved, are a witness or have sufficient medical training. Freeways are extremely dangerous because of the heavy flow of high-speed traffic. Even under ideal conditions, driver fatigue or inattentiveness, high speeds and short distances between vehicles often make it impossible to stop a vehicle from striking stationary objects. If you must stop on a freeway, pull out of traffic and onto distress lanes. Exercise extreme caution to protect yourself. Don't add to the traffic problem. Instead, radio for help.

Search and Rescue

Amateurs helping search for an injured climber use repeaters to coordinate the rescue. A small airplane crashes, and amateurs direct the search by tracking from its Emergency Locator Transmitter. No matter what the situation, it's reassuring to team up with local search-and-rescue organizations who have familiarity with the area. Once a victim is found, the hams can radio the status, autopatch for medical information, guide further help to the area and plan for a return transportation. If the victim is found in good condition, Amateur Radio can bolster the hopes of base-camp personnel and the family of the victim with direct communications.

Even in cities, searches are occasionally necessary. An elderly person out for a walk gets lost and doesn't return home. After a reasonable time, a local search team plans and coordinates a search. Amateurs take part by providing communications, a valuable part of any search. When the missing person is discovered, there may be a need to radio for an ambulance for transportation to a nearby hospital.

Hospital Communications

Hospital phones can fail. For example, when a construction crew using a backhoe may accidentally cut though the main trunk line supplying telephone service to several hundred users, including the hospital. Such major hospital telephone outages can block incoming emergency phone calls. In addition, the hospital staff cannot telephone to discuss medical treatment with outside specialists.

Several hand-held-radio equipped amateurs can first handle emergency calls from nursing homes, fire departments and police stations. They can also provide communications to temporarily replace a defective hospital paging system. Next, they can help restore critical interdepartmental hospital communications and, finally, communications with nearby hospitals.

Preparation for hospital communications begins by cooperating with administrators and public-relations personnel. You'll need their permission to perform inside signal checks, install outside antennas or set up net control stations in the hospital.

Working with local hospitals doesn't always involve extreme situations. You may simply be asked to relay information from the poison control center to a campsite victim. Or you may participate in an emergency exercise where reports of the "victim's" condition are sent to the hospital from a disaster site. One typical drill involved a simulated crop-duster plane crash on an elementary school playground during recess. The doctors and officials depended on communications to find casualties who were contaminated by crop-dusting chemicals. Again, never give the names of victims or fatalities over the air; this information must be handled only by the proper agency.

Toxic-Chemical Spills and Hazardous Materials

A toxic-chemical spill suddenly appears when gasoline pours from a ruptured bulk-storage tank. A water supply is unexpectedly contaminated, or a fire causes chlorine gas to escape at an apartment swimming pool. On a highway, a faulty shut-off valve lets chemicals leak from a truck, or drums of chemicals fall onto the highway and rupture. Amateur communications have helped in all these situations.

Caution: don't rush into a Hazardous Materials (HAZMAT) incident area without knowing what's involved, or you may well become a victim yourself. Vehicles carrying 1000 pounds or more of a HAZMAT are required by Federal regulations to display a placard bearing a four-digit identification number. From a safe distance radio the placard number to the authorities and they will decide whether to send HAZMAT experts to contain the spills.

Follow directions from those in command. Provide communications to help them evacuate residents in the immediate area and coordinate between the spill site and the shelter buildings. Hams also assist public service agencies by setting flares for traffic control, helping reroute motorists and so on. We're occasionally asked to make autopatch calls for police or fire-department workers on the scene as they try to determine the nature of the chemicals.

The National Transportation Safety Board, the Environmental Protection Agency and many local police, fire, and emergency government departments continue to praise ARES volunteers in their assistance with toxic spills.

MUTUAL AID (ARESMAT) CONCEPT

Most disasters are local and of relatively short duration, which is why the traditional county and Section-based ARES approach is appropriate most of the time. However, disasters do not conform to state and ARRL Section boundaries. Disasters that are truly national-level catastrophes require national-level coordination. Regional disasters of less magnitude than, say, the 2005 Gulf coast hurricanes, do not require national coordination but may need well-organized responses from several adjacent ARRL Sections.

At the present time, relatively few ARRL Sections have formal, written agreements with neighboring Sections spelling out how emergency communications cooperation would be structured and managed. The ARRL National Emergency Response Planning Committee (NERPC) recommended that Section Managers should consider developing such agreements with one or more neighboring Sections, depending on the disaster hazards likely in their parts of the country. These agreements would become appendices to existing Section emergency plan documents.

The NERPC suggested that the following points should be among those considered in the mutual aid planning process and the development of formal agreements:

1) Share current phone numbers, postal addresses and e-mail addresses for the Section Manager, Section Emergency Coordinator and Section Traffic Manager in each adjacent section.

2) List major likely hazards in each Section.

3) List available resources Sections have that can be used to assist adjacent Sections. If ARESMAT are available, then list locations, points of contact, and capabilities.

4) If ARESMAT resources are needed, then Section leadership should be familiar with and utilize ARESMAT information and requirements in EC-003 and the PSCM.

The Long Beach (CA) ARES/RACES communications van is ready to go at a moment's notice. (*WB6GXS photo*)

5) List the major served agencies in each Section, whether or not a written support agreement exists, and the point of contact for each. Identify any volunteer insurance coverage, credentialing, and expense reimbursement which may be available from these agencies.

6) Describe the activation authority and the process for requesting and providing out-of-Section mutual assistance in each Section.

7) List or summarize Section currently-installed emergency communications capabilities and points of contact.

8) List Sections' major VHF and HF routine, operations and traffic net frequencies.

9) List Sections' Web site addresses.

10) It is suggested that the agreement should specify that mutual assistance can be invoked only by Section Managers, Section Emergency Coordinators, or specific designees.

11) It is recommended that the agreement should require certain documentation be kept when the agreement has been invoked. For example: daily documentation and logbook for SITREPS (situation reports), after-action reports, and notes on future needs.

12) It is recommended that the agreement should require each Section Manager who requests or provides mutual assistance to prepare a written after-action report which summarizes each mutual assistance activation. This report should be sent to the involved SMs and to the ARRL Field and Educational Services Manager no later than 30 days following the stand-down from each mutual assistance activation.

13) Plans should be reviewed by each SM, SEC and STM annually, and updated as necessary.

INTERNATIONAL EMERGENCY COMMUNICATIONS

Many disaster situations transcend national boundaries, and that is especially true in this hemisphere. Emcomm radio amateurs are often involved in such international scenarios.

The International Amateur Radio Union Region 2 (comprising the Americas) Emergency Coordinator (abbreviated as EMCOR) is an international coordinating, planning and organizational position who is familiar with the international organization of emergency management and communications, and the emergency communications structure of his/her nation. He/she is also aware of the emergency communications structure and resources of the various Region 2 countries through continuing liaison with the Member Societies. A data-base for all Region 2 Member Societies together with up-to-date contact information is published on-line at **iaru-r2emcor.net** that includes the capacity and capabilities of emergency facilities of each Member Society.

The EMCOR's objective is to develop compatible international norms and standard operating procedures and ensure their acceptance and adherence by all Region 2 Member Societies, which includes the US and ARRL. The Region 2 EMCOR is supported by an Emergency Coordination Advisory Group (ECAG), which has a representative from each of the Areas of Region 2. The purpose of this group is to aid and support the EMCOR in his/her work and to represent him/her as liaisons within each group member's Area, in order to support the emergency organizations of the Member Societies.

REFERENCES

ARRL EMcomm and Public Service Resources
www.arrl.org/public-service
www.arrl.org/ares-el
www.arrl.org/media-and-public-relations

Training

ARRL training courses: **www.arrl.org/emergency-communications-training**

Red Cross training courses: **www.redcross.org/flash/course01_v01/**

FEMA training courses: **training.fema.gov/IS/**

FEMA National Incident Management System: **www.fema.gov/nims/**

IARU Emergency Communications: **www.iaru.org/emergency/**

IARU Region 2 Emergency Communications: **www.iaru-r2emcor.net**

Major Amateur Radio Emergency Communications Nets

Hurricane Watch Net: **www.hwn.org**

Maritime Mobile Service Net: **www.mmsn.org**

Salvation Army (SATERN) Net: **www.satern.org**

Waterway Net: **www.waterwayradio.net**

VoIP SKYWARN/Hurricane Net: **www.voipwx.net**

Served Agencies and Other Organizations

ARRL/Served Agency Memoranda of Understanding: **www.arrl.org/served-agencies-and-partners**

National Volunteer Organizations Active in Disaster: **www.nvoad.org**

American Red Cross: **www.redcross.org**

National Weather Service: **www.nws.noaa.gov**

Department of Homeland Security — Citizen Corps , FEMA: **www.citizencorps.gov**, **www.dhs.gov**, **www.fema.gov**

Association of Public-Safety Communications Officials — International: **www.apcointl.org**

National Communications System: **www.ncs.gov**

National Association of Radio and Telecommunications Engineers: **www.narte.org**

Salvation Army: **www.salvationarmyusa.org**

Society of Broadcast Engineers: **www.sbe.org**

Quarter Century Wireless Association: **www.qcwa.org**

Radio Emergency Associated Communication Teams: **www.reactintl.org**

SKYWARN: **www.skywarn.org**

Sections of this chapter are based on the Emergency Communications chapter by Richard Regent, K9GDF, in the 8th edition of the ARRL Operating Manual.

Maria Evans, KT5Y

chapter 5

Traffic Handling — Getting the Message Through

For just pennies a day, you can protect you and your family from all sorts of catastrophic illnesses with the Mutual of Podunk health care policy. . . .

Yes, at the amazing low price of $9.95, you can turn boring old potatoes, carrots and okra into culinary masterpieces with the Super Veggie-Whatchamadoodler — a modest investment for your family's mealtime happiness. . . .

Tired of all that ugly fat on your otherwise-beautiful body? Our Exer-Torture home gym will trim those thunder thighs in 30 days or your money back. . . .

Ah, those pitches. Everybody is trying to sell something — even the participants in the specialty modes of Amateur Radio. Our eyes light up thinking about all those wondrous gizmos that digitize, packetize and equalize. Those kinds of specialty modes are easily remembered and can quickly gain popularity. Most people, though, forget about the oldest specialty mode in Amateur Radio — traffic handling.

Admittedly, it's hard for traffic handlers to compete with other specialty modes because it just doesn't look exciting. After all, tossing messages from Great Uncle Levi and Grandma Strauss sure doesn't put you on the leading edge of our high-tech hobby, does it? Yet, hundreds of nets are members of the ARRL National Traffic System (NTS), probably one of the most highly organized special interests of Amateur Radio. Today's traffic handlers are at this very moment setting new standards for traffic handling via digital modes — as well as using traditional modes. If you enjoy emergency-communications preparation, traffic handling is for you. Sure, it's true that over 90% of all messages handled via Amateur Radio are of the "at the state fair, wish you were here" or the "happy holidays" variety — certainly not life-and-death stuff. But consider this: Your local fire department often

conducts drills without ever putting out a real fire, your civil defense simulates emergencies regularly, and many department stores hire people to come in and pretend to be shoplifters to check the alertness of their employees. Similarly, when real emergencies rear their ugly heads, traffic handlers just take it all in stride and churn messages out like they always do.

Traffic handling is also an excellent way to paint a friendly picture of Amateur Radio to the nonamateur public. What sometimes seems to be unimportant to us is seldom unimportant to that person in the address block of a message. Almost every traffic handler can relate stories of delivering a Christmas message from some long-lost friend or relative that touched the heart of the recipient such that they could hear the tears welling up at the other end of the phone. Those happy recipients will always mentally connect Amateur Radio traffic handling with good and happy things, and often this is the most satisfying part of this hobby within a hobby.

Next time you go to a hamfest, see if you can spot the traffic handlers. They are almost always reveling in a big social cluster, sharing stories and enjoying a unique camaraderie. Traffickers always enthusiastically look forward to the next hamfest, because it means another chance to spend time with their special friends of the airwaves. These friendships often last a lifetime, transcending barriers of age, geographical distance, background, and gender or physical ability.

Young or old, rural or urban, there's a place reserved for you on the traffic nets. Young people often can gain respect among a much older peer group and obtain high levels of responsibility through the traffic nets, good preparation for job opportunities and scholarships. "Nine to fivers" on a tight schedule can still manage to get a regular dose of Amateur Radio in just 15 to 30 minutes of net operation

Handling traffic is a valuable skill that you'll need to know when an emergency arises. Whether you operate SSB, CW or digital modes, there are plenty of opportunities for you to join in and learn how.

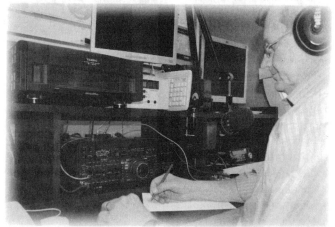

— a lot of hamming in a little time. Retired people can stay active in an important activity and provide a service to the general public.

Even if you live in the sticks, where you rarely get a delivery, you can still perform a vital function in NTS as a net control station (NCS) or as a representative to the upper echelons of NTS. You don't have to check in every night (a popular myth about traffic handling — if you can donate time just once a week you are certainly welcome on NTS). You don't need fancy antennas or huge amplifiers, and you don't even need those ARRL message pads. For the cost of a pad or paper and a pencil, you can interface with a system that covers thousands of miles and consists of tens of thousands of users. A world of fun and friendship is waiting for you in traffic handling. You only have to check into a net to become part of it.

MAKING THE BIG STEP: CHOOSING A NET AND CHECKING INTO IT

Checking into a net for the first time is a lot like making your first dive off the high board. It's not usually very pretty, but it's a start. Once you've gotten over the initial shock of hitting the water that hard, the next one comes a lot easier. But, like a beginning dive you can do a little advance preparation that will get you emotionally prepared for your first plunge.

Before you attempt to interface with the world of NTS, you need the right "software." Go online and find the ARRL Net Search page from the links at **www.arrl.org/FandES/ field/nets/**. While you're visiting the ARRL site, download two free ARRL operating aids — FSD-3, the list of ARRL numbered radiograms, and FSD-218, the "Q-signals for nets and message form" card. These are available via **www.arrl.org/ FandES/field/forms/**. The *Public Service Communications Manual* (PSCM) is also recommended reading (**www.arrl.org/ FandES/field/pscm/**). After you have a basic understanding of the materials, you're ready to pick out a net in your ARRL section/state that suits you.

Go through the net listings and match up your time schedule with the nets in your section/state. Your section/state slow-speed CW net is a good choice (or your neighboring section, if yours doesn't have one). But if you still don't have the confidence to try the "big" CW section net, don't feel embarrassed about checking into a slow-speed net. Slow-speed nets are chockfull of veterans that help with NCS and NTS duties, and they're willing to help you, too. Perhaps you'd like to try the section phone net or weather net or a local 2-meter net. At any rate, you are the sole judge of what you want to try first.

Once you've chosen a net, it's a good idea to listen to it for a few days before you check in. Although this chapter will deal with a generalized format for net operation, each net is "fingerprinted" with its own special style of operation, and it's best to become acquainted with it before you jump in. If you have a friend who checks into the net, let your friend "take you by the hand" and tell you about the ins and outs of the net.

When the big day arrives, keep in mind that everybody on that net had to check into the net for the first time once. You aren't doing anything different than the rest of them, and this, like your first QSO, is just another "rite of passage" in the ham world. You will discover that it doesn't hurt, and that many other folks will be pleased, even happy, that you checked in with them.

How to be the Kind of Net Operator the Net Control Station (NCS) Loves

As a net operator, you have a duty to be self-disciplined. A net is only as good as its worst operator. You can be an exemplary net operator by following a few easy guidelines.

1) Zero beat the NCS. The NCS doesn't have time to chase all over the band for you. Make sure you're on frequency, and you will never be known at the annual net picnic as "old so-and-so who's always off frequency." Double-check that RIT control if your radio has one.

2) Don't be late. There's no such thing as "fashionably late" on a net. Liaison stations are on a tight timetable. Don't hold them up by checking in 10 minutes late with traffic.

3) Speak only when spoken to by the NCS. Unless it is a bona fide emergency situation, you don't need to "help" the NCS unless specifically asked. If you need to contact the NCS, make it brief. Resist the urge to help clear the frequency for the NCS or to "advise" the NCS. The NCS, not you, is boss.

4) Unless otherwise instructed by the NCS, transmit only to the NCS. Side comments to another station in the net are out of order.

5) Stay until you are excused. If the NCS calls you and you don't respond because you're getting a "cold one" from the fridge, the NCS may assume you've left the net, and net business may be stymied. If you need to leave the net prematurely, contact the NCS and simply ask to be excused (QNX PSE on CW).

6) Be brief when transmitting to the NCS. A simple "yes" (C) or "no" (N) will usually suffice. Shaggy dog tales only waste valuable net time.

7) Know how the net runs. The NCS doesn't have time to explain procedure to you while the net is in session. After you have been on the net for a while, you should already know these things.

8) Before the net begins, get yourself organized. Have all the materials you will need to receive traffic at hand. If you have messages to send, have them grouped by common destination according to the procedure of the net you're participating in. Nothing is more frustrating to the other operators — especially the one waiting to take your traffic — than being told "Wait a minute, I've got it here somewhere."

9) When receiving traffic and you have a question about the accuracy of anything passed in the message, don't tie the net up with discussions about ZIP codes, telephone area codes, etc. Just tell the NCS that you would like discuss message number 123 with the sending station after the net, or request to be allowed to move off frequency to clear up the matter. Remember, only the originating station can change the message — with the exception of the word count — between the number and the signature. Any suggested changes can be added as an "Op Note" if necessary.

10) Have a current copy of the Public Service Communications Manual and read it.

11) Don't "freelance" your traffic. Wait your turn to pass your messages as directed by the NCS.

(See accompanying sidebar for general recommendations on how to make your NCS love you!)

On CW

First, we'll pay a visit to a session of the Missouri CW Net, not so long ago, on an 80-meter frequency not so far away. KØSI is calling tonight's session, using that peculiar CW net shorthand that we aren't too used to yet.

KØSI: MCWN MCWN MCWN DE KØSI KØSI KØSI QND QNZ QTC? K

(Translation: Calling the Missouri CW Net, calling the Missouri CW Net. This is KØSI. This is a directed net, zero beat me. Any traffic? Over)

In the meantime, NDØN, K2ONP and WØOUD are waiting in the wings to check in. Since each is an experienced traffic handler, each listens carefully before jumping in, so as to not step on anyone.

NDØN: N

KØSI: N

(Notice that NDØN just sent the first letter of his suffix, and the NCS acknowledged it. This is common practice, but if you have the letter E or T or K as the first letter of your suffix, or if it is the same as another net operator's first letter, you might use another letter. It's not a hard-and-fast rule.)

NDØN: DE NDØN GE PETE QTC SOUTH CORNER 1 AIØO 1 K

(NDØN has one piece of traffic for South Corner, and one for AIØO.)

KØSI: NDØN DE KØSI GE JOHN R $\overline{AS}$

(Good evening, John, roger (I acknowledge) your traffic list. Wait/standby)

K2ONP: M

KØSI: M

K2ONP: DE K2ONP GE PETE TEN REP QRU K

(K2ONP is representative to the NTS Tenth Region Net tonight, and he has no traffic.)

KØSI: K2ONP DE KØSI HI GEO TU $\overline{AS}$

WØOUD: BK

KØSI: BK

ARRL QN Signals for CW Net Use

QNA*	Answer in prearranged order.
QNB*	Act as relay Between_____ and _____.
QNC	All net stations Copy.
	I have a message for all net stations.
QND*	Net is Directed (controlled by net control station.)
QNE*	Entire net stand by.
QNF	Net is Free (not controlled.)
QNG	Take over as net control station.
QNH	Your net frequency is High.
QNI	Net stations report In.
	I am reporting into the net. (Follow with a list of traffic or QRU.)
QNJ	Can you copy me?
QNK*	Transmit messages for_____ to_____.
QNL	Your net frequency is Low.
QNM*	You are QRMing the net. Stand by.
QNN	Net control station is _____.
	What station has net control?
QNO	Station is leaving the net.
QNP	Unable to copy you.
	Unable to copy _____.
QNQ*	Move frequency to ____ and wait for _____ to finish handling traffic. Then send him traffic for _____.
QNR*	Answer_____ and Receive traffic.
QNS	Following Stations are in the net.* (Follow with list)
	Request list of stations in the net.
QNT	I request permission to leave the net for _____ minutes.
QNU	The net has traffic for you. Stand by.
QNV*	Establish contact with _____ on this frequency. If successful, move to ____ and send him traffic for _____.
QNW	How do I route messages for ___?
QNX	You are excused from the net.*
	Request to be excused from the net.
QNY*	Shift to another frequency (or to __ kHz) to clear traffic with _____.
QNZ	Zero beat your signal with mine.

*For use only by the Net Control Station.

Notes on use of QN Signals

The QN signals listed here are special ARRL signals for use in amateur CW nets only. They are not for use in casual amateur conversation. Other meanings that may be used in other services do not apply. Do not use QN signals on phone nets. Say it with words. QN signals need not be followed by a question mark, even though the meaning may be interrogatory.

These "Special QN Signals for New Use" originated in the late 1940s in the Michigan QMN Net, and were first known to Headquarters through the then head traffic honcho W8FX. Ev Battey, W1UE, then ARRL assistant communications manager, thought enough of them to print them in *QST* and later to make them standard for ARRL nets, with a few modifications. The original list was designed to make them easy to remember by association. For example, QNA meant "Answer in Alphabetical order," QNB meant "Act as relay Between ...," QNC meant "All Net Copy," QND meant "Net is Directed," etc. Subsequent modifications have tended away from this very principle so that some of the less-used signals could be changed to another, more needed, use.

Since the QN signals started being used by amateurs, international QN signals having entirely different meanings have been adopted. Concerned that this might make our use of QN signals with our own meanings at best obsolete, at worst illegal, ARRL informally queried FCC's legal branch. The opinion then was that no difficulty was foreseen as long as we continued to use them only in amateur nets.

WØOUD: DE WØOUD GE PETE QRU K
KØSI: WØOUD DE KØSI GE LETHA QNU TU $\overline{AS}$

(Good evening, Letha, the net has traffic for you. Please stand by.)

(Since Letha lives in South Corner, the NCS is going to move WØOUD and NDØN off frequency to pass the South Corner traffic.)

KØSI: ØN?
NDØN: HR

(HR [here], or C [yes] are both acceptable ways to answer the NCS, who will usually use only your suffix from here on out to address questions to you.)

KØSI: OUD?
WØOUD: C
KØSI: NDØN ES WØOUD QNY UP 4 SOUTH CORNER K

(Go up 4 kHz and pass the South Corner traffic.)

NDØN: GG (going)
WØOUD: GG

(When two stations go off frequency, the receiving station always calls the transmitting station. If the NCS had said WØOUD QNV NDØN UP 4 GET SOUTH CORNER, WØOUD would have called NDØN first on frequency to see if she copied him. This is done often when conditions are bad. If they don't make connection, they will return to net frequency. If they do make connection, and pass the traffic, they will return as they are done.)

AIØO: O
KØSI: O
AIØO: DE AIØO GE PETE QRU K
KØSI: AIØO DE KØST GE ROB QNU UP 4 AIØO WID
　　　NDØN AFTER WØOUD THEN BOTH QNX 73 K

(Good evening, Rob, the net has traffic for you. Please go up 4 and get one for you from NDØN [WID means "with"] after he finishes with WØOUD. Then, when you are both finished, you and NDØN are both excused from the net. 73!)

AIØO: 73 GG

As you can see, it doesn't take much to say a lot on a CW net. Now that all the net business is taken care of, the NCS will start excusing other stations. Since K2ONP has a schedule to make with the Tenth Region Net, he will be excused first.

KØSI: K2ONP DE KØSI TU GEO FER QNI NW QRU QNX
　　　TU 73 K
K2ONP: TU PETE CUL 73 DE K2ONP $\overline{SK}$
WØOUD: OUD

(Letha is back from receiving her traffic.)

KØSI: OUD TU LETHA NW QRU QNX 88 K
WØOUD: GN PETE CUL 88 DE WØOUD $\overline{SK}$

Now, the NCS will close the net.

KØSI: MCWN QNF [the net is free] GN DE KØSI CL

When you check into a CW net for the first time, don't worry about speed. The NCS will answer you at about the speed you check into the net. You will discover that everyone on a CW net checks in with a different speed, just as everyone has a different voice on SSB. It's nothing to be self-conscious about. As the saying goes, "We're all in this together." The goal is to pass the traffic correctly, with 100 percent accuracy, not burn up the ether with our spiffy fists. Likewise, don't hesitate to slow down for someone else. Remember, when handling traffic, 100 percent accuracy is the minimum acceptable performance level!

On SSB

Now, let's tune in a session of the Missouri Single Sideband Net.

As we look in on KØPCK calling tonight's session, keep in mind these few pointers:

1) The net preamble, given at the beginning of each session, will usually give you the information you need to survive on the net. Method of checking in varies greatly from net to net. For instance, some section nets have a prearranged net roll, some take checking by alphabetical order, or some even take check-ins by geographical area. Don't feel intimidated by a prearranged net roll. Those nets will always stand by near the end of the session to take stations not on the net roster.

2) As you listen to a net, you will find that on phone, formality also varies. Some SSB nets are strictly business, while others are "chattier." However, don't always confuse lack of formality with looseness on a net. There is still a definite net procedure to adhere to.

3) Once, on a close play, the catcher asked umpire Bill Klem, "Well, what is it?"

"It ain't nothin' till I call it," he growled.

By the same token, you need to keep in mind that the NCS is the absolute boss when the net is in session. On CW nets, this doesn't seem to be much of a problem to the tightness of operation, but on phone nets, sometimes a group of "well-meaners" can really slow down the net. So don't "help" unless NCS tells you to.

Since net time is upon us, let's get back to the beginning of the Missouri Single Sideband Net.

"Calling the Missouri Single Sideband Net, calling the Missouri Single Sideband Net. This is KØPCK, net control. The Missouri Single Sideband Net meets on 3963 kHz nightly at 5:45 PM for the purpose of handling traffic in Missouri and to provide a link for out-of-section traffic through the ARRL National Traffic System. My name is Ben, Bravo Echo November, located in Toad Lick. When I call for the letter corresponding to the first letter of the suffix of your call, please give your call sign only."

"Any low-power, mobile or portable stations wishing to check in?"

(wait 5 seconds)

"Any relays?"

(wait 5 seconds)

"This is KØPCK for the Missouri Sideband Net. Do we have any traffic?"

"KØORB traffic"

"KØORB, Good evening Bill. List your traffic, over."

"Good evening, Ben. Two out-of-state."

"Very good. Who is our Tenth Region Rep tonight?"

"Good evening, Ben. This is NIØR, Ten Rep."

"NIØR, this is KØPCK. Hi, Roger. Please call KØORB, move him to 3973 and get Bill's out-of-state traffic."

"KØORB, this NIØR. See you on 73."

"Going. KØORB."

Now, let's sit back and analyze this. As you can see, the format is pretty much identical except that it takes more words. Oh, yes, one other difference . . . you may have noticed that not one single Q-signal was used! Q-signals should not be used on

Who Owns the Frequency?

Traffic nets sometimes have difficulties when it comes time for the call-up, and a ragchew is taking place on the published net frequency. What to do? Well, you could break in on the ragchew and ask politely if the participants would mind relinquishing the frequency. This usually works, but what if it doesn't? The net has no more right to the frequency than the stations occupying it at net time, and the ragchew stations would be perfectly within their rights to decline to relinquish it.

The best thing to do in such a case is to call the net near, but not directly on, the normal frequency — far enough (hopefully) to avoid causing QRM, but not so far that net stations can't find the net. Usually, the ragchewers will hear the net and move a bit farther away — or even if they don't, the net can usually live with the situation until the ragchew is over.

It is possible to conceive of a situation, especially on 75-meter phone, in which the net frequency is occupied and the entire segment is loaded with ongoing QSOs. In any case, it is not productive to argue about who has the most right to a certain frequency. Common courtesy says that the first occupants have, but there are many extenuating circumstances. Avoid such controversies, especially on the air.

Accordingly, net frequencies should be considered "approximate," inasmuch as it may be necessary for nets to vary their frequencies according to band conditions at the time. Further, no amateur or organization has any preemptory right to any specific amateur frequency.

phone nets. Work hard at avoiding them, and you will reduce the "lingo barrier," making it a little less intimidating for a potential new check in.

Two Special Cases

HF digital operations are almost identical to CW nets, except for the method of transmission, but you need to remember this: It is always important to zero-beat, but here it is crucial!

The other "exception to the rule" is the local 2-meter FM net. Many 2-meter nets are designed for ragchewing or weather spotting, so often if you bring traffic to the net, be prepared to coach someone in the nuances of traffic handling.

A few other things to remember:

1) Unlike a "double" on CW or SSB, where the NCS might even still get both calls, a "double" on an FM repeater either captures only one station, or makes an ear-splitting squeally heterodyne. Drag your feet a little before you check in, so you are less likely to double.

2) Be especially aware to wait for the squelch tail or courtesy beep. More people seem to time out the repeater on a net than at any other time!

3) Remember that a lot of people have scanners, many with the local repeater programmed in on one of the channels. Design your behavior in such a way that it attracts nonhams to Amateur Radio. In other words, don't do anything you wouldn't do in front of the whole town!

MAKING IT, TAKING IT AND GIVING IT AWAY: MESSAGE HANDLING AND MESSAGE FORM

By this stage, you have probably been checking into the net for a while, and things have started to move along quite

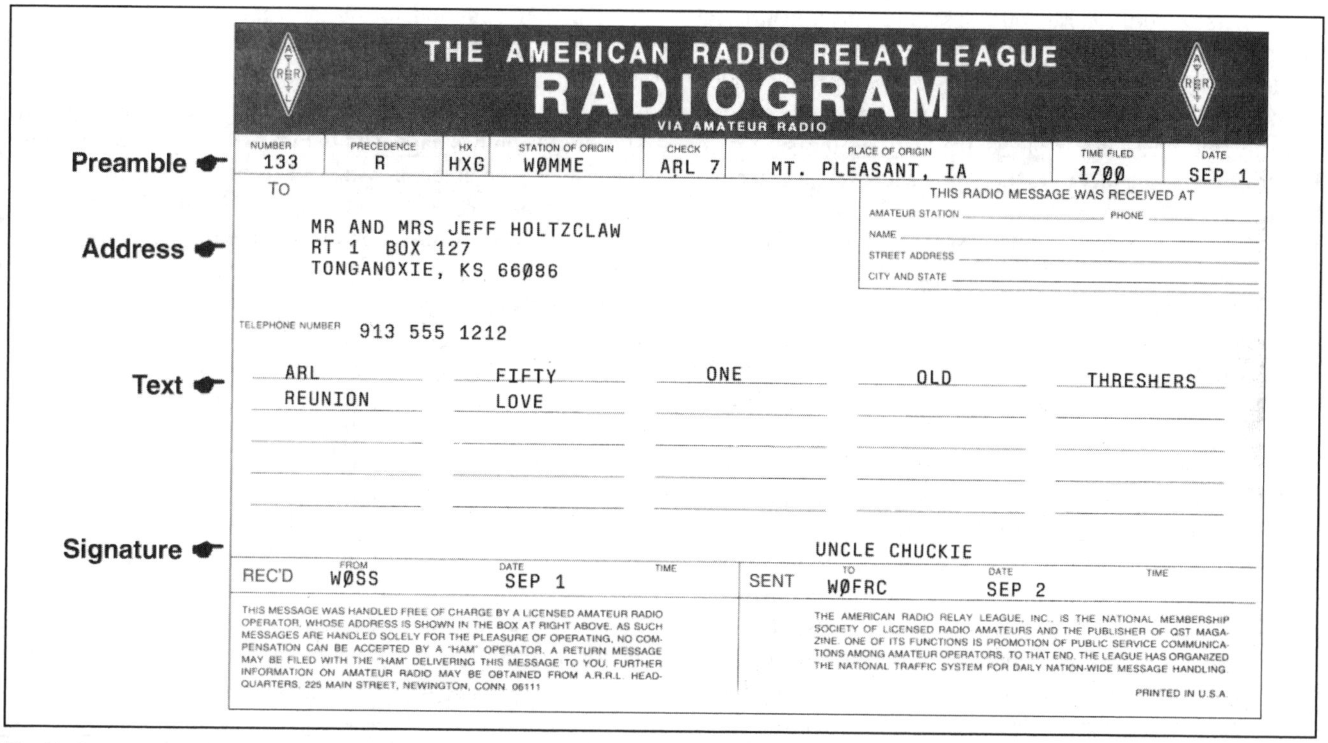

THE AMERICAN RADIO RELAY LEAGUE
RADIOGRAM
VIA AMATEUR RADIO

NUMBER	PRECEDENCE	HX	STATION OF ORIGIN	CHECK	PLACE OF ORIGIN	TIME FILED	DATE
133	R	HXG	WØMME	ARL 7	MT. PLEASANT, IA	17ØØ	SEP 1

TO
MR AND MRS JEFF HOLTZCLAW
RT 1 BOX 127
TONGANOXIE, KS 66Ø86

THIS RADIO MESSAGE WAS RECEIVED AT
AMATEUR STATION ____ PHONE ____
NAME ____
STREET ADDRESS ____
CITY AND STATE ____

TELEPHONE NUMBER 913 555 1212

ARL FIFTY ONE OLD THRESHERS
REUNION LOVE

UNCLE CHUCKIE

REC'D FROM WØSS DATE SEP 1 TIME
SENT TO WØFRC DATE SEP 2 TIME

THIS MESSAGE WAS HANDLED FREE OF CHARGE BY A LICENSED AMATEUR RADIO OPERATOR, WHOSE ADDRESS IS SHOWN IN THE BOX AT RIGHT ABOVE. AS SUCH MESSAGES ARE HANDLED SOLELY FOR THE PLEASURE OF OPERATING, NO COMPENSATION CAN BE ACCEPTED BY A "HAM" OPERATOR. A RETURN MESSAGE MAY BE FILED WITH THE "HAM" DELIVERING THIS MESSAGE TO YOU. FURTHER INFORMATION ON AMATEUR RADIO MAY BE OBTAINED FROM A.R.R.L. HEADQUARTERS, 225 MAIN STREET, NEWINGTON, CONN. 06111

THE AMERICAN RADIO RELAY LEAGUE, INC., IS THE NATIONAL MEMBERSHIP SOCIETY OF LICENSED RADIO AMATEURS AND THE PUBLISHER OF QST MAGAZINE. ONE OF ITS FUNCTIONS IS PROMOTION OF PUBLIC SERVICE COMMUNICATIONS AMONG AMATEUR OPERATORS. TO THAT END, THE LEAGUE HAS ORGANIZED THE NATIONAL TRAFFIC SYSTEM FOR DAILY NATION-WIDE MESSAGE HANDLING.

PRINTED IN U.S.A.

Fig 5-1 — Example message properly entered on the ARRL message form.

smoothly on your journey as a traffic handler. But in the life of any new traffic op, the fateful day comes along when the NCS points RF at you and says those words that strike fear in almost every newcomer: "Go up four, get Cornshuck Hollow."

Now what? You could suddenly have "rig trouble" or a "power outage" or a "telephone call," or just bump your dial and disappear. After all, it has been done before, and everyone that didn't do it sure thought of it the first time they were asked to take traffic! Of course, there is a more honorable route — go ahead and take it! Chances are you will be no worse than anyone else your first time out.

To ease the shock of your first piece of traffic, maybe it would be a good idea to go over message form "by the book" — ARRL message form, that is.

ARRL Message Form — The Right Way, and the Right Way

A common line of non-traffickers is, "Aw, why do they have to go through that ARRL message-form stuff? It just confuses people and besides, my message is just a few words or so. It's silly to go through all that rigamarole."

Well, then, let's imagine that you are going to write a letter to your best friend. What do you think would happen to your letter if you decided that the standardized method the post office used was "silly," so you signed the front, put the addressee's address where the return address is supposed to go, and stamped the inside of the letter? It would probably end up in the Dead Letter Office.

Amateur message form is standardized so it will reach its destination speedily and correctly. It is very important for every amateur to understand correct message form, because you never know when you will be called upon in an emergency. Most nonhams think all hams know how to handle messages, and it's troublesome to discover how few do. You can completely change the meaning of a piece of traffic by accident if you don't know the ARRL message form, and as you will see later, this can be a real "disaster." Learn it the right way, and this will never happen.

If you will examine the sample message in **Fig 5-1**, you will notice that the message is essentially broken into four parts: the preamble, the address block, the text and the signature. The preamble is analogous to the return address in a letter and contains the following:

1) The number denotes the message number of the originating station. Most traffic handlers begin with number 1 on January 1, but some stations with heavy volumes of traffic begin the numbering sequence every quarter or every month.

2) The precedence indicates the relative importance of the message. Most messages are Routine (R) precedence — in fact, about 99 out of 100 are in this category. You might ask, then why use any precedence on routine messages? The reason is that operators should get used to having a precedence on messages so they will be accustomed to it and be alerted in case a message shows up with a different precedence. A Routine message is one that has no urgency aspect of any kind, such as a greeting. And that's what most amateur messages are — just greetings.

The Welfare (W) precedence refers to either an inquiry as to the health and welfare of an individual in the disaster area or an advisory from the disaster area that indicates all is well. Welfare traffic is handled only after all emergency and prior-

ity traffic is cleared. The Red Cross equivalent to an incoming Welfare message is DWI (Disaster Welfare Inquiry).

The Priority (P) precedence is getting into the category of high importance and is applicable in a number of circumstances: (1) important messages having a specific time limit, (2) official messages not covered in the emergency category, (3) press dispatches and emergency-related traffic not of the utmost urgency, and (4) notice of death or injury in a disaster area, personal or official.

The highest order of precedence is EMERGENCY (always spelled out, regardless of mode). This indicates any message having life-and-death urgency to any person or group of persons, which is transmitted by Amateur Radio in the absence of regular commercial facilities. This includes official messages of welfare agencies during emergencies requesting supplies, materials or instructions vital to relief of stricken populace in emergency areas. During normal times, it will be very rare.

3) Handling Instructions are optional cues to handle a message in a specific way. For instance, HXG tells us to cancel delivery if it requires a toll call or mail delivery, and to service it back instead. Most messages will not contain handling instructions.

4) Although the station of origin block seems self-explanatory, many new traffic handlers make the common mistake of exchanging their call sign for the station of origin after handling it. The station of origin never changes. That call serves as the return route should the message encounter trouble, and replacing it with your call will eliminate that route. A good rule of thumb is never to change any part of a message.

5) The check is merely the word count of the text of the message. The signature is not counted in the check. If you discover that the check is wrong, you may not change it, but you may amend it by putting a slash bar and the amended count after the original count. See the "Checking Your Message" sidebar for additional information on the message check.

Another common mistake of new traffickers involves "ARL" checks. A check of ARL 8 merely means the text has an ARL numbered radiogram message text in it, and a word count of 8. It does not mean ARRL numbered message no. 8. This confusion has happened before, with unpleasant results. For instance, an amateur with limited traffic experience once received a message with a check of ARL thirteen. The message itself was an innocuous little greeting from some sort of fair, but the amateur receiving it thought the message was ARRL numbered message thirteen — "Medical emergency situation exists here." Consequently, he unknowingly put a family through a great deal of unnecessary stress. When the smoke cleared, the family was on the verge of bringing legal action against the ham, who himself developed an intense hatred for traffic of any sort and refused to ever handle another message. These kinds of episodes certainly don't help the "white hat" image of Amateur Radio!

6) The place of origin can either be the location (City/State or City/Province) of the originating station or the location of the third party wishing to initiate a message through the originating station. Use standard abbreviations for state or province. ZIP or postal codes are not necessary. For messages from outside the US and Canada, city and country is usually used.

7) The filing time is another option, usually used if speed

of delivery is of significant importance. Filing times should be in UTC or "Zulu" time.

8) The final part of the preamble, the date, is the month and day the message was filed — year isn't necessary.

Next in the message is the address. Although things like ZIP code and phone number aren't entirely necessary, the more items included in the address, the better its chances of reaching its destination. To experienced traffic handlers, ZIP codes and telephone area codes can be tip-offs to what area of the state the traffic goes, and can serve as a method of verification in case of garbling. For example, all ZIP codes in Minnesota start with a 5. Therefore, if a piece of traffic sent as St Joseph, MO, with a ZIP of 56374 has been garbled along the way, it conceivably can be rerouted. So, when it comes to addresses, the adage "the more, the better" applies.

The text, of course, is the message itself. You can expedite the counting of the check by following this simple rule — when copying by hand, write five words to a line. When copying with a typewriter, or when sending a message via a digital mode, type the message 10 words to a line. You will discover that this is a quick way to see if your message count agrees with the check. If you don't agree, nine times out of 10 you have dropped or added an "X-ray," so copy carefully. Another important thing to remember is that you never end a text with an "X-ray" — it just wastes space and makes the word count longer.

When counting messages, don't forget that each "X-ray" (instead of period), "Query" and initial group counts as a word. Ten-digit telephone numbers count as three words; the ARRL-recommended procedure for counting the telephone number in the text of a radiogram message is to separate the telephone number into groups, with the area code (if any) counting as one word, the three-digit exchange counting as one word, and the last four digits counting as one word. Separating the telephone number into separate groups also helps to minimize garbling. Also remember that closings such as "love" or "sincerely" (that would be in the signature of a letter) are considered part of the text in a piece of amateur traffic.

Finally, the signature. Remember, complimentary closing words like "sincerely" belong in the text, not the signature. In addition, signatures like "Dody, Vanessa, Jeremy, Ashleigh, and Uncle Porter," no matter how long, go entirely on the signature line.

At the bottom of our sample message you will see call signs next to the blanks marked "sent" and "received." These are not sent as the message, but are just bookkeeping notes for your own files. If necessary, you could help the originating station trace the path of the message.

Keeping It Legal

In the FCC rules under the "Prohibited transmissions" heading (§97.113), it states that no amateur station shall transmit "Communications for hire or for material compensation, direct or indirect, paid or promised, except as otherwise provided in these rules."

The FCC rules also have a section directly addressing traffic handling — §97.115, "Third party communications," which reads as follows:

(a) An amateur station may transmit messages for a third party to:

Checking Your Message

Traffic handlers don't have to dine out to fight over the check! Even good ops find much confusion when counting up the text of a message. You can eliminate some of this confusion by remembering these basic rules:

1) Punctuation ("X-rays," "Queries") count separately as a word.

2) Mixed letter-number groups (1700Z, for instance) count as one word.

3) Initial or number groups count as one word if sent together, two if sent separately.

4) The signature does not count as part of the text, but any closing lines, such as "Love" or "Best wishes" do.

Here are some examples:

- Charles J McClain — 3 words
- W B Stewart — 3 words
- St Louis — 2 words
- 3 PM — 2 words
- SASE — 1 word
- ARL FORTY SIX — 3 words
- 2N3904 — 1 word
- Seventy three — 2 words
- 73 — 1 word

Telephone numbers count as 3 words (area code, prefix, number), and ZIP codes count as one. ZIP + 4 codes count as two words. Canadian postal codes count as two words (first three characters, last three characters.)

Although it is improper to change the text of a message, you may change the check. Always do this by following the original check with a slash bar, then the corrected check. On phone, use the words "corrected to."

Book Messages

When sending book traffic, always send the common parts first, followed by the "uncommon" parts. For example:

R NØFQW ARL 7 BETHEL MO SEP 7 $\overline{BT}$

ARL FIFTY ONE BETHEL SHEEP FESTIVAL LOVE $\overline{BT}$
PHIL AND JANE $\overline{BT}$

NR 107 TONY AND LYN CALHOUN $\overline{AA}$
160 NORTH DOUGLAS $\overline{AA}$
SPRINGFIELD IL 62702 $\overline{BT}$

NR 108 JOE WOOD AJØX $\overline{AA}$
84 MAIN STREET $\overline{AA}$
LAUREL MS 39440 $\overline{BT}$

NR 109 JEAN WILCOX $\overline{AA}$
1243 EDGEWOOD DRIVE $\overline{AA}$
LODI CA 95240 N

Before sending the book traffic to another operator, announce beforehand that it is book traffic. Say "Follows book traffic." Then use the above format. On CW, a simple HR BUK TFC will do.

(1) Any station within the jurisdiction of the United States.

(2) Any station within the jurisdiction of any foreign government when transmitting emergency or disaster relief communications and any station within the jurisdiction of any foreign government whose administration has made arrangements with the United States to allow amateur stations to be used for transmitting international communications on behalf of third parties. No station shall transmit messages for a third party to any station within the jurisdiction of any foreign government whose administration has not made such an arrangement. This prohibition does not apply to a message for any third party who is eligible to be a control operator of the station.

(b) The third party may participate in stating the message where:

(1) The control operator is present at the control point and is continuously monitoring and supervising the third party's participation; and

(2) The third party is not a prior amateur service licensee whose license was revoked or not renewed after hearing and re-licensing has not taken place; suspended for less than the balance of the license term and the suspension is still in effect; suspended for the balance of the license term and re-licensing has not taken place; or surrendered for cancellation following notice of revocation, suspension or monetary forfeiture proceedings. The third party may not be the subject of a cease and desist order which relates to amateur service operation and which is still in effect.

(c) No station may transmit third party communications while being automatically controlled except a station transmitting a RTTY or data emission.

Note that emergency communications is described in §97.403 as providing "essential communication needs in connection with the immediate safety of human life and immediate protection of property when normal communications systems are not available."

It's self-explanatory. Every amateur should be familiar with these rules. Also, while third-party traffic is permitted in the US and Canada, this is not so for most other nations. A special legal agreement is required in each country to make such traffic permissible, both internally and externally (except if the message is addressed to another amateur). More information about these "third-party agreements" may be found in Chapter 11.

Such third-party agreements specify that only unimportant, personal, nonbusiness communications be handled — things that ordinarily would not utilize commercial facilities. (In an emergency situation, amateurs generally handle traffic first and face the possible consequences later. It is not unusual for a special limited-duration third-party agreement to be instituted by the affected country during an overseas disaster.) The key point here is, particularly under routine day-to-day nonemergency conditions, if we value our privileges, we must take care not to abuse any regulations, whether it be on the national or international level.

Some Helpful Hints About Receiving Traffic

1) Once you have committed the format of ARRL message form to memory, there's no need to use the "official" message

Handling Instructions

HXA — (Followed by number.) Collect landline delivery authorized by addressee within ____ miles. (If no number, authorization is unlimited.)

HXB — (Followed by number.) Cancel message if not delivered within _____ hours of filing time; service originating station.

HXC — Report date and time of delivery (TOD) to originating station.

HXD — Report to originating station the identity of station from which received, plus date and time. Report identity of station to which relayed, plus date and time, or if delivered report date, time and method of delivery.

HXE — Delivering station get reply from addressee, originate message back.

HXF — (Followed by number.) Hold delivery until_____ (date).

HXG — Delivery by mail or landline toll call not required. If toll or other expense involved, cancel message and service originating station.

An HX prosign (when used) will be inserted in the message preamble before the station of origin, like this: NR 207 R HXA50 W1AW 12 . . . (etc).

If more than one HX prosign is used, they can be combined if no numbers are to be inserted, like this: NR 207 R HXAC W1AW . . . (etc).

If numbers are inserted, the HX should be repeated: NR 207 R HXA50 HXC W1AW . . . (etc).

On phone, use phonetics for the letter or letters following the HX, to ensure accuracy.

pads from ARRL except for deliveries. Traffic handlers have many varied materials on hand for message handling. Some just use scrap paper. Many buy inexpensive tablets available at stationery stores.

2) Don't say "QSL" or "I roger number . . . " unless you mean it! It's not "Roger" unless you've received the contents of the message 100%. It's no shame to ask for fills (repeats of parts of the message). Make sure you have received the traffic correctly before going on to the next one.

3) Full (QSK) or semi-breakin can be very useful in handling traffic on CW. If you get behind, saying "break" or sending a string of dits will alert the other op that you need a fill.

4) You can get a fill by asking for "word before" (WB), "word after" (WA), "all before" (AB), "all after" (AA) or "between" (BN).

Sending the Traffic

Just because you've taken a few messages, don't get the notion that being good at receiving traffic makes you a good sender, too. Good traffic operators know they have to learn the nuances of sending messages as well as getting them. Your ability to send can "make or break" the other operator's ability to receive traffic in poor conditions. You must be careful to send your traffic at a comfortable speed for the receiving op, and use standardized protocol (standard ARRL message form). As you will see, these are slightly different for phone and CW, with even a couple of other deviations for HF digital or packet operations.

Sending the Traffic By CW

Someone once remarked, "The nice thing about CW traffic handling is that you have to spell it as you go along, so you don't usually have to spell words over." Also, the other main difference in CW traffic handling is that you tell someone when to go to the next address line or message section by use of the prosigns $\overline{AA}$ or $\overline{BT}$. Keeping this in mind, let's show how our sample message would be sent:

NR 133 R HXG WØMME ARL 7 MOUNT PLEASANT IA
1700Z SEP 1
MR MRS JEFF HOLTZCLAW
ROUTE 1 BOX 127 $\overline{AA}$
TONGANOXIE KS 66086
TEL 913 555 1212 $\overline{BT}$
ARL FIFTY ONE OLD THRESHERS REUNION LOVE $\overline{BT}$
UNCLE CHUCKIE $\overline{AR}$ N (if you have no more messages) or
$\overline{AR}$ B (if you have further messages)

Now, let's examine a few points of interest:

1) You don't need to send "preamble words" such as precedence and check. The other operator is probably as familiar with standard ARRL form as you are (maybe more!).

2) The first three letters of the month are sufficient when sending the date.

3) In the address, always spell out words like "route" and "street."

4) Do not send dashes in the body of telephone numbers; it just wastes time.

5) Always, always, always spell out each word in the text! For example, "ur" for "your" could be misconstrued as the first two letters of the next word. Abbreviations are great for ragchewing, but not for the text of a radiogram.

6) Sometimes, if you have sent a number of messages, when you get to the next-to-last message, it's a good idea to send $\overline{AR}$ 1 instead of $\overline{AR}$ B to alert the other station that you have just one more.

7) If the other operator "breaks" you with a string of dits, stop sending and wait for the last word received by the other side. Then, when you resume sending, start up with that word, and continue through the message.

Becoming a proficient CW traffic sender is tough at first, but once you've mastered the basics, it will become second nature — no kidding!

Sending the Traffic By Phone

Phone traffic handling is a lot like the infield fly rule in baseball — everyone thinks they know the rule, but in truth few really do. Correct message handling via phone can be just as efficient as via CW if and only if the two operators follow these basic rules:

1) If it's not an actual part of the message, don't say it.

2) Unless it's a very weird spelling, don't spell it.

3) Don't spell it phonetically unless it's a letter group or mixed group, or the receiving station didn't get it when you spelled it alphabetically.

Keeping these key points in mind, let's waltz through our sample message. This is how an efficient phone traffic handler would send the message:

"Number one hundred thirty three, routine, Hotel X-ray Golf, WØ Mike Mike Echo, ARL SEVEN, Mount Pleasant, Iowa, seventeen hundred Zulu, September one."

"Mr and Mrs Jeff Holtzclaw, route one, box twenty seven, Tonganoxie, T-O-N, G-A-N, O-X, I-E, Kansas, six six zero eight six. Telephone Nine one three, five five five, one two, one two. Break." You would then let up on the PTT switch and give the operator any fills needed in the first half of the message.

"ARL FIFTY ONE Old Threshers Reunion Love
Break Uncle Chuckie. End, no more" (if you have no more messages), "more" (if you have more messages).

Notice that in phone traffic handling, a pause — or with difficult addresses, "next line" — is the counterpart for AA. Also notice the lack of extraneous words. You don't need to say, "check," or "signature," or "Jones, common spelling." (If it's common spelling, why tell someone?) You only spell the uncommon. Most importantly, you speak at about half reading speed to give the other person time to write. If the receiving operator types, or if you have worked with the other op a long time and know his capabilities, you can speak faster. Always remember that any fill slows down the message more than if you had sent the message slowly to begin with!

Oh, Yes . . . Those Exceptions

Once again, HF digital and FM provide the exceptions to the rules. Digital traffic is very much like CW traffic. Use three or four lines between messages. This allows you to get four or five average messages on a standard sheet of paper.

When sending a message over your local repeater, remember that you often will be working with someone who isn't a traffic handler. It may be necessary to break more often (between the preamble and the address, for instance). Also, always make sure they understand about ARL numbered radiogram texts, and if they don't have a list, tell them what the message means. (The complete list of ARRL numbered radiogram texts is part of FSD-3 that we mentioned at the start of this chapter.) FM is a quiet mode, so you can get away with less spelling than you do on SSB.

If you yourself are already into traffic, don't try to force-feed correct traffic procedure in the case of someone just starting out; ease the person into it a little at a time. You will give a nontrafficker a more positive impression of traffic handling and may even make someone more receptive to joining a net. After all, our goal as traffic handlers is to have fun while being trained in accurately passing message traffic and enjoying it.

DELIVERING A MESSAGE

Up to now, all our traffic work has been carried out on the air. All of this changes, though, when we get a piece of traffic for delivery. Now we're tasked with contacting the general public with this message and expected to give it to someone. Unfortunately, many hams don't realize the importance of this action and miss an opportunity to engrave a favorable impression of Amateur Radio on nonhams. It's ironic that many hams can chat for hours on the air, but can't pick up the telephone and deliver a 15-word message without mumbling, stuttering or acting embarrassed. Delivering messages should be a treat, not a chore.

Let's go through a few guidelines for delivery, and if you keep these tips in mind, you and the party on the other end of the phone will enjoy the delivery.

1) Introduce yourself. Don't you hate phone calls from people you don't know and don't bother to give a name? Chances are they're trying to sell you something, and you brush them off. Most people have no idea what Amateur Radio is about, and it's up to you to make a good first impression.

2) Ask for the person named in the message. If he or she is not home, ask the person on the phone if they would take a message for that person.

3) Tell who the message is from before you give the message. Since the signature appears at the end of the message, most hams give it last, but you will hold the deliveree's attention longer if you give it first. When you get letters in the mail, you check out the return addresses first, don't you? Then you open them in some sort of order of importance. Likewise, the party on the phone will want to know the sender of the message first.

A good way to start off a delivery is to say something like, "Hi, Mr/Mrs/Miss so-and-so, my name is whatever, and I received a greeting message via Amateur Radio for you from wherever from such-and-such person." This usually gives you some credibility with your listener, because you mentioned someone they know. They will usually respond by telling such-and-such is their relative, college friend, and so forth. At that point, you have become less of a stranger in their eyes, and now they don't have to worry about you trying to sell them some vinyl siding or a lake lot at Casa Burrito Estates. Make sure you say it's a greeting message, too, to allay any fears of the addressee that some bad news is imminent.

4) When delivering the message, skip the preamble and just give the text, avoiding ARL text abbreviations. Chances are, Grandma Ollie doesn't give two hoots about the check of a message, and thinks ARL FORTY SIX is an all-purpose cleaner. Always give the "translation" of an ARL numbered text, even if the message is going to another ham.

5) Ask the party if they would like to send a return message. Explain that it's absolutely free, and that you would be happy to send a reply if they wish. Experienced traffickers can vouch that it's easy to get a lot of return and repeat business once you've opened the door to someone. It's not uncommon for strangers to ask for your name or phone number once they discover Amateur Radio is a handy way to communicate with friends and relatives.

6) Notices of death and/or serious injury should only be handled as communication between emergency preparedness, Red Cross, Salvation Army or other relief agency officials and only in the absence of alternate commercial facilities. Radio amateurs should never, repeat never, be responsible for notifying individuals, third-party or otherwise, of death or serious injury. These should always be handled through the appropriate relief agencies.

To Mail Or Not To Mail

Suppose you get a message that doesn't have a phone number, or the message would require a toll call. Then what? If you don't know anyone on 2 meters that could deliver it, or Directory Assistance is of no help, you are faced with the de-

cision whether to mail it or not. There is no hard and fast rule on this (unless, of course, the message has an HXG attached). Always remember that since this is a free service, you are under no obligation to shell out a stamp or track someone down just because you accepted the message.

Many factors may influence your decision. If you live in a large urban area, you probably have more deliveries than most folks, and mail delivery could be a big out-of-pocket expense that you're not willing to accept. If you live out in the wide open spaces, you may be the only ham for miles around, and probably consider mail delivery more often than most. Are you a big softie on Christmas or Mother's Day? If so, you may be willing to use a few stamps during those times of the year when you wouldn't otherwise. At any rate, the decision is entirely up to you.

Although you may be absolved from the responsibility of mailing a message, you don't just chuck the message in the trash. You do have a duty to inform the originating station that the message could not be delivered. A simple ARL SIXTY SEVEN followed by a brief reason (no listing, no one home for three days, mail returned by post office, and so forth) will suffice. This message always goes to the station of origin, not the person in the signature. The originating station will appreciate your courtesy.

NOW THAT YOU'RE MOVING UP IN THE WORLD

By now, you are starting to get a grasp of the traffic world. You've been checking in to a net on a regular basis, and you're pretty good at message form. Maybe you've even delivered a few messages. Now you are ready to graduate from Basic Traffic 101 and enroll in Intermediate Traffic 102. Good for you! You have now surpassed 80 percent of your peers in a skillful specialty area of Amateur Radio. However, there's still a lot to learn, so let's move on.

Book Messages

Over the years, book messages have caused a lot of needless headaches and consternation among even the best traffic handlers. Many hams avoid booking anything just because they think it's too confusing. Truthfully, book messages are fairly simple to understand, but folks tend to make them harder than they actually are.

So, just what are book messages? Book messages are merely messages with the same text and different addresses. They come in two categories — ones with different signatures, and ones with the same signatures. Often you will see book messages around holiday times and during fairs or other public events.

Oh, yes . . . one other thing about book messages. When you check into a net with a bunch of book messages, give the regular message count only. Don't say, "I have a book of seven for Outer Baldonia." Say instead, "Seven Outer Baldonia." Then, when you and the station from Outer Baldonia go off frequency to pass the traffic, tell him that it is book traffic. When he tells you to begin sending, give common parts first, then the "uncommon" parts (addresses and possibly signatures.) By following this procedure, you will avoid a lot of confusion.

Suppose you get a book of traffic on the NTS Region net bound for your state, but to different towns. When you take them to your section net, you will not be able to send them as a book, since they must be sent to different stations. Now what? Simply "unbook" them, and send them as individual messages. For instance, let's say you get a book of three messages for the Missouri section from the region net. Two are for Missouri City, and one is for Swan Valley. Simply list your traffic as Missouri City 2 and Swan Valley 1, for a total count of 3. Books aren't ironclad chunks of traffic, but a stepsaver that can be used to your advantage. They can be unbooked at any time. Use them whenever you can, and don't be afraid of them.

BECOMING NCS AND LIVING TO TELL ABOUT IT

Some momentous evening in your traffic career, you may be called upon to take the net. Perhaps the NCS had a power failure, or is on vacation, or perhaps a vacancy occurred in the daily NCS rotation on your favorite net. Should this be the case, consider yourself lucky. Net Managers entrust few members with net-control duties.

Of course, you probably won't be thinking how lucky you

Are You a Type-NCS Personality?

As net control station (NCS), it pays to remember that the net regulars are the net. Your function is to preside over the net in the most efficient, businesslike way possible so that the net participants can promptly finish their duties and go on to other ones. You must be tolerant and calm, yet confident and quick in your decisions. An ability to "take things as they come" is a must. Remember that you were appointed NCS because your Net Manager believes in you and your abilities.

1) *Be the boss, but don't be bossy.* It's your job to teach net discipline and train new net operators (and retrain some old ones!). You are the absolute boss when the net is in session, even over your Net Manager. However, you must be a "benevolent monarch" rather than a tyrant. Nets lose participation quickly one night a week when it's Captain Bligh's turn to call the net. If the net has a good turnout every night but one, that tells something about its NCS.

2) *Be punctual.* Many of the net participants have other commitments or nets to attend to; liaison stations are often on a tight schedule to make the NTS region or area net. If you, as NCS, don't care when the net starts, others will think it's okay for them to be late, too. Then traffic doesn't get passed in time, and someone may miss his NTS liaison. In short, the system is close to breaking down.

3) *Know your territory.* Your members have names — use them. They also live somewhere — by knowing their locations you can quickly ascertain who needs to get the traffic. As NCS, it's your responsibility to know the geography of your net. You also need to understand where your net fits into the scheme of NTS.

4) *Take extra care to keep your antennas in good shape.* An NCS can't run a net with a "wimpy" signal. Although you don't have to be the loudest one on the net, you do have to be heard. You will discover that the best way to do this is to have a good antenna system. A linear amplifier alone won't help you hear those weak check ins!

5) *The NCS establishes the net frequency.* Just because the ARRL Net Search lists a certain frequency doesn't give you squatters rights to it if a QSO is already in progress there. Move to a nearby clear frequency, close enough for the net to find you. QRM is a fact of life on HF, especially on 75/80 meters, so live with it.

6) *Keep a log of every net session.* Just because the FCC dropped the logging requirements doesn't mean that you have to drop it. It's a personal decision. The Net Manager may need information about a check in or a piece of traffic, and your log details can be helpful to him in determining what happened on a particular night.

7) *Don't hamstring the net by waiting to move the traffic.* Your duty is to get traffic moving as quickly as possible. As soon as you can get two stations moving, send them off to clear the traffic. If you have more than one station holding traffic for the same city, let the "singles" (stations with only one piece for that city) go before the ones with more than one piece for that city. The quicker the net gets the traffic moved, the sooner the net can be finished and the net operators can be free to do whatever they want.

are when the Net Manager says "QNG" and sticks your call after it. Once again, just like your first check-in or your first piece of traffic, you will just have to grit your teeth and live through it. However, you can make the jump easier by following these hints long before you are asked to be a net control:

1) Become familiar with the other stations on the net. Even if you never become NCS, it pays to know who you work with and where they live.

2) Pay close attention to the stations that go off frequency to pass traffic. What frequencies does the net use to move traffic? Which stations are off frequency at the moment? You will gain a feel for the net control job just by keeping track of the action.

3) Try to guess what the NCS will do next. You will discover many dilemmas when you try to second-guess the NCS. Often different amounts of traffic with equal precedence appear on the net, and a skillful NCS must rank them in order of importance. For instance, if you follow the NCS closely, you will discover that traffic for the NTS rep, such as out-of-state traffic, gets higher priority than one for the NTS rep's city. Situations like these are fun to second-guess when you are standing by on the net and will better prepare you for the day you might get to run the net.

Should that day arrive, just keep your cool and try to implement the techniques used by your favorite net-control stations. After a few rounds of NCS duties, you will develop your own style, and who knows? Perhaps some new hopeful for NCS will try to emulate you some day! See accompanying sidebars for further hints on developing a "type-NCS" personality and on proper net-control methods.

HANDLING TRAFFIC AT PUBLIC EVENTS

A very special and important aspect of message handling is that of how to handle traffic at public events. If the event is of any size, like a state fair, it doesn't take long to swamp a group of operators with traffic. Only by efficient, tight organization can a handful of amateurs keep a lid on the backlog.

No matter what size your public event, the following points need to be considered for any traffic station accessible to the public:

1) Often, more nontraffic handlers than traffic handlers will be working in the booth. This means your group will have to lay out a standard operating procedure to help the nontraffickers assist the experienced ops.

Jobs such as meeting the public, filling out the message blanks, sorting the "in" and "out" piles, and keeping the booth tidied up, can all be performed by people with little or no traffic skill, and is a good way to introduce those people into the world of traffic.

2) If you plan to handle fairly large amounts of traffic, the incoming traffic needs to be sorted. A good system is to have an "in-state" pile, an "in-region" pile, and an area pile for the three levels of NTS. After the traffic has been sent, it needs to be stacked in numerical order in the "out" pile. Keeping it in numerical order makes it easier to find should it need to be referred to.

Since your station will be on a number of hours, plan to check into your region and area, as well as your section, net. Another good idea is to have "helpers" on 2 meters who can also take some of your traffic to the region and/or area net. These arrangements need to be worked out in advance.

Handy Hints for Handling Traffic at Fairs or Other Public Events

1) Although you may only be there a day or two, don't compromise your station too much. Try to put up the most you can for an antenna system because band conditions on traffic nets in the summer can really be the pits! Usually, you will be surrounded by electrical lines at fairs, so a line filter is a must. An inboard SSB or CW filter in your rig is a definite plus, too, and may save you many headaches.

2) Don't huddle around the rigs or seat yourself in the back of the booth. Get up front and meet the people. After all, your purpose is to "show off" Amateur Radio to perk the interest of nonhams.

3) Most people will not volunteer to send a piece of traffic, nor will they believe a message is really "free." It's up to you to solicit "business." Be cheerful.

4) Always use "layman's language" when explaining Amateur Radio to nonhams. Say "message," not "traffic." Don't ramble about the workings of NTS or repeaters; your listener just wants to know how Aunt Patty will get the message. "We take the message and send it via Amateur Radio to Aunt Patty's town, and the ham there will call her on the phone and deliver it to her," will do.

5) Make sure your pencils or pens are attached to the booth with a long string, or you will be out of writing utensils in the first hour!

6) Make sure there are plenty of instructions around for hams not familiar with traffic handling to help them "get the hang of" the situation.

7) Make sure your booth is colorful and attractive. You will catch the public's eye better if you give them something to notice, such as this suggested poster idea.

3) Make up your radiogram blanks so that most of the preamble is already on them, and all you need to fill in is the number, check and date. In the message portion, put only about 20-word lines to discourage lengthy messages. Try to convince your "customer" to use a standard ARL text so you can book your messages.

A real time- and headache-saver in this department is to fill out the message blank for the sender. This way, you can write in the X-rays and other jargon that the sender is unaware of.

4) Most importantly, realize that you sometimes have to work at getting "customers" as much as if you were selling something! Most people have no concept of Amateur Radio at all, and don't understand how message handling, works. ("How can they get it? They don't have a radio like that" is a very common question!)

Use posters to make your booth appealing to the eye. Make sure one of the posters is of the "How your message gets to its destination" variety, such as the one shown in this section. Don't go over someone's head when answering a question — explain it simply and succinctly.

Finally, don't be afraid to "solicit" business. Get up in front of the booth and say "hi" to folks. If they say "hi" back, ask them if they would like to send a free greeting to a friend or relative anywhere in the US (grandparents and grandchildren are the easiest to convince!). Even if they decide not to send a message, your friendliness will help keep our image of "good guys in white hats" viable among the general public, which is every bit as great a service as message handling. For further hints, see accompanying sidebar.

THE NATIONAL TRAFFIC SYSTEM — MESSAGE HANDLING'S "ROAD MAP"

Although you probably never think about it, when you check into your local net or section net, you are participating in one of the most cleverly designed game plans ever written — the National Traffic System (NTS). Even though the ARRL conceived NTS way back in 1949, and it has grown from one regular cycle to two or more, NTS hasn't outgrown itself and remains the most streamlined method of traffic handling in the world. (During this discussion, please refer to the accompanying Section/Region/Area map in **Fig 5-2**, the NTS Routing Guide in **Table 5-1** and the NTS Flow Chart in **Fig 5-3**.)

Actually, the National Traffic System can trace its roots to the railroad's adoption of Standard Time back in 1883, when radio was still only a wild dream. Three of the Standard Time Zones are the basis for the three NTS areas — Eastern Area (Eastern Time Zone), Central Area (Central Time Zone) and Pacific Area (Mountain and Pacific Time Zones). Within these areas are a total of 12 regions. Why not just break it up into 10 regions, one for each US call-sign district? Ah, but check the map. You will discover that NTS not only covers the US, but our Canadian neighbors as well. Then, of course, the region nets are linked to section/local nets.

The interconnecting lines between the boxes on the flow chart represent liaison stations to and from each level of NTS. The liaisons from area net to area net have a special name, the Transcontinental Corps (TCC). In addition to the functions shown, TCC stations also link the various cycles of NTS to each other.

The clever part about the NTS setup, though, is that in any

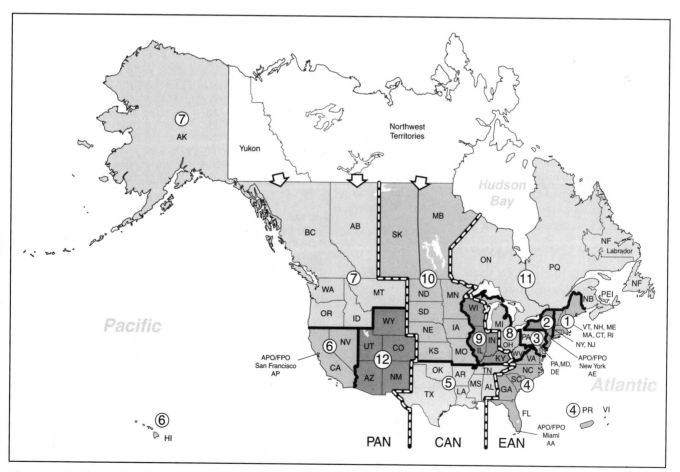

Fig 5-2 —National Traffic System Area and Region map.

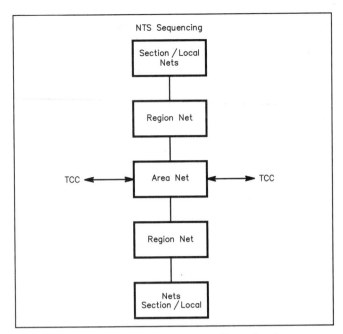

Fig 5-3 —National Traffic System flow chart. See text.

Table 5-1
National Traffic System Routing Guide

State/Province	Abbrev.	Region	Area
Alaska	AK	7	PAN
Alabama	AL	5	CAN
Alberta	AB	7	PAN
Arizona	AZ	12	PAN
Arkansas	AR	5	CAN
British Columbia	BC	7	PAN
California	CA	6	PAN
Colorado	CO	12	PAN
Connecticut	CT	1	EAN
Delaware	DE	3	EAN
Dist. of Columbia	DC	3	EAN
Florida	FL	4	EAN
Georgia	GA	4	EAN
Guam	GU	6	PAN
Hawaii	HI	6	PAN
Idaho	ID	7	PAN
Illinois	IL	9	CAN
Indiana	IN	9	CAN
Iowa	IA	10	CAN
Kansas	KS	10	CAN
Kentucky	KY	9	CAN
Labrador	LB	11	EAN
Louisiana	LA	5	CAN
Maine	ME	1	EAN
Manitoba	MB	10	CAN
Maryland	MD	3	EAN
Massachusetts	MA	1	EAN
Michigan	MI	8	EAN
Minnesota	MN	10	CAN
Mississippi	MS	5	CAN
Missouri	MO	10	CAN
Montana	MT	7	PAN
Nebraska	NE	10	CAN
Nevada	NV	6	PAN
New Brunswick	NB	11	EAN
New Hampshire	NH	1	EAN
New Jersey	NJ	2	EAN
New Mexico	NM	12	PAN
New York	NY	2	EAN
Newfoundland	NF	11	EAN
North Carolina	NC	4	EAN
North Dakota	ND	10	CAN
Nova Scotia	NS	11	EAN
Ohio	OH	8	EAN
Oklahoma	OK	5	CAN
Ontario	ON	11	EAN
Oregon	OR	7	PAN
Pennsylvania	PA	3	EAN
Prince Edward Is.	PEI	11	EAN
Puerto Rico	PR	4	EAN
Quebec	PQ	11	EAN
Rhode Island	RI	1	EAN
Saskatchewan	SK	10	CAN
South Carolina	SC	4	EAN
South Dakota	SD	10	CAN
Tennessee	TN	5	CAN
Texas	TX	5	CAN
Utah	UT	12	PAN
Vermont	VT	1	EAN
Virginia	VA	4	EAN
Virgin Islands	VI	4	EAN
Washington	WA	7	PAN
West Virginia	WV	8	EAN
Wisconsin	WI	9	CAN
Wyoming	WY	12	PAN
APO New York	APO NY	2	EAN
APO San Francisco	APO SF	6	PAN

given cycle of NTS, all nets in the same level commence at approximately the same local time. This allows time for liaisons to the next level to pick up any outgoing traffic and meet the next net. In addition, this gives the TCC stations at least an hour before their duties commence on another area net or their schedule begins with another TCC station.

The original NTS plan calls for four cycles of traffic nets, but usually two cycles are sufficient to handle a normal load of traffic on the system. However, during the holiday season, or in times of emergency, many more messages are dumped into the system, forcing NTS to expand to four cycles temporarily. The cycles of normal operation are Cycle Two, the daytime cycle, which consists primarily of phone nets, and Cycle Four, the nighttime cycle, made up mostly of CW nets. In addition, Cycle One has been implemented in the Pacific Area and Cycle Three in the Eastern Area. Now that the rudiments of NTS have been covered, let's see where you fit in.

NTS and You

Before the adoption of NTS, upper-level traffic handlers worked a system called the "trunk line" system, where a handful of stations carried the burden of cross-country traffic, day in day out. Nowadays, no one has to be an "iron man" or "iron woman" within NTS if they choose not to. If each liaison slot and TCC slot were filled by one person, one day a week, this would allow over 1000 hams to participate in NTS! Unfortunately, many hams have to double- and triple-up duties, so there is plenty of room for any interested amateur.

An NTS liaison spot one day (or night) a week is a great way to stay active in the traffic circuit. Many hams who don't have time to make the section nets get satisfaction in the traffic world by holding a TCC slot or area liaison once a week. If you would enjoy such a post, drop a note to your Section Traffic Manager or

Fame and Glory: Your Traffic Total, PSHR Report and Appointments

Even if you handle only one message in a month's time, you should send a message to your ARRL Section Traffic Manager (STM) or ARRL Section Manager (SM) reporting your activity. Your report should include your total originations, messages received, messages sent and deliveries.

An origination is any message obtained from a third party for sending from your station. If you send a message to Uncle Filbert on his birthday, you don't get an origination. However, if your mom or your neighbor wants you to send him one with her signature, it qualifies (it counts as one originated and one sent). The origination category is essentially an "extra" credit for an off-the-air function. This is because of the critical value of contact with the general public and to motivate traffickers to be somewhat more aggressive in making their message-handling services known to the general public.

Any formal piece of traffic you get via Amateur Radio counts as a message received. Any message you send via Amateur Radio, even if you originated it, counts as a message sent. Therefore, any time you relay a message, you get two points: one received and one sent.

Any time you take a message and give it to the party it's addressed to, on a mode other than Amateur Radio, you are credited with a delivery. (It's okay if the addressee is a ham.) As long as you deliver it off the air (eg, telephone, mail, Internet/e-mail, in person), you get a delivery point.

Your monthly report to your STM, if sent in radiogram format, should look something like this:

```
NR 111 R NIØR 14 ST JOSEPH MO NOV 2
BLAIR CARMICHAEL WBØPLY
MISSOURI STM
FULTON MO 65251
OCTOBER TRAFFIC ORIG 2 RCVD 5 SENT 6 DLVD 1
TOTAL 14
73
ROGER NIØR
```

If you have a traffic total of 500 or more in any month, or have over 100 originations-plus-deliveries in a month, you are eligible for the Brass Pounders League (BPL), even if you did all that traffic on SSB! Make sure you send your traffic totals to your STM or SM.

Another mark of distinction is the Public Service Honor Roll (PSHR). You don't have to handle a single message to get PSHR, so it's a favorite among traffickers in rural areas. You can receive points for activities such as checking into public service nets and handling emergency traffic. Candidates for PSHR need to report their monthly PSHR point total to their STM or SM. See the *QST* Public Service column for particulars or www.arrl.org/FandES/field/pshr/.

If you are an ARRL member, you can also become eligible for an Official Relay Station appointment in the ARRL Field Organization. (For details concerning the ARRL Field Organization, see www.arrl.org/FandES/field/org/.)

The local radio amateur community and your section leadership officials are ready to help you get involved in traffic handling. To contact your Section Manager, see the list near the front of any recent *QST* or visit the information page for your section on the ARRL Web site (www.arrl.org/sections/).

Net Manager. They will be happy to add another to their fold.

However, remember that the area and region net are very different from your section or local net in one aspect. The function of the section or local net is to "saturate" its jurisdiction, so the more check ins, the better. On the upper-level nets, though, the name of the game is to move the traffic as quickly and efficiently as possible. Therefore, additional check ins — other than specified liaisons and stations holding traffic — only slow down the net. (If you are a station holding traffic to be moved, you can enter NTS at any level to pass your traffic, even if you've never been on an upper-level net before. Entering the system at the section or local level is preferred.)

If you are interested in finding out more about the "brass tacks" of the workings to NTS, get a copy of the *Public Service Communications Manual*, available online as described at the beginning of this chapter. Every aspect of NTS is explained, as well as information about local net operating procedure, RACES and ARES operation. The PSCM will also orient you with net procedure of region and area NTS nets. It takes a little more skill and savvy to become a regular part of NTS, but the rewards are worth the effort. If you have the chance, go for it!

So There You Have It

Although this chapter is by no means a complete guide to traffic handling, it should serve as a good reference for veterans and newcomers alike. If you've never been involved in message handling, perhaps your interest has been piqued. Should that be the case, don't put it off. Find a net that's custom-made for you and check into it! You'll find plenty of fine folks that will soon become close friends as you begin to work with them, learn from them, and yes, even chat with them when the net is over.

The roots of traffic handling run deep into the history of Amateur Radio, yet its branches reach out toward many tomorrows. Our future lies in proving our worth to the nonham public, and what better way to ensure the continuance of our hobby than by uniting family and friends via Amateur Radio? Sure, it takes some effort, but a trafficker will tell you he stays with it because of the satisfaction he gets from hearing those voices on the other end of the phone say, "Oh, isn't that nice!" We've plenty of room for you — come grow with us!

The following ARRL NTS Officials helped with the revision of this chapter: Bill Thompson, W2MTA, Jim Leist, KB5W, Robert Griffin, K6YR, and Nick Zorn, N4SS.

DXing — Contacting Those Faraway Places

What is DX? An abbreviation for "distant station" or "signal from a distant station," DX is at the core of Amateur Radio. The excitement of contacting ever more distant stations has attracted amateurs of all types from the very earliest days of radio. The goal of spanning larger and larger distances has driven many technological advances. Whether DX means to you, as it does to HF DXers, a contact somewhere outside your own country, or to VHF+ DXers, a faraway grid square or hilltop, all of us get a thrill out of pushing the limits of our own skill and equipment. That's what "DXing" really means — extending your radio range and abilities.

Most amateurs don't begin their ham radio activity as a DXer. We start by making local contacts with friends and club members and gradually become aware of radio's broader possibilities. Even experienced hams have discovered DXing after years of local and regional contacts. The spark may be a visit to a DXer's station or seeing a presentation on DX, but is most likely to be an unexpected contact over a long distance. Perhaps a DX station answers your CQ one evening or you encounter an unexpected call sign while tuning the band. Even bringing up your favorite repeater while far from home on a hike or drive is DXing! This is the "magic of radio" writ large and it has been known take hold of one's ham radio interests with a lifetime's tenacity.

DXing is even more fun if you become skilled at it! That's the purpose of this chapter — to introduce beginners to DXing and help those with some experience at the DX game get better at it. The sections cover Beginning and Intermediate DXing, followed by a section on DX activities. Propagation, so important to DXers, is covered on a band-by-band basis. DXpeditions and QSLing conclude the chapter. See you in the pileups!

BASIC DXING

If you've made a few DX contacts (or would like to) and are interested in making DX a part of your regular ham radio diet, you've come to the right place! In many ways, this is the most exciting part of your DX career. Every time you turn on the radio, you'll experience something new and every contact is as exciting as it can possibly be! So enjoy this time and make it fun, as it lays the foundation for everything that follows.

Let's set a timeline of one year for you to learn the basics of DXing. What should you have learned during that one trip around the Sun? Why one year? You'll get to know HF or VHF+ propagation during all of the seasons and have a chance to work numerous DXpeditions and contests. This translates to invaluable experience that you wouldn't have had a year before. You'll put a year of practice in your log, along with a bunch of exotic calls and QSLs on the wall.

As a beginning DXer, you will have the exalted title of "Little Pistol." Even if you have a lot of fancy equipment, you'll still be learning the ropes and getting used to the techniques and procedures of DXing. This section assumes that if you will be engaging in HF DXing, you have a General or Amateur Extra license.

Basic DXing Equipment

Relax! You don't have to take out a second mortgage to get into the world of DXing! In fact, you may have most of the gear already. You may be surprised to learn that most of the DX stations you encounter on HF will be using equipment very similar to yours. It's how you operate it that will make the difference. For entry-level HF DXing, you'll need equipment similar to that described below.

HF Transceiver

Almost any modern 100 W HF transceiver (160-10 meters) less than 10 years old will give perfectly adequate performance. The receiver should be equipped with both SSB (2.0 or 2.4 kHz) and CW receive (400 or 500 Hz) filters. You should invest in a comfortable set of communications quality (200 to 4000 Hz is sufficient) headphones — you'll be wearing them a

Jon, DU9/NØNM, provided DXers with many QSOs with the Philippines over the course of several years of living there. He was especially active on the low bands.

lot — and a high-quality microphone. Headphones with an attached boom mike (called a *boom set*) are a good choice. The radio should support computer control. Radios with a second receiver are quite useful for DXing. The transceiver should have at least two VFOs (usually shown as VFO A and VFO B) that are easy to access and select. If you are just learning CW, learn to use a *paddle* with your rig's internal keyer or use an external electronic keyer.

The combination of headphones and lightweight microphone makes extended hours of operating a breeze. Choosing a microphone element designed for maximum intelligibility and proper positioning of the boom really makes a difference on the other end of the QSO.

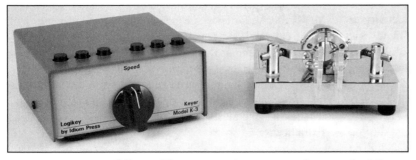

Learn to use a paddle and keyer to raise your code speed while dramatically lessening the effort required to send CW.

HF Antennas

For the high bands above 10 MHz, dipoles 20 feet off the ground or higher will work fine. A multiband vertical (with plenty of ground plane radials for ¼-wavelength antennas) will also work. On the low bands below 10 MHz, a vertical wire antenna (such as an inverted-L), dipoles at heights of 40 to 50 feet or more and multiband verticals will do the job. A copy of the *ARRL Antenna Book* with its many antenna designs and information on antenna systems is an invaluable addition to your station reference materials. For a wide selection of antenna projects, check out *Simple and Fun Antennas for Hams* by Chuck Hutchinson, K8CH, and Dean Straw, N6BV, also published by ARRL.

Dipoles generally work best with both ends at about the same height although an inverted-V configuration is acceptable. They may also be mounted in a sloping position, with one end much higher than the other. This is often done for DXing on 40, 80 and 160 meters. Many variations on the dipole and other similar wire antennas may be found in the

ARRL book *ON4UN's Low-Band DXing* by John Devoldere, ON4UN.

If a ground-mounted vertical is used, at least 16 radials should be installed and more if possible. If the vertical is elevated, such as on a roof or mast, it is best to provide at least four radials for each desired band. Excellent references for installation of radial systems for verticals may be found in *The ARRL Antenna Book*, *The Antenna Compendium Volume 5*, and *Vertical Antenna Classics* (all available from ARRL).

Use low-loss coax, such as RG-8 or RG-213, and trim the antennas to resonance near the bottom end of the General frequency allocations. If impedance matching is required, invest in good quality equipment.

Computer and Software

You'll find a lot of resources on the Internet, so you should be able to make use of your computer at the same time you're on the air. A dial-up connection is fine. Most ham programs are not "resource hogs" so you won't need a top-of-the-line computer, either. The computer should have at least one USB or serial port available to connect to your radio's control port. The majority of ham programs are *Windows*-based, but there is a growing community of *Linux* and Macintosh users.

As you begin logging DX stations, it's a good idea to start a computerized logbook. There are a number of programs available — ask other local hams, particularly DXers, what they are using. A DXer will want features like QSL label printing, award status tracking, and the ability to export log data as ADIF formatted files for electronic QSLing. The major programs have Web sites to explain the program features and functions. It is not recommended that you write your own software or use a spreadsheet or word processor since your log won't be compatible with other common programs.

Ward, NØAX, has used this simple low-power/QRP station to reach DXCC Honor Roll status. All of the equipment fits on a computer cart and small rolling cabinet that make it easy to do station maintenance, as well as comfortable to use.

The availability of all-band, all-mode rigs like the IC-7000 shown here make it easy to operate mobile or portable, in HF or VHF+ contests.

VHF+ Equipment

On VHF+, one of the many fine 50 W or higher "all-band" rigs is more than sufficient to get you started. You will be primarily operating on 6 and 2 meters. A CW filter is a "nice to have" on the VHF+ bands, but not critical. For antennas, you can get started with dipoles or loops, but there are many inexpensive 2- or 3-element 6-meter antennas available. For 2 meters, a Yagi with five or more elements is easy to mount and rotate, and will yield much better results than an omnidirectional antenna. You can try building your own antenna from the plans in *Simple and Fun Antennas for Hams* or from the Internet.

Use horizontally polarized antennas because that is the standard on VHF+. Low-loss coax is a must — every dB lost in the feed line is very hard to make up! And a higher antenna is usually a better antenna.

Height is important on VHF+ to increase the distance to your radio horizon. If you aren't in an advantageous location, consider an effective portable or "rover" installation that you can drive to a nearby hilltop — even the roof of a parking garage will do!

Basic DX Operating

As you begin to take DXing seriously, the most important thing is not to learn how to transmit but how to listen! Listen, listen, listen! Even in this age of computer networks and instantaneous worldwide connections, there is no substitute for being able to tune the band, understanding what you hear. As you become more experienced, you'll learn what the bands sound like when they're open. You'll get to know the characteristic sound of a signal that originated far away, what a pileup sounds like, how to hear the DX station under all that QRM, and so forth. But if you jump right in and start transmitting, you'll never get a chance to learn. The oldest DX saying in the book is, "You can't work 'em if you can't hear 'em!" The moral of that story is that if you want to make your transmissions count, learn how to receive.

Another important aspect of learning any activity is to have reasonable expectations. After all, if you begin an exercise program, you don't expect to start winning races right away, do you? It's important to expect you'll have successes — savor them! But expecting too much — such as working DXCC in a month or working more DX than the local Big Gun — is a sure recipe for disappointment. What DX you can expect to work

depends a great deal on where you live and solar conditions, but if you keep your expectations modest, you'll find DXing will continue to be enjoyable day after day.

In line with reasonable expectations, it's also unreasonable to start DXing with too little power. A 100 W transceiver will generate a solid, mid-level signal capable of working many DX stations. QRP (5 W output or less on CW) places a premium on the operator skills that you are trying to acquire. So avoid the frustrations of QRP for the time being. Once you are more skilled, turn the power down and enjoy the pleasures of QRP operating.

Timely and up-to-date information is even more important than signal power. There are a few tools and references that every DXer should have close at hand:

• ARRL DXCC List and ITU call sign prefix reference. You can find this information in *The ARRL DXCC List* booklet or online at **www.arrl.org/awards/dxcc/**. As you spend time on the bands, you'll gradually memorize the common prefixes, but special and unfamiliar ones will keep you guessing for a while. Keep this list handy and consult it often.

• World map showing CQ zones, DXCC entities, and most common prefixes. Mount it on the wall so that you can see it easily from your operating position. An azimuthal equidistant map centered on your location will also tell you the direction to each country at a glance. The ARRL offers nice wall maps of the world and of North America.

• Weekly ARRL propagation bulletins or monthly propagation predictions. These are available at no charge to ARRL members via W1AW, by email, or from the ARRL Web page.

By having these three pieces of reference information close at hand you will learn how to predict what you will hear on the air and understand what you hear. For example, if the propagation bulletin predicts good conditions to Japan at a certain time of day, the map also lets you know to listen for signals from UAØ (Asiatic Russia), HL (Korea), BY (China), and so forth. If you

The ARRL DXCC Handbook by Jim Kearman, KR1S, offers useful advice and tips in an easy-to-read format for beginners and veteran DXers alike.

are fortunate to hear a station with the JD1 prefix, the DXCC List confirms that this is station from Ogasawara or Minami Torishima. Both are considerably less common than mainland Japanese stations and possibly a new DXCC entity for you!

What about CW? This is also a great time to start learning CW if you don't already use it. As a Little Pistol, you'll want to maximize the effectiveness of your station and CW allows you to do just that. Veteran DXers will confirm that it is a lot easier to make a contact on CW than on phone, regardless of power level. CW signals pack their power into a narrow bandwidth instead of spreading it out over a couple of kilohertz. This allows you to "get through" when conditions aren't good or noise levels are high, as they are on the lower bands. Start now and you'll be knee-deep in the CW pileups before you know it!

Operating a Receiver

While operating a transmitter is certainly important, the success of a DXer more often depends on the ability to get the most out of a receiver on crowded and noisy bands where weak DX signals lurk. Your rig's operating manual will tell you a lot about what the various controls do, but not a lot about the effect using them will have on what you hear. It's worth repeating the old adage "You can't work 'em if you can't hear 'em!" Here's how to hear 'em better.

Let's start with passband tuning, IF shift, variable bandwidth or similar controls. All of these allow you to avoid interference by shifting the receive filter frequency without changing the VFO or filter bandwidth. Because the different manufacturers often implement these features slightly differently, read the radio's manual and experiment with the controls to observe their effect.

Digital signal processing (DSP) has become nearly standard in modern rigs. Top of the line radios do the filtering digitally, allowing tremendous flexibility in selecting filter shape and width. Noise reduction features also help remove annoying noise. Learning how to use the DSP functions effectively is a useful exercise.

You might be surprised to learn that your RF gain control is not locked in the full-on position! Maximum RF gain makes your receiver very sensitive, but also leaves your IF (and sometimes the RF) amplifiers susceptible to overloading by strong signals common on the DX bands. Experiment by reducing RF gain to see if it improves your receiver's performance in a strong signal environment. Even during casual operating, backing off the RF gain can dramatically reduce background noise. Experiment by changing the AGC settings. You can even turn AGC off and use the RF gain control manually to control volume. Using the minimum amount of receiver gain necessary can really clean up what comes out of the headphones or speaker!

The attenuator can be your biggest friend when dealing with strong nearby signals. It's surprisingly easy for a strong signal to overload a receiver's RF amplifier or mixers, creating spurious distortion products that can mask weaker signals. As you add attenuation you may find that interference drops dramatically when your receiver is no longer being overloaded. Using 10 dB of attenuation cures a surprising number of ailments at the cost of just a couple of S units of signal strength. Remember that the goal is to maximize signal-to-noise ratio, not necessarily absolute signal strength.

Two receiver functions actually make strong-signal performance *worse* when they are activated. The biggest villain is the noise blanker (not noise reduction — a DSP function). Most operate by sensing wide-bandwidth pulses in the receiver's IF. They look at the entire band, not just what is coming through the narrow

filters further down the receiver's signal path. A strong nearby signal can confuse a noise blanker to the point of nearly shutting down a receiver or causing what sounds like severe overmodulation over many kHz. Unless you have really strong local line noise, turn your noise blanker off. If the band is full of strong signals, noise blankers are useless or worse.

The second villain is the preamplifier (preamp). It's rarely useful on the lower HF bands and only occasionally of use on 12 and 10 meters. Preamps are much more useful at VHF and higher frequencies. By increasing the incoming signal strengths, it becomes much easier to overload a receiver as described above. Keep the preamp off unless absolutely necessary to hear the desired signal.

By effectively using the capabilities of a modern receiver, you will surely find that the band is quieter and nearby signals less disruptive. In fact, you will find yourself making better use of your receiver's controls every day!

The following description of receiver characteristics was written by ARRL Lab Engineer Mike Gruber, W1MG. A full description of receiver performance tests is included in recent editions of *The ARRL Handbook for Radio Amateurs*. The regular transceiver product reviews in *QST* show how to compare specifications from radio to radio.

CW and SSB Sensitivity

One of the most common sensitivity measurements you'll find for CW and SSB receivers is *minimum discernible signal* (MDS). It indicates the minimum signal level that can be detected with the receiver (although an experienced operator can often copy somewhat weaker signals). MDS is the input level to the receiver that produces an output signal equal to the internally generated receiver noise. Hence, MDS is sometimes referred to as the receiver's "noise floor."

You'll find MDS expressed in most spec sheets as μV or dBm. The lower the number in μV, or more negative the number in dBm, the more sensitive the receiver. (For example, a radio with an MDS of −139 dBm (0.022 μV) is more sensitive than one with an MDS of −132 dBm (0.055 μV).)

When making sensitivity comparisons between radios, keep in mind that more is not always better. Atmospheric and other radio noise on the band (not the receiver noise) often sets the practical limit below 20 MHz. If the receiver can hear external noise, greater sensitivity simply amplifies it. Also, too much sensitivity may make the receiver more susceptible to overload and decrease dynamic range.

A typical modern HF transceiver has an MDS of between −135 and −140 dBm (or 0.0398 to 0.0224 μV). You can easily make a dB comparison between two radios if the MDS is expressed in dBm. Simply subtract one MDS from the other. If, for example, one has an MDS of −132 and the other −139 dBm, the latter radio has a sensitivity that is 7 dB better than the first — if both measurements are made at the same receive bandwidth.

Dynamic Range

Dynamic range is a measure of the receiver's ability to tolerate strong signals outside of its passband. Essentially, it's the difference between the weakest signal a receiver can hear and the strongest signal a receiver can accommodate without noticeable degradation in performance. Two types are considered in *QST* product reviews: blocking dynamic range (BDR) and third-order intermodulation distortion dynamic range (IMD DR).

Blocking dynamic range (also called blocking gain compression) describes a receiver's ability to not become desensitized by a strong undesired signal on a different frequency while tuned to a desired signal. IMD dynamic range, on the other hand, is an indication of a receiver's ability to not generate false signals as a result of the two strong signals on different frequencies outside the receiver's passband. Both types of dynamic range are normally expressed in dB relative to the noise floor.

As in the case of our hypothetical receiver, the IMD DR is usually 20 dB or more below the BDR. This means false signals will usually appear well before sensitivity is significantly decreased. It's not surprising that IMD DR is often considered to be one of the more significant receiver specifications. It's generally a conservative evaluation for other effects that may or may not be specified. Meaningful dynamic range comparisons can only be made when the unwanted signals are equally spaced from the desired signal. Wider spacings generally result in better (higher) DR figures.

Third Order Intercept Point

Another parameter used to measure receiver performance in *QST* product reviews is the third-order intercept point (IP3). This is the extrapolated point (specified in dBm) at which the desired signal and the false signals caused by third-order IMD become equal in strength. Higher levels for IP3 indicates better receiver performance.

Second Order IMD Dynamic Range and Intercept Point

Second-order IMD distortion dynamic range, like third-order products, also are generated within a receiver. Strong signals (f1, f2) cause the offending products at frequencies of f1 ± f2. In today's busy electromagnetic environment, they can become truly offensive under certain conditions.

Consider the case of two strong shortwave stations, on two different bands, that sum to the frequency of the weak DX you're trying to copy. If their intermodulation product is strong enough, you may not be able to copy the station through the interference. As an example, a high seas coast telephone station on 4400 kHz might sum with a shortwave broadcast station on 9800 kHz to produce an intermod product on 14200 kHz.

IF and Image Rejection

A station transmitting at a receiver's IF frequency can be truly offensive if its signal is strong enough and the radio's IF rejection is insufficient. The station will then be heard on all frequencies! This is called an image. Be sure to consider IF rejection when considering a receiver if a nearby transmitter is located on its IF frequency.

When testing IF rejection, we first measure the level that causes the unwanted signal to be received with a strength equal to the MDS. The difference between the unwanted signal's strength and the MDS is then the IF rejection in dB.

Collecting Information

Gathering information is as important to a DXer as any other facet of operating, because knowledge really is power. In fact, it's *better* than power because it doesn't matter how strong your signal is if you're operating on the wrong frequency or at the wrong time!

A DX newsletter, such as *Daily DX* or *QRZ DX*, really helps the DXer in the search for new stations. A DXer or DX club may set up a Web site and begin keeping a chart of the activities of DX operators by using QSN (heard on ___ kHz) reports. For example, you may note that a VKØ on Macquarie Island is beginning to show up on a certain band, on or near a certain frequency, and usually around the same time of day. Further charting may observe that this occurs on the same day, but every other week. Thus, there's a high probability that if the DXer is there at the right time on the next likely day, there will be a chance of working that rare entity.

Keep track of national holidays and customs in your area of interest. Know when the DXer from other lands might be taking his cup of coffee (or whatever) into the shack to enjoy a few minutes of radio before or after work. Read a newspaper or Web news service with a good international section to keep track of world events that may affect DXing.

DX spotting networks are another important tool. In fact, it has been said that many owe their DXCC Honor Roll plaques to them. Add spot filtering software that alerts the operator if a needed station comes on the air, and you have a most formidable tool.

The DX spotting network now stretches around the world through Internet connections. It's possible to see what's being worked in Italy or Japan. This is actually more useful than you may think. First, it's possible to know that stations from certain areas are actually on the air. It's also possible to identify these stations, and even request schedules. Sometimes, depending on propagation, spots from another area of the country actually can be used. Spots can help you work stations at times that you would not have even listened. And spots have tipped operators to band openings not thought possible before. Real time spotting is probably the most superior method of intelligence gathering for ongoing operations currently in use. It is a truly amazing system, and the hybrid radio/Internet system is one of the best forms of useful ham ingenuity.

Receiving and Transmitting

Bill Kennamer, K5NX, offered some advice on operating in the 8th edition of this book that is just as pertinent today as it was a few years ago. Let's follow Bill as he grabs a cup of coffee and heads for the DX bands for a typical morning of DXing…

Suppose it is morning, during a period when the sunspots are low to moderate. For these conditions, the band of choice would be 20 meters. Begin on SSB, near the bottom of the band. You do have your headphones on, don't you? Remember now, we're just listening, so it doesn't matter where we are in the band. Of course, when transmitting it will be necessary to be in the part of the band authorized for your license class.

Tune slowly up the band. Listen to the QSOs going on. If the signals are steady, and the accent sounds like your own countryman, pass it up now, and move slowly up the band. A signal is heard speaking in accented English. Stop here and listen. The signal may be strong and steady, or it may be strong

Pirates and Police, Lids and Jammers
By Bill Kennamer, K5NX

The DXer does encounter a few problems in the pursuit of his avocation. Those nefarious denizens named in the title of this sidebar are not there to make life easier for the DXer. However, all DXers will ultimately have in common the fact that they have overcome and persevered through the jungle created by the antics of these creatures of the ether. These cretinous individuals should not diminish the pleasure of the DXer, but allow him to puff out his chest with pride, as he overcomes the obstacles put into his path by such miscreants.

Pirates have been with us always. We can't be sure if Marconi heard one when he first fired up, but certainly the first signal received across the Atlantic by Godley was one. Probably the most famous pirate was named Slim. At a time when a volcanic island had popped up out of the sea near Iceland, Slim turned up from Cray Island as 8X8AA, claiming that the island had just popped up in the North Atlantic, and would qualify for a new country. He held forth for several days, then disappeared forever. Since then, many pirates over the years have been tagged as Slim. So, if an operation comes onto the air, and it's so improbable as to be suspect, it may be Slim, back for another run.

One thing the DXer must do when encountering suspected pirates: *Work Them!* Yes, always work them, because sometimes the improbable is true. The rule is *Work 'em First, Worry Later (WFWL).* Two things are accomplished by doing so: first, the DXer can practice pileup technique, and second, if it is for real, it's in the log. If it's suspect, the QSL need not be sent until later. But if it's not in the log, it's hard to get a QSL. Some pirates and bootleggers do QSL, so it's not unusual to get cards rejected for awards credit. Everybody does, so it's best to continue working stations until one sticks.

Every pileup will have police and jammers. The police may be well-meaning souls, but they really are in the same category as the jammers. They just do it in a less sophisticated way. The DX is calling, working a hundred an hour by split frequency. Meanwhile, on the DX operater's transmit frequency, the lids, police and jammers may be all heard at once, each pursuing DX infamy. The lid will start with "Who's the DX?" or "Where's he listening?" or the inevitable, "Is the frequency in use?" All these questions could be answered by listening a little, but either the lid's time is too valuable, or intelligence level is too low to think of that.

This is, of course, an excuse for the police to jump in, with varying responses. Ten police will, one after the other (never in unison) give all the information anyone would care to know about the DX station, meanwhile totally obliterating the DX station and stopping the pileup in its tracks. This is immediately followed by 10 more who attack the lid, questioning their parentage or intelligence level. Finally come the last 10, who are telling the previous ones and the lid to just shut up. Ah yes, the musical chaos of the pileup!

Did we say music? That must be the cue for the jammer to appear, as music is one form of jamming. The "laughing box" is also good, although not in much use in recent years. Finding someone calling in the pileup and recording it and replaying it on the DX frequency is also a frequently used technique. Sometimes the call of their favorite DX net control is used this way. Most jammers these days are not that sophisticated. Now it's mostly just tuning up or calling CQ on the DX frequency, or running a couple of minutes of white noise onto the air. One of the easiest ways for the jammers to enjoy themselves is to just ask who the DX is, and get the police started.

Meanwhile, the DXer can rejoice in the fact that, although all these obstacles are placed in the way, she's still working the DX! So let the others moan and groan, let them complain to the utmost. The fact remains, those who learn their skills well will succeed.

---

but occasionally dipping in strength. This may well be a DX station. Stick around long enough for them to send a call sign or otherwise give a clue as to location. If it is a European, then you know the band is open in that direction, for example

Determine the style of operating. If the DX is in a QSO, record the frequency and call signs. Don't call until the contact is definitely finished. To do otherwise would be rude, and usually only lids are rude. You can check back in a few minutes.

Keep moving up slowly. Be sure to pay attention to weak signals. Many times they are passed over because people either can't hear them through their speakers (but you're wearing headphones, remember?) or think they're too weak to be workable. More than once a rare DX station has appeared on the band, called a few CQs with no response, and gone away. With 100 W and a simple antenna, it's to your advantage to try to find stations before anyone else is calling and the pileup starts. It's likely that the DX station may be running 100 W to a dipole, sometimes even an indoor dipole. If you can hear the DX, they can most likely hear you, too, especially if no one else is calling.

The important thing while you're tuning is to listen to as many different DX stations as possible. Notice the sound, the

accents, the audio quality. With a little practice, you can tune the band quickly, and immediately identify the DX stations. Later, you will be able to do the same thing on CW.

Now it's time to begin calling some of the DX stations you've been hearing. You hear the DX station sign off. You know the call sign. Now call! If it's a station that has been working short QSOs, give their call one time only (they *know* their call!), and yours twice, using standard phonetics. Then wait. If you're lucky, the DX will come back to you! If the DX comes back to someone else, wait patiently until he's finished. DXing is a game of patience. But turn off your VOX while waiting, Tripping your VOX while waiting on the frequency is the behavior of a lid.

You're lucky!! The DX station came back to you! You're now in QSO with the DX station. The first QSO with a DX station can be somewhat like dancing. They lead, you follow. As a rule, on your first transmission work by a formula. Give your name, state and signal report. A good form would be, "My name is Bill, in the state of Arkansas. Your report is 5 by 9, over." The DX station's English may be limited, they may be working many stations, or may be waiting on frequency for a schedule. In

Using Spotting Networks

Once (and still) simply referred to as "packet," DX spotting networks have become a significant force in DXing. Since the early days of DXing, local DXers have banded together to share information about what stations are on the air. Before packet radio, DXers listened on a VHF frequency (usually on 2 meters) that was kept quiet except for announcements about DX stations. For example, you might hear, "TZ6ZZ is on 14024, listening up two, K6ABC clear" Helping each other has a long and honorable history in DXing.

Packet radio became popular in the early 1980s and DXers naturally migrated to it. Instead of a voice announcement, the example above might have looked like "K6ABC A TZ6ZZ on 14024 QSX up 2," with the 'A' signifying an announcement to be sent to all connected stations. Bulletin board systems appeared, based on similar systems used over landline computer networks. Soon PacketCluster software adapted the bulletin board to the DX-centric format used today. Local stations connected via VHF or UHF and stayed connected, receiving a steady stream of information that could be stored and reviewed, if so desired.

As the Internet became ubiquitous, the packet radio link gave way to a dial-up or broadband connection. By that time, the format for data and commands for PacketCluster operating were in widespread use and so were replicated on Web-based versions. Today, a worldwide system incorporates users linked by packet radio, Telnet, or Web-based interfaces. If desired, you can sit in your shack and watch a steady stream of DX station information and announcements flow by, posted by stations from all over the world!

This is a "good news, bad news" situation. The good news is, of course, that there is so much information for DXers. More DX QSOs and entities are being logged by more DXers than ever. What could be wrong with that? The bad news is that there is so much information that the need to actually tune the band for yourself is reduced. Without putting your ears to work, you lose the opportunity to gain hard-won knowledge of propagation and band characteristics. You will also find that the posted information is not 100% reliable, as well, leading to the "busted call" or dreaded "not in the log" result.

DX spots also create the original version of a "smart mob," known as a "packet pileup" to DX operators. As information about the DX station filters out across the world's spotting networks, dozens to literally hundreds of DXers can descend on a single frequency, hoping for a QSO! It's important to remember that a DXer relying on spotting information to do his or her tuning will *never* be the first to find a DX station on the bands!

Nevertheless, as long as an appropriate amount of caution is applied and you remember that spotting networks are an aid and not an end in themselves, the information can be a great boon. Learn as much as you can about the spotting system you choose to use. Use the information to help you find the DX first instead of rushing madly about as spots pop up on your computer screen.

You can find local spotting networks by inquiring of your local or regional DX club. A list of spotting systems worldwide, Internet spotting sites and many other useful spot-related links is available at **www.dxcluster.info** and at **www.ng3k.com**. Once connected, be sure to use the Help functions of the system to find out how to operate it correctly. Remember that the information you post will likely be seen around the planet within a few minutes!

When Montenegro attained independence, it became a new addition to the DXCC Entity List and was sought after by DXers the world over. Here we see Nicola YZ9AMD making the first QSO of the 4O3T DXpedition.

any case, the next transmission will determine whether they will say 73 or want to have an hour's discussion of the state of the fishing where you live. Just follow the DX station's lead and enjoy the QSO, no matter how long or short. Yes, you'll want to QSL. We'll talk about that later.

Many times you'll hear DX stations running stations at a fairly high rate. They'll answer each station with call sign and signal report, then go on to the next station. When calling a running station, sign your call sign *one time*, using phonetics. If you're beaten in the pileup, wait until the next opportunity and call again. Don't ask the station for QSL information in this type of pileup — listen until it's given or look it up on the Internet or in a newsletter.

While you're listening to the pileup and trying to find the frequency at which the DX station is working callers, you'll notice many stations just seem to call over and over, never listening. Why do they do that? Others respond to the DX station, no matter what the call sign of the requested station. Why do they do that? No one really knows, but it certainly slows down the operation, doesn't it? Certainly, it makes it impossible for them to find where the DX station is listening and reduces their chances of getting in the log dramatically. Don't be a pileup lid — respond only when the DX station is calling for a call sign close to yours. Spend your time listening and you'll be able to say, "Got 'em in just one call!"

Goals for the Little Pistol DXer

The world of DXing can be overwhelming at first. There is so much to learn and so much to do! All around are experienced veterans who have been around seemingly since the days of spark and who have worked everything dozens of times. To cut the problem down to size, set five modest goals for your first stage of DXing and accomplish them. Here are five suggestions for the Little Pistol:

• Learn to operate your transceiver well.

• Learn to tune the bands and find propagation opportunities — don't get hooked on DX spots.

• Learn how to operate split and how to find the DX station's transmit frequency.

- Start computer logging and register for Logbook of the World (see the section on QSLing later in this chapter).
- Work 75 or more different DXCC entities or VUCC grids.

BEYOND THE BASICS

When can you graduate from being a Little Pistol? Whenever you want! You'll know when you've become a "Medium Gun" because you feel confident on the bands, you have enough contacts for an award or two (even if you choose not to apply for them), and you begin to recognize the sounds of DXing. You can discern the bands opening and closing, identify the characteristics of DX signals, and know how to make DX QSOs.

This is really the most exciting and enjoyable period of any DXer's "career" because there are plenty of "New Ones" to put in the log. You're now skilled enough to be successful on a regular basis, but not so experienced that you don't get surprised now and then! Enjoy being a Medium Gun because it's fun!

Eventually you'll approach some rarified air — 300 DXCC entities or 200 grids or band-mode-zone totals that seemed unattainable not so long ago. Remember? You've become a Big Gun! As such, you should be writing this chapter, congratulations! Don't forget what it was like to be a Little Pistol and the magic spell of even the most garden variety DX QSO. Your assignment? Be an Elmer and a friend to an up-and-coming Little Pistol so that they will become a Big Gun someday, just like you!

DXing Equipment — The Next Step

As a DXer with some experience in the log, you'll have used your station enough to have found some of its weak spots and have a list of features you need. Now's the time to upgrade! Before you do, make a list of what your station can and cannot do. Get the advice of more experienced DXers to see if you're missing something important or are yearning for a feature or gadget that really doesn't make much difference.

A cautionary note — there is no substitute for being on the air! All the gear in the world and all the Internet bandwidth won't put your call in the DX log. It's easy to get lost in the gadgetry of DXing. As you improve your station's capabilities, build for reliability. A fancy, but broken, amplifier or antenna doesn't make any QSOs! Your goal should be to put out a solid signal every time you operate and to get plenty of "chair time."

HF Transceiver

A transceiver with 100 W of RF output remains adequate. Upgrade to one of the rigs that uses advanced DSP technology to create the IF filters or purchase a complete set of filters for your radio. Cascaded crystal filters (one in each IF stage) can be a very powerful listening tool! Other DSP functions,

such as several levels and styles of noise reduction and auto-notch filters will be useful, as well. The second receiver is no longer an option — you'll definitely want to have one while chasing DX stations with large pileups.

Accessories, such as the microphone and paddle, should be selected to fit your operating preferences. Evaluate different types of microphone elements on the air to find the one that gives you punchy but crisp and clear audio. For DXing, high and low frequency response is secondary to intelligibility over difficult paths and in pileups. As your CW competency and speed increase you may want a paddle with a lighter touch. An external keyer with message buffers may make operating more convenient. Don't be afraid to start trying different styles of these very important interfaces between you and the radio!

As you pursue rarer DX over more difficult paths, obtaining an amplifier will prove to be a good step. It needn't be a top-of-the-line, 1500 W continuous-duty model. Amps that put out 1000 W or so are perfectly adequate. There are lots of used amplifiers that will give plenty of good service. A footswitch will help you avoid excessive wear and tear on the amplifier's transmit/receive relay.

HF Antennas

You'll want to consider some sort of tower and beam antenna. This is a great investment, one of the best the DXer could ever make. A small *tribander* (a rotatable antenna that operates on 20-15-10 meters) at 40 to 50 feet will provide a noticeable improvement over wire antennas on both transmit and receive. Wires may still be used for the low bands, or the tower itself may be fed as a vertical.

The 30, 17 and 12 meter bands become increasingly important as the DX becomes rarer. Be sure to at least have wire antennas for these bands, particularly for 30 and 17 meters. If you can obtain a beam antenna for 17 and 12 meters, it will make a big difference because those bands often provide a contact with a DXpedition or rare station when 20, 15 and 10 meters are too crowded.

Pay particular attention to your feed lines and associated accessory equipment. Don't give away your hard work and expense by using inferior cable, connectors or construction technique. Pay attention to the details and "do it right." Individual fractions of a dB saved by careful assembly of station components can add up to significant differences on the air.

VHF+ Equipment

The biggest bang for your ham radio buck at this stage is to install bigger antennas mounted higher above ground. Propagation is often marginal on 6 and 2 meters, particularly after you've worked all of the nearby grids and those common on

Ann, WA1S, is a top contester and DXer. Here she is seen operating from a beachfront tent on Kure Atoll during the 2005 K7C DXpedition. (*AD6E photo*)

sporadic-E or whatever tropospheric propagation is common in your area. Antennas with longer booms and more elements — for example, a 4 or 5 element Yagi on 6 meters and 10 elements or more on 2 meters — often make the crucial difference in being heard when signals are weak and openings very brief.

Power amplifiers and mast-mounted preamps on the higher bands will pay dividends by increasing your ability to take advantage of marginal openings. You'll also begin to hear and work weaker stations, increasing the number of stations available for you to contact. Feed line and connector quality is crucial for VHF+ DXing, so don't scrimp here. Ask for advice from veteran VHF+ DXers.

Taming the Pileup

You've learned the basics by now. DX signals are recognized by their sound and tuned in quickly. You are comfortable competing with other stations and have learned the appropriate timing of making your call. The bands feel like home to you. Now it's time to tackle the most difficult DXing task — the pileup. Once again, Bill Kennamer, K5NX, has some valuable lessons to impart, useful on HF or VHF+.

There are two kinds of pileups, transceive (or simplex) and split frequency. These are exactly what their names imply — transceive means working stations on the same frequency for both transmit and receive. Split means using one frequency for transmitting and another for listening. Both are easily manageable if proper technique is used. For medium to large-sized pileups, split is actually quite preferable. It's important to listen and see how other operators apply that technique from either end of the pileup!

Tuning the band, a DX station is heard passing out rapid fire QSOs — signal reports only or grid squares. As a rule, you should listen for a moment or two to see who it is. If needed, great, get ready to make your call. If not, stick around for some time to listen. The pileup builds, almost to the point of getting unmanageable. Notice who's getting through and who's not.

The stations transmitting just part of their call signs or just their last two letters on phone seem to be having a more difficult time. That's because many DX stations these days give priority to a full call sign. So, even with a good signal, sending the "last two" leads to spinning your wheels to some degree. Full calls are always best. On CW this isn't much of a problem.

Notice that occasionally you will hear a station giving a call sign while extraneous information is being given to the DX station. This may be something like a second station signing his call on top of the signal report. This is a technique called *tailending*. Although it is a good technique if you get the timing right, you need to listen to a few good practitioners of the art, for it is an art, before trying it. Otherwise it can cause QRM

and makes you sound like a lid. Notice that often the calling station is on a slightly different frequency and uses a different speed on CW. Sometimes he's weaker. Some practitioners of the art actually turn off their amplifier before trying this because that avoids being obnoxious. Notice also that if the station trying the technique tries it once or twice and it doesn't work, it isn't tried again. To continue could annoy the DX station, and she may be deliberately not taking tailenders when they call, but one or two calls later just to keep everyone from trying it at once. A pileup can quickly turn into bedlam if two or three tailenders are taken in a row.

Continue listening to the pileup and see where callers are positioning themselves in the pileup. On CW, they may be sending higher by 100 to 200 Hz from where the last caller was worked to make their signal stand out. Sometimes slower speed is better if everyone else is fast. This also works somewhat on phone. By adjusting the XIT (transmitter incremental tuning) on SSB, it's possible to make your voice take on a different pitch that may cut through the pileup.

If you don't hear anyone coming back to the DX station, yet the signal reports keep on coming, the DX station is obviously working callers split on a different frequency. This is when that second receiver pays for itself. Split frequency operation can be, and is, done most frequently with two VFOs, but can be even more effective when done with two receivers. On CW, start looking for the stations calling about 1 kHz up. Tune higher from the DX station until the calling stations are found. The pileup may be as much as 5 to 10 kHz away and is almost always higher in frequency.

Once you've found the pileup, start tracking the stations that are working the DX station to see how far, and in which direction, they are tuning between QSOs. Listen to see if tailenders are getting through (easier to do while split than transceive). Do the same thing on SSB if it's a phone pileup.

Listen carefully to what the DX station is saying. If you can't hear, don't call until you can. Surprisingly, when these pileups get really loud and poorly behaved, the DX station will often call out a specific spot frequency where no one is calling. Those who are listening will catch it. Those who don't hear will continue to call in vain. Look also for operators who operate at or below the edge of the announced calling frequency range. Sometimes DX stations will announce something like "200 to 210." At that moment, they may have tuned down to 200 to start tuning up again. Often a caller at 199.5 can get the QSO because of the difference in pitch, or because sidebands from the signal make it difficult to hear on 200. This only works once. If the DX moves away from 200, then it's back to square one. Find and follow, then get ahead.

Have you heard the operator at the DX club who comes into

DXpeditions take hams to the far ends of the Earth to make thousands of DXers happy. This photograph shows one of the operating tents on the glaciers of Peter I Island during the 3YØX operation of 2006. (photo courtesy 3YØX expedition)

DXing, DXpeditioning and . . . Contesting!

By Wayne Mills, N7NG

Wayne has been a DXer and contester for over 40 years. He is currently at the top of the DXCC Honor Roll and holds WAZ and 5BDXCC awards as well. After participating in contests for many years from home, Wayne began his ventures to offshore locations in the late1980s. Since then he has been involved in numerous world-class contest operations including several world records in multioperator classes and has a single operator world record as well. Since 1985, he has partici-pated in numerous major DXpeditions to every continent of the world, including ZA1A—the operation that launched the Amateur Radio service in Albania, and significant operations from Myanmar, Pratas Island, Scarborough Reef and the Temotu Province of the Solomon Islands. Wayne was elected to the CQ DX Hall of Fame in May 1999. More information on contesting can be found in Chapter 7 of this book.

Braving stiff seas and relentless crabs, the FOØAAA team activated Clipperton Island off the coast of Mexico. (*K6SGH photo*)

This chapter offers excellent insight into how to become a seasoned DXer. Learning, however, is best accomplished by doing. Practice with the lessons of this chapter can be obtained by participating in contests. Contesting offers a great opportunity to practice DXing skills. Contesting can also point to ways to improve your station. DXing is an art, which requires considerable skill, skill that often is acquired only after years of practice, practice and more practice. The more you work at it, the more proficient you will become. Contesting can help the DXer gain important operating skills and increased sta-tion effectiveness.

Many years of experience as a DXer and contester convinces me that this is true. My contesting experiences began shortly after I began DXing. Contests created many opportunities to practice chasing relatively non-rare DX in a short period of time. The skills acquired in the course of many contest efforts have made DXing easy for me. Emulating the contester who is successful leads to greater efficiency on your part. Listening is a particularly important ability. Paying attention to what is happening and deciding how to approach a pileup is particularly important. Is the DX working split? Is there a distinctive listening pattern? Where and when should I call next? In major pileups, it is easy to spot those who lack the tech-niques to be successful. I credit contesting with teaching me the timing, placement and rhythm to be a successful DXer.

From home, contesting offers many opportunities to snag a rare DX station in a major-league pileup. You may be competing with some of the largest stations in the country, so it's not necessarily easy. However, this is great practice for getting through to the very rare DX, and it's also a good gauge of your abilities and your station's capabilities. At the same time, pileups in a contest are not always as large and as unruly as those on the rarest of DX stations. Because there are so many DX stations in a contest, many DXers are off chasing one or the other, leaving this one for you.

Elementary contesting is often learned at a local club's ARRL Field Day site. Field Day includes many of the elements of contesting and DXpeditioning. For many hams, the ARRL Field Day is their introduction to contest-ing. The ARRL Sweepstakes Contest is a great next step since good results can be had with a smaller station and

antenna system. For the DXer, the ultimate experience is the DX contest. In addition to providing DXing experi-ence, DX contests can add many counters to your DX to-tal. Success in these contests may require bigger signals and a good deal of skill, but good results can still be had with a modest station.

Success in contests requires a high quality station. The stronger signal you can deliver to the DX station, the better your chance to bust the pileup. Big power isn't always necessary, and good antennas are often better than power, as antenna gain improves receiving as well as transmitting. Knowledge of propagation often substi-tutes for high power. Calling when propagation favors your area will likely result in success. All of these factors, which are crucial to successful contesting, will make you a better DXer.

When you feel comfortable participating in contests from home, you may be ready to graduate to participat-ing in contests outside the 48 states. At some point, many DXers wonder what it would be like to operate at the other end of a pileup. With travel to distant points on the globe easier than ever before, the opportunity to operate at "the other end" is a reality for many DXers. If you would like this type of activity, why not take your spouse on a va-cation to the Caribbean and spend a weekend working a DX contest? You will probably find yourself inundated with callers in a way you have never have heard. Read some of the literature beforehand, though. Such an effort will give you experience in logistics, licensing, and travel as well as DXpeditioning operating. Setting up a station in a remote hotel accommodation can be an experience. This can be a low-pressure affair designed to give you a real DXpedition experience. Have you learned the basics? When the action starts, you will soon find out!

Want to learn DXpeditioning? Just what exactly do you need to know to be a DXpeditioner? One of the best places to start learning is in a DX contest. Contesting offers the opportunity to operate on the other end of the pileup. As a DXpeditioner, you need to learn how to dig call signs out of big pileups while maintaining control and minimizing the impact on the band. You need to know how to work specific regions when everyone from

CQ Hall of Fame members Roger, G3SXW, and Nigel, G3TXF, are seen here as they depart to French Guyana (FY) for another of their many DXpeditions. (*G3SXW photo*)

everywhere is calling you. Stamina, you'll need *lots* of stamina! Most successful DXpeditioners are also well-known contesters.

DXpeditioning requires different types of ability. Rather than putting your signal in the right place at the right time, you must identify signals in that huge mess we call a pileup. You must not only pick out a call, but you must do it quickly, with a predictable pattern and rhythm. DXpeditioning is mostly about operating. To some extent, the name of the game is *rate*. How many stations can you work in an hour? For rare locations, it may also be about how to work as many different stations as possible. At the operating position of a DXpedition, you will usually find a DXer who is also a contester. Contesters have the operating skills required to be successful DXpeditioners. For DXpeditioning, you must also set up a station in some far-off place, often with few resources. Everything is done "Field-Day" style. Logistics and planning are very important. Most of all, however, you must be familiar with working a pileup. This is DXpeditioning.

If you are getting the idea that contesting can help in developing your DXing and DXpeditioning skills, you are right. There are two steps in contesting that can help develop these skills. The first is simply to become familiar with contest-style operating by participating in contests from home. Many of the skills required can be learned by observing how it is done. This experience will greatly enhance your DXing skills. The second step, which is the easy and fun way to learn DXpeditioning, is to actually participate in contests from a location "off shore." Contesting offers a condensation of DXing opportunities into a number of short but highly concentrated operating periods throughout the year. For intense experience, practice in breaking pileups and developing DXing skills, try contesting!

the discussion on the latest big DXpedition? "Yep, worked them with one call." You'll can almost bet that a half an hour or more was spent using the techniques above to set up that one call.

Goals for the Medium Gun DXer

Now is the time to develop "DX muscles" by expanding your expertise and building up your station to work the rarest DX reliably. You will begin your quest for the top echelons of DXCC or VUCC. These goals will take time and effort to achieve, but the journey is its own reward. Your QSL collection will begin to swell with numerous cards from around the world. Don't ignore the social aspects of the hobby — take in a DX convention or two and meet some of those faces behind the signals you hear (and compete against) in the pileups! They'll be glad to meet you, too, and maybe a few lifelong friendships will begin.

- Improve your station capabilities to reach another level of DX stations or grids.
- Study unusual propagation opportunities or propagation on an unfamiliar band.
- Hone your pileup technique in large and difficult pileups.
- Log DXpeditions on as many bands or from as many grids as possible.
- Start working toward 5BDXCC and 5BWAZ. On VHF+, keep logging new grids and investigate new modes.

DX AWARD PROGRAMS AND CONTESTS

It is completely natural to take an interest in extending your station's range. Getting the most out of your equipment and personal skills delivers a well-deserved sense of accomplishment. DXing can be treated as a casual activity focused on making overseas friends or as competitive as you wish. Many DXers enjoy a relaxed chat with someone in a different country just for the sheer pleasure of establishing contact. You may elect to work DX and never submit an award application or submit a DX contest log — that's fine! Or you may try to reach #1 DXCC Honor Roll by verifying contacts with every entry on the DXCC List. Find your DX comfort level and enjoy!

To encourage and reward improved operating and station construction, many organizations sponsor DX-oriented awards. The ARRL, *CQ* Magazine, the Radio Society of Great Britain (RSGB), and many other organizations sponsor DX award programs for both HF and VHF+. There are literally thousands of awards! Let's take a brief look at some of the most popular award programs. (Look for more information in the **Operating Awards** chapter of this book.)

WAC and WAS

WAC (Worked All Continents) and *WAS* (Worked All States) are the gateway to DXing for many hams. Complete information on these two awards is available at **www.arrl.org/awards/wac** and **www.arrl.org/awards/was**, respectively.

WAC is a great "first" HF DX certificate to hang on the wall, signifying contact with each of the six main continents: North and South America, Europe, Asia, Africa and Oceania. WAC is available on VHF+ bands, too — a real achievement!

WAS on HF often requires both high- and low-band contacts to complete, along with a pair of "real" DX countries: Hawaii (KH6) and Alaska (KL7). Completing a QSO with your "last" state will be an unforgettable thrill! WAS on VHF+ is much

The DXCC Challenge award encourages DXers to expand their capabilities to all bands. The basic award is for 1000 entities worked on a combination of bands. Bob, W4DR, has been at the top of the award's ranking since its inception and was also the first to achieve 5BDXCC.

The Islands On the Air program (www. rsgbiota.org) has grown to become one of the world's most popular DXing awards programs. Focusing on saltwater islands, IOTA chasers have a nearly never-ending supply of New Ones to put in the log. (Another program, the US Islands program, includes inland and river islands. See www.usislands. org.)

harder because of the limits of propagation above the HF bands.

Both programs offer endorsements for completing the required contacts on multiple bands, too. Depending on solar conditions, the multiple band WAC or WAS can be a worthy challenge. Once you've qualified for WAC or WAS, you're well on your way to DX adventures.

DXCC Program

Undoubtedly the premier DX award program on either HF or VHF+, *DXCC* was initiated in the 1930s when amateur equipment and techniques were just beginning to enable regular intercontinental contacts. (The first transatlantic QSOs were made in 1923.) After World War II, the program was restarted and modern DXing began in earnest. Through the years, DXCC (**www.arrl. org/awards/dxcc**) has come to be the standard for DX achievement around the world. In fact, to become a full member of some DX clubs, the applicant must have achieved DXCC!

The DXCC award is based on the *DXCC List* of recognized "entities" that may or may not be countries in the traditional sense. Currently 337 entities count for DXCC credit. Some are "regular" countries like France or Japan while some are tiny islands far from the beaten track or geographical oddities tucked away in obscure corners of the world.

The DXCC program recognizes many different types of operating. Along with single and multiple band endorsements, the program recognizes CW, Phone, and RTTY DXCC — even DXCC from contacts via amateur satellites! Serious DXers can also participate in the *DXCC Challenge*, working DX entities on every band and mode they can.

CQ DX Award Program

CQ Magazine (**www.cq-amateur-radio.com**) has promoted DXing for many years and sponsors a number of popular DX awards along with an active HF and VHF+ contest program. These complement DXCC very well and most DXers participate in both CQ and ARRL awards programs. The list of CQ DX Awards includes:

• *CQ DX* — similar to DXCC with its own *CQ DX Country List*.

• *CQ DX Field* — based on Maidenhead Grid Fields around the world.

• *CQ iDX* — recognizes contacts made via Voice Over Internet Protocol (VOIP) systems.

• *WAZ* (Worked All Zones) — contact all of the 40 zones recognized by CQ.

• *WPX* (Worked Prefixes) — counts different call sign prefixes worldwide.

VUCC

VHF+ DXers think of grid locators in the way HF DXers think of countries and entities. The ARRL's *VUCC* (VHF-UHF Century Club) award is based on contacts with the 2° by 1° Maidenhead grid locators (**www.arrl.org/locate/gridinfo. html**) anywhere in the world. There are 32,400 of these regions, many rarely traveled, so it is unlikely anyone will "work 'em all" any time soon.

As with the DXCC award, the VHF+ DXer must contact 100 grid locators or "grids" as they're called on the air. With modest equipment, VUCC takes about the same amount of effort as DXCC for an HF DXer. You can find out all about the VUCC program at **www.arrl.org/awards/vucc**.

IOTA and US Islands

It's a rare DXer that hasn't imagined operating from a deserted island under a tropical Sun with the whole world calling in! The *Islands On the Air* program, sponsored by the RSGB (**www.rsgbiota.org**) caters to that imaginative impulse. Island groups are identified by continent, such as NA-001 or OC-050. There are 18 separate IOTA awards, beginning at making contact with 100 different island groups.

Where IOTA only counts "saltwater" islands, the US Islands program (**www.usislands.org**) includes all of the islands in the United States. As you might imagine, some of these can be as difficult to contact as rare DXCC entities! There are a number of special island award programs. Links to the appropriate Web site can be found by entering "ham radio island awards" into an Internet search engine.

DX Contests

Occasionally you will turn on the radio to find the band

crammed full of loud signals from all over the planet. Operators will be exchanging short messages, such as a signal report, contact number or location codes. What's this? It's a DX contest! Some DX contests are of an "everybody works everybody" format — truly a worldwide DX event! Others restrict contacts to those with a specific country, region, or continent. Most focus on a single mode such as CW or phone. (That means the portion of the band for the "other" mode is relatively quiet if you prefer a more relaxed radio environment.) These competitions are almost always open to all operators and encourage contacts with stations that aren't in the competition directly. Listen a little to get a feel for what information is being exchanged and then jump in!

DX contests are a terrific way to make a lot of short QSOs with DX stations, particularly for beginning DXers. For more information on contesting, check out that chapter in this book. There is also a sidebar on contesting and DXing by Wayne Mills, N7NG, elsewhere in this chapter.

PROPAGATION

DXing is an activity that can span several sunspot cycles. The bands will change dramatically as the solar conditions change. While you may eventually discover a "favorite band," the DXer should know how each band works in order to take advantage of what is offered. After all, there's DX to be worked on at least one of the bands almost all the time, whether there are 50 spots on the Sun's disc or none at all. The choice is not whether to chase DX, but on which bands to chase it! Three excellent Web sites for radio propagation information are **www.hfradio.org**, **www.spaceweather.com**, and **dxworld.com**.

While it's important to understand the effects of solar phenomena, the key is to be on the air to find DX signals and put them in your log, no matter if the conditions are good or poor. After all, the DXpedition is going to be on the air and the DX contest will begin regardless of how the bands sound. Read and learn as Bill Kennamer, K5NX, takes us on a tour of each DX band in the following sections.

10 Meters

If you're new to the HF bands, you may be wondering why there is such a fuss about 10 meters. Unfortunately, when sunspots are low as they were when this book was written in 2007, 10 meters is hibernating with only an occasional flash of greatness. That's why it is necessary to know all its propagation well. Of all the HF bands, 10 meters has more propagation modes than any other. Each has its place, depending upon the time of year, time of the sunspot cycle or time of day.

During low sunspots, 10 meters often opens in the *sporadic E* mode. E-layer clouds form rather quickly, and often break up just as fast. While sometimes intense enough to even provide propagation on 20 meters, it is most noticeable on 10 and 6 meters. Openings can be from 1500 to 3000 miles, depending upon whether the cloud is formed well enough to permit one or two hops. Sporadic E often occurs during the summer, and sometimes in mid-winter. Openings can last as long as 24 hours. When this occurs, it's likely to be open all night long. Summertime openings can provide openings to Europe or the Pacific, and can occur at either low or high sunspot numbers. The best seasons are May through early August, and December.

Scatter is another form of 10-meter propagation. Using high power and high antennas, stations from 400 to 800 miles away can be worked, albeit with weak signals. Occasionally the ping of a meteor can be heard or an airplane may be positioned just right, as signal strengths jump suddenly, then fall. Scatter occurs during high sunspot or low sunspot periods.

Another form of scatter involves beaming away from the desired direction. Often called *sidescatter*, this propagation mode can be used by beaming southeast in the morning, and southwest in the afternoon. At the early stages of a sunspot cycle, this is a main propagation path to Europe, open when the direct path never does. It will sometimes seem that all signals come from this one direction. When in doubt about which way to point the beam, this is the mode to try. Don't hesitate to try directions other than the direct path to the DX station!

Backscatter is still another of the scatter modes that can be useful. Sometimes 10 meters is an extreme long distance band. At times like that, it's often difficult to work close-in stations. Backscatter can be used for these situations. To use this mode, *both* stations should point their antennas in the *same* direction. The stations then receive each other's signals as they are reflected from the ground or from the ionosphere itself. The band needs to be somewhat quiet for this to occur. As an example, suppose a station in Texas wants to work a station in Mexico. The Mexican station is working the East Coast or Europe. The Texan's best chance is to turn his antenna in the direction of the stations being worked by the Mexican station.

During periods of high sunspots, the preferred propagation mode is via the F layer. This produces the best long distance propagation of all. Due to the nature of 10 meters and the long skip involved, there is less interference from stations on the same frequency. This can be deceptive, as the DXer is often beaten in pileups by stations he can't hear at all! Still, this is preferable to hearing the pileup hammer his ears and it makes hearing the DX station a lot easier.

As sunspot Cycle 24 begins its upward climb, there will be more and more 10 meter openings. Near the peak of the cycle, during a contest it may well be impossible to find a clear frequency from 28.300 MHz all the way to 29.000 MHz! Band openings during these periods are incredible, although worldwide band openings are somewhat more rare. Yet it is possible to cover the world, and with low power, when conditions are right.

North-south transequatorial propagation is available at almost any time in the sunspot cycle. From North America, it is possible to work Africa, New Zealand, Australia or South America at almost any time of the sunspot cycle. Paths south of 90° or 270° are open weakly throughout most of the sunspot cycle.

With its unique characteristics, 10 meters gets attention from amateurs of all interests. When 10 meters is open again, most of the DX will be here most of the time.

12 Meters

As you might expect, 12 meters closely resembles 10 meters. It is lower in frequency, so it is open more often than 10, but slightly less than 15 meters. If 15 is open, it is worthwhile to try 12. As the sunspot numbers begin to climb, 12 meters will become increasingly popular.

15 Meters

This is somewhat of a transition band. It has many of the

characteristics of 20 meters at times, including possible long path openings, and in addition some of the characteristics of 10 meters. It often provides very long distance openings, and would be a good choice for working Africa in the afternoon during times of moderate to good solar activity. At times of low sunspots, it may not open at all on east-west paths, but is usually open to the south.

Typically 15 opens after sunrise, if it is going to open. At the bottom of the sunspot cycle, openings are likely to be of very short duration. During cycle peaks, openings are likely to last from sunrise to long after sunset. Propagation moves noticeably from east to west, with absorption around local noon often making signal levels go down for a while, only to return later in the afternoon. The band will begin to open to the west as the Sun moves across the Pacific.

At times of high solar activity, 15 meters will provide openings to Asia as late as local midnight. However, at times of low solar activity, the band isn't likely to open to Asia at all, unless the DXer happens to live on the West Coast. When the bands are open, no band provides more access to exotic DX than 15 meters.

17 Meters

Sandwiched between 15 and 20, 17 meters has many of the characteristics of 15 meters. It's lower in frequency, so it's open more often and for longer periods, especially during times of low sunspots. Again, look for morning openings from the east, and evening openings to the west. Tuning down the bands, you will begin to notice more atmospheric noise as you move from 15 to 17 meters.

20 Meters

The undisputed King of the DX bands is 20 meters, which supports long distance propagation at any time of the sunspot cycle. During low sunspots, it's likely to be the *only* band open for DX during the daytime. At sunspot maximums, 20 will be open to somewhere almost 24 hours each day. Almost every form of propagation can be found here.

During the winter, 20 will open to the east at sunrise. The opening will last until stations at the eastern end of the path are past sunset. In the early afternoon, the opening will extend to the south and to the southwest. Early evening should find the band opening to the west to northwest. In the spring and fall, long-path propagation exists, with openings to the east coming from a southwesterly to westerly path just after sunrise, and lasting for several hours. In the evening, the path opens to the southeast. It is not unusual to find long-path openings to areas of the world that are actually stronger than the short-path opening.

Summertime often finds openings to the Far East in the mornings, while European openings continue through the early evening and on into the night. There is always a southern path, extending well into the night after other paths have closed. The band may seem to close, then open up again later, around midnight, on certain paths.

This single band is so productive that more than a few serious DXers restrict their antenna choice to one large monoband 20-meter antenna. All DX operates on 20 meters at some point; it's impossible to be a truly effective DXer without it.

30 Meters

If ever there was a DX band that provided 24 hour DXing at any stage of the sunspot cycle, 30 meters would be it. It shares many of the characteristics of 20 and 40 meters, with long nighttime openings, while providing DX throughout most of the daytime as well. Propagation is hard to describe because of this, as 30 meters can almost be open to anywhere at anytime as the seasons change. The DXer should check this band frequently for some pleasant surprises.

40 Meters

If 20 meters is the King of DX bands, then 40 meters surely must be the Queen. While affected by many of the same conditions as 80, absorption by the D-layer is reduced because of the shorter wavelength, and it becomes possible to work intercontinental DX during the late afternoon. In fact, at the sunspot minimum, it's possible to hear DX all day long, and some of it may be worked if your signals are not absorbed too severely.

In the late afternoon, the band is likely to provide good long path openings to the southeast. Openings are again basically toward the east until well after eastern sunrise. Afterward, the opening will swing south, then toward the west as sunrise approaches. An opening to the southwest is very common in the morning, and stations that would normally be found with a northwest Great Circle path will be found there, with no opening at all to the northwest! An example of this is the USA to Hong Kong path, which will often be open at a heading of 210-225°, rather than the expected 330°.

DXing on 40 meter phone is often difficult because of interference from shortwave broadcast stations located outside ITU Region 1. These megawatt transmitters make sharing the band difficult, if not impossible. This situation is due to begin changing in 2009 as broadcasters begin to vacate their 40 meter frequencies, creating a worldwide allocation for amateurs.

60 Meters

Just as 30 meters shares the characteristics of both 20 and 40 meters, 60 meters features aspects of its adjacent bands, 80 and 40 meters. Currently restricted to a handful of fixed-frequency channels, DX is still occasionally found on this band. DXing is limited because not all amateurs have access to 60 meters in their home countries. Furthermore, the amateur allocation in the US is secondary to government stations. Be careful when transmitting so as not to create unnecessary interference to the primary users! Because of the limitations on 60 meters, DXing is not really encouraged here.

80 Meters

Propagation on 80 meters shares many characteristics with 160 meters, described below. Auroral zones, D-layer absorption, and thunderstorm activities all have limiting effects on this band. It usually begins to open in the early afternoon. The band opening is to the east and will continue until after sunrise at the eastern end of the path, then to the south, finally ending with westerly openings as sunrise approaches.

DXing on 80 meters is seasonal, with better conditions in the wintertime, but with DX still available in the summer. In times of low sunspots, 80 (or 75, as the phone part of the band

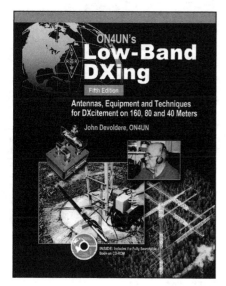

Aficionados of the bands below 20 meters keep a copy of ON4UN's Low-Band DXing handy at all times. It contains detailed information on antennas, propagation and operating for these challenging, but rewarding, bands.

is commonly called) becomes the prime nighttime phone band, as 20 closes and 40 turns into a morass of broadcast stations. While used less often in times of high sunspots, it's still open, although usually later in the evening.

160 Meters

Often called the "Top Band," 160 offers one of the great DX challenges. Openings are sometimes very short in duration, and usually provide shorter distance openings than other bands. During high sunspot levels, the band is open, often with greater intensity. But the Sun's activity causes an increase in noise level, and absorption of signals increases as the D layer, forming at sunrise and dissipating at sunset, is more intense in years of high solar activity. This effect is somewhat lessened during times of low sunspot activity, but for the most part, 160 meters is still a nighttime band. There is even an e-mail reflector dedicated to 160 meter operation: **topband@contesting.com**. It deals exclusively with 160 meter information such as DXing, antennas, propagation and band conditions.

Propagation on 160 begins in the late afternoon to early evening, in the direction of the approaching darkness. As stations in the east approach their sunrise, there will likely be a short but noticeable increase in their signal strength called the *dawn enhancement*. This is the opportunity to work the longest distances. Propagation continues to flow east to west, as the DXer follows the Sun. As the Sun rises, the DXer can expect to work stations to his west until they finally sink into the noise as the D layer begins to absorb the signal again.

Also worth more than a little mention are the auroral zones that are ring-shaped regions centered on the magnetic poles. Charged particles discharged by the Sun follow the Earth's magnetic field and are guided to the magnetic poles. Along with creating the visual displays known as aurora, the particles flowing down through the ionosphere create a vertical region that attenuates signals passing through it. The longer the wavelength, the greater the attenuation. Thus, low band signals are affected more than others by the auroral zones. This will be apparent on northerly paths, as stations in the Yukon and Alaska often report one way propagation where they can hear stations to the south, yet are not able to be heard by them.

Shorter periods of sunlight and less thunderstorm activity make 160 meter propagation better in the fall and winter. Don't overlook possible openings to the Southern Hemisphere in the summer, as the seasons are reversed, and those in the Southern Hemisphere are experiencing their best propagation of the year.

The VHF DX Bands
6 Meters

A DX band? Yes! It can provide some of the most fun DX of any band. Again, many modes of propagation are available, but sporadic E is probably the most popular. Occurring in the spring and early summer, and again in December, sporadic E can provide DX contacts up to 4000 miles, and sometimes more. At the peak of the solar cycle, 6 meters provides worldwide communication via the F layer.

This band is the lowest practical frequency for EME (moonbounce) operations. Stations utilizing four or more high gain antennas and high power have been able to communicate internationally even though the band is closed for other propagation modes. No longer a curiosity, 6 meters is a legitimate DX band. Many stations have DXCC totals well over 100 on this band.

2 Meters

Two meters is also a DX band. Through the use of meteor scatter, many Europeans have earned credits for their Mixed DXCC on 2 meters before upgrading their license and finishing up on the HF bands. However, most DXers who have earned DXCC on 2 meters did so through the use of EME.

Pick a Band, From 160 to 2

This is not a scientific guide to propagation on the DX bands. It is only to alert the DXer to the possibilities of the DX bands and how to use them. The DXer should note the time of day, solar activity, and the direction of the DX, and make a band choice that may give him an opportunity to find the DX. No attempt has been made to fully explain any phenomenon, only to point out that it does exist, and the DXer should plan for the various possibilities. For example, you may have to calculate the Sun's position at the other end of the desired path in order to make a band choice. The important thing to remember is that the DXpedition doesn't usually sit at home waiting for the Sun. So propagation doesn't matter; how to use it does.

Special Propagation
Beacons

Any guide to propagation can only educate so much. The final test is to listen for yourself whenever you can. Don't just watch DX spots roll in off the Internet — tune for yourself! There are many beacon stations around the world that transmit low-power carriers and CW identification to alert stations to band openings.

The best known set of beacons is operated by the Northern California DX Foundation on the 20, 17, 15, 12 and 10 meter bands. Each beacon operates in sequence at a series of power levels so that you can gauge the conditions. Complete information on the beacons is available at **www.ncdxf.org** along with tutorial information about them.

There are also many beacons stations on the 10 meter band

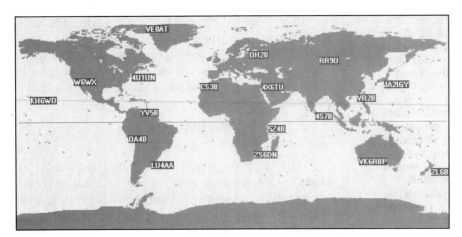

The beacons of the NCDXF/IARU beacon network allow HF DXers to check conditions on the 20, 17, 15, 12 and 10 meter bands from any where in the world.

between 28.190 and 28.225 MHz. When solar flux is low, such as at the bottom of the sunspot cycle, beacons are very useful propagation tools. A list of such stations is available on the Ten-Ten Web site (an organization that promotes activity on 10 meters) at **www.ten-ten.org/beacons.html**.

Long path

Any of the HF bands can support long-path propagation at some point during the sunspot cycle. Because of the extra distance involved, signals are generally weaker and the openings much shorter. Making contacts via the long path is exciting and worth the extra effort.

The conditions that support long-path propagation vary depending on the band. For the "low bands" (those below 10 MHz), long path most often occurs along the gray line (see below) near sunrise and sunset. The openings are short — often just a few minutes. Because of atmospheric noise on these bands, working DX long path usually requires a good location and capable station. Above 10 MHz, long path requires solar illumination instead of darkness so that the MUF (maximum useable frequency) is high enough to support propagation all the way along the route. Watch for long path openings to the southeast in the morning and to the southwest in the afternoon.

Long path most often occurs over paths that pass over the oceans because the lower losses of reflection by salt water keep signal strengths usable at longer distances. A special form of long path is *round-the-world* (RTW) propagation. If you hear an echo of your signal delayed by about 1/7th of a second, your signal may be traveling completely around the Earth!

Gray Line

Because the D layer is the lowest layer of the ionosphere, it remains non-illuminated for longer than the higher layers. Thus, it forms after all the other layers and is the first one to dissipate. The result is a region along the *terminator* — the dividing line between light and dark areas — in which absorption from the D layer is reduced. Propagation along the terminator is called *gray line* propagation. Gray line propagation may be especially useful at the beginning of an opening. A good antenna system and output power will maximize the success of gray line contacts. Use your favorite Internet search engine to locate information

on software that generates gray line maps for the different seasons.

Tropospheric

Although unknown at HF, tropospheric propagation or "tropo" can be a regular source of DX QSOs on the VHF+ bands. Most common at 2 meters and shorter wavelength bands, propagation can occur along discontinuities and weather features in the atmosphere. The two most common sources of tropo are weather fronts and temperature inversions. You can watch for tropo by monitoring the FM broadcast band for signals from distant stations.

DXPEDITIONS

These short-term operations have been mentioned several times so far in this chapter. From the DXer's perspective, they provide an exciting change to the everyday bands. Suddenly there are big pileups on different bands and modes — everyone wants a contact before they shut down! Their QSLs are often spectacular and there may be a video or convention presentation to enjoy. With radios and antennas more compact and efficient than ever, there are more DXpeditions on the air than ever, too! While most active on HF, more and more DXpeditions take gear for 6 meters, even moonbounce!

And what DXer could resist daydreaming about being on "the other end" of the pileup? Hundreds of stations calling, pileups around the clock day and night, thousands of contacts logged at high rates. This could be you! What's to stop you from putting together a small station and hopping on the next plane for somewhere with sandy beaches and not much radio activity? Not much, actually!

This section talks about DXpeditions from both ends — how to work them and the basics of going on one. They are a

Vlad, UA4WHX, has operated extensively from Africa and the Middle East, putting over 310,000 QSOs from 21 countries into the logs of anxious DXers.

A Micro-lite Penguin Point of View on DXing

By Lew Sayre W7EW/W7AT for the Micro-lite Penguins

Years ago, do you remember the excitement and thrill of tuning a band, hearing a weak signal, realizing it was real DX and then working that station? We want that type of experience to remain active for as long as hams are able to propagate their calls around the world.

What is different about the Micro-lite Penguin philosophy of DXing? We think that the onus for working a DX station should be squarely upon the shoulders of the ham who is looking to make the DX contacts. The DX is not responsible for the contact — the ham at home should be responsible! Technology has made it very easy for a radio operator to get on the Internet, scan the spotting systems and see what is currently being spotted. Then that ham can use the computer interface to drive the radios, amplifiers, tuners and antennas to QSO the DX for another step on the DXCC ladder.

How easy is that? Way too easy, in our opinion. This shift to technology makes the operating skill factor much less relevant. Why tune and listen to figure out the DX station's pattern, when you can simply punch the computer button to spread your call repeatedly over the pile-up so that you might get into the DX log?

Human nature places a higher value on something that you have to work for rather than something you are given. Developing the DXing skills, and then applying them to snag that rare DX, makes a QSO much more valuable than working a massive DXpedition signal that anyone could work.

The Micro-lite Penguin philosophy celebrates simple antennas such as verticals and dipoles. We typically use 100 W. That is enough to put a workable signal into any corner of the Earth. We'll use 500 to 800 W on the very low bands because of the nasty QSB and QRM that are prevalent on those frequencies. We are experienced operators who tend to work the weak ones first and the strong ones last. We try not to give advance notice when we embark on a Micro-lite DXpedition. In short, we appreciate the skills it takes to make contact with the DX station and wish to encourage the advancement of the art of DXing.

The rising cost of fuel will make major DXpeditions less frequent. Compared to large, pre-announced expeditions, Micro-lite Penguins carry much less gear — no beam antennas or multiple amplifiers. This means we are much more likely to be putting on a spot rare in the DXing world as compared to different types of DXpeditions where they do everything except turn on your radio for you.

If you've worked VP8THU, VP8GEO, FT5XO or ZL8R you've utilized the philosophy and skills of the Micro-lite Penguins. Developing your skills as a DXer provides better enjoyment and satisfaction during your Amateur Radio activities.

The MicroLite DXpedition team landed on both South Georgia (VP8GEO) and South Sandwich (VP8THU) in 2002. The team travels with small radios and lightweight antennas, relying on the ears of DXers to pull their signals through.

Ralph, KØIR. has been a key player on several major DXpeditions, beginning with the 1995 VKØIR Heard Island operation. Ralph is seen here operating from South Sandwich as VP8THU. (*K5TR photo*)

big part of the spice of DXing — bringing geography home in a way a textbook simply can't.

Working DXpeditions

You won't be able to work DXpeditions unless you know they're on the air. Furthermore, you may have to make arrangements to be on the air at the right time for propagation to your area. After all, the expeditioners aren't going to wait for you to get home from work! Most DXpeditions are 24/7 operations, following the bands with the Sun.

The first thing is to learn about the trip and who is taking it. This is where newsletters and DX Web sites are most helpful. They'll alert you to upcoming expeditions and answer questions such as, when will the operation begin and end? Who are the operators? What bands and modes will they use? Will they be using specific frequencies or will you need to be looking for them? It's a good thing that there are Web sites and newsletters to

provide the information. Write down all the necessary information on paper and post it at your station for easy reference. You might also want to let other family members know that you'll be operating at odd times in pursuit of these rare birds!

You'll find that there is a wide variety in the capabilities of DXpeditions. Some are one-operator holidays with operating time, bands and modes limited to the interests and schedule of the individual taking the trip. At the other end of the scale is the "mega" DXpedition with a dozen operators or more, lots of equipment, continuous operation, and loud signals wherever they choose to tune. These big operations, so to speak, often have supporting resources such as on-line logs and pilot stations that provide feedback and guidance to the expeditioners.

Once the expedition is on the air, listen to the pileups and decide on a strategy. If your station has strong capabilities in that part of the world, you might enjoy jumping in at the beginning. If not, take the opportunity to listen and learn the operating styles being used. You can wait until the pile thins out or try to catch them as they change bands or modes. The risk of waiting is, of course, that something might go wrong — generator failure or a storm — and cause an early shutdown. Toward the end of even the largest expeditions, however, the pileups thin out and it becomes easier to make contact.

Medium Gun DXers may take as a goal to have a single, solid contact in the DXpedition's log on each band and mode in which they have an interest. It's usually not necessary to make several "insurance" QSOs to be sure of having one good one. If the DX sent your call clearly and you were able to hear the entire QSO without confusion as to timing, you should be in the log. If not, make a second QSO. Avoid being one of the "DX hogs" who make duplicate QSOs just because they can. It denies other stations an opportunity to make possibly their first QSO with the expedition and maybe the first ever with that entity! On-line logs are particularly helpful in this regard. Once your call is confirmed, you can relax.

After the expedition is over, be sure to QSL according to the directions of the operators or their QSL manager. Manage your expectations for a quick confirmation. Most DXpeditions give their logs a careful check before responding to QSL requests. Gear has to be unpacked, cleaned, and sorted or shipped. The expedition members have to get their personal lives back in order. QSLs have to be printed. It may be weeks or more likely months before your QSL request is processed. If patience is difficult to come by, get on the air and work some more DX!

During the days of chasing an elusive DXpedition QSO you may become frustrated. The operators may switch to another area just as propagation to yours is building. They may operate on bands with poor propagation to you or spend time on your favorite mode. There may be times when the operator has a hard time controlling the pileup or working stations at a decent rate. At times like this, don't let your frustrations get the better of you. The expeditioners are likely operating under stress. They're hot, cold, thirsty, smelly, being bitten by insects or crabs, and wondering why it was that they sailed, flew, or drove all the way to whatever bizarre location it is. It's your relatively easy job to remain calm and follow their instructions. Give them the benefit of the doubt, since they have gone to great lengths for your benefit.

Going on a DXpedition

It's a rare DXer indeed who hasn't listened to a DXpedition and imagined being at the "other end" with the headphones on, picking out calls one by one from a sandy beach or mountaintop location. Surely, we've all thought, "I could do that!" as we listen to contacts stream by. The answer is that you can certainly give it a try! There is no guarantee of success, of course, but it's a lot easier to be the DX than you might think.

You need to start simple, of course. Good practice is surprisingly easy to come by — operate from an IOTA island or operate from a portable location in the next contest. Read articles or Web sites about the experiences of other DXpedition operators. Learn what gear you require and develop a package of equipment that works. Get used to operating away from your comfortable shack. Become skilled at packing, transporting, deploying, and repacking your equipment.

Once you're ready to become "real DX," choose a reasonable first location. You wouldn't want to try for a really difficult destination on the first time out. Difficulty can mean transportation or licensing. Remember that you'll need all the proper permissions for your operation to count for most award programs! It's best to start at with easier location where licensing and transportation and accommodations are not problem. After a couple of "shakedown cruises" you can set your sights higher. Is your passport up to date? Let's go then!

There are a number of Web sites that can assist you in finding the necessary information. The ARRL Web site has a good section on international licensing at **www.arrl.org/FandES/ field/regulations/io/#us**. One of the better sites is DX Holiday (**www.dxholiday.com**). Not only is there "how to" information on the mechanics of DXing, but on locations around the world for you to browse and select. Don't overlook operators who have operated from your chosen location before. Most are quite willing to help you out by answering questions and even making recommendations or introductions. Soon you'll have airline tickets and your gear packed for the trip!

An alternative to figuring it all out on your own is to join forces with a group making a trip of their own. If one of your club members has gone on DXpeditions, that's a good place to start your inquiries. They may be planning another trip, or know someone who is, and be willing to make an introduction. You can also contact DXpedition operators from teams that have made recent trips, perhaps by approaching them after a presentation. If you're enthusiastic and keep at it, you should be able to eventually find a team in need of another operator. Here's where your practice trips will come in handy as experience the group will value. You'll have to fit in with their plans and style, contributing and assisting as requested. Nevertheless,

---

Operating Permission and Documentation

Once a DXpeditioner starts to get off the beaten track, the issue of operating permission becomes more important. That's particularly for uninhabited locations that may be under some kind of access restriction, such as a wildlife preserve. In many cases, operating permission consists only of the necessary landing permits. For example, some French and American possessions have limited access, but no need for a special license. These destinations will require special landing permission, and it must be in writing from the proper agency. This may be a difficult task, but it is not insurmountable, as proven by the fact that it has been done before. But it may take many letters and a few visits before the goal is accomplished. Nothing difficult is ever easy by definition!

The copies of operating and landing permissions will document that the DXer had permission to be there for the purpose of Amateur Radio. There is a need, however, to further document presence at the location. Documents may consist of transportation receipts, ship's logs or certifications signed by the captain, and pictures of the operators at known locations. Postcards mailed to the DXCC desk from the location, or if that's impossible, from the nearest port, also help document the operation. If there is any doubt as to what constitutes the appropriate documentation for a DXpedition, contact the administrator of the appropriate awards program and find out!

the experience will be invaluable to you.

Describing the process of conducting a DXpedition is well beyond the scope of this book. Every trip is both different and the same, but all require a lot of detailed and painstaking effort to be successful. Start small, work your way up, soak up information from every source available, and someday we'll see your face on the cover of our favorite magazine with a weathered, but happy, smile!

Supporting DXpeditions

As you will find out if you go on a DXpedition, they can be expensive undertakings! To put a team of operators on a rock in the middle of the ocean or on an ice floe near one of the Earth's poles — and get them back home again safely — requires a lot of resources and planning. Recent DXpeditions to some of the rarest islands have operating budgets of more than $100,000! Needless to say, not all of this expense is borne by the operating team. Sponsors are required. Manufacturers often donate or loan equipment to DXpeditions, but that won't pay for a boat!

DXers are encouraged to support the DXpedition by making a donation as requested and encouraging your DX club to do the same. While it is most helpful to donate before the DXpedition hits the airwaves, it is also acceptable to make a donation with your QSL request.

The following are just a few of the organizations that raise money to support DXpeditions and who are themselves supported themselves by the donations of individual DXers: European DX Foundation (EUDXF, **www.eudxf.de**); German DX Foundation (GDXF, **www.gdxf.de**); INDEXA (**www.indexa. org**); Northern California DX Foundation (**www.ncdxf.org**).

CONFIRMING THE CONTACT — QSLING

For DXers who are pursuing awards, confirming the contact is almost as important as the contact itself. The paper QSL has been a part of Amateur Radio and DXing for as long as radio itself has existed. Electronic confirmation systems, such as ARRL's Logbook of the World, complement paper QSLs. In either case, they provide the confirmation that actually proves the contact. After all, without a confirmation the DXer might never know that he or she had worked a pirate or a bootlegger!

Electronic QSLing

Why, in the this 21st century age of instantaneous communication and digital information, are there not systems to confirm a QSO electronically? Why, there are! As of early 2007, the two most-used systems are eQSL (**www.eqsl.cc**) and the ARRL's Logbook of the World (**www.arrl.org/lotw**). Both systems require a registration process and that you upload an electronic copy of your logbook.

Not all awards programs yet accept electronic QSLs. For example, the ARRL does not accept eQSLs for its awards, although Logbook of the World confirmations are accepted. Each system publishes a list of awards for which electronic QSLs are accepted. There are complete instructions for using the system and descriptions of how the system works on their respective home pages.

Electronic QSLs are unlikely to ever completely replace paper QSLs because the experience of exchanging QSLs remains very enjoyable. A collection of paper QSLs built up over

a lifetime contains many beautiful souvenirs. It is likely that DXers will continue to exchange a paper card for initial contacts and use electronic QSLing for subsequent confirmations and for contest QSOs.

Paper QSLs

It's important to realize that a DX station receives a lot more incoming cards than he or she really needs. Therefore, it's really important for DXers to make it easy for their cards to be answered.

First, the card itself should be designed for the convenience of the DX station or QSL manager. After processing 20,000 to 30,000 QSLs, it's easy to understand how a manager could get a little upset with having to hunt for information around the card or on both sides. QSL card design doesn't make the chore totally painless, but can at least prevent the manager or DX station from learning the DXer's call sign in a negative context! So, the QSL card should have all the information on one side only. It should be easy to read, and in a logical order.

There is certain information required on a QSL card that is to be submitted for DXCC credit, the standard for DX awards programs. Confirmation for two-way communication must include the call signs of both stations, the DXCC entity, mode, date, time and the frequency band used. For VUCC, the station's grid square should be included. Desirable information includes the county and if the DXer lives on an island, an Islands on the Air (IOTA) identifier. This way, if DX stations happen to be pursuing awards, they will be able to use the DXer's QSL card for their own purposes.

The card should have the information printed plainly on the card. Avoid optical illusion cards or ones with overly embellished lettering. Save them for non-DX purposes. Plain lettering on a plain card is much better. If a picture card is desirable, it may be better to have the picture on the front and the information in plain print on the back. Print your call on *both* sides of the card. That way the card can be displayed by the DX station, but processed rapidly as well.

There are three ways to get a card to its destination: By bureau, by QSL service and direct mail. Each has its advantages, although there are some differences in the speed. There are also some differences in how a DX station will handle them. The method the DXer uses depends upon his or her own personal requirements.

The ARRL Outgoing QSL Service (see the end of this chapter) provides economical service to the countries that have incoming bureaus. While slow, with turnaround time sometimes exceeding a year or more, still this may be considered an efficient and cost effective method for QSLing. This is especially true when compared with postal pilferage of direct QSLs in some parts of the world. The disadvantages of the bureau system are that in some countries served by bureaus, only the cards of members are delivered. The bureau system is highly recommended when QSLing North and South America, Japan, Europe, Russia and the former CIS entities.

A somewhat faster method is a QSL service, such as the WF5E QSL Service (**www.qsl.net/wf5e**). For a small amount per card, the QSL service will send the cards by the bureau, direct, or to a manager. Cards are returned via the DXer's own incoming bureau unless special arrangements are made. The DXer will notice the cards coming back this way, as they are usually marked with the service's stamp. Turnaround time is improved as cards are sent to bureaus in smaller quantities, and cards are sent to managers with return postage. In some cases, it isn't even necessary to know the manager, as the QSL service keeps track of managers, and will get the card to the right place. The success rate over time with this method is very good.

Direct QSLs

Direct QSLing is used by many DXers. QSLing direct isn't cheap, so be prepared to spend some money if this method is used. Presentation is worth a lot when QSLing direct, so carefully prepare the card and envelopes to maximize the chance of a response. This method is generally best not used for resident amateurs if a bureau is available. The bureau is often more convenient for resident amateurs.

Direct QSLing starts with a good address. Sometimes the station will give a complete address over the air. If not, then one of the call sign lookup sites on the Internet or available by CD-ROM may have the information. Try entering "qsl route" or something similar into your favorite search engine, or visit **www.ac6v.com/callbooks.htm**. The Internet sites often have newer addresses for stations who have recently been active. It is best to get the complete name of the operator, as it is always best that call signs *not* be placed on the envelope.

The envelopes themselves are important. Other countries do not use the same envelope sizes that are commonly found in the United States. This means that using a standard US #10 envelope will create the undesirable situation of sending something through the mail that attracts unwanted attention and possible theft. It is far better to obtain the proper size envelope for the job at hand rather than trying to make do. The best size is a $4\frac{3}{4} \times 6\frac{1}{2}$ inch outer Air Mail envelope, and a $4\frac{1}{2} \times 6\frac{1}{4}$-inch inner Air Mail envelope for returns. If possible, the addresses should be typed directly on the envelope, or printed labels. It is important to remember that *no* call signs should go on the outside of any envelope, again to avoid unwanted attention. The envelope should look as ordinary as possible.

Inside the flap of the return envelope the DXer should put their call and date, time, and mode of the QSO. In the event the card gets separated from the return envelope, it is still possible for the manager to look up the QSO and send the card. Also, either cards or a list of all QSOs made with the station, if a DXpedition, should be sent so that the manager won't have to guess about whether to provide cards for all QSOs found in the log. Chances are the manager *won't* if not asked!

Return Postage

The old saying "The final courtesy of a QSO is a QSL" should be changed to "It is discourteous to send a QSL card *without* return postage provisions." QSL cards aren't cheap these days, with even the cheapest around 5 cents each. As this is written, inside the United States it costs 41 cents for mailing in an envelope or 26 cents without. Multiply this by a thousand, and you'll find that QSLing could easily cost $400 to $500! Make it air mail, and the price jumps even further. Then consider that United States postal rates are among the cheapest in the world, which could put the tab for a thousand QSLs without return postage well over $1000! That's an lot of money for something the DX station likely doesn't need! It should be easy to see why there is poor or no response to cards received without return postage. A word to the wise: If you really want that QSL card, be sure that return postage is provided in whatever form is necessary.

The best way to provide return postage these days is the International Reply Coupon (IRC). They may be obtained from a Post Office, and are redeemable for the lowest Air Mail rate in any Universal Postal Union (UPU) country. IRCs can often be obtained from a QSL manager in the DXer's own country. IRCs purchased this way trade somewhere between the value of new IRCs and the redemption value. At the present, in the US this is around $1.50. IRCs are often available at discount rates from QSL managers.

Be aware that in some countries, the lowest Air Mail rate won't provide enough postage to return an envelope and QSL card. Sometimes it takes two. For example, until recently, Germany's lowest Air Mail rate provided for less weight than the average QSL card and envelope. So it became necessary to go to the next highest rate, and it takes two IRCs to provide enough postage.

Another way to provide return postage is through the use of mint stamps from the DX station or QSL manager's country with sufficient value to provide return postage. This allows the manager to fill out the card and put it in the envelope without converting money or redeeming IRCs. Purchase postage and affix it to the envelope. It also removes the temptation to keep the IRCs or money, returning the card later, if at all. If this method is used, it's best to put the postage on the return envelope so that it may only be used for returning the DXer's cards.

Some DXers prefer to provide return postage by sending

a ubiquitous "Green Stamp", the United States one dollar bill. There are several problems associated with using Green Stamps, not the least of which is mail pilferage. Even mail passing through the US is not immune to it, and in some countries if the envelope is identified as going to an Amateur Radio operator, it is almost certain to disappear. In addition to exchange problems at the country of destination, there are some countries around the world where hard currency is so controlled it is illegal to have US currency.

In other countries, Green Stamps trade much like IRCs; that is, they are not exchanged at all, but traded for the amateur's own QSLing needs. They are often sent with visitors from the US back to the States to buy US postage and forward the cards on from there. One Green Stamp no longer will buy sufficient postage in many countries. So two are required if the DXer expects to get a return. Green Stamps are used mostly for convenience, but the price paid may well be loss of the card.

Preparation is Key

With the QSL card, return postage in whatever form, and envelopes, the DXer is ready to prepare the QSL for mailing. First be sure the QSL is completed properly, with all QSOs made with the station listed on the card. The card should then be inserted into the envelope, which should have the DXer's return address typed or printed on it. Be sure that the country name is the bottom line of the return address. If a Green Stamp or IRC is used, insert that into the return envelope. The idea is to make as flat a package as possible.

If the card is going to an area of high humidity, putting a piece of waxed paper under the return envelope flap can prevent it from sticking together before it is used. All this should then be placed into the outer envelope and sealed. Remember, no call signs or references to Amateur Radio should be on the outer envelope. With some luck, the DXer will see a desired rare QSL coming back in a few weeks or months.

One word about QSL turnaround: Many DXers have much too high an expectation about how fast they should receive QSLs from DXpeditions. It depends upon the operation and whether a special effort is put into quick turnaround, but six months is very reasonable for QSL return. Whereas the larger DXpeditions may have a small army of helpers to complete the QSLing, most smaller DXpeditions depend upon one individual. If an operation made 10,000 QSOs, allowing 3 minutes per card for opening, finding and checking the log entry, writing or attaching a label to the card, inserting the card and sealing the envelope, and obtaining and affixing stamps, figure on the manager handling 100 cards per day. That's five hours per day for 100 days without a break! If the manager also had a full time job and family, you can see where a little time off from this routine would be desired. Allow a minimum of at least six months before even thinking about a second QSL, even if friends are receiving theirs. A card may just have been near the bottom of the pile.

Also, the DXer shouldn't send a request via the bureau at the same time as sending the direct card. QSL managers note all cards received and sent in the log. When they find a DXer using this practice, they make a note of the call sign. The next time, that DXer's card often goes out with the last batch mailed, or through the bureau.

THE ARRL OUTGOING QSL SERVICE

Note: The ARRL QSL Service cannot be used to exchange QSL cards within the 48 contiguous states. All prices in this section are current as of June 2007. For the latest information on this service, check **www.arrl.org/qsl/qslout.html** or via e-mail to **buro@arrl.org**

One of the greatest bargains of ARRL membership is being able to use the Outgoing QSL Service to conveniently send your DX QSL cards to overseas QSL Bureaus. You just need to provide proof of ARRL Membership and include payment following the fee schedule below. The potential savings over sending direct QSL cards with return postage are huge. Your cards are sorted promptly by the Outgoing Service staff, and cards are on their way overseas usually within a week of arrival at HQ. Approximately one million cards are handled by the Service each year!

QSL cards are shipped to QSL Bureaus throughout the world, which are typically maintained by the national Amateur Radio Society of each country. In the case of DXpeditions and/or active DX stations that use US QSL managers, a better approach is to QSL directly to the QSL manager.

How to Use the Outgoing QSL Service

1) Presort your DX QSLs alphabetically by parent call-sign prefix (AP, C6, CE, DL, ES, EZ, F, G, JA, LY, PY, UN, YL, 5N, 9Y and so on with numeric prefixes last). Canadian and Australian cards should be sorted by numerical call sign (VE1, VE2, VE3; VK1, VK2, VK3 etc). Some countries have a parent prefix and use additional prefixes. When sorting countries that have multiple prefixes, keep that entity's prefixes grouped with the parent prefix in your alphabetical stack. For example, G is the parent prefix, but M, 2E, 2I, 2M and 2W cards should be grouped with the G station cards. Use the ARRL DXCC List as your guide to parent prefixes. Addresses are not required. Do not separate cards with paper clips, rubber bands, slips of paper or envelopes.

2) Enclose proof of current ARRL Membership. This can be a photocopy of the address label from your current copy of *QST*, or you can write your membership information from the label on a slip of paper. A copy of your current Membership card is also acceptable.

3) Members (including International Members, QSL managers or managers for DXpeditions) should enclose payment of $5.00 for the first ½ pound of cards or portion thereof — approximately 75 cards weigh ½ pound. One pound costs $10.00 and the fee rate then increases at the rate of $5.00 for each additional ½ pound (a package containing 1.5 pounds of cards is $15.00, and so on). A package of 10 cards or fewer costs only $1.50. For 11 to 20 cards it's $2.50. For 21 to 30 cards, $3.75. Please pay by check (or money order) and write your call sign on the check. Send cash at your own risk. Don't send postage stamps or IRCs. Please make checks payable to The ARRL Outgoing QSL Service. DXCC credit cannot be used toward the QSL Service fee.

4) Include only the cards, proof of membership and fee in the package. Wrap the package securely and address it to the ARRL Outgoing QSL Service, 225 Main St, Newington, CT 06111.

5) Family members may also use the service by enclosing their QSLs with those of the primary member. Include the appropriate fee with each individual's cards and indicate "family membership" on the primary member's proof of membership.

Table 6-1

DXCC Entities Not Served by the ARRL Outgoing QSL Service

A3	Tonga
A5	Bhutan
A6	United Arab Emirates
C2	Nauru
C5	Gambia
C6	Bahamas
CN	Morocco
D2	Angola
E3	Eritrea
E5	North & South Cook Is.
HH	Haiti
HV	Vatican
J5	Guinea-Bissau
J8	St. Vincent
KG4	Guantanamo Bay
KH0	Mariana Is.
KH1	Baker & Howland Is.
KH4	Midway Island
KH5	Palmyra & Jarvis Is.
KH7K	Kure Island
KH9	Wake island
KP1	Navassa Island
KP5	Desecheo Island
P2	Papua New Guinea
P5	North Korea
PZ	Suriname
S0	Western Sahara
S7	Seychelles
S9	Sao Tome & Principe
ST	Sudan
SU	Egypt
T2	Tuvalu
T3	Kiribati
T5	Somalia
T8	Palau
TJ	Cameroon
TL	Central African Rep
TN	Congo
TT	Chad
TY	Benin
V3	Belize
V4	St. Kitts & Nevis
V6	Micronesia
VP2E	Anguilla
VP2M	Montserrat
XU	Cambodia
XW	Laos
XZ	Myanmar
YA	Afghanistan
Z2	Zimbabwe
ZD9	Tristan da Cunha
3B	Agalega, Mauritius, Rodrigues
3C0	Pagalu Island
3C	Equatorial Guinea
3DA	Swaziland
3W	Vietnam
3X	Guinea
4J	Azerbaijan
4W	Timor- Leste
5A	Libya
5R	Madagascar
5T	Mauritania
5U	Niger
5V	Togo
7O	Yemen
7P	Lesotho
7Q	Malawi
8Q	Maldives
9L	Sierra Leone
9N	Nepal
9U	Burundi
9X	Rwanda

6) Blind members who do not receive *QST* need only include the appropriate fee along with a note indicating the cards are from a blind member.

7) ARRL affiliated-club stations may use the service when submitting club QSLs by indicating the club name. Club secretaries should check affiliation papers to ensure that affiliation is current. In addition to sending club station QSLs through this service, affiliated clubs may also "pool" their members' individual QSL cards to effect an even greater savings. Each club member using this service must also be a League member. Cards should be sorted "en masse" by prefix, and proof of Membership enclosed for each ARRL member.

Recommended QSL Card Dimensions

The efficient operation of the worldwide system of QSL Bureau requires that cards be easy to handle and sort. Cards of unusual dimensions, either much larger or much smaller than normal, slow the work. Most cards fall in the following range: Height, 2¾ to 4¼ inches and width, 4¾ to 6¼ inches. Cards in this range can be easily sorted, stacked and packaged. Cards outside this range create problems. Larger cards often cannot be handled without folding or otherwise damaging them. IARU Region 2 (which includes the US) has suggested that 3½ inches height and 5½ inches width are optimum.

Entities Not Served By the Outgoing QSL Service

Approximately 225 DXCC entities are served by the ARRL Outgoing QSL Service. As noted previously, cards are forwarded from the ARRL Outgoing Service to a counterpart Bureau in each of these entities. In some cases, there is no Incoming Bureau in a particular entity and cards therefore cannot be forwarded. However, QSL cards can be forwarded to a QSL manager, for example, ZB2FX via G3RFX. The ARRL Outgoing Service cannot forward cards to the entities shown in **Table 6-1**.

The QSL bureaus in some countries will only forward QSL cards to members of that country's national radio society. That restriction applies to cards bound for Denmark, France, Germany, Hungary, Italy, Japan, Monaco, Norway, Poland, Portugal, Russia, South Africa, Sweden and Zambia.

Additional Information

When sending cards to non-US QSL managers, be sure to clearly indicate the manager's call sign and sort the cards according to the manager's call sign, rather than the station worked. SWL cards can be forwarded through the QSL Service. The Outgoing QSL Service cannot forward stamps, IRCs or cash to the foreign QSL bureaus.

THE ARRL INCOMING QSL BUREAU SYSTEM

Within the US and Canada, the ARRL DX QSL Bureau System is made up of numerous call area bureaus that act as central clearing houses for QSLs arriving from other countries. These incoming bureaus are staffed by volunteers. The service is free and ARRL membership is not required. (Canadian amateurs can use the Radio Amateurs of Canada's incoming QSL bureau.)

How it Works

Most countries have "outgoing" QSL bureaus that operate

in much the same manner as the ARRL Outgoing QSL Service. The members send cards to the outgoing bureau where they are packaged and shipped to the appropriate countries.

A majority of the DX QSLs are shipped directly to the individual incoming bureaus where volunteers sort the incoming QSLs by the first letter of the call sign suffix. An individual may be assigned the responsibility of handling one or more letters of the alphabet.

With the many vanity calls on the air, what bureau should you use? The answer is to use the bureau that handles QSLs for the district represented by the number in your call sign. If your call is NØAX, use the tenth district bureau, no matter where you operate from. If you operate portable or mobile from another district, QSLs will still be sent to your home district's bureau — don't use the "portable" bureau. If you operate from an entity outside the US and it has a bureau, make the necessary arrangements for your QSLs to be mailed to you, otherwise they may be discarded.

Claiming Your QSLs

Check with your incoming bureau to see what procedure they follow. Some incoming bureaus prefer that you send them a supply of self-addressed, stamped envelopes (SASEs), while other prefer that you send money which will be used for envelope and postage credits. Check with your bureau for the preferred method.

In the absence of instructions to the contrary, SASEs should be 5 × 7.5 or 6 × 9 inches. Neatly print your call sign in the upper

left corner of the envelope. Place your mailing address on the front of the envelope. A suggested way to send envelopes is to affix First Class postage for 1 ounce and clip extra postage to the envelope. Then, if you receive more than 1 ounce of cards, they can be sent in a single package. (Check with your local post office for the correct rates.)

Helpful Hints

Good cooperation between the DXer and the bureau is important to ensure a smooth flow of cards. Remember that the people who work in the area bureaus are volunteers. They are providing you with a valuable service. With that thought in mind, please pay close attention to the following DOs and DON'Ts.

DOs

• DO keep self-addressed 5 × 7.5 or 6 × 9 inch envelopes on file at your bureau, with your call in the upper left corner, and affix at least one unit of first-class postage. Or send enough money to keep credits on hand.

• DO send the bureau enough postage to cover SASEs on file and enough to take care of possible postage rate increases.

• DO respond quickly to any bureau request for SASEs, stamps or money. Unclaimed card backlogs are the bureau's biggest problem.

• DO notify the bureau of your new call as you upgrade. Please send SASEs with new call, in addition to SASEs with old call.

• DO include a SASE with any information request to the bureau, or communicate via e-mail or the bureau's Web site.

• DO notify the bureau in writing if you don't want your cards.

• DO inform the bureau of changes in address.

DON'Ts

• DON'T send your outgoing DX cards or domestic US-to-US cards to your call-area bureau.

• DON'T expect DX cards to arrive for several months after the QSO. The process takes time to work. Many cards coming from overseas bureaus are over a year old.

• DON'T send SASEs to your "portable" bureau. For example, NØAX/7 sends SASEs to the WØ bureau, not the W7 bureau.

• DON'T send SASEs or money credits to the ARRL Outgoing QSL Service.

• DON'T send SASEs larger than 6 × 9 inches. SASEs larger than 6 × 9 inches require additional postage surcharges.

Incoming QSL Bureau Addresses

Note that bureaus occasionally change managers or addresses or Web pages. Check the ARRL Web site at **www.arrl. org/qsl/qslin.html** for the latest information.

First Call Area

W1 QSL Bureau
YCCC
PO Box 7388
Milford, MA 01757-7388
This QSL bureau accepts money credits only. No SASEs.

For specific information on the W1 incoming bureau, please e-mail **w1qsl@yccc.org**. This address can also be used to send comments or general questions to the W1 QSL Bureau Manager. See **www.yccc.org/Resources/w1qslburo.htm**.

Second Call Area

ARRL 2nd District QSL Bureau
NJDXA
PO Box 599
Morris Plains, NJ 07950

This bureau accepts money credits only. No SASEs. For detailed information on the W2 Incoming QSL Bureau, please contact Douglas Rue, W2EN, **w2en@njdxa.org**. See **www.njdxa.org/**.

Third Call Area

National Capitol DX Association
NCDXA
PO Box 1149
Clinton, MD 20735-5149

Comments or questions on this bureaus operation may be directed to **NC3DX@arrl.net**. See **www.qsl.net/ncdxa/ncdxa_third_call_area_bureau_revised.html**.

Fourth Call Area

Because of the large number of fourth-district hams, there are two incoming QSL bureaus for this district. One bureau handles single-letter prefixes (K4, N4, W4) and the second handles the remaining two-letter prefix calls.

Single-letter prefixes (K4, N4, W4):
Mecklenburg Amateur Radio Club
Call Box DX
Charlotte, NC 28220

Comments or questions on this bureau's operation may be directed to **k4dxa@bellsouth.net**. See **w4bfb.org/qsl.html**.

Two-letter prefixes (AA4, KB4, NC4, WD4, etc):
Sterling Park Amateur Radio Club
Call Box 599
Sterling, VA 20167

Comments or questions on this bureau's operation may be directed to **rwmaylott@aol.com**. See **www.qsl.net/sterling/QSLBuro4/QSLBuro4.html**.

Fifth Call Area

The ARRL W5 QSL Bureau
OKDXA
PO Box 10
Hobart, OK 73651

Comments or questions on this bureau's operation may be directed to: **k5yaa@okdxa.org**. See **www.okdxa.org/buro**.

Sixth Call Area

ARRL 6th District DX QSL Bureau
PO Box 970
Fairfax, CA 94978-0970

Comments or questions on this bureau's operation may be directed to **kc6awx@arrl.net**. See **www.QSLBureau.org**.

DX Is! What It's All About
By Bill Kennamer, K5NX

"DX Is!" (Hugh Cassidy, WA6AUD)

If it were not for the desire to send a signal over the hill, then over the water, then across the oceans, and around the world, Amateur Radio, or even wireless itself would probably have been dismissed as a useless laboratory phenomenon. But that first DXer, Guglielmo Marconi, put the signals over the hill, across the oceans, and around the world, and the world hasn't been the same since. It isn't an overstatement to say that worldwide communication owes everything to DXing, and to Marconi, the original DXer and DXpeditioner.

The history of DXing is long and varied. Of course it starts with those early efforts of Marconi, who very early turned to commercial development. It continued with amateurs whose experimentation allowed them to work stations farther and farther away. But the real dream was to bridge the oceans. The ARRL had a part in that dream. At the Board of Directors meeting at the first National

The birthplace of Guglielmo Marconi is now the home of the Guglielmo Marconi Foundation station IY4FGM. While never licensed as an amateur, Marconi keenly appreciated and understood their drive to span ever greater distances via radio.

Convention in Chicago in 1921 Traffic Manager Fred Schnell presented a plan that would give the best possible chance for radio signals being heard across the Atlantic. For the transatlantic receiving test scheduled in the late fall, Paul Godley, 2XE, considered to be the foremost receiving expert in the United States at the time, and a member of the ARRL Technical Committee, was dispatched across the Atlantic with his best receiving equipment. Setting up in a tent on the coast of Scotland, Godley began his tests. By December 7, 1921, he was ready. Tuning across the bands, he began to hear a spark signal on 270 meters. The operator's call sign, 1AAW, was clearly heard! (But 1AAW turned out to be a pirate! Even at the beginning pirates were one of the hazards of DXing.) The signals of more than 30 American amateurs were heard during this series of tests, waiting only for a two-way contact to be completed.

Even then, the experimenting and modernization spurred by a desire for better DX performance was apparent. Godley reported that of the signals heard, over 60% had used CW rather than spark, and with less power. The death knell for spark had been sounded, and the future of tube transmission was ensured. All because of the desire for DX.

In late 1921 and early 1922, Clifford Dow, 6ZAC, located in Hawaii, heard signals from the western United States. He announced this in a letter to *QST*, and said if he could get some transmitting equipment, he believed he could make it across the Pacific. A group from the West Coast sent him the needed transmitter, and two-way contact was established on April 13, 1922, between Dow and 6ZQ and 6ZAF in California. Thus was yet another tradition of DXing established, that of providing equipment to activate a "new one."

Léon Deloy, 8AB, of France, had participated in the transatlantic tests of early 1923. His signal had been one of several heard by US amateurs, but no two-way communication resulted. During the summer, he studied American receiving methods, and even came to Chicago for the National Convention. He returned to France with American receiving equipment, determined to be the first to make the transatlantic crossing.

After setting up and testing, by November Deloy was ready. He cabled ARRL Traffic Manager Schnell that he would transmit on 100 meters from 9 to 10 PM, beginning November 25. He was easily heard. By November 27, Schnell had secured permission for use of the 100-meter wavelength at 1MO and the station of John Reinartz, 1XAM. The two of them waited for Deloy.

For an hour Deloy called and sent messages. Then he signed. The first DX pileup began as Schnell and Reinartz both called. Deloy asked Reinartz to stand by, and worked first Schnell and then Reinartz for the first transatlantic QSOs. The age of DXing had finally truly begun.

From these small beginnings, to the later exploits of such as Bill Huntoon, Danny Weil, Gus Browning, Martti Laine, and groups that travel to lonely islands and mountain kingdoms, DXing has grown. While the early days were marked by exploration and discovery, we now recognize that we have the equipment, power and antennas to hear a pin drop on the other side of the world and respond to it. While some discovery is still involved, and that mostly on the VHF/UHF bands, for most of us DXing takes the form of Radiosport at its zenith, a ritual of great importance to some, and a source of friendship and occasional enjoyment to others. DX Is!. . .no doubt about it, the essence of Amateur Radio.

Not for nothing is tiny Scarborough Reef (BS7H) known as "Scaffold Reef"! Bob W6RGG is shown operating from one of the four exposed rocks during the 2007 BS7H expedition, giving many DXers the QSO they need to have "worked 'em all!" (*photo courtesy W6RGG*)

Seventh Call Area

Willamette Valley DX Club Inc
PO Box 555
Portland, OR 97207

Comments or questions on this bureau's operation may be directed to **w7qsl@cs.com**. See **wvdxc.org/dotnetnuke/QSLBureau/tabid/59/Default.aspx.**

Eighth Call Area

8th Area QSL Bureau
PO Box 307
West Chester, OH 45071-0307

Comments or questions on this bureau's operation may be directed to **k4zle@arrl.net**. See **www.greatlakes.arrl.org/gldburo.html.**

Ninth Call Area

Northern Illinois DX Assn.
PO Box 273
Glenview, IL 60025-0273

Comments or questions on this bureau's operation may be directed to **k9qvb@sbcglobal.net**. See **qsl.nidxa.org**.

Tenth Call Area

WØ QSL Bureau
PO Box 907
Florissant, MO 63032

Comments or questions on this bureau's operation may be directed to **ac0n@arrl.net**. See **www.zeroburo.com**.

Hawaii

KH6 QSL Bureau
Big Island ARC
Attn: Barbara Darling
PO Box 1938
Hilo, HI 96721-1938

Comments or questions on this bureau's operation may be directed to **nh7fy@yahoo.com**.

Alaska

Alaska QSL Bureau
PO Box 520343
Big Lake, AK 99652

Comments or questions on this bureaus operation may be directed to **trygve@mtaonline.net**. There is no Alaska Bureau Web page at this time.

Puerto Rico

Puerto Rico QSL Bureau
PO Box 9021061
San Juan, PR 00902-1061

Comments or questions on this bureaus operation my be directed to **kp4wi@arrl.net**. There is no Puerto Rico Bureau Web page at this time.

US Virgin Islands

Virgin Islands QSL Bureau
PO Box 25782
Christiansted, St Croix

US Virgin Islands, VI 00824

Comments or questions on this bureau's operation may be directed to **kp2yl@arrl.net**. There is no US Virgin Islands Bureau Web page at this time.

Guam

Guam QSL Bureau
Marianas Amateur Radio Club
PO Box 445
Agana, Guam 96932

Comments or questions regarding this Bureau may be directed to Danny Pobre, KH2JU, **Pobre@guam.net**. There is no Guam Bureau Web page at this time.

All US SWL Calls

SWL QSL Bureau
Mike Witkowski, WDX9JFT
4206 Nebel St
Stevens Point, WI 54481

DXING HISTORY

For a DXer to truly appreciate the awards and achievements of the DXing community, it is necessary to also appreciate the long history of DXing with the Amateur Radio tradition.

With the explosion of interest in ham radio during the 1950s came a corresponding interest in DX. Sunspot Cycle 19 peaked in 1959 — the most intense cycle on record. Hams were working DX with a few watts and a bit of wire thrown out the window! With all that DX to be worked came legendary call signs still discussed in reverent tones today. As a beginning DXer, you will enjoy knowing more about these ham radio icons, all Silent Keys. Here is a little information (only a little!) about these historic figures. Entering their call signs into an Internet search engine will provide hours of entertaining reading — perfect while waiting for that New One to appear on the bands!

• **Gus Browning, W4BPD**: Gus hailed from South Carolina and activated quite a number of rare countries in the early and mid-1960s. He is best known for being the first to activate Bouvet Island (LH4C in 1962), but was a legendary solo DX-peditioner.

• **The Colvins: Lloyd, W6KG and Iris, W6QL**: The Colvins traveled extensively through the 1960s, 1970s and 1980s, operating from well over 100 DXCC entities! Their QSL collection numbered well over one million cards.

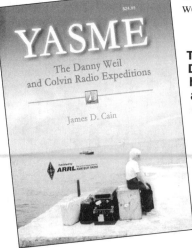

The adventures of Danny Weil, VP2VB, as he sailed the Yasme around the world are chronicled in this detailed book by Jim Cain, K1TN. Sponsored by the YASME Foundation, Jim also tells the story of the Colvins (Lloyd, W6KG, and Iris, W6QL), two very famous call signs in DX history.

Lloyd and Iris set up the YASME Foundation (**www.yasme. org**), whose mission is to further Amateur Radio DXing.

• **Bob Dennison, WØDX/VP2VI**: At one time an ARRL President and indisputably the father of the DXpedition, Bob started with an expedition to the Bahamas in 1948 as VP7NG. He was the first to activate Clipperton Island (FO8X) and other previously inactive countries.

• **Ernst Krenkel, RAEM**: That's no error in the call sign, Ernst was the only amateur ever to hold a call without a number. He received that call as recognition for his efforts as the radio operator of a Russian polar expedition in 1938, saving the lives of more than 100 explorers adrift on an ice floe. It is for Ernst that the RAEM series of contests and awards are named.

• **Charlie Mellen, W1FH**: Mellen was the first to achieve DXCC after WWII, obtaining Mixed-Mode and Phone certificates #1. His competition with Don Wallace W6AM (see below) to stay atop the DXCC listings ran for decades. He had the highest total of DXCC entities worked of any operator.

• **Katashe Nose, KH6IJ**: An operator of extraordinary skill, Katashe was for many years the best-known and most-heard station from the central Pacific. He was a dominant figure in DXing and DX contesting through the 1980s.

• **Stew Perry, W1BB**: 160 meters was considered too local a band for DXing but W1BB demonstrated that it was just a matter of education and technique. Stew (for whom the Stew Perry Topband Distance Challenge contest is named) almost single-handedly opened up the 160 meter band and coined the phrase "The Gentleman's Band."

• **Don Wallace, W6AM**: It was Don who made the rhombic antenna famous with his 120 acre "farm" of 16 full-sized rhombics, each usable in either direction. Second only to W1FH (see above), Don set the standard for DXing from the West Coast.

• **Danny Weil, VP2VB**: While sailing around the world, Danny activated many rare DXCC entities and made over 100,000 contacts up until his final expedition to Wallis Island (FW8FW) in 1963. It is his sailboat, *Yasme*, for whom the YASME Foundation is named.

For more historic information on DXing, you are encouraged to read Clinton DeSoto's *200 Meters and Down*. DeSoto created the concept of the DXCC program in the 1930s. To learn more about post-WWII DXing, *YASME — The Danny Weil and Colvin Radio Expeditions* by Jim Cain, K1TN, is an excellent source of biographical information about some of the major figures on the DX scene through the 1980s. Cain also annotates all of the W6KG/W6QL and VP2VB expeditions. If you can find a copy, *Don C. Wallace, W6AM, Amateur Radio's Pioneer* by Jan Perkins, N6AW, bridges the gap between DeSoto and Cain quite nicely.

RESOURCES FOR DXERS

Books and Magazines

• *The Complete DXer* by Bob Locher, W9KNI — an excellent tutorial to turn a Little Pistol into a Medium Gun. Available from Idiom Press, **www.idiompress.com**.

• *Up Two!* by Roger Western, G3SXW — stories of G3SXW and his many one- and two-man DXpeditions to rare spots around the globe. Available from Idiom Press.

• *The ARRL DXCC Handbook* by Jim Kearman, KR1S — tips, techniques and encouragement for those chasing DXCC. Available from the ARRL Bookstore.

• *Where Do We Go Next?* By Martti Laine OH2BH — the personal history of one of modern Amateur Radio DXing and contesting's towering figures. Available from the CQ Bookshelf, **www.cq-amateur-radio.com**.

• DX columns are included each month in *QST*, *CQ Magazine*, and *WorldRadio* magazines.

DX Clubs

• A list of links to DX club Web sites around the world is available from **www.ac6v.com/clubs.htm#DX**.

• To find local or regional DX clubs affiliated with the ARRL, check **www.arrl.org/find-a-club**.

DX Awards

• For a comprehensive list of links to Amateur Radio awards, primarily DX oriented, **visit www.ac6v.com/ hamawards.htm**.

• A Web site devoted to awards, including K1BV's directory of more than 3000 Amateur Radio awards, can be found at **www.dxawards.com**.

DX News Services

• *The Daily DX,* **www.dailydx.com**
• *QRZ DX* and *The DX Magazine,* **www.dxpub.com**
• *425 DX Bulletin,* **www.425dxn.org**
• *OPDXA Bulletin,* **www.papays.com/opdx.html**
• New Jersey DX Assn *DX Reflector,* **www.njdxa.org/ dx-tools/dx-news.php**.

chapter 7

Contesting —
Competitive Wireless

Sorting through the mail, one large envelope stood out, white with green stripes around the edges, marked "Do Not Bend." It was from Newington, Connecticut, although nothing had been ordered from the ARRL. The letter opener's work done, fingers reached inside and pulled out…a certificate! First Place, Missouri, Low-Power, Mixed-Mode in the ARRL 10 Meter Contest! That the contest had been entered was almost forgotten, the log submitted as an afterthought. That cold and snowy December Saturday made the ham shack and coffee a lot more inviting than outside chores. The 10 meter band had been full of signals with one contact leading to another and then maybe a few more states could be worked and maybe get some of those DX stations and…wow, *a certificate*? It *had* been a lot of fun, but who would have thought of it being a winning entry? What contests are going on this weekend?

Across town, just a couple of weeks before, a flat, heavy box from ARRL Headquarters had been delivered to a residence sporting a tower and beams in the back yard. Waiting on the kitchen table, it was immediately spotted and opened with gusto. Removed from the protective packing, there it was — a gleaming brass plate on a dark walnut panel. The ARRL November Sweepstakes plaque read, "First Place, Midwest Division, High-Power, Phone." As light played across the polished surface, it was a dream come true. That previous November weekend, from the moment the clock rolled over to 2100Z signaling the start of the contest, everything had gone just right. The "clean sweep" of all 80 sections had been logged before midnight with a pair of VE8 stations a particularly good omen. Of

course, neighboring Arkansas had to have been the final section! After years of practice and station improvements and suffering through Murphy-bites, at last the goal had been reached. Could the Top Ten be reached this year? With the plaque mounted over the operating position, it just might!

It wasn't long before the plaque was delivered that two friends were comparing notes from the just-completed ARRL International DX Contest. In the shadow of the Gateway Arch, making their way through plates of toasted ravioli and marinara, the conversation jumped from topic to topic. "How did you work S92SS so quick? When I got there the pileup was a mob, but I heard 'em give your call and you were outta there!" "Oh, Charles likes to listen up about half a kilohertz — it works every time. So what's up with your 80 meter mults? You got me by at least 10!" "Yeah, that new pair of half-slopers really works — a lot better than the old inverted-V they're made from, ha ha! Were you able to run much or was it pretty much search-and-pounce like last year? Quit hoggin' the breadsticks." "Sometimes I could run. If I found a hole while I was tuning, I'd call CQ and got up to a 60 rate once or twice. You?" "I couldn't hold a frequency on 20, but I got to 15 at just the right time and had a real nice hour from about 1430Z or so. Did your rig give you any trouble this time?" "Nope, got it fixed. Found a flaky connector on my keying interface and that was the whole problem. The new version of the logging software was great." "Oh, that automatic band mapping? Yeah, it really helped!" And so on, comparing triumphs and failures, two friends motivating each other to do a better job with every competition, regardless

The HC8N contest station is one of the top-scoring stations in the world, holding several record scores from its equatorial location directly south of the US. In this photo, NØAX is working 20 CW in the background, while K9NW (center) and KM3T work on the 15 meter pileups.
(N6TV photo)

There's nothing like the first DX contest as shown by the smile on W5AN's face assisted by Bruce, AA5B, as contest "Elmer." (Bob Ayre, N5LVR photo)

of who comes out ahead.

There are many reasons to engage in contesting, also known as *radiosport* around the world. Just as there are many levels of athletes, from the occasionally engaged to the devoted aficionado, so does contesting attract many types of entrants. For some hams, contesting is their primary interest. They build highly capable stations, travel thousands of miles to desirable locations or assemble a skilled team of master operators. Most contesters, whether they are on the air for an hour or a weekend, operate just for the pleasure of reaching out and touching so many other hams in so many other places so quickly.

Along with the most common phone and CW contests, there are plenty of specialty contests intended to foster interest and activity from a particular region, in a specific mode or as a style of operating. There is a contest featuring every state (these are usually called "QSO Parties"). Other contests feature the VHF+ bands and even here some specialty contest themes include EME, meteor scatter or the new digital modes tailored for those bands. On the HF bands, contesting on RTTY and other digital modes is growing rapidly and there are contests for contacting everything from islands to lighthouses to countries. On both VHF+ and HF, short contests known as *sprints* are becoming more popular all the time.

Contests are held throughout the year. Looking to work some DX to build up your totals? The major DX contests are the ARRL International DX Contest, with the CW weekend in February and Phone in March; the IARU HF World Championships in July; and the CQ World Wide DX Contest, which holds its Phone weekend in October and CW weekend in November. If you are chasing states for your Five-Band WAS award, you should be checking out the ARRL November Sweepstakes. The CW weekend is always the first weekend and Phone the third weekend in November.

COOPERATION

Every contest has something for all levels of hams and something unique in almost all of sport — cooperation! To succeed in contesting, participants must cooperate with each other as they make contacts. Even archrivals need to put each other in the log! The best contesters are those who have figured out

Contesting History

Contests have their genesis in the early days of message handling when the ability to relay messages quickly and accurately was the hallmark of a good operator. Even in the days of spark, there were a number of exercises that attempted to move messages across the country as quickly as possible. The signature of message handling is writ large across contesting today. Many of today's top operators got started as traffic handlers in the National Traffic System (NTS). If you look at the information exchanged during the ARRL Sweepstakes — number, category, call, check and section — you'll recognize the header of an ARRL Radiogram. The characteristics of a good traffic handler remain the attributes of a top contester: accurate, efficient, flexible, capable.

The first formal on-the-air competition was the 1927 International Relay Contest, sponsored by the ARRL as an extension to the annual "tests" in which stations attempted to make contact with stations outside the US and Canada. This event has changed names several times, growing into the ARRL International DX Contest we know and love today. The need also grew for a *domestic* contest emphasizing shorter distances within the North American continent. The result was the creation of the ARRL Sweepstakes contest in 1930. Contesting on the VHF and higher bands got its start in 1948 and the first radioteletype contest was held in 1957.

Contest History Who's Who

W9IOP, Larry LeKashman — In the late 1950s and early 1960s, ARRL Sweepstakes was the contest and W9IOP's call sign was never far from first place (as was W2IOP in previous years). Later a president of ElectroVoice, W9IOP is also famous for his pre-PC "Second Op" operating aid.

W4KFC, Vic Clark — His yearly Sweepstakes battles with W9IOP were the stuff of legend. Vic was a master contester and pioneered the use of two separate sets of equipment to make better use of available time. A past president of the ARRL (1982-83), Vic was also a Big Gun in DXing.

K2GL, Buz Reeves — Buz single-handedly created the multi-operator, multi-transmitter category of operating with a superb station and a crack team of operators. For years, K2GL was the standard setting station, inspiring present-day operations such as KC1XX, K3LR and W3LPL.

W7RM, Rush Drake — W7RM brought competitive multi-multi operating to the Northwest, building a station at Foulweather Bluff known not only for signal strength, but the ability to hear well. His teams of operators include many top West Coast contesters active today.

LU8DQ, Jorge Humberto Bozzo — Widely considered one of the best CW operators of all time and certainly the best ever from South America, Jorge held four world records and had won every major contest at least once.

Why Contest?

By Dan Henderson, N1ND

Why does it seem there is always a contest on the air? Almost every IARU national society sponsors at least one event during the year. Generally intended to achieve the same goals as ARRL contests, they promote activity among the licensed amateurs in those countries and encourage the development of operating skills. You can also find listings of upcoming contests monthly in *QST*, linked from the ARRL Contest Branch homepage (www.arrl.org/contests) and at the on-line contest calendars listed in the Resources section of this chapter.

What inspires normally mild-mannered hams to develop a "warrior" mentality during contest weekends? There are no cash prizes or awards. What causes even casual operators to join the crowd during certain times of the year? What motivates otherwise normal operators to plan a year in advance to build and erect new antennas, add station equipment and clear time to participate in these on-the-air events?

Thousands of hams in the US and around the globe spend some time during the year contesting. Why go to the effort? The answers to that are as varied as their operators. There is no single reason, but most responses will fall into one of several categories.

Honing Operator Skills

Contesting is a great way to develop and hone operating skills. Contests require accuracy on both the sending and receiving side. With modern computer techniques to verify contacts made in a contest, accuracy and thoroughness are requirements to be a top-flight contester. Where do you find these operators in emergencies? They can be found using their experience and stations to assist with emergency traffic and communications. Many of the top contesters hold ARRL Field Organization appointments, placing their talents at the disposal of communities in crisis.

Demonstrating Use of Amateur Frequencies

Contesting, especially on the VHF, UHF and microwave bands, is a valuable means of demonstrating the use of our frequencies and the need to preserve allocation of those parts of the radio spectrum. In today's age of frequency auctions and increasing commercial demand for spectrum, activity on the higher amateur bands provides a good argument for protecting and preserving our allocation. By encouraging the use of microwave bands during contest periods and providing an increased, concentrated period of activity during contest weekends, contesting increases both our use and knowledge of this valuable radio spectrum.

Advancing Amateur Technological Development

Contesting has been the inspiration for some of the technological advances during recent years. Many hams today use spotting networks as a regular part of their daily station operation. From spotting rare DX to putting out the word about band openings on 6 and 2 meters, these networks are an important part of amateur activity. But how many hams know that the original PacketCluster was created to allow contesters to "spot" contest multipliers? From antenna designs and station enhancements to integration of computer technology in the shack, you can see the work of members of the contest community in many areas of technological improvements in the hobby.

It's Fun!

Despite the value of technological advancements and developing operating skill, maybe the best reason amateurs contest is the simplest: it's FUN! Whether they are running stations at a rate of 120 per hour during the ARRL International DX Contest or experimenting with earth-moon-earth communications during the annual ARRL EME Competition, thousands of hams annually use contesting as their outlet to enjoy the hobby. The invested hours of study to earn your license and the dollars you spend in building and improving your shack and equipment come back to you with the rewards of enjoying a successful contest.

how to cooperate most effectively with the largest number of other hams. It is not enough to have just the strongest signal or the fastest fist. The tension between competing and needing to cooperate makes radiosport difficult enough to be interesting, but not so difficult that strategy and skill can't win the game.

That richness of possibilities brings a wide variety of operators to the ham bands during a contest. During an hour's tuning or calling, you'll encounter every level of ham from one just getting started to an expert who has been at the top of the heap for 50 years or more. Browsing the scores takes you to every corner of the Earth and from grade schoolers coached by a parent in Kids Day to old-timers startling the operator at the other end by sending a Sweepstakes check (the year first licensed) in the 1930s. So it doesn't matter that you're not super skilled or just getting started. Jump in and discover the possibilities of competitive wireless!

Coexisting With Contests

Is contesting allowed everywhere on the amateur bands? Sometimes it sure sounds like it! In reality, there are plenty of kilohertz without contest activity. On the HF bands, by general agreement there is no contest activity on 60, 30, 17 or 12 meters. On the VHF+ bands, almost all contest activity takes place in the so-called "weak signal" segments at the lower edge of the bands.

Of the larger contests, very few allow operation on more than one mode, so you'll just find normal activity on the other portion of the band. Even though there may be more than one contest scheduled during a weekend, most are small enough that activity is clustered around a handful of frequencies. If you choose not to participate, tune around or change bands and you'll likely be able to avoid contest activity. Just as planning ahead in real life avoids frustration, there are plenty of contest

Contesting — Competitive Wireless 〉 **7-3**

calendars to check for potential conflicts with your favorite non-contest activity.

Just because a contest is going on doesn't mean other contacts can't be made, either! Even during the biggest contests, you'll hear non-contest QSOs taking place — how do they manage so well? The key is to make the most of your station's capabilities, primarily the receiver. Most receivers are very sensitive — too sensitive for a band full of big contest signals. Turn down the RF gain, turn off the preamp and noise blankers and maybe add a little attenuation. Help your receiver operate linearly and you may be surprised at how clean the band sounds as a result! If you have a rotatable antenna, you may be able to point it in a direction that minimizes QRM, but leaves plenty of signal for a comfortable QSO. Remember, you're trying to maximize the ratio of signal to noise plus interference, not necessarily the absolute signal level. Choosing frequencies towards the high end of the band segment, away from the lower portions where signals are stronger, will also help. There are usually plenty of opportunities to coexist with a contest.

CONTESTING BASICS

So what is a contest anyway? If you encounter someone calling "CQ Contest" on the air, what should you do? If you've found a contest that looks interesting, how can you determine the proper way of operating? Let's start with the basics.

The Contest QSO

A contest is a competition between stations to make as many contacts as possible according to the theme of the contest within the time period defined by the contest rules. Each contact will be as short as possible, while satisfying the rules of contest. Remember, this is a competition so what constitutes a contact is different than during regular day-to-day operating. During a contest, include a minimum of non-contest information.

Each contact consists of five steps that are just like a regular contact, but greatly abbreviated:
- One station calls CQ (CQing is known as *running*).
- A caller responds to the CQ.
- The CQing station acknowledges the call sign of calling station and sends the required information.
- The caller acknowledges receiving the information and sends information back in return.
- The CQing station acknowledges receiving the caller's exchange and ends the contact.

At any point, should one of the stations not receive a call sign or exchange properly, the information is repeated until received correctly. We'll go over that process later in this section.

The Contest Exchange

During each contact, specific information must be exchanged and logged. This information is called your *exchange*. In some contests, the exchange is very simple. For example, in the North American QSO Party contests, the exchange is your name and state, province or country. (Because "state, province or country" is so commonly used in contesting, it is often abbreviated SPC or S/P/C.) ARRL November Sweepstakes, mentioned earlier, has a lengthy exchange. Most contests keep the exchange simple, beginning with signal report (RST) and

adding other information in line with the contest's theme. Here are some common types of information you'll find in contest exchanges:
- *ITU or CQ Zone* — there are 88 ITU (**www.iaru.org/ituzonesc.gif**) and 40 CQ Zones (**www.cq-amateur-radio.com/wazrules.html**).
- *Serial Number* — the number of the contact in the contest. For your fifth contact, your serial number would be 5 (sometimes sent as 05 or 005 for clarity).
- *Name* — just your first or most common name. Nicknames are acceptable.
- *Member Number* — for contests sponsored by an organization, this is the membership number of the control operator.
- *Power* — up to three digits specifying your transmitter power ("KW" or "kilowatt" is sometimes sent instead of "1000"). Some operators don't add the "W" since that is understood.
- *Location code or abbreviation* — for contests that target a specific country or region, this is an abbreviation (such as "TN" for Tennessee in contests that use states) or numeric identifier. It can also be an abbreviated county name, ARRL section or a grid square in VHF+ contests. The contest sponsor Web site will define these exactly.

There are other types of information that might be needed in a contest exchange, but these cover most contests. When in doubt, check the contest sponsor's Web site.

If you encounter a contester calling CQ, but don't know the exchange information, just ask "What do you need?" or on CW or digital "INFO?". The CQing station will respond with something like, "I need your number and ARRL section" or on CW "PSE NR ES ARRL SEC." If it's your first contact in the contest and you live in the Pittsburgh, Pennsylvania, area you would respond "You're my number 1 in Western Pennsylvania" or on CW "NR 1 WPA." That's it! Contesters want and need your QSO, so don't hesitate to ask them for help with the QSO.

One common question from new contesters is "Why are signal reports always 59 or 599?" During a non-contest QSO, accurate signal reports help both stations gauge the clarity of

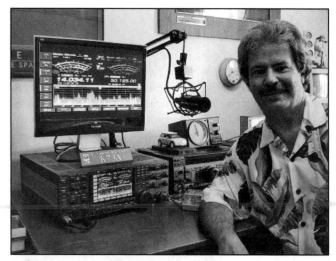

Well-known contester, Chip, K7JA, operates from his suburban Los Angeles QTH when not on a contest expedition to the Caribbean.

communications during the QSO. Since contest QSOs are so short, typically 10 seconds or less, there is little need for an accurate report. If the contester can hear you, 59 or 599 is just as good as any other report and removes uncertainty from what is sent. It also cues you to mentally prepare to copy the rest of the exchange. On CW, most contesters send 599 as 5NN. The "N" is a form of *cut number* where an abbreviation for a numeral is sent to save time. Other common cut numbers are "A" for 1 and "O" or a dash for zero. You are expected to convert the cut number character to a real numeral when you enter it into your log, even a computer log.

Contest Scoring

The final score is a combination of the total number of contacts and the number of contacts with different locations or attributes, according to the theme of the contest. The usual calculation begins with adding up points from each contact, called *QSO points*. The total is then multiplied by the sum of the different locations or attributes, called *multipliers*. Since each contest has a different system (*vive la difference!*), check the sponsor's rules to compute your score.

All contacts may have the same QSO point value or the points may vary by band or distance or mode. Here are some examples:

• *North American QSO Party* — each contact counts for 1 point.

• *ARRL 10 Meter Contest* — phone contacts count for 2 points and CW or digital contacts 4 points. Contacts with Novice or Technician stations on CW count 8 points.

• *CQ World Wide DX* — contacts between stations on different continents are worth 3 points. Contacts between stations in different countries on the same continent count for 1 point, except contacts between stations in different North American countries count for 2 points. Contacts within one's own country do not count for points, but can count for multiplier credit.

• *Stew Perry Topband Distance Challenge* — points for each contact are calculated based on the distance between the stations.

Multipliers are really the spice of the contest! If contesting were just about working a large number of stations, it would be a rather simple game and quickly lose its novelty. When the requirement to make contacts with special stations or locations is added, things begin to get really interesting. For example, a station might have a "pipeline" to Japan. If all of the contacts count for the single JA country multiplier, would it be better to work stations from Europe at a slower rate, but pick up many more country multipliers? Is it better to call CQ in the ARRL 160 Meter Contest and hope that stations from the different ARRL and RAC sections respond or should you go looking for them? There are many aspects to consider, with the capabilities of one's station and propagation being the most important.

Check the rules for each contest to find out how multipliers are defined and then go hunting! You'll want to know if each multiplier counts only once or whether you can count multipliers from each band or mode. For example, in the ARRL Sweepstakes each section counts once and only once — you can work a maximum of 80 section multipliers. In the ARRL DX Contest, though, each different DXCC entity counts as a separate multiplier on each band. There may be different types

of multipliers besides locations. The IARU HF Championship also recognizes stations operating from IARU radio society headquarters as multipliers.

Along with QSO points and multipliers some contests offer special bonus points or power multipliers. Many state QSO parties (contests that require contacts with a specific state or states) have bonuses for working the sponsor's club or other special stations. Power multipliers are applied after the basic score is calculated, but before bonuses are added. The QRP Amateur Radio Club International contests, for example, multiply the score by 10 if the output power is 1 W or less! As always, check the sponsor's rules for the exact scoring.

Typical Rules

Now that you're familiar with the basic ideas behind contesting, let's take a close look at a typical contest rule summary that might be found in a newsletter or on a Web site. Here's the listing for the CQ WPX SSB Contest, held at the end of March every year with reference numbers ([#]) added:

CQ WW WPX Contest — SSB, sponsored by CQ Magazine from [1] 0000Z Mar 24 - 2400Z Mar 25 (CW is May 26-27). Frequencies: [2] 160 – 10 meters. Categories: [3] SOAB, SOSB, SO-Assisted, HP, LP and QRP, MS (10-min rule), M/2, MM, SO-Rookie, SO-Tribander-and-Single-Wire. [4] SO operate 36 hours max with off times at least 60 min. Exchange: [5] RS(T) + serial number. QSO Points: [6] different continents — 3pts (14-28 MHz) and 6 pts (1.8-7 MHz), with North America — 2 pts (14-28 MHz) and 4 pts (1.8-7 MHz), with own country — 1 pt. Score: [7] QSO points × prefixes worked (ie, N8, KA1, HG73, JD1) counted only once. For more information: [8] **www. cqwpx.com**. Logs due [9] May 1 (CW, Jul 1) to **ssb@cqwpx. com** (**cw@cqwpx.com**).

[1] The time period is always specified in UTC. No contest QSOs outside these times are permitted.

[2] The contest will be held on all HF bands, except 60, 30, 17 and 12 meters as noted previously. Smaller contests often specify a list of frequencies to concentrate activity so that participants can more easily make QSOs. Unless otherwise noted, you can work stations on all bands and modes permitted by the contest.

[3] If you are unfamiliar with the abbreviations — for example, SOAB means "single operator, all-band" — check the sponsor's rules for exact definitions.

[4] There may be special rules about required breaks or restrictions on changing bands.

[5] This is the information to be exchanged in each contact.

[6] The rules carefully spell out the value of each contact.

[7] This is the formula for calculating your score. Note that the multipliers (call sign prefixes) are counted only once during the contest, not once on each band.

[8] Check the Web site for complete rules, since a summary leaves out details and conditions that affect how you should operate.

[9] Logs must be sent to the sponsors by this date or they may be used as *checklogs* not listed in the final results.

This information can also be used "in reverse" to find out

in which contest a station is participating. For example, let's say that one October Saturday you turn on the radio and hear a station calling "CQ Contest" on CW. The exchange seems to be a signal report and some kind of state-number combination, such as "WA060." Turning to *QST* and looking in the Contest Corral column, you find six contests listed for that date — not an unusual number for a fall weekend. They are the Illinois QSO Party, US/VE Island QSO Party, QRP Fall QSO Party, Worked All Germany, JARTS RTTY Worldwide and Delaware Valley FM contests. Rule out the RTTY and FM contests right away. Of those remaining, all allow CW contacts and the exchange includes RST. The Illinois QSO Party exchange includes a county or SPC abbreviation. QRP contest QSOs require power and member number. Worked All Germany participants exchange a serial number or a DOK code (like a US Zip code). Clearly, the station must be calling from a US or Canadian island and is giving out a state or province abbreviation followed by the island designator! This sort of confusion is a good reason to clearly indicate which contest you are operating as part of your CQ!

Making a Contest QSO

You're ready to make a few contest QSOs! How about an example to show how it's done? Let's start with a typical QSO in the Washington State QSO Party (also known as "The Salmon Run"). In this example, we'll assume you are operating from W1AW in Connecticut.

On voice, the contact sounds like this:

W7DX: CQ Washington State QSO Party from Whisky Seven Delta X-ray
[W7DX is making it clear which contest he is operating.]
W1AW: Whiskey One Alpha Whiskey
[Just give your call once, phonetically.]
W7DX: W1AW you're five nine in Chelan county
[This identifies the caller and gives the exchange.]
W1AW: Thank you, you're five nine in Connecticut
[You acknowledge that you've received W7DX's information and give yours.]
W7DX: Thank you, CQ Salmon Run from W7DX
[This acknowledges receiving W1AW's information and starts the cycle again. See how easy it is?]

Here's the same contact on CW:
W7DX: CQ SR DE W7DX
["SR" stands for Salmon Run; it could also be WAQP for Washington QSO Party.)
W1AW: W1AW
[Again, just your call sign. No K or BK is required.]
W7DX: W1AW 5NN CHE
[Note the use of the cut number N to abbreviate 9. "CHE" is the abbreviation for Chelan County. Most QSO Party sponsors publish a list of approved abbreviations to keep everyone on the same page.]
W1AW: R 5NN CT
[A simple "R" confirms that you received his information; then send yours. Again, no BK needed.]
W7DX: TU CQ SR DE W7DX
[The TU acknowledges receiving W1AW's information and starts the cycle again.]

Edu, EA8URL, enjoys operating from the Canary Islands during the IARU HF World Championships contest. He made about 700 contacts during the 24-hour contest.

That's pretty snappy operating! No wasted characters or unnecessary information. If this was emergency traffic, isn't that how you would want it to flow? Remember that even in a small contest, efficiency is important. You can ragchew with the station some other day, although it's perfectly okay to quickly say hello if you know the operator. Just don't launch into a conversation in the middle of a contest QSO!

There is more to making contest QSOs than this simple example, but that format will get you started. If you'd like to know more, the following sections are an introduction to real contest operating.

OPERATING BASICS: YOUR FIRST CONTESTS

You may have happened upon several contests and even made a few contest QSOs. It was fun, wasn't it? Are you ready to try entering one for real? Let's go! Your QSOs will be welcomed by everyone, especially the serious participants. They are always looking for additional contacts and most will guide you through your first contest QSOs.

Choosing a Contest

Contests generally fall into three categories, each having a different group of stations you should work. Contests that only allow point credit for working stations in the same country or region are called *domestic contests*. For an ARRL domestic contest, stations may work other stations in the US or Canada (known in contest lingo as W/VE.). The ARRL November Sweepstakes is an example of a W/VE domestic contest. In contrast, a European domestic contest limits QSOs to those between European stations.

There are two types of *DX contests*. Targeted DX contests require that contacts be between a specific region or DXCC entity and stations located elsewhere. Contacts in the ARRL International DX Contest, for example, must be between the contiguous 48 US states or a Canadian province and stations outside W/VE, including KH6, KL7 and US possessions. Non-W/VE stations cannot contact each other in this contest. Some targeted DX contests do allow contacts between stations in the targeted area. Check the rules to be sure.

The other type of DX contest is called *everybody-works-everybody* where all QSOs are allowed for some amount of credit. The ARRL 10-Meter Contest, IARU HF Championship, CQ WPX and CQ World Wide (WW) contests are all examples of this type of contest. As you might imagine, these are the largest contests of all, attracting thousands of participants worldwide.

Remember to check the rules for mode of operation. Some contests, such as the ARRL November Sweepstakes and ARRL International DX Contest have separate weekends for CW and phone operation. For the ARRL 10 Meter Contest and IARU HF World Championships, you work both CW and phone during the same weekend. In the ARRL RTTY Round-Up, you can operate using any digital mode, from Baudot to packet to PSK31. ARRL VHF/UHF contests allow QSOs on any mode — CW, phone or digital — during the same event.

For your first few contests, assess your personal and station capabilities as well as what type of contacts you'd like to make. If you have a modest station and are just beginning, look for the state QSO parties. These low-key events are great opportunities to get your feet wet and chase the Worked All States award. Run by groups in the various states, the goal is to encourage activity among the hams of that particular state. Some state QSO parties offer interesting prizes. Be a winner in the California state QSO party and you may find yourself with a bottle of vintage California wine for your efforts. Top scoring stations in another state QSO party may receive jams, apples or even salmon (as well as some beautiful certificates to hang on the wall).

If you would rather try for some DX contacts, the ARRL DX Contest, IARU HF Championship and CQ WPX or WW contests put lots of loud signals on the band that you can probably work in a few calls. Don't be afraid to jump into almost any contest you find. You will pick up the rhythm and techniques quickly.

Read the Rules

To find a contest and be ready to operate, check the *Contest Corral* column in the current issue of *QST* for available contests and pick one that looks interesting. Check the sponsor's Web site for the complete rules and more information about the contest, including awards and special operating requirements. Being familiar with the rules will make operating more comfortable, smooth and enjoyable.

Knowing the rules also will help you plan your operating times. You should know when the event starts and how long you are allowed to operate. Does the contest require *off-times* during the event? Is it a 12, 24 or 48 hour contest? Not knowing the rules beforehand could require you to delete multipliers and QSOs worked late in a contest because you exceeded the maximum permissible operating time.

After you choose a contest, learn the exchange. This is the most important thing to know for every contest you enter, no matter how much experience you have. By memorizing the exchange, it becomes so automatic you'll find you can do other things while sending your exchange, without even thinking about it. That ability will become valuable in future contesting. After you've learned the exchange, you're ready to go on the air!

Search and Pounce Technique

What a great term! "Search and Pounce" (S&P) describes exactly the technique of tuning up and down a band for new stations (searching), then working them (pouncing). As you tune, you'll hear some stations calling "CQ Contest" or simply "CQ Test." To get up to speed just listen for a while. Observe how the louder, busy stations do it, making each call quickly and crisply. They send the exchange smoothly without extra syllables, words or characters and without unnecessarily repeating information.

If you find it helpful, prepare by writing the contest exchange on "cheat sheets" to guide you through each QSO without getting flustered. (This is also helpful when mentoring

Field Day — Not A Contest?

First held in 1933 as an emergency exercise Field Day is a *non-contest* in a contest-like environment. It incorporates all modes, including satellite communications and both HF and VHF/UHF bands — the only ARRL contest to touch so many parts of ham radio. More US licensed amateurs participate in Field Day annually than any other on-the-air operating event. It allows contacts with any station worldwide, on any mode and on all bands (except 60, 30, 17 and 12 meters). Even diehard non-contesters seem to enjoy participating in this all-inclusive operating event.

Field Day occupies a special place in the hearts of many contesters because it is during these outings that many get their first taste of competitive operating. Perhaps at the elbow of a more experienced operator, logging and listening, inexperienced operators gain invaluable experience during a single operating shift.

If you are new to contesting, take advantage of Field Day's smorgasbord to sample different styles of operating. Make sure to listen as a contest veteran tunes the bands or holds a frequency. Take a turn yourself! If you're an experienced ham, be sure to return the favor of those that taught you by showing a new contester "how it's done". You'll make a lifetime friend and help keep radiosport going!

Field Day isn't a contest, but many organizations approach it with a competitive attitude! Here Connie, K5CM, and his daughter Melissa, N5KK, tackle 40-meter CW duties at the Muskogee Amateur Radio Club site.

a new operator or a youngster making the first QSOs.) Practice giving your exchange along with a QSO being made on the air, but without transmitting. Here's a tip: In a phone contest take a full breath before replying to a station. Give all of your exchange the same way every time in a single, uninterrupted statement. Your voice will be natural and unforced — you'll sound and feel much more confident.

Once you're ready, how do you give yourself the best chance of getting through? What's the best way to call? On phone, make the most of your transmissions by speaking clearly and distinctly. Don't speak so slowly that the running station responds to someone else before you're finished. Don't mumble or run the phonetics all together. Use standard phonetics that are easy to speak (remember, you'll be saying them a lot!) and easy to understand. If you're unsure about your technique, practice with a friend on a quiet band until you get it right. On CW, send your call cleanly with the characters spaced properly. Using a computer program or CW keyer is a good way to send your call correctly every time. Send at a speed you'll feel comfortable receiving.

Give your full call one time and one time only, using phonetics on phone. Why the full call? Because sending only a partial call (such as the poor practice of giving only the "last two" letters) requires at least one extra set of transmissions to get your complete call sign. This slows down the running station — a breach of etiquette. And why only one time? Because if you're heard, you'll get through with only one call. If you're not heard, the extra calls are just interference. Listen for the running station's response and respond appropriately. If another station is called, wait until the contact is completed and try again. Or if you think too many other stations are calling, store the frequency in one of your rig's VFOs or memories or even write the frequency and call on paper so that you can come back later and try again.

Stick with standard or commonly used phonetics. You should know three sets of common ones because in marginal conditions it pays to be able to change to a more easily understood word for better comprehension.

Another problem for operators new to contesting is keeping up with the speed at which contacts are conducted. A running station may only listen for two seconds before starting another CQ. You have to start your call during that short window to be heard. Don't put the microphone down or take your hand off the key! By the time you get ready to transmit, it will be too late. Be ready to transmit as soon as the running station's transmission ends. You don't have to send your entire call in two seconds because the running station will pause as soon as your transmissions are heard. It's only important that you start in time to be heard. Just think of contesting as "DXing speeded up" and you'll quickly adapt.

Efficiency is the name of game in contesting. There's no need to give the running station's call before yours — after all, they already know their call! Don't append information to your call unless it's necessary to identify your station. Don't add "/QRP" or your location, for example. It adds nothing to identify you and just creates more work for the station you're calling.

If the running station hears you, be ready to copy the response. Most contacts will happen just as shown in the example given earlier. What happens if there is QRM, QRN, QSB or any number of other problems that cause errors? What if the

running station gets your call sign wrong?

Let's start with getting your call correct. The best time to fix it is as the running station responds to you. Don't give your exchange — a tacit acceptance of the incorrect call — until your call is given correctly by the running station. Here's an example (imagine that both stations are using phonetics in this phone example):

OH8X: CQ Contest from OH8X
KD8ABC: KD8ABC
OH8X: KD8APZ you are 59 15
[He has the call wrong and gave you the exchange 59 zone 15. Usually you don't say "zone" — it's understood.]
KD8ABC: KD8ABC KD8ABC
[Just say your call sign, phonetically, no exchange yet.]
OH8X: KD8ABZ?
KD8ABC: KD8ABC, last letter is C
[Here's your chance to try a different phonetic for the difficult letter.]
OH8X: KD8ABC QSL, 59 15
KD8ABC: Thank you, 59 4
[Now that he has your call sign and you have his exchange, you give your exchange. KD8ABC is in zone 4.]
OH8X: Thank you, CQ Contest OH8X

What if part of the exchange is lost? Request a repeat immediately, before giving your information as shown in this CW example for a VHF+ contest:

W8ABC: KD8ABC [static crash]
KD8ABC: GRID?
W8ABC: KD8ABC EM99
KD8ABC: R EN81

There are many variations on making corrections. The important thing is to let the other station know there is a problem before sending information back to them. If you implicitly accept the incorrect information by responding with your exchange, it's confusing and takes longer to correct the error.

As you give your exchange information, don't add any

Scott, K7ZO, and Joe, NK7U, work together not only on the air but between contests to assemble and organize a winning multi-operator team from Joe's station in Baker, Oregon. (*N0AX photo*)

extra words or phrases. Just give the information in the same order used by the running station. There is no need for phrases such as "please copy" or "you are" or to say what each bit of information is. Do not repeat the exchange you've received. Just rattle off your information in a string and the running station will be perfectly happy.

Don't say or send anything twice. Don't repeat any information unless requested or you are absolutely sure the running station won't copy everything on the first try — you might be surprised! Just send your information — once — as smoothly and as efficiently as possible. You will be pleased with how effective this technique is and how it builds your confidence.

If you are asked for a repeat, give only the information requested. If you are asked for your prefix, give only your prefix. If asked for your suffix or any letter of your call sign or report, give only what is asked. The receiving station already has most of what of the information or will confirm a full call sign after getting a partial. To send anything extraneous may cause confusion under marginal receiving conditions.

Now that you have all of the information, log the QSO time and date in UTC, the band and the complete exchange. Then continue to tune, chasing more contest contacts. There's still a lot to learn, but the basic fun of contesting begins right now!

INTERMEDIATE CONTEST OPERATING

After you find out how easy it is to have fun in a contest, you may want to get a little more serious about participating. You don't have to go all-out as a serious contester to enjoy some success, but it will take a little effort to get good results. You'll want to submit a log to the sponsors, see your standings in the final results and possibly even contribute your score to a contest club. This is good stuff! Even if you never get more serious about radiosport than casual contesting, it will be amazing how much you learn about operating and propagation while simultaneously extending your station's capabilities.

Part of being successful lies in managing your expectations. Unreasonable expectations lead to frustration that can really diminish your enjoyment of contesting. Don't expect to place in the national Top Ten until you've spent some time gaining experience. If your QTH is challenging — such a valley location, a high noise area or limited by antenna restrictions — it will be difficult to make a big score from home. In any case, plan an operating strategy by which you could reach some reasonable goals. Get creative to develop your radio skills! Operating from a portable location or mobile is an option getting more popular every year.

Be prepared to handle the QRM that comes naturally in a contest. The bands will be much more crowded than during a normal weekday. Don't expect quiet, clear frequencies in the middle of the activity. This is where your listening skills become very important. Contesting develops an operator's ability to copy information through noise, fading and interference from nearby signals. How you handle contest QRM is one of the most important contest skills.

Calling CQ

You may have tried an occasional CQ in a contest as a beginner, but as a more serious participant you'll want to CQ or *run*, as much as possible. Experienced contesters know that if they have a good signal, the overall rate at which they can make contacts will be at least as good as from tuning the band. More importantly, they also know that the multipliers will eventually tune by *them*. Learning to call CQ and hold a run frequency is an important contest skill.

To decide whether or not to call CQ, you have to decide whether your signal is strong enough in the target area. One way to find out is to tune the band searching and pouncing. If you are working stations on the first call, you're probably loud enough to get answers to a CQ. You can also ask stations that you work about your signal strength. If you decide you're loud enough, the next step is to find an unoccupied frequency.

A good way to find a frequency is to tune from one end of the band (usually the high end) and look for "holes" between stations calling CQ. When you find one, ask if the frequency is in use (send your call once on CW to avoid unidentified transmissions, although just "?" is common) and listen for responses. On phone, you will need to be at least 1.5 kHz from adjacent stations. On CW, at least 300 Hz. Don't expect a channel without QRM in a big contest. If you can hear just the high frequency crackle or low-frequency rumble of nearby signals, that's about as good as you can expect.

Assuming you got no response to your inquiry (and remember to listen for non-contest QSOs), it's time for a CQ. Think of each CQ as casting a fishing lure into a lake with fish swimming by. Your lure has to be in the water if a fish is going to bite, so keep the channel occupied with short listening periods between calls. On phone or CW, leave two to three seconds between CQs. Short CQs work best on busy bands — too long a CQ and impatient contest stations will tune right by.

Here are some examples of reasonable contest CQs on phone. Note the use of phonetics at least once in each CQ:

"CQ Contest CQ Contest from Whiskey One Alfa Whiskey, Whiskey One Alfa Whiskey, Contest"

"CQ CQ Contest this is Kilo Delta Seven Delta Quebec Oscar, KD7DQO, over"

Team Canada is all smiles as John, VE3EJ, and Jim, VE7ZO, are congratulated by WRTC-2006 Chairman Atilano Oms, PY5EG. The World Radiosport Team Championships (WRTC) bring the best operators from around the world together in one spot and place them at equivalent stations for head-to-head competition during the IARU HF World Championships contest. Team Canada was the first non-US team to win the WRTC in the five competitions held since 1990. (K1IR photo)

Computers in Contests

By Bill Kennamer, K5NX

I can still remember the dark ages of contesting. No computers. An automatic pencil with a fresh supply of lead was the high-tech logging device. The routine was simple: Call the station, write the call in the log, send the report, write the call in the dupe sheet, hit the CQ button on the keyer (or keep talking) and scratch off another multiplier. Then spend a week after the contest rechecking the dupes to avoid the dreaded additional three-QSO penalty for leaving duplicate contacts in the log. Scores bandied about just after the contest were only a rough approximation and the real ones weren't known for days or weeks.

Progress came when the home computer arrived and after-the-contest duping programs were developed. As part of the N5AU contest crew "back in the day," we used a program for the Apple II called *SoDups*, developed for us by Bruce Hubanks, WD5-FLK. The procedure was simple: I would read the calls to Randy, K5ZD and he would type them into the computer. This easily saved us at least a week in log preparations for a large multi-multi operation, but it still didn't give us the real time scores and multiplier checks we wanted.

Around 1988, Ken Wolff, K1EA, began developing a contest program called *CT*. This program was designed for real-time logging on an IBM PC and it was apparent almost from the start that users of this program had a significant advantage in the contest over those who weren't using it. The program at that time was developed only for DX contests, so Dave Pruett, K8CC, developed a program having the look and feel of *CT* for domestic contests. Dave called his program *NA*. Eventually both programs were developed for more contests and had some different functions, so even though the screens were similar, each program had some features the other one did not. Larry Tyree, N6TR, then developed a program called *TR Log* that had a different look and feel and used the logical sequence of events in a contest to determine keystrokes. By then, contest logging had become a reality, with most serious competitors using computers to their best advantage.

Your Advantage

So why should you use a computer and what can it do for you? The easiest answer is that it will improve your score and relieve you of after-the-contest paperwork. Given two options like that, it's hard to imagine why anyone would want to operate without one.

To begin using a computer, you should buy one of the popular contest logging programs. These programs are developed by very active (and usually high scoring) contesters who know how to use a computer to improve their scores. They not only log contacts, but also help you manage your time during the contest and offer many special features to help you improve your score.

A general-purpose logging program is just not efficient enough to even consider. Use one of those for your general logging and buy a real contest program for contesting. Install the program on your hard drive and be ready for increased enjoyment and scores.

The contest program will step you through the set up routine for a particular contest. Just follow the instructions. It's important to do this correctly since several things that can happen during the contest are based upon the data input at set up. Be especially sure to complete the name, address and most importantly the information about the location from which you are participating. These are important for the exchange information in the contest, as well as for the contest sponsor to know where to send your contest award.

You may have to configure your computer COM, parallel and USB ports and sound card for the program to use. On CW, one of the ports can be used to key the radio. In some programs, a keyer paddle can be connected through the same port and the computer will function as an electronic keyer for those who prefer sending non-repetitive data with a paddle. COM and USB ports may also control frequencies on the radio, a rotator, keyers, a packet TNC, Internet connection or antenna relays — all from the keyboard. This is a significant advantage, especially in split-frequency phone operations. The ports can even control two radios with one computer or be networked together to share log information in a multi-multi operation.

During the Contest

Once the setup is complete and the contest begins, the software really starts to shine. On CW, all exchanges are sent by the computer, allowing the contester to spend more time with things other than sending. For SSB, a voice keyer may be set up to save your voice. On RTTY, some programs generate the transmitted tones and decode the received tones. This allows operation to be almost totally automatic.

To log a contact, enter the call sign of the station you're about to work into the call sign field. Most contest software will check to see if it's a duplicate contact or a new multiplier. You can usually see if you've worked that station during the contest on other bands (or modes), and whether or not the station is a needed multiplier on other bands.

And on CW:
CQ TEST DE VE7SV VE7SV TEST
CQ SS CQ SS K4RO K4RO SS (SS is for Sweepstakes)
TEST K1TO (if QSOs are really moving along quickly)

Instead of "Contest" you can substitute the name of the contest if you are participating in one of the smaller contests. That attracts the attention of stations tuning by.

Each CQ should be brisk and crisp, not slurred or tentative. Think of each CQ as a small advertisement for your station that makes another operator want to answer you. Your voice should be friendly but businesslike.

As long as we're on the subject, calling CQ is an excellent reason why contest audio is so important. While you tune the bands, make note of stations with good and bad audio. What

When the other station sends you the exchange, enter the needed information. The software automatically fills in the date, time and frequency. For contests requiring a signal report, the software assumes 59 or 599 for every contact although you can change that if needed.

Pressing another key sends your exchange information (if you have the CW key line or a voice keyer hooked up) and logs the contact, then moves on to the next line, ready for the next contact. In most programs, the contact is entered into a *band map* that lists the stations on the band by frequency (including incoming call sign spots, if connected), allowing those stations to be skipped on subsequent S&P passes. The band map can be loaded with calls to be worked later. Some programs allow this to happen with a simple key stroke or mouse click.

Having trouble copying a call sign? The *check partial and super check partial* functions allow you to be prompted with possible calls after entering two or more letters of a call sign. Don't use these cues to guess, though. Using the partial call features is much like finding a picture hidden in a picture—once you know the pattern, it's easier to find. This feature can often help when conditions are marginal.

Want to know how you're doing? The *rate meter* will tell you what your rate looks like over whatever time period you specify. The score summary can always be displayed. A multiplier table will show missing multipliers. All of these things will improve your score over what might be possible without using the software.

After the Contest

After the contest, the logging program will prepare your log for you. While you do need to review it for typos, the preparation itself is automatically taken care of by the program. No need to second guess; the programmers know what is needed by the sponsors and how to prepare the log files as requested by the sponsors. If you send the proper file, there's no need to worry about what the log form looks like. Just use the file created by the program.

After the contest, *data mining* is useful for future contest operations. The logging program facilitates this with information about QSO rates per hour (including what bands were being used), points per hour, when each multiplier was worked for the first time, continent and country breakdowns for DX contests and all manner of important information for after-contest review. Carefully studying these results files should help devise strategies for improved future contest scores.

Contest logging programs are sometimes available as demos of obsolete or unsupported versions so that a contester may try them and make a decision on which new version to buy. The original programs were designed

for *DOS* programs and are unlikely to run properly under *Windows*. The latest programs are designed for *Windows*, but you should carefully check the requirements to make sure they work with your computer and the version of *Windows* you're running.

You can check out *CT* at www.k1ea.com. You can download the latest version of *CT* as freeware (unsupported). Note the hardware requirements. The dominant version runs under *DOS* and there is a *Windows* version available as *CTWin*.

Information about *NA* software may be found at www.datomonline.com. It may be ordered from the Radio Bookstore, PO Box 209, Rindge NH 03461, tel 800-457-7373, fax 603-899-6826. This is a *DOS* program.

TR Log information is found at www.qth.com/tr. A free trial version is available for download and it may be purchased from the Web site. This is also a *DOS* program.

N3FJP's set of *Contest Log* programs are designed for inexpensive entry-level contesting with a simple user interface. Each contest is supported by a different version of the program. There is a companion Amateur Contact Log program for general purpose logging. The software requires *Windows* and can be downloaded from www.n3fjp.com.

Writelog for Windows is supported at www.writelog.com. This is a *Windows* only program that can use the soundcard for RTTY or as a voice keyer. Ordering information is on the Web site.

The *N1MM Logger* is an open-source, freeware program supported as a cooperative development effort by volunteer programmers. The program requires *Windows*. It supports RTTY and PSK modes via the computer sound card. The program is available at pages.cthome.net/n1mm.

WinTest is a European contest logger that runs on *Windows*. It has many features and places special emphasis on SO2R (single-op, two-radio) contesting. It can be obtained at www.win-test.com. As a shareware program, it can be used for a short trial before purchase is required.

Super-Duper by EI5DI is another *DOS* based program for contest logging. It is a single-op program, with many edit features and separate modules for many different contests. It covers the DX side of many contests very well and some versions are available for download from the website as freeware. Information and online ordering may be done at www.ei5di.com.

Contest software is always evolving. To find out the latest information, check the *National Contest Journal, QST* ad pages or visit www.contesting.com and check out the Contest Links area.

---

is it about the good audio that got your attention? It was probably punchy, with crisp mid-to-high frequency response, just enough low frequencies and not noisy or distorted. Strive for those qualities. Get together on a dead band with a friend between contests and adjust your mic gain and speech processor settings for that same quality of audio. If you use a voice keyer, do the same for its messages. You'll recall some stations whose

audio is so distorted, over-compressed or contaminated with background noise that they're hard to understand. Why make it difficult for your audience to understand you?

Let's assume that you find a frequency and you're calling CQ. If you get a steady stream of callers, there's nothing better in contesting! Be consistent and smooth in your responses. Give directions or make requests calmly — no need to shout!

Make sure of the other station's call sign and exchange before calling CQ again.

Improve your running rate by learning to get the full call sign sent to you the first time, every time. Repeats not only take time, but stations waiting to work you may move on. Learn to receive a call sign phonetically and give it back to the other station without phonetics. This only works, however, when you're absolutely, positively sure that you have the call sign correct. Remember that contest sponsors remove points for incorrect call signs.

What if you don't get many callers? How long should you continue to call CQ? There is no set answer, but you should be doing whatever maximizes your contact rate. Most contesters will try a reasonably clear frequency for two or three minutes without callers before tuning away. If in the past hour, you were able to work stations at a rate of 30/hour (most contest logging software will display your "last hour" rate), then calling CQ should be expected to generate that rate or better. If you get a stream of callers that eventually dries up, a good rule of thumb is to continue calling CQ for at least twice the interval between your S&P QSOs. For example, if your S&P rate was 30/hour or one station every two minutes, you should call CQ for four minutes before deciding to return to S&P. This is not a hard and fast rule. As you gain experience, your intuition will begin to tell you when to CQ and when to tune.

If you're not getting answers to your calls or are being asked for repeats a lot, think about why this might be. Are you sending too fast on CW? Are you transmitting clear, undistorted audio on SSB? Either can prevent you from making QSOs, so it's counterproductive to have poor audio or to send too fast. On CW, it's sometimes more productive to go slower late in the contest, when you've already worked most of the active contesters. Remember, you cannot win many contests by working only the hardcore, experienced contesters. You have to also work casual operators who turn on their radios, make a few contacts and go off to enjoy other pursuits. Temper your voice or keying speed to what you're trying to accomplish at that minute. If you have a large pileup, go fast so callers will know they have a chance and stick around. If you're getting only one or two calls per minute, be slower and friendlier.

If you have multiple or directional antennas, don't forget to try different directions or antennas. As bands open and close, the vertical and horizontal angles at which signals arrive can change dramatically. An antenna that was hot as a pistol when the band first opened may be the wrong one an hour later. The band may also open to another area. For example, from the Midwest in a domestic contest such as Sweepstakes, fading rate to the 1-2-3 districts may be a cue that it's time to turn your antennas west.

You might also lose your frequency to another station. Two stations in each other's skip zones can call CQ right on top of each other without ever hearing the other station! You can tell this is happening when stations seem to be calling, but the timing isn't "right." You may also hear the other station faintly via backscatter. When this happens, if you feel you're the louder station, you might want to stay and battle it out. If you think sticking around will hurt your contact rate too badly, by all means look for another frequency.

Occasionally another station will ask if the frequency is in use, not hear your reply and proceed to call CQ. You can try to convince them to move or your can move yourself. It depends on your interpersonal skills and signal strength. Another station may try to squeeze in between you and the next station up or down the band when there really isn't room. You'll just have to decide whether to hold your ground, slide up or down the band a little bit to accommodate the newcomer, or look for a new frequency. In any of these cases, don't lose your temper and get into an argument or worse, intentionally interfere with the other station. Life is too short for that stuff. And if you're arguing with another station, you're not making QSOs and you're losing the contest!

Advanced Search and Pounce

As a more serious competitor, you'll want to make better use of the time you spend tuning around the band. A good operator can work stations at a rate of 60/hour on a "fresh" band with lots of stations calling CQ. This requires a radio with two VFOs and bandstacking registers and either a good personal memory or a pencil and paper. Practicing this technique or some variation of it can make a big improvement over tuning up the band one station at a time.

Start at one end of the band on VFO A. Tune until you find a station and call them. If you work them right away, keep tuning. If you don't, set VFO B = VFO A and tune to the next station and call them. You now have two running stations in the two VFOs. Alternate between the VFOs until one station is worked, then keep tuning with that VFO. Flip back to the other VFO and call that station as they end a contact. By alternating between the VFOs you can be in two pileups at once all the way down the band! If the pileup on a station is just too big, store the frequency in a bandstacking register or a memory and make a note of the call and frequency. Revisit the frequency in a few minutes and you'll often find a big pileup is now a little pileup and you get right through. Watching a skilled operator S&P through a band this way is quite an experience as they hop from frequency to frequency.

Don't just tune from loud signal to loud signal. Listen carefully where there seems to be a small gap or a weak signal. Stations with small antennas, such as those from operators on vacation or operating Field Day-style, may have weak signals and be unable to attract a large pileup. They can probably hear you just fine, however — if you don't tune past them!

Many logging programs offer a feature called a *band map*. This is a linear scale along one edge of the display showing call signs and frequencies. Call signs are added to the band map as you work them, by manually entering them into the band map or from a spotting network. It's usually possible to configure the band map to show only multipliers, only stations not yet worked or even all stations. As you tune, some programs will even put the call of a station on the band map at the current frequency into the call window, ready for you to give your call and work them!

As you develop these quick-tuning skills, you'll find a quick scan of the band to be a valuable way to grab points quickly as you change bands or between periods of CQing.

Spotting Networks

As an intermediate contester, you'll be using your computer for contest logging as explained in the sidebar, "Computers

James, 9V1YC, is a good bet to be your Singapore multiplier in a DX contest. His pileup management skills and superb video filming and editing techniques also make him a valuable addition to major DXpeditions.

in Contests." Besides automating many of the housekeeping functions of logging, the computer can also connect you to information from other contesters. This requires you to enter the Single Operator Assisted (SOA) category as described in the sidebar. (In some events it's called the Single Op Unlimited category.) The rules differ from the Single Operator category in one way — the entrant may use information from DX spotting networks (also called "packet" because the original computer-based spotting networks used *PacketCluster* software running over packet radio links). To be clear, with few exceptions, getting such information from *any* source other than your own ears — whether from packet or 2-meter voice nets — *requires* you to submit your log in the SOA category. (In contests without an SOA category, you usually — but not always — have to enter in a multioperator category if you use spotting assistance.)

Connecting your computer to the Internet and your radio is a powerful combination that is used through two features of the logging software, the *announce window* and the *band map*. The band map was introduced in the Advanced Search and Pounce section. Logging software can use information from the spotting network to populate the band map automatically, filling it with stations spotted around the world. It's like having the whole world tuning for you! As you tune, the computer senses the new frequency and scrolls the band map along with your receive frequency.

The announce window shows each spot individually. This is important because additional information may be posted by the spotter, such as "listening up 2" or "QSX 7167" for a DX station on 40 meter phone who is transmitting below 7100 kHz and listening up in the US phone band. The band map and announce window features can usually be configured to show only stations you haven't yet worked or only those that are new multipliers. It may be able to show the different types of information in different colors, to help you quickly make sense of it.

You will find that spots from stations far away from your location are often not much use, since propagation is probably quite different in that location. Even spots from across the US are often of no value. Learn how to use the spotting network

filters to prevent unworkable spots from cluttering up your band map and spot windows. It's easy to remove spots from bands and modes not included in your current contest. Some systems can also filter spots based on the location of their origin. Programs like VE7CC's *CC Cluster* act as a "smart" spotting network client with special filtering and display functions.

Spotting networks have had a big effect on intermediate contesting — not all good. The fun side of spotting is that casual participants have more fun by finding more stations to work. This increases their score, as well as their club's aggregate score, and they may work some new stations toward an award. The problem arises when the spotting information begins to *replace* tuning and operating skill instead of *assisting* the operator.

The rush of stations to work a newly spotted station creates what are known as "packet pileups." DX operators know instantly when they've been "spotted" as their pileup grows suddenly from a handful of callers to dozens or more. The sudden rush of stations is confusing to everyone, causing the pileups to get out of sync with the DX station, reducing contact rate for everyone. Don't contribute to the mob mentality — if you grab a spot to work a station, wait until you can hear them before calling and use good pileup discipline. Sometimes it's more productive to wait a while before chasing a spot, giving the packet pileup a chance to subside.

Don't become dependent on spotting network assistance. Use it to aid you and your own abilities. Make sure that you copy each call sign you work. Spots are helpful, but the call signs given may be — and frequently are — wrong or *busted*. By not copying the call sign and exchange for yourself, and simply trusting the spotting network, you run the risk of having the incorrect QSO removed from your log, along with a penalty!

CONTEST STRATEGY

As an intermediate contester, you have progressed from struggling to tune the bands and work stations one by one to being able to quickly search and pounce your way through a thicket of stations. You're probably even calling CQ and holding your own! You're ready to start thinking about strategy.

Pre-Contest Preparation

Start by making sure you know the contest rules well enough to perform properly during the contest. This includes knowing whom to work during the contest and how the scoring system works. All of these will play a part in strategic planning for the contest. The exchange should be memorized to the point that you could send the exchange while concentrating on some other contest chore, such as logging, checking multipliers or equipment conditions. You should know your grid square, CQ zone, ITU zone, state, county, section or anything else required for any contest you might enter. A seasoned contester knows the exchange for all of the major contests.

Develop an operating plan, even if just a simple one. Without some kind of plan, it is difficult to be successful in any contest. While there are some experienced contesters who seem to never have a plan, that's not really true. It's just that their experience is such that before the contest starts they can estimate where they will be at various points along the way, what multipliers they will need, and what kind of QSO totals will be required.

Select an operating category based on your station limitations, operating time available and personal capabilities. If propagation is good, you might want to try QRP or leave the amplifier off for the weekend and try low power. Single-band categories are often a great way to really learn about propagation and pursue single-band DXCC or other single-band awards. If you are a serious certificate collector, you may find little competition in the more obscure categories.

Even if the category is one where you do not think you will win, you should still have some sort of plan and goals

---

Single Operator Assisted: Using Packet Radio Power for Higher Scores

By Charles Fulp, K3WW

Many contests have added a Single Operator Assisted (SOA) or Unlimited (SU) category. We'll just call it SOA here. This category usually has the same rules at the Single Operator category with one major exception. The entrant may use spotting nets such as the DX PacketClusters. Spotting nets have opened up a whole new world for many contesters, allowing access to information about band conditions and stations and multipliers available during the contest like never before.

The SOA category allows operators who enjoy monitoring their spotting network for new countries to participate in contests without missing anything. Other operators like working cooperatively with their friends while operating contests. Still others feel that the use of spotting networks can help them score more points for their club by increasing their multiplier totals. Being part of the network can keep some operators motivated to push on to bigger scores. Being "connected" in many ways makes SOA closer to a multi-op category than single op.

The only special equipment necessary to participate in the SOA category is a link to a spotting network. Originally, the links were by VHF radio. Later, contest software was developed to integrate VHF packet networks. Today, it is possible for those in remote areas to connect by the Internet. Many VHF cluster systems are connected to the Internet, as well. Most logging programs will accommodate packet connections and will interact with the radio, computer and logging in such a way that getting to a spot is only a mouse click or keystroke away.

SOA Station Setup

If you decide to try to make the best scores you can, some station design features can help you and make SOA much more fun. The first thing you should have is a transceiver that can be controlled by your contest logging program. This allows you to move quickly to work new multipliers and back to your original frequency, where you can resume your tuning or calling CQ.

You may choose to use an amplifier, since most SOA categories do not have a separate low power division. An auto-tuning amplifier and automatic antenna switch allows you to quickly jump from one band to another. Some operators just bypass the amplifier when making a quick contact on another band.

As in the Single-Op category, the use of a second radio can improve your performance as an SOA entrant. If your station is capable of running at good rates on some bands, you can use the second station to study spots. When the opportunity is right, make quick contacts between answers to your CQ. Since many SOA stations are not the biggest on the bands, being able to stay on a frequency and catch some extra multipliers without leaving for more than a few seconds at a time can help you get the most out of your station. Having a second radio also decreases the importance of auto-tuning amplifiers and rapid band change antenna switching. Of course the more automated everything is, the more flexible your station can be.

Too Much Information

Historically the top Single Op entrants usually out-score the top SOA. There are several reasons for this. Traditionally the top operators with stations capable of winning at the highest levels enter the Single Op category. After competing in the SOA category for a few years and watching

Chas, K3WW, operates in the Single Op Assisted category from his well organized ham shack. You can count on him to finish in the top 10.

set before the contest. Find the results of last year's contest and see what it took to win your section, division or call area. Then see what the leaders in your chosen category did in last year's version of the contest. Evaluate this year's potential by the expected propagation. For example, on HF when sunspots are rising, expect 10 meters to be better than the year before. As sunspots decline, expect 10 meters to be worse. The other bands should see an increase or decrease in activity, based upon what 10 meters will do. Most single-operator, all-band (SOAB) participants will naturally migrate to the highest band open.

Along with evaluating the probable propagation on each band, check previous contest *breakdowns* of other stations in your category — the number of multipliers and QSOs on each band. It's best to pick a station near to you and with similar the performance of other participants, I coined the term "Single Op Distracted."

There are many elements involved in building a big score and access to spotting information is only one. Being distracted by all the spots is the biggest nemesis of the serious SOA entrant. If you are actually trying to make the best score you can, reverting to being a DXer can ruin your effort. In order to chase spots, it is usually necessary to give up some of the other activities that can build a big score. Even if you work every spot with one call, you will lose running time chasing them.

Most operators will find it difficult to hold a run (CQ) frequency and simultaneously enter a lot of large pile-ups. It is very easy to become distracted by all of the information available on the spotting networks and end up forgetting to do all the other things that Single Ops do to make big scores. At some point, you must be able to ignore beautiful, hard-to-work multipliers and con-centrate on making lots of easy-to-make contacts. On the other hand, you may set a goal of working the most multipliers possible and not be concerned about optimiz-ing your score.

Knowing your objective, regardless of your entry category, is important in establishing a game plan for any category. If you want to work some new countries or make a clean sweep, monitoring the spotting nets can improve your chances. If you want to make more points for your club, you will need a different strategy. Here's the most effective game plan for the SOA entrant: Do every-thing that you would do as a Single Op, while judiciously picking up extra multipliers without detracting from your most efficient practices.

Calling CQ is still the fastest way to build a large QSO total for most operators. When we can't run effectively, searching and pouncing can produce good QSO totals. With spotting, S&P can be even more effective. As you tune the band, you can skip over duplicates quickly and the spots may help in identifying some of the stations you come to.

Making the Best Use of Spots

It pays to tune in an orderly manner, even if you do run off to a different portion of the band or even to another band to grab a new multiplier. Most software now dis-plays a band map, which lets you see many of the calls as you tune your radio. This visual display permits you to know who you can probably skip and who you probably need to work. You can click your mouse and go to new multipliers directly from the band map, as well as from the window that lists the most recent spots.

Early in the contest I tend to just display new multi-pliers but use the band map to make tuning on my second radio while running on my primary radio a quicker job. Later in the contest it may be more productive to work through the band map jumping from one needed station to the next, especially if you cannot hold a good run frequency.

Listen carefully to be sure the spots are accurate! If you have already worked a lot of QSOs, the ones that show up as "needed" may well be bad calls. If you only have one radio, but it has two receivers, you can still try to maintain a run and listen on the second radio to the spots in your band map. I find this more efficient than trying to tune the second receiver on the same band that I am running with no help from the spotting network.

On some bands you will find stations working split. An unfortunate complication of spotting networks is that many stations now announce their listening frequency less often. For the SOA operator this information is often available from the network, making it faster to work these stations while Single Ops have to wait for the DX station to say the listen-ing frequency.

Another situation involves stations that do not identify very often. There is a strong temptation to as-sume that the spot is correct and work these stations without ever hearing the call. This is a risky proposi-tion, as a fair percentage of spots are wrong. Even when they are correct, sometimes a different station is on the frequency when you arrive.

Information from the spotting network will let you know which bands are most active and should allow you to choose the best band at any given time. Noth-ing replaces knowledge of what is going on around you.

It is important to be patient, especially early in the contest when there are large numbers of spots for stations that will be active throughout the weekend and much easier to work later in the contest. Unless you especially like the challenge of entering pileups with many of the biggest stations in your area, you may find it easier to wait for the smoke to clear before you go after a new multiplier.

If a station in an area where you have long periods of propagation is spotted early and the pileup is large, don't waste time unless you have an incredible signal. Even if you do, it may be more productive to wait until later to pick up many of these stations.

If you want to maximize your enjoyment of the en-tire contest experience, give the Single Op Assisted category a try.

Sometimes it's nice to have someone to share the contest experience with. This group put Michigan State University club station W8SH on the air for ARRL November Sweepstakes.

equipment for this evaluation. Breakdown information can be found on the 3830 e-mail reflector archives at **www.contesting.com** or in the detailed online contest results from ARRL and other contest sponsors. Make an estimate for QSOs and multipliers for each band. It's good to have goals, even though things will likely change during the contest.

Breakdowns from last year's contest can be used to prepare for this year's contest. Use those breakdowns to set goals for this year's contest. It's often helpful to compare the rate from the previous year to find out where you were and what you were doing as the contest progressed, especially if you made a wrong move last year.

By studying the band breakdowns and looking at your own goals, you can determine the probability of meeting them and make an educated guess as to what to do if you need to correct something in your operation. You should strive to stay ahead of last year's score, even to the point of computing how much you want to be ahead in this year's contest. Watching last year's rate sheet will keep you on track for an increased performance. Improvement is always the name of the game in contesting and results analysis will help get you there.

Finally, make the necessary plans to prevent interruptions to your contest effort. Be at the station at the start of the contest period and stay there as much as possible during the contest. As described later in this chapter, food preparation should be such that there is sufficient food available, but you should not plan on having a sit-down dinner during the contest. Try to get as much rest as possible in the days leading up to the contest. Sleep time will be minimal, and the sleeping area should be close by and comfortable. Be sure to have a good alarm clock (or two!) and be able to motivate yourself to get out of bed when it goes off.

Getting a Fast Start

Beginning on the highest band expected to be open at the start of the contest is the best thing to do. Getting some success by working stations in the first few minutes of the contest is important to your overall success. While you can't win a contest in the first few minutes, getting off to a good start will have a positive effect on your attitude for the whole weekend.

If you start by doing search-and-pounce, don't sit on a frequency waiting to be someone's first QSO unless you're in contact as the contest begins. There are probably others lurking on frequency trying to do the same thing and you'll find yourself in a big pileup right away. You'll have better results by making a quick sweep through the band to make a few contacts before settling in. Make a band map as you go and then get down to business. After the first 30 minutes of the contest, you'll settle down and the band will even out as everyone finds a comfortable rhythm. You may have to make a couple of band changes right away to find the best band for making contacts.

You may decide to start by trying to establish a run frequency. This is a good strategy if you know you have a good signal where the band is open. Unless you're a Big Gun, aim for higher in the band where the crowding won't be so intense. Although the adrenaline will be flowing, don't start at extremely high speed. Work a few stations and assess what the conditions and activity will bear. Don't be too impatient for a high rate because it takes everyone a little while to get rolling.

QSO Rate Versus Multipliers

Any contest should be considered as something similar to a scavenger hunt. The object is to collect a lot of something (QSOs in this case) while also acquiring as many items from a list (multipliers) as possible. Each contest has a different theme (list) with different strategies as a result. For example, in working a DX contest from the US the most active, available multipliers are in Europe. In the eastern US, the most QSOs will also be found in Europe. Thus, if you live in the eastern US, you would concentrate your operating hours on Europe. If you live in the western US, you are likely to work the most QSOs in Asia, but there are fewer active multipliers there. So, you would have to try to work European multipliers, but plan on making a lot of QSOs by working Asia. This requires an entirely different operating strategy.

In some contests, you may make most of your QSOs by S&P. That means the time you spend calling in a pileup is important. The less time required per QSO the better. A big pileup is harder to crack than a small one. But a G or JA station has the same multiplier value to you as a much rarer P29 station, if you haven't already worked one on that band. The G or JA may have a smaller pileup, so you'll log the multiplier quickly. Remember, the object is to work as many countries *and* QSOs as possible on each band, not to work the rarest ones. All multipliers are equal!

If your goal is to achieve a certain score, you should try for a reasonable balance between QSOs and multipliers. For example, you can score 50,000 points in the CQ WW contests with 300 three-point QSOs and 55 multipliers spread across several bands. This score is a reachable goal for most stations.

If you work a station that would be a multiplier on another band and you think propagation would support a QSO on that band, you can ask the station to move to that band for a quick contact. This is called *moving multipliers* and can make a dramatic improvement in your score. It's probably not a good idea to ask a station to move if they are *really* busy, but this technique can be effective when things are slow.

If the station prefers not to move or if propagation is not good on other bands at the moment, try making a schedule for

The Contest Club

If you've tried a contest or two and liked it, you might want to consider rubbing shoulders with like-minded individuals. One of the most important resources available to today's amateur is the Contest Club. While such clubs have been around for many years, the formation of new clubs has been on the upswing. What better way to improve your operating and contesting skills, to learn the tricks of the trade or to gain knowledge and experience in contesting than by joining together with other amateurs with the same interests? In every region of the country you will find solid contest clubs, all working toward a similar goal: being the best at what is called in some parts of the world *radiosport*.

Meetings of a contest club, such as the Yankee Clipper Contest Club shown here, are excellent opportunities to pick up valuable operating and technical information, as well as providing the opportunity to meet other contesters from your area. (K1IR Photo)

Just as different hams have different interests, you will find a wide variety of contest clubs, each with a special focus. Some clubs concentrate their efforts on VHF, UHF and microwave events. These clubs often form portable multi-op expeditions or seek to have Rover stations active during the contest. They can often provide technical assistance, perhaps helping you to get on a new microwave band for the contest.

Other clubs concentrate on HF events and possibly have DXing as an additional focus of the group. Some of these clubs specialize in DX contests, while others specialize in domestic contests. More than a few of these clubs also sponsor some specialty contests of their own, such as state QSO parties. Meeting programs often show new and simple ideas for improving station or operator capabilities.

Club Competition

What challenges these clubs to compete? The ARRL sponsors affiliated club competition in seven major operating events: the January VHF Sweepstakes, the International DX Contest, the June and September VHF QSO Party, the November Sweepstakes, the 160 Meter Contest and the 10 Meter Contest. Each year dozens of clubs — in Local, Medium or Unlimited categories depending on their size — enlist their members to "win one for the club." If your club isn't already competing, check out the criteria for the ARRL Affiliated Club Competition published on the ARRL Web. Clubs may also compete against one another in other major contests, such as the CQ World Wide DX Contest.

Join the Group, Improve Your Score

At meetings of the contest club, you'll have the opportunity to meet individuals at all experience levels. Many clubs have some sort of program for helping new contesters. Most clubs have one or more multi-operator stations that need a supply of operators. It's valuable to get onto a multi-op crew to learn contesting from experienced individuals. Camaraderie in a contest club makes the contester feel like part of the group, and sharing contest experiences at meetings (official and otherwise) helps bring the contester along to new heights.

Many clubs also run some sort of intra-club competition to help foster higher club scores. This allows contesters within a club to compete for awards that might not be available on a national level and provides motivation for sticking with it. For example, the club award program may reward certain score levels, numbers of QSOs or even time operated — anything to encourage club members to "stay in the chair" and contribute to the club score. The value of a contest club to the individual contester cannot be denied and it is rare that anyone is found in the Top Ten of any contest who is not a member of a recognized contest club.

You can find local and regional contest clubs by using the ARRL Club search Web page at **www.arrl.org/FandES/ field/club/clubsearch.phtml**. Enter "contest" in the window for "Show clubs by name or call sign". You can also contact your representative on ARRL Division's Contest Advisory Committee (**www.arrl.org/contests/cac.html**).

---

later in the contest. If you overhear another station making a schedule or moving a juicy multiplier to another band, try to follow the move or show up on the schedule and work that multiplier, too. Always be listening and thinking during the contest.

Whether you decide to S&P, call CQ, or change bands will depend on how far along the contest is. If it's the first day and other bands are open, you might want to S&P on another band, especially if you're running low power or the band is too crowded for you to hold a run frequency. The decision of when to chase multipliers or to stay with calling CQ largely depends on both the contact rate and the point value of a new multiplier.

Ellen White, W1YL, in a 1955 *QST* article, stated a formula that still works well today. This formula can help determine whether it's more worthwhile to work a multiplier or a new QSO. The formula is: Value of Multiplier (in equivalent QSOs) = Number of Contacts Worked ÷ Number of Multipliers worked + 1.

As an example, in a DX contest, 20 QSOs ÷ 10 Mults + 1 = 3, so 1 new multiplier is equivalent to 3 QSOs. In another example, 1200 QSOs ÷ 350 Mults + 1 = 4.4, so the multiplier is equivalent to 4.4 QSOs. As you can see, the further into the contest you go, the greater value of a multiplier. You can also calculate how much time can be spent in pursuit of one multiplier versus continuing to work QSOs. In the second example, if your contact rate was 30/hour (one every 2 minutes), you could spend $2 \times 4.4 = 8.8$ minutes chasing the new multiplier and keep your score increasing at the same rate. Many contest logging programs will actually do this calculation for you in real-time.

Band Planning

Band plans are hour-by-hour strategies for operating on different bands to different areas. To make a band plan, spend some time with a propagation prediction program and logs from other similar contests at the same time of year and look for openings to the various areas of the world. This is a good time to ask an experienced contester for help. They will tell you how much planning is useful and what part of the plan is the most important. As you build experience, it will be helpful to have some guidelines throughout the contest to remind you to check other bands, look for openings and maintain a balance between CQing and tuning for multipliers.

Although you may have a general feel for propagation, the wide variability of propagation with the seasons and solar conditions require a custom plan for each contest. Even then, it could all go out the window on any given weekend if conditions and participation don't cooperate. The good contest operator develops a strategic awareness of what is happening nearby during the contest and changes strategy as necessary. This is where experience comes into play and helps you adapt.

Many operators have gone into a contest with a game plan and stubbornly stayed with it even if it wasn't working. During the contest you must be flexible. If 15 meters was your band plan choice and nothing is happening for you there, go to 10 or 20 or possibly even lower. If 10 meters works best, don't try to force 15. Check the other bands from time to time to be aware of how propagation is changing. Either a marked lessening of your rate or a lack of new stations to work is a sign that you need to change to a different band.

Considering Population

A reliable strategy requires determining where the populations centers are for the contest of interest and maximizing efforts to reach those centers. For a DX contest from the East Coast of the US, the most important population center is Europe. For the West Coast, the most reachable population centers are in Asia and Oceania, but some time must be devoted to working Europe. The Mid-South often has the best of both worlds, but with shorter openings to either. For domestic contests, the object is to work the population centers of the eastern seaboard while getting multipliers from the west, and running California when possible. This even applies to eastern stations that often devote more time to lower bands. Fix your strategy on contacting the population centers. If you need help deciding which population centers are most important, check out past contest results and see where the entries come from.

By the same token, pointing your antennas away from a population center for extended periods of time will not increase your contest scores. Yet valuable multipliers often come from less-populated directions. The best solution to that problem is determining when there is a high likelihood of working a station in that direction, devoting a few minutes to the pursuit of multipliers and returning to the primary direction. As an example, 10 meters often opens for Northern Hemisphere stations in a southerly direction around local noon.

AFTER THE CONTEST

You've put a lot of effort into making contacts and working multipliers — don't sell yourself short by not submitting your log to the contest sponsors! If you're a contest club member, you will want to be sure your club receives credit for your score, as well. Even if you've just entered the contest casually and made a handful of QSOs, go ahead and submit a log. The sponsor will appreciate your efforts and it allows them to more accurately gauge contest activity.

Contest sponsors have criteria for submitting entries for their events. You should know what forms or electronic files the sponsor requires for an official entry. Each contest has a submission deadline. For all ARRL contests, the deadline is 30 days after the end of the event. The deadline for other contests may be found in the rules announcement on the sponsor's Web site. It's usually not more than 30 days, and sometimes less, so plan to submit as soon as possible after the contest ends. The amount of work involved in processing and verifying/checking entries is considerable, so contest sponsors are strict about meeting the log submission deadlines. Make certain that your entry is either e-mailed or postmarked by the deadline date.

As soon as the contest is over, start the log preparation process by making a backup copy of the log file before you do anything else. You're probably tired and anxious to relax — this is when mistakes happen, so be careful about naming and storing the file! There is no feeling worse than losing your just-completed contest log.

If you're really tired, go no further! Wait until you're fresh to edit your computer log. Make any changes you've noted on paper during the contest. For example, if you made a mistake in copying a station's exchange and made a note to yourself to fix it, now is the time. Many logging programs allow the operator to embed notes in the log. Collect all of your notes and make any necessary log changes. Most operators will also review the log for typos, such as entering double or extra characters. Finding typographical errors is the responsibility of the contest operator, not the contest sponsor. Remember, the log you submit is the log that will be checked.

What about duplicate QSOs — should they be removed? If you are submitting your log in Cabrillo format, leave them in the log. The sponsor's software will automatically only count one of the QSOs. You won't be penalized for duplicate QSOs because the sponsor calculates QSO points for you. If you are submitting an ASCII or paper log, leave the QSOs in the log file, but enter zero for QSO points.

Ethics

Before manipulating the log any further, there are ethical considerations to be weighed. How much editing is appropriate? What should you do if the information you've logged "looks" wrong? These questions (and more) are addressed in the ARRL's "HF Contesting — Good Practices, Interpretations and Suggestions" at **www.arrl.org/contests/hf-faq.html**. Here's what it says about log editing:

"It's possible to 'sanitize' a log after the contest, but... the contest is over at the time the rules say it's over. Examples of post-contest log manipulation include editing times, correcting band changes, checking calls against the call book, checking against…spots, looking through logs from other contesters, confirming calls and exchanges with your buddies, reading DX and contesting reflectors for news about rare calls and even posting questions like, 'did anyone get QSL info for that VQ0?'

"There are wide ranging opinions about the acceptability of editing your log after the contest. The most conservative and always acceptable answer is that no editing of any sort is permissible. Some feel you have until the log submission deadline to do anything you want to the log. Most contesters would agree that if you made a note during the contest about an error, it's OK to fix it afterwards. Furthermore, it is generally OK to make a quick pass through the log immediately after the contest looking for 'obvious' typos such as entering CT as CTT or changing 'o' to '0' — in fact, most logging software does such a check before creating the final log file. Correcting syntax errors reported by a log acceptance robot, such as improper dates or multiplier abbreviations is also acceptable. Once you step over the line into making changes to what you think you 'should' have logged, that's going too far.

"Reviewing your log is completely appropriate to help improve your operating accuracy and look for ways to improve strategy — in the *next* contest. In fact, many top operators regularly review their logs and even record parts of contests in order to review and improve their operating practices. For example, when you get your log-checking report, you can go back to review busted calls and see what the other station really sent. This is an excellent way to discover where your weak spots are. A quick scan of last year's log will refresh your memory about when and where you worked those rare multipliers, too!"

LOG SUBMISSION

When you are satisfied with your log, prepare a copy for the contest sponsor. The rules will usually specify the format in which the log should be submitted. The log format is the arrangement of information in the submitted computer file. The two most common are Cabrillo and ASCII and most logging software can create log files in both of these formats. Again, carefully check the rules to see what file type(s) are accepted. If you don't send the right one, chances are your log won't be accepted and your score won't show up in the results.

Cabrillo: A Contest Log Standard

The most common file format used by contest sponsors is Cabrillo. (Pronounced ca-BREE-oh, the name refers to Cabrillo College near the home of Trey Garlough, N5KO, author of the Cabrillo format specification.) *All* electronic files for ARRL (and many other)

Table 7-1
ARRL Contest Log E-Mail Addresses

10 GHz and Up Contest	10GHZ@arrl.org
ARRL 10 Meter Contest	10Meter@arrl.org
ARRL 160 Meter Contest	160Meter@arrl.org
August UHF Contest	AugustUHF@arrl.org
ARRL International DX CW Contest	DXCW@arrl.org
ARRL International DX Phone Contest	DXPhone@arrl.org
International EME Contest	EMEContest@arrl.org
Field Day	Fieldday@arrl.org
IARU HF World Championships	IARU@iaru.org
January VHF Sweepstakes	JanuaryVHF@arrl.org
June VHF QSO Party	JuneVHF@arrl.org
RTTY Round-UP	RTTYRU@arrl.org
September VHF QSO Party	SeptemberVHF@arrl.org
November Sweepstakes CW	SSCW@arrl.org
November Sweepstakes Phone	SSPhone@arrl.org
Straight Key Night	Straightkey@arrl.org

contests *must* be in the Cabrillo format. All of the major contest logging programs will generate a valid Cabrillo file.

Cabrillo files are composed of ASCII characters, and the log information is in fixed-position columns. See the example in **Fig 7-1**. Cabrillo also adds a number of standardized "header" lines that contain information about the log, such as the operator's name, call and location, contest category, power and so forth. The Cabrillo format allows sponsors to automate the process of log collection, sorting and checking even though entrants use many different programs to generate the submitted log files. The Cabrillo log file should be named **yourcall.cbr** (for example, **n0ax.cbr**). You can read up on Cabrillo at **www. kkn.net/~trey/cabrillo**.

If you have created an electronic Cabrillo format log file for submission, the next step is to e-mail it to the sponsors. The rules will provide the address to use. Attach your log to an e-mail

```
START-OF-LOG: 2.0
ARRL-SECTION: NH
CALLSIGN: K1RO
CATEGORY: SINGLE-OP 160M LOW CW
CLAIMED-SCORE: 47320
CLUB:
CONTEST: ARRL-160
CREATED-BY: WriteLog V10.43F
NAME: Mark Wilson
ADDRESS: 77 Anderson Rd
ADDRESS: Newport, NH 03773
OPERATORS: K1RO
SOAPBOX:
QSO:  1836 CW 2006-12-02 0043 K1RO      599 NH   K0TV       599    NH
QSO:  1839 CW 2006-12-02 0045 K1RO      599 NH   K4ZA       599    MDC
QSO:  1840 CW 2006-12-02 0045 K1RO      599 NH   AA1SU      599    VT
QSO:  1805 CW 2006-12-02 0047 K1RO      599 NH   N8II       599    WV
QSO:  1806 CW 2006-12-02 0048 K1RO      599 NH   VE3MIS     599    ON
QSO:  1809 CW 2006-12-02 0049 K1RO      599 NH   K1EO       599    EMA
QSO:  1810 CW 2006-12-02 0050 K1RO      599 NH   N2MM       599    SNJ
QSO:  1812 CW 2006-12-02 0052 K1RO      599 NH   K1GU       599    TN
QSO:  1814 CW 2006-12-02 0052 K1RO      599 NH   K3ZO       599    MDC
QSO:  1815 CW 2006-12-02 0053 K1RO      599 NH   N4IR       599    TN
QSO:  1817 CW 2006-12-02 0053 K1RO      599 NH   W3BGN      599    EPA
QSO:  1864 CW 2006-12-02 0056 K1RO      599 NH   K1EP       599    EMA
QSO:  1860 CW 2006-12-02 0057 K1RO      599 NH   W4PM       599    VA
QSO:  1859 CW 2006-12-02 0057 K1RO      599 NH   NB1B       599    EMA
```

Fig 7-1 — Here is the header and first few QSOs from a Cabrillo file ready for submission to the contest sponsor. The header contains all the information that the sponsor needs to include the entry in the right category and send awards if earned. Each QSO is reported on a separate line in a consistent format. Because the Cabrillo format is the same no matter which logging program was used during the contest, log data can easily be loaded into a master database for cross-checking.

RTTY Contesting

By Ed Muns, WØYK

RTTY contesting is the fastest growing segment of radiosport. Each year, participation in the major RTTY contests increases dramatically. New Hams as well as veteran CW and phone contesters are jumping into the fun. Unlike RTTY operation a few decades ago, today you can set up this digital mode with a minimum of additional equipment beyond a basic CW/phone station. Transmitting and receiving can be easily done with most modern transceivers, an old PC and simple cables. Most contesters already have a computer integrated with their station, so getting on RTTY can be very quick.

Gearing Up

The majority of RTTY contests use the traditional 60 WPM (45.45 Baud) 5-bit Baudot code consisting of sequences of "marks" and "spaces" that are simply two tones at 2125 and 2295 Hz, respectively. On receive, the audio output of the receiver is connected to the sound card input on the PC where the RTTY demodulator software decodes it into text on the screen. Alternatively, the receiver audio can be connected to a hardware RTTY modem which in turn is connected to the computer via a standard RS-232 cable. It is a good idea to use an audio isolation transformer, such as RadioShack p/n 273-1374, in-line between the receiver audio output and the PC sound card or RTTY modem.

To transmit, a standard serial keying interface cable is connected from the computer to the FSK input of the transmitter. If a hardware RTTY modem is being used instead, its output can connect to the transmitter's FSK input. A third transmitting alternative is to use AFSK (Audio Frequency Shift Keying) and connect the PC's sound card output to the transmitter's mic input, using LSB mode. Again, an audio isolation transformer is recommended.

More details of these connections can be found in the "Getting Started on RTTY" Web page, authored by Don Hill, AA5AU at aa5au.com/rtty.html. He also developed and maintains a robust RTTY contesting Web site at www.rttycontesting.com. An experienced and successful RTTY competitor, Don gives an excellent overview all aspects of RTTY contesting. Although his Web site is based on the *Writelog* contest software, much of the information is equally applicable to setups using other programs. There are also links to many other sources of information for new and experienced RTTY contesters alike.

There are several choices for software, but most people starting out today choose *MMTTY*, a freeware RTTY PC program for receiving and transmitting. While the RTTY modulation and demodulation capability is superb, the contest logging aspect of *MMTTY* is far less than what most contesters will want. For RTTY contest logging, three programs are most popular: *Writelog, N1MM Logger* and *Win-Test*. *MMTTY* can be integrated with each of these so that RTTY encoding/decoding is available with contest logging in a single optimized package.

RTTY Operating Skills

In contrast to CW contesting where the operator's brain is timeshared between decoding CW and other tasks, in RTTY contesting the computer does all the decoding for you. When a RTTY signal is properly tuned in on the receiver, the result is clear "printing" of the transmitted characters on the computer screen. The good news is that this frees up the operator to attend to other details of contest operation, including very effective use of SO2R (single-op, two-radio) operating. The bad news is that until the receiver is tuned very close to the correct frequency of the incoming signal, only gibberish is available on the screen. Thus, many RTTY contesters use a narrow 250 Hz IF filter. Starting out, you may want to use a 500 Hz filter until you are accustomed to quickly tuning in a RTTY signal. With practice, your ears will be able to help you tune in the signal to within a few Hertz. RTTY decoding software and RTTY modems have tuning indicators to facilitate precise tuning of the signal.

Once you have basic RTTY receiving and transmitting working and integrated with your choice of contest logging software, you will want to focus on making your system as streamlined as possible for the most efficient RTTY contest operation. Basic to this are the message buffers used almost exclusively for all RTTY contest transmissions. While it is easy to go into "keyboard mode" and be able to type free text, it is far more efficient to use message buffers, just as in CW contesting. Message buffers should be kept as short as possible to reliably convey the necessary information. Each message should be preceded with a Line Feed and ended with a Space. This sets off your transmission within the screen of the receiving station in case there are gibberish characters around it as there often are.

You will soon learn that some "gibberish" is actually numbers that were falsely decoded as letters. For example, "TOO" is "599" when this occurs. If you suspect a letter group is really a number, as in a contest exchange, look at the keyboard and translate the letters to numbers by mapping the key above and to the left of each letter key.

Efficient RTTY contest operation for high rates also requires minimum keystrokes for each of (hopefully!) hundreds or thousands of contacts. Thus, it is important to study your logging software features to understand how to accomplish each phase of a RTTY contest QSO with the fewest keystrokes.

In many loggers, each phase can be achieved with a single keystroke. For example, software using a call sign database will capture and highlight valid call signs out of incoming transmissions. Properly configured, the logger will grab the most recent call sign that is a new multiplier or a new band-station, drop it in the call sign field of the entry window, call the station and send your exchange...all as a result of pressing a single key on the keyboard! As the return exchange comes in, use the mouse to click on any part of the exchange that is not already pre-filled in the entry window. At the end of the station's transmission, you can press another key to send a TU, QRZ message.

Single Op, Two Radios

With the RTTY fixed speed of 60 WPM, it quite feasible to achieve hourly QSO rates in excess of 120/hour with a properly configured and tuned SO2R RTTY contesting station. Because the operator does not need to expend brainpower on decoding the signal, more attention can be given to tuning and operating each radio. In fact, this characteristic leads veteran CW contester K5ZD to point out that RTTY contesting is the ideal training ground for SO2R skill development in general.

As with SO2R contesting in the other modes, there is a choice to be made. Do you use a single computer to control both radios and both sets of RTTY hardware/software, or do you use two networked computers, one for each radio/RTTY setup? Basically, this is a Multi-Two setup with transmit interlock to guarantee transmission by only one radio at a time. Currently, the vast majority of SO2R contesters use the single-computer system on all modes — CW, phone and RTTY.

There are a number of advantages to the two-computer model. With the ready availability of PCs suitable for ham applications these days, it is quite practical. Furthermore, in RTTY contesting very little typing actually need be done, so two mini-keyboards (full size, but minus the number pad area) and trackballs/mice can be conveniently arranged at the operating position along with two displays. As explained earlier, only two key strokes and perhaps a trackball movement are all that is required for most contest QSOs in a properly configured RTTY contest station.

So jump in and have a blast with RTTY contesting! While there are many similarities to CW and phone contesting, there are also a number of unique differences. This can add diversity and excitement to your overall contesting experience. Be aware of direct comparisons to your current favorite mode of contesting and keep an open mind while learning RTTY contesting.

RTTY contesting is the most rapidly growing part of radiosport. Operators like Ed, WØYK, are enjoying working many new calls, with over 1550 unique call signs logged in a recent contest!

with the subject line containing just the call you used during the contest, nothing else. The e-mail may be processed by a human or by a software "robot" program that automatically scans the received log files. Before sending the e-mail, double-check the attached file to be sure it is the file you intended to send!

Where do you send the e-mail? Each ARRL contest has a specific e-mail address and only entries for that contest should be sent there (see **Table 7-1**). Other contests will have submission addresses in their published rules. There may also be a Web page that you can use to simplify the log upload process.

If a person handles your log file, you will probably receive an acknowledgement within a day or two. The sponsor may also add your call to a list of "Logs Received" on a Web site. If you don't receive an acknowledgement and your call doesn't appear on the list with other calls, resend the log and send a *separate* e-mail to the sponsors.

If a software robot accepts your log, it will scan the log immediately. The robot looks to be sure that it understands everything in the log. The robot does *not* perform any QSO crosschecks with other logs. The robot will tell you if your dates are wrong or if you've picked a category that doesn't exist for that contest or if your contest club isn't recognized, for example. You can then correct any problems in the log file, resubmit it to the robot and wait for the reply. You can send your log to the robot any number of times. Each subsequent version will overwrite the previous version.

When the robot is happy with the information in your log (remember, that doesn't mean your QSOs are okay, just that the information is properly formatted) you will receive a message that the log has been accepted and you may be given a numeric "receipt" or reference number. Save the robot's e-mail and all reference numbers for possible later use.

While all this sounds terribly complicated, logging software usually makes the process very simple. If there is not much log editing to be performed, it's not uncommon to have a complete log submitted to the sponsors within 15 minutes after the contest! This is a vast improvement from the Old Days when it would take at least a week to go through the hand-printed paper logs. Once you've walked through this process a couple of times, it won't be a problem.

ASCII

The other common log submission format is ASCII. ASCII refers to the type of characters and means that the log should be a text file that only contains printable information. If you view this type of log file with a text editor, you will see the information arranged in fixed-position columns. Do not send the "binary" database file that your logging software uses during the contest.

Your logging software will probably have a file generation utility that creates ASCII or text files. Name the output log file **yourcall.txt** or **yourcall.asc** (for example, **n0ax.txt** or **n0ax.asc**). If you are going to submit an ASCII log file, you'll also need to generate a Summary Sheet file — name it **yourcall.sum**.

ASCII logs are usually e-mailed to the sponsor as described in the previous section.

Logs on Paper or Disk

If you are unable to e-mail your log file to the sponsor, copy it onto a 3.5 inch diskette or a CD-ROM and mail it to the address where paper logs are sent. Do not include any other files with a Cabrillo log file. If you are sending an ASCII log file, include the Summary Sheet file as well. The disk label should show your name, call sign and the name and year of the contest. Be sure to check the rules carefully, as not all sponsors will accept entries by postal mail.

Speaking of paper logs, if you hand-logged during the contest, as part of your preparations you should have acquired copies of the official contest entry forms, usually known as summary sheets. Summary sheets are a necessary part of your entry. Without them, the contest sponsor may not be able to determine how you intend to enter the contest. Don't rely on photocopies of forms you have from the same contest several years earlier. Contest rules change and those changes will be reflected on the summary sheets. Even though the number of paper logs is declining, they continue to be accepted by the sponsors of most contests.

Make certain you legibly complete the forms, including all information. If you don't complete the required forms, your entry is going to be difficult to process by the contest sponsor. If you don't include the little things, such as a correct entry category or power level, the sponsor may have no alternative but to assign your entry to default categories. For example, your failure to include the fact that you were QRP in the contest may mean your entry is treated as high power — and could cost you a chance at a certificate!

The mailing address for ARRL contest entries is: ARRL Contest Branch, 225 Main St, Newington, CT 06111. Please write the name of the contest on the outside of the envelope. You may also use that postal address to request copies of the latest contest summary sheets, log sheets and rules. Please include an SASE with sufficient postage to cover your request (about one unit per 4 sheets of information). These forms are also available for download from the ARRL Web site. Perhaps a friend or family member can download the files for you if you don't have Internet access.

While it is tempting, *don't* submit entries for more than one contest in the same envelope or e-mail. Contest sponsors are looking for a single entry in each envelope or e-mail. If you include more than one in a submission, it can be overlooked or stapled together as a single entry and can be misfiled. When the error is finally discovered, it could be well past the submission or publication deadline for one of the contests.

LOG CHECKING

What happens next varies from contest to contest, but the overall process is more or less the same as in the following oversimplified description. Your log is inspected to be sure that it has all the necessary information, that the dates are correct and so forth. The logs are then sorted by category and the cross-checking begins.

If the contest is of small to medium size, the cross-checking may be done manually and a detailed inspection only done on logs competing for awards. A committee of volunteers then makes the necessary corrections to scores and publishes the results. This may take from a few weeks beyond the submission deadline to several months.

For larger contests, including those sponsored by the ARRL, the automated process is much more thorough. All logs, once accepted by the robot or checked by hand, are combined into a master database. Special software then compares each of the submitted QSOs with the log of the corresponding station and looks for errors. If there are errors, the appropriate penalties are assessed. Following the crosscheck of all QSOs, the scores for all participants are then computed and compiled for the sponsor, who then publishes the results. The results for larger contests are generally available in a few months to a year.

The automated log checking process also generates a report for each log containing information on what the process found. This is called a *log checking report* (LCR) or a *UBN report*, where "UBN" stands for Unique, Busted or Not-In-the-Log. (See the Glossary at the end of this chapter.) Log checking reports are full of valuable information, generally containing complete information on every QSO in which errors were found.

Errors that can be attributed to you (miscopying calls or exchange information) will result in penalties defined by the sponsors. In general, you'll lose credit for the QSO, including any multiplier credit claimed. (If you worked the multiplier again later in the contest, you'll still get credit for it.) Some contests also assess an additional penalty to discourage fast-but-sloppy operating. You're not being accused of cheating, just penalized for making a mistake to encourage better performance next time!

Errors not attributed to you (the other station busting your call or information) are still valuable because they highlight possible shortcomings in your transmissions. For example, if a lot of stations are miscopying the H in your call as S or 5, you may not be sending your call cleanly. Even so, you are rarely penalized for errors by "the other guy."

Once the log checking is complete, the scores are compiled and the sponsor determines the winners. Results are usually published on the Web and sometimes in magazines such as *QST* or *National Contest Journal* (*NCJ*). That the results are ready is generally made known through popular e-mail reflectors or magazines. Awards and certificates are mailed after results publication.

Results Analysis

After the contest, results can be analyzed to see what might have been done differently. Comparing notes with friends is a good idea, as you will often find they did something totally different from you and it may come in handy to have the benefit of their experience in the future.

Assuming you used computer logging, you'll find that most programs have several post-contest features for use in log analysis. One of the best is the simple *rate chart*. This chart shows your hourly rate for each hour of the contest and the bands used during that hour. Log files often show the frequency used for each contact so you can tell if you were CQing (contacts on the same frequency) or using S&P. Other breakdowns will show the general area where the contacts came from, the first contact for a particular multiplier or how many contacts came from each individual multiplier.

A *points-per-hour sheet* may also be found as part of most analysis packages. Using this data, you can draw a graph to see how the score progressed hourly or which hours seem to be most productive. You will also notice that the score rises

VHF+ Contesting

By Jon Jones, N0JK

VHF contests offer an exciting and challenging experience for the HF contester. (Most of these events include VHF, UHF and microwave bands, but they're usually just called "VHF contests.") The single-band 10 meter and 160 meter contests are perhaps the most like VHF Contests. At the solar minimum, 10 meters behaves a lot like 6 meters at the solar maximum. Ionospheric F2 propagation can make an appearance in the September and January VHF Contests. E-skip, aurora and meteor scatter are propagation modes used both on 10 and 6 meters. Working weak signals on the higher VHF bands is much like digging out weak DX amid the static on 160 meters.

Station Equipment

You may already have a transceiver that will get you started in VHF contesting. With HF/VHF/UHF radios such as the ICOM IC-706 series and IC-7000, the Kenwood TS-2000 and Yaesu's FT-847 and FT-897 becoming common, casual participants can get their feet wet on 6 and 2 meters and 70 cm in the VHF contests. Even more radios offer 6 meter coverage along with HF, which will get you started in VHF contests as a single-band 6 meter entry. For higher bands and 222 MHz, transverters are usually necessary. These are commercially available and usually require only a little special knowledge to set up and use.

Although you can start with a dipole or your 2-meter FM antenna, you'll quickly find that the contest is more fun with a horizontally polarized Yagi of some sort. The good news is that VHF/UHF antennas are compact, so you can put them on a mast, roof tripod or light duty tower and turn them with a small rotator. You might even have some extra room in between your HF antennas. Be sure to use a good quality feed line. Common HF cables like RG-213 have quite a bit of loss at higher frequencies.

Portable operation is popular and encouraged in the VHF contests. For the antenna-restricted or apartment operator, the Single Operator Portable and Rover categories let you operate on a competitive basis with many of the well equipped home stations. A 10 W portable station on a mountaintop can be louder than a high power station down in a valley.

Multi-operator groups operating stations such as K8GP and W2SZ/1 take high-power stations and large antennas for all bands to high mountaintops to extend their reach. They're like beacons, operating with big signals and sensitive receivers on several bands simultaneously and giving many VHF operators their first far-away contacts.

Operating a VHF Contest

Grid locators, often called "grid squares," are usually the multipliers in VHF contests. Grid squares aren't actually square. They are 1° latitude by 2° longitude rectangles that measure approximately 70 × 100 miles in the continental US. A grid square is indicated by two letters (the field) and numbers (the square). For example, the grid square for W1AW in central Connecticut is FN31. In most VHF contests, grid squares are the only information (other than call signs) that must be exchanged. See www.arrl.org/locate/gridinfo.html or Chapter 3 of this book for more information on grid locators.

VHF contests are often casual when conditions are slow. Operators work at a leisurely pace and may take several tries to finish a contact with a weak station. Things change if the band opens, though. During a tropo or E-skip opening, the VHF bands can be as busy as 40 meters on Saturday evening in the phone Sweepstakes! Several stations made over 1100 contacts on 6 meters in the June 2006 VHF QSO Party, with peak rates of over 200 contacts per hour.

Strategy is important to achieving a high score. Operating as many bands as possible and making sure to work stations on all available bands is the way to maximize your score. A 432 MHz QSO is worth twice as many points as one on 6 or 2 meters. On 1296 MHz a contact is worth 3 times as much, plus the grids are counted as new multipliers on each band. So scores can increase exponentially as stations are moved from band to band.

Just as in an HF contest, balance your efforts between working new grids and making more QSO points to maximize your score. If a band is open to an unusual area, stick with it to expand your multiplier and QSO count. It may not be open later. For example, stick with 6 and 2 meters in the ARRL June VHF QSO Party as long as they are open, and work the higher bands at a later time. In the January VHF Sweepstakes, when 6 meters is often dead, changing bands frequently and moving stations to needed bands as you run across them is the way to improve your score.

Always remember that on VHF and above, enhanced propagation can occur when you least expect it. For example, E-skip can appear in January — as it did in the 2007 VHF Sweepstakes on Saturday evening. QRP ops KA6AKH and N0JK made 6 meter contest E-skip contacts with ease. When 6 meters is open, low power and a dipole or whip can make 1000-mile contacts. So stay alert and "expect the unexpected" in VHF Contests — this is often what make them fun and interesting to operate in.

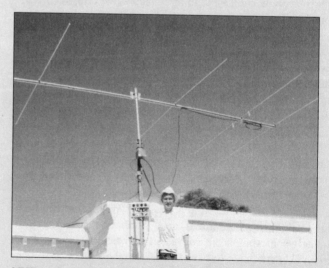

VHF+ contesters can go on expeditions, too! Jon, N0JK, traveled to Bermuda (VP9) for the June ARRL VHF QSO Party. From this location, E-skip (E_s) propagation is common into the Eastern seaboard and even across the US on 6 meters if conditions are good. Other VHF+ contesters head for the Caribbean, beaming northwest across the entire US and Canada.

at a faster rate the farther into the contest you look. The more contacts, the more total point value to multiply and the score starts to increase geometrically. This is further graphic proof that it pays to keep working at making contacts.

CONTEST EQUIPMENT

Just as a knowledgeable driver can't win a race without a good car, the radiosport operator will find it hard to make a good score without solid radio gear. Start by purchasing good-quality equipment and work your way up, learning how to make the most out of every item. Step by step, you'll build your way to a capable, effective station.

Basic Equipment

A good receiver is needed for even the casual contester. Most modern radios have good receivers that can handle the big signals you'll encounter on contest weekends. High dynamic range is essential. (See the section on Equipment in Chapter 6, DXing) Install good-quality filters if they are available: 500 Hz for CW and 2.0 kHz for phone. Headphones are a must, as you just can't catch all of the weak calls in the QRM without them. Others near your operating position will appreciate their use too.

The transmitter should have a good, properly adjusted speech processor and the microphone should have a contest element that trades wide response for emphasis on the mid-range speech components. Some popular mikes have a switch for contest/DX use or casual conversation. Remember that overdriving your transceiver or amplifier is not only bad manners but also hurts your intelligibility on the air. It is important to have a crisp, clear signal.

A memory keyer or a computer with a keying interface is a must for CW. Configure the memories to send as much of the CQ and exchange information as possible. Using the memories leaves you time for housekeeping chores, such as keeping up a band map, reviewing a multiplier sheet or other things that will contribute to raising your score, while the computer or keyer does the work of sending CQs or your exchange.

Full sized antennas are preferred. A dipole at modest height gives great "bang for the buck" performance. If you can't install it high, then try sloping it from as high as possible on one end and lower on the other end. If you use a vertical antenna, make sure you install a good ground system and keep it clear of obstacles to radio waves. Both antennas will probably work better than you'd expect — don't be afraid to call anyone you can hear. They'll probably hear you better than you can hear them. Tribanders (beams that operate on 20, 15 and 10 meters) and other gain antennas are more desirable.

Without recommending a specific type of antenna, one thing will always hold true: Proper installation is the key. Ultimately contesting is the true test of any station's potential. It doesn't do any good to have the best, highest antenna in the world if it's fed with a piece of junk coaxial cable and unsoldered connectors. Make sure that the antenna is properly built and tuned, that you use good quality feed line and that all connectors are installed correctly and waterproofed.

Intermediate Equipment

As you become more engaged in contesting, take every opportunity to optimize the radio station as much as possible within your budget. A contest station can be as cheap or expensive as you want to make it, but continue to purchase top quality equipment.

Contesters often talk in terms of "layers" of stations. Making an improvement is often intended to allow the station to reach a new group — or layer — of stations that are currently too weak to work effectively. By improving an antenna, receiver or transmitted signal those stations can be worked and you will find a lot of new calls in your log. Each layer seems to require approximately one S-unit's worth of improvement (6 dB, nominally) on receive *and* transmit. They have to hear you and you have to hear them. When you plan upgrades — lowering a radiation angle, lowering a noise floor or raising power — think in terms of layers of improvement.

Receiver improvements at this level revolve around better performance in crowded conditions, not necessarily more memories or wider coverage. You'll want to take every opportunity to listen to different receivers. Can the receiver clearly reproduce a weak signal squeezed in between two domestic titans calling CQ? If many stations are calling, does the receiver allow you hear individual signals or do they merge into one big mess? How does the receiver sound when the DSP functions are operating? Most modern receivers are quite good and significant improvements are often subtle. Take the time to learn about them because you'll be using a receiver every time you're on the air!

The ability to hear through QRM makes the difference between good scores and great ones. The better you can hear, the better the results. Use the receive attenuator to prevent overload. A receiver's AGC can be overpowered by strong nearby signals — try reducing the RF gain as this often will help you hear weak signals through strong signals. Use the variable bandwidth or IF shift controls. Turn off the noise blanker. Experiment with the settings in the face of QRM, but remember the original settings so that you can return to them.

Install several filters if available, especially on CW. There are two schools of thought on wide and narrow CW filters. One says that it is better to hear stations calling if they are not exactly on your frequency, while the other school feels that in crowded band conditions it's better to use the narrow filters. If you have both filters available, you can switch between them to suit the circumstances. DSP filtering is becoming the norm in contest radios and can be tailored to suit almost any conditions. Just remember that while you're messing around with the filter settings, you're not making QSOs!

A contest-grade transceiver with dual receive may be the ultimate weapon. The second receiver allows you to work two pileups simultaneously or search for multipliers while running stations. If you don't have such a transceiver, it's possible to use an outboard second receiver (perhaps your old rig?) with a two-port power divider coupled through the external antenna port of the main transceiver. Two receivers are effective for finding new stations to work on the same band or on different bands or for working split frequency pileups on 40 and 75 meter phone. Remember that you still have to listen for ongoing QSOs on the split transmit frequency before calling the other station!

Amplifiers

Adding an amplifier to a transceiver is definitely a way

Two-Radio Contesting

The use of two radios in a single-operator station (SO2R or single-op, two-radios) has been around for many years, but has spread significantly in recent years. Coupled with innovations in logging software, it is almost necessary for the winning single-op contester to use two radios.

This subject could almost be a book in itself. Design of a station capable of two-radio contesting is similar to the design of a multi-multi station. One transceiver might listen on one band while the second is transmitting on another. The use of bandpass filters and harmonic suppression stubs is necessary for successful high-power operation. If adequate separation is available between antennas, a two-radio station can be as simple as adding another transceiver and a dipole or vertical antenna. There is an advantage to using the second station. The degree of the advantage depends on the operator and how he uses the station.

The purpose of the second radio is to allow an operator who might be calling CQ on one band to be listening for activity or multipliers on another band. Once found, a multiplier may be called and worked on the second station during a listening period for the first station. Over the course of the contest, a neophyte to SO2R operation may add up to 100 QSOs. An accomplished operator can add as many as 400 QSOs, including multipliers that may not otherwise be worked. Needless to say, this is a tremendous advantage in close competitions. As with any contesting skill, effective SO2R operation requires practice. Until you learn how to do it well, trying to manage a second radio may actually slow you down when you should be concentrating fully on a high-rate run.

There are several ways to listen to the second radio. Some listen to one radio in one ear, the other in the other ear on a stereo headset. Others like to mix the audio into both ears, but with one radio running a higher volume. A third and less confusing method is to shut off the monitor on the main radio and listen to the second radio only during transmit periods for the first radio. This can be done with a relay to switch the audio.

Designs for two-radio switching systems have appeared in the *National Contest Journal* in recent years. Several manufacturers offer "SO2R controllers" and there are numerous Web sites that provide information on operating with two radios.

You don't have to have a room full of equipment to be effective at single-operator, two-radio contesting. This compact and straightforward SO2R station operated by Pete, N4ZR, can often be heard from West Virginia.

to reach a new level or two of stations. A small amplifier with 500 to 1000 W output will make a big difference in your signal and allow you to hold a frequency under challenging conditions. Going to a "full gallon" at 1500 W output is better yet. Remember that you may need to upgrade your antenna system and feed line components to handle the higher power level. You may also have to run a sufficiently heavy electrical service to the shack. It's generally unnecessary in contesting to require full break-in (QSK) capabilities of the amplifier, but if you like that style of operating it may be worth the extra expense.

Amplifiers should be chosen for high duty cycle usage. Cooling is important, so don't expect the fan to be quiet. Whatever its output rating, a good amplifier for contest use should be able to loaf along at full rated output power because it's likely to be turned on for an entire contest — up to 48 hours at a time. If you are buying a used amplifier, check availability and price of the amplifier tubes and components that may need to be replaced, such as the TR relays.

HIGH BAND ANTENNAS

Antennas for serious contesting are usually bigger, higher and more efficient than for any other use in Amateur Radio. The antenna system is where more improvement can be made than anywhere else in the station.

This discussion will focus on the needs of the single-operator, all-band operator. Those needs are different from the single-band operator or multi-op station. For example, the single band or multi-multi operator needs antennas capable of getting through during band openings and closing and marginal openings, as well as providing good coverage during the peak band openings. The single-operator all-band operator needs antennas that provide good coverage during the peak band openings, but not necessarily during the marginal band openings and closings. The single operator needs to be working lots of QSOs on an open band rather than chasing marginal openings.

Most intermediate contesters begin their high-band (20, 15 and 10 meter) antenna systems with a large Yagi antenna at least

60 feet in the air. These antennas should have at least three full-size elements active on each band, providing gain above that available from smaller or shortened three-element antennas. Front-to-back ratio will improve by an S-unit or more, which is helpful in reducing interference from nearby stations. A station using an amplifier and such an antenna in an average or better location should be able to hold a run frequency under most conditions.

Planning Your Antennas

To improve beyond this level requires some thought and planning so that money and effort are not wasted. The place to start in planning a contest antenna system is *The ARRL Antenna Book*. The propagation chapter and the companion disk provide tables of radiation angles at which openings occur with maximum probability for most areas of the world. By using that information, you can develop an effective antenna building strategy for your location. For example, the path from Cincinnati, Ohio, to Europe on 20 meters always requires an arrival angle between 1° and 28°. However, 90% of the time, the angle is from 3° to 12°. The peak signal angle is 8°, which occurs 26% of the time, so an antenna system for working Europe on 20 meters should be designed to radiate at angles at or near 8°. This study can be carried out for each band of interest and antennas optimized to provide patterns within the range of angles specified in the tables for your area.

Choosing a site for your antenna is also important. If you are considering a move, use modeling to evaluate the new location as a candidate for hosting a contest station antenna farm. Even if you're working with an existing location, some properties are large enough that antenna placement could make a difference. Check out the section on effects of the Earth in *The ARRL Antenna Book*. There you will find information about site selection and the use of the *YT* program included in the book. Using this program, a USGS 7.5 minute topographical map of your QTH and the files of arrival angles for the various bands and regions, you can determine the most useful angles for propagation for your area. You can then apply those studies to generate ideas for your own antenna farm. If you can't choose a site, at least you can check the potential of your present site.

Returning to our Cincinnati example, a 20-meter antenna should provide a take-off angle of 8° for peak propagation to Europe on 20 meters. Using a profile for your terrain (and each QTH is different), you might find that for equivalent antennas at 100 feet your terrain is actually almost 2 dB better at 8° than flat terrain. Maybe the analysis shows that your terrain has a disadvantage, instead. Try moving the antenna to a different location on the site or adjusting the height of the antenna to

Bob, N6TV, puts out a powerful contest signal from this city lot in San Jose, California. His stack of antennas on a crank-up tower are competitive on all bands, 160 through 10 meters. (NØAX photo)

change the antenna's radiation pattern to peak at the most favorable angle.

How High?

Higher is not always better. You may find that raising an antenna actually hurts performance! In the previous example, changing the antenna from 100 to 150 feet lowers performance at the optimum angle of 8° by about 1 dB and the overall pattern is hurt even more, with the introduction of higher angle lobes and suppression of radiation at some angles between 8° and 15°! On the other hand, a multi-multi or single-band station would want at least one antenna this high or maybe even higher, for use during band openings and closings, plus other antennas at different heights for use under other conditions.

Comparisons of antenna heights should of course be made based on the topography of the site. But what differences can one expect by changing antenna heights given the same terrain? Given a flat ground site, moving the antenna to 100 feet from 70 feet results in an advantage of about 2 dB at the optimum radiation angle. Similarly, the difference between 100 feet and 50 feet over flat ground can be almost 5 dB, and it's around 2 dB between 50 and 70 feet. That is not the case on all types of terrain. For example, it is possible to show that steeply sloping terrain in front of the antenna can provide such an advantage that a 50 foot high antenna will perform almost as well as a 100 foot high antenna. However, both will be outperformed by an antenna at 70 feet — exactly the perfect height for that terrain.

Antenna type also makes a difference in choice of heights. A dipole over flat ground at 70 feet would have a gain of approximately 7.7 dBi at 14°. A three-element beam at the same height would have a gain of 14.2 dBi at 14°. At the desired angle of 8°, the dipole's apparent gain would have dropped to 5.8 dBi, while the beam's gain would be 12.1 dBi. The beam has a substantial gain difference at the same height as the dipole and would equal it from a lower height. To have the advantage at 8°, the beam could be as low as 40 feet and still be marginally better than a dipole at 70 feet. However, a high dipole may be shown to be as good as a low beam. Using modeling programs and studying the angles can help with choice of antenna type.

Multiple Antennas

Stacked antennas are now almost standard equipment for the competitive contest station. A "stack" is two or more antennas for the same band placed at different heights on the tower. Usually they can be fed together or independently.

Not only do stacked antennas allow choices of height and direction, they also broaden the footprint of the transmitted signal and provide anywhere from 1 to 3 dB extra gain. For contest stations, "loud is good" (N2AA), so it's worth studying the possible gains available from stacked antennas. Look at different numbers of antennas (usually 2, 3 or 4) at varying heights when considering station improvements.

Many contest operators have successfully stacked tribander Yagis, so the limitations of using only monobanders no longer exists. Using stacked tribanders on a city lot will often increase the flexibility and competitiveness of smaller contest stations.

Obviously some compromises must be made in antenna selection and antenna heights, but these choices should be made from an informed position and not without some understanding of the basic principles involved.

LOW-BAND ANTENNAS

The low bands (160, 80 and 40 meters) require just as much study as the high bands. You may, however, have fewer practical options because of the physical size antennas for these bands. Even if you're on a city lot rather than acreage out in the country, it is still possible to get out a decent signal if you pay attention to detail.

For 40 meters, the easiest solution these days seems to be the two-element shortened beam, often called the "shorty forty." Offered by several companies, these antennas work well at 70 feet or higher. Phased verticals can also be used, and a simple vertical radiator can be made of push-up TV mast with a base insulator. If your property has suitable trees, wire antennas such as a Bobtail curtain or wire beam are often excellent choices.

You'll find that 80 and 160 meters are similar — it's just the size of the antenna that's different. While three-element 80-meter beams are nice, the odds of competing with one in a pileup are slim. Many contesters are putting up phased verticals or four-square arrays on these bands. (A "four-square" is an array of four vertical antennas in a square box configuration with switching circuitry to provide gain in several directions.) Another popular option is a switched array of sloping dipoles suspended from a tower. You can be competitive with well planned, but simple, arrays.

Again, take into consideration the desired wave angles, then do what it takes to maximize performance at the optimum angles. In most cases on the low bands, that's likely to mean vertical antennas, but not always. You would do well to buy a copy of *ON4UN's Low Band DXing* written by John Devoldere, ON4UN, and published by ARRL. This book has everything you need to know about low-band transmit and receive antennas. The winning contester has a copy and studies it and you should too.

Roving — operating on the move or from several choice locations — has become a very popular operating style for VHF+ contesters. Jerry, W7IEW, has converted this VW bus to a capable multi-band station. *(W7IEW photo)*

VHF/UHF ANTENNA SYSTEMS

A beginning VHF+ contester likely has a beam of several elements for 2 meters and possibly a dipole or small beam on 6 meters. Unlike FM antennas, those used for SSB/CW operation and contesting are horizontally polarized. It is easy to improve antenna gain and pattern at VHF+ in ways impossible at lower frequencies.

Big improvements in gain are available simply by increasing the number of elements on a long-boom Yagi antenna. It's not unusual to see Yagis with 20 elements or more at 2 meters and higher frequencies, nor are 7 element Yagis uncommon on 6 meters. These antennas can have more than 10 dB of gain in free space — the same as an amplifier! (Be careful around this antennas because of the increased levels of RF exposure at high power!)

Beyond simply increasing the boom length and number of elements, building arrays of multiple long-boom Yagis create some truly awesome gain and pattern performance. They take some careful planning to get the mechanical and electrical details right, but the results are impressive.

Another area of improved antenna system performance at VHF+ frequencies is in feed line loss. In a run of 100 feet of feed line, a change to surplus Hardline (½ inch or larger) can save several dB over the best flexible coax. This is a "free" improvement, requiring no rotator and no power supply. Losses are simply reduced — you'll hear better and be heard better.

One aspect of high-performance VHF+ antenna building not available to HF operators is for roving or portable operation. If you can't build a powerhouse antenna system at home, make one you can move and take it on the road! VHF+ antenna systems can be mounted on a vehicle or trailer and taken to a hilltop or other advantageous location — make your own propagation!

STATION ACCESSORIES

In addition to basic equipment like transceivers, amplifiers and antennas, most contest operators gradually add accessories and tools that make operation more efficient.

Integrating the Computer and Station

Once just a tool for entering log information, the computer is integrated into nearly all phases of the modern contest station.

The computer sends voice and CW messages. It reads and sets the operating parameters of the radio. Digital mode contesting is virtually impossible without it. Through interfaces, it can control nearly all of the station equipment. All this allows the operator to remain focused on making QSOs instead of fiddling with various pieces of equipment.

Assuming you are running contest logging software and can use the computer to send CW (and possibly voice) messages, you'll next need to connect the computer to the radio through its control port. The two standard radio control interfaces are RS-232 and ICOM's CI-V interface, a variation of RS-232. USB interfaces are not yet part of the amateur transceiver as of 2007. Ethernet interfaces are available on a handful of transceivers. The data protocols used to interact with radios vary with manufacturer and model, so be sure your logging software will support your radio and that your computer has the correct interface for it. Since most new laptop PCs do not have an RS-232 port, you'll have to use a USB-to-RS-232 adapter or get a computer-to-transceiver interface designed for USB operation.

If you plan on entering Assisted, Unlimited or Multi-operator categories, connection to the Internet spotting networks is required. The amount of data received is not great, so dial-up connections are quite acceptable. You can even use instant messaging services to chat with other operators during the contest! As a pure Single-Op, you are still permitted to take advantage of propagation bulletins, weather information and other useful Internet services.

There are a number of accessory programs that augment the logging software. Propagation prediction and frequency maps can be very helpful in deciding when to change bands and look for secondary band openings. A gray line program will remind low-band operators when to look for sunrise and sunset openings.

Headphones and Microphones

Headphones are the only choice for the serious contester. Anything that sounds good is fine. Some prefer headphones with a restricted audio range, while others prefer hi-fi type phones with a good low frequency response for hearing low pitched CW signals. Some operators like to switch the audio in one ear so that it is out of phase with audio in the other ear, giving the signals a spatial quality of perception. You will need stereo headphones if you have a dual channel receiver.

An important consideration: Headphones must be comfortable to wear for long periods of time. While some operators prefer the lightweight foam padded headsets, most prefer the full muff headsets that help reduce sounds from outside the radio. Sometimes it's a good idea to be able to change headphones when you feel like your head is in a vise or when a set rubs too long on one patch of skin.

A headset/boom microphone combination is best for SSB operation. Fatigue is always a factor in any contest and not having to keep your head in a certain position to use the microphone can provide great relief. Some prefer the freedom of movement that VOX control permits. Others rely on a footswitch so that they only transmit when they want, not whenever they talk or cough.

Stubs and Filters

As you build a more sophisticated station, you'll reach the point where you want to tune around for new stations and

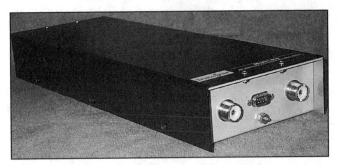

Multi-band bandpass filters, such as the Dunestar Model 600 shown here, help minimize interference and prevent receiver damage during SO2R or multi-operator competitions. Such filters are most effective when they are set up to switch automatically as the transceiver changes bands.

multipliers on one band while you're CQing on another. With the transmitting and receiving antennas in such close proximity, it's inevitable that noise and signals from the transmitter will challenge your ability to receive on another band at the same time. Most contest stations employ a combination of bandpass filters and transmission line stubs to clean up the transmitter and limit the signals the receiver has to deal with.

Bandpass filters are available in single-band or multi-band models. The multi-band models can be switched manually or automatically by an interface device connected to the radio. Most stations do the filtering between the transceiver and amplifier, although the larger stations also build high-power bandpass filters that can handle the full amplifier output.

Stubs are used to remove harmonics and out-of-band signals at specific frequencies. *The ARRL Antenna Book* discusses how to construct and apply stubs. An excellent reference on this topic is *Managing Interstation Interference* by George Cutsogeorge, W2VJN, and available from International Radio (**www.qth.com/inrad**). Stubs can provide 20 dB or more of attenuation at low cost and effort.

Filter and Switch Control

The complexity of a full-blown contest station makes it very difficult for the human operator to control all of the equipment manually. There are multiple antenna switches, filters, stubs and amplifiers to be reset at every band change. If the operator is using two radios at once to CQ on one band and tune for mults on another, audio to the headphones needs to be switched, as well.

Most of the information to make the necessary changes is available in the band and frequency information the radio can supply through its data and band ports. Control interfaces can read the radio's information and then change antenna and filter switches accordingly. Given the expense of repairing or replacing a blown filter, amplifier output or receiver input, these controllers are a good investment once station complexity begins to exceed the operator's ability to keep track of all the settings. You can tell when it has become time for automated interface control when you find yourself making mistakes in the heat of the contest or become confused when tired or busy.

The interfaces can be driven by the radio directly or by the station computer. The computer is assumed to be connected to

The information available from contest-grade transceivers allows the rig to control external devices such as filters and switches. To convert the rig's information into switch closures a decoder is required, such as the Top Ten device shown here.

Antenna switching schemes can quickly become quite complex and difficult to operate properly. Automated accessories, such as the WXØB Six Pack, keep switching functions simply and less likely to be operated improperly.

the radio from which it acquires the band and frequency information. It is hard to add switch and filter control automation "halfway." If you are considering adding these functions to your station, it's best to do the whole job at once. The interface manufacturers provide a wealth of information on their Web sites to assist you in designing your new system and selecting equipment. Articles in *National Contest Journal* and information in *The ARRL Antenna Book* and *The ARRL Handbook* show you how to build this equipment yourself, if you prefer.

ERGONOMICS

Ergonomics is the study and practice of human engineering in station design. Simply put, if you're not comfortable, you won't stay in the chair and operate. If you don't stay in the chair, you won't be competitive. This section touches on some of the important aspects of station ergonomics, but for more complete information and guidelines, read up on workplace ergonomics. The requirements are much the same as for a radio operating position. Enter "office ergonomics guidelines" into an Internet search engine for numerous references on placement of equipment, products, exercises and so forth. Over the course of a contest, ergonomics and the comfort factor can make a big difference in your alertness and energy!

Speaking of chairs, what you sit on can make or break your weekend. Choose an office chair designed for someone who works at a computer keyboard all day. It should be firm but comfortable, adjustable for height and back support and sturdy enough to last. You'll find that big, padded and expensive executive model is too cushy for long-term sitting. A firm, adjustable chair allows you to change positions for variety through the contest. Chairs have been the subject of discussion on the CQ-Contest Reflector and it might be worth digging through some archives on the Internet at **www.contesting.com/_cq-contest**. You spend hundreds (or thousands) of dollars on your radio, so don't scrimp on another piece of equipment you'll be using every minute the rig is on!

Arranging Your Operating Desk

The operating desk's surface should be large enough to hold all of your operating equipment, usually with multiple tiers for holding the various items in their most convenient locations. Arrange equipment so that everything used frequently during the contest is immediately at hand or in front of you. The keyboard, radio and monitor should be central, with all peripheral equipment surrounding the operator in accordance with how it will be used. Place the keyboard, radio and CW paddle short distances apart to minimize unnecessary hand and arm movement. In general, if you're uncomfortable while operating, move the equipment around until you are comfortable.

Your desk or table will usually be 29 inches high. That's the standard for office furniture in the US and an ideal height for a working surface. The standard height for a typing surface is 26 inches. That's the height you would want for a computer keyboard. It's important that the keyboard be lower to prevent repetitive motion injuries and to prevent fatigue from using a keyboard at the wrong height. Many operators prefer the style of keyboard that has the function keys down the side rather than on top. To lower the keyboard, try attaching a keyboard tray or shelf underneath the operating surface. As a bonus, that gives you more room on the desktop. Remember to use a pad to support your wrists and forearms.

The computer is a major factor in today's contest operation. Place the computer monitor directly in front of the operating chair, since that's where you will be looking most of the time. Don't place the monitor to the side or so high that you have to raise your head to look at it. The monitor should be at the right distance for comfortable viewing. If you wear glasses, consider a pair of glasses specifically for watching a computer screen. Place the computer case completely off the desktop since it shouldn't have to be touched during contest.

Rotator control boxes and antenna switches should be easy to reach, although consideration should be given to having these items controlled by the radio or computer. Rotator control boxes are available with preset controls that don't require a hand to be on them throughout rotation. It's tiring to hang onto a rotator control box throughout a contest, trying to remember when to release the switches while you're concentrating on making QSOs. Some antenna switches, such as for high/low or stacks, are probably best controlled by hand, but the band-by-band switching of antennas can be performed by an interface controller driven by the radio or logging computer. Wattmeters should be placed in visual range so that you can monitor the functions of the transmitter and antennas during the course of the contest.

Unless your amplifier has automatic band switching, mark the dials so that you can quickly set the controls when you make band changes. Amplifiers should be placed where you can see the meters and indicator lights to check for proper operation and where you can reach the controls for occasional adjustments. Since the adjustments and band changes aren't made frequently, amps can be placed off to the side or above the radios and monitor.

Place a clock at the operating position, even though the computer clock will actually be the one used. The separate clock provides a reference for checking the computer time throughout the contest.

To save wear and tear on your voice, phone operators should definitely consider a voice keyer of some sort — particularly for calling CQ. The best option might be using the computer's sound card to record messages that can be replayed from the computer keyboard under control of the logging software. This integrates voice and logging functions so that your hands do not need to continually move back and forth between the keyer and keyboard.

PERSONAL PREPARATION

Whether you are just making contest QSOs now and then, for a few hours at a time or spending the whole weekend at it, you need to be alert and clear-headed to make and record QSOs accurately and operate your equipment properly. To do so means that you should also take care of that very important piece of equipment — the operator!

Sleep

The number one consideration to taking care of yourself during long contest weekends is getting enough sleep. Some contesters can "do 48 in the chair" but they have to prepare themselves first. They stock up on sleep throughout the week before the contest and often try to sleep in the hours just before the contest starts. That means no tower or antenna work on contest day! By building up a reserve of sleep, they start the contest refreshed, making it a lot easier to get through that first 24 hours. The second night is tough for everybody and about impossible if you were running on empty during the first night.

How many operators actually operate all 48 hours? Not many! Look at the contest results to see if hours of operation are listed. Most of the top scorers in a 48 hour contest put in between 40 and 46 hours of operating time. They grab short periods of sleep during slow hours, trading the loss of a few QSOs against mental acuity the following day. Again, look at logs and ask other operators to find out when you should do the same.

How long should you sleep? The answer varies from person to person, but there are a number of references that indicate the brain works on a 90-minute sleep cycle. According to those researchers, sleeping for one such cycle leaves you more refreshed and satisfied than one hour or two hours. Two 90-minute naps every 24 hours results in 42 hours of operating time. (See

"Sleep — A Contest Prescription," by T. Scott Johnson, KC1JI, in Nov/Dec 1988 *NCJ* and "A Sleep Strategy for DX Contesting," by Randall A. Thompson, K5ZD, in Sep/Oct 1994 *NCJ*.)

Another popular strategy is to catnap for a few minutes right at the operating position whenever you need a bit of sleep. The trick is to wake back up before too much time goes by. A long nap in the operating chair can be uncomfortable, as well.

When should you sleep? Analysis of your hourly rate from previous contests shows when it is most productive to sleep if you can't stay awake for the entire contest. For example, if your rate went to 5 per hour at 0800 UTC and only one of those contacts was a multiplier, perhaps an hour's rest would have helped you more the next day. Another good idea is to check out a rate sheet from a multi-multi station from the 3830 reflector archives and look for their times of lowest activity on the various bands. Those may be good times for you to sleep.

Food and Fitness

There as many opinions about the right food for contesting as there are contest operators. In general, contesters prefer light fare during the contest that's easy to digest and keeps blood sugar levels topped off. Some operators like to "carbo-load" before the contest, just like for a bike race. Experiment with different favorites to see what keeps you nourished without making you drowsy. Eat lightly to avoid a post-meal "low."

Another consideration is the mechanics of eating while you're operating. CW and digital contests have a built-in advantage over voice as you aren't trying to eat and operate with the same apparatus! Perhaps that's why CW contesting remains popular and digital contesting is becoming more popular? Without trying to tell you what to eat, finger foods and drinkable soups are great contest meals! Another tip: Crunchy foods create a huge amount of local QRM in headphones.

What about coffee and energy drinks? Caffeine and herbal "boosters" do pick up your mental energy for a while, but the fall off afterwards can be worse than not having the beverage in the first place. Many contesters try not to use any kind of

Celebrations erupt as the operators at the Missouri University of Science and Technology club, WØEEE, put the final section in the log for an ARRL Sweepstakes "Clean Sweep"!

stimulant until the second day of a contest when the boost is really needed. Try to go into a contest refreshed and caught up on sleep. Don't try to coffee or cola your way through.

While contesting doesn't require a lot of physical activity — just the opposite — it certainly does burn a lot of calories. Being physically fit does have a measurable effect on one's stamina and the ability to remain alert and focused. Prepare for big contest efforts with regular exercise and attention to your diet. You'll be more comfortable and able to maintain high performance levels longer.

Breaks

Would you subject yourself to a 48-hour airplane flight without breaks or the opportunity for some activity? Of course not, so why do it in the ham shack? Sitting in one position for long periods of time is not healthy. You need to get up every once in a while and stretch. A short walk is recommended, but even operating from a standing position can help. Use headphones with a cord long enough to permit bending and stretching. Let the computer do the work while you limber up.

There are very few contests in which you can't take a few minutes every few hours to get a little exercise. Activity is often the perfect tonic when you're dragging at oh-dark-thirty with a slow QSO rate. To find the right times for breaks, take a look at logs from previous years and ask other contesters. Make reminders to yourself so that those breaks happen as they should.

Bathroom breaks can be managed by managing your liquid intake. Be sure to stay hydrated, but avoid having a continuously full beverage glass. You'll wind up visiting the facilities way too often! Note that leaving the keyer in beacon mode while you take a pit stop is considered bad contest manners!

MULTI-OPERATOR CONTESTING

Nowhere in Amateur Radio will you find the camaraderie that exists in operating a multi-op station. Shared experiences are always more enjoyable and there's no better way to share the contest experience than with a group of enthusiastic friends.

Multi-ops provide an ideal training ground for operators new to contesting, allowing the new operator to learn from contesters having years of experience. Often contest careers are prolonged by multi-ops, allowing those who have neither the time nor the endurance, but still have the desire and skills, to participate in a competitive entry.

There are generally two types of multi-ops: the multi-op, single-transmitter (MS or MOST) and the multi-op multi-transmitter (MM). The multi-op, two-transmitter (M2) class is actually an offshoot of the multi-single class designed for those stations who are capable of putting two signals on the air at the same time. Each contest's multi-single rules are different and should be studied carefully before operating the contest.

Multi-Single and Multi-Two

The multi-single class was originally conceived as a way to keep a single station on the air for the entire contest by allowing more than one operator. It has evolved over time into a very competitive category. In many cases more than one station is used during the course of the contest — a "run station" that strives for the maximum of QSOs and a "mult station" that searches for multipliers. Strategy plays an important part in

the planning and operation of the multi-single station. The key is to determine how a second station and operator can be used for maximum effectiveness.

Multi-single stations are generally limited to a certain number of band changes per hour or are required to spend a minimum amount of time on a particular band before changing bands. The multi-single participant must use those band changes strategically. For example, before a band change is made for purposes of working a multiplier, the operator manning the multiplier station should make a band map of stations to work before changing bands. The operator might even record those stations in the memories of the transceiver. At the band change, the mult station becomes the run station for a few minutes (usually at least 10 minutes). Any multipliers in his band map are worked, along with any other QSOs possible. He might even call CQ for a while on the new band. Control then returns to the hot band and the run station. This process repeats again and again on the same or other bands, wherever the operators decide it is worthwhile to make the band change.

While the limitations on the multi-single stations (and multi-two) may seem somewhat restrictive, they create a class of competition for multi-op stations that are not set up with individual stations for every band. Multi-single has been a popular category over the years. Easing of the restrictions would definitely raise the level of equipment required to be competitive. Recent winners in multi-single categories use two or three independent stations at one QTH.

Multi-two category rules are very similar to multi-single, with the addition of a second run station and a single mult station trading off band changes between the two run stations. The strategy to maximize output of a multi-two station is an interesting challenge and often requires four complete stations to really maximize the score.

Multi-Multi

The multi-multi station does exactly what the name implies, many operators, many transmitters, with only one transmitting on any band at one time. Successful multi-multi stations often

Piloting one of the most capable contest stations on the planet, the K3LR team is on its way to the US multi-multi title. Some of the top names in contesting make the trip to Western Pennsylvania to operate Tim's station. *(K3LR photo)*

have two-station capability on each band. One chases multipliers on the band while the other one calls CQ throughout the contest. Only one transmitted signal per band at any time is allowed, but that's easy to work out between the operators. It's no wonder that these stations make very high scores in the contests where the category is permitted.

These stations provide excellent training grounds for new operators, as staffing a multi-multi is one of the more difficult tasks in contesting. You can frequently get "chair time" at one if you make the acquaintance of one of the regular operators. You may be calling "CQ Canada" on 160 meters during the daytime from Texas, but it's worth it to gain the experience. You'll always value the opportunity to watch and hear the operators go about their business at a top multi-op.

The multi-multi is also useful to the beginning operator for learning what is possible on each band. The successful multi-multi is required to work all bands almost all the time. By doing so, one can learn about those midnight over-the-Pole openings on 15 or 20, how early 40 meters opens to Asia, how 80 meters opens before sunset and stays open an hour or two after sunrise, and what contacts might be possible at those times. It's a great way to gain useful experience in every phase of contesting, operating under fire with experienced teachers of the contest art.

PROPAGATION

When it's all said and done, the fact is that the contest starts at the given date and time and regardless of the propagation, you still have to compete. Knowing what's likely to happen will give you an edge, however. (You may want to start by reviewing the Propagation section of Chapter 6 — DXing elsewhere in this book.)

In general, your antenna on 10 and 15 meters should follow the sun. It should be east to southeast at the morning band opening, moving south by local noon, then west, southwest and northwest until after sunset. Openings to the east may last longer, so use discretion. Twenty meters will open to the west at sunrise, but may be more productive to the east. The lower the sunspot activity, the more important 20 will be.

All three nighttime bands (160, 80 and 40) may open at sunset, generally to the east, but sometimes to the southeast. The southeast opening may yield some Asian or Africans in a DX contest. Nighttime is the right time for Asia and Oceania on these bands. In the morning, the bands will be open to the west, although a southwesterly path will again yield Asian DX. At European sunrise the low bands will be open in that direction, with 160 and 80 closing before 40, which is likely to stay open much longer.

Twenty meters will often share characteristics with both the low and high bands. It is more likely to be like the high bands in periods of low sun activity and like the low bands during high sunspot activity.

Someday, you will experience a Sudden Ionospheric Disturbance (SID) from a solar flare, especially during times of high solar activity. If that happens, it will feel as though someone turned the bands off with a switch. If you experience an SID, try going to a higher band and possibly beaming south. Sometimes nothing works until the band comes back, but more often than not you may find that there is less absorption on the higher

bands and maybe some propagation to somewhere. Take heart in the knowledge that it's just as bad for everybody else! Wait it out and don't give up.

Develop your band plans from experience, from the previous year's logs and by listening to the bands at different times in the weeks leading up to a contest. See who's coming in on which band and how the band sounds. The spotting networks are invaluable for this, since you can review the spots for a week or two, learning what bands seem to be working to various areas of the world at a given time.

REMEMBER, CONTESTING IS FUN!

Of course there are many good reasons for contest participation, all of them perfectly valid. But the main reason it is so popular (and when did you ever hear as much activity on the bands as during a contest?) is that it's *fun*. Over the years, you'll find that you work a lot of the same people each year and it's fun to say hello by giving them a contact. You'll develop new topics of conversation as you run into them on the air between contests. Meeting other contesters in person adds another dimension to contesting. It provides the opportunity to see the faces of your on-air friends and builds a special camaraderie. Try it and see!

GLOSSARY

Alligator — a station whose signal is loud, but cannot hear calling stations well

Bonus — extra points added to a score for making a specific type of QSO, for contacting specific stations or operating in a specified way

Breakdown — a table showing the QSOs and multipliers worked on each band

Busted — an incorrect spot, call sign or exchange

Cabrillo — a log file format specification

Checklog — submitted logs that are only used in the log checking process and are not listed in the results for competitive purposes

Cut Numbers — letter abbreviations for Morse numerals, such as N for 9, A for 1, T for zero, and so forth

DQed — disqualified, the result of rules violations

Dupe — duplicate contact, a station that has been worked before and can't be contacted again for point credit

Exchange — the information that must be exchanged in a contest QSO

Hired gun — a guest operator, usually referring to someone highly skilled

Hold — in reference to a frequency, to maintain a presence on a frequency by calling CQ

LCR — Log Checking Report, the output of the log checking process for a submitted log

MO, MS, MM, M2 — Multi-Operator; Multi-Operator Single-Transmitter; Multi-Operator Multi-Transmitter; Multi-Operator Two-Transmitter

Move — to coordinate a change to another band to contact a station for additional multiplier credit

Mult — shorthand for *multiplier*

Not In the Log (NIL) — a QSO that can not be cross-referenced to an entry in the log of the station with which the QSO is claimed

Off-time — enforced periods of non-operation during a contest

Penalty — points removed during the log checking process in response to errors

QSO points — the point credit for a specific QSO

Rate — the equivalent number of stations that would be worked in an hour, based on various time periods (last hour, last 10 minutes, last 10 stations, last 100 stations, and so forth)

Robot — a software program that processes logs submitted by e-mail

Rover — a mobile station that operates while in motion or from multiple locations in a contest

Run — to work stations by calling CQ; a run also means a steady stream of callers in response to CQs

S&P — search-and-pounce, the technique of tuning for stations to work instead of calling CQ

Serial Number — the sequential number of the contact in the contest — first contact, second contact, 199th contact, and so on

SO, SOAB, SOAB — Single Operator; Single-Operator All-Band; Single-Operator Single Band

SPC or S/P/C — State, Province, Country, the most common three location-based types of multipliers

Spot — an announcement of a station's call and frequency via a spotting network

Sprint — a short contest, usually six hours or less

Sunday Driver — casual operators who appear late in the contest (usually Sunday afternoon) to make a few QSOs

UBN — Unique, Busted, Not In Log; the three ways in which a QSO can be declared invalid

Unique — a call sign that was not in any other submitted log

10-minute rule — refers to a limit on the number of band changes permitted in an hour or how long a station is required to operate on a band after making a band change

RESOURCES
Magazines & Newsletters

ARRL *Contest Update* —
   www.arrl.org/the-arrl-contest-update

National Contest Journal —
   www.ncjweb.com

Contest Columns appear regularly in
CQ Magazine —
   www.cq-amateur-radio.com

Web Sites & E-Mail Reflectors

ARRL Contest Branch —
   www.arrl.org/contests

World Wide Young Contesters —
   www.wwyc.net

   www.contesting.com — a general site about contesting

3830 score reporting —
   lists.contesting.com/mailman/listinfo/3830

Online Contest Calendars

ARRL Contest Corral —
   www.arrl.org/contests (also monthly in *QST*)

N2CQ QRP Contest Calendar —
   www.amqrp.org/contesting/contesting.html

SM3CER Contest Service —
   www.sk3bg.se/contest

WA7BNM Contest Calendar —
   www.hornucopia.com/contestcal

HF Digital Communications

We tend to think of the HF bands in terms of voice (SSB and AM) and CW activity. With the ubiquity of the personal computer, however, digital communication has seen an increasing HF presence as well. This has been particularly true for amateurs who are forced to operate in restricted situations using such things as hidden antennas and low output power. They've discovered that a few watts with a digital mode can still take them considerable distances, even around the world.

EVOLUTION AND REVOLUTION

Radioteletype, better known as *RTTY*, was one of the first Amateur Radio digital modes. Hams began using it in the late 1940s and the technology remained essentially unchanged for more than 30 years. If you had visited an amateur RTTY station prior to about 1980, you probably would have seen a hulking mechanical teletype machine, complete with rolls of yellow paper. The teletype would be connected to the transceiver through an interface known as a *TU*, or *terminal unit*. An oscilloscope would probably have graced the layout as well. Oscilloscopes were necessary for proper tuning of the received signal. The entire RTTY conversation was printed on, and had to be read from, an endless river of paper.

The first serious change occurred when affordable microprocessor technology appeared in the late 1970s. That's when we started to see TUs that included their own self-contained keyboards and displays, making the mechanical teletype (and all that paper!) obsolete. When personal computers debuted in the early 1980s, they became perfect companions for the new TUs. The PC functioned as a "dumb terminal," displaying the received data *from* the TU and sending data *to* the TU for transmission. Some TUs of this era offered ultra-sharp receive filters that allowed hams to copy weak signals even in the midst of horrendous interference. TU models such as the HAL Communications ST-8000 were renowned for their perfor-

mance. Some RTTY operators still use ST-8000s to this day.

In the late 1980s, conventional terminal units began to yield to sophisticated devices known as *multimode controllers*. As the name suggests, these compact units handle several different digital modes in one package, typically RTTY, packet, AMTOR and PACTOR. The Kantronics KAM, AEA PK-232 and MFJ-1278 are well-known examples. Like TUs, multimode controllers are standalone devices that communicate with your personal computer. When using a multimode controller, your computer is, once again, acting as a dumb terminal — all of the heavy lifting is being done by the controller and its self-contained software known as *firmware*. These controllers functioned as radio modulators/demodulators, or *modems*, converting data to modulated audio signals for transmission and also converting received signals back to data for display.

The winds of change began to stir again in the early 1990s when sound cards appeared as accessories for personal computers. At first, sound cards were used for little more than…well… *sound*. They made it possible for computer users to enjoy music, sound effects in their computer games and other applications. But as sound cards became more powerful, hams began to realize their potential. They discovered that with the right software a sound card could function as a modem, too.

Peter Martinez, G3PLX, exploited the potential of the sound-card-as-modem when he created an entirely new amateur digital mode known as *PSK31*. It was not only a new mode, but a new way of using sound cards. The sound card not only decoded the received signal, it created the transmitted signal too. The only piece of hardware necessary (other than the transceiver, of course!) was a simple interface that allowed the computer to switch the radio from receive to transmit, and vice versa.

In the years that followed, sound cards became more powerful and versatile. They also began showing up as sound *chips* on personal computer motherboards and inside deluxe interfaces. Hams responded by devel-

Jose, YV6BTF, is often heard on RTTY.

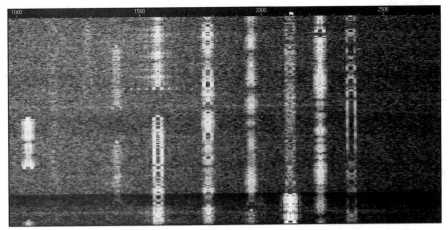

Fig 8-1 — A typical waterfall display. This one shows several PSK31 signals (represented by the vertical lines).

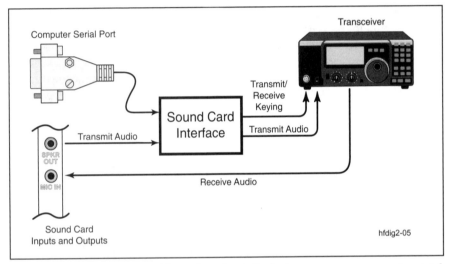

Fig 8-2 — The sound card interface installs between your computer and your HF transceiver. Its primary function is to allow your computer to switch your radio between transmit and receive, but many models perform additional functions such as providing audio isolation.

computers on eBay and elsewhere that meet this requirement at a cost of less than $500.

Your software selections are easy and affordable, too. There are excellent multimode applications that, as the term implies, provide many HF digital modes in a single program. Among the most popular are…

MixW for *Windows* at **www.mixw.net**

MultiPSK for *Windows* at **f6cte.free.fr/index_anglais.htm**

Multimode for *MacOS* at **www.black-catsystems.com**

Cocoamodem for *MacOS* at **homepage.mac.com/chen/index.html**

Fldigi for *Linux* at **www.w1hkj.com/Fldigi.html**

All of these sound card applications, and many others, work by taking the receive audio from your radio and creating a visual representation of the detected signals on your computer monitor, usually in what is known as a *waterfall*. You can see an example of a typical waterfall display in **Fig 8-1**. To decode a signal, all you have to do is click your mouse cursor on the signal's pattern in the waterfall.

Finally, you'll need a sound card interface to tie everything together. The sound card interface acts as the link between your computer and your transceiver (see **Fig 8-2**). It's most basic function is to allow your computer to switch your radio between transmit and receive. Many interfaces also allow you to set the transmit and receive audio levels. Interface manufacturers include MFJ (**www.mfjenterprises.com**), West Mountain Radio (**www.westmountainradio.com**), microHAM (**www.microham.com**), TigerTronics (**www.tigertronics.com**), MixW RigExpert (**www.rigexpert.net**) and more. **Fig 8-3** shows a typical unit. See the advertising pages of *QST* magazine for more information on specific devices.

oping more new digital modes to go with them. At the time this book went to press, there were well over a dozen sound-card HF digital modes with more in their pre-release stages.

The hardware multimode controllers are still with us, but they are primarily used for modes like PACTOR that require more processing muscle and precise timing than a typical personal computer can provide on its own. All of the other Amateur Radio HF digital modes have gone the way of the sound card.

YOUR HF DIGITAL STATION

You can explore most HF digital modes with little more than a sound-card-equipped computer and an SSB transceiver.

The computer doesn't need to be particularly powerful unless you intend to explore processor-intensive applications such as digital voice or software-defined radios. A 1 GHz processor and 500 Mbytes of RAM should be adequate for most purposes. Low-priced computers available today are far more powerful than this and you can pick up used

Fig 8-3 — Some transceiver interfaces such as the MixW RigExpert Standard include extra features. This model has a built-in sound card chip set for digital modes and even includes a CW keyer.

Sound card interfaces connect to your computer through the serial (COM) port or via a USB port. You can make the radio connections at the microphone and external speaker jack, or more conveniently, at the rear-panel "accessory" jack. The interface manual will explain all this in detail.

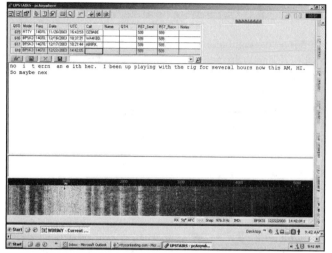

MixW multimode HF digital software.

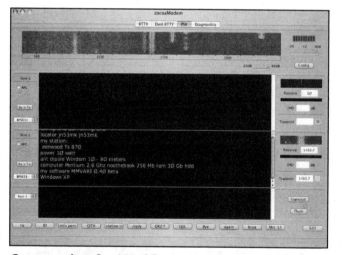

Cocoamodem for MacOS.

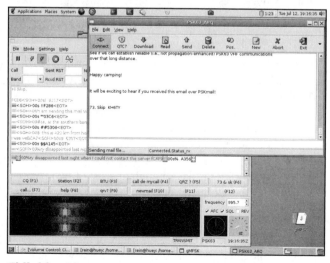

Fldigi for Linux.

Which Sound Card is Best?

This is one of the most popular questions among HF digital operators. After all, the sound device is second only to the radio as the most critical link in the performance chain. A poor sound device will bury weak signals in noise of its own making and will potentially distort your transmit audio as well.

Before you dash out to purchase a costly high-end sound card, ask yourself an important question: How do you intend to operate? If you have a modest station and intend to enjoy casual chats and a bit of DXing, save your money. An inexpensive sound card, or the sound chipset that is probably on your computer's motherboard, is adequate for the task. There is little point in investing in a luxury sound card if you lack the radio or antennas to hear weak signals to begin with, or if they cannot hear you.

On the other hand, if you own the station hardware necessary to be competitive in digital DX hunting or contesting, a

Keeping Everything on the Level

One of the perennial problems with sound devices is the fact that optimum audio levels have a tendency to differ depending on the software you are using. The sound card input and output levels you set correctly for one application may be wildly wrong for another. And what happens when another family member stops by the computer to listen to music or play a game? They're likely to change the audio levels to whatever suits them. When it comes time to use the computer again for HF digital operating, you may get an unpleasant surprise.

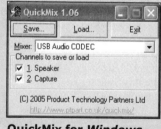

QuickMix for Windows.

The common sense answer is to simply check and reset the audio levels before you operate. However, what if you can't quite remember the settings? At the very least, you'll have to go back through and tweak for best receive and transmit audio. Fortunately, there are some software applications that will "remember" your audio settings and reapply them for you. One example is *QuickMix* for *Windows*, which is available free on the Product Notes section of the ARRL Web. Go to **www.arrl.org/product-notes** and scroll down to the Operating Manual section. *QuickMix* takes a "snapshot" of your sound card settings and saves them to a file that you name according to the application (for example, "PSK31"). To use *QuickMix* you simply open the program, click the LOAD button and select the settings you need. *QuickMix* instantly adjusts your sound card according to the configuration snapshot you saved. *QuickMix* is for *Windows 98*, *ME* and *XP* only.

Don't Overdrive Your Transceiver!

When you're setting up your rig for your first PSK31 transmission, the temptation is to adjust the output settings for "maximum smoke." This can be a serious mistake because overdriving your transceiver in PSK31 can result in a horrendous amount of splatter, which will suddenly make your PSK31 signal much wider than 31 Hz — and make you highly unpopular with operators on adjacent frequencies.

As you increase the transmit audio output from your sound card or multimode processor, watch the ALC indicator on your transceiver. The ALC is the automatic level control that governs the audio drive level. When you see your ALC display indicating that audio limiting is taking place, you are feeding too much audio to the transceiver. The goal is to achieve the desired RF output with little or no activation of the ALC.

Unfortunately, monitoring the ALC by itself is not always a sure bet. Many radios can be driven to full output without budging the ALC meter. You'd think that it would be smooth sailing from there, but a number of rigs become decidedly nonlinear when asked to provide SSB output beyond a certain level. (Sometimes this nonlinearity can begin at the 50% output level.) We can ignore the linearity issue to a certain extent with an SSB voice signal, but not with PSK31 because the immediate result, once again, is splatter.

So how can you tell if your PSK31 signal is really clean? Unless you have the means to monitor your RF output with an oscilloscope, the only way to check your signal is to ask someone to give you an evaluation on the air. The PSK31 programs that use a waterfall audio spectrum display can easily detect "dirty" signals. The splatter appears as rows of lines extending to the right and left of your primary signal. (Overdriven PSK31 signals may also have a harsh, clicking sound.)

If you are told that you are splattering, ask the other station to observe your signal as you slowly decrease the audio level from the sound card or processor. When you reach the point where the splatter disappears, you're all set. Don't worry if you discover that you can only generate a clean signal at, say, 50 W output. With PSK31 the performance differential between 50 W and 100 W is inconsequential.

good sound card can give you a substantial edge. This is particularly true if you are using a software-defined radio. Sound card performance is critical for this application.

In 2007 the ARRL undertook an evaluation of 11 common sound card models. The study was performed by Jonathan Taylor, K1RFD, and the results were published in the "Product Review" section of the May 2007 issue of *QST*. As you'd expect, the high-end sound cards came out on top, but think carefully before you reach for your wallet. *All* of the sound cards tested delivered adequate performance for digital mode applications. Don't buy more performance than you really need.

SO WHAT'S OUT THERE?

What can you do with your new HF digital station? More than you might imagine. There are more than a dozen different HF digital modes on the air today, but only a handful are used extensively. Let's concentrate on the modes you're most likely to encounter.

RTTY

Good old radioteletype (RTTY) is still holding its ground on the HF bands. In fact, it is still the most popular digital mode for contests and DXpeditions (where groups of hams travel to rare DX Century Club locations to operate).

As with so many aspects of Amateur Radio, it is best to begin by listening. **Table 8-1** shows where to find digital mode activity on the various HF bands. There's almost always something happening on 20 meters, so try there first. Tune between 14.070 and 14.095 MHz and listen for the long, continuous *blee-blee-blee-blee* signals of RTTY. What you are hearing are the two alternating *mark* and *space* signals that RTTY uses in its binary *Baudot* coding scheme.

Depending on your transceiver and interface, you may use *audio frequency shift keying (AFSK)* or *frequency shift keying (FSK)* to transmit RTTY. The end result sounds the same on the air.

In AFSK, the audio tones for mark and space are generated by the computer and/or interface and fed into your transceiver's microphone input. For AFSK, make sure your transceiver is set for lower sideband (LSB). That is the RTTY convention.

Your rig may have an FSK mode (sometimes labeled DATA or RTTY). Many hams prefer operating this way because it allows them to use the transceiver's narrow IF filters to screen out interference. Just like on CW, with RTTY you can use 500 Hz or narrower filters to get rid of nearby signals. When you operate in FSK mode, your computer is not generating the mark and space tones. It is merely sending data pulses to the radio and the radio is creating its own mark and space signals. (This often requires a special connection to the transceiver. Consult your manual.)

A good time to observe RTTY activity is during a contest. There is at least one RTTY contest every month. See the sidebar "HF Digital Contesting."

With your software in the RTTY mode, tune across a RTTY signal. Your software likely includes some kind of tuning indicator to help you line up the mark and space signals correctly so that the software can start decoding. The tuning indicator may be part of a waterfall display. It might consist of two parallel lines that line up with mark and space, or it could even be a simulated oscilloscope display. Check your software manual and experiment with any variable settings. With some experience, you will be able to correlate the sound of the RTTY signal with the visual indicator and quickly tune in a new signal.

As you tune in the signal, you should see letters marching

Table 8-1
Popular HF Digital Frequencies

Band (Meters)	Frequencies (MHz)
10	28.070–28.120
12	24.920–24.930
15	21.070–21.110
17	18.100–18.110
20	14.070–14.099
30	10.130–10.140
40	7.070–7.125
80	3.570–3.600
160	1.800–1.810

HF Digital Contesting

Some hams shun contesting because they assume they don't have the time or hardware necessary to win — and they are probably right. But winning is not the objective for most contesters. You enter a contest to do the best you can, to push yourself and your station to whatever limits you wish. The satisfaction at the end of a contest comes from the knowledge that you were part of the glorious frenzy, and that you gave it your best shot!

Contesting also has a practical benefit. If you're an award chaser, you can work many desirable stations during an active contest. During the ARRL RTTY Roundup, for example, some hams have worked enough international stations to earn a RTTY DXCC. Jump into the North American RTTY QSO Party and you stand a good chance of earning your Worked All States in a single weekend.

Contest Software

No one says you have to use software to keep track of your contest contacts, but it certainly makes life easier! One of the fundamental elements of any contest program is the ability to check for duplicate contacts or dupes. Working the same station that you just worked an hour ago is not only embarrassing, it is a waste of time. The better contest programs feature immediate dupe checking. When you enter the call sign in the logging window, the software instantly checks your log and warns you if the contact qualifies as a dupe. The more sophisticated programs "know" the rules of all the popular digital contests and they can quickly determine whether a contact is truly a dupe under the rules of the contest in question. Some contests, for example, allow you to work stations only once, regardless of the band. Other contests will allow you to work stations once per band.

A good software package will also help you track multipliers. It will display a list of multipliers you've worked, or show the ones you still need to find.

One of the most widely used contest software packages in the HF digital world is *Writelog* for *Windows*, which you'll find at www.writelog.com. *Writelog* has built-in RTTY and PSK31 modules. Another digital contest favorite is the free *N1MM Logger* at pages.cthome.net/n1mm/. *N1MM* by itself does not have RTTY capability, but you can add this functionality by installing the free *MMTTY* RTTY application, which is available at mmhamsoft. amateur-radio.ca/mmtty/.

For more information about contesting, see Chapter 7.

Digital Contest Calendar

See *QST* or the *National Contest Journal* for complete rules and to check dates.

Month	Date	Contest
January	1st	SARTG New Year's RTTY Contest
January	First full weekend	ARRL RTTY Roundup
January	Fourth full weekend	BARTG RTTY Sprint
February	First full weekend	NW QRP Club Digital Contest
February	Second weekend	CQ WW RTTY WPX Contest
February	Last full weekend	North American RTTY QSO Party
March	Second full weekend	*NCJ* RTTY Sprint
March	Third weekend	BARTG Spring RTTY Contest
April	First full weekend	EA WW RTTY Contest
April	Third weekend	TARA PSK31 Rumble
April	Fourth full weekend	SP DX RTTY Contest
May	First full weekend	ARI International DX Contest
May	Second weekend	VOLTA WW RTTY Contest
July	Third weekend	North American RTTY QSO Party
July	Fourth full weekend	Russian WW RTTY Contest
August	Third weekend	SARTG WW RTTY Contest
August	Last full weekend	SCC RTTY Championship
September	First full weekend	CCCC PSK31 Contest
September	Last full weekend	CQ WW RTTY Contest
October	First full weekend	TARA PSK31 Rumble
October	First full weekend	DARC International Hellschreiber Contest
October	Second Thursday	Internet RTTY Sprints
October	Second full weekend	*NCJ* RTTY Sprint
October	Third weekend	JARTS WW RTTY Contest
November	Second weekend	WAE RTTY Contest
December	First full weekend	TARA RTTY Sprints
December	Second weekend	OK RTTY DX Contest

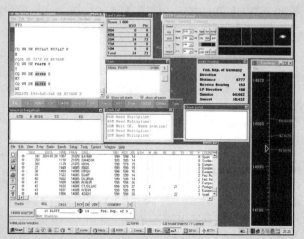

Writelog contest software.

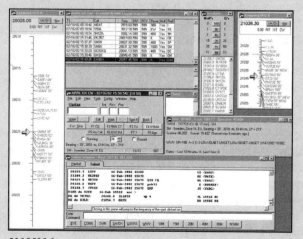

N1MM Logger.

across your screen. If you've stumbled across a contest, you may see something like this…

AA5AU 599 CT CT 010 010 DE WB8IMY K

In this instance, AA5AU is receiving a 599 signal report from WB8IMY in the state of Connecticut. This is also WB8IMY's tenth contact during the contest (that's the repeated "010"). The letter "K" means "over to you."

Most contest operators create "canned" messages, called *macros*, in their software. A macro can be set up to place your radio in the transmit mode, send a string of text, then return the radio to receive. Macros eliminate the need to type the same thing over and over, which comes in handy in a contest where you may be making hundreds of contacts.

Let's assume that you have a contest CQ stored in a macro right now. Tap the appropriate key (or click your mouse on the designated button) and your RTTY macro will do the rest…

(The radio enters the transmit mode)

CQ CONTEST CQ CONTEST DE WB8IMY WB8IMY K

(The radio returns to receive)

Of course hams still enjoy chatting on RTTY, just like they do on SSB or CW, and you may see them exchanging names, locations, antenna descriptions and other items of interest. RTTY DXing is popular too, and so you may run across "pileups" on DX stations. If the DX station is rare, the QSOs may just be rapid-fire exchange of signal reports and call signs, just like on voice or CW.

PSK31

PSK31 is the most widely used HF digital communications mode on the HF bands today. Most PSK31 activity involves casual conversation, although there are a few PSK31 contests as well.

The "PSK" stands for Phase Shift Keying, the modulation method that is used to generate the signal; "31" is the bit rate. Where RTTY uses two specific frequencies to communicate the binary data, PSK31 does the same thing by creating an audio signal that shifts its phase 180° in sync with the 31.25 bit-per-second data stream. A 0 bit in the data stream generates an audio phase shift, but a 1 does not. The technique of using phase shifts (and the lack thereof) to represent binary data is known as Binary Phase-Shift Keying, or *BPSK*. If you apply a BPSK audio signal to an SSB transceiver, you end up with BPSK modulated RF. At this data rate the resulting PSK31 RF signal is only about 50 Hz wide, which is actually narrower than the average CW signal.

With such a narrow bandwidth, PSK31 makes the most of a very small amount of spectrum. Transmit power is highly concentrated, meaning that you don't need a lot of power to communicate over great distances. (Most PSK31 operators use less than 50 W output.) At the receiving end, the PSK31 software uses digital signal processing to detect the phase changes, even in very weak signals. The result is that PSK31 rivals or exceeds the weak-signal performance of CW.

Its terrific performance not withstanding, PSK31 will not always provide 100% copy; it is as vulnerable to interference as any digital mode. And there are times, during a geomagnetic storm for example, when ionospheric propagation will cause slight changes in the frequency of the signal you're trying to copy. (When you are trying to receive a narrow-bandwidth, phase-shifting signal, frequency stability is very important.) This effect is almost always confined to the polar regions and it shows up as very rapid flutter, which is deadly to PSK31. The good news is that these events are usually short-lived.

If you are operating your transceiver in SSB without using narrow IF or audio-frequency filtering, the bandwidth of the receive audio that you're dumping to your sound card is about 2000 to 3000 Hz. With a bandwidth of only about 50 Hz, a lot of PSK31 signals can squeeze into that spectrum. Your software acts like an audio spectrum analyzer, sweeping through the received audio from 100 to 3000 Hz and showing you the results in a waterfall display that continuously scrolls from top to bottom. What you see on your monitor are vertical lines of various colors that indicate every signal the software can detect. Bright yellow lines represent strong signals while blue lines indicate weaker signals.

Most of the PSK31 signals on 20 meters are clustered around 14.070 MHz. You'll also find PSK31 activity on 3.580, 7.070 and 21.070 MHz. PSK31 signals have a distinctive sound unlike any digital mode you've heard on the ham bands. You won't find PSK31 by listening for the *deedle-deedle* of a RTTY signal, and PSK31 doesn't "chirp" like the TOR modes. PSK31 signals *warble*.

Start by putting your radio in the USB (upper sideband) mode and parking it on or near a PSK31 frequency (tune until you see a number of lines in the waterfall). Do not touch your rig's VFO again. Just boot up your software and get ready to have fun.

It is not at all uncommon to see several strong signals (the audible ones) interspersed with wispy blue ghosts of very weak "silent" signals. Click on a few of these ghosts and you may be rewarded with text (not error free, but good enough to understand what is being discussed).

As you decode PSK31 signals, the results will be a conversation on your monitor…

Yes, John, I'm seeing perfect text on my screen, but I can barely hear your signal. PSK31 is amazing! KF6I DE WB8IMY K

I know what you mean, Steve. You are also weak on my end, but 100% copy. WB8IMY DE KF6I K

If you find a station calling CQ and you want to reply, don't worry about tuning your radio. The software will use your sound card to generate the PSK31 transmit signal at exactly the same audio frequency as the received signal. When applied to your radio, this audio signal will create an RF signal that is exactly where it needs to be.

Some PSK31 programs and processor software offer type-ahead buffers, which allow you to compose your response "off line" while you are reading the incoming text from the other station. Just type what you wish to send, then press the keyboard key or click on the software "button" to transmit.

MFSK16

An MFSK signal consists of 16 tones, sent one at a time at

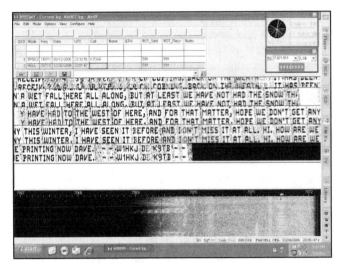

Fig 8-4 — Hellschreiber signals are displayed in repeating lines that look like an old-fashioned dot-matrix printer.

15.625 baud, and they are spaced only 15.625 Hz apart. Each tone represents four binary bits of data. With a bandwidth of 316 Hz, the signal easily fits through a narrow CW filter. MFSK16 has a distinctive musical sound that some compare to an old-fashioned carnival calliope.

MFSK16 can be tricky to tune. You must place the cursor at exactly the right spot on the signal pattern in the waterfall display. It takes some skill and patience to tune MFSK, but the results are worth the effort. MFSK offers excellent weak-signal performance and is a conversational mode like PSK31. Listen for the "music" of MFSK just above the PSK31 frequencies.

Hellschreiber

Are the Hellschreiber modes really HF digital? Or, are they a hybrid of the analog and digital worlds? Check out **Fig 8-4**.

Some argue that the Hellschreiber modes are more closely related to facsimile since they display text on your computer screen in the form of images (not unlike the product of a fax machine). On the other hand, the elements of the Hellschreiber "image text" are transmitted using a strictly defined digital format rather than the various analog signals of true HF fax or SSTV.

The Hellschreiber concept itself is quite old, developed in the 1920s by Rudolf Hell. Hellschreiber was, in fact, the first successful direct printing text transmission system. The German Army used Hellschreiber for field communications in World War II, and the mode was in use for commercial landline service until about 1980.

As personal computers became ubiquitous tools in ham shacks throughout the world, interest in Hellschreiber as an HF mode increased. By the end of the 20th century amateurs had developed several sophisticated pieces of Hellschreiber software and had also expanded and improved the Hellschreiber system itself.

Like PSK31, the Hellschreiber modes are intended for live conversations. Most of the activity is found on 20 meters, typically between 14.076 and 14.080 MHz. As with other conversational modes, you simply type and send your text. The main difference involves what is actually seen on the receiving end.

Feld-Hell is the most popular Hellschreiber mode among HF digital experimenters. It has its roots in the original Hellschreiber format, adapted slightly for ham use. Each character of a Feld-Hell transmission is communicated as a series of dots, with the result looking a bit like the output from a dot-matrix printer. A key-down state is used to indicate the black area of text, and the key up state is used to indicate blank or white spaces. One hundred and fifty characters are transmitted every minute. Each character takes 400 ms to complete. Because there are 49 pixels per character, each pixel is 8.163 ms long.

Most multimode software packages offer Hellschreiber. You won't find many Hell signals on the air, but conversing in this mode is a unique experience. Listen for odd "scratchy" signals just above the PSK31 frequencies.

PACTOR

Unlike the sound card modes we've discussed so far, PACTOR is a burst mode. That is, it sends and receives data in segments or bursts rather than in a continuous stream. When a burst of data arrives, the receiving station quickly checks for

---

The Need for Speed

When you're operating the burst modes such as PACTOR and Clover, your success will be largely measured by how fast your transceiver can switch from transmit to receive.

For example, a PACTOR station transmits a 960-ms long data block, then waits up to 170 ms for a 120-ms ACK or NAK signal from the receiving station. If the ACK or NAK fails to arrive before this 170-ms window closes, the data block will be repeated. PACTOR's patience is not endless though. If the ACKs or NAKs still fail to arrive after a certain number of repeated data blocks, your processor will declare the link "broken."

With this critical timing in mind, it's important to understand that the time it takes for your SSB transceiver to switch from transmit to receive is deducted from the 170-ms window. This has a substantial effect on how far you can communicate with PACTOR.

Let's say that your rig is a bit on the slow side. It switches from transmit to receive at a lazy 90 ms. Deduct 90 from 170 and you'll see that your window has suddenly shrunk to 80 ms.

Now deduct the delays at the receiving station. Let's be generous and say that his rig can switch within 40 ms. Now your window has collapsed to 40 ms. A radio signal can travel approximately 3700 miles — roundtrip — in 40 ms. This means that the maximum range of your PACTOR station would be roughly 4000 miles.

It is best to shop for an SSB transceiver that has the fastest transmit/receive turnaround. *QST* Product Reviews often publish this information in their data tables. Look for it and let it guide you to the best choice. When in doubt, the fewer milliseconds, the better!

errors caused by noise, interference or fading. If the data is corrupted, the receiving station transmits a brief signal known as a NAK (nonackowledgment) and the data burst is repeated. If the data arrives intact, or if the receiving station has enough information to "repair" any errors, an ACK (acknowledgment) is sent and the next block of data is on the way. This system of rapid-fire data bursts, ACKs and NAKs guarantees a 100% error-free information exchange between stations.

PACTOR and Winlink 2000

More than 50 HF digital stations worldwide have formed a remarkably efficient Internet information exchange network, including e-mail, binary file transfer and global graphic WX reporting. Running *Winlink 2000* software and using PACTOR, PACTOR II or PACTOR III protocols, these facilities transfer information between HF stations and the Internet. They also share information among themselves using Internet forwarding.

The network evolved in the 1990s from the original AMTOR-based *APLink* system, authored by Vic Poor, W5SMM. APLink was a network of stations that relayed messages to and from each other and the VHF packet network. As PCs became more powerful, and as PACTOR and Clover superceded AMTOR, a new software system was needed. That need brought about the debut of *Winlink*, again authored by Vic Poor, W5SMM, with additions from Peter Schultz, TY1PS. *Winlink* itself evolved with substantial enhancements courtesy of Hans Kessler, N8PGR. To bring the Internet into the picture *Winlink* stations needed an e-mail "agent" to interface with cyberspace. To meet that requirement Steve Waterman, K4CJX enlisted the help of Jim Jennings, W5EUT and Rick Muething, KN6KB, to add *NetLink*.

Early in 2000 the system took the next evolutionary leap, becoming a full-featured Internet-to-HF gateway system known as *Winlink 2000* or "WL2K." Jim Corenman, KE6RK, concurrently developed software called *AirMail* (available on the Web at **www.winlink.org**), which is the end-user portion of *Winlink 2000*. *Winlink 2000* is a network of participating stations (PMBOs); all connected to a central server (CMBO), which is the "hub" for Internet connectivity to Internet e-mail and position reporting.

Thanks to these advancements, an HF digital operator at sea, for example, can now connect to a *Winlink 2000* participating network station using *AirMail*, and exchange Internet e-mail with non-ham friends and family. He can also exchange messages with other amateurs by using the *Winlink 2000* network stations as a traditional global "mailbox" operation.

Most *Winlink 2000* participating stations scan a variety of HF digital frequencies on a regular basis, listening on each frequency for about two seconds. By scanning through frequencies on several bands, the *Winlink 2000* stations can be accessed on whichever band is available to you at the time.

Using *AirMail, Winlink 2000* features include…

• Text-based e-mail with binary attachments such as DOC, RTF, XLS, JPG, TIF, GIF, BMP or other files.

• Position inquiries accessible from both the Internet graphically via APRS and YotReps, e-mail, or radio to track the mobile user.

• Graphic and text-based weather downloads from a list of over 400 weather products, covering the entire globe.

• Pickup and delivery of e-mail regardless of the participating station accessed.

• End-user control of which services and file sizes are transmitted from the participating stations, including the ability for each user to redirect incoming e-mail messages to an alternate e-mail address.

• The ability to use the Internet via Telnet instead of a radio transmission.

• The ability to use any Web browser to pick up or deliver mail over *Winlink 2000*.

• The inclusion of a propagation program in *AirMail* to predict the best band for connection to any *Winlink 2000* participating station.

Hardware and Software Requirements

In addition to your HF SSB transceiver, you'll need a multimode processor that is capable of communicating in binary mode with either PACTOR I, PACTOR II or PACTOR III. At the time this book was published, only the "PTC" processors manufacturered by SCS (**www.scs-ptc.com**) met this requirement. See **Fig 8-5**.

Fig 8-5 — The SCS PTC-II is the only multimode communication processor that offers PACTOR II or III.

Accessing a Winlink 2000 Station

Information about operating procedures may be found at **www.winlink.org**, or within the *AirMail* help files. *AirMail* can operate your radio if you set it up properly. Just choose a station, pick a frequency and push "SEND." All information transfer is automatic and would be set up prior to the actual transmission just like any other e-mail agent. A continually updated list of stations and a catalog containing weather as well as other helpful information may be automatically maintained through *AirMail*.

Remember that *Winlink 2000* stations usually scan through several frequencies. If you can't seem to connect, the *Winlink 2000* station may already be busy with another user, or propagation conditions may not be favorable on the frequency you've chosen. Either try again later, or use the built-in propagation feature to connect on another band.

Sending E-mail To and From the Internet

From the Internet side of *Winlink 2000*, friends and family can send e-mail to you just as they would send e-mail to anyone else on the Net. In fact, the idea of *Winlink 2000* is to make HF e-mail exchanges look essentially the same as regular Internet e-mail from the user's point of view. Internet users simply address their messages to **<your call sign>@winlink.org**. For example, a message addressed to **wb8imy@winlink.org** will be available when WB8IMY checks into *any Winlink 2000* station.

Through the *AirMail* software the ham user can address messages to non-hams, or to other hams, for that matter, by using the same format used in any other e-mail program.

Although *Winlink 2000* supports file attachments, remember that the radio link is *very* slow (especially compared to the Internet). Sending an attachment of more than 40,000 bytes is usually not a good idea. Text, RTF, DOC, XLS, JPG, BMP, GIF, WMO, GREB and TIF files are permitted as long as they are small enough to comply with the particular user-set limit. Where possible, *Winlink 2000* compresses files. For example, a 400,000 byte BMP file may be compressed to under 15,000 bytes. However, this is an exception rather than the rule. Also, the transmission protocol provides additional compression of approximately 35 percent. Speed depends on the PACTOR protocol used. PACTOR II is approximately 4-to-6 times faster than PACTOR I. Some *Winlink* stations are now using PACTOR III, which is even faster.

Position Reports

Another fascinating feature of *Winlink 2000* is the ability to provide position reports for mobile users. Through the use of *AirMail*, they may be manually entered or sent electronically to *AirMail* from a GPS with an "NMEA" port (most have such a port.)

There are two ways in which a family member or friend may query position reports and determine where you are (or at least where you *were* at the last report). The first method of obtaining a graphic position report of a mobile user on a series of maps is to request it from the Automatic Position Reporting System, APRS. Simply go to the *Winlink 2000* home page **www.winlink.org** and click on "APRS." Then input the call of the station you are locating and push "Display." You are shown a Worldview and successive views down to 250 feet! In US territories, you may also see a satellite photo of the site!

The second method, which can provide historical tracking is to send an e-mail message addressed to **qth@winlink.org** requesting the report. The subject line of the message must be "Position Request" (without the parentheses). The body of the message contains the call letters of interest (one call letter per line.)

For example:

To: qth@winlink.org
Subject: Position Request

W4NWD ← Message Body.
KG8OP 6 ← Last 6 reports.
KF4TVU 999 ← All existing reports for last 30 days.
REPLY: SMTP:jblow@yahoo.com ← Additional e-mail address to receive report.
W5CTX ← Sent to this user over the Radio using *Winlink 2000*.

In the above example, for the entries in the position reports table for W4NWD, only the *most recent* report will be sent back. No number after the call letters is the default. For KG8OP, the *last 6* most recent reports will be returned, and for KF4TVU, 999 will return *all* the position reports for KF4TVU. In addition to the originator of the position request message, a reply

will also be sent to e-mail address **jblow@yahoo.com**, and W5CTX, a radio user. Again, in all cases a reply will be sent to the originating e-mail address. Be patient when you send requests — it can take about 15 minutes to receive a reply.

Telnet

Another important supplement to using the radio for accessing *Winlink 2000* stations is the use of a "telnet session." Through a facility in *AirMail*, a direct connection to the Internet just like any other Internet connection will provide entry into the *Winlink 2000* system. Its look and feel is exactly the same as it would be over the radio, but, of course, it is about 100 times faster for a typical Internet connection. Once again, only radio users have access to this password protected service.

HF DIGITAL VOICE

Hams have made significant strides in the use of HF digital voice technology. It's been a difficult challenge, though. Amateur HF allocations are relatively narrow and crowded, so any digital voice or image system has to share the same territory with traditional analog modes such as SSB.

The digital systems must also be compatible with common Amateur Radio hardware, which means an SSB transceiver with a bandwidth of 3 kHz or less. Even so, hams have achieved a surprising amount within a 3-kHz bandwidth. Today's amateur HF digital voice technology produces FM-repeater-quality audio and it isn't confined to voice alone. You can also exchange images and other data during the same conversation.

It is the Content that Matters

It's interesting to note that Part 97 of the FCC Rules, the portion of the rules that govern the Amateur Radio Service, treats digital communication in an odd way. If the information being communicated is sent from a keyboard, or otherwise contains an exchange of data, it is deemed "digital." Such communication must take place in the portions of the bands reserved for CW and "data." So far so good. However, if the transmission contains voice or image information, *even if it is a digital transmission by any other reasonable description*, it must take place in the portions of the bands reserved for voice (phone) and image. In other words, it is the *content* of the transmission that matters most.

If you think this regulation is convoluted and strange, you're right. It was written before the appearance of the personal computer and the digital revolution that followed. Back then, a clear line separated data (RTTY) and voice/image (AM, SSB, slow scan TV and fax) on the HF bands. Today that line is blurred beyond recognition, but we're still governed by rules written in a simpler time. That's why HF digital voice communications must take place in the *voice* portions of our HF bands. We know they are really digital transmissions, and so does the FCC, but the old rules regulate by content and they are not likely to change any time soon.

AOR and AMBE

The AOR Corporation was the first ham manufacturer to arrive on the scene with an HF digital voice and data "modem" in 2004. The fundamental design of their model ARD9800 is based on a Vocoder protocol created by Charles Brain, G4GUO.

His protocol involves the use of *advanced multi-band excitation,* better known as *AMBE,* a proprietary speech coding standard developed by Digital Voice Systems. Brain's protocol operates at 2400 bit/s, with forward error correction (FEC) added to effectively produce a 3600 bit/s data stream. This data stream is then transmitted on 36 carriers, spaced 62.5 Hz apart, at 2 bits/symbol, 50 symbols/sec using QPSK. This gives the protocol a total RF bandwidth of approximately 2250 Hz (compared to 2700-3000 Hz for an analog SSB transmission).

The ARD9800 is designed to be as "plug and play" as possible. You simply plug your microphone into the front-panel jack and then plug the modem into the microphone input of your transceiver. A front panel switch selects digital encoding or analog transmission, so the unit can be kept in the line when not used for digital conversations. On the receive side, the modem automatically detects the synch signal of an AMBE transmission and switches to digital mode automatically. In addition to voice, the ARD9800 has the capability to send digital data (typically images).

AOR on the Air

AOR digital voice is clear and quiet, an unusual thing to hear on an HF frequency! Tune around 14.236 MHz and you're likely to hear AOR AMBE signals. They sound like rough hissing noises.

During *QST* Product Review testing in 2004, the ARRL Lab discovered that decoding was solid down to about 10 dB S/N. Digital voice is an all-or-nothing proposition, however, and below that level the signals begin to break up. The result is absolute silence during those periods. Interference produced a similar outcome.

The common approach on the air is to begin the conversation in analog SSB, then switch to digital. Each transmission starts with a one-second sync burst after the push-to-talk button is pressed. If the other station misses the sync signal, the audio doesn't decode and the transmission sounds like analog white noise. This means that for successful communication you must be on the correct frequency and ready to receive at the beginning of the transmission. However, if there is fading or interference during the sync transmission, you still may be unable to decode the signal that follows.

There are an additional few steps you can take to improve your odds of success with AOR modems…

• Make sure that you and your partner are on exactly the same frequency. The AOR units tolerate some discrepancy, but not much.

• Set your IF receive filters to 3 kHz or wider.

• Don't overdrive the modem audio input.

• Turn off your transceiver speech compression.

• Don't overdrive your radio. If the ALC meter shows any activity, turn down the output from the modem.

It is important to note that your transceiver duty cycle will be substantially higher when you're operating digital voice compared to normal SSB. To avoid damaging your radio, it is a good idea to reduce your output by 25 to 50%.

Because of its $550 price tag, adoption of the ARD9800 has been somewhat slow. In recent years AOR released the ARD9000MK2 (**Fig 8-6**), a pared-down unit (it cannot send digital images like the '9800) at a price of $350. Both modems

Fig 8-6 — Front and rear views of the AOR ARD9000MK2.

are compatible with each other, but they cannot converse with the other HF digital voice protocol in use today: *DRM.*

WinDRM

WinDRM began with a "Dream." The *Dream* I'm alluding to is an ingenious piece of open-source software developed by Volker Fisher and Alexander Kurpiers at the Darmstadt University of Technology in Germany. It was designed to decode Digital Radio Mondiale (DRM), a relatively new digital shortwave broadcast format. If you've tuned outside the amateur HF bands you've likely heard DRM on the air. It is a wide signal that sounds like the bellow of an enraged chain saw. A commercial DRM signal is capable of carrying high-quality audio along with text and occasional images.

DRM works its magic through Coded Orthogonal Frequency Division Multiplexing (COFDM) with Quadrature Amplitude Modulation (QAM). COFDM uses a number of parallel subcarriers to carry all the information, which makes it a reasonably robust mode for HF use.

Not long after *Dream* debuted, Francesco Lanza, HB9TLK, began adapting it for Amateur Radio. He redesigned *Dream* to support DRM transmission and reception within a 2.5-kHz SSB transceiver bandwidth. That meant sacrificing some audio quality, along with the ability to simultaneously send images and other large chunks of information. Despite the difficulties, Francesco's ingenuity prevailed and *WinDRM* was born.

As the name implies, *WinDRM* is a *Windows* application. It is designed to use your computer sound card (or on-board sound chipset) to send and receive amateur DRM on HF, or wherever you choose to use it. Best of all, *WinDRM* is utterly *free of charge.* All you need to explore amateur DRM is a radio, a computer (preferably with a 1 GHz processor or faster) and one of the sound-card interfaces we discussed earlier.

Listening with *WinDRM*

You start by visiting the Web site of Jason Buchanan, N1SU, and downloading the *WinDRM* software (**n1su.com/windrm/**). While you're visiting the site, be sure to get the tutorial, which will help you to install and configure the software. Most *WinDRM* enthusiasts are using the MELP codec, so make sure to download the latest MELP version of *WinDRM* along with a copy of the MELP codec and the TUNE audio WAV file. All of these download links are on the same Web page. If you intend to swap digital images with *WinDRM,* you'll also need to download and install the free *InfranView* software at **www.infranview. com/**. *InfranView* is a nice little application that allows you to view and edit a huge variety of digital images.

If your objective is to simply receive amateur DRM, all you need is a cable between the audio output of your radio and the LINE INPUT of your sound card (see **Fig 8-7**). You may need

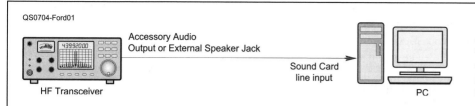

Fig 8-7 — Listening to a DRM digital voice conversation with *WinDRM* is as easy as connecting an audio cable between your radio and your computer sound card.

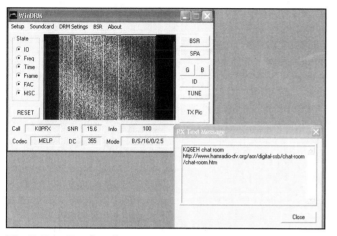

Fig 8-8 — Tuning in an amateur DRM signal amounts to little more than lining up the three vertical lines under the red markers at the top of the waterfall window. Watch the column of "state" indicators along the left side of the waterfall display. When they all go black, you should hear audio. If the station is sending text, a separate window will open to display it (if you've enabled that function in *WinDRM*).

to get into your sound card control software and boost the LINE INPUT gain. Using the *Windows* audio mixer, which you can access within *WinDRM*, bring up the RECORDING CONTROL panel and make sure LINE is selected and that the "slider" control is up. If the *WinDRM* waterfall display is too bright, reduce the gain control.

WinDRM users tend to hang out around 14.236 MHz USB, although you'll find them on other bands as well. When this book went to press, the *WinDRM* portion of the Weekend Digital Voice Net was meeting on Saturdays and Sundays at 14.236 MHz from 2000 to 2100 UTC. This might be a good opportunity to test your receive capability.

Listen for the jet turbine noise and then tune your receiver until you have three vertical lines in the waterfall display. The lines must be centered beneath the red markers at the top of the waterfall window (**Fig 8-8**). You'll know you are in the sweet spot when you see the "state" indicators along the left side of the window lighting up in sequence from top to bottom. When the MSC (Main Status Channel) indicator blinks on at the bottom, you should be hearing audio through your PC speakers or headphones.

If you can't get all the indicators to light, (A) the signal isn't tuned correctly, (B) you don't have enough audio going to the sound card or the software or (C) the received signal is too weak. When you finally achieve success, the result is an astonishing thing to hear. The voice sounds like it is coming to you through a local FM repeater. Look in the lower left corner of the *WinDRM* window and you will see the call sign of the transmitting station. If the station is sending text, a separate window will pop open to display the text if you've enabled that function in *WinDRM*.

Ready to Transmit?

Transmitting with *WinDRM* is not as straightforward as listening, especially if you have only one sound card. The reason is easy to understand when you think about it. The audio output from your sound card must be applied to your headset or PC speakers for receiving, but the *same* output must also feed your transceiver for transmitting.

The easiest approach is to use two separate sound cards as shown in **Fig 8-9**. The second sound card doesn't need to be expensive. In fact, it doesn't even need to be installed inside your computer. You can use an inexpensive USB sound card for this application.

As with the AOR modems, be careful not to overdrive your transceiver. If you see the ALC meter moving, you're sending too much audio to the radio.

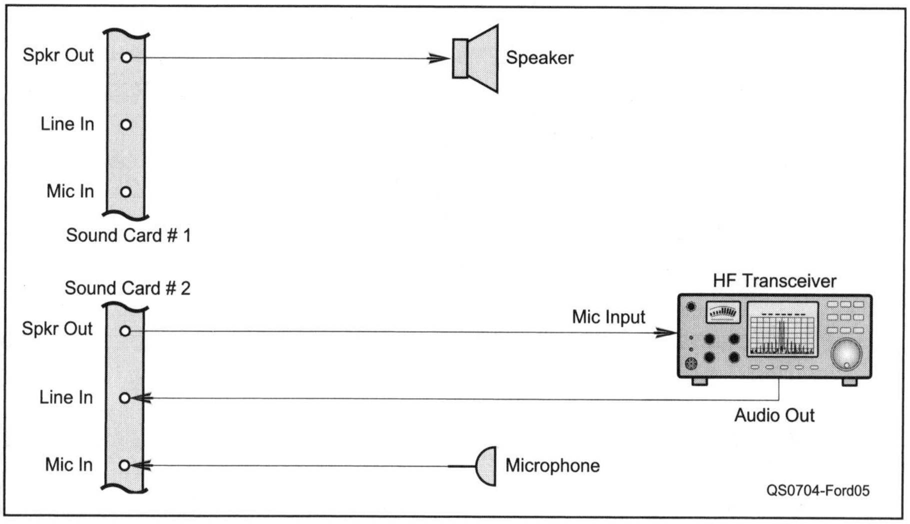

Dreaming on the Air

This is new technology on the ham bands and the operating prac-

Fig 8-9 — Two sound cards offer the most elegant approach to getting on the air with *WinDRM*.

tices are very much in flux. Some digital voice *aficionados* operate amateur DRM exclusively; they never switch to analog during the conversation. Others begin their CQs in analog SSB like this: "WB8IMY calling CQ in digital voice using the MELP codec." After that short analog preamble, they jump to DRM and call a long digital voice CQ. Most amateur DRM activity takes place on the 20-meter band, primarily around 14.236 MHz.

Remember that *WinDRM* uses a completely different protocol than that used by the AOR devices. You can't use *WinDRM* to talk to a station using an AOR voice modem, or vice versa. *WinDRM* also cannot decode commercial DRM broadcasts.

ATV: **Art Towslee, WA8RMC**
SSTV/Fax: **Dennis Bodson, W4PWF**
and Steven L. Karty, N5SK

chapter 9

Image Communications

As Amateur Radio operators, we communicate via radio. That's what our hobby is about. A natural extension to radio communication is television or image communication. Sound interesting? That's what this chapter is all about.

Thousands of Amateur Radio operators in the USA have ventured beyond *talking* and regularly transmit and receive pictures on the ham bands using modes such as slow scan television (SSTV), facsimile (FAX) and other experimental digital forms. In the first part of this chapter, we will concentrate on what is called Fast Scan Amateur Television (FSATV) or simply ATV for short. Did you know that at least 5000 hams find enjoyment in ATV?

If you're skeptical, you may ask "What practical use does ATV have, and why would I ever want to do it?" Why communicate via ham radio when you can simply call a person on the phone? It doesn't *have* to be practical, but it is indeed practical — and fun to boot! Are you interested in public safety and emergency communications? You can assist with security by transmitting video of local events such as parades, marathons, airport disaster drills, and so forth. Maybe you'd like to share videos with fellow ATVers. Perhaps you would just like to see how many video contacts you can make.

In general, ATV is like the television that broadcasters have been transmitting for over 50 years. However, much simpler equipment is used. At first you may think that ATV is overly complex and expensive, but it is quite the contrary on both counts. Yes, it is rather complex, but it is easy and not too expensive mainly because of commercially available home-entertainment equipment.

For ATV, you may already own two of the three main components in a beginner's station — the receiver and camera. Your standard cable-ready TV set will work as a receiver without modification of any kind. The required camera is the same camcorder that you use to record your family and vacation memories.

How about the ATV transmitter? Well, *that* can be the hardest part because usually there are no ATV transmitters in use for other purposes. More about that later.

Admittedly, there is one down side. ATV requires a large bandwidth signal to reproduce the picture with sufficient detail and in color. For that reason, among other factors, the communication distance is usually no greater than an average TV broadcast signal in your area. It is important for you to understand this now so you don't create an ATV station with hopes of regularly communicating thousands of miles. But even with the normally limited range of around 50 miles or less, there's a lot of fun and

Fred Magliacane, KF4VRS, sets up an ATV transceiver atop a luxury box at the Daytona Speedway. Members of the Volusia Amateur Radio Emergency Communications Service volunteered to assist Daytona city officials during the annual Race Week and used ATV to monitor traffic conditions.

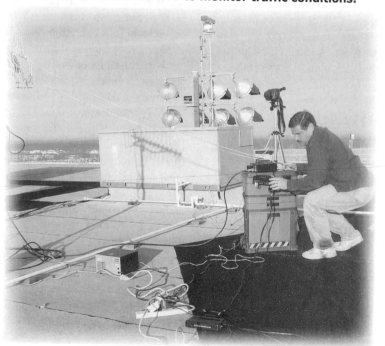

satisfaction to be had if there are other ATV-equipped stations in your area. When UHF propagation is enhanced and that 100-500 mile DX rolls in, the excitement becomes intense.

The most popular ATV band, by far, is 70 cm (420-450 MHz) where 439.25 MHz (cable channel 60) sees the most activity. To check for local activity, you can monitor this frequency with a cable-ready TV set connected to an outside UHF antenna. It's best if you can locate someone in your area who will transmit an ATV picture to you first. The 910-920 MHz (33 cm), 1250-1280 MHz (23 cm) or 2410-2450 MHz (13 cm) segments are also in use in many areas, but reception is slightly more involved. A detailed description will follow later.

Hams don't use the same high power levels nor do they have the same antenna heights that the broadcasters use. Therefore, we must use creativity to help make up some of the difference. While the broadcasters use hundreds of thousands of watts of power and antennas a thousand feet or so above ground, a typical ATV station uses less than 50 W with antenna heights of less than 50 feet.

Broadcasters use omnidirectional antennas with less than 10 dB gain; hams can build directional antennas with more than 16 dB gain — at each end. This, combined with the fact that they are usually willing to be satisfied with less than a snow-free signal most of the time, makes two-way communication feasible. In fact, given the overall circumstances, it is surprising how good the communication link can be. If it were not for the challenge of achieving a good two-way communication link, it wouldn't be nearly as much fun. Without doubt this is the challenge that motivates most ATVers.

HOW TO GET STARTED

What comes first? Well, that depends. Many factors influence where you go from here so no one can tell you exactly how to go about it. Instead, the best way is to outline the information resources available so you can choose the best avenue. After all, the best help is to know where to find information, and you'll learn a lot along the way. Here are some places to start for details.

1) **The Internet.** This is a wonderful resource of activity, because many ATV clubs post activity details on their Internet homepage. Area activity, as well as frequencies used, provides details of where and when to look for signals. Some of the most active Web sites are:
Columbus, Ohio ATCO Group:
   www.atco.tv/homepage/index.htm
Baltimore, Maryland BRATS Group:
   www.bratsatv.org
Houston, Texas HATS Group:
   www.hats.stevens.com
Detroit, Michigan DATS Group:
   www.detroitatvrepeater.com
Amateur Television Directory: **atv-tv.org**

2) **Hamfests.** Check *QST* magazine or visit **www.arrl.org/hamfests.html** for a list of hamfests or ham conventions in your area. Most of the larger hamfests post signs about ATV activity and have ATV forums.

3) *ARRL Repeater Directory.* Check this annual reference for ATV repeater listings.

4) **Local Ham Store.** Ask about ATV activity in the area.

Most ATVers are well known in these places so a list of individual hams involved in ATV can be compiled. Contact these individuals. Most active ATVers are willing to help newcomers and frequently invite potential ATVers to their ham shack to see firsthand what it is all about.

5) **ATV Equipment Dealers.** Many are willing to share information about where their equipment is sold. If you are interested in a given manufacture's equipment, ask about it and who owns that item in your area. Most will help you. A few of the larger original equipment ATV dealers that have been in business for a number of years are:
PC Electronics — Transmitters, receivers, preamps
   www.hamtv.com
Downeast Microwave — Transmitters, converters, preamps
   downeastmicrowave.com
Directive Systems — Antennas
   www.directivesystems.com
M² — Antennas
   www.m2inc.com
MFJ — Transmitters, preamps, Mirage amplifiers
Wyman Research — Transmitters, receivers
   www.svs.net/wyman

6) **Ham Magazines.** Check *QST* and other ham magazines for ATV related articles and advertising. *ATVQ* magazine is dedicated solely to amateur television. Check **www.hampubs.com/atvq.htm** for details. *The ARRL Handbook* ATV section also contains good reference information.

That should keep you busy for awhile. But sooner or later, a transition from planning to implementation must be made. So, a recommendation is in order at this point. Start by *receiving* an ATV signal. After all, if you own a cable ready TV set and an outside UHF antenna that can be turned, you're ready for action. Tune in and enjoy. The rest will follow.

LICENSING, LIMITS, RESTRICTIONS

ATV can be used by any ham with a Technician license or higher on any ham band 420 MHz and above. Some regional limitations exist for frequency and power levels in parts of the United States, so check the *ARRL Repeater Directory* or local sources before operating. Activity concentrates on different frequencies in different parts of the USA. However, most ATV activity can be found in the 420-440 MHz portion of the 70-cm band. ATV repeaters usually transmit on 421, 426 or 427 MHz and receive on 434 or 439 MHz (cable channel 59 or 60). A few ATV repeaters transmit on 439 MHz and receive on 421, 426 or 427 MHz. If you prefer simplex operation, 439.25 MHz is the most popular transmit and receive frequency.

The only formal FCC imposed frequency restriction is that no operation is allowed outside the allocated ham bands. That includes sideband energy, so it is important to know that television requires a large bandwidth. If not adequately suppressed with appropriate filters, it may extend beyond the band limits. Insufficient space is available here to define and detail the specifics of the various modulation types, so be sure you know the characteristics of your signal before selecting an operating frequency. For example, many ATV repeaters transmit on 421.25 MHz. The lower band limit here is 420.0 MHz so special filtering of the sound/color subcarrier is required to prevent the signal from extending below the 420-MHz limit.

ATV History

ATV generally appeals to hams more interested in the technical portion of the hobby. Therefore, many have little concern with contests but lean toward building, modifying and working on equipment. Initially, if you didn't build it, you weren't successful in ATV because there was very little affordable and readily available commercial equipment. Today that's changed dramatically so more and more non-technical people are entering this fascinating side of Amateur Radio and learning to be quite technical as they progress.

Back in the 1950s, very few people experimented with amateur television. Those who did tended to be TV broadcast engineers who had the knowledge and equipment to get started.

In the '60s there was very little commercial equipment available. Most of the experienced ATVers were busy converting the transmitter portion of taxicab UHF radios and trying to squeeze those extra few milliwatts out of a 2C39 or 5894 tube. They got, if they were lucky, a few watts of RF. Feed lines were lossy, so if a watt was delivered to the antenna, that was good.

On the receiving side, the situation was even more difficult. The only way to use commercially available stuff was to modify (retune) a UHF tube-type tuner so that it would cover 439 MHz. Bell Telephone had a special low-noise tube known as the 416B that could be used for a receiving preamp if one of these could be found. If located, you then had to find a machinist willing to fabricate a socket and housing for the circuitry.

Transmitters and receivers were difficult enough but the real stumbling block was the camera. Black and white vidicon cameras were available but generally not on the surplus market. The cheapest way to generate video was with a photo multiplier tube using a TV raster as the scanning device (another story for another day). This method *only* produced still pictures.

The '70s introduced widespread use of those tiny solid-state devices called transistors

and a new era of experimentation began. Many types of low-noise devices became available, but not necessarily affordable for all. Numerous ATV articles appeared in ham magazines for both transmitting and receiving equipment. Black and white vidicon cameras were now becoming more available.

The '80s and early '90s were transitional, as more and more modifiable commercial units became available, as well as some gear designed specifically for the ham market. When this happened, more hams got involved because it no longer required an engineer to make things work.

Today, individual transistors of earlier times are reduced dramatically in size, combined into entire circuits on a single integrated circuit (IC) and packaged into complete radios. Even more dramatic is the cost reduction. A complete radio circuit is cheaper now than a single transistor was in the '70s. As a result, low-cost, high-efficiency circuitry for ATV without modification is available to everyone. Those expensive color camcorders of the '80s and early '90s are now available at hamfests for $25 or less.

Twenty years ago, no one even dreamed this could happen. So what's next? Have we approached the limit? No, we're still on a nearly vertical learning curve with many more exciting things yet to come. Total digital processes are now emerging, so get involved and join the excitement of the adventures of amateur television.

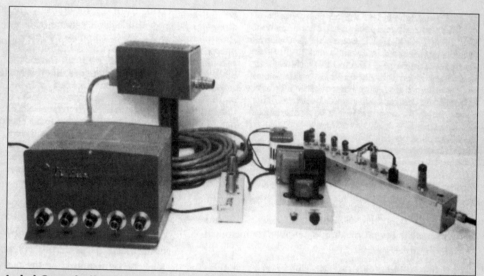

Laird Campbell, W1CUT, described this 70 cm ATV transmitter in November 1962 *QST*. Typical of early ATV stations, it uses a combination of homebrew and commercial equipment. Getting a UHF amateur television station up and running in this era was quite an achievement!

Although the full legal limit of 1500 W is allowed on any of these bands (check for some local exceptions), very few operators exceed about 50 W. One quickly learns that the complexity, technical expertise, mechanical ability and cost all go up exponentially past this point so don't get carried away. There's plenty of time to dream later!

Other than the FCC imposed restrictions, the remaining allocations are mostly by *gentleman's agreement* or locally agreed to band plans. If the local frequency coordinators have assigned a repeater frequency within a given ATV segment to someone else, it should be honored. Cooperation is necessary. As the operating frequency is increased to the higher ham bands

Nick Klos, AC6Y, worked with local amateurs to develop an airborne ATV station that hams could use to assist the Corona, California, police department during emergencies. The complete portable system includes a 70 cm ATV transceiver, ID generator, LCD television, 2 m/70 cm FM transceiver and antenna duplexer. A 12 V, 18 Ah battery provides power.

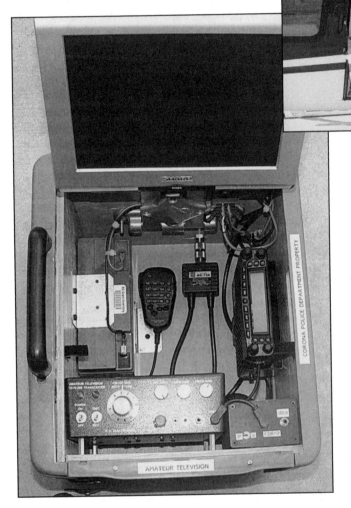

(33, 23 or 13 cm) interference becomes less of a problem because of directivity, activity and losses. If it becomes too crowded in your area, serious consideration should be given to one or more of these higher bands.

One last note on the interference issue — ATV is a wideband signal with energy dispersion that decreases rapidly as it departs from center carrier. The ATV receiver must tune this entire bandwidth, so it will see all signals within its passband. Therefore, someone else's narrow-band signal is much more likely to interfere with an ATV signal than the other way around, so be understanding. We must all share.

SIGNAL DETAILS...A BROADCAST STANDARD COMPARISON

At this point, we need a brief description of the type of signals we are dealing with for ATV. The description is broken into two parts, as there are two basic transmission modes in common use.

Amplitude Modulation

The first mode is called *vestigial sideband* and is a form of amplitude modulation. This is most common and is used by all broadcast TV stations. In this system, an all white screen will generate a minimum RF signal. An all-black screen is a maximum RF signal. Therefore, if you are transmitting a signal and put your hand over the lens, the average power level will be greater than if you display a bright scene.

The amplitude-modulated signal has upper and lower sidebands plus the carrier frequency in the middle. The sidebands result from the modulation process, which produces the sum and difference of the carrier and video frequencies. Only one of these sidebands is needed for picture reconstruction because each is identical.

In broadcasting, the lower sideband is *partially* eliminated to conserve spectrum space. Because part of it remains, it is called vestigial sideband. However, if the lower sideband wasn't partially suppressed, the TV receiver would ignore it anyway. Since the sideband suppression process tends to be complex and expensive, ATV transmitters that hams commonly use rarely do it since the receiver doesn't care.

Amplitude modulated ATV signals can be detected with relatively low transmitted power levels (compared to FM ATV signals, discussed in the next section). However, it does take a very strong signal to get a snow-free picture. If you receive a signal that is just discernible (sync bars are visible but the content is not recognizable) and the power level at the transmitter end is 0.1 W (100 mW), the transmitted signal must be boosted by 30 dB — to roughly 100 W — to obtain a snow-free signal. Likewise, the received signal can be improved by using better feed line, a better antenna or a more sensitive receiver.

A transmitted AM ATV signal is relatively easy to create (if you don't use vestigial sideband like the broadcasters). It's also easy to receive on the 70-cm band mainly because it allows the use of a standard TV receiver for reception without modification of any kind.

Frequency Modulation

The second mode is FM (frequency modulation), and it is employed with almost all satellite systems. If you watch satellite TV (either 4-GHz C band or the newer 11/12-GHz Ku band systems) the signal is first downconverted and then FM detected at a 70-MHz intermediate frequency. The resulting video is either fed directly to an ATV video input or used to modulate a signal on TV channel 2 or 3 for reception on your TV set. Because of this, a number of commercially available converters can be used for ATV.

As discussed earlier, a weak AM signal can be detected easily. It is not so with FM. As the FM signal strength is increased, nothing is seen until the limiter circuit in the receiver sees a significant signal. Once that limiter threshold is crossed, from the point of signal recognition to snow-free is, in many cases, only 6-8 dB. As in the earlier example, instead of 100 mW producing the barely recognizable signal, 25 W would be needed if 100 W produced a snow-free picture. In practice, the comparison may or may not be quite as dramatic, but hopefully you get the point.

There are many variables involved, so true comparisons are difficult. On the up side, an FM signal tends to produce a higher resolution picture. However, quality is mainly limited by the monitor you use. It is also less subject to fading than its AM counterpart. Also, since noise is fundamentally AM, the FM detection process results in lower noise. Haven't you noticed static crashes on your AM radio but not on FM?

There's no free lunch. Each system has its advantages and disadvantages. You may want to experiment and determine for yourself, if both are used in your area or if you have a friend or two who is willing to work with you.

Because of increased available bandwidths, FM systems dominate the 2.4 GHz and higher bands while 902 and 1240 MHz bands are mixed. By contrast, 420 MHz is the only place where AM enjoys exclusive use.

The differences are shown in the experience of the ATCO (Amateur Television in Central Ohio) ATV group. They originally used 920 MHz with AM modulation for a repeater link. That link is located in a metropolitan area plagued with intermodulation problems from nearby TV broadcast and FM commercial radio transmitters. The link suffered from fading, herringbone bars in the picture and frequent noise bursts. They changed to FM, and the improvement was miraculous — even though the power levels remained about the same! If power levels were reduced, there would have been a point where AM could have been recognized and FM wouldn't. The rule is if you have adequate power, are willing to spend more money for increased complexity and want a better quality picture...use FM.

Signal Reports

When you watch an ATVer's picture, you want to tell the sender how well it is being received. You could say, "Your picture is 20% snow." But that terminology is vague and wordy. The only exceptions are "I can't see it at all," or "You're perfectly snow-free," which we all understand. It's analogous to the digital 1s or 0s indicating on or off, but it's the shades of gray that become a bit more arbitrary. To solve this the *P system* was developed for AM signal reception. It goes like this: P stands for picture level and is divided into six levels from P0 to P5.

A signal received as P0 is recognizable as to its existence only. No detail is discernible and usually only sync bars can be seen in the snow. Since the minimum recognizable signal change is about 3 dB, 6 dB steps are easily recognized and they represent a convenient increment. The numbers continue in 6 dB steps from P0 to P5, which is a snow-free signal and 30 dB greater than P0.

Beyond that, we tend to say "P5 plus," or "broadcast quality." Everyone likes compliments and ATVers are no exception, so if you like what you see, tell the sender about it. Try not to overdo it, though.

P-unit reporting is universal across the USA and in other countries as well. This system is accurate only for AM because of the near-linear levels. P-unit reporting of FM signals can be used as long as it's understood that it will not be 6 dB per P unit because of the non-linear nature of the receiver detection system. For a visual representation of what the AM signal for each P-unit level looks like, see **Fig 9-1**.

BUILDING THE STATION

Let's start putting something together. If you have convinced the rest of the family to relinquish the main TV set, let's hope you have been able to see an ATV picture. In any case, now you need equipment for the ham shack . . . The receiver is a good start.

Receiving Equipment

There are many receiver possibilities and combinations available, mainly depending on which band you want to receive. Let's start with 70 cm (420-450 MHz) because it's the easiest to receive and, universally, most popular.

70 cm

This band is home to much more than ATV operation, but as a rule parts of the segment from 420 to 440 are used for ATV. Of this segment, 439.25 MHz (cable channel 60) is the most popular ATV frequency for simplex and repeater inputs, while 434.25 MHz (cable channel 59) is used for simplex and repeater inputs to a lesser extent. Most repeater outputs are 421.25 (cable channel 57), 426.25 (receivable on cable channel 58) and 427.25 (cable channel 58). Other frequencies are in use, but they're generally avoided to preserve most band plans. If there's no established ATV activity in your area, be sure to study the band plans and avoid frequencies set aside for EME, weak signal, beacon, auxiliary and satellite operation (generally 432-438 MHz).

ATV signals in the 70-cm band usually are horizontally polarized. This came about from two main factors: Existing broadcast TV antenna systems are horizontal and many early ATVers were weak signal DXers first. They used horizontal antennas exclusively. In addition, horizontally polarized 439.25 MHz signals are better neighbors to the vertically polarized FM voice repeaters in the 440-450 MHz segment because of cross polarization isolation. If you also plan 70-cm narrowband FM activity, consider a cross-polarized antenna, separate antennas or a polarization rotator so vertical and horizontal signals can be accommodated.

One type of 70-cm ATV receiver is the cable-ready TV itself. Almost all TVs manufactured since 1990 are cable ready, so if you own one you have a good start! ATV activity on cable channels 57, 58, 59 and 60 is no coincidence; it is the result of the cable ready sets. Most tuners in these sets are quite good

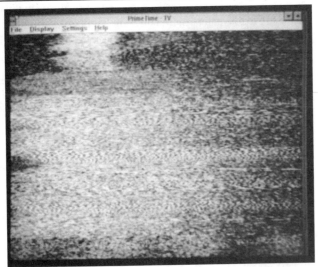

P0 — Picture is barely recognizable. Only sync bars can be seen.

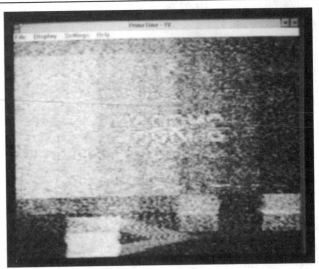

P1 — 6 dB > P0. Picture is recognizable, but extremely snowy.

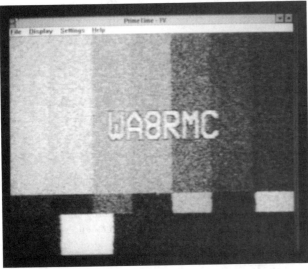

P2 — 12 dB > P0. Picture is easily recognizable, but lacks detail and still is quite snowy.

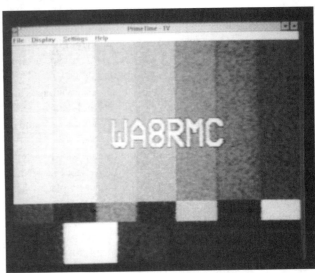

P3 — 18 dB > P0. Picture detail is much better, but snow is still visible

P4 — 24 dB > P0. Picture detail is better with very little snow.

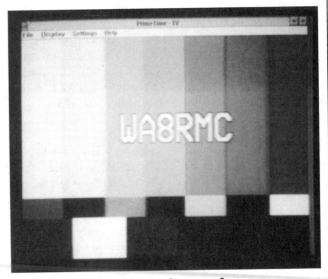

P5 — 30 dB > P0. Picture is snow free.

Fig 9-1 — P-Level Reporting System

and will suffice to start, but usually they are not as good as a separate receiver made specifically for ATV reception.

A preamp for any receiver is a good idea, but if you decide to purchase a separate receiver, it may already contain an acceptable preamp. Most preamps today are constructed with a GaAsFET transistor, which is a good idea for intermodulation rejection characteristics and almost a must for wideband operation. Simple GaAsFET preamps are not expensive, and on this band it's easy to achieve low-noise operation. Expensive microwave devices won't buy anything extra. A good preamp can be had for $25 (kit — assembled by you in your box) or $100 (assembled by manufacturer in a box with connectors).

When buying a preamp, make sure it has a tuned input (filter on the incoming line). This will help deal with the interference and overloading that is apt to occur in metropolitan areas because of narrowband FM activity nearby. Consider the purchase of an *interdigital* type of filter if interference is experienced. This filter has the wide passband characteristics needed for ATV while maintaining steep passband skirts for maximum rejection of unwanted out-of-band signals. The cost is about $100 for a 4-pole unit.

You may ask, "If I buy a good preamp, can I mount it at the antenna and use cheap coax to go to the receiver?" Well, it *might* be a good idea, but let's continue with the receiver discussion first. More on that later.

If you purchase a separate receiver or use your existing TV, think about an additional factor. Sooner or later you are going to want to transmit. Therefore, some means is necessary to disconnect the receiver while transmitting and vice versa. This is usually accomplished with a coaxial relay. If a self-contained receiver/transmitter package is purchased, this feature is usually built in so that issue is simplified and may be more desirable even though the cost is higher. See a typical receiver/transmitter combined package in **Fig 9-2**. If you like to build things and are handy with tools, don't forget about the antenna relay. When the transmitter and receiver are purchased separately, this little item is often forgotten.

33 cm

This band (902-928 MHz) offers no easy opportunity to utilize unmodified commercial equipment. For that reason, building expertise is generally required. Surplus 850-MHz cellular equipment is available that could be modified for use on 902-928, but all of this equipment is for narrow-band FM so it may not work satisfactorily. RadioShack stores used to market "Rabbit radio" units that operate with low power on 910 MHz. Some people have used these low-cost units with limited success but only for short ranges. If you're serious about trying ATV on this band, check out the Amateur Radio FM receiver and transmitter units from the ATV vendors.

23 cm

This band (1240-1300 MHz) offers the best opportunity for those who want to get away from the sometimes-crowded 70-cm band. ATV operation here is primarily FM but there are some old timers still using AM. Check for activity in your area.

If AM is chosen, a suitable downconverter that takes 1250 MHz and converts it to a suitable VHF TV channel is the best choice. Several are available. The overall activity on this band

Fig 9-2 — A complete 20-W 70-cm receiver transmitter combination ideal for the beginner, if an all-in-one package is desired. Its 20-W output may eliminate the need for a final amplifier. (Photo courtesy of PC Electronics, Inc.)

largely depends upon your location, but in general, narrowband SSB and CW are found around 1290-1300 MHz. Simplex and repeater FM ATV inputs can be found around 1270-1280 MHz. FM ATV repeater outputs are generally located below this at around 1250-1270 MHz. Localities with UHF TV station channels 39 to 44 sometimes have second harmonic energy strong enough to cause interference in this band, so ATV activity is usually away from these signals.

The ideal receiver for FM ATV reception is a surplus LNB (low-noise block converter), the type used for a satellite receiver. These units sometimes have acceptable sensitivity, tune the entire band and output video directly for connection to a TV monitor or modulated channel 3 or 4 for connection to a standard TV set. The best part is the cost. They are rarely priced above $30 and if you're lucky, hamfest $5 bargains could happen! Here are some things to look for when searching for these units at your favorite hamfest or garage sale.

The bad news. Some don't work, which may be why they're there in the first place. Now, here's the good news. Most do, and the ones that are bad usually have defective satellite rotator/polarizer circuitry not needed anyway. If you can, power it before purchase. If it lights, it's probably okay for ATV use.

Make sure the unit that you choose has a switch on either the front or rear panel for *inverted video* operation. In its intended use, the LNB amplifier on the satellite dish converts the 3.8-4.2 GHz incoming signal to a 950-1450 MHz output frequency, inverting the signal. It is then fed into the LNB receiver. When it is used for 1250-MHz ATV, the signal from the antenna goes directly to the receiver. No signal inversion takes place, so the receiver must be in the inverted video mode if used for ATV. Some receivers don't have this switch and if not, it's useless for ATV use unless an inverting amplifier is added to the video output.

There are two types of LNB receivers: those that tune 950-1450 MHz (which is what you *do* want) and those that tune 450-950 MHz (which you *don't* want, unless you use it for the 33-cm band). It's nearly impossible to tell which is which if it isn't marked on the rear of the unit at the input connector. Fortunately, very few 450-950 MHz units were in service, so it's very unlikely that you will get one by mistake. (Nevertheless, WA8RMC found one of these disguised as an *ideal* unit.)

Select a unit with manual switch or pushbutton tuning if possible. Nothing fancy is needed, so don't get one with a lot of bells and whistles. These features will only be bothersome.

Look at the unit closely. There are many look-alikes with only a 70-MHz input intended to operate with LNA satellite dish voltage-tunable converters. These won't work. (WA8RMC also made that mistake once.)

Most LNB receivers are equipped to provide 12-18 V dc to power the LNB converter on the dish. They usually provide this dc voltage on the center conductor of the incoming coax, so check for this voltage at the input connector. If found, it must either be removed or disabled, or a dc isolator inserted to prevent a short when the antenna or preamp is connected.

These receivers are intended for use with an LNB satellite dish low-noise amplifier/converter, which has high signal amplitude output. Therefore, the input sensitivity will probably be low. Search for an IF gain control and turn it up if it has one. If not, an input preamp may be needed.

Most of the previous discussion about 70-cm preamps applies here also. However, many have untuned front ends and these require an input filter of some type for acceptable operation. Some people have reported that when an untuned preamp was first tried, the results were poorer than with no preamp at all. This usually results from front-end signal overload caused by out-of-band signals. A simple cavity filter will usually fix the problem. Again, the preamps are not expensive and run about the same price as the 70-cm ones.

13 cm

This band has grown very rapidly in popularity ever since RadioShack introduced the Wavecom/Wavecom Jr. short-range video extender units. Other manufacturers have similar ones. They are purchased as a receiver/transmitter pair and operate on 1 of 4 pushbutton selected frequencies of 2411, 2434, 2453 and 2473 MHz. Since two of the channels are in the ham band, they're ideal for 2.4 GHz experiments and short range ATV communication. These units are also modifiable in a number of ways to increase power in the transmitters and provide more available frequencies. Quite a few ATV dealers stock these units as well as modification kits. If you like to experiment, here is a wonderful opportunity to have some fun at minimum cost. The only bad part is the limited range. It is difficult to increase the transmitter power beyond 50 mW or so because of available devices and high cost, so this usually becomes a *buddy project* with normal ranges being a mile or so (and then only if a good line-of-sight path is available).

However, because of the receiver/transmitter compactness, Wavecoms have become the favorite for remote control projects such as radio-controlled airplanes, radio-controlled cars and balloons. Here the low power is an advantage because a very good signal can be achieved with a small and lightweight package. The line-of-sight restriction is not normally a problem because it's a good idea to be able to see these devices while operating or bad things could happen.

Above 2400 MHz

Very little ATV activity is found on the bands above 2400 MHz. They are generally reserved for the more experienced and dedicated ATVer. Most activity is centered around 10 GHz because of the availability of Gunnplexer units. You may have seen some of these at hamfests sold as brake-light testers because they can generate signals that activate automotive radar detectors.

In any case, these bands are generally reserved for experienced hams willing to experiment.

Transmitting Equipment

Let's investigate transmitter possibilities. As before, let's start with 70 cm.

70 cm

A number of ATV manufacturers make transmitters both in kit and preassembled form. Your choice depends upon your level of expertise. For this band, the *minimum* usable power level is approximately 100 mW. Coupled to a reasonably large antenna with 50 feet or less of low-loss feed line, 100 mW will yield a communication range of about 5 miles over flat terrain. Many entry-level transmitters run 2 to 5 W. This is a good starting point because a reasonable picture can be transmitted about 20 miles. In addition, if you decide to add more power later, most high power amplifiers (50 to 100 W) require about 2-5 W of drive. If you settle on a 10-15 W unit now and later want to add a power amp, you may have to attenuate the signal a bit to be compatible with the maximum allowable power level into the amplifier. That varies from unit to unit, though.

Solid state final amplifiers that output up to 100 W usually operate from a 13.8-V dc power supply. For power output levels beyond that, tubes and associated high-voltage power supplies are normally used. If this range interests you, bear in mind that you'll probably have to build it yourself or buy a home-brew unit from someone else. Amplifiers with one or two 4CX250 tubes are common and can output up to 500 W (for 2 tubes). Beyond about 75 W, the cost goes up exponentially with improved signal strength. As mentioned previously, doubling the power level will only yield ½ P-unit better picture at the other end. Most hams start with 5-10 W transmitters and then get solid state power amps later to boost the signal to 50-60 W (but seldom beyond that).

33 cm

There's not too much to say about this band for the beginner as far as transmitting equipment is concerned. A few manufacturers provide FM transmitters with outputs in the 1-5 W range and additional amplifiers with outputs in the 15 W range but not much beyond that. It's possible to convert surplus cellular transmitting equipment for use on this band, but most are designed for narrowband service and converting them to accept a 5-MHz-wide video signal may be quite a chore. As mentioned earlier, Rabbit transmitters are available, but the output power of a couple of milliwatts puts them in the toy category.

23 cm

Now here's a neat band with lots of opportunity for adventure. Unfortunately, again there are few, if any complete packaged solutions; only individual modules are available. A few manufacturers have put together units for security purposes that can output up to 100 mW. They are great for ham use because they're either within the amateur band as is or they can be switched there. This is an excellent starting point because with the availability of higher gain antennas, a transmission distance up to 20 miles is possible. Inexpensive FM power amps that require 100 mW or so of drive and output 10-15 W are relatively easy to obtain.

Higher power on this band is not very common and again you must use tubes, with the 2C39 variety the most common. If you go this route, most likely you're going to have to roll your own.

13 cm

At the present, this band presents a real transmitter challenge if power levels in the 1 W range and higher are desired. For the beginner, stick with the Wavecom or equal units and be happy. The unmodified Wavecoms output about 0.5 mW but a simple internal attenuator modification will bring the output up to approximately 3 mW. Add an internal MMIC amplifier to easily boost it to about 50-60 mW. At that level, it serves as a very good transmitter for short-range communications of up to 1 mile. The required modifications are easily found in a number of ATV publications as well as on the Internet and are not difficult, even for the beginner.

Above 2400 MHz

Although a number of articles are written about transmitters in this range, little exists for ATV applications except for 10 GHz. These bands are normally reserved for the serious, experienced individuals and definitely not beginner material. They always are buddy projects because of the short ranges involved.

Antennas

What a potentially huge subject! This is an area where a lot of us like to experiment and rightfully so, because there are more articles on this subject than any other in the Amateur Radio field. You can find antenna designs of almost every imaginable size and shape with emphasis on many variables for a variety of reasons.

Size is probably the most important factor. For example, many of us live in apartments or in antenna-restricted locations so a small one is anticipated. Then again some lucky people live in rural areas and the spouse doesn't mind looking outside at a tower with multiple antennas on it, so a much larger array may be your choice.

Whatever the size, try to stay with one designed for 50 Ω transmission lines, as they are most popular and will make the transmission line choice much easier. Let's summarize the things to look for when selecting an antenna specifically for ATV.

Antennas for 70 cm ATV

Concentrate on 70-cm antennas first because that's where most start. Most ATV signals in this band are horizontally polarized. Antennas with gains below 10 dBd (gain referenced to a dipole) should not be considered unless repeater-only operation in a metropolitan area is anticipated. These Yagi antennas are compact, with boom lengths of about 6 feet or less. Antennas with gains of 10 to 15 dBd are considered intermediate and are most common (8-14 foot booms). Gains greater than 15 dBd are found only on very large antennas with boom lengths in the 15-20 foot category. **Fig 9-3** shows a typical installation.

Beware of gain claims that sound too good to be true — most likely they are. With the widespread availability of accurate antenna modeling software, it's much easier for hams to know what a given antenna will do. As a result, outrageous gain claims are pretty much a thing of the past, but it's still possible to stretch the truth. For instance, check the reference for gain figures. Some specifications are referenced to an isotropic radiator, which is about 2 dB less than a dipole. Therefore, 10 dBi is about the same as 8 dBd but it looks much better if dBi values are listed on the data sheet. Sometimes gain is just stated as 10 dB so you can guess whether they mean dBi or dBd.

Without a doubt, the Yagi is the antenna of choice for most ATV applications on 70 cm. Yagis are easy to build if you like that sort of thing, but many good ones are available commercially. Just try to keep these things in mind:

1) Yagis can be high-Q antennas. That is, they're sensitive to construction variables, surrounding objects and weather conditions for consistent optimum performance. Some designs don't do well in the rain. The SWR goes up and performance goes down.

2) Because of the inherent narrow bandwidth properties of most Yagis, they probably won't be acceptable for optimum ATV use on both 421 MHz and 439 MHz. If a compromise must be made here, optimize for 439 MHz (your transmit and simplex receive frequency) and take whatever you get at 421 MHz (repeater transmit frequency).

3) The bandwidth limitation at a given frequency *may* degrade ATV performance but usually is not a consideration. Be more concerned about the achievable communication distance than signal quality. If the signal at the receive end is 50% snow (about P3) it won't matter if the resolution is good or fair. In fact, a narrower bandwidth antenna generally has a higher gain for a given size.

4) The physical size is relatively small for a given gain. However, if a really large Yagi is used to get as much gain as possible, you may have difficulty keeping it intact because of wind and ice-loading problems.

Fig 9-3 — W8SJV's antenna arrays. Sandwiched between his HF beam (below) and his 2-meter Yagi (above) is a 21-element 15-dBd Yagi on a 14-foot boom. John uses this for his ATV work, and has reported excellent results.

5) Polarization arrangements are easily accommodated. You can mount a polarization rotator on the boom of most reasonably sized antennas. Or you can simply use two antennas, one vertical and one horizontal, mounted on the same mast.

The next most popular 70-cm ATV antenna is the collinear or broadside array. This antenna is not usually found commercially so home construction is in order. *The ARRL Antenna Book* and other publications contain good designs. There are rewards for rolling your own, so this avenue should not be ignored. Here are some of the pros and cons:

1) Broadside arrays are low-Q antennas. As a result, construction errors, nearby objects and tolerances generally are not critical. In fact, it's a good idea to stagger the element lengths slightly in construction to help broaden the bandwidth with no significant gain sacrifice. Neat huh?

2) Rain has little impact on its performance.

3) It is more difficult to erect because of vertical construction. It looks similar to bedsprings standing on end fastened to the mast. It takes a lot of vertical mast area, which many folks don't have, but it is very tolerant of nearby antennas.

4) This antenna is very broadband and usually works well for the *entire* 70-cm band. In fact, it is an acceptable antenna for UHF commercial television up to about channel 20 so it can be used to check for band openings by watching the lower UHF TV station signal strength.

5) If all antennas with equal claimed gain are compared, this one will perform better because of its increased capture area.

A number of other antennas stand out for particular individual situations or for the desire to just try something new but are normally not used for ATV purposes. For instance, omnidirectional antennas are commonly employed for ATV repeaters, but shouldn't be used by an individual because of low gain. Remember that you don't get something for nothing. For a given desirable feature, something else must be sacrificed. The loop Yagi and helical antennas are also used but primarily on the higher bands.

Antennas for 33 and 23 cm

The 902 and 1240-MHz bands have more antenna choices because designs that are too large on 70 cm work just fine here. The Yagi is the first choice, but it usually shows up in a slightly different configuration. One of the most popular designs uses elements made from flat aluminum strips folded into a circle to form loops. Called a *loop Yagi*, this antenna is actually a variation on the quad. WA8RMC has used them on both the 902 and 1240 bands with good success.

The helix antenna is worth noting at this point because of its circular polarization properties. Because it's circularly polarized, a 3-dB cross-polarization loss will occur when transmitting to or receiving from a vertically or horizontally polarized antenna. That's considerably less than the cross polarization loss normally associated with vertical and horizontal antennas. So, if a single antenna must be selected for both polarizations and it can't be rotated for polarity, the 3-dB loss for each could be the better choice.

The collinear or broadside array also can be used on this band, and in many cases is easier to construct because of the small size. The supports for the elements can be fashioned from ¼-inch dowel rods — if you like to construct model airplanes

Richard Logan, WB3EPX, is an active ATV operator. His station is designed with space limitations in mind.

and cars, this is for you. The bad news is that there are very few published articles on this; the good news is they can be scaled down from existing lower frequency designs.

Antennas for 2400 MHz are similar to 900 and 1200 MHz ones except they are smaller. Loop Yagis dominate this band and are now small enough to be placed inconspicuously almost anywhere. Parabolic dishes are also sometimes used here but the size on this band tends to be rather large. However, as the frequency goes up, the antenna gain must also go up to maintain the same signal level. With all other factors equal, if the frequency is tripled, the antenna gain at each end must be increased by about 5 dB to maintain the same signal strength.

Feed Lines

All too often the feed line is not considered, or if it is, not nearly enough emphasis is put on its importance. Since the coax passes energy from the antenna to the receiver as well as from the transmitter, any losses here will be noticed on both transmitting and receiving. Therefore, buy the best coax you can afford, as it will improve both. *The ARRL Antenna Book* treats feed line theory and detailed applications very well, but here's what you should know about selecting for the UHF bands.

Regular RG-8 cable has quite a bit of loss at UHF, so you should only use it as a last resort. Belden, Times Microwave and others make coaxial cable that looks similar to RG-8 on the outside but is designed for lower loss at higher frequencies. Times LMR400 and Belden 9913 are popular part numbers, but check the *QST* ads for similar products. As the frequency goes up the losses get worse, so look for something better for 902 MHz and up or even for runs longer than 50 feet or so at 70 cm.

An improvement is surplus 75-Ω CATV Hardline with a solid aluminum outer jacket. It is available in ½-inch, ¾-inch and larger sizes. There are a few drawbacks. First, the fittings are a little hard to find. Second, the impedance probably doesn't match your normal 50 Ω ham antenna, so it will introduce a mismatch if not compensated. Fortunately, most 50 Ω antennas can be reasonably matched to 75 Ω line. If both coax and fittings are *free*, (ATVers love that word) because it was discarded by the local cable company, go ahead and use them. Even without the matching sections, it is good stuff. If you have to pay, buy something better.

Next we move up to the Heliax category. This 50 Ω cable, made by Andrew Corp, has a ribbed solid copper outer conductor and vinyl jacket and is readily available on the surplus market in both ½-inch and ⅞-inch sizes. It's used commercially for industrial communications including police, fire and cellular applications. The cable is shipped on huge rolls, and the end pieces that are too short to be used for a commercial run are often available at bargain prices. The connectors are not easy to work with but they are manageable so be careful and patient. They can be pricey, but used connectors will work and can be found much more reasonably. If you're investing in Heliax, try to get the ⅞-inch size. The losses are considerably lower, especially on 1200 MHz and up, so the investment is well worth it.

When planning your ATV antenna system, it's worth doing a little planning and research. Measure out your cable runs and look up the losses for various feed lines at the frequencies you'll be using. You can find this information in the *ARRL Antenna Book* or on manufacturer and dealer Web sites.

Oh yes, here's a short message about connectors. Try, if at all possible, to use type N connectors and not the PL-259 type. PL-259 connectors are okay for HF, but they have objectionable losses at 70 cm and above. Also, the N connectors have gaskets to make them waterproof. Do yourself a favor and get the best from the start. They don't cost that much more.

ATV PROJECTS

Here's where it gets fun. After the station is built and a number of contacts have been made, the imagination starts to roam. "What else can I get involved in?" After all it's great talking with and seeing the ATVers but sometimes that's not enough. Many other activities could use ATV involvement; but they sometimes just don't know it! That helps form groups and then clubs dedicated to helping other activities. After all, it's a hobby so it's supposed to be fun. Get involved and make it just that.

Balloon launches are now becoming popular. Hams fill up a 6-foot, or larger, weather balloon with helium, attach an ATV camera with transmitter, put in some avionics and direction locating equipment and launch it. These balloons can reach heights beyond 100,000 feet (19 miles) and usually send back spectacular pictures of Earth's curvature and near outer space. Also, at that altitude the reception distance extends beyond 500 miles, so it provides a show for many viewers. It's exciting, but it's also expensive.

If ballooning is not your fancy, try radio controlled airplanes with a camera and ATV transmitter aboard. The transmitters available in the Wavecom units mentioned earlier operate in the 2.4 GHz band. They are small enough to fit quite nicely inside a typical model plane and consume little power so small batteries can be used. The antenna is also small so this item is seldom a problem. I've seen the monitor video from a model

airplane and it's just like being in a real one. The range with this configuration can exceed a mile!

Don't like planes but cars are your bag? Easier yet! Radio controlled cars don't have as much of a weight restriction, so more hardware can be incorporated. A car constructed by N8QPJ from the Detroit Amateur Television Society (DATS) uses a camera connected to an ATV transmitter for the *eyes* and *ears* (the Wavecom units transmit stereo sound also). It has a 2-meter hand-held receiver for the *voice* so he can literally drive the car around the block and talk to people as it goes. Many were surprised and astounded that this unit could actually communicate with them with no one else around.

Want a club activity? It's fun and constructive to supply surveillance video of public-service events such as marathons, airport disaster drills and 4th of July celebrations. To provide police with video at these events is a valuable service to the community. It helps to draw new hams into this segment of the hobby and makes the general public aware of the existence of this hobby. Oh by the way, it's lots of fun for the participants too.

Are you interested in being a weather spotter? You know, they are the people who chase tornadoes to give the local weather service details about the incoming storm. Well, chasing severe weather is not what many consider fun, but ATVers frequently provide video to assist the spotters.

Here is an activity that a local ATV amateur repeater group can get involved with. More on ATV repeaters later but this too can be a group project.

Engineering students at the Temple University ARC (K3TU) built this radio- controlled Earth-bound version of a Mars Rover to put their knowledge to use in solving a practical design problem. Equipped with GPS, sensors and telemetry, the Rover includes a camera and 70 cm ATV transmitter so the operator can see where the Rover is headed.

The ATV group in central Ohio (ATCO) provides this service by retransmitting local TV station radar on the ATV repeater upon command to assist the weather spotters with up to date video of an incoming storm. When not in service, any ATVer can bring up the radar signal on command to check on weather conditions.

Here's another one for you. N8UDK attached a camera and transmitter to a miniature blimp (about 6 feet long) and flew it inside a shopping mall. He used a monitor to show mall-goers what it looks like from the ceiling. It's quite an attention getter.

ATV AND COMPUTERS

Computers are now part of our daily lives. So, why not use them for ATV? For many years we've used cards with the call sign or graphics on them in front of a camera lens for the identification mechanism. Now, an unlimited variety of computer graphics is available for the same job. It's now possible at a fraction of the cost of studio commercial equipment needed for this task only a few years ago. Things are surely changing.

Most ATVers own and use a computer to generate identification graphics. No special program is required specifically for the purpose, only a standard graphics program commonly used for presentation purposes. That way, a slide show of sorts can be shown. It has been my experience to witness competition in this area among various ATVers who compete for the best and most unusual graphic presentation.

The problem, then, is not how to do the graphics razzle dazzle but how to convert the VGA monitor output to NTSC (USA TV broadcast standard) video for ATV transmission. A number of suppliers have come to the rescue with VGA-to-video converter units. They're not specifically to assist the ATVers but to supply those who want a remote monitor typically needed in the classroom. As these became affordable (purchase price under $100), we started using them for ATV purposes also. So, here again is another inexpensive way to enhance ATV video quality.

ATV REPEATERS

Here is a subject of great interest among the ATVers. The design, construction and cost of ATV repeaters is beyond the scope of the beginner, but communicating through them is simple and can be quite exciting. A number of groups, clubs and individuals around the country have decided to construct and operate a repeater to receive ATV signals and retransmit them at higher power to an omnidirectional antenna mounted in a high location. (This is the same way FM repeaters operate with your hand-held radio. The difference is that video and audio signals are repeated instead of just the audio.) A list of ATV repeaters is available on many Internet homepages or in *The ARRL Repeater Directory*. You might want to check if any exist in your area before starting station construction. The first ATV signal you see most likely will come to you through a repeater.

It also is a great tool to use for fine tuning your transmitter because you can transmit on one frequency and, at the same time, watch your signal on the repeater output frequency. Some repeaters have outputs on different bands specifically for this purpose because it's often very difficult to transmit and receive on the same band without interference problems. In Columbus,

Ohio for instance, the ATCO repeater has an ATV input on 439.25 MHz and ATV output on 427.25 MHz with auxiliary ATV outputs on 1250 MHz FM and 2433 MHz FM. A signal sent to it on 439 MHz can easily be watched on 1250 or 2400 with only a very small separate antenna pointed toward the repeater during the 439 MHz signal transmission. Neat huh?

Once you become involved with the people using the repeater, you'll find that help with equipment selection, troubleshooting and all around technical information will be plentiful. These individuals are willing to assist because quite often they had to learn the hard way. There was no help available for them. It's gratifying to be able to help others who are just starting. So make yourself known to the others — the rewards are great.

Once an ATV repeater is located, look for a talk frequency because most repeaters have a 2 meter or 440-MHz FM frequency to serve as a discussion channel and act as a function control for the ATV repeater. The frequency varies from locality to locality but the most popular national frequency is 144.34 MHz simplex. Most areas monitor more than one frequency, so check for others also. For instance, in the Columbus, Ohio area, 147.45 MHz is the primary local talk frequency, which many monitor most of the time. When the band opens up, however, 144.34 MHz becomes primary for out-of-town signals.

DIGITAL ATV

As the name implies, Digital Amateur Television, or *D-ATV*, involves the transmission of video images as data, not analog signals. The image signal from the analog TV camera is turned into digital information and then specially encoded for over-the-air transmission. At the receiving end, the signal is decoded and the video information is extracted and displayed on the TV monitor.

If you have digital cable at home, you're watching digital TV right now. The data is sent through the cable system and decoded by your cable converter (or by your TV if you own a

Crisp, clear digital ATV through the ATCO WR8ATV repeater.

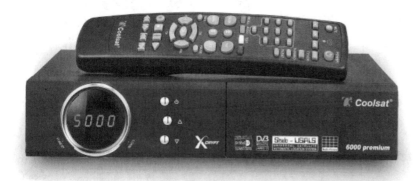

A CoolSat Free-to-Air satellite receiver. Receivers like these are favorites among amateur digital television experimenters.

set that can decode digital cable directly). The same is true if you subscribe to satellite TV.

You may also be watching terrestrial digital TV over the air, either through a digital-ready television or a digital-TV converter. The Federal Communications Commission has mandated a deadline of February 2009 for all broadcasters to switch from analog to digital television. There are three digital TV standards currently in use.

DVB-T

DVB-T was developed for terrestrial digital television communication and is used by US broadcast television stations for digital and HDTV. Known best as *8VSB modulation* (8 quadrant Vestigial Sideband), it is designed to overcome the effects of multipath reflections that cause "ghosts" in analog TV reception. DVB-T employs a very complex signal and a high data rate. This is fine for broadcast television, but the necessary hardware is expensive and impractical for ham use.

DVB-C

DVB-C was developed for cable digital television transmission using QAM modulation. A cable environment is a relatively protected from distortion and multipath effects, so a DVB-C signal is relatively straightforward as digital TV signals go. It is this very simplicity (and poorer over-the-air performance)

that makes it a weak choice for amateur digital television.

DVB-S

The DVB-S standard is developed for satellite digital television transmission using QPSK modulation (Quadrature Phase Shift Keying), which is a type of FM modulation. DVB-S is also the standard of choice for many amateur digital TV enthusiasts. It offers very good performance without taking up more bandwidth than an analog TV signal.

Amateur Experimentation

D-ATV is still largely an experimental activity among Amateur Radio operators. A group of Dutch hams pioneered an innovate DVB-S system using an MPEG-2 encoder and a DVB-S I/Q board. This system has since been widely adopted in the D-ATV community. You'll find more details online at **www.d-atv.nl/**.

Using the Dutch approach, the Amateur Television in Central Ohio (ATCO) group placed the first US D-ATV repeater on the air in 2006. ATCO repeater users are able to receive and view the D-ATV images using so-called Free To Air (FTA) satellite receivers. These devices are designed to receive unencrypted satellite TV signals that use MPEG-2 encoding, which makes them easily compatible with D-ATV.

FTA receivers should *not* be confused with the received used for satellite TV services such as DirectTV. Manufacturers of FTA satellite receivers include Viewsat, Pansat, Coolsat, Fortec, BlackBird, UltraStar, Ariza, MultiStar, Digiwave and Twinhan. They are often for sale on auction sites such as eBay.

Summary

With the information presented here and that gathered from other sources, including the Internet, you will be well on the road toward a successful ATV station. It's a lot of fun and you'll amaze your friends with your capability.

Special thanks to the many folks who helped with needed information and assistance in the preparation of this material.

SLOW-SCAN TELEVISION

Nestled among the CW, phone and RTTY operators in the Amateur Radio bands is a sizable following of hams who regularly exchange still pictures in a matter of seconds virtually anywhere on Earth. They are using a system called slow-scan television (SSTV), which was originally designed in the early 1960s by an amateur — Copthorne Macdonald, VE1BFL. Over the years, the amateur community has been continually refining and improving the quality of SSTV. Amateur success with SSTV for almost four decades has led to its application by the military and commercial users as a reliable long-range, narrow-bandwidth transmission system. The worldwide appeal of SSTV is evident by the many DX stations that are now equipped for this type of picture transmission. Several amateurs have even

This slow-scan television (SSTV) picture is displayed on a standard TV set using a digital scan converter.

Table 12-1 SSTV Formats

Mode	Designator	Color Type	Scan Time (sec)	Scan Lines	Notes
AVT	24	RGB	24	120	D
	90	RGB	90	240	D
	94	RGB	94	200	D
	188	RGB	188	400	D
	125	BW	125	400	D
Martin	M1	RGB	114	240	B
	M2	RGB	58	240	B
	M3	RGB	57	120	C
	M4	RGB	29	120	C
	HQ1	YC	90	240	G
	HQ2	YC	112	240	G
Pasokon TV	P3	RGB	203	16+480	
	P5	RGB	305	16+480	
	P7	RGB	406	16+480	
Robot	8	BW	8	120	A,E
	12	BW	12	120	E
	24	BW	24	240	E
	36	BW	36	240	E
	12	YC	12	120	
	24	YC	24	120	
	36	YC	36	240	
	72	YC	72	240	
Scottie	S1	RGB	110	240	B
	S2	RGB	71	240	B
	S3	RGB	55	120	C
	S4	RGB	36	120	C
	DX	RGB	269	240	B
Wraase SC-1	24	RGB	24	120	C
	48	RGB	48	240	B
	96	RGB	96	240	B
Wraase SC-2	30	RGB	30	128	
	60	RGB	60	256	
	120	RGB	120	256	
	180	RGB	180	256	
Pro-Skan	J120	RGB	120	240	
WinPixPro	GVA 125	BW	125	480	
	GVA 125	RGB	125	240	
	GVA 250	RGB	250	480	
JV Fax	JV Fax Color	RGB	variable	variable	F
FAX 480	Taggart	B&W	138	480 (512 Pixels)	
	Truscan	B&W	128	480 (546 (Pixels)	H
	Colorfax	RGB	384	480 (546 Pixels)	I

Notes
RGB—Red, green and blue components sent separately.
YC—Sent as Luminance (Y) and Chrominance (R-Y and B-Y).
BW—Black and white.
A—Similar to original 8-second black & white standard.
B—Top 16 lines are gray scale. 240 usable lines.
C—Top 8 lines are gray scale. 120 usable lines.
D—AVT modes have a 5-second digital header and no horizontal sync.
E—Robot 1200C doesn't really have B&W mode but it can send red, green or blue memory separately. Traditionally, just the green component is sent for a rough approximation of a b&w image.
F—JV Fax Color mode allows the user to set the number of lines sent. The maximum horizontal resolution is slightly less than 640 pixels. This produces a slow but very high resolution picture. SVGA graphics are required.
G—Available only on Martin 4.6 chipset in Robot 1200C.
H—Vester version of FAX 480 (with Vertical-Interval-Signaling instead of start signal and phasing lines).
I—Trucolor version of Vester Truscan.

fill the screen. Additionally, the vertical resolution of SSTV is 480 lines or less compared with 525 lines for fast scan. These disadvantages are offset by the fact that SSTV requires a very tiny fraction of a fast-scan TV's bandwidth. Thus, the FCC permits it in any amateur phone band.

The basic SSTV format represents a tradeoff among bandwidth, picture rate and resolution. To achieve practical HF long-distance communications, the SSTV spectrum was designed to fit into a standard 3-kHz voice bandwidth through a reduction in picture resolution and frame rate. Thus, SSTV resolution is lower than FSTV and is displayed in the form of still pictures.

Extraordinary new developments are emerging from the amalgamation of consumer color cameras, digital techniques and personal computers. The greatest advancements currently being made in the realm of color SSTV are increased resolution and improved noise immunity. These efforts have spawned over 40 SSTV modes that are not interoperable. For that reason interface and software developers are designing products with a multiple mode capability. **Table 9-1** lists many of the formats. Scottie and Martin are the two most popular modes.

OPERATING FREQUENCIES

Since SSTV operation is restricted to the phone bands, license requirements are identical to those for voice operations. While most activity occurs on HF using SSB, it is also well suited to FM at VHF or UHF frequencies. In the US, slow-scan TV using double-sideband AM or FM on the HF bands is not permitted.

The commonly accepted SSTV calling frequencies are 3.845, 7.171, 14.230, 14.233, 21.340, 28.680 and 145.5 MHz.. Traditionally, 20 meters has been the most popular band for SSTV operations, especially on Saturday and Sunday mornings. A weekly international SSTV net (International Visual Communications Association, IVCA), is held each Saturday at 1500 UTC on one of the active 14-MHz frequencies. Many years ago, when SSTV was first authorized, the FCC recommended that SSTVers not spread out across the band even though it was legal to do so. A *gentlemen's agreement* has remained to this day that SSTVers operate as close as possible to the above calling frequencies to maintain problem-free operation.

Identifying

On SSTV, the legal identification must be made by voice

worked more than 100 DXCC entities on SSTV!

Just as the name implies, SSTV is the transmission of a picture by slowly transmitting the picture elements, while a television monitor at the receiving end reproduces it in step. The most basic SSTV signal for black and white transmission consists of a variable frequency audio tone from 1500 Hz for black to 2300 Hz for white, with 1200 Hz used for synchronization pulses. Unlike fast-scan television, which uses 30 frames per second, a single SSTV frame takes at least eight seconds to or CW. Sending "This is N5SK" on the screen is not sufficient. Most stations intersperse the picture with comments anyway, so voice ID is not much of a problem. Otherwise SSTV operating procedures are quite similar to those used on SSB.

EQUIPMENT

All you need to get started is an Amateur Radio transceiver and a computer. Like RTTY, SSTV is a 100%-duty-cycle transmission. Most sideband rigs will have to run considerably below their voice power ratings to avoid ruining the final amplifier or power supply.

Early SSTV monitors used long-persistence CRTs much like classical radar displays. In a darkened environment, the image remained visible for a few seconds while the frame was completed. This type of reception is no longer used, and has been replaced with computer sound-card based software.

Most of the software packages for SSTV are designed around *Windows* PCs, but there are some very nice packages for *Mac OS* and *Linux* as well. See the sidebar, "SSTV Sound Card Software." You don't need an ultra-fast, sophisticated machine. Most any modern computer will do.

SSTV on a PC is more than just software, though. We have to translate analog SSTV tones into digital data the computer can understand. When it's time to transmit, the same process must occur in reverse. So we need an interface to bridge the gap between the digital and analog worlds. Sound cards are perfectly suited for this task — analog-to-digital conversion (and vice versa) is what they do best. That's why you'll find SSTV software written for PCs equipped with sound cards.

The wiring to and from your transceiver is best accomplished through a device known as a *sound card interface*. These boxes simply match the transmit and receive audio levels, and provide some form of transmit/receive switching (so that your software can "command" your radio to transmit). Sound card interfaces come in a variety of sizes and prices. Check the ads in *QST* for the latest models. Once you set up a sound card interface for SSTV, you will be able to use the same hardware to operate many other digital modes including PSK31, RTTY, MFSK16 and others.

How Do We Make an SSTV Picture?

Receiving an SSTV image is easy and fun, but eventually you'll want to start sending images of your own. The first step is to create a picture. There are many ways to do this.

With any digital camera, you can snap a picture, dump the

SSTV Sound Card Software

ChromaPIX:
www.barberdsp.com/cpix/chroma.htm

MMSSTV:
http://hamsoft.ca

Multimode (for Macintosh):
www.blackcatsystems.com/software/multimode.html

QSSTV (for *Linux*):
users.telenet.be/on4qz/

An SSTV image received from the International Space Station.

image data to your PC, and send the data over the air. Or you can use a hand-held or flatbed color scanner to convert paper photos and artwork to images you can transmit.

If you're running Microsoft *Windows*, chances are you have *Paint* on your PC. Did you know that you can use *Paint* to create artwork that you can transmit via SSTV? Of course, if you own more sophisticated software such as *Photoshop*, *Paint Shop Pro* or any of the many popular image editing programs you can really get cooking!

By the way, most SSTV programs have a text function that lets you place "type" on the image to add information, comments or simply your call sign. These functions, however, are often limited in choices of fonts, colors and so on. You're probably better off using *Paint* or other software to dress up your images.

And what kind of images can you send? Anything is fair game, as long as it isn't offensive or in poor taste. Show the world your rig, antenna, your home, your family or...yourself.

Operating

Prior to sending a picture, it is important to announce the specific SSTV mode that will be used. Many operators then follow with descriptive verbal comments about the picture.

An SSTV signal must be tuned in properly so the picture will come out with the proper brightness and synchronization. If the signal is not *in sync*, the picture will appear wildly skewed. The easiest way to tune SSTV is to wait for the transmitting operator to say something on voice and then fine tune for proper pitch. With experience, you may find you are able to zero in on an SSTV signal by listening to the sync pulses and by watching for proper synchronization on the screen. Many SSTV computer programs display built-in tuning aids.

WB5UZR - 1.4W   WB8DQT - 4.6W

The results of a QRP contact on SSTV between Ralph Taggart, WB8DQT, in Michigan and Robert McSpadden, WB5UZR, in Texas.

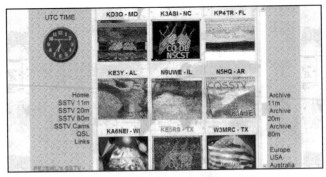

Fig 9-4 — The Web site at pe2swl.sprinterweb.net/ worldwide-sstv-servers.htm displays SSTV images captured from hams all over the world in "real time." You can use this and similar sites to check your own signal and keep an eye on what your fellow SSTV enthusiasts are doing.

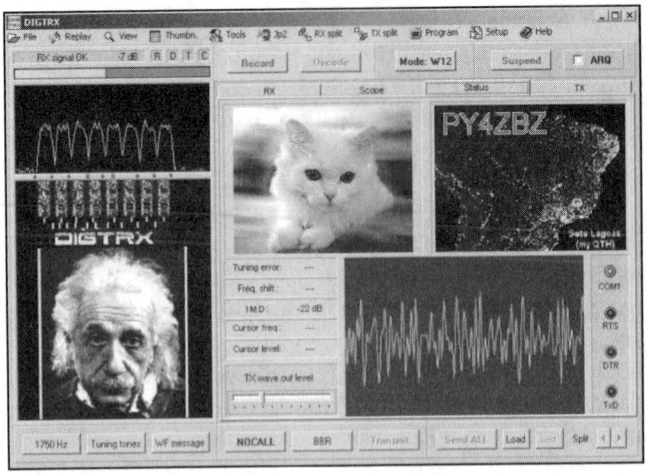

Fig 9-5 — *DigTRX* software uses your computer sound card and SSB transceiver to send and receive Digital SSTV images.

SSTV on the Web

Perhaps you've heard of so-called *remote receivers* that monitor specific HF frequencies and stream their audio over the Internet. A number of hams have established these around the world and they are convenient tools for checking how well your signal is reaching various destinations.

Now the same remote reception ability is available for SSTV. Enthusiasts refer to it as "live" SSTV, or "SSTV cam."

If you know your away around Internet file transfers, setting up an SSTV monitoring station is straightforward. KE5RS wrote a *Windows* application that automatically grabs received SSTV images and uploads them to your personal Web page, or any other Web page. You'll find it at **www.ke5rs.com/sstv/create. html**. All a monitoring station needs is a receiver connected to a sound-card equipped computer running SSTV software. KE5RS's application takes care of the rest. Since everything is handled automatically, the monitoring station can operate unattended.

Each time the monitoring station receives an SSTV image, the KE5RS application immediately transfers it to the Web. Depending on the Web page design, you may see a single image frame that is "refreshed" with new images as they are received. Or, you may see a page that archives multiple images received over, say, the last hour. There are even Web sites such as the one maintained by PE2SWL at **pe2swl.sprinterweb.net/ worldwide-sstv-servers.htm** that display "live" image captures from a dozen stations or more. See **Fig 9-4** for a sample. Web sites like these are a great way to check your signal, and to see what other SSTV enthusiasts are doing on the air.

DIGITAL SSTV

Until the early years of the 21st century, if you wanted to exchange images on the HF bands, SSTV was the only game in town. Although computers and software made modern SSTV possible, the mode was still analog in nature.

The great leap to digital came as a result of the creative effort of Barry Sanderson, KB9VAK, and the enthusiastic work of a number of experimentally inclined amateurs who helped turn it into a practical image transmission system. The KB9VAK modulation/signal format is known as *RDFT* (redundant digital file transfer). The next advancement was the ham adaptation of Digital Radio Mondiale, or DRM. The result is Digital SSTV, or simply D-SSTV.

The advantage of D-SSTV is that the received images are crystal clear, unlike the distortion seen in analog SSTV images resulting from noise or interference. D-SSTV accomplishes this within the voice bandwidth of an SSB transceiver, just like analog SSTV. In fact, D-SSTV uses the same sound-card techniques and interfaces described in Chapter 8.

The free *WinDRM* digital voice software discussed in Chapter 8 will send and receive D-SSTV images. There are also applications dedicated specifically to HF image communications using DRM, such as *HamPAL* and *DigTRX*. *DigTRX* (**Fig 9-5**) was created by PY4ZBZ and *HamPAL* was developed by VK4AES. Both applications are based on sound-card technology and all applications are cross compatible. *HamPAL* is available at **www.kb1hj.com/vk4aes.html**. *DigTRX* can be downloaded at **paginas.terra.com.br/lazer/py4zbz/hdsstv/ HamDRM.htm**.

Digital image transmission uses the JPEG2000 (JP2) file format. Depending on how you've set up the software, you may see nothing until the image is completely received, or you may see a distorted image that will "clean up" when all the data segments are received.

Of course, fading, noise and interference are likely to cause loss of data during a transmission. If this is the case, you typically have the option to send a "Bad Segment Report" (BSR) to the transmitting station. It is basically a list of all the missing segments. Assuming that the transmitting station receives the BSR intact, he can resend the missing segments at the click of a button!

Digital image enthusiasts often exchange D-SSTV on 14.233 MHz. Like analog SSTV operators, the D-SSTV operators usually begin their conversations on SSB voice, then switch to digital to send pictures.

FACSIMILE

Facsimile (fax) is a method for transmitting very high-resolution still pictures using voice-bandwidth radio circuits. The narrow bandwidth of the fax signal, equivalent to SSTV, provides the potential for worldwide communications on the HF bands. Fax is the oldest of the image-transmitting technologies and has been the primary method of transmitting newspaper photos and weather charts. Facsimile is also used to transmit high-resolution cloud images from both polar-orbit and geostationary satellites. Many of these images are retransmitted using fax on the HF bands.

The resolution of typical fax images greatly exceeds what can be obtained using SSTV or even conventional television (typical images will be made up of 800 to 1600 scanning lines). This high resolution is achieved by slowing down the rate at which the lines are transmitted, resulting in image transmission times in the 4 to 10-minute range. Prior to the advent of digital technology, the only practical way to display such images was to print each line directly to paper as it arrived. The mechanical systems for accomplishing this are known as *facsimile recorders* and are based on either photographic media (a modulated light source exposing film or paper) or various types of direct printing technologies including electrostatic and electrolytic papers.

Modern desktop computers have eliminated bulky fax recorders from most amateur installations. Now the incoming image can be stored in computer memory and viewed on a standard TV monitor or a high-resolution computer graphics display. The use of a color display system makes it entirely practical to transmit color fax images when band conditions permit.

The same computer-based system that handles fax images is often capable of SSTV operation as well, blurring what was once a clear distinction between the two modes. The advent of the personal computer has provided amateurs with a wide range of options within a single imaging installation. SSTV images of low or moderate resolution can be transmitted when crowded band conditions favor short frame transmission times. When band conditions are stable and interference levels are low, the ability to transmit very high-resolution fax images is just a few keystrokes away!

Hardware and Software

In the past few years, electromechanical fax equipment has been replaced by personal computer hardware and software. This replacement allows reception and transmission of various line per minute rates and indices of cooperation by simply pressing a key or clicking a mouse. Many fax programs are available as either commercial software or shareware. Usually, the shareware packages (and often trial versions of the commercial packages) are available by downloading from the Internet.

Amateur Satellites

Hams were present at the dawn of the Space Age, creating the first amateur satellite in 1961, and we've been active on the "final frontier" ever since. Even so, satellite-active hams compose a relatively small segment of our hobby, primarily because of an unfortunate fiction that has been circulating for many years — the myth that operating through amateur satellites is difficult and expensive.

Like any other facet of Amateur Radio, satellite hamming is as expensive as you allow it to become. If you want to equip your home with a satellite communication station that would make a NASA engineer blush, it will be expensive. If you want to simply communicate with a few low-Earth-orbiting birds using less-than-state-of-the-art gear, a satellite station is no more expensive than a typical HF or VHF setup.

What about difficulty? Prior to 1982, hams calculated satellite orbits using an arcane manual method that many people found unfathomable. In truth, the manual method taught you a great deal about orbital mechanics, but it was viewed by some as being too difficult. Today computers do all of the calculations for you and display the results in easy to understand formats (more about this later). Satellite equipment also has become much easier for the average ham to use.

SATELLITES: ORBITING RELAY STATIONS

Most amateurs are familiar with repeater stations that retransmit signals to provide coverage over wide areas. Repeaters achieve this by listening for signals on one frequency and immediately retransmitting whatever they hear on another frequency. Thanks to repeaters, small, low-power radios can communicate over thousands of square miles.

This is essentially the function of an amateur satellite as well. Of course, while a repeater antenna may be as much as a few thousand meters above the surrounding terrain, the satellite is hundreds or thousands of kilometers above the surface of the Earth. The area of the Earth that the satellite's signals can reach is therefore much larger than the coverage area of even the best Earth-bound repeaters. It is this characteristic of satellites that makes them attractive for communication. Most amateur satellites act either as analog repeaters, retransmitting CW and voice signals exactly as they are received, or as packet store-and-forward systems that receive whole messages from ground stations for later relay.

Linear Transponders

Several analog satellites are equipped with *linear transponders*. These are devices that retransmit across a band of frequencies, usually 50 to 100 kHz wide, known as the *passband*. Since the linear transponder retransmits the entire band, many signals may be retransmitted simultaneously. For example, if four SSB signals (each separated by 20 kHz) were transmitted to the satellite, the satellite would retransmit all four signals — still separated by 20 kHz each. Just like a terrestrial repeater, the retransmission takes place on a frequency that is different from the one on which the signals originally were received.

In the case of amateur satellites, the difference between the transmit and receive frequencies is similar to what you might encounter on a crossband terrestrial repeater. In other words, retransmission occurs on a different *band* from the original signal. For example, a transmission received by the satellite on 2 meters might be retransmitted on 70 cm. This crossband operation allows the use of simple filters in the satellite to keep its transmitter from interfering with its receiver.

Some linear transponders invert the uplink signal. In other words, if you transmit to the satellite at the *bottom* of the uplink passband, your signal will appear at the *top* of the downlink passband. In addition, if you transmit in upper sideband (USB), your downlink signal will be in lower sideband (LSB). Transceivers designed for amateur satellites usually include features that cope with this confusing flip-flop.

Linear transponders can repeat any type of signal, but those used by amateur satellites are primarily

Two Field Day operators rise early to get their chance at working a satellite.

designed for SSB and CW. The reason has to do with the problem of generating power in space. Amateur satellites rely on batteries that are recharged by solar cells. "Space rated" solar arrays and batteries are expensive. They are also heavy and tend to take up a substantial amount of space. Thanks to meager funding, hams don't have the luxury of launching satellites with large power systems such as those used by commercial birds. We have to do the best we can within a much more limited "power budget."

So what does this have to do with SSB or any other mode?

Think of *duty cycle* — the amount of time that a transmitter operates at full output. With SSB and CW the duty cycle is quite low. A linear transponder can retransmit many SSB and CW signals while still operating within the power generating limitations of an amateur satellite. It hardly breaks a sweat.

Now consider FM. An FM transmitter operates at a 100% duty cycle, which means it is generating its *full output* continuously during every transmission. Imagine how much power a linear transponder would need to retransmit, say, a dozen FM signals — all demanding 100% output!

Having said all that, there *are* a few FM repeater satellites, and we'll discuss them in this chapter. However, these are very low-power satellites (typically less than 1 W output) and they do not use linear transponders. They retransmit only one signal at a time, not many signals simultaneously.

FINDING A SATELLITE

Before you can communicate through a satellite, you have to know when it is available. Computers make this task very easy. First, however, we need to understand a little bit about how ham satellites behave in orbit.

Amateur satellites, unlike many commercial and military spacecraft, do not travel in geostationary orbits. Satellites in geostationary orbits cruise above the Earth's equator at an altitude of about 22,000 miles. From this vantage point the satellites can "see" almost half of our planet. Their speed in orbit matches the rotational speed of the Earth itself, so the satellites appear to be "parked" at fixed positions in the sky. They are available to send and receive signals 24 hours a day over an enormous area.

Of course, amateur satellites *could* be placed in geostationary orbits. The problem isn't one of physics; it's money and politics. Placing a satellite in geostationary orbit and keeping it there costs a great deal of money — more than any one amateur satellite organization can afford. An amateur satellite group could ask similar groups in other areas of the world to contribute funds to a geostationary satellite project, but why should they? Would you contribute large sums of money to a satellite that may never "see" your part of the world? Unless you are blessed with phenomenal generosity, it would seem unlikely!

Instead, all amateur satellites are either low-Earth orbiters (LEOs), or they travel in high, elongated orbits. Either way, they are not in fixed positions in the sky. Their positions relative to your station change constantly as the satellites zip around the Earth. This means that you need to predict when satellites will appear in your area, as well as what paths they'll take as they move across your local sky.

A bare-bones satellite-tracking program will provide a schedule for any satellite you choose. A very simple schedule might look something like this:

Date	Time	Azimuth	Elevation
10 OCT 07	1200	149°	4°
10 OCT 07	1201	147°	8°
10 OCT 07	1202	144°	13°
10 OCT 07	1203	139°	20°

The date column is obvious: 10 October 2007. The time is usually expressed in UTC. This particular satellite will appear above your horizon beginning at 1200 UTC. The bird will "rise" at an azimuth of 149°, or approximately southeast of your station. The elevation refers to the satellite's position above your horizon in degrees — the higher the better. A zero-degree elevation is right on the horizon; 90° is directly overhead.

By looking at this schedule you can see that the satellite will appear in your southeastern sky at 1200 UTC and will rise quickly to an elevation of 20° by 1203. The satellite's path will curve further to the east as it rises. Notice how the azimuth shifts from 149° at 1200 UTC to 139° at 1203.

The more sophisticated the software, the more information it usually provides in the schedule table. The software may also

Table 10-1
Consistently Active Amateur Satellites: Frequencies and Modes

Satellite	Uplink (MHz)	Downlink (MHz)
SSB/CW		
VuSAT-OSCAR 52	435.220-435.280	145.870-145.930
FM Voice Repeaters		
AMSAT-OSCAR 51	145.920	435.300
AMRAD-OSCAR 27	145.850	436.795

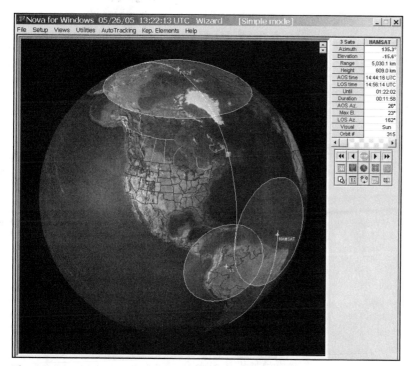

Fig 10-1 — This is one of several tracking displays provided by the *Nova* satellite-tracking software (available from AMSAT).

3 Sats	HAMSAT
Azimuth	135.3°
Elevation	-15.6°
Range	5,030.1 km
Height	609.0 km
AOS time	14:44:16 UTC
LOS time	14:56:14 UTC
Until	01:22:02
Duration	00:11:58
AOS Az.	26°
Max El.	23°
LOS Az.	162°
Visual	Sun
Orbit #	315

Fig 10-2 — You can also find satellite pass predictions on the Web at www.amsat.org/amsat-new/tools/predict/.

display the satellite's position graphically as a moving object superimposed on a map of the world. Some of the displays used by satellite prediction software are visually stunning! See **Fig 10-1** for an example.

Satellite prediction software is widely available on the Web. Some of the simpler programs are freeware. A great place to start is the AMSAT-NA site at **www.amsat.org**. They have the largest collection of satellite software for just about any computer you can imagine. AMSAT software isn't free, but the cost is reasonable and the funds support amateur satellite programs.

You can even dispense with software altogether and use the pass predictor on the AMSAT-NA Web site to set your schedule.

You'll find it at **www.amsat.org/amsat-new/tools/predict/** (see **Fig 10-2**).

Whichever approach you choose, you must provide two key pieces of information before you can obtain pass predictions:

1) *Your position.* The software must have your latitude and longitude before it can crank out predictions for your station. The good news is that your position information doesn't need to be extremely accurate. Just find out the latitude and longitude and plug it into the program. You can obtain the longitude and latitude of your town by calling your public library or nearest airport. It is also available on the Web at **geonames.usgs.gov/pls/gnis/web_query.gnis_web_query_form**.

2) *Orbital elements.* This is the information that describes the orbits of the satellites. You can find orbital elements (often referred to as *Keplerian elements*) at the AMSAT Web site, and through many other sources on the Internet. You need to update the elements every few months. Many satellite programs will automatically read in the elements if they are provided as ASCII text files. The less sophisticated programs will require you to enter them by hand. The automatic-update software helps to avoid typing mistakes with manual entries. Note that if you use the AMSAT-NA online satellite pass predictor, you do *not* need to supply orbital elements.

Table 10-1 shows the amateur satellites that were consistently active when this book went to press. Check **www.amsat.org** for the latest status of these and other birds.

GETTING STARTED WITH FM REPEATER SATELLITES

Would you like to operate through an FM repeater with a coverage area that spans an entire continent? Then check out the AMSAT-OSCAR 51 FM repeater satellite (**Fig 10-3**). From its near-polar orbit at altitudes of approximately 500 miles, this satellite can hear stations within a radius of 2000 miles in all directions. OSCAR 51's FM repeater has one channel with an uplink frequency of 145.920 MHz and a downlink frequency of 435.300 MHz, both plus/minus the Doppler effect (sidebar "Down with the Doppler"). You must also use a 67-Hz subaudible (CTCSS) tone on the uplink, just like many terrestrial repeaters.

You can operate through OSCAR 51 with a basic dual-band FM transceiver with 25 W output or more. Assuming that the transceiver is reasonably sensitive, you can use an omnidirectional antenna such as a dual-band collinear ground plane or something similar. Some amateurs even have managed to work it with handheld transceivers, but to reach an FM satellite with a handheld you'll need to use a multi-element directional antenna. Of course, this means that you'll have to aim your antenna at the satellites as they cross overhead.

Start by booting up your satellite tracking software, or

Fig 10-3 — This solar-cell-covered box is OSCAR 51, a popular FM repeater satellite.

Fig 10-4 — A view of OSCAR 52 just prior to launch. (It is the small, dark cube below and to the right of the large commercial satellite above.)

Down with the Doppler

The relative motion between you and the satellite causes *Doppler shifting* of signals. As the satellite moves toward you, the frequency of the downlink signals will increase by a small amount. As the satellite passes overhead and starts to move away from you, there will be a rapid drop in frequency of a few kilohertz, much the same way as the tone of a car horn or a train whistle drops as the vehicle moves past the observer.

The Doppler effect is different for stations located at different distances from the satellite because the relative velocity of the satellite with respect to the observer is dependent on the observer's distance from the satellite. The result is that signals passing through the satellite transponder shift slowly around the calculated downlink frequency. Your job is to tune your uplink transmitter — *not your receiver* — to compensate for Doppler shifting and keep your frequency relatively stable on the downlink. That's why it is helpful to hear your own signal coming through the satellite. If you and the station you're talking to both compensate correctly, your conversation will stay at one frequency on the downlink throughout the pass. If you don't compensate, you will drift through the downlink passband as you attempt to "follow" each other's signals. This is highly annoying to others using the satellite because your drifting signals may drift into their conversations.

Doppler shift through a transponder becomes the sum of the Doppler shifts of both the uplink and downlink signals. In the case of an inverting type transponder (as in OSCAR 52), a Doppler-shifted increase in the uplink frequency causes a corresponding decrease in downlink frequency, so the resultant Doppler shift is the **difference** of the Doppler shifts, rather than the **sum**. The shifts tend to cancel.

---

grabbing a schedule from the AMSAT-NA online predictor. Check for a pass where the satellite rises at least 45° above your horizon. As with all satellites, the higher the elevation, the better. If you plan to operate outdoors or away from home, either print the schedule or jot down the times on a piece of scrap paper that you carry with you.

When the satellite comes into range, you'll be receiving its signal about 10 kHz higher than the designated downlink frequency, thanks to Doppler shifting. So, begin listening there. At about the midpoint of the pass you'll need to shift your receiver down 10 kHz or more. As the satellite is heading away, you may wind up stepping down to as much as 10 kHz below the downlink frequency. Some operators program these frequencies into memory channels so that they can compensate for Doppler shift at the push of a button.

These satellites behave just like terrestrial FM repeaters. Only one person at a time can talk. If two or more people transmit simultaneously, the result is garbled audio or a squealing sound on the output. The trick is to take turns and keep the conversation short. Even the best passes will only give you about 15 minutes to use the satellite. If you strike up a conversation, don't forget

that there are others waiting to use the bird.

It is also a good idea to check the OSCAR 51 schedule on the Web at **www.amsat.org/amsat-new/echo/ControlTeam.php**. The bird occasionally changes its operating mode for experiments.

The FM repeater satellites are a great way to get started. They are easy to hear and easy to use. Once you get your feet wet, however, you'll probably wish you could access a satellite that wasn't so crowded, where you could chat for as long as the bird is in range.

MOVING UP TO VUSAT-OSCAR 52

The FM repeater satellites are a fun way to get your feet wet, but soon you'll want to graduate to satellites that offer the luxury of longer conversations and minimal interference — such as VuSAT-OSCAR 52. Shown on **Fig 10-4**, OSCAR 52 is a linear-transponder bird that listens on 70 cm and repeats everything it hears on the 2-meter band. (This is called "Mode U/V" in satellite jargon. See the sidebar, "Satellite Modes Demystified.")

OSCAR 52 — Hardware

To set up a station for OSCAR 52 you'll need either (A)

The modest satellite antennas of VE3VRW are mounted on a small az/el rotator.

an SSB/CW transceiver that can operate on 2 meters and 70 cm in full duplex, (B) an SSB/CW transmitter on 70 cm and a separate 2-meter receiver or (C) an SSB/CW transmitter on 70 cm and a 2-meter receive converter attached to a 10 meter receiver. Let's look at each option.

(A) VHF/UHF all-mode transceivers designed for satellite operating are available, although the newer radios usually come with price tags around $1500. Despite the cost, these radios are good investments if you intend to expand your satellite operating.

(B) Many popular HF/VHF transceivers today feature 2-meter SSB/CW capability, so using one of those radios for your downlink isn't a problem. SSB/CW transmitters or transceivers for the 70-cm uplink are less common, but some HF/VHF+ transceivers include this band.

(C) The least expensive way to enjoy OSCAR 52 is to use a UHF SSB/CW transceiver for the uplink and a 2-meter receive converter with a separate HF (10-meter) receiver for the downlink. These receive converters are relatively inexpensive and they are available from a number of vendors.

You can use omnidirectional antennas such as ground-planes, eggbeaters and others to work OSCAR 52, but the results may be disappointing. If you choose this approach, you may find that you need to run substantial power on the 70-cm uplink (about 100 W) and a preamplifier on the 2-meter downlink antenna to achieve consistent results.

If you can afford it, the better choices by far are directional antennas on 2 meters and 70 cm (such as Yagis). With directional antennas you'll enjoy solid signals throughout each pass. Of course, this raises the issue of how you will track the satellites with your antennas — either by hand or by using an az/el (azimuth and elevation) rotator (**Fig 10-5**). The decision to invest in an az/el rotator will probably hinge on whether you plan to try other VHF and/or UHF satellites in the future.

If you are using directional antennas, you will find that you'll need to readjust their positions every couple of minutes.

Attempting to do this manually while carrying on a conversation (and compensating for Doppler) can be quite a juggling act. In this situation, an az/el rotator is particularly attractive. And if you're using satellite-tracking software that supports rotator control, a computer rotator control interface is also worth considering. This turns the job of antenna aiming over to your computer, leaving you free to concentrate on the radios.

OSCAR 52 — Operating

When you're ready to make contacts through OSCAR 52, you'll discover an interesting twist: this satellite uses an *inverting transponder*. This means that the downlink passbands are inverted mirror images of the uplink passbands. If you transmit to the satellite in the *lower* portions of the uplink passband (435.220 to 435.280 MHz), your signal will appear on the *upper* portion of the downlink passband (145.870 to 145.930 MHz)! In addition, if you transmit to the satellites in *lower* sideband (LSB), your signal will be repeated on the downlink in *upper* sideband (USB).

Here's an example: You're transmitting at: 435.230 MHz LSB and you hear your signal from the satellite at: 145.920 MHz USB. Notice the "upside down" relationship? Your LSB signal on the uplink has become USB on the downlink. Your downlink signal appears 10 kHz *below* the *top* end of the downlink passband because you transmitted 10 kHz *above* the *bottom* end of the uplink passband.

Many VHF/UHF transceivers that are intended for satellite operating include a feature that allows you to lock the uplink and downlink VFOs so that they'll track in reverse. Using our example above, as you begin tuning the downlink VFO *downward* from 145.930 to 145.870 MHz, the uplink VFO will automatically increment *upward* from 435.220 to 435.280 MHz. This takes a lot of the confusion out of working satellites that use inverting transponders. The convention with

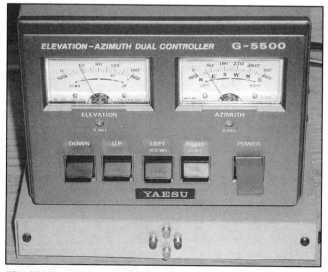

Fig 10-5 — An azimuth/elevation (az/el) rotator has two motors. One moves the antenna array from side to side, while the other moves it up and down. The controller usually has two sets of controls and two position displays so you know exactly where the antenna is pointed. Some controllers have computer interfaces so that tracking software can automatically update antenna position during a pass.

OSCAR 52 is to transmit in LSB so that your signal is USB on the downlink.

Wear a pair of headphones so that you can monitor your own signal on the downlink. Find a quiet spot in the passband and say (or send) your call sign repeatedly. Tune your downlink receiver above and below where you think your signal should be. In time you'll learn the knack and be able to "find yourself" quickly. If you're using a transceiver with reverse-tracking VFOs, it is best to disable the auto-tracking function until you locate your signal.

If you hear someone calling CQ, do a rough calculation of the necessary uplink frequency and begin calling the other station repeatedly, tuning your *uplink* radio until you hear yourself (unlock your auto-tracking VFOs if you have them). The other station will no doubt be tuning around as well. Once the conversation is established, change only your *downlink* frequency setting to compensate for the Doppler Effect.

Considering the substantial Doppler frequency shifting that takes place on the downlinks, it's best to use short exchanges to minimize the amount of uplink re-tuning necessary at the beginning of each transmission.

Keep your transmissions short. That'll make it easier for the other station to compensate for Doppler. Operating on OSCAR 52 is casual; you'll enjoy 15 to 20 minutes of talking time during each pass.

THE PACSATS

If you enjoy packet operating, you'll love the PACSATs! The PACSATs work like temporary mail boxes in space. You upload a message or a file to a PACSAT and it is stored for a time (days or weeks) until someone else — possibly on the other side of the world — downloads it. Many PACSATs are also equipped with on-board digital cameras. They snap fas-

cinating images of the Earth which are stored as files that you can download and view.

Which PACSAT is Best?

You can divide the PACSATs into two types: The 1200- and 9600-baud satellites. OSCAR 16 is presently the only operational 1200-baud PACSAT. You transmit packets to it on 2-meter FM and receive on 435-MHz SSB. The remaining PACSATs operate at 9600 baud. You send packets to them on 2-meter FM and receive on 435-MHz FM.

So which PACSATs are best for beginners? There's no easy answer for that question. You can use any 2-meter FM transceiver to send data to a 1200-baud PACSAT, but getting your hands on a 435-MHz SSB receiver (or transceiver) could put a substantial dent in your bank account. In addition, you need a special PSK (*phase-shift keying*) terminal node controller (TNC). These little boxes are not common and could set you back about $250.

So the 9600-baud PACSATs are best for the newbie, right? Not so fast. It's true that you don't need a special packet TNC. Any of the affordable 9600-baud TNCs will do the job. The catch is that not any FM transceiver is usable for 9600-baud packet. Both the 2-meter *and* 440-MHz FM radios must be capable of handling 9600-baud signals; and not all 440-MHz FM rigs can receive down to 435 MHz.

Broadcasting Data

Despite the huge amounts of data that can be captured during a pass, there is considerable competition among ground stations about exactly *which* data the satellite should receive or send! There are typically two or three dozen stations within a satellite's roving footprint, all making their various requests. If you think this sounds like a recipe for chaos, you're right.

The PACSATs produce order out of anarchy by creating two *queues* (waiting lines) — one for uploading and another for downloading. The upload queue can accommodate two stations and the download queue can take as many as 20. Once the satellite admits a ground station into the queue for downloading, the station moves forward in the line until it reaches the front, whereupon the satellite services the request for several seconds.

For example, let's say that OSCAR 32 just accepted me, WB8IMY, into the download queue. I want to grab a particular file from the bird, but I have to wait my turn. OSCAR 32 lets me know where I stand by sending an "announcement" that I see on my monitor. It might look like this:

WB8ISZ N1OJS N1ND WB8IMY

WB8ISZ is at the head of the line. The satellite will send him a chunk of data, then move him to the rear.

N1OJS N1ND WB8IMY WB8ISZ

Now there are only two stations ahead of me. When I reach the beginning of the line, I'll get my share of "attention" from the satellite.

Unless the file you want is small, you won't get it all in one shot. If the satellite disappears over the horizon before you receive the complete file, there's no need to worry. Your PACSAT software "remembers" which parts of the file you still need from the bird. When it appears again, your software can request that these "holes" be filled.

And while all of this is going on, *you're receiving data that other stations have requested!* That's right. Not only do

---

Satellite Modes Demystified

In the amateur satellite community, we use a kind of shorthand when we talk about which bands satellites use for uplinks and downlinks. Satellite operators aren't trying to be mysterious, just concise. For example . . .

(1) OSCAR 52 presently listens on 70 cm and repeats on 2 meters.

(2) OSCAR 52 is presently in Mode U/V.

Sentence #2 is clearly less of a mouthful. Say "Mode U/V" and everyone understands what you mean.

Each amateur satellite band has a letter designator:

21 MHz = H
29 MHz = A
145 MHz = V
435 MHz = U
1296 MHz = L
2400 MHz = S
5600 MHz = C
10000 MHz = X
24000 MHz = K

In a "Mode" expression, the first letter is the uplink band and the second letter is the downlink band.

You can get started with a simple, homemade satellite antenna like this one. Rick Rogers, K5RCR, described it, along with his very basic station setup, in November 2004 *QST*.

you get the file you wanted, you also receive a large portion of the data that other hams have requested. You may receive a number of messages and files without transmitting a single watt of RF. All you have to do is listen. That's why they call it "broadcast" protocol.

Station Software

You must run specialized software on your station PC if you're going to enjoy any success with the PACSATs. If your computer uses DOS only, you need a software package known as *PB/PG*. *PB* is the software you'll use most of the time to grab data from the satellite. *PG* is only used when you need to upload.

If you're running Microsoft *Windows* on your PC, you'll want to use *WISP*. *WISP* is a *Windows* version of *PB/PG* that includes such features as satellite tracking, antenna rotator control and more. Both software packages are available from AMSAT at the address mentioned elsewhere in this chapter. While you're contacting AMSAT, pick up a copy of the *Digital Satellite Guide*. It gets deep into the details of PACSAT operation far beyond the scope of what we can discuss here.

Legally, Safely, Appropriately — The FCC Rules and You

Legally — Safely — Appropriately. These are the three hallmarks that allow each radio amateur to fully enjoy their on-the-air experience.

It is the responsibility of each amateur to operate their station within the rules governing the Amateur Radio Service (legally). The second responsibility is to take precautions to ensure that their activity doesn't pose harm to themselves or others (safely). And finally, each amateur is charged with making sure that their activities on the air are in keeping with the operating standards set by the rules, as well as those standards that have developed within the amateur community over time (appropriately).

This chapter is intended to answer most of the common questions posed by active hams and to guide you to other resources for more information about the rules and regulations. To get the most from this material, you'll need a current copy of the FCC rules and regulations. They are available from several sources in booklet form, or you can look on the ARRL Web site at **www.arrl.org/FandES/field/regulations/news/part97/**.

THE AMATEUR RADIO SPECTRUM

The electromagnetic spectrum is a limited resource. Every kilohertz of the radio spectrum represents precious turf that is blood sport to those who lay claim to it. Fortunately, the spectrum is a resource that cannot be depleted — if misused, it can be restored to normal as soon as the misuse stops. Every minute of every hour of every day, we have a fresh chance to use the spectrum intelligently.

Although the radio spectrum has been used in a certain way in the past, changes are possible. Needs of the various radio services evolve with technological innovation and growth. There can be changes in the frequency bands allocated to the Amateur Service, and there can be changes in how we use those bands.

Amateur Radio is richly endowed with a wide range of bands starting at 1.8 MHz and extending above 300 GHz. Thus, we enjoy a veritable smorgasbord of bands with propagation "delicacies" of every type. To our benefit, radio propagation determines how far a signal can travel. Specific frequencies may be reused numerous times around the globe.

WHERE DO THE RULES COME FROM?

International Regulation of the Spectrum

Amateur Radio frequency band allocations don't just happen. Band allocation proposals must first crawl through a maze of national agencies and the International Telecommunication Union (ITU) with more adroitness than a computer-controlled mouse. Simultaneously, the proposals affecting Amateur Radio have to run the gauntlet of competing interests of other spectrum users.

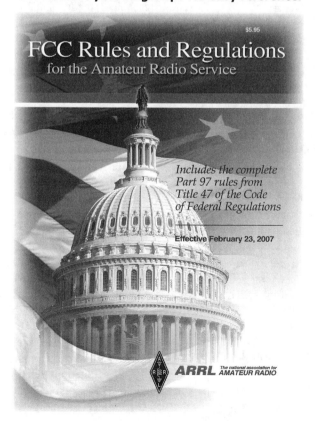

A current copy of the FCC rules is a must for every station. A booklet such as *FCC Rules and Regulations for the Amateur Radio Service*, published by the ARRL, is a great way to keep the rules at your fingertips for easy reference.

$5.95

FCC Rules and Regulations
for the Amateur Radio Service

Includes the complete Part 97 rules from Title 47 of the Code of Federal Regulations

Effective February 23, 2007

ARRL The national association for AMATEUR RADIO

Treaties and Agreements

To bring some order to international relationships of all sorts, nations sign treaties and agreements. Otherwise (with respect to international communications) chaos, anarchy and bedlam would vie for supremacy over the radio spectrum. Pessimists think we already have some of that, but they haven't any idea how bad it could be without international treaties and agreements.

International Telecommunication Union

The origins of the ITU trace back to the invention of the telegraph in the 19th century. To establish an international telegraph network, it was necessary to reach agreement on uniform message handling and technical compatibility. Bordering European countries worked out some bilateral agreements. This eventually led to creation of the ITU at Paris in 1865 by the first International Telegraph Convention, which yielded agreement on basic telegraph regulations.

World Radiocommunication Conferences (WRCs), conducted by the ITU, are held every few years to amend the international Radio Regulations. At the 2003 conference, after years of preparatory work we were successful in achieving a realignment of 40 meters to increase the worldwide Amateur Radio allocation to 7000-7200 kHz effective in 2009. Initial debates on the realignment were held in this Sub Working Group at the conference and the proposal worked its way through the process to become reality.

Plenipotentiary Conferences

The ITU has Plenipotentiary Conferences every four years. A "Plenipotentiary" is a conference that is fully empowered to do business. The conferences determine general policies, review the work of the Union and revise the Convention if necessary. The conferences also elect the Members of the Union to serve on the ITU Council, and elect the Secretary-General, Deputy Secretary-General, the Directors of the Bureaus and members of the Radio Regulations Board.

World Radiocommunication Conferences

ITU World Radiocommunication Conferences (WRCs) are held every two years with agendas agreed at the previous WRC and confirmed by the ITU Council. Various issues related to Amateur Radio may come up at these conferences. For example, amateur frequency allocations may be made or modified (such as the creation of the 30, 17 and 12 meter bands in 1979). In addition, changes made to the primary allocations of another service may affect the secondary status of Amateur Radio allocations.

Inter-American Telecommunication Commission (CITEL)

CITEL is the regional telecommunication organization for the Americas. It is a permanent commission under the Organization of American States (OAS), with a secretariat in Washington, DC. The CITEL Assembly meets every four years, while its committees meet one or more times yearly. ARRL and IARU Region 2 are active participants in Permanent Consultative Committee no. 3 (PCC.III — Radiocommunications).

TELECOMMUNICATIONS REGULATION WITHIN THE UNITED STATES

Practically from the day you started studying for your first Amateur Radio license, you encountered two terms that brought home the significance of the responsibilities that accompany an Amateur Radio license. Those two terms are FCC and Part 97.

FCC of course refers to the Federal Communications Commission, the agency of the US government responsible for making and enforcing the rules for the Amateur Radio Service. This five-person commission is charged with writing the rules that govern the licensing process for the various radio services in the US — commercial and private. The FCC oversees services as diverse as broadcast television and radio; communications services, such as wireless technologies; and wired services, such as cable television and telephone carriers. The FCC is charged with determining the standards for obtaining a federal license for the various services, as well as determining the privileges and technical standards that must be adhered to by each licensee.

Assisting the Commissioners in this task are hundred of employees. These experts help develop the standards and criteria for licensing and for operating under a Commission license. They also handle enforcement issues when rules are violated.

Code of Federal Regulations

The full FCC rules are found in *Code of Federal Regulations* (*CFR*). The 50 "titles" of the CFR contain the laws and regulations of the United States. Those laws and regulations dealing with telecommunications are found in Title 47 of the CFR.

Title 47 is further divided into three general subsections, each including additional sections known as "Parts." The three main subsections include the rules and responsibilities for the three units of the federal government that are responsible for some area of national telecommunication policy. The first subsection, which includes Parts 0 through 199 are the rules for the Federal Communications Commission. The remaining two subsections are the regulations for the Office of Science and Technology Policy and National Security Council (under direction of the White House), and for the National Telecommunications and Information Administration (NTIA), under the Department of Commerce.

The functions relating to assignment of frequencies to radio stations belonging to, and operated by, the United States Government are assigned to the Assistant Secretary of Commerce for Communications and Information (Administrator, NTIA). Among other things, NTIA:

1) Coordinates telecommunications activities of the Executive Branch;

2) Develops plans, policies and programs relating to international telecommunications issues;

3) Coordinates preparations for US participation in international telecommunications conferences and negotiations;

4) Develops, in coordination with the FCC, a long-range plan for improved management of all electromagnetic spectrum resources, including jointly determining the National Table of Frequency Allocations; and

5) Conducts telecommunications research and development.

Obviously, the FCC and the NTIA work closely together on many issues relating to radio spectrum. Many Amateur Radio bands, especially the UHF and higher frequency bands, are shared with a variety of government agencies. As long as we remain good sharing partners, these agencies can be powerful advocates for protecting Amateur Radio frequencies from other users.

For the most part, the rules for the Amateur Radio Service are contained in CFR Title 47, Part 97. That's why the term "Part 97" is used when referring to the rules for Amateur Radio. It is important to note that sections of Title 47 other than Part 97 do impact the Amateur Radio Service in some way. For example, Part 2 contains specific information on geographic areas where amateur operations are restricted, such as power limitations around certain US military sites. Part 15 contains standards for unlicensed low-power devices that could cause potential interference to amateur bands. The best resource to view the current versions of these related parts is online at **ecfr. gpoaccess.gov**. This is the official online version of the CFR, maintained by the National Archives.

Why We are Here

The five basic principles for the Amateur Radio Service are clearly established at the very beginning of the rules:

§97.1 Basis and purpose.

The rules and regulations in this part are designed to provide an amateur radio service having a fundamental purpose as expressed in the following principles:

(a) Recognition and enhancement of the value of the amateur service to the public as a voluntary noncommercial communication service, particularly with respect to providing emergency communications.

(b) Continuation and extension of the amateur's proven ability to contribute to the advancement of the radio art.

(c) Encouragement and improvement of the amateur service through rules which provide for advancing skills in both the communication and technical phases of the art.

(d) Expansion of the existing reservoir within the Amateur Radio service of trained operators, technicians, and electronics experts.

(e) Continuation and extension of the amateur's unique ability to enhance international goodwill.

Though often referred to as a hobby, Amateur Radio crosses many boundaries. The licensees of the Amateur Service play important roles in public service and emergency communications as well as the development of new and innovative technological advancements. They function as trained communicators available to assist others, but they also participate to enjoy camaraderie and fun with the new friends they meet on the airwaves. Some amateurs seek new operating challenges or pursue hands-on opportunities to learn new things about radio or electronics. The rules recognize that amateurs have distinct talents that they make available to serve their communities.

OVERVIEW OF THE PART 97 SUBPARTS

Part 97 is divided into six distinct subparts, A through F. Each subpart deals with rules and content in specific areas. Taken together, the subparts comprise the knowledge each licensee needs to legally, safely and appropriately operate on the air. Let's start with a brief overview of the parts and then jump into the details of each one.

Subpart A deals with the broad *general provisions* of what an individual is required to do when operating. It also includes specific definitions (§97.3) of various terminology used through the rules. Subpart A covers license grants, call signs and general requirements for becoming a Commission licensee. It also includes certain requirements and protections regarding your station location and antennas.

Subpart B discusses *station operation standards*. These include the responsibilities of the licensee and the control operator of any amateur station. Subpart B details permitted and prohibited transmissions, proper station identification, third party and international communications, and restricted operations.

Amateur stations are allowed special types of operations, and these are covered in **Subpart C**. Included in this portion of the rules are the regulations that govern how some of the most popular methods of amateur communications are carried out. At some point, almost every amateur will be involved with one or more of these *special operations*. They include basic repeater operation or message forwarding systems, as well as more "exotic" operations such as satellite communications or remote control of amateur stations.

The *technical standards* of how we operate are found in **Subpart D**. Each amateur is responsible for the technical quality of their transmissions and for making sure that signals are transmitted only on frequencies authorized by their license. The frequency allotments, signal emission standards and power limitations for each US license class can be found here.

As one of the basic purposes of the Amateur Radio Service, each licensee has a role to play in *supporting and providing emergency communications*. The guidelines for this, found in **Subpart E,** are the reason many of today's licensees got involved.

Unlike some other radio services authorized by the FCC, each person seeking to become an amateur operator must pass one or more written examinations. **Subpart F** delineates the *qualifying examination systems* through which individuals may obtain and upgrade their operating privileges.

Don't be confused or overwhelmed by the scope or magnitude of Part 97. Though some areas may be a bit complex or difficult to understand, the six subparts work together to provide the basic framework for each amateur to operate legally, safely and appropriately.

Table 11-1
Currently Issued Amateur Operator Licenses†

Class	Written Examination	Privileges
Technician	Technician-level theory and regulations. (Element 2)*	All amateur privileges above 50.0 MHz. Some CW privileges on 80, 40, 15, 10 meters. Some SSB and data privileges on 10 meters.
General	Technician and General theory and regulations. (Elements 2 and 3)	All amateur privileges except those reserved for Advanced and Amateur Extra.
Amateur Extra	Technician and General theory, plus Extra-class theory (Elements 2, 3 and 4)	All amateur privileges.

†A licensed radio amateur must pass only those elements that are not included in the examination for the amateur license currently held. Novice and Advanced licenses are no longer being issued but may be renewed. No Morse code test is required for any license.
*If you hold an expired Technician license issued before March 21, 1987, you can obtain credit for Element 3. You must be able to prove to a VE team that your Technician license was issued before March 21, 1987 to claim this credit.

SUBPART A — GENERAL PROVISIONS
Your Amateur Radio License

Your journey into Amateur Radio begins with a single important piece of paper — your license. This grant from the FCC is actually two licenses in one — your station license and your operator license. This document is your authorization to transmit on the amateur bands and it conveys your operating privileges.

An individual who becomes a Commission licensee is granted one — and only one — operator/station license. To qualify, you must pass one or more written examinations administered by a team of Volunteer Examiners (VEs) who conduct exams under the auspices of an accredited Volunteer Examiner Coordinator (VEC). **Table 11-1** gives an overview, and exam requirements are covered in more detail later in this chapter.

Anyone, except for a representative of a foreign government, is eligible to hold a US amateur license. You must have a valid US mailing address, though [§97.5(b)(1)]. Remember that it is your responsibility to keep your mailing address current with the FCC. Failure to do so can result in the suspension or revocation of your license [§97.23].

Your station license designates your call sign — a prized possession for most hams. When you receive your initial license, you will be assigned a call sign from the Sequential Call Sign Assignment System. Many amateurs choose to participate in the Vanity Call Sign program [§97.19], which allows licensees to pick their own call sign following the guidelines for their license class. More on call signs in a bit.

Keep in mind that a station license — your call sign — is only an identifier. A station license does not convey any operator privileges. All operating privileges come to you through the license class you have earned through your examinations.

The FCC maintains all licensee information in a central database known as ULS, the Universal Licensing System. As soon as your information appears in the ULS you are considered licensed and may operate using your assigned call and privileges. When you are issued your license, or when you renew (if you have renewed since December 3, 2001), you are also issued a Federal Registration Number (FRN). Any modification, renewal or upgrade of a license must includes the licensee's FRN, which in most cases for newer licenses is printed on the license itself. You can also find your FRN using the FCC ULS online search at **www.fcc.gov/wtb/uls** or ARRL's call sign lookup, available at **www.arrl.org.**

License Renewals and Updates

The FCC prefers that you renew your license or make modifications (update information such as your address) online using ULS. It's still possible to conduct business with the Commission "the old fashioned way" — by filing paper forms — but you should know the following:

1) ARRL members may use NCVEC Form 605 for everything except requests for new vanity call signs. This is not an FCC form, but it is accepted by the FCC if it is processed by an accredited VEC. You can download a copy from **www.arrl.org/fcc/forms.html**. The ARRL VEC processes renewals or modifications via NCVEC Form 605 as a free membership service. Amateurs may also deal directly with the FCC using FCC Form 605, found at **www.fcc.gov/Forms/Form605/605main.pdf**.

2) ARRL members using the NCVEC Form 605 should send it to the ARRL VEC, 225 Main St, Newington, CT 06111. Do not send NCVEC Form 605 to the FCC; it won't be accepted. Amateurs using the FCC Form 605 must send it to the FCC, 1270 Fairfield Rd, Gettysburg, PA 17325. There is no fee for renewing your amateur license at this time, unless your call sign was issued under the Vanity Call Sign Program.

3) The FCC will not process renewal applications received more than 90 days prior to the license expiration date.

4) It's a good idea to make a copy of your renewal application as proof of filing before your expiration date. If your application is processed before the expiration date, you may continue to operate until your new license arrives. Otherwise, you may not operate until your renewal is processed.

5) If your license has already expired, it is still possible to renew since there is a two-year grace period. If it has been expired more than two calendar years, you will have to take the current license test(s) to regain your amateur privileges.

6) You are required to keep your mailing address up to date. The FCC may cancel or suspend a license if their mail is returned as undeliverable.

For more information, see **www.arrl.org/arrlvec/**. You can

Table 11-2
FCC-Allocated Prefixes for Areas Outside the Continental US

Prefix	Location
AH1, KH1, NH1, WH1	Baker, Howland Is.
AH2, KH2, NH2, WH2	Guam
AH3, KH3, NH3, WH3	Johnston Is.
AH4, NH4, NH4, WH4	Midway Is.
AH5K, KH5K, NH5K, WH5K	Kingman Reef
AH5, KH5, NH5, WH5 (except K suffix)	Palmyra, Jarvis Is.
AH6,7 KH6,7 NH6,7 WH6,7	Hawaii
AH7, KH7, NH7, WH7	Kure Is.
AH8, KH8, NH8, WH8	American Samoa
AH9, KH9, NH9, WH9	Wake Is.
AHØ, KHØ, NHØ, WHØ	Northern Mariana Is.
ALØ-9, KLØ-9, NLØ-9, WLØ-9	Alaska
KP1, NP1, WP1	Navassa Is.
KP2, NP2, WP2	Virgin Is.
KP3,4 NP3,4 WP3,4	Puerto Rico
KP5, NP5, WP5	Desecheo

also contact the VEC staff or Regulatory Information Branch at ARRL HQ for information on ULS and keeping your license current.

Call Sign Structure

The International Telecommunication Union (ITU) is an international organization that, among other things, sets the standards for the prefixes and formation of call signs in the various radio services worldwide. According to the ITU Radio Regulations, an amateur call sign must start with one or two letters as a prefix, although sometimes the first or second character might be a number (as in 8P for Barbados). The prefix is followed by a number indicating a call sign district (or "call area"), and then a suffix of not more than three letters. You can find the current allocated prefixes for each country online at **www.arrl.org/awards/dxcc/itucalls.html**.

Every US Amateur Radio station call sign is a combination of a 1 or 2-letter prefix, a number and a 1, 2 or 3-letter suffix. The first letter of every US Amateur Radio call sign will always be K, N or W, or from the AA-AL double letter block. Some examples: KA9XYZ, NN1N, WB2OSQ, KN4AQ, AB6ZZ, W3ABC. Certain prefixes are reserved for stations that are under FCC jurisdiction but located outside the continental US. Common examples are KP2 for the US Virgin Islands or KH6 for Hawaii. See **Table 11-2** for details.

The mailing address that you use when obtaining your initial sequential call sign determines the number used. The 10 call sign districts for the continental US are illustrated in **Fig 11-1**. So the call sign W1AW indicates a US station (from the prefix W). The call sign was initially assigned to that station while it was located in the first US call area (indicated by the number 1). The letters AW comprise the assigned suffix, completing the identification of that station.

Vanity Call Signs

Under the Vanity Call Sign Program, individual amateurs and club stations may select a distinctive call sign to replace the one assigned by the sequential system. There are many reasons for doing so. Some operators want shorter call signs, or call signs that are easy to say or send. A popular choice is a suffix with the initials of your name. Others may want to recapture a former call sign or that of a departed friend or family member. Some operators just grow tired of their current call sign and want to try something new.

Although there was a period in the 1970s when Amateur Extra licensees could select "1 × 2" call signs (N2CQ, K8MR and so forth), the current Vanity Call Sign Program is much broader. Beginning in 1996 amateurs could select any available call sign valid for their license class for a fee. The exact amount is subject to change each year, but it has always been reasonable considering that the term is 10 years. In addition to paying the fee when the Vanity Call Sign is issued, note that you must pay whatever fee is in effect at your scheduled license renewal. The number in a vanity call sign does not have to indicate the call area in which you reside.

Changing Locations

Over time, you may move to another state and find that the number in your call sign no longer matches the district of your current residence. Not a problem. You have the option of keeping your call sign even though you have changed districts, and many amateurs choose to do just that. At one time you were required to turn in your old call sign for a new one that matched your current district, but the FCC dropped this rule in the 1970s.

It's routine to hear stations on the air using call signs that do not correspond to their locations. You are not required by Part 97 to identify your station as portable or mobile, fixed or temporary, but it is certainly allowed and sometimes helps listeners understand your location. For example, N1ND operating in North Carolina might send N1ND/4 on 6 meters to help others point their beams in the right direction.

You will occasionally hear a station identify as "marine mobile" or "maritime mobile" This simply indicates that the station is being operated from onboard a boat or ship. Finally you may hear a station identify as "aeronautical mobile" indicating operation from on board an airplane. While these are legal IDs, remember that operation onboard a ship or airplane must be approved by the captain of the vessel or pilot of the plane.

Antennas and Support Structures

A growing concern for many hams is the placement and location of Amateur Radio antennas and supporting structures, typically towers. Amateurs understand that the effectiveness of their stations and communications ability centers on the type and quality of their antennas. Not everyone views antennas the same way, and amateurs occasionally are drawn into disputes with the neighbors and town officials over the height and placement of antennas and support structures.

In the 1980s, the FCC recognized that amateurs sometimes need assistance in dealing with local governments and zoning boards to pursue the privileges granted by their FCC license. From this was born a powerful tool — known as PRB-1 — that grants amateurs a limited federal preemption of local zoning ordinances and regulations. The purpose is to protect amateurs from outright prohibitions or unreasonable restrictions placed on antenna support structures.

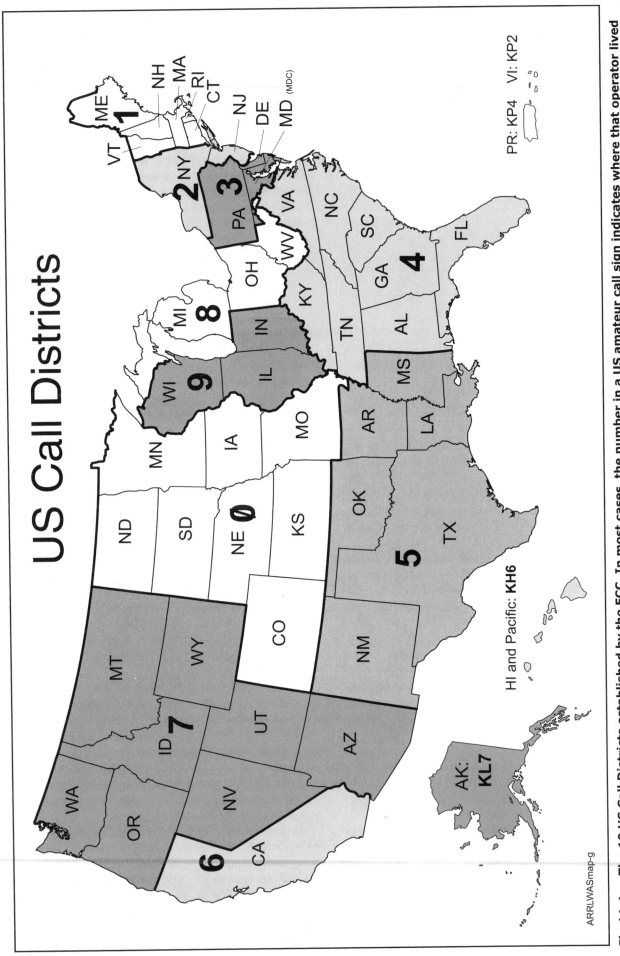

US Call Districts

PR: KP4 VI: KP2

HI and Pacific: **KH6**

AK: **KL7**

ARRLWASmap-g

Fig 11-1 — The 10 US Call Districts established by the FCC. In most cases, the number in a US amateur call sign indicates where that operator lived when the FCC first issued that call sign. Alaska is part of the seventh call district, but has its own set of prefixes: AL7, KL7, NL7 and WL7. Hawaii is part of the sixth call district but also has its own set of prefixes: AH6, KH6, NH6 and WH6.

PRB-1 has been incorporated into §97.15(b) and states: "Except as otherwise provided herein, a station antenna structure may be erected at heights and dimensions sufficient to accommodate amateur service communications. [State and local regulation of a station antenna structure must not preclude amateur service communications. Rather, it must reasonably accommodate such communications and must constitute the minimum practicable regulation to accomplish the state or local authority's legitimate purpose. See PRB-1, 101 FCC 2d 952 (1985) for details.]"

In addition to being part of the FCC rules, as of October 2007 a total of 25 states have incorporated PRB-1 protections into state as well. You can find complete information on PRB-1 and links to the specific pieces of state legislation adopting PRB-1 at **www.arrl.org/FandES/field/regulations/PRB-1_Pkg/index.html**

There are two things to remember as far as PRB-1 goes. First, PRB-1 does not give amateurs *carte blanche* to do what they wish in regard to antennas and support structures. PRB-1 requires local authorities to work with the amateurs to satisfy communications needs with the minimum amount of regulation needed to meet the legitimate needs of the local authority. Local regulators may not reject *all* amateur antennas, but they don't have to allow a structure either of a certain size, either.

The second important item to remember is that at this time PRB-1 applies only to regulation by local government officials. Many amateurs face similar (and sometimes more stringent) restrictions when dealing with what are known as CC&Rs — covenants, conditions and restrictions. Sometimes called simply "deed restrictions," CC&Rs are restrictions that are placed on property and deed, usually by the builder of a housing development or by a homeowner's association.

CC&Rs typically include limitations or guidelines for property appearance and use and may require approval of things such as site plan, building design and colors, placement of fences, landscaping and so on. Of concern to amateurs, CC&Rs often limit or prohibit outdoor antennas or supports. You should make it a point to find out about CC&Rs before entering into a real estate contract. They run with the property and you will have to abide by them once you're the owner.

The FCC has ruled that PRB-1 does not apply to CC&R situations. CC&Rs are private contacts, not public law or policy implemented by state or local government. For a good overview of the differences between PRB-1 issues and CC&R issues, see "What Should I Do Now?" from May 2007 *QST* and available online at **www.arrl.org/FandES/field/regulations/hender.pdf**.

SUBPART B — STATION OPERATION STANDARDS

When teaching license classes or speaking about my passion, I often say that your license is only the *second* most important piece of paper you receive in Amateur Radio. Of course you must have a license to get on the air, but I believe that your first QSL card (a written confirmation from another station that you have completed a two-way contact with them) is *the* most important "document" you receive.

Why do I believe that? Your first QSL card shows that you not only learned what you needed to pass the license exam,

Getting permission from local government to put up antennas and antenna supports can be a problem in some areas. FCC's PRB-1 grants limited pre-emption of local zoning regulations and requires reasonable accommodation of amateur antennas.

but also put that knowledge to use, got on the air and actively participated. Getting on the air is the point of the exercise, right? To do this successfully, Subpart B — Station Operation Standards — is critical to your pursuing Amateur Radio legally, safely and appropriately.

Thou Shall Not...

Front and center in Subpart B, §97.101(a) may well be the most important rule of all because it lays out the overriding responsibility of each amateur licensee: "In all respects not specifically covered by FCC Rules each amateur station must be operated in accordance with good engineering and good amateur practice."

This simple sentence underscores the responsibility of each operator to use good judgment and common sense when pursuing their interests. It means each licensee must continue to learn how stations interact properly, cooperate with fellow amateurs and treat each operator on the air with respect.

In many ways Subpart B is a laundry list of "do's and don'ts" that enable hundreds of thousands of amateurs on the air to share our limited bandwidth. Take the time to familiarize yourself with Subpart B. By following the letter and spirit of these rules, you can maximize your enjoyment while reducing potential problems or complaints on the air. A considerate operator will apply the rules and standards found in this section to his or her daily operation.

Sharing Our Spectrum

One of the most common hassles we experience on the air is crowded conditions. For example, trying to find a clear frequency on 20 meter SSB on a busy weekend morning can be a challenge. Effective spectrum use requires the cooperation of each and every operator. That's equally true during years of low solar activity when poor high-band propagation drives everyone to the low bands, or during years of high solar activity when the bands are filled with hams coming out of the woodwork to enjoy the great conditions. Remember we all share these frequencies: No one individual or group is assigned a frequency for exclusive use [§97.101(b)].

Over the years, to promote the orderly sharing of frequencies, some "gentleman's agreements" have emerged. Known as *voluntary band plans*, these are not hard and fast FCC rules, but rather guidelines for what type of amateur activity should take place in various parts of the spectrum. For example, a station trying to work the popular PSK31 digital mode would want to operate around frequencies where that mode is generally found. Remember "good amateur practice?" Band plans are a good example.

Band plans vary from region to region, especially on the VHF and higher bands. It's worth taking the time to learn about and follow band plans for the activities, modes and bands that interest you. When everyone works cooperatively and follows the guidelines, it allows each of us to better enjoy the time we spend on the air. Current ARRL Band Plans are at **www.arrl.org/FandES/field/regulations/bandplan.html**. The "Considerate Operators Guide" shown here is a great quick reference to keep handy in your station.

One of the most overlooked areas of good amateur practice is found in §97.313(a): "An amateur station must use the minimum transmitter power necessary to carry out the desired communications." Follow this important rule and you'll be able to conduct your QSO while reducing interference to others on crowded bands.

Many amateurs have an interest in emergency communications and public service. It is one of the core principles of Amateur Radio previously mentioned. It is the responsibility of each licensee to give priority to stations handling emergency communications [§97.101(c)]. Good amateur practice in this area suggests that, in an emergency, you should not transmit

---

The Considerate Operator's Frequency Guide

The following frequencies are generally recognized for certain modes or activities (all frequencies are in MHz) during normal conditions. These are not regulations and occasionally a high level of activity, such as during a period of emergency response, DXpedition or contest, may result in stations operating outside these frequency ranges.

Nothing in the rules recognizes a net's, group's or any individual's special privilege to any specific frequency. Section 97.101(b) of the Rules states that "Each station licensee and each control operator must cooperate in selecting transmitting channels and in making the most effective use of the amateur service frequencies. No frequency will be assigned for the exclusive use of any station." No one "owns" a frequency.

It's good practice — and plain old common sense — for any operator, regardless of mode, to check to see if the frequency is in use prior to engaging operation. If you are there first, other operators should make an effort to protect you from interference to the extent possible, given that 100% interference-free operation is an unrealistic expectation in today's congested bands.

Frequencies	Modes/Activities	Frequencies	Modes/Activities
1.800-2.000	CW	14.230	SSTV
1.800-1.810	Digital Modes	14.285	QRP SSB calling frequency
1.810	CW QRP calling frequency	14.286	AM calling frequency
1.843-2.000	SSB, SSTV and other wideband modes	18.100-18.105	RTTY/Data
		18.105-18.110	Automatically controlled data stations
1.910	SSB QRP	18.110	IBP/NCDXF beacons
1.995-2.000	Experimental		
1.999-2.000	Beacons	21.060	QRP CW calling frequency
		21.070-21.110	RTTY/Data
3.500-3.510	CW DX window	21.090-21.100	Automatically controlled data stations
3.560	QRP CW calling frequency	21.150	IBP/NCDXF beacons
3.570-3.600	RTTY/Data	21.340	SSTV
3.585-3.600	Automatically controlled data stations	21.385	QRP SSB calling frequency
3.590	RTTY/Data DX		
3.790-3.800	DX window	24.920-24.925	RTTY/Data
3.845	SSTV	24.925-24.930	Automatically controlled data stations
3.885	AM calling frequency	24.930	IBP/NCDXF beacons
3.985	QRP SSB calling frequency		
		28.060	QRP CW calling frequency
7.030	QRP CW calling frequency	28.070-28.120	RTTY/Data
7.040	RTTY/Data DX	28.120-28.189	Automatically controlled data stations
7.070-7.125	RTTY/Data	28.190-28.225	Beacons
7.100-7.105	Automatically controlled data stations	28.200	IBP/NCDXF beacons
7.171	SSTV	28.385	QRP SSB calling frequency
7.285	QRP SSB calling frequency	28.680	SSTV
7.290	AM calling frequency	29.000-29.200	AM
		29.300-29.510	Satellite downlinks
10.130-10.140	RTTY/Data	29.520-29.580	Repeater inputs
10.140-10.150	Automatically controlled data stations	29.600	FM simplex
		29.620-29.680	Repeater outputs
14.060	QRP CW calling frequency		
14.070-14.095	RTTY/Data	ARRL band plans for frequencies above 28.300 MHz are shown in	
14.095-14.0995	Automatically controlled data stations	*The ARRL Repeater Directory* and on **www.arrl.org**.	
14.100	IBP/NCDXF beacons		
14.1005-14.112	Automatically controlled data stations		

unless you can be of direct assistance. While we all wish to be helpful, sometimes the best help in an emergency is to listen, rather than transmit.

Interference

A combination of FCC-mandated and voluntary restrictions are intended to keep us out of one another's way help, but these cannot completely eliminate interference between amateur stations — nor should we expect them to.

Let's put interference into perspective. Note that we're referring only to interference from one amateur station to another, not RFI/TVI or to non-amateur intruders into exclusive ham bands.

Except when it concerns emergency communications, amateur-to-amateur interference is not, in and of itself, illegal. Each amateur station has an equal right to operate; just because you've used the same frequency since 1947 doesn't mean you have any more legal right to it than the person who received their license in the mail five minutes ago. The rules specifically prohibit willful or malicious interference [§97.101(d)].

What's malicious interference? Here's an example. If two hams, or groups of hams, find themselves on the same frequency pursuing mutually exclusive objectives, that's happenstance, not malicious interference. On the other hand, if one moves to another frequency and the other follows for the purpose of continuing to cause QRM to the first, the second has crossed the line. If he does it enough, he'll put his license in jeopardy. Of course, what sometimes happens is that they'll all sit on one frequency and argue about who has more right to be there. All it accomplishes is to keep the frequency from being used by anyone for anything worthwhile.

Radio amateurs have the right to pursue legitimate objectives within the privileges conveyed by their licenses, but they also have the obligation to minimize the inconvenience and loss of enjoyment hams cause to others. If there's a tiny segment of a band used for international communication, it's not too much to ask that local rag chews take place elsewhere. If establishing a beacon in the middle of a densely populated area is going to cause interference to nearby weak-signal enthusiasts, an amateur can find another place to put it. And surely, in such cases amateurs don't need the FCC to tell us what growing up in a civilized society should already have taught us to do.

Control Operator Responsibility

Under all circumstances it is the station licensee (or trustee for a club station) who is ultimately responsible for the correct and proper station operation. If the station licensee has designated a control operator, the rules consider both to be equally responsible for the correct operation [§97.103(a)]. This means that the control operator must make certain that the station is being operated properly at all times [§97.105(a)]. If you, as the licensee or control operator, are in doubt as to whether the station is being operated according to the rules and good amateur practice, it is your responsibility to immediately cease the transmissions. Don't transmit again until you are certain the station can resume legal, safe and appropriate operation.

Reciprocal Operating Within the US

Under many circumstances it is legal for licensed amateurs from foreign countries to get on the air while visiting the US. To do so, several criteria must be in order.

1) There must be a current reciprocal operating agreement between the US and their home country. This agreement must be either through a multilateral treaty such as CEPT or IARP (see below) or a direct bilateral agreement between the US and their home country.

2) The foreign licensee must not hold a US amateur license and call sign. If they do, they must operate under the terms of the US license and are not eligible to operate under a reciprocal license agreement.

3) The visitor must not be a US citizen. US citizens must hold a US license to operate and may not operate in the US under any type of reciprocal agreement.

The operating privileges that a visiting amateur may use while in the US depends on several factors. Visitors operating in the US under the European Conference of Postal and Telecommunications Administrations (CEPT) agreement, or under CITEL's International Amateur Radio Permit (IARP) Class 1 agreement, enjoy the full privileges of the Amateur Extra license [§97.301(a)(b)]. Holders of an IARP license other than Class 1 are entitled to VHF and up privileges [§97.301(a)].

Visitors from Canada are entitled to whatever operating privileges they hold at home, but they may not exceed the privileges of the Amateur Extra license [§97.107(a)]. This means that where their Canadian privileges differ from the US allocations (different limits on the phone operating frequencies, for example) they must stay within the privileges for US Amateur Extra licensees.

A visiting amateur who is not from Canada, or is from a country that is not party to CEPT or IARP, may operate if there is an existing bilateral agreement between the US and their home country. They may operate up to the limit of their own privileges back home, again not exceeding Amateur Extra operating privileges.

A visiting amateur from a country with which the US does not hold a reciprocal agreement of any sort may not operate. There is no citizenship requirement for obtaining a US amateur license, though, so any visitor may take the US license exams and then operate with a US call sign. They must provide a permanent US mailing address.

Reciprocal Operating By US Licensees Visiting Other Countries

US licensed amateurs benefit from reciprocal operating agreements when they travel outside the US. As a party to the CEPT agreement, US amateurs visiting most European countries and other countries that are signatories to the CEPT treaty have relatively easy reciprocal operating privileges. In most cases, all you need is to take your US amateur license and a copy of the CEPT agreement (which can be downloaded from **www.arrl.org/FandES/field/regulations/io/cept-ral.pdf**) and you are set to operate. You simply use the appropriate prefix designator before your FCC-issued call sign (for example, DL/N1ND during a visit to Germany).

CITEL's IARP certificate is the basic document necessary for operating in eight Latin/South American countries. IARP does not necessarily grant you instant operating privileges, but it does facilitate the ease of licensing in the countries where it is accepted. To apply for an IARP, download the application from **www.arrl.org/FandES/field/regulations/io/iarp-app. pdf** and submit it, along with the processing fee indicated in the instructions, to the ARRL VEC, 225 Main St, Newington CT 06111. Please allow 2-3 weeks for processing and return mail. Expedited processing is available. Contact the ARRL VEC for more information.

For non-CEPT countries, it is usually necessary for you to make some kind of direct notification or application to the licensing authority in the country you are visiting before you can begin operating. Do not assume that you can simply begin operating even if there is a reciprocal agreement in place. With the cooperation of Veke Komppa, OH2MCN, the ARRL works to maintain a detailed list of requirements for visiting each country in the world. Details are available at **www.arrl.org/ FandES/field/regulations/io/recip-country.html**. If you're planning a trip, it's always a good idea to review the material and start the process early.

Visit **www.arrl.org/FandES/field/regulations/io/faq. html** for the most up-to-date information on reciprocal licensing.

Authorized Transmissions

Normal communications via Amateur Radio are two-way in nature and according to §97.111(a) include:

1) Transmissions necessary to exchange messages with other stations in the amateur service, except those in any country whose administration has notified the ITU that it objects to such communications. The FCC will issue public notices of current arrangements for international communications;

2) Transmissions necessary to meet essential communication needs and to facilitate relief actions;

3) Transmissions necessary to exchange messages with a station in another FCC-regulated service while providing emergency communications;

4) Transmissions necessary to exchange messages with a United States government station, necessary to providing communications in RACES; and

5) Transmissions necessary to exchange messages with a station in a service not regulated by the FCC, but authorized by the FCC to communicate with amateur stations. An amateur station may exchange messages with a participating United States military station during an Armed Forces Day Communications Test.

Practically speaking, you may contact stations in the US and around the world that are authorized to conduct communications with stations in the Amateur Service. Your conversations should be confined to comments of technical or a personal nature when talking to amateurs outside the US [§97.117]. While you may communicate in languages other than English, you are re-

Reciprocal operating agreements and multilateral treaties like CEPT and IARP make it easier for hams to pack up portable stations and get on the air from other countries. (VK7MO photo)

quired to identify your station in English if using voice modes. If using CW or digital communications, it is permissible to send your station identification in that mode [§97.119(a)].

Amateurs may engage in a few types of short duration, one-way transmissions spelled out in §97.111(b):

1) Brief transmissions necessary to make adjustments to the station;

2) Brief transmissions necessary to establishing two-way communications with other stations;

3) Telecommand;

4) Transmissions necessary to providing emergency communications;

5) Transmissions necessary to assisting persons learning, or improving proficiency in, the international Morse code;

6) Transmissions necessary to disseminate information bulletins; and

7) Transmissions of telemetry.

Prohibited Communications

While a wide range of communications are legal for Amateur Radio operations, there are also some specific prohibitions. Many of the misunderstandings and disputes among Amateur Radio operators stem from these areas. Although most prohibitions are clear and simple, a few rely on each amateur to decide how to employ good amateur practice. One of the hallmarks of the Amateur Service is the commitment of the licensees to "self-police" our frequencies. A little thought about what we are about to transmit usually keeps us in line.

Certain types of communication are strictly forbidden. These are found in §97.113. For starters, you are never allowed to use the amateur service for business communication. This is defined in §97.113(a)(3) as "Communications in which the station licensee or control operator has a pecuniary interest, including communications on behalf of an employer." The rules do allow on-air swap nets where you can notify other hams of station equipment and accessories for sale — as long as you don't engage in that activity on a regular basis. (The rules don't define "regular basis" so here's a situation where individual amateurs must apply common sense and good amateur practice.)

One of the most frequently asked questions in relation to business communication rules is "Can I, as a paid employee of an emergency response service (such as a hospital, fire department or emergency dispatch office) be 'on the clock' while communicating via Amateur Radio during an emergency?" The FCC clarified this specific area in December 2006, in their Report and Order on Docket 04-140. The Commission's answer is that in their view, in an emergency a responder is being paid for their services as an emergency worker, not as an Amateur Radio operator. Keep in mind that this is specific to emergencies, not routine day-to-day operations.

Another frequently posed question relates to the use of a repeater autopatch to conduct business. The FCC view is that it is permissible to use the autopatch to do such routine tasks as order a pizza or call your doctor's office to tell them you are running late for an appointment. Remember, though, that a repeater owner or trustee may set more stringent standards for the use of their repeater and autopatch than required by the FCC. A good rule of thumb is "if in doubt — don't."

Amateurs provide communications free of charge and may not accept compensation for their services [§97.113(a)(2)]. Occasionally hams ask if they may accept T-shirts, hats and the like from organizers of events where hams provide public service communications. The answer is, you cannot be paid directly (money or goods) or indirectly (publicity, advertising, and so on) for your service. If the organizers supply you with T-shirts, hats or other incidental items to identify you while providing your services, that's not considered material compensation. Such items may be accepted, provided the communications would have been provided whether you had received the incidental item or not. This can be one of those "gray areas," so, if in doubt, don't.

Certain transmissions are always prohibited [§97.113(a)(4)]. You may never intentionally transmit music or obscene or indecent words or language on the amateur frequencies. You must not use the amateur frequencies in connection with any criminal activity. You may not transmit information via Amateur Radio in a code or cipher that obscures or hides the meaning of the transmission. False or deceptive messages or station identification are also prohibited. These prohibitions are clear and precise, and the FCC seriously enforces them.

Communications, on a regular basis, that could reasonably be furnished using another radio service are also prohibited [§97.113(a)(5)]. For example, you might help out your local firefighters during an emergency, but they need to rely on authorized public safety frequencies and radios for their day-to-day operations.

Broadcasting

Can you broadcast traffic reports and similar information on the local repeater? The answer is a resounding *no*! Part 97.113(b) is clear: Broadcasting is not permitted on the amateur bands. The FCC defines broadcasting as "transmissions intended for reception by the general public, either direct or relayed" [§97.3(a)(10)]. You may think it is helpful as a public service to relay or retransmit traffic reports or newscasts on the local repeater, but Amateur Radio transmissions are not intended to be transmitted to and received by the general public. Even allowed one-way amateur transmissions, such as code practice or HF propagation bulletins, are intended for an audience of licensed Amateur Radio operators, not the general public.

Along these lines, you are not allowed to retransmit commercial AM or FM radio broadcasts or television audio or video. The two allowed specific retransmissions are weather bulletins transmitted by US government stations (such severe weather alerts from the various NOAA weather radio stations) and, with permission, NASA manned space communications. In both cases, remember that you may not conduct such transmissions on a routine basis.

Amateur Radio's reputation for providing accurate information means that amateur transmissions are occasionally used as a source of information by local television and radio stations. Broadcasters are aware of SKYWARN and other emergency activities and will occasionally use information from Amateur Radio communications to help with news programming. There is a fine line between what is acceptable and what is not in this area.

In an emergency, Amateur Radio can be used to directly provide news information if several conditions are met:

1) The information must be directly related to the event;

2) It must involve the immediate safety of life or property; and

3) No other means of communications is available at the time of the event.

The general rule is that Amateur Radio is not to be used for newsgathering for production purposes by the media [§97.113(b)]. This is an important protection intended to stop encroachment by commercial news media who may see Amateur Radio as an inexpensive alternative to other communications systems.

Remember as well that the FCC rules provide some flexibility to allow the amateur community to meet its basic purpose of providing emergency communications. In a disaster or emergency, it is your responsibility as a licensed amateur to provide whatever assistance you can with emergency communications.

Third Party Communications

In many cases it is permissible for a licensed amateur to provide communications on behalf of someone other than the control operator or station licensee. This is known as *third party communications* and is defined in §97.3(a)(46) as "A message from the control operator (first party) of an amateur station to another amateur station control operator (second party) on behalf of another person (third party)."

Third party communications usually fall into one of three main types:

1) *Third party messages* — written messages generally sent via traffic nets or Amateur Radio message-handling services (packet or radio e-mail);

2) *Telephone interconnection* — autopatch or phone patch communications;

3) *Direct participation* — where the third party actively participates in transmitting the message.

FCC licensed amateurs may conduct third party traffic if specific conditions are met [§97.115]. A US amateur station may transmit third-party communications to another amateur station in the US. Third party traffic is permitted with stations in foreign countries for the purpose of emergency or disaster relief communications. For routine (non-emergency) third party communications, though, there must be an agreement between the US and the government of the country where the other amateur station is located. A current list of countries with which the US has third party agreements is found in **Table 11-3**.

The control operator must always be present at the control point when third party communications are being conducted, and the control op must continuously monitor and supervise the transmissions. Third party communications may not be

Table 11-3
Third-Party Traffic Agreements List

Countries that share third-party traffic agreements with the US:

Occasionally, DX stations may ask you to pass a third-party message to a friend or relative in the States. This is all right as long as the US has signed an official third-party traffic agreement with that particular country, or the third party is a licensed amateur. The traffic must be noncommercial and of a personal, unimportant nature. During an emergency, the US State Department will often work out a special temporary agreement with the country involved. But in normal times, never handle traffic without first making sure it is legally permitted.

US Amateurs May Handle Third-Party Traffic With:

C5	The Gambia	XE	Mexico
CE	Chile	YN	Nicaragua
CO	Cuba	YS	El Salvador
CP	Bolivia	YV	Venezuela
CX	Uruguay	ZP	Paraguay
D6	Federal Islamic Rep. of the Comoros	ZS	South Africa
DU	Philippines	3DA	Swaziland
EL	Liberia	4U1ITU	ITU - Geneva
GB	United Kingdom	4U1VIC	VIC - Vienna
HC	Ecuador	4X	Israel
HH	Haiti	6Y	Jamaica
HI	Dominican Republic	8R	Guyana
HK	Colombia	9G	Ghana
HP	Panama	9L	Sierra Leone
HR	Honduras	9Y	Trinidad and Tobago
J3	Grenada		
J6	St Lucia		
J7	Dominica	*Notes:*	
J8	St Vincent and the Grenadines		
JY	Jordan		
LU	Argentina		
OA	Peru		
PY	Brazil		
TA	Turkey		
TG	Guatemala		
TI	Costa Rica		
T9	Bosnia-Herzegovina		
V2	Antigua and Barbuda		
V3	Belize		
V4	St Kitts and Nevis		
V6	Federated States of Micronesia		
V7	Marshall Islands		
VE	Canada		
VK	Australia		
VP6	Pitcairn Island*		

Notes:

*Since 1970, there has been an informal agreement between the United Kingdom and the US, permitting Pitcairn and US amateurs to exchange messages concerning medical emergencies, urgent need for equipment or supplies, and private or personal matters of island residents.

Please note that Region 2 of the International Amateur Radio Union (IARU) has recommended that international traffic on the 20 and 15-meter bands be conducted on 14.100-14.150, 14.250-14.350, 21.150 -21.200 and 21.360-21.450 MHz. The IARU is the alliance of Amateur Radio societies from around the world; Region 2 comprises member-societies in North, South and Central America and the Caribbean.

At the end of an exchange of third-party traffic with a station located in a foreign country, an FCC-licensed amateur must transmit the call sign of the foreign station as well as his own call sign.

Current as of January 2007; see **www.arrl.org/FandES/field/ regulations/io/3rdparty.html** for the latest information.

---

conducted on behalf of anyone whose US license has been revoked; is currently suspended; or has been surrendered in lieu of revocation, suspension or monetary forfeiture. Nor may third-party communications be conducted on behalf of anyone subject to a cease-and-desist-order relating to Amateur Radio operations [§97.115(b)(2)]. Also, no station may transmit third party communications while under automatic control unless that station is using RTTY or data emissions [§97.115(c)].

Station Identification

There is a simple reason why stations must transmit their call sign — so people will know who they are talking to. In addition, unidentified transmissions are prohibited. The rules are straightforward in this area. Part 97.119(a) states: "Each amateur station, except a space station or telecommand station, must transmit its assigned call sign on its transmitting channel at the end of each communication, and at least every 10 minutes during a communication, for the purpose of clearly making the source of the transmissions from the station known to those receiving the transmissions. No station may transmit unidenti-

fied communications or signals, or transmit as the station call sign, any call sign not authorized to the station."

You will hear a wide range of comments and opinions and variations on this simple rule. But under FCC rules you are required to give your call sign every 10 minutes during active communications and at the end of the contact you are finishing. You are not *required* to give your call sign at the start of a contact. (Common sense suggests that during routine operation you would probably want to send your call sign at the start of the contact so that the other station knows who is talking to them.) You do not have to ID your station in a roundtable discussion every 10 minutes if you haven't transmitted since the last time you identified.

A few additional rules apply to station identification requirements:

1) You should transmit your station ID using the mode in which you are communicating.

2) When conducting an international third party contact, you must give both the call sign of the station with which you are communicating and your own call sign.

3) If you are transmitting the station ID of an automatically controlled station using CW, the speed may not exceed 20 WPM.

4) If you have upgraded your license recently, you must sign the correct temporary designator, such as "temporary AG" or "temporary AE" until your upgrade is processed by the FCC and appears in the ULS database.

SUBPART C — SPECIAL OPERATIONS

As your experience grows and as your interests change, you may want to become involved in more specialized activities. These are not different "modes" of operation — they are different "uses" for Amateur Radio stations. When you are talking on or controlling a local repeater, sending or receiving messages through a message forwarding system such as radio e-mail or packet, or communicating through one of the Amateur Radio satellites, you are participating in a special operation, and special rules apply to your activities.

Auxiliary Stations

Amateur Radio stations are sometimes set up and controlled remotely via an RF link. A station involved in this type of activity is defined under §97.3(a)(7) as an *auxiliary station*. Auxiliary stations are often set to perform such tasks as controlling or linking repeaters or performing station control tasks, such as changing operating parameters of a remote base station. The stations that these auxiliary stations control, as well as the auxiliary stations themselves, become what the FCC refers to as a "system of cooperating stations."

Auxiliary stations have some specific operating guidelines that enable them to carry out their function while holding to the principle of effective use of our Amateur Radio spectrum. They may operate only on frequencies in the 2-meter band or higher, with the exception of these specific segments: 144.0-144.5, 145.8-146.0, 219-220, 222.00-222.15, 431-433 and 435-438 MHz [§97.201(b)]. Auxiliary stations may be automatically controlled and may transmit one-way communication [§97.201(d)(e)]. Holders of a Technician or higher license may be an auxiliary station or serve as control operator for such a system [§97.201(a)]. Finally, in cases where there is interference between two auxiliary stations, both are equally responsible to resolve the issue, unless one of the stations has been coordinated by a frequency coordinating body. In that case, the non-coordinated auxiliary station has primary responsibility to resolve the issue [§97.201(c)].

Remote Operation and Links

In today's time of deed and antenna restrictions, many amateurs find it convenient or even necessary to employ a *remote base station*. While not defined in Part 97, a remote base uses a form of auxiliary operation to both control and use the station. As such, they must follow the rules for auxiliary operation as well as those for remote control of a station. Remote control is defined in §97.3(a)(38) as "The use of a control operator who indirectly manipulates the operating adjustments in the station through a control link to achieve compliance with the FCC Rules."

Remote bases are not the same as repeaters. In a remote base system, the user is part of the system, whereas in a repeater system, a user is not part of the system. This means that the person transmitting on a remote base must be a control operator of the system, or working directly under the supervision of a control operator. This is different from a repeater where individual users do not have to be able to control the operation of the repeater itself.

With the advent of the modern multiband VHF/UHF radios, it has become common for individuals to use those radios for "crossband repeating." Most often, operation as a crossband repeater is actually operation as a remote base, and as such must meet the remote base rules.

Until the rules changed in December 2006, auxiliary stations were required to operate on frequencies above 222.15 MHz. It is now legal to operate an auxiliary station on the 2-meter band with the exception of 144.0-144.5 MHz and 145.8-146.0 MHz. This makes it easier to legally operate these multiband radios as remote bases. They must still have some sort of system for a control link (remember, all stations must be controlled by some legal mechanism). They must also have some sort of timer or means of shutting down the system after three minutes should the control link fail [§97.213]. But with auxiliary stations now allowed on 2 meters, the user's ID over both sides of the link serves to legally ID the remote station when operating as a crossband repeater.

It is also common to link repeaters to one another or to an Internet connection (such as IRLP, EchoLink or simply a computer gateway). This linking of radio constitutes a system of cooperating stations and involves the concepts of remote bases and auxiliary stations. The auxiliary station rules apply. One of the big concerns to keep in mind when participating in interconnection to the Internet is to ensure that there is no access

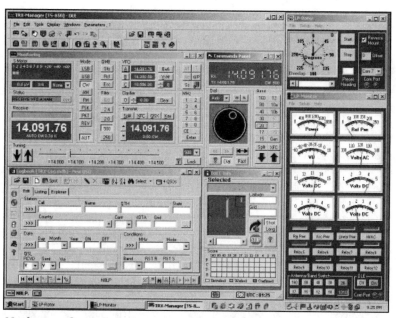

Modern software and computer-controlled radios make remote operation easier than ever, but you need to follow the rules. Be sure to review the requirements in Subpart C for details on auxiliary and remote base operation.

to Amateur Radio via the Internet by a non-amateur without an appropriate control operator. As with all amateur communications, the Part 97 rules for station identification, interference and other normal operating issues apply.

Repeater Stations

Almost every ham uses repeaters at one time or another. A repeater is defined in §97(a)(39) as "An amateur station that simultaneously retransmits the transmission of another amateur station on a different channel or channels." Any station owned by a Technician or higher licensee may operate as a repeater on 6 meters and up, and General or higher licensees may also operate as a repeater on 10 meters. Repeater operation is not allowed in these segments of those bands: 28.0-29.5, 50.0-51.0, 144.0-144.5, 145.5-146.0, 222.0-222.15, 431.0-433.0 and 435.0-438.0 MHz [§97.205(b)].

By their nature, repeaters tend to be placed in locations that are not easily accessible, such as mountaintops or tall buildings. This means they are frequently controlled remotely. Remote control can be achieved through several means. A dedicated wireline or non-published telephone line is permissible. If the repeater also has an autopatch interface to the telephone line, there must be an additional control link. That's needed because it would not be possible to terminate operation of the repeater via the telephone line if the problem was being caused by the failure of that line. You may also use a radio control link through an auxiliary station as a means of remote control for the repeater station. It is also permissible for a repeater to be under automatic control [§97.205(d)]. It is important to remember that regardless of the type of control, the licensee is *always* responsible for the proper operation of the repeater.

One of the most common repeater problems involves repeater users who transmit communications that violate the rules — obscene material or music, for example. While the rules state that the control operator is not accountable when such actions occur [§97.205(g)], it is still their responsibility to ensure that the repeater is being operated under the rules. In such cases the control operator should shut down the repeater until the problem is resolved. If necessary to ensure proper operation of the repeater, it is permissible for the repeater owner to limit its use to only certain stations [§97.205(e)]. A repeater is not a "public utility." No licensee has the automatic right to use a specific repeater. Repeater owners may always make rules for use of their equipment that are more stringent than those imposed by Part 97. Failure to abide by those additional rules can lead to the revocation of your privilege to use that specific repeater.

You won't have to spend much time on the VHF and UHF bands to realize that they are crowded. To deal with this congestion, a series of frequency coordinating groups have developed to try and manage the repeater spectrum. From §97.3(A)(22): A frequency coordinator is "An entity, recognized in a local or regional area by amateur operators whose stations are eligible to be auxiliary or repeater stations, that recommends transmit/receive channels and associated operating and technical parameters for such stations in order to avoid or minimize potential interference."

These coordinating groups work on local or regional policies to maximize the efficient use of the available spectrum as well as minimize interference issues or problems. The National Frequency Coordinator's Council (NFCC) certifies most frequency coordinating groups. Each group develops procedures for a designated territory and maintains an accurate database of coordinated repeaters within that area.

When repeater owners experience harmful interference, coordinators assist in resolving the problems. If an interference issue involves a coordinated and uncoordinated repeater, §97.205(c) states that the primary responsibility for resolving the issue rests with the uncoordinated repeater.

Message Forwarding Systems

Improvements in technology mean changes in our ability to communicate with new methods. As with any operating method — new or old — we need to ensure that we adhere to the rules. Part 97.3(a)(31) defines a message forwarding system as "A group of amateur stations participating in a voluntary, cooperative, interactive arrangement where communications are sent from the control operator of an originating station to the control operator of one or more destination stations by one or more forwarding stations." These systems now operate on HF, VHF and UHF and often a message may pass among several frequency bands as it makes its way to the recipient.

The licensee of the originating station of a message is always primarily accountable for any message content that violates FCC rules [§97.219(b)]. But the responsibility does not stop there. The first forwarding station must make sure that the originator of a message is authorized to send messages over the system and must take responsibility for any messages it retransmits into a system. In essence it has the responsibility to act as a "filter" to protect other stations down the line [§97.219(d)(1),(2)]. However subsequent forwarding stations also have the responsibility to terminate any message they are aware of that is in violation of the rules, even though they are not responsible for it reaching them [§97.219(3)].

Remember that Part 97 rules apply at all times. The rules regarding third-party traffic, business communications, obscene and indecent materials, and so forth apply to messages sent via message forwarding systems just as they do to "real time" amateur communications.

Two or more unattended HF digital stations that are connected may be automatically controlled while transmitting RTTY or data emissions, but they are restricted to specific frequencies. There are no restrictions at 6 meters and above. On HF, only these segments are allowed: 28.120-28.189, 24.925-24.930, 21.090-21.100, 18.105-18.110, 14.0950-14.0995, 14.1005-14.112, 10.140-10.150, 7.100-7.105 and 3.585-3.600 MHz [§97.221(b)].

Automatic control is authorized only if the station is responding to an interrogation from a station under local or remote control. In addition, no transmission from an automatically controlled system may occupy a bandwidth of more than 500 Hz [§97.221(c)(1),(2)].

An automatically controlled station may still be placed on a frequency outside of the allowed fully automated sub-bands as long as a manually controlled station (a real person) initiates or "turns on" the station. Until that happens, it must remain silent.

SUBPART D — TECHNICAL STANDARDS

Many amateurs find this subpart of the rules to be the most confusing — or least interesting. It's an important section because here you will find the specifics rules that determine the frequencies, transmitter power and emission types you may use. This subpart also governs the quality of the signals you are allowed to transmit.

License Classes

Currently there are three levels of Amateur Radio license issued in the US — Technician, General and Amateur Extra. Each level of license requires you to pass an examination administered by a team of at least three Volunteer Examiners (VEs) working under the direction of an FCC-certified Volunteer Examiner Coordinator (VEC).

The Technician license requires that you correctly answer a minimum of 26 questions on a 35-question written test. To earn the General license, you pass the Technician exam and then an additional 35-question General exam (again with 26 correct answers minimum). The Amateur Extra license requires that you pass the Technician and General examinations, as well as a 50-question Amateur Extra exam (with at least 37 correct answers).

The written exam questions cover rules and regulations, radio and electronic theory, antennas, safety, operating techniques and other amateur practices. The FCC no longer requires candidates to pass a Morse code examination for any amateur license.

There are two additional US license classes — Novice and Advanced. No new Novice or Advanced licenses have been issued since April 15, 2000. Current Novice and Advanced licensees may continue to renew at expiration and use frequencies, modes and power levels for that license as allowed in the rules.

Table 11-4

The Electromagnetic Spectrum with Amateur Service Frequency Bands by ITU Region

Wavelength	Frequency	Nomenclature	Metric Band	Amateur Radio Bands by ITU Region		
				Region 1	Region 2	Region 3
1 mm	300 GHz	EHF Millimetric	1 mm	241-250	241-250	241-250
			2 mm	142-149	142-149	142-149
			2.5 mm	119.98-120.02	119.98-120.02	119.98-120.02
			4 mm	75.5-81	75.5-81	75.5-81
			6 mm	47-47.2	47-47.2	47-47.2
1 cm	30 GHz	SHF Centimetric	1.2 cm	24-24.25	24-24.25	24-24.25
			3 cm	10-10.5	10-10.5	10-10.5
			5 cm	5.65-5.85	5.65-5.925	5.65-5.85
			9 cm		3.3-3.5	3.3-3.5
10 cm	3 GHz	UHF Decimetric	13 cm	2.3-2.45	2.3-2.45	2.3-2.45
			23 cm	1240-1300	1240-1300	1240-1300
			33 cm		902-928	
			70 cm	430-440	430-440	430-440
1	300 MHz	VHF Metric	1.25 m		222-225	
			2 m	144-148	144-148	144-148
			6 m		50-54	50-54
10	30 MHz	HF Decametric	10 m	28-29.7	28-29.7	28-29.7
			12 m	24.89-24.99	24.89-24.99	24.89-24.99
			15 m	21-21.45	21-21.45	21-21.45
			17 m	18.068-18.168	18.068-18.168	18.068-18.168
			20 m	14-14.350	14-14.350	14-14.350
			30 m	10.0-10.150	10.1-10.150	10.1-10.150
			40 m	7-7.1	7-7.3	7-7.1
			80 m	3.5-3.8	3.5-4	3.5-3.9
100	3 MHz	MF Hectometric	160 m	1.81-1.85	1.8-2	1.8-2
1000	300 kHz	LF Kilometric				
10,000	30 kHz	VLF Myriametric				
100,000	3 kHz					

Note: This table should be used only for a general overview of where Amateur Service and Amateur-Satellite Service frequencies by ITU Region fall within the radio spectrum. They do not necessarily agree with FCC allocations; for example, the 70-cm band is 420-450 MHz in the United States.

Subpart D is the Technical Standards section. This subpart includes rules governing FCC Certification of certain types of Amateur Radio equipment, including power amplifiers.

Frequency Bands

Bands of frequencies are allocated to the Amateur Service from 1800 kHz (73 kHz in the UK) to over 300 GHz. **Table 11-4** gives an overview of the radio spectrum and shows the Amateur Service bands allocated in the International Telecommunication Union (ITU) Radio Regulations.

Development of band plans is an ongoing process. It requires planners to research, invite and digest comment from amateurs, arrive at a mix that will serve the diverse needs of the amateur community, and adopt a formal band plan. This is a process that can take a year or more on the national level and a similar period in the International Amateur Radio Union (IARU). Nevertheless, new communication modes or changes in the popularity of existing ones can make a year-or-two-old band plan look obsolete.

Such revolutionary change has taken place in the past decade with the popularity of new digital modes. Changes of this magnitude cause the new users to scramble for frequencies and some of the existing mode users to draw their wagons in a circle. The national societies (such as ARRL), their staffs and committees, and the IARU have the job of sorting out the contention for various frequencies and preparing new band plans. Fortunately, we have not exhausted all possible ways of improving our management of the spectrum so that all Amateur Radio interests can be accommodated.

Here are some band-by-band highlights:

The 160-Meter Band

The 160-meter band, 1800-2000 kHz, provides some excellent DX opportunities in addition to local operations. The basic problem with allocations in this band has been competition with the Radiolocation Service. New pressures are possible as a result of planned expansion of the medium-frequency broadcast band in the 1605-1705 kHz range.

The 80-Meter Band

While US amateurs enjoy the use of 3500-4000 kHz, not all countries allocate such a wide range of frequencies to the 75/80-meter band. There are fixed, mobile and broadcast opera-

tions, particularly in the upper part of the band.

The 60-Meter Band

The FCC has granted amateur *secondary* access on upper sideband (USB) *only* to five discrete 2.8-kHz wide channels at the following frequencies:

Channel Center	Amateur Tuning Frequency
5332 kHz	5330.5 kHz
5348 kHz	5346.5 kHz
5368 kHz	5366.5 kHz
5373 kHz	5371.5 kHz
5405 kHz	5403.5 kHz

While the center channel is the allocated frequency, on USB, amateurs must set their transceivers to the amateur tuning frequency. *This is very important.* General, Advanced and Amateur Extra licensees may operate on these channels with no more than 50 W PEP ERP (effective radiated power). In this case, ERP is calculated by multiplying transmitter power by antenna gain relative to a dipole. That means 50 W to a dipole is the maximum allowed, but if you use an antenna with more gain than a dipole you must reduce transmitter power accordingly. If you use an antenna other than a dipole, you must include information about its gain characteristics in your station log [§97.303(s)].

The 40-Meter Band

The 40-meter band has a big problem: International broadcasting occupies the 7100-7300 kHz band in many parts of the world. That changes on March 29, 2009, when the 7100-7200 kHz band will become amateur exclusive. International broadcast stations will no longer be allowed in this segment — clearer frequencies on this band are coming.

During the daytime, particularly when sunspots are high, broadcasting does not cause much interference to US amateurs. At night, however, especially when sunspot activity is low, the broadcast interference is heavy. Some countries allocate only the 7000-7100 kHz band to amateurs. Others, particularly in Region 2, allocate 7100-7300 kHz as well, which at times is subject to interference. The result is that there is a great demand for frequencies in the 7000-7100 kHz segment. The effect is that there are two band plans overlaid on each other: ours, spread out over 7000-7300 kHz and another one that compresses everything into 7000-7100 kHz. The pending changes in 2009 will help resolve some of this compression, giving the amateur community worldwide more spectrum.

The 30-Meter Band

The 30-meter band, 10100-10150 kHz, is excellent for CW and digital modes. The only problem is that US amateurs must not cause harmful interference to the fixed operations outside the US. This restricts transmitter power output to 200 W and is one reason for not having contests on this band.

The 20-Meter Band

The workhorse of DX is undoubtedly the 20-meter band, 14000-14350 kHz. It offers excellent propagation to all parts of the world throughout the sunspot cycle and is virtually clean of interference from other services.

The 17-Meter Band

The 18068-18168 kHz band was awarded to amateurs on an exclusive basis, worldwide, at WARC-79. It was made available for amateur use in the US in January 1989. It shares propagation characteristics with 15 and 20 meters.

The 15 and 12-Meter Bands

The 21000-21450 and 24890-24990 kHz bands are excellent for DX during the high part of the sunspot cycle. They also offer some openings throughout the rest of the sunspot cycle.

The 10-Meter Band

Spanning 28000-29700 kHz, this is an exclusive amateur band worldwide. Its popularity rises and falls with sunspot numbers and propagation.

The VHF and Higher Bands

The 6-meter band is not universal, but the trend seems to be toward allocating it to amateurs as TV broadcasting vacates the 50-54 MHz band. It is also excellent for amateur exploitation of meteor-scatter communications using various modes including digital.

Two meters is heavily used throughout the world for CW, EME (moonbounce), SSB, FM and packet radio. The allocation is 144-148 MHz. Satellites occupy the 145.8-146 MHz segment.

US amateurs have a primary allocation at 222-225 MHz, which is largely used for repeaters. The Commission has allocated 219-220 MHz to the Amateur Radio Service on a secondary basis, only for stations participating in fixed, point-to-point digital messaging systems. There are special provisions to protect domestic waterways telephone systems using that band.

The 70-cm band is prime UHF spectrum. The 430-440 MHz band is virtually worldwide, whereas the 420-430 MHz and 440-450 MHz bands are not. Frequencies around 432 are used for weak-signal work, including EME, and the 435-438 MHz band is for amateur satellites. The 70-cm band is the lowest frequency band that can be used for fast-scan television and spread spectrum emissions.

The 33-cm band (902-928 MHz) is widely shared with other services, including Location and Monitoring Service (LMS), which is primary, and ISM (industrial, scientific and medical) equipment applications. A number of low-power devices including spread spectrum local area networks operate in this band under Part 15 of the FCC's Rules.

The 1240-1300 MHz band is used by Amateur Radio operators for essentially all modes, including FM and packet. By regulation, the 1260-1270 MHz segment may be used only in the Earth-to-space direction when communicating with amateur satellites.

Amateur Radio is primary at 2390-2417 MHz. While the Amateur Service has a secondary allocation in the 2300-2450 MHz band in the international tables, in the United States the allocation is 2390-2400 MHz and 2390-2417 MHz primary, and 2300-2310, and 2417-2450 secondary. Most of the weak-signal work in the US takes place around 2304 MHz, while much of the satellite activity is in the 2400-2402 MHz segment.

The remaining microwave and millimeter bands are the territory of amateur experimenters. It is important that the Amateur Service and the Amateur Satellite Service use these bands, and contribute to the state-of-the-art in order to retain them. There is growing interest on the part of the telecommunications industry and the space science community to fully exploit the 20-95 GHz spectrum.

It is important to remember that we share frequency allocations on many of our bands above 420 MHz. For example, while we have a frequency allocation between 420 and 450 MHz, we are only the secondary user (with the Radiolocation Service designated as primary). In any case where an amateur station as a secondary user causes harmful interference to the primary user (regardless of band), it is the sole responsibility to mitigate or eliminate that interference.

Frequency Allocations and Emission Types

Part 97.301 lays out the specific frequency allocations for each type of amateur license, and §97.305 delineates the types of emissions that are permissible on each portion of each band. The chart in **Fig 11-2** summarizes this information.

Emission Standards

In keeping with the principle of good amateur practice, it is important that the signals transmitted by an amateur station be "clean." But it is for more than on-the-air aesthetics — good signal quality reduces interference and problems on the bands, which in turn makes our operating time more enjoyable and easier.

The rules are clear about signal quality. No station should occupy more bandwidth than is necessary for the type of communication being conducted [§97.307(a)]. Your modulated signal must not exceed the band segments authorized for your license [§97.307(b)]. Spurious emissions must be reduced as much as possible and corrected if they are causing harmful interference [§97.307(c)]. The remaining paragraphs of 97.307 deal with specifications for various modes.

Certification and Standards for External RF Power Amplifiers

Certain types of Amateur Radio equipment are required to have FCC Certification (formerly known as type-acceptance). Primarily this is done to combat the modification of Amateur Radio gear for illegal use on frequencies in and around the Citizen's Band Radio Service frequencies (commonly referred to as 11 meters). New RF power amplifiers are required to exhibit no amplification between 26 and 28 MHz, and they may not be designed to allow easy modification to do so [§97.317(a)(3) and (b)].

SUBPART E — PROVIDING EMERGENCY COMMUNICATIONS

Providing emergency communications is one of the basic purposes of the Amateur Radio service. Because of its importance, Part 97 devotes a small but significant Subpart to special rules for use during emergencies.

Emergency communication means "essential communication needs in connection with the immediate safety of human life and immediate protection of property when normal communication systems are not available" [§97.403(b)]. This rule section in essence states when life or property are at risk, nothing in the

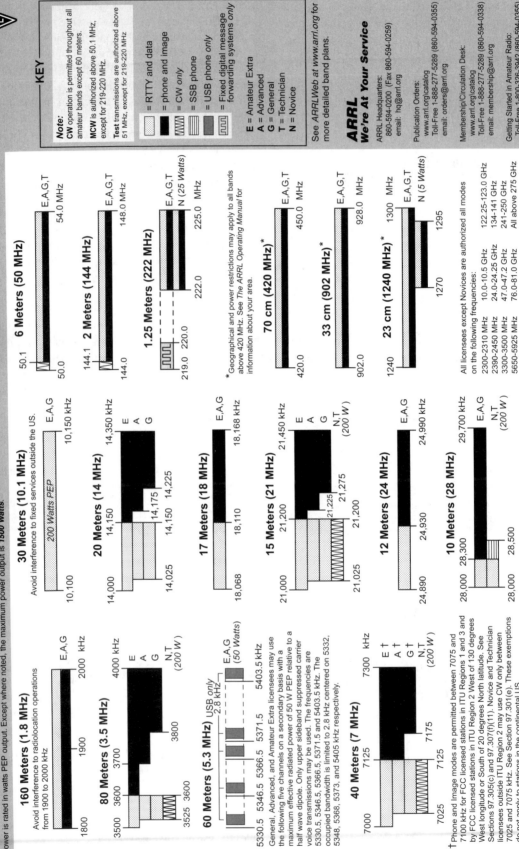

Fig 11-2 — US amateur operating privileges.

Volunteer Examiner (VE) teams make it possible for you to take license exams. Whether you're going for your first license or an upgrade, you can find the nearest exam session on the ARRL Web site at www.arrl.org/arrlvec/examsearch.phtml.

Emergency communications is important enough that it warrants its own section, Subpart E. Amateur Radio volunteers may be found out in the field, or they may assist at Emergency Operations Centers, like this one activated in the aftermath of a hurricane.

Part 97 rules prevents the licensee from using Amateur Radio to try to obtain the help or relief needed. Part 97.405 goes further when it states that a station in distress should use *any means at its disposal* to "attract attention, make known its condition and location, and obtain assistance." As FCC officials have stated, "In a real emergency — do what is necessary."

This isn't a responsibility to be taken lightly. The FCC records are full of enforcement actions involving stations that "cried wolf" or made false claims. The trust that the FCC places in the amateur community gives us a lot of latitude during emergencies, but it is a trust that each licensee must responsibly bear.

Often when participating in an emergency (or when practicing for them through drills, nets or public service events) you may use self-assigned "tactical" call signs during your communications. While these are not prohibited by Part 97, remember that you are still required to give your FCC-assigned call sign at least every 10 minutes during the contact and at the end of your communications.

SUBPART F — QUALIFYING EXAMINATION SYSTEMS

As discussed previously, the FCC delegates most of the Amateur Radio examination process to the amateur community itself, through the Volunteer Examiner (VE) program. The FCC maintains the standards for what classes of license are available in the US [§97.501] and what is necessary to pass the various examinations [§97.503]. The actual content, preparation and administration of exams are determined by Volunteer Examiner Coordinators (VECs).

The individual VECs are responsible for training and certifying qualified Amateur Radio operators to serve as Volunteer Examiners. They are also responsible for implementing the FCC guidelines for administration of exams and filing the results of those exams electronically with the FCC.

The individual VECs across the US work jointly through the National Conference of Volunteer Examiner Coordinators (NCVEC). The NCVEC is responsible, through its Question Pool Committee, to maintain a common question pool for each license class [§97.523].

SUMMARY

The wide variety of Amateur Radio bands, modes and activities available to you can be overwhelming at times. At every step you have to ensure that you are operating your station legally, safely and appropriately — no small task! While the regulations can seem daunting, the answers to most rules and regulations questions and issues can be determined from a good review of Part 97.

This chapter was not intended to provide an exhaustive discussion of every rule and regulation. Rather, it's intended to answer the most commonly asked questions. Each amateur is encouraged to have a copy of the current rules handy.

Steve Ford, WB8IMY

chapter 12

Operating Awards

Awards hunting is a significant part of the life-support system of Amateur Radio operating. It's a major motivating force behind many of the contacts that occur on the bands day after day. It takes skillful operating to qualify, and the reward of having a beautiful certificate or plaque on your ham-shack wall commemorating your achievement is very gratifying. If you've been on the air for a while, you can probably get a good start by pulling out your shoebox of QSLs on a cold, winter afternoon to see what gems you already have on hand.

Aside from expanding your Amateur Radio-related knowledge, chasing awards is also a fascinating way to learn about the geography, history or political structure of another country, or perhaps even your own. This chapter provides information on awards sponsored by ARRL plus some other awards that may be of interest to you.

AWARD BASICS

There are some basic considerations to keep in mind when applying for awards. Always carefully read the rules, so that your application complies fully. Use the standard award application if possible, and make sure your application is neat and legible, and indicates clearly what you are applying for. Official rules and application materials are available directly from the organization sponsoring the par-

Hams enjoy exchanging QSL cards and collecting them to count for various awards. Whether you're chasing DX countries, US states, grid locators, call sign prefixes or counties, the QSL card is the foundation upon which most awards are based. In recent years, hams have gravitated toward ARRL's electronic Logbook of The World to help bolster DXCC and WAS totals, but everyone loves to receive a colorful QSL card in the mail from a "rare one."

ticular award. You can often find the needed information and forms on the Web. If you need to get something by postal mail, always include an SASE (self-addressed, stamped envelope) or, in the case of international awards, a self-addressed envelope with IRCs (International Reply Coupons, available from your local Post Office) when making such requests. Sufficient return postage should also be included when directing awards-related correspondence to Awards Managers. Many (if not most) are volunteers. Above all, be patient!

As to QSL cards, if they are required with your application, send them the safest possible way and always include sufficient return postage for their return the same way. It is vital that you check your cards carefully before mailing them. Make sure each card contains your call and other substantiating information (band, mode, and so on). Never send cards that are altered or have information crossed out and marked over, even if such modifications are made by the amateur filling out the card. Altered cards, even if such alterations are made in "good faith," are not acceptable for awards. If you are unsure about a particular card, don't submit it. Secure a replacement.

None of the above is meant to diminish your enthusiasm for awards hunting. These are just helpful hints to make things even more fun for all concerned. Chasing awards is a robust facet of hamming that makes each and every QSO a key element in your present or future Amateur Radio success.

ARRL AWARDS

To make Amateur Radio QSOs more enjoyable and to add challenge, the League sponsors awards for operating achievement, some of which are the most popular awards in ham radio. Except for the Code Proficiency awards, US applicants must be League members to apply. It is advisable to always check the current fee schedule found online at **www.arrl.org/awards**.

Code Proficiency (CP)

You don't have to be a ham to earn this one. But you do have to copy one of the W1AW qualifying runs. (The current W1AW operating schedule is printed in *QST*, listed on **www. arrl.org** or available from ARRL HQ for an SASE.) Twice a month, five minutes worth of text is transmitted at the following speeds: 10-15-20-25-30-35 WPM. For a real challenge, W1AW transmits 40 WPM twice yearly.

To qualify at any speed, just copy one minute solid. Your copy can be written, printed or typed. Underline the minute you believe you copied perfectly and send this text to ARRL HQ along with your name, call (if licensed) and complete mailing address. Your copy is checked directly against the official W1AW transmission copy, and you'll be advised promptly if you've passed or failed. If the news is good, you'll soon receive either your initial certificate or an appropriate endorsement sticker. Check **www.arrl.org/awards** for the current fee schedule.

Worked All States (WAS)

The Worked All States (WAS) award is available to all amateurs worldwide who submit proof of having contacted each of the 50 United States. The WAS program includes 10 different awards for working all states on various bands and modes, as well as endorsement stickers for working various kinds of stations.

To earn the basic WAS award, establish two-way communication on the amateur bands with each state. There is no minimum signal report required. Any or all amateur bands and modes may be used for general WAS. The District of Columbia may be counted for Maryland.

Contacts must all be made from the same location or from locations no two of which are more than 50 miles apart. Club-station applicants, please include clearly the club name and call sign of the club station (or trustee).

Contacts may be made over any period of years. Contacts must be confirmed in writing, preferably in the form of QSL cards. Original confirmations must be submitted (no photocopies). Confirmations must show your call and indicate that two-way communication was established. Specialty awards and endorsements must be shown as two-way (2×) on that band and/or mode. Contacts made with Alaska must be dated January 3, 1959 or later, and with Hawaii dated August 21, 1959 or after.

ARRL's online Logbook of the World (LoTW) also supports the WAS program. If you are an LoTW participant, you can upload your logs and track your progress on various WAS awards and endorsements. When you have gathered the LoTW confirmations needed for an award, you can even apply online. Details on LoTW are given later in this chapter.

Specialty awards (numbered separately) are available for OSCAR Satellite, SSTV, 432 MHz, 222 MHz, 144 MHz, 50 MHz and 160 meters. The Digital award, issued for working any digital mode (PSK3, AMTOR, PACTOR, RTTY, G-TOR and so forth) is also available. The Digital and Phone awards are dated but not numbered, except RTTY.

Endorsement stickers for the basic mixed mode/band award and any of the specialty awards are available for CW, Novice, QRP, Packet, EME and any single band. The Novice endorsement is available for the applicant who has worked all states as a Novice licensee. QRP is defined as 5 W output as used by the applicant (the station you work does not need to be running QRP as well), and is affirmed by signature of the applicant on the application.

Contacts made through "repeater" devices or any other power relay method cannot be used for WAS confirmation. (A separate WAS is available for OSCAR satellite contacts.) All stations contacted must be "land stations." Contact with ships (anchored or otherwise) and aircraft cannot be counted. The only exception is permanently docked exhibition ships, such as the Queen Mary and other historic ships. Those are considered land based in the state where they are docked.

All US applicants must be ARRL members to participate in the WAS program. DX stations are exempt from this requirement.

HQ reserves the right to "spot call" for inspection of cards (at ARRL expense) of applications verified by an HF Awards Manager. The purpose of this is not to question the integrity of any individual, but rather to ensure the overall integrity of the program. More difficult-to-be-attained specialty awards (222 MHz WAS, for example) are more likely to be so called. Failure of the applicant to respond to such a spot check will result in non-issuance of the WAS certificate.

Disqualification: False statements on the WAS application or submission of forged or altered cards may result in

disqualification. ARRL does not attempt to determine who has altered a submitted card; therefore do not submit any marked-over cards. The decision of the ARRL Awards Committee in such cases is final.

Application Procedure (please follow carefully): Confirmations (QSLs) and application form (MSD-217) may be submitted to an approved ARRL Special Services Club HF Awards Manager for checking. If you can have your application verified locally, you need not submit your cards to HQ. If you cannot have your application verified locally, send your application, cards, and required fees to HQ, as indicated on the application form. You can search for the nearest ARRL HF Awards Manager by following the link from **www.arrl.org/awards/was/**.

Forms and the latest rules for WAS are available online at **www.arrl.org/awards/was/**. You can also obtain forms from Special Requests, ARRL HQ, 225 Main St, Newington, CT 06111 (please be specific in your request and include an SASE).

Be sure that when cards are presented for verification (either locally or to HQ) they are sorted alphabetically by state, as listed on the back of application form MSD-217.

All QSL cards sent to HQ must be accompanied by sufficient postage for their safe return, and the required fee (see **www.arrl.org/awards/was/**). A WAS pin is available.

Five-Band WAS (5BWAS)

This award is designed to foster more uniform activity throughout the bands, encourage the development of better antennas and generally offer a challenge to both newcomers and veterans. The basic WAS rules apply, including cards being checked in the field by HF Awards Managers. In addition, 5BWAS carries a start date of January 1, 1970, and contacts before that do not count. Unlike WAS, 5BWAS is a one-time-only award; no band/mode endorsements are available. Contacts made on 10/18/24 MHz are not valid for 5BWAS. Forms and the latest rules for WAS are available online at **www.arrl.org/awards/was/**.

All QSL cards sent to HQ must be accompanied by sufficient postage for their safe return, and the required fee (see **www.arrl.org/awards/was/**). A special 5BWAS pin and 5BWAS plaque are also available.

Pins

Special pins for WAS and 5BWAS may be purchased through the ARRL Publication Sales Department (**www.arrl.org/catalog**). These attractive, colorful lapel pins let others know that you have earned the awards.

Worked All Continents (WAC)

In recognition of international two-way Amateur Radio communication, the International Amateur Radio Union (IARU) issues Worked All Continents (WAC) certificates to Amateur Radio stations around the world. WAC is issued for working and confirming 2-way contacts with all six continents (North America, South America, Oceania, Asia, Europe and Africa) on a variety of bands and modes. The ARRL DXCC List includes a continent designation for each DXCC country.

QSL cards are examined and verified the International Secretariat, or a Member-Society of the IARU. All contacts must be made from the same country or separate territory within the same continental area of the world. All QSL cards (no photocopies) must show the mode and/or band for any endorsement applied for.

The following WAC certificates are available: Basic Certificate (mixed mode); CW Certificate; Phone Certificate; SSTV Certificate; RTTY Certificate; FAX Certificate; Satellite Certificate; 5-Band Certificate.

The following WAC endorsements are available: 6-Band endorsement; QRP endorsement; 1.8-MHz endorsement; 3.5-MHz endorsement; 50-MHz endorsement; 144-MHz endorsement; 432-MHz endorsement; any higher-band endorsement.

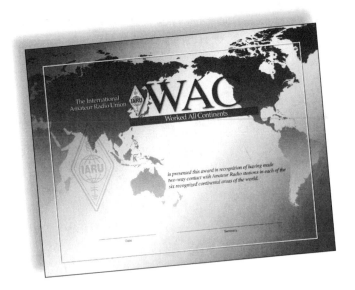

judgment and courtesy. You must be recommended for the certification independently by two amateurs who already are A-1 Ops. This honor is unsolicited; it is earned through the continuous observance of the very highest operating standards.

Amateur Extra Class Radio Operator

Reminiscent of the *original* FCC Amateur Radio Extra Class License Certificate (no longer available), this beautiful certificate allows the Amateur Extra licensee to display evidence of his achievement. The Amateur Extra Class Radio Operator certificate indicates the name and call sign of the operator as well as the date he or she achieved this top grade. Send your name (exactly as you wish it to appear) and address and the date you were issued your Amateur Extra license (the year is close enough) to the Awards Branch at ARRL HQ. Check **www.arrl. org/awards/** for current processing fees for this certificate.

Contacts made on 10/18/24 MHz or via satellites are not allowed for the 5-band certificate and 6-band sticker. All contacts for the QRP endorsement must be made on or after January 1, 1985, while running a maximum power of 5 W output.

Current rules and forms are available online at **www.iaru. org/wac/**. For amateurs in the United States or countries without IARU representation, applications and QSL cards should be sent to the ARRL Awards Manager, 225 Main St, Newington, CT 06111. After verification, the cards will be returned, and the award sent soon afterward. Check **www.iaru.org/wac/** for the current fee schedule. Sufficient return postage for the cards, in the form of a self-addressed, stamped envelope or funds is required. US amateurs must have current ARRL membership. All other applicants must be members of their national Amateur Radio Society affiliated with IARU and must apply through the Society only.

A-1 Operator Club (A-1 OP)

Only the best operators can qualify for membership in the A-1 Operator's Club. Members must demonstrate superior competence and performance in the many facets of Amateur Radio operation: CW, phone, procedures, copying ability,

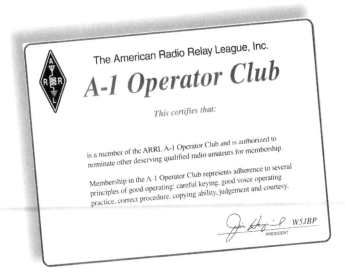

VHF/UHF Century Club Award

The VHF/UHF Century Club (VUCC) is awarded for contacts on 50 MHz and above with stations located in Maidenhead 2° × 1° grid locators. Grid locators are designated by a combination of two letters and two numbers (for example, W1AW is in FN31 in central Connecticut). More information on grid locators can be found in the VHF/UHF Operating chapter. The *ARRL Amateur Radio Map of North America*, *The ARRL World Grid Locator Atlas* and the *ARRL Grid Locator for North America* are available from **www.arrl.org/catalog** and show grid locators in the US.

The VUCC certificate and endorsements are available to amateurs worldwide. ARRL membership is required for US hams, possessions and Puerto Rico. The minimum number of grid locators needed to qualify for a certificate is as follows: 50 MHz, 144 MHz and Satellite — 100 credits; 222 MHz and 432 MHz — 50 credits; 902 MHz and 1296 MHz — 25 credits; 2.3 GHz — 10 credits; 3.4 GHz, 5.7 GHz, 10 GHz,

24 GHz, 47 GHz, 75 GHz, 119 GHz, 142 GHz, 241 GHz and Laser (300 GHz) — 5 credits.

Endorsements are available for additional contacts at these levels: 50 MHz, 144 MHz and Satellite — 25; 222 MHz and 432 MHz — 10 credits; 902 MHz and above 5 credits

Contacts must be dated January 1, 1983, and later to count. Separate bands count for separate awards. Repeater and/or crossband contacts are not permitted except for Satellite awards. Contacts with aeronautical mobile stations do not count, but maritime mobiles are okay.

For VUCC awards on 50 through 1296 MHz and Satellite, all contacts must be made from locations no more than 200 km apart. For SHF awards, contacts must be made from a single location, defined as within a 300-meter diameter circle.

Application procedure (please follow carefully): Confirmations (QSLs) and application forms (MSD-259 and MSD-260) must be submitted to an approved VHF Awards Manager for certification. You can download the most current rules and forms, as well as search for the nearest ARRL VHF Awards Manager, by following the links from **www.arrl.org/awards/vucc/**. You can also obtain forms from Special Requests, ARRL HQ, 225 Main St, Newington, CT 06111 (please be specific in your request and include an SASE). Foreign VUCC applications should be checked by the Awards Manager for their IARU Member Society in their respective country. Do not send cards to HQ, unless asked to do so.

For the convenience of the Awards Manager in checking cards, applicants may indicate in pencil (pencil *only*) the grid locator on the address side of the cards that do not clearly indicate the grid locator. The applicant affirms that he/she has accurately determined the proper location from the address information given on the card by signing the affirmation statement on the application. Cards must be sorted alphabetically by field and then numerically from 00 to 99 within that field. (For example, DM03, DM04, EN42, FN20, FM29 and so on.)

Where it is necessary to mail cards for certification, sufficient postage for proper return of all cards and paperwork, in addition to appropriate fees, must be included along with a separate self-addressed mailing label. An SASE is not necessary when a certificate will be issued, since a special mailing tube is used. ARRL accepts no responsibility for cards handled by mail to and from VHF Awards Managers and will not honor any claims.

Enclosed with the initial VUCC certificate from HQ will be a computer printout of the original list of grid locators for which the applicant has received credit (MSD-259). When applying for endorsements, the applicant will indicate in RED on the right hand side of the page those new grid locators for which credit is sought, and submit cards for certification to an Awards Manager. A new updated computer printout will be returned with appropriate endorsement sticker(s). Thus, a current list of grid locators worked is always in the hands of the VUCC award holder, available to the VHF Awards Manager during certification, and a permanent historical record always maintained at HQ.

Complete information on the VUCC Program can be found **www.arrl.org/awards/vucc/**. This includes all the forms, rules, current fees and copy of the January 1983 *QST* article.

DX Century Club (DXCC)

DXCC is the premier operating award in Amateur Radio. The DXCC certificate is available to League members in the US and possessions, and Puerto Rico, and all amateurs in the rest of the world. There are several DXCC awards available and fall roughly into four categories:

Mixed bands and modes: Mixed

Mode specific: Phone, CW, RTTY, Satellite

Band specific: All contacts on 160, 80, 40, 30, 20, 17, 15, 12, 10, 6 or 2 meters.

The basic award level is 100 DXCC entities. Endorsements are available in specific increments beyond the 100 entity level. The DXCC Honor Roll is awarded to those participants who are closing in on working all current entities, and the #1 Honor Roll plaque is available when you work them all.

The complete DXCC rules are quite lengthy. You can download the most current rules and forms, as well as search for the nearest DXCC Card Checker following the links from **www.arrl.org/awards/dxcc/**. Also see the References chapter of this book for more details on DXCC and the DXCC List.

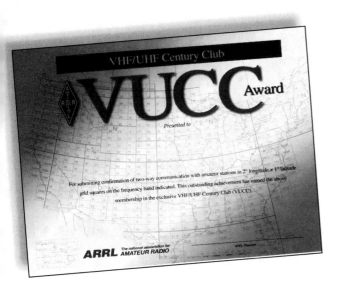

5BDXCC

For those who enjoy the thrill of the hunt on more than one band, the 5-Band DXCC (5BDXCC) award is a formidable accomplishment. This award encourages more uniform DX activity throughout the amateur bands, encourages the development of more versatile antenna systems and equipment, provides a challenge for DXers, and enhances amateur-band occupancy.

The 5BDXCC certificate is issued after the applicant submits QSLs representing two-way contact with 100 different DXCC countries on each of the 80, 40, 20, 15 and 10-meter Amateur Radio bands. 5BDXCC is endorsable for additional bands: 160, 30, 17, 12, 6 and 2 meters. In addition to the 5BDXCC certificate, a 5BDXCC plaque is available at an extra charge.

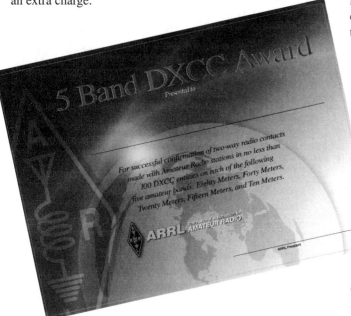

DXCC List Criteria

The ARRL DXCC List is the result of progressive changes in DXing since 1945. Each entity on the DXCC List contains some definable political or geographical distinctiveness. While the general policy for qualifying entities for the DXCC List has remained the same, there has been considerable change in the specific details of criteria which are used to test entities for their qualifications. See the DXCC rules at **www.arrl.org/awards/dxcc/** for the most current information.

QRP DXCC

In recognition of the popularity of QRP (low power) operating, the ARRL offers the QRP DX Century Club, or QRP DXCC. The award is available to amateurs who have contacted at least 100 DXCC entities (see the list at **www.arrl.org/awards/dxcc/**) using 5 W output or less, and standard DXCC rules apply. Contacts may have been made at any time since November 15, 1945, and no QSLs are required.

The QRP DXCC is a one-time award and is non-endorsable. Certificates will be dated, but not numbered. This award is separate and distinct from the traditional DXCC award program. Credits are not assigned to other DXCC awards.

The DXCC Challenge

The DXCC Challenge Award is given for working and confirming at least 1000 DXCC Entities on any Amateur bands, 1.8 through 54 MHz. The Challenge award is in the form of a plaque, which can be endorsed in increments of 500. Entities for each band are totaled to give the Challenge standing. Deleted entities do not count for this award. All contacts must be made after November 15, 1945. QSOs for the 160, 80, 40, 30, 20, 17, 15, 12, 10 and 6 meter bands qualify for this award. Bands with less than 100 contacts are acceptable for credit for this award. Check **www.arrl.org/awards/dxcc** for fees and more information.

The DeSoto Cup is presented to the DXCC Challenge leader as of the 30th of September each year. The DeSoto Cup is named for Clinton B. DeSoto, whose definitive article in October 1935 *QST* forms the basis of the DXCC award. Only one cup will be awarded to any single individual. A medal will be presented to the winner in subsequent years. Medals will also be awarded to the second and third place winners each year.

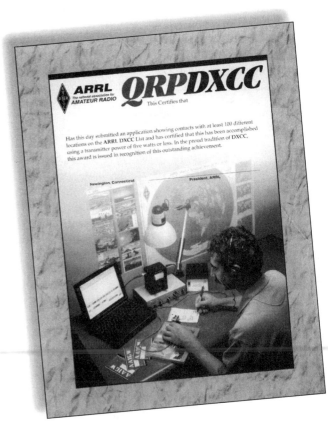

The award is available to amateurs worldwide, and you do not have to be an ARRL member to qualify. To apply for the QRP DXCC, just send a list of your contacts including call signs, countries/entities and contact dates. Do not send QSLs. The list must also carry a signed statement from you that all of the contacts were made with 5 W RF output (as measured at the antenna system input) or less.

Along with your contact list, include the application fee (see **www.arrl.org/awards/**). Make sure to indicate your mailing address and your name as you want it to appear on the certificate. Mail everything to: QRP DXCC, ARRL, 225 Main St, Newington, CT 06111.

RSGB ISLANDS ON THE AIR — IOTA

The IOTA Program was created by Geoff Watts, a leading British shortwave listener, in the mid-1960s. When it was taken over by the RSGB in 1985 it had already become, for some, a favorite award. Its popularity grows each year and it is highly regarded among amateurs worldwide. The information given here is just a summary of the program. Full information, rules and forms may be found at **www.rsgbiota.org**.

The IOTA Program consists of 21 separate certificates. They may be claimed by any licensed radio amateur eligible under the General Rules, who can produce evidence of having made two-way communication, since November 15, 1945, with the required number of Amateur Radio stations located on the islands both worldwide and regional. Part of the fun of IOTA is that it is an evolving program with new islands being activated for the first time.

The basic award is for working stations located on 100 is-

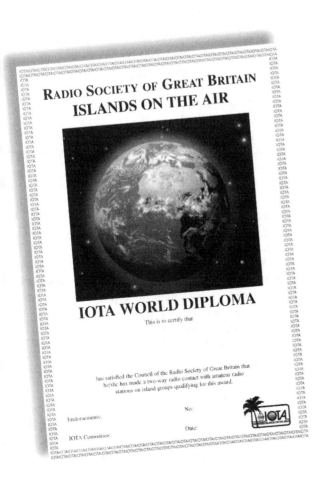

lands/groups. There are higher achievement awards for working 200, 300, 400, 500, 600, 700, 800, 900 and 1000 islands/groups. In addition there are seven continental awards (including Antarctica) and three regional awards — Arctic Islands, British Isles and West Indies — for contacting a specified number of islands/groups listed in each area. The IOTA World Diploma is available for working 50% of the numbered groups in each of the seven continents. A Plaque of Excellence is available for confirmed contacts with at least 750 islands/groups. Shields are available for every 25 further islands/groups. The IOTA 1000 Islands Trophy is available for contacting 1000 IOTA groups. Mini plates are available for 1025 to 1175 IOTA groups in increments of 25.

The rules require that QSL cards be submitted to nominated IOTA checkpoints for checking. Although paper applications may be used, on-line applications are strongly encouraged. These checkpoints are listed in the *RSGB IOTA Directory and Yearbook*.

A feature of the IOTA program is the annual Honor Roll which appears each Spring on the official RSGB IOTA Web site.

RSGB IOTA Directory

The official source of IOTA information is the *RSGB IOTA Directory*. This publication lists thousands of islands, grouped by continent and indexed by prefix, details the award rules, and provides application forms and a wealth of information and advice for the island enthusiast. The colorful new IOTA certificates are also shown. The latest *RSGB IOTA Directory* is an essential purchase for those interested in island-chasing. Copies are available from the ARRL at **www.arrl.org/catalog**.

CQ MAGAZINE AWARDS
Worked All Zones (WAZ)

The CQ WAZ Award will be issued to any licensed amateur station presenting proper QSL cards as proof of contact with the 40 zones of the world. QSL cards may be checked by any authorized CQ checkpoint or sent directly to the WAZ Award Manager, Floyd Gerald, N5FG, 17 Green Hollow Rd, Wiggins, MS 39577, e-mail **n5fg@cq-amateur-radio.com**. Many of the major DX clubs in the United States and Canada and most national Amateur Radio societies abroad are authorized CQ checkpoints. Check the CQ Web site, **www.cq-amateur-radio. com**, for the current rules, zone lists, forms, checkpoints, processing fees and payment information. Paper copies of zone maps, rules and application forms are available from the WAZ Award Manager or CQ Communications, 25 Newbridge Rd, Hicksville, NY 11801. Send a business-size (4 × 9-inch), self-addressed envelope with two units of First-Class postage or $2 (US stations), or a self-addressed envelope and 3 IRCs (non-US stations).

The official CQ WAZ Zone Map and the printed zone list will be used to determine the zone in which a station is located. Confirmation must be accompanied by a list of claimed zones, using CQ Form 1479, showing the call letters of the station contacted within each zone. Form 1479 should also clearly show the applicant's name, call letters and complete mailing address, as well as the award being applied for (such as Mixed, SSB, single band, and so forth).

All contacts must be made with licensed, land-based, amateur stations operating in authorized amateur bands, 160-10 meters. Any legal type of emission may be used, providing communication was established after November 15, 1945.

All contacts submitted by the applicant must be made from within the same country. It is recommended that each QSL clearly show the station's zone number. When the applicant submits cards for multiple call signs, evidence should be provided to show that he or she also held those call letters. Any altered or forged confirmations will result in permanent disqualification of the applicant. Decisions of the CQ DX Awards Advisory Committee on any matter pertaining to the administration of this award will be final.

All applications should be sent to the WAZ Award Manager after the QSL cards have been checked by an authorized CQ checkpoint.

WAZ By Mode and Band

In addition to the basic Mixed Mode award, certificates are available for these modes: AM, SSB, CW. RTTY, SSTV and Digital (any digital mode except RTTY). (For these awards, all contacts must be two-way in that mode and so indicated on the QSL cards.)

WAZ awards are also issued for various bands: 160 Meters (mixed only, contacts starting January 1, 1975); 80, 40, 20, 15 or 10 meters (any single mode, contacts starting January 1, 1973); 30, 17 or 12 meters (any single mode, contacts starting January 1, 1991); Satellite (mixed only, contacts starting January 1, 1989); and 6 Meters and EME (mixed only, contacts starting January 1, 1973). Applications and cards for Digital, 160 Meters, Satellite, 6 Meters and EME must be submitted directly to the WAZ Manager, not through checkpoints.

The 160 Meter WAZ Award requires that the applicant submit QSL cards from at least 30 zones. Stickers for 35, 36, 37, 38, 39 and 40 zones can be obtained from the WAZ Manager upon submission of the QSL cards and payment of the appropriate fees.

The Satellite and 6 Meter WAZ Awards require that the applicant submit QSL cards from at least 25 zones. Stickers for 30, 35, 36, 37, 38, 39 and 40 zones can be obtained from the WAZ Manager upon submission of the QSL cards and payment of the appropriate fees.

5 Band WAZ

CQ offers a most challenging DX award — 5 Band WAZ. Applicants who succeed in presenting proof of contact with the 40 zones of the world on these five HF bands — 80, 40, 20, 15 and 10 meters (for a total of 200) — will receive a special certificate in recognition of this achievement.

Contacts must be made after January 1, 1979, using any combination of modes (CW, SSB, RTTY). The award is available for Mixed Mode only. The first plateau, where the initial certificate is issued, requires a total of 150 of the possible 200 zones on a combination of the five bands. Applicants should use a separate sheet for each frequency band, using CQ Form 1479. Endorsements in increments of 10 are issued until the full 200 zone level is reached. A plaque is available at the 200 zone level.

Initial applications of up to 170 cards may be checked at an authorized checkpoint. Cards for all endorsements must be checked only by the WAZ Award Manager.

A regular WAZ or Single Band WAZ is a prerequisite for a 5 Band WAZ certificate. All applications should show the applicant's WAZ number. All applications should be sent to the WAZ Award Manager. The 5 Band WAZ Award is governed by the same rules as the regular WAZ Award and uses the same zone boundaries.

The CQ DX Awards Program

The CQ DX Award is issued in three categories: SSB, CW and RTTY. Each award requires proof of contact with 100 or more countries using that mode. All QSOs must be 2× SSB, 2× CW or 2× RTTY. Cross-mode or one-way QSOs are not valid for the CQ DX Awards. All contacts must be with licensed land-based amateur stations working in authorized amateur bands. Contacts with ships and aircraft cannot be counted. QSLs must be listed in alphabetical order by prefix, and all QSOs must be dated after November 15, 1945. The application (Form 1067B) and full rules and current fees are available from the CQ Web site, **www.cq-amateur-radio.com**.

QSL cards must be verified by one of the authorized checkpoints for the CQ DX Awards or must be included with the application and sent to the CQ DX Awards Manager, Billy Williams, N4UF, PO Box 9673, Jacksonville, FL 32208. In all cases, include adequate funds for return postage.

Endorsement stickers are issued for 150, 200, 250, 275, 300, 310 and 320 countries. The ARRL DXCC List constitutes the basis for the CQ DX Award country status. Deleted countries will not be valid for the CQ DX Awards. If a DXCC country is deleted, it will automatically be deleted from CQ award records and totals readjusted accordingly. Special endorsement stickers are available for 3.5/7 MHz and 28-MHz (100 countries); 1.8 MHz, QRP, Mobile, SSTV and Satellite (50 countries each).

The CQ DX Honor Roll lists all stations with a total of 275 countries or more. Separate Honor Rolls are maintained for SSB and CW. To remain on the Honor Roll, a station's country total must be updated annually.

Other CQ DX Awards

CQ also offers several other DX awards. Check **www. cq-amateur-radio.com** for details and forms.

The CQ WPX Award is for working different Amateur Radio prefixes around the world (NN1, DL7, JA6, 9J2 and so on). Awards start at 400 prefixes for Mixed Mode (CW and SSB/phone only) and 300 prefixes for 2×CW and 2×SSB.

The CQ DX Field Award rewards contacts with the 324 Maidenhead Grid Fields (10° latitude by 20° longitude rectangles lettered AA through RR). There are four categories — Mixed, CW, SSB and Digital — and 50 confirmed QSOs are required for the initial award. Endorsements are available at various levels up to the full 324 Fields. Special endorsement stickers are available for various bands and modes.

County Hunting: USA-CA Program

The United States of America Counties Award (USA-CA), also sponsored by *CQ*, is issued for confirmed two-way radio contacts with specified numbers of US counties. Full rules, forms and current fees are available from **www.cq-amateur-radio.com**.

The USA-CA is issued in seven different classes. Higher levels are awarded as endorsement seals the basic certificate. Also, special endorsements will be made for all one band or mode operations subject to the rules.

Class	Counties Required	States Required
USA-500	500	Any
USA-1000	1000	25
USA-1500	1500	45
USA-2000	2000	50
USA-2500	2500	50
USA-3000	3000	50
USA 3077	ALL	50

USA-CA is available to all licensed amateurs everywhere in the world. You can accumulate contacts toward the USA-CA Award with any call sign you have held, and from any operating QTHs or dates. All contacts must be confirmed by QSL, and such QSLs must be in your possession for examination by USA-CA officials. QSL cards must not be altered in any way. QSOs via repeaters, satellites, moonbounce and phone patches are not valid for USA-CA. So-called "team" contacts, where one person acknowledges a signal report and another returns a signal report, while both amateur call signs are logged, are not valid for USA-CA. Acceptable contact can be made with only one station at a time.

The National Zip Code & Directory of Post Offices will be helpful in some cases in determining identity of counties of contacts as ascertained by name of nearest municipality. Publication No. 65, Stock no. 039-000-00264-7, is available from the Superintendent of Documents, US Government Printing Office, Washington, DC 20402, but will be shipped only to US or Canada.

Unless otherwise indicated on QSL cards, the QTH printed on cards will determine county identity. For mobile and portable operations, the postmark shall identify the county unless other information is stated on QSL card to positively identify the county of operation In the case of cities, parks or reservations not within counties proper, applicants may claim any one of adjoining counties for credit (once).

The USA-CA program is administered by a *CQ* staff member acting as USA-CA Custodian, and all applications and related correspondence should be sent directly to the custodian at his or her QTH. Decisions of the Custodian in administering these rules and their interpretation, including future amendments, are final.

The scope of USA-CA makes it mandatory that special Record Books be used for application. For this purpose, *CQ* provides a 64-page 4.25 × 11-inch Record Book that contains application and certification forms and provides record-log space meeting the conditions of any class award and/or endorsement requested.

A completed USA-CA Record Book constitutes the medium of the basic award application and becomes the property of *CQ* for record purposes. On subsequent applications for either higher classes or for special endorsements, the applicant may

use additional Record Books to list required data or may make up his own alphabetical list conforming to requirements. Record Books are available from *CQ*, 25 Newbridge Rd, Hicksville, NY 11801. It is recommended that two be obtained, one for application use and one for personal file copy.

Make Record Book entries necessary for county identity and enter other log data necessary to satisfy any special endorsements (band-mode) requested. Have the certification form provided signed by two licensed amateurs (General or higher) or an official of a national-level radio organization or affiliated club verifying the QSL cards for all contacts as listed have been seen.

The USA-CA custodian reserves the right to request any specific cards for any reason. In such cases, the applicant should send sufficient postage for return of cards by registered mail. Send the original completed Record Book (not a copy) and certification forms and handling fee to Ted Melinosky, K1BV, 12 Wells Woods Rd, Columbia, CT 06237. For later applications for higher-class seals, send the Record Book or self-prepared list per rules and handling fee. For application for later special endorsements (band/mode) where certificates must be returned for endorsement, send certificate and handling fee.

County hunter activity may be found daily on these frequencies: 14.336 MHz SSB, 14.066.5 MHz CW and 10.122.5 MHz CW.

INFORMATION ON OTHER AWARDS

One of the handiest reference books for the awards chaser is *The K1BV DX Awards Directory*. The latest edition comprises 330 pages and is available on paper or online. You'll find information for more than 3000 different awards from 122 DXCC countries. *The K1BV DX Awards Directory* also contains a special chapter with hints and suggestions for both the beginning and advanced collector of awards. For further information and current pricing, visit **www.dxawards.com** or contact Ted Melinosky, K1BV, 12 Wells Woods Rd, Columbia, CT 06237. You can also

LOGBOOK OF THE WORLD

Note: As this book went to press, some changes to Logbook of The World procedures were under development. Please check **wwww.arrl.org/lotw** *for the latest details and more information.*

By the mid to late nineties, the electronic transmission of QSO confirmations was a concept whose time had come. In some senses, Internet technology was rendering the time-honored methods of QSLing obsolete. As postage and printing costs rose and delivery difficulties and delays increased, many people were asking "why not the Internet?" At the July 2000 ARRL Board meeting, staff presented a concept of Internet-based QSLing. But the proposal for confirming QSOs went in a direction that many people didn't expect.

When the term "electronic QSL" hit the streets as early as 1998, most people envisioned sending e-mail images of a QSL card to one another. Some even suggested that these e-mail exchanges would include digital signatures to assure the integrity of the information. But the proposal to the Board in 2000 was to create *a depository of QSO information* that would allow participants to submit radio logs containing digitally signed QSO records. Logs from all participants would be

collected in a secure, central database, where they could be scanned for matching confirmations. If a pair of matching QSO records were to be found, the resulting confirmation could be sent to the appropriate award system, where awards credit for both participants could be automatically recorded. After some discussion, Delta Division Director Rick Roderick, K5UR, spoke up and said, "So, this is like a Logbook of the World?" It is, and the name stuck.

Digital security experts, and active DXers/contesters Dick Green, WC1M, and Ted Demopoulos, KT1V, were hired to write the specifications for Logbook of The World (usually called LoTW or just Logbook). After some months pinning down system details, ARRL programmers and volunteers led by ARRL Web/Software Development Manager Jon Bloom, KE3Z, began writing the software for this complex and challenging project. Logbook of The World went "live" in September 2003. By mid-2007, the system had more than 17,000 users worldwide, had received more than 137 *million* QSOs, and had made nearly *10 million* confirmations. Several users had confirmed DXCC on 9 bands, with Mixed DXCC totals as high as 250 entities, using only QSOs confirmed in LoTW!

Trustworthy Data

Logbook of The World is designed to generate QSO confirmations that can be used for awards credits. That is to say, when you submit a log, your data is compared to all of the existing data in the database. If the log data you submit matches that in another station's record, the result is a confirmed QSO record. Either you or the other operator may then apply that confirmed QSO credit to various awards. All of this data is handled electronically, from the submission of the original logs to placement of the credit in an award database.

Creating a paper QSL card based on this electronic QSO data is *not* part of LoTW, although other services could be employed to perform that service. LoTW goes a step or two beyond the conception of a QSL card. A single QSL card is a one-sided request for a confirmation from the other side of the QSO. LoTW begins by verifying that a QSO has occurred between two stations, based on the "signed" data submitted by each.

In order for participants to have confidence in an electronic QSL system, they must be assured that each confirmation submitted to the system is authentic — that it comes from the true owner of the associated call. Until recently, such assurance would have been impossible. With the advent of digital signature technology, however, it is now possible for an Amateur Radio operator to indelibly "mark" QSO data with a signature connected to his/her call. The Logbook of The World system uses digital signatures to ensure the authenticity of every QSO record. Digital signatures utilize a technology called *Public Key Infrastructure* or *PKI*. These signatures cannot be forged, and the QSO data cannot be altered without detection. This not only ensures that we know the origin of the data, but also assures us that the data has not been altered anywhere along the way.

A Digital Certificate

In order to be able to submit your log to Logbook of The World, you will need to obtain a *digital certificate*. A digital certificate ties the identity of a participant to a digital key pair, which allows a electronic message to be signed.

Of course, in order for digital signatures to be trusted, we must be sure of the identity of each person to whom a certificate is assigned, so we will need to verify you are who you say you are. The security of the entire system depends heavily on the method used for verifying the user's identity. This process is called *Authentication*. Authentication for US calls relies on a combination of information in the *FCC license database* and postal mail addresses. Authentication for non-US calls relies on photocopies of a radio license and an official identification document. You can find out more about how to obtain a certificate by visiting the ARRL Logbook of The World Web site (**www.arrl.org/lotw/**).

You'll need to apply for, receive and install the digital certificate on your system to become a registered LoTW user and start submitting QSOs. The program *TQSLCert*, downloadable from the LoTW Web site, is for used generating requests for digital certificates and storing the resulting digital certificates that you receive from ARRL.

The Hows and Whens

To get started you should visit the LoTW Web site at **www.arrl.org/lotw/** where you can find directions, updates, news and tips. This system will be, to use a term from the World Wide Web, "always under construction" as we add software updates, additional capabilities and more user information. Once you have received and installed your digital certificate, another piece of software found on the LoTW Web site is are key to the process: *TQSL* is the utility program used to prepare log data for submission to LoTW.

Anyone with a suitable computer can submit data to LoTW as soon as they have received a digital certificate from ARRL. LoTW will accept signed logs in either ADIF (Amateur Data Interchange Format) or Cabrillo (contest log) format, which are standard in most commercial logging software. Log files are "signed" using a digital certificate. The signing process is a mathematical operation that will work best on a computers with a fast, modern processor, but older computers will work. At present, you need to use a computer with a *Windows, Linux* or *Mac OS* operating system to run *TQSL* and *TQSLCert*. Access to an Internet connection is necessary.

You may send in QSO information from your logs as far back in time as 1945. Computer logging really got going only in the late '80s and early '90s, so it is not going to be likely that

you will find confirmations for QSOs farther back than that. But many people have typed their old logs into logging programs, so one never knows. You can query the system to determine if a certain station has submitted a log.

Although there may be cases when you will want to use *TQSL's* ability to manually enter a submission for a small group of QSOs (perhaps just the ones you need), the best method will be to submit all of your contacts to give others credit for your QSO even if you have no interest in theirs. The first time, submit your whole log. After that, submit that portion created since you last submitted (resubmitting *all* of your QSOs just slows down the system and is of no benefit to you).

A number of popular logging and contesting programs include built-in support for LoTW. That makes it easier to select a group of QSOs and prepare them for submission. Some logging programs automate the process completely, digitally signing the QSOs with your certificate, generating the appropriate file for submission, and calling up your e-mail program to send the file to ARRL.

How am I going to receive awards credit? Look for links to "Awards" on the LoTW Web site. Here you can find out what countries or states you have confirmed in the system and follow the directions to select the ones that you would like to use for credit for your DXCC or WAS award. You can also link your existing DXCC records to your Logbook account to see what credits you already have and where the new Logbook credits fit in. You can even see which awards you earned while you were busy working the necessary stations!

One very important point: *ARRL will not be the "QSL Manager" for the stations submitting logs to Logbook of the World*. If a contact is not in the log, you will need to work it out with the station involved. We will not search the log for your contact. If you can't submit a match, you won't be able to receive a credit. Broken calls and incorrect QSO information won't be acceptable. A time window will allow some leeway to allow for variations in time keeping, however.

What does it cost? Everyone is invited to submit data — Logbook wants all logs! For this reason, there will be *no charge for submitting logs*. This all takes time and money, of course, and LoTW is being paid for initially by ARRL members, so there is be a per-QSO charge for each *credit used toward an award*. Check the LoTW Web site for the current fee schedule — you will be pleasantly surprised to see how much less expensive it is than the cost to print paper cards and exchange them via postal mail. Detailed instructions for using LoTW credits toward DXCC and WAS are shown on the Web site.

While we hope everyone will use and enjoy Logbook of The World, we realize that there will be those who cannot, or will not, use it. ARRL will *always* accept traditional QSL cards for its awards using the same applications and methods now in place. We do anticipate the nature of QSLing will change. We are confident that everyone will find their own "best" way to make use of this new technology. Most people use a combination of Logbook and traditional QSLing methods. Others have started "from scratch" and built credits for awards that in the past would have taken many years and hundreds or thousands of dollars in postage and printing costs to achieve. Some of those who have avoided operating because of the resulting QSL responsibilities have become more active. Will you be one of them?

Chapter 13

References

Item	Page
ARRL DXCC Rules	13-2
ARRL DXCC List	13-7
Allocation of International Call Sign Series	13-19
Morse Code Character Set	13-21
Morse Code for Other Languages	13-22
Spanish Phonetics	13-22
Morse Abbreviated ("Cut") Numbers	13-22
DX Operating Code	13-23
ARRL Procedural Signals (Prosigns)	13-24
Q Signals	13-24
The RST System	13-25
CW Abbreviations	13-26
ITU Recommended Phonetics	13-26
ARRL Numbered Radiograms	13-27
ARRL Field Organization Map	13-28
ARRL Grid Locator Map (North America)	13-29
KØOST Ham Outline Maps	
California Counties	13-30
South American Countries	13-31
Antarctica and Offshore Islands	13-32
European Countries	13-33
African Countries	13-34
Asian Countries	13-35
Chinese Provinces	13-36

Item	Page
ARRL Field Organization	13-37
K5ZI Azimuthal Equidistant Maps	
W1AW	13-46
Eastern USA	13-47
Central USA	13-48
Western USA	13-49
Alaska	13-50
Hawaii	13-51
Caribbean	13-52
Eastern South America	13-53
Southern South America	13-54
Antarctica	13-55
Western Europe	13-56
Eastern Europe	13-57
West Africa	13-58
East Africa	13-59
Southern Africa	13-60
Near East	13-61
Southern Asia	13-62
Southeast Asia	13-63
Far East	13-64
Australia	13-65
South Pacific	13-66

INTRODUCTION

The DXCC List is based upon the principle espoused by Clinton B. DeSoto, W1CBD, in his landmark 1935 *QST* article, "How to Count Countries Worked, A New DX Scoring System." DeSoto's article discussed problems DXers had in determining how to count the DX they had worked. He presented the solution that has worked successfully for succeeding generations of DXers.

In DeSoto's words, "The basic rule is simple and direct: *Each discrete geographical or political entity is considered to be a country.*" This rule has stood the test of time — from the original list published in 1937 to the *ARRL DXCC List* of today. For more than 60 years, the *DXCC List* has been the standard for DXers around the world.

DeSoto never intended that all DXCC "countries" would be countries in the traditional, or dictionary, meaning of the word. Rather, they are the distinct geographic and political Entities which DXers seek to contact. Individual achievement is measured by working and confirming the various Entities comprising the DXCC List. This is the essence of the DXCC program.

DXCC activity was interrupted by World War II. In 1947, the program started anew. Contacts are valid from November 15, 1945, the date US amateurs were authorized by the FCC to return to the air.

Over time, the criteria for the List has changed. However, Entities are not removed when changes are made. The List remains unchanged until an Entity no longer satisfies the criteria under which it was added. Thus, today's *DXCC List* does not fully conform with today's criteria.

SECTION I. BASIC RULES

1. The DX Century Club Award, with certificate and lapel pin is available to Amateur Radio operators throughout the world (see #15 for the DXCC Award Fee Schedule). ARRL membership is required for DXCC applicants in the US, its possessions, and Puerto Rico. ARRL membership is not required for foreign applicants. All DXCCs are endorsable (see Rule 5). There are 18 separate DXCC awards available, plus the DXCC Honor Roll:

a) Mixed (general type): Contacts may be made using any mode since November 15, 1945.

b) Phone: Contacts must be made using radiotelephone since November 15, 1945. Confirmations for cross-mode contacts for this award must be dated September 30, 1981, or earlier.

c) CW: Contacts must be made using CW since January 1, 1975. Confirmations for cross-mode contacts for this award must be dated September 30, 1981, or earlier.

d) RTTY: Contacts must be made using radioteletype since November 15, 1945. (Baudot, ASCII, AMTOR and packet count as RTTY.) Confirmations for cross-mode contacts for this award must be dated September 30, 1981, or earlier.

e) 160 Meter: Contacts must be made on 160 meters since November 15, 1945.

f) 80 Meter: Contacts must be made on 80 meters since November 15, 1945.

g) 40 Meter: Contacts must be made on 40 meters since November 15, 1945.

h) 30 Meter: Contacts must be made on 30 meters since November 15, 1945.

i) 20 Meter: Contacts must be made on 20 meters since November 15, 1945.

j) 17 Meter: Contacts must be made on 17 meters since November 15, 1945.

k) 15 Meter: Contacts must be made on 15 meters since November 15, 1945.

l) 12 Meter: Contacts must be made on 12 meters since November 15, 1945.

m) 10 Meter: Contacts must be made on 10 meters since November 15, 1945.

n) 6 Meter: Contacts must be made on 6 meters since November 15, 1945.

o) 2 Meter: Contacts must be made on 2 meters since November 15, 1945.

p) Satellite: Contacts must be made using satellites since March 1, 1965. Confirmations must indicate satellite QSO.

q) Five-Band DXCC (5BDXCC): The 5BDXCC certificate is available for working and confirming 100 current DXCC entities (deleted entities don't count for this award) on each of the following five bands: 80, 40, 20, 15, and 10 Meters. Contacts are valid from November 15, 1945.

The 5BDXCC is endorsable for these additional bands: 160, 30, 17, 12, 6, and 2 Meters. 5BDXCC qualifiers are eligible for an individually engraved plaque (at a charge of $40.00 US plus shipping).

r) The DXCC Challenge Award is given for working and confirming at least 1,000 DXCC band-Entities on any Amateur bands, 1.8 through 54 MHz (except 60 meters). This award is in the form of a plaque. Certificates are not available for this award. Plaques can be endorsed in increments of 500. Entities for each band are totaled to give the Challenge standing. Deleted entities do not count for this award. All contacts must be made after November 15, 1945. The DXCC Challenge plaque is available for $79.00 (plus shipping). QSOs for the 160, 80, 40, 30, 20, 17, 15, 12, 10 and 6 meter bands qualify for this award. Bands with less than 100 contacts are acceptable for credit for this award.

s) The DeSoto Cup is presented to the DXCC Challenge leader as of the 31st of December each year. The DeSoto Cup is named for Clinton B. DeSoto, whose definitive article in October, 1935 *QST* forms the basis of the DXCC award. Only one cup will be awarded to any single individual. A medal will be presented to the winner in subsequent years. Medals will also be awarded to the second and third place winners each year.

t) Honor Roll: Attaining the DXCC Honor Roll represents the pinnacle of DX achievement:

i) Mixed—To qualify, you must have a total confirmed entity count that places you among the numerical top ten DXCC entities total on the current DXCC List (example: if there are 337 current DXCC entities, you must have at least 328 entities confirmed).

ii) Phone—same as Mixed.

iii) CW—same as Mixed.

iv) RTTY—same as Mixed.

To establish the number of DXCC entity credits needed to qualify for the Honor Roll, the maximum possible number of current entities available for credit is published monthly on the ARRL DXCC Web Page. First-time Honor Roll members are recognized monthly on the ARRL DXCC Web Page. Complete Honor Roll standings are published annually in *QST*, usually in the August issue. See DXCC notes in *QST* for specific information on qualifying for this Honor Roll standings list. Once recognized on this list or in a subsequent monthly update of new members, you retain your Honor Roll standing until the next standings list is published. In addition, Honor Roll members who have been listed in the previous Honor Roll Listings or have gained Honor Roll status in a subsequent monthly listing are recognized in the DXCC Annual List. Honor Roll qualifiers receive an Honor Roll endorsement sticker for their DXCC certificate and are eligible for an

Honor Roll lapel pin $6 (plus shipping) and an Honor Roll plaque ($40 plus shipping). Write the DXCC Desk for details or check out the Century Club Item Order Form in the back of this book or at http://www.arrl.org/awards/dxcc/

v) #1 Honor Roll: To qualify for a Mixed, Phone, CW or RTTY Number One plaque, you must have worked every entity on the current DXCC List. Write the DXCC Desk for details. #1 Honor Roll qualifiers receive a #1 Honor Roll endorsement sticker for their DXCC certificate and are eligible for a #1 Honor Roll lapel pin ($6) and a #1 Honor Roll plaque ($55 plus shipping).

2. Written Proof: Except in cases where the rules of Section IV apply, proof of two-way communication (contacts) must be submitted directly to ARRL Headquarters for all DXCC credits claimed. Photocopies and electronically transmitted confirmations (including, but not limited to fax, telex and telegram) are not currently acceptable for DXCC purposes. Exception: Confirmations created and delivered by ARRL's Logbook of the World system are acceptable for DXCC credit.

The use of a *current* official DXCC application form or an approved facsimile (for example, **exactly** reproduced by a computer program) is required. Such forms must include provision for listing callsign, date, band, mode, and DXCC entity name. Complete application materials are available from ARRL Headquarters. Confirmations for a total of 100 or more different DXCC credits must be included with your first application.

Cards contained in the original received envelopes or in albums will be returned at applicant's expense without processing.

3. The ARRL DXCC List is based on the DXCC List Criteria.

4. Confirmation data for two-way communications must include the call signs of both stations, the Entity name as shown in the DXCC List, mode, and date, time and band. Except as permitted in Rule 1, cross-mode contacts are not permitted for DXCC credits. Confirmations not containing all required information may be rejected.

5. Endorsement stickers for affixing to certificates or pins will be awarded as additional DXCC credits are granted. For the Mixed, Phone, CW, RTTY, 40, 30, 20, 17, 15, 12 and 10-Meter DXCC, stickers are provided in exact multiples of 50, i.e. 150, 200, etc. between 100 and 250 DXCC credits, in multiples of 25 between 250 and 300, and in multiples of 5 above 300 DXCC credits.

For 160-Meter, 80-Meter, 6-Meter, 2-Meter and Satellite DXCC, the stickers are issued in exact multiples of 25 starting at 100 and multiples of 10 above 200, and in multiples of 5 between 250 and 300. Confirmations for DXCC credit may be submitted in any increment, but stickers and listings are provided only after a new level has been attained.

6. All contacts must be made with amateur stations working in the authorized amateur bands or with other stations licensed or authorized to work amateurs. Contacts made through "repeater" devices or any other power relay methods (other than satellites for Satellite DXCC) are invalid for DXCC credit.

7. Any Amateur Radio operation should take place only with the complete approval and understanding of appropriate administration officials. In countries where amateurs are licensed in the normal manner, credit may be claimed only for stations using regular government-assigned call signs or portable call signs where reciprocal agreements exist or the host government has so authorized portable operation. Without documentation supporting the operation of an amateur station, credit will not be allowed for contacts with such stations in any country that has temporarily or permanently closed down Amateur Radio operations by special government edict or policy where amateur licenses were formerly issued in the normal manner. In any case, credit will be given for contacts where adequate evidence of authorization by appropriate authorities exists, notwithstanding any such previous or subsequent edict or policy.

8. All stations contacted must be "land stations." Contacts with ships and boats, anchored or underway, and airborne aircraft, cannot be counted. For the purposes of this award, remote control operating points must also be land based. *Exception*: Permanently docked exhibition ships, such as the Queen Mary and other historic ships will be considered land based.

9. All stations must be contacted from the same DXCC Entity. The location of any station shall be defined as the location of the transmitter. For the purposes of this award, remote operating points must be located within the same DXCC Entity as the transmitter and receiver.

10. All contacts must be made using callsigns issued to the same station licensee. Contacts made by an operator other than the licensee must be made from a station owned and usually operated by the licensee and must be made in accordance with the regulations governing the license grant. Contacts may be made from other stations provided they are personally made by the licensee. The intent of this rule is to prohibit credit for contacts made for you by another operator from another location. You may combine confirmations from several callsigns held for credit to one DXCC award, as long as the provisions of Rule 9 are met. Contacts made from club stations using a club callsign may not be used for credit to an individual's DXCC.

11. All confirmations must be submitted exactly as received by the applicant. The submission of altered, forged, or otherwise invalid confirmations for DXCC credit may result in disqualification of the applicant and forfeiture of any right to DXCC membership. Determinations by the ARRL Awards Committee concerning submissions or disqualification shall be final. The ARRL Awards Committee shall also determine the future eligibility of any DXCC applicant who has ever been barred from DXCC.

12. Conduct: Exemplary conduct is expected of all amateur radio operators participating in the DXCC program. Evidence of intentionally disruptive operating practices or inappropriate ethical conduct in *any* aspect of DXCC participation may lead to disqualification from all participation in the program by action of the ARRL Awards Committee.

Actions that may lead to disqualification include, but are not limited to:

a) The submission of forged or altered confirmations.

b) The presentation of forged or altered documents in support of an operation.

c) Participation in activities that create an unfavorable impression of amateur radio with government authorities. Such activities include malicious attempts to cause disruption or disaccreditation of an operation.

d) Blatant inequities in confirmation (QSL) procedures. Continued refusal to issue QSLs under certain circumstances may lead to disqualification. Complaints relating to monetary issues involved in QSLing will generally not be considered, however.

13. Each DXCC applicant, by applying, or submitting documentation, stipulates to:

a) Having observed all pertinent governmental regulations for Amateur Radio in the country or countries concerned.

b) Having observed all DXCC rules.

c) Being bound by the DXCC rules.

d) Being bound by the decisions of the ARRL Awards Committee.

14. All DXCC applications (for both new awards and endorsements) must include sufficient funds to cover the cost of returning all confirmations (QSL cards) via the method selected. Funds must be in US dollars using US currency, check or money order made payable to the ARRL, or credit card number with expiration date. Address all correspondence and inquiries relating to DXCC awards and all applications to: ARRL Headquarters, DXCC Desk, 225 Main St., Newington, CT 06111, USA, or send an e-mail to dxcc@arrl.org

15. Fees. All amateurs applying for their very first DXCC Award will be charged a one-time registration fee. For ARRL Members this fee is $12. For foreign non-ARRL members this fee is $22.

All first time applicants will receive one free DXCC certificate and lapel pin. Applicants must provide adequate return postage for QSL cards.

a) A $12.00 fee will be charged for each additional DXCC certificate issued, whether new or replacement.

b) Applications may be presented in person at ARRL HQ, and at certain ARRL conventions. When presented at conventions in this manner, such applications shall be limited to 120 QSOs maximum, and an additional $7.00 fee will apply. Applications processed "while-you-wait" at ARRL HQ will be accessed an additional $9.00 fee.

c) Each ARRL member will be charged $12.00 plus postage for the first submission of the year, up to 120 QSOs.

d) Foreign non-ARRL members will be charged $22.00 plus postage for their first submission in a calendar year. Fees in 15. a), 15. b), and 15. d), and 15. f) also apply.

e) A $0.15 fee will be charged for each QSO credited beyond the limits described in 15. b), 15. c), and 15. f).

f) DXCC participants who wish to submit more than once in a calendar year will be charged an additional $10 fee for each second or subsequent application. The fees for a second or subsequent submission in a calendar year are $22 for ARRL members and $32 for foreign non-ARRL members. *For a limited time, no Additional $10 fee is charged for second and subsequent applications if LoTW credits are included.* The $12 application fee still applies. Return postage must be provided by applicant. Charges from 15. a), 15. b) and 15. d) apply.

16. The ARRL DX Advisory Committee (DXAC) requests your comments and suggestions for improving DXCC. Address correspondence, including petitions for new listing consideration, to ARRL Headquarters, DXAC, 225 Main St., Newington, CT 06111, USA. The DXAC may be contacted by e-mail via the DXCC Desk at **dxcc@arrl.org Correspondence on routine DXCC matters should be addressed to the DXCC Desk, or by e-mail to dxcc@arrl.org**

SECTION II. DXCC LIST CRITERIA

Introduction:

The ARRL DXCC List is the result of progressive changes in DXing since 1945. Each Entity on the DXCC List contains some definable political or geographical distinctiveness. While the general policy for qualifying Entities for the DXCC List has remained the same, there has been gradual evolution in the specific details of criteria which are used to test Entities for their qualifications. The full DXCC List does not conform completely with current criteria, for some of the listings were recognized from pre-WWII or were accredited with earlier versions of the criteria. In order to maintain continuity with the past, as well as to maintain a robust DXCC List, all Entities on the List at the time the 1998 revision became effective were retained.

Definitions:

Certain terms occur frequently in the DXCC criteria and are listed here. Not all of the definitions given are used directly in the criteria, but are listed in anticipation of their future use.

Entity: A listing on the DXCC List; a counter for DXCC awards. Previously denoted a DXCC "Country."

Event: An historical occurrence, such as date of admission to UN or ITU, that may be used in determining listing status.

Event Date: The date an Event occurs. This is the Start Date of all Event Entities.

Event Entity: An Entity created as the result of the occurrence of an Event.

Discovery Entity: An Entity "Discovered" after the listing is complete. This applies only to Geographic Entities, and may occur after a future rule change, or after an Event has changed its status.

Discovery Date: Date of the rule change or Event which prompts addition of the Entity. This is the Start Date for a Discovery Entity.

Original Listing: An Entity which was on the DXCC List at the time of inception.

Start Date: The date after which confirmed two-way contact credits may be counted for DXCC awards.

Add Date: The date when the Entity will be added to the List, and cards will be accepted. This date is for administrative purposes only, and will occur after the Start Date.

Island: A naturally formed area of land surrounded by water, the surface of which is above water at high tide. For the purposes of this award, it must consist of connected land, of which at least two surface points must be separated from each other by not less than 100 meters measured in a straight line from point to point. All of the connected land must be above the high tide mark, as demonstrated on a chart of sufficient scale. For the purposes of this award, any island, reef, or rocks of less than this size shall not be considered in the application of the water separation criteria described in Part 2 of the criteria.

Criteria:

Additions to the DXCC List may be made from time to time as world conditions dictate. Entities may also be removed from the List as a result of political or geographic change. Entities removed from the List may be returned to the List in the future, should they requalify under this criteria. However, an Entity requalified does so as a totally new Entity, not as a reinstated old one.

For inclusion in the DXCC List, conditions as set out below must be met. Listing is not contingent upon whether operation has occurred or will occur, but only upon the qualifications of the Entity.

There are five parts to the criteria, as follows:
1. Political Entities
2. Geographical Entities
3. Special Areas
4. Ineligible Areas
5. Removal Criteria

1. Political Entities:

Political Entities are those areas which are separated by reason of government or political division. They generally contain an indigenous population which is not predominantly composed of military or scientific personnel.

An Entity will be added to the DXCC List as a Political Entity if it meets one or more of the following criteria:

a) The entity is a UN Member State.

b) The entity has been assigned a callsign prefix bloc by the ITU[1]. A provisional prefix bloc assignment may be made by the Secretary General of ITU. Should such provisional assignments not be ratified later by the full ITU, the Entity will be removed from the DXCC List.

c) The Entity contains a permanent population, is administered by a local government, and is located at least 800 km from its parent. To satisfy the "permanent population" and "administered by a local government" criteria of this sub-section, an Entity must be listed on either (a) the U.S. Department of State's list of "Dependencies and Areas of Special Sovereignty" as having a local "Administrative Center," or (b) the United Nations list of "Non-Self-Governing Territories."

New Entities satisfying one or more of the conditions above will be added to the DXCC List by administrative action as of their "Event Date."

Entities qualifying under this section will be referred to as the "Parent" when considering separation under the section "Geographical Separation." Only Entities in this group will be acceptable as a Parent for separation purposes.

2. Geographic Separation Entity:

A Geographic Separation Entity may result when a single Po-

---

[1] The exceptions to this rule are international organizations, such as the UN and ICAO. These Entities are classified under Special Areas, 3. a); and Ineligible Areas, 4. b).

litical Entity is physically separated into two or more parts. The part of such a Political Entity that contains the capital city is considered the Parent for tests under these criteria. One or more of the remaining parts resulting from the separation may then qualify for separate status as a DXCC Entity if they satisfy paragraph a) or b) of the Geographic Separation Criteria, as follows.

a) Land Areas:

A new Entity results when part of a DXCC Entity is separated from its Parent by 100 kilometers or more of land of another DXCC Entity. Inland waters may be included in the measurement. The test for separation into two areas requires that a line drawn along a great circle in any direction from any part of the proposed Entity must not touch the Parent before crossing 100 kilometers of the intervening DXCC Entity.

b) Island Areas (Separation by Water):

A new Entity results in the case of an island under any of the following conditions:

i) The island is separated from its Parent, and any other islands that make up the DXCC Entity that contains the Parent, by 350 kilometers or more. Measurement of islands in a group begins with measurement from the island containing the capital city. Only one Entity of this type may be attached to any Parent.

ii) The island is separated from its Parent by 350 kilometers or more, and from any other island attached to that Parent in the same or a different island group by 800 kilometers or more.

iii) The island is separated from its Parent by intervening land or islands that are part of another DXCC Entity, such that a line drawn along a great circle in any direction, from any part of the island, does not touch the Parent before touching the intervening DXCC Entity. There is no minimum separation distance for the first island Entity created under this rule. Additional island Entities may be created under this rule, provided that they are similarly separated from the Parent by a different DXCC Entity and separated from any other islands associated with the Parent by at least 800 km.

3. Special Areas:

The Special Areas listed here may not be divided into additional Entities under the DXCC Rules. None of these constitute a Parent Entity, and none creates a precedent for the addition of similar or additional Entities.

a) The International Telecommunications Union in Geneva (4U1ITU) shall, because of its significance to world telecommunications, be considered as a Special Entity. No additional UN locations will be considered under this ruling.

b) The Antarctic Treaty, signed on 1 December 1959 and entered into force on 23 June 1961, establishes the legal framework for the management of Antarctica. The treaty covers, as stated in Article 6, all land and ice shelves below 60 degrees South. This area is known as the Antarctic Treaty Zone. Article 4 establishes that parties to the treaty will not recognize, dispute, or establish territorial claims and that they will assert no new claims while the treaty is in force. Under Article 10, the treaty States will discourage activities by any country in Antarctica that are contrary to the terms of the treaty. In view of these Treaty provisions, no new Entities below 60 degrees South will be added to the DXCC List as long as the Treaty remains in force.

c) The Spratly Islands, due to the nature of conflicting claims, and without recognizing or refuting any claim, is recognized as a Special Entity. Operations from this area will be accepted with the necessary permissions issued by an occupying Entity. Operations without such permissions, such as with a self-assigned (e.g., 1S) callsign, will not be recognized for DXCC credit.

d) Control of Western Sahara (S0) is currently at issue between Morocco and the indigenous population. The UN has stationed a peacekeeping force there. Until the sovereignty issue is settled, only operations licensed by the RASD shall count for DXCC purposes.

e) Entities on the 1998 DXCC List that do not qualify under the current criteria remain as long as they retain the status under which they were originally added. A change in that status will result in a review in accordance with Rule 5 of this Section.

4. Ineligible Areas:

a) Areas having the following characteristics are not eligible for inclusion on the DXCC List, and are considered as part of the host Entity for DXCC purposes:

i) Any extraterritorial legal Entity of any nature including, but not limited to, embassies, consulates, monuments, offices of the United Nations agencies or related organizations, other inter-governmental organizations or diplomatic missions;

ii) Any area with limited sovereignty or ceremonial status, such as monuments, indigenous areas, reservations, and homelands.

iii) Any area classified as a Demilitarized Zone, Neutral Zone or Buffer Zone.

b) Any area which is unclaimed or not owned by any recognized government is not eligible for inclusion on the DXCC List and will not count for DXCC purposes.

5. Removal Criteria:

a) An Entity may be removed from the List if it no longer satisfies the criteria under which it was added. However, if the Entity continues to meet one or more currently existing rules, it will remain on the List.

b) An Entity may be removed from the List if it was added to the List:

i) Based on a factual error (Examples of factual errors include inaccurate measurements, or observations from incomplete, inaccurate or outdated charts or maps); and

ii) The error was made less than five years earlier than its proposed removal date.

c) A change in the DXCC Criteria shall not affect the status of any Entity on the DXCC List at the time of the change. In other words, criteria changes will not be applied retroactively to Entities on the List.

SECTION III. ACCREDITATION CRITERIA

1. Each nation of the world manages its telecommunications affairs differently. Therefore, a rigid, universal accreditation procedure cannot be applied in all situations. During more than 50 years of DXCC administration, basic standards have evolved in establishing the legitimacy of an operation.

It is the purpose of this section to establish guidelines that will assure that DXCC credit is given only for contacts with operations that are conducted with proper licensing and have established a legitimate physical presence within the Entity to be credited. Any operation that satisfies these conditions (in addition to the applicable elements of SECTION I., Rules 6, 7, 8, and 9) will be accredited. It is the intent of the DXCC administration to be guided by the actions of sovereign nations when considering the accreditation of amateur radio operation within their jurisdiction. DXCC will be reasonably flexible in reviewing licensing documentation. Conversely, findings by a host government indicating non-compliance with their amateur radio regulations may cause denial or revocation of accreditation.

2. The following points should be of particular interest to those seeking accreditation for a DX operation:

a) The vast majority of operations are accredited routinely without a requirement for the submission of authenticating documentation. However, all such documents should be retained by the operator in the unlikely event of a protest.

b) In countries where Amateur Radio operation has not been permitted or has been suspended or where some reluctance to authorize amateur stations has been noted, authenticating documents may be required before accrediting an operation.

c) Special permission may be required from a governmental agency or private party before entering certain DXCC Entities for the purpose of conducting amateur radio operations even though the Entity is part of a country with no amateur radio restrictions. Examples of such Entities are Desecheo I. (KP5); Palmyra I. (KH5); and Glorioso Islands (FR/G).

3. For those cases where supporting documentation is required, the following can be used as a guide to identify those documents necessary for accreditation.

a) Photocopy of license or operating authorization.

b) Photocopy of passport entry and exit stamps.

c) For islands, a landing permit and a signed statement of the transporting ship's, boat's, or aircraft's captain, showing all pertinent data, such as date, place of landing, etc.

d) For locations where special permission is known to be required to gain access, evidence of this permission must be presented.

e) It is expected that all DXpeditions will observe any environmental rules promulgated by the administration under whose authority the operation takes place. In the event that no such rules are actually promulgated, the DXpedition should leave the DXpedition site as they found it.

4. These accreditation requirements are intended to preserve the integrity of the DXCC program and to ensure that the program does not encourage amateurs to "bend the rules" in their enthusiasm, possibly jeopardizing the future development of Amateur Radio. Every effort will be made to apply these criteria uniformly and to make a determination consistent with these objectives.

5. The presentation in any public forum of logs or other representations of station operation showing details of station activity or other information from which all essential QSO elements (time, date, band, mode and callsign) for individual contacts can be derived creates a question as to the integrity of the claimed QSOs with that station during the period encompassed by the log. Presentation of such information in any public forum by the station operator, operators or associated parties is not allowed and may be considered sufficient reason to deny ARRL award credit for contacts with any station for which such presentations have been made. Persistent violation of this provision may result in disqualification from the DXCC program.

SECTION IV. FIELD CHECKING OF QSL CARDS

QSL cards for new DXCC awards and endorsements may be checked by a DXCC Card Checker. This program applies to any DXCC award for an individual or station, except those specifically excluded.

1) Entities Eligible for Field Checking:

a) All cards dated ten years or less from the calendar year of the application may be checked, except for those awards specifically excluded from the program. 160 meter cards are currently excluded from this program. QSLs for years more than ten calendar years from the application date must be submitted directly to ARRL Headquarters. All deleted entities must be submitted to ARRL HQ.

b) The ARRL Awards Committee determines which entities are eligible for Field Checking.

2) DXCC Card Checkers:

a) Nominations for Card Checkers may be made by:

i) The Section Manager of the section in which the prospective checker resides.

ii) An ARRL affiliated DX specialty club with at least 25 members who are DXCC members, and which has DX as its primary interest. If there are any questions regarding the validity of a DX club, the issue shall be determined by the division director where the DX club is located. A person does not have to be a member of a nominating DX club.

iii) By Division Director.

b) Appointments are limited to one per section, one per DX club and one per division.

c) Qualifications:

i) Those nominated as a card checker must be of known integrity, and must be personally known to the person nominating them for appointment.

Recent Changes to the DXCC List

Prefix	Entity	Start Date	Add Date
YT-YU, YZ	Montenegro	6/28/06	6/28/06
KH8	Swains I.	7/22/06	10/1/06

ii) Candidates must be ARRL members who hold a DXCC award endorsed for at least 150 entities.

iii) Candidates must complete an open book test about DXCC rules concerning QSL cards and the Card Checker training guide.

iv) The applicant must be willing to serve at reasonable times and places, including at least one state or Division ARRL Convention each year.

v) The applicant must have e-mail and Internet capabilities, and must maintain current e-mail address with DXCC Desk.

d) Approval:

Applications for DXCC Card Checkers are approved by the Director of the ARRL Division in which they reside and are appointed by the Membership Services Manager.

e) Appointments are made for a two year period. Retention of appointees is determined by performance as determined by the DXCC Desk.

3) Card Checking Process:

a) Only eligible cards can be checked by DXCC Card Checkers. An application for a first time ever award shall contain a minimum of 100 QSL confirmations from the list and shall not contain any QSLs that are not eligible for this program. Additional cards may not be sent to HQ with field checked applications. The application may contain any number of cards, subject to eligibility requirements and fees as determined by Section I, Basic, 15.

b) It is the applicant's responsibility to get cards to and from the DXCC Card Checker.

c) Checkers may, at their own discretion, handle members' cards by mail.

d) The ARRL is not responsible for cards handled by DXCC Card Checkers and will not honor any claims.

e) The QSL cards may be checked by one DXCC Card Checker.

f) The applicant and DXCC Card Checker must sign the application form. (See Section I no. 11 regarding altered, forged or otherwise invalid confirmations.)

g) The applicant shall provide a stamped no. 10 envelope (business size) addressed to ARRL HQ to the DXCC Card Checker. The applicant shall also provide the applicable fees (check or money order payable to ARRL-no cash, credit card number and expiration date is also acceptable).

h) The DXCC Card Checker will forward completed applications and appropriate fee(s) to ARRL HQ.

4) ARRL HQ involvement in the card checking process:

a) ARRL HQ staff will receive field-checked applications, enter application data into DXCC records and issue DXCC credits and awards as appropriate.

b) ARRL HQ staff will perform random audits of applications. Applicants or members may be requested to forward cards to HQ for checking before or after credit is issued.

c) The applicant and the DXCC Card Checker will be advised of any errors or discrepancies encountered by ARRL staff.

d) ARRL HQ staff provides instructions and guidelines to DXCC Card Checkers.

5) Applicants and DXCC members may send cards to ARRL Headquarters at any time for review or recheck if the individual feels that an incorrect determination has been made.

ARRL DXCC LIST

All entities on the current list are eligible for field checking.

Note: * Indicates current list of entities for which QSLs may be forwarded by the ARRL Membership Outgoing QSL Service.

Note: † Indicates entities with which US Amateurs may legally handle third-party message traffic.

Prefix	Entity	CONTINENT	ZONE ITU	ZONE CQ	MIXED	PHONE	CW	RTTY	SAT	160	80	40	30	20	17	15	12	10	6
	Spratly Is.	AS	50	26															
1A[1]	Sov. Mil. Order of Malta	EU	28	15															
3A*	Monaco	EU	27	14															
3B6, 7	Agalega & St. Brandon Is.	AF	53	39															
3B8	Mauritius	AF	53	39															
3B9	Rodriguez I.	AF	53	39															
3C	Equatorial Guinea	AF	47	36															
3CØ	Annobon I.	AF	52	36															
3D2*	Fiji	OC	56	32															
3D2*	Conway Reef	OC	56	32															
3D2*	Rotuma I.	OC	56	32															
3DA†	Swaziland	AF	57	38															
3V*	Tunisia	AF	37	33															
3W, XV	Vietnam	AS	49	26															
3X	Guinea	AF	46	35															
3Y*	Bouvet	AF	67	38															
3Y*	Peter 1 I.	AN	72	12															
4J, 4K	Azerbaijan	AS	29	21															
4L*	Georgia	AS	29	21															
4O[47]*	Montenegro	EU	28	15															
4S*	Sri Lanka	AS	41	22															
4U_ITU†*	ITU HQ	EU	28	14															
4U_UN*	United Nations HQ	NA	08	05															
4W[44]	Timor - Leste	OC	54	28															
4X, 4Z†*	Israel	AS	39	20															
5A	Libya	AF	38	34															
5B, C4, P3*	Cyprus	AS	39	20															
5H-5I*	Tanzania	AF	53	37															
5N*	Nigeria	AF	46	35															
5R	Madagascar	AF	53	39															
5T[2]	Mauritania	AF	46	35															
5U[3]	Niger	AF	46	35															
5V	Togo	AF	46	35															

Prefix	Entity	CONTINENT	ITU	CQ	MIXED	PHONE	CW	RTTY	SAT	160	80	40	30	20	17	15	12	10	6
5W*	Samoa	OC	62	32															
5X*	Uganda	AF	48	37															
5Y-5Z*	Kenya	AF	48	37															
6V-6W4*	Senegal	AF	46	35															
6Y†*	Jamaica	NA	11	08															
7O5	Yemen	AS	39	21, 37															
7P	Lesotho	AF	57	38															
7Q	Malawi	AF	53	37															
7T-7Y*	Algeria	AF	37	33															
8P*	Barbados	NA	11	08															
8Q	Maldives	AS/AF	41	22															
8R†*	Guyana	SA	12	09															
9A6*	Croatia	EU	28	15															
9G7†*	Ghana	AF	46	35															
9H*	Malta	EU	28	15															
9I-9J*	Zambia	AF	53	36															
9K*	Kuwait	AS	39	21															
9L†	Sierra Leone	AF	46	35															
9M2, 48*	West Malaysia	AS	54	28															
9M6, 88*	East Malaysia	OC	54	28															
9N	Nepal	AS	42	22															
9Q-9T*	Dem. Rep. of Congo	AF	52	36															
9U9	Burundi	AF	52	36															
9V10*	Singapore	AS	54	28															
9X9	Rwanda	AF	52	36															
9Y-9Z†*	Trinidad & Tobago	SA	11	09															
A2*	Botswana	AF	57	38															
A3	Tonga	OC	62	32															
A4*	Oman	AS	39	21															
A5	Bhutan	AS	41	22															
A6	United Arab Emirates	AS	39	21															
A7*	Qatar	AS	39	21															
A9*	Bahrain	AS	39	21															
AP*	Pakistan	AS	41	21															
B*	China	AS	(A)	23,24															
BS711	Scarborough Reef	AS	50	27															
BU-BX*	Taiwan	AS	44	24															
BV9P12	Pratas I.	AS	44	24															
C2	Nauru	OC	65	31															
C3*	Andorra	EU	27	14															

Prefix	Entity	CONTINENT	ITU	CQ	MIXED	PHONE	CW	RTTY	SAT	160	80	40	30	20	17	15	12	10	6
C5†	The Gambia	AF	46	35															
C6	Bahamas	NA	11	08															
C8-9*	Mozambique	AF	53	37															
CA-CE†*	Chile	SA	14,16	12															
CEØ†*	Easter I.	SA	63	12															
CEØ†*	Juan Fernandez Is.	SA	14	12															
CEØ†*	San Felix & San Ambrosio	SA	14	12															
CE9/KC4▲*	Antarctica	AN	(B)	(C)															
CM, CO†*	Cuba	NA	11	08															
CN	Morocco	AF	37	33															
CP†*	Bolivia	SA	12,14	10															
CT*	Portugal	EU	37	14															
CT3*	Madeira Is.	AF	36	33															
CU*	Azores	EU	36	14															
CV-CX†*	Uruguay	SA	14	13															
CYØ*	Sable I.	NA	09	05															
CY9*	St. Paul I.	NA	09	05															
D2-3	Angola	AF	52	36															
D4	Cape Verde	AF	46	35															
D6[13]†*	Comoros	AF	53	39															
DA-DR[14]*	Fed. Rep. of Germany	EU	28	14															
DU-DZ, 4D-4I†*	Philippines	OC	50	27															
E3[15]	Eritrea	AF	48	37															
E4[43]	Palestine	AS	39	20															
E5	N. Cook I.	OC	62	32															
E5	S. Cook I.	OC	62	32															
E7[29]†*	Bosnia-Herzegovina	EU	28	15															
EA-EH*	Spain	EU	37	14															
EA6-EH6*	Balearic Is.	EU	37	14															
EA8-EH8*	Canary Is.	AF	36	33															
EA9-EH9*	Ceuta & Melilla	AF	37	33															
EI-EJ*	Ireland	EU	27	14															
EK*	Armenia	AS	29	21															
EL†*	Liberia	AF	46	35															
EP-EQ*	Iran	AS	40	21															
ER*	Moldova	EU	29	16															
ES*	Estonia	EU	29	15															
ET*	Ethiopia	AF	48	37															
EU-EW*	Belarus	EU	29	16															
EX*	Kyrgyzstan	AS	30,31	17															

Prefix	Entity	Continent	ITU	CQ	MIXED	PHONE	CW	RTTY	SAT	160	80	40	30	20	17	15	12	10	6
EY*	Tajikistan	AS	30	17															
EZ*	Turkmenistan	AS	30	17															
F*	France	EU	27	14															
FG, TO*	Guadeloupe	NA	11	08															
FH, TO13*	Mayotte	AF	53	39															
FJ, TO49*	Saint Barthelemy	NA	11	08															
FK, TX*	New Caledonia	OC	56	32															
FK, TX45	Chesterfield Is.	OC	56	30															
FM, TO*	Martinique	NA	11	08															
FO, TX16*	Austral Is.	OC	63	32															
FO, TX*	Clipperton I.	NA	10	07															
FO, TX*	French Polynesia	OC	63	32															
FO, TX16*	Marquesas Is.	OC	63	31															
FP*	St. Pierre & Miquelon	NA	09	05															
FR/G, TO17*	Glorioso Is.	AF	53	39															
FR/J, E, TO17*	Juan de Nova, Europa	AF	53	39															
FR, TO*	Reunion I.	AF	53	39															
FR/T, TO*	Tromelin I.	AF	53	39															
FS, TO*	Saint Martin	NA	11	08															
FT/W*	Crozet I.	AF	68	39															
FT/X*	Kerguelen Is.	AF	68	39															
FT/Z*	Amsterdam & St. Paul Is.	AF	68	39															
FW*	Wallis & Futuna Is.	OC	62	32															
FY*	French Guiana	SA	12	09															
G, GX, M*	England	EU	27	14															
GD, GT, MD*	Isle of Man	EU	27	14															
GI, GN, MI*	Northern Ireland	EU	27	14															
GJ, GH, MJ*	Jersey	EU	27	14															
GM, GS, MM*	Scotland	EU	27	14															
GU, GP, MU*	Guernsey	EU	27	14															
GW, GC, MW*	Wales	EU	27	14															
H4*	Solomon Is.	OC	51	28															
H4Ø18*	Temotu Province	OC	51	32															
HA, HG*	Hungary	EU	28	15															
HB*	Switzerland	EU	28	14															
HBØ*	Liechtenstein	EU	28	14															
HC-HD†*	Ecuador	SA	12	10															
HC8-HD8†*	Galapagos Is.	SA	12	10															
HH†	Haiti	NA	11	08															
HI†*	Dominican Republic	NA	11	08															

Prefix	Entity	CONTINENT	ITU	CQ	MIXED	PHONE	CW	RTTY	SAT	160	80	40	30	20	17	15	12	10	6
HJ-HK, 5J-5K†*	Colombia	SA	12	09															
HK0†*	Malpelo I.	SA	12	09															
HK0†*	San Andres & Providencia	NA	11	07															
HL, 6K-6N*	Republic of Korea	AS	44	25															
HO-HP†*	Panama	NA	11	07															
HQ-HR†*	Honduras	NA	11	07															
HS, E2*	Thailand	AS	49	26															
HV	Vatican	EU	28	15															
HZ*	Saudi Arabia	AS	39	21															
*	Italy	EU	28	15, 33															
S0, IM0 *	Sardinia	EU	28	15															
2*	Djibouti	AF	48	37															
J3†*	Grenada	NA	11	08															
J5	Guinea-Bissau	AF	46	35															
6†*	St. Lucia	NA	11	08															
7†*	Dominica	NA	11	08															
J8†	St. Vincent	NA	11	08															
A-JS, 7J-7N*	Japan	AS	45	25															
D1 19*	Minami Torishima	OC	90	27															
D1 20*	Ogasawara	AS	45	27															
T-JV*	Mongolia	AS	32,33	23															
W*	Svalbard	EU	18	40															
X*	Jan Mayen	EU	18	40															
Y†*	Jordan	AS	39	20															
K,W, N, AA-AK†	United States of America	NA	6,7,8	3,4,5															
KG4†	Guantanamo Bay	NA	11	08															
KH0†	Mariana Is.	OC	64	27															
KH1†	Baker & Howland Is.	OC	61	31															
H2†*	Guam	OC	64	27															
KH3†*	Johnston I.	OC	61	31															
KH4†	Midway I.	OC	61	31															
KH5†	Palmyra & Jarvis Is.	OC	61,62	31															
KH5K†	Kingman Reef	OC	61	31															
KH6, 7†*	Hawaii	OC	61	31															
H7K†	Kure I.	OC	61	31															
H8†*	American Samoa	OC	62	32															
H8 48†*	Swains I.	OC	62	32															
H9†	Wake I.	OC	65	31															
L, AL, NL, WL*	Alaska	NA	1, 2	1															
P1†	Navassa I.	NA	11	08															

Prefix	Entity	Continent	ZONE ITU	ZONE CQ	MIXED	PHONE	CW	RTTY	SAT	160	80	40	30	20	17	15	12	10	6
KP2[†][*]	Virgin Is.	NA	11	08															
KP3, 4[†][*]	Puerto Rico	NA	11	08															
KP5[22][†]	Desecheo I.	NA	11	08															
LA-LN[*]	Norway	EU	18	14															
LO-LW[†][*]	Argentina	SA	14,16	13															
LX[*]	Luxembourg	EU	27	14															
LY[*]	Lithuania	EU	29	15															
LZ[*]	Bulgaria	EU	28	20															
OA-OC[†][*]	Peru	SA	12	10															
OD[*]	Lebanon	AS	39	20															
OE[†][*]	Austria	EU	28	15															
OF-OI[*]	Finland	EU	18	15															
OHØ[*]	Aland Is.	EU	18	15															
OJØ[*]	Market Reef	EU	18	15															
OK-OL[23][*]	Czech Rep.	EU	28	15															
OM[23][*]	Slovak Rep.	EU	28	15															
ON-OT[*]	Belgium	EU	27	14															
OU-OW, OZ[*]	Denmark	EU	18	14															
OX[*]	Greenland	NA	5, 75	40															
OY[*]	Faroe Is.	EU	18	14															
P2[24]	Papua New Guinea	OC	51	28															
P4[25][*]	Aruba	SA	11	09															
P5[26]	Dem. People's Rep. Korea	AS	44	25															
PA-PI[*]	Netherlands	EU	27	14															
PJ2[50][*]	Curacao	SA	11	09															
PJ4[51]	Bonaire	SA	11	09															
PJ5, 6[52]	Saba, St. Eustatius	NA	11	08															
PJ7[53][*]	St. Maarten	NA	11	08															
PP-PY, ZV-ZZ[†][*]	Brazil	SA	(D)	11															
PPØ-PYØF[†][*]	Fernando de Noronha	SA	13	11															
PPØ-PYØS[†][*]	St. Peter & St. Paul Rocks	SA	13	11															
PPØ-PYØT[†][*]	Trindade & Martim Vaz Is.	SA	15	11															
PZ	Suriname	SA	12	09															
RI/F[*]	Franz Josef Land	EU	75	40															
RI/M[*]	Malyj Vysotskij I	EU	29	16															
SØ[1,27]	Western Sahara	AF	46	33															
S2[*]	Bangladesh	AS	41	22															
S5[6][*]	Slovenia	EU	28	15															
S7	Seychelles	AF	53	39															
S9	Sao Tome & Principe	AF	47	36															
SA-SM[7S,8S][*]	Sweden	EU	18	14															
SN-SR[*]	Poland	EU	28	15															
ST	Sudan	AF	47, 48	34															

Prefix	Entity	CONTINENT	ZONE ITU	ZONE CQ	MIXED	PHONE	CW	RTTY	SAT	160	80	40	30	20	17	15	12	10	6
SU	Egypt	AF	38	34															
SV-SZ, J4*	Greece	EU	28	20															
SV/A*	Mount Athos	EU	28	20															
SV5, J45*	Dodecanese	EU	28	20															
SV9, J49*	Crete	EU	28	20															
T2[28]	Tuvalu	OC	65	31															
T3Ø	W. Kiribati (Gilbert Is.)	OC	65	31															
T31	C. Kiribati (Brit. Phoenix Is.)	OC	62	31															
T32	E. Kiribati (Line Is.)	OC	61,63	31															
T33	Banaba I. (Ocean I.)	OC	65	31															
T5, 6O	Somalia	AF	48	37															
T7*	San Marino	EU	28	15															
T8[21]	Palau	OC	64	27															
TA-TC†*	Turkey	EU/AS	39	20															
TF*	Iceland	EU	17	40															
TG, TD†*	Guatemala	NA	12	07															
TI, TE†*	Costa Rica	NA	11	07															
TI9†*	Cocos I.	NA	11	07															
TJ	Cameroon	AF	47	36															
TK*	Corsica	EU	28	15															
TL[30]	Central Africa	AF	47	36															
TN[31]	Congo (Republic of)	AF	52	36															
TR[32]*	Gabon	AF	52	36															
TT[33]	Chad	AF	47	36															
TU[34]	Côte d'Ivoire	AF	46	35															
TY[35]	Benin	AF	46	35															
TZ[36]*	Mali	AF	46	35															
UA-UI1,3,4,6 RA-RZ*	European Russia	EU	(E)	16															
UA2, RA2*	Kaliningrad	EU	29	15															
UA-UI8, 9, Ø RA-RZ*	Asiatic Russia	AS	(F)	(G)															
UJ-UM*	Uzbekistan	AS	30	17															
UN-UQ*	Kazakhstan	AS	29-31	17															
UR-UZ, EM-EO*	Ukraine	EU	29	16															
V2†*	Antigua & Barbuda	NA	11	08															
V3†	Belize	NA	11	07															
V4[37]†	St. Kitts & Nevis	NA	11	08															
V5*	Namibia	AF	57	38															
V6[38]†	Micronesia	OC	65	27															
V7†*	Marshall Is.	OC	65	31															
V8*	Brunei Darussalam	OC	54	28															
VA-VG, VO, VY†*	Canada	NA	(H)	1-5															

Prefix	Entity	CONTINENT	ZONE ITU	ZONE CQ	MIXED	PHONE	CW	RTTY	SAT	160	80	40	30	20	17	15	12	10	6
VK, AX†*	Australia	OC	(I)	29,30															
VKØ†*	Heard I.	AF	68	39															
VKØ†*	Macquarie I.	OC	60	30															
VK9C†*	Cocos (Keeling) Is.	OC	54	29															
VK9L†*	Lord Howe I.	OC	60	30															
VK9M†*	Mellish Reef	OC	56	30															
VK9N*	Norfolk I.	OC	60	32															
VK9W†*	Willis I.	OC	55	30															
VK9X†*	Christmas I.	OC	54	29															
VP2E37	Anguilla	NA	11	08															
VP2M37	Montserrat	NA	11	08															
VP2V37*	British Virgin Is.	NA	11	08															
VP5, VQ5*	Turks & Caicos Is.	NA	11	08															
VP6†*	Pitcairn I.	OC	63	32															
VP646*	Ducie I.	OC	63	32															
VP8*	Falkland Is.	SA	16	13															
VP8, LU*	South Georgia I.	SA	73	13															
VP8, LU*	South Orkney Is.	SA	73	13															
VP8, LU*	South Sandwich Is.	SA	73	13															
VP8, LU, CE9, HF0, 4K1*	South Shetland Is.	SA	73	13															
VP9*	Bermuda	NA	11	05															
VQ9*	Chagos Is.	AF	41	39															
VR*	Hong Kong	AS	44	24															
VU*	India	AS	41	22															
VU4*	Andaman & Nicobar Is.	AS	49	26															
VU7*	Lakshadweep Is.	AS	41	22															
XA-XI†*	Mexico	NA	10	06															
XA4-XI4†*	Revillagigedo	NA	10	06															
XT39*	Burkina Faso	AF	46	35															
XU	Cambodia	AS	49	26															
XW	Laos	AS	49	26															
XX9*	Macao	AS	44	24															
XY-XZ	Myanmar	AS	49	26															
YA, T6	Afghanistan	AS	40	21															
YB-YH40*	Indonesia	OC	51,54	28															
YI*	Iraq	AS	39	21															
YJ*	Vanuatu	OC	56	32															
YK*	Syria	AS	39	20															
YL*	Latvia	EU	29	15															
YN, H6-7, HT†*	Nicaragua	NA	11	07															
YO-YR*	Romania	EU	28	20															

Prefix	Entity	CONTINENT	ZONE ITU	ZONE CQ	MIXED	PHONE	CW	RTTY	SAT	160	80	40	30	20	17	15	12	10	6
YS, HU†*	El Salvador	NA	11	07															
YT-YU*	Serbia	EU	28	15															
YV-YY, 4M†*	Venezuela	SA	12	09															
YVØ†*	Aves I.	NA	11	08															
Z2	Zimbabwe	AF	53	38															
Z3⁴¹*	Macedonia	EU	28	15															
ZA	Albania	EU	28	15															
ZB*	Gibraltar	EU	37	14															
ZC4⁴²*	UK Sov. Base Areas on Cyprus	AS	39	20															
ZD7*	St. Helena	AF	66	36															
ZD8*	Ascension I.	AF	66	36															
ZD9	Tristan da Cunha & Gough I.	AF	66	38															
ZF*	Cayman Is.	NA	11	08															
ZK2*	Niue	OC	62	32															
ZK3*	Tokelau Is.	OC	62	31															
ZL-ZM*	New Zealand	OC	60	32															
ZL7*	Chatham Is.	OC	60	32															
ZL8*	Kermadec Is.	OC	60	32															
ZL9*	Auckland & Campbell Is.	OC	60	32															
ZP†*	Paraguay	SA	14	11															
ZR-ZU†*	South Africa	AF	57	38															
ZS8*	Prince Edward & Marion Is.	AF	57	38															

Notes

[1] Unofficial prefix.

[2] (5T) Only contacts made June 20, 1960, and after, count for this entity.

[3] (5U) Only contacts made August 3, 1960, and after, count for this entity.

[4] (6W) Only contacts made June 20, 1960, and after, count for this entity.

[5] (7O) Only contacts made May 22, 1990, and after, count for this entity.

[6] (9A, S5) Only contacts made June 26, 1991, and after, count for this entity.

[7] (9G) Only contacts made March 5, 1957, and after, count for this entity.

[8] (9M2, 4, 6, 8) Only contacts made September 16, 1963, and after, count for this entity.

[9] (9U, 9X) Only contacts made July 1, 1962, and after, count for this entity.

[10] (9V) Contacts made from September 16, 1963 to August 8, 1965, count for West Malaysia.

[11] (BS7) Only contacts made January 1, 1995, and after, count for this entity.

[12] (BV9P) Only contacts made January 1, 1994, and after, count for this entity.

[13] (D6, FH8) Only contacts made July 6, 1975, and after, count for this entity.

[14] (DA-DR) Only contacts made with DA-DR stations September 17, 1973, and after, and contacts made with Y2-Y9 stations October 3, 1990 and after, count for this entity.

[15] (E3) Only contacts made November 14, 1962, and before, or May 24, 1991, and after, count for this entity.

[16] (FO) Only contacts made after 23:59 UTC, March 31, 1998 count for this entity.

[17] (FR) Only contacts made June 25, 1960, and after, count for this entity.

[18] (H4Ø) Only contacts made after 23:59 UTC, March 31, 1998, count for this entity.

[19] (JD) Formerly Marcus Island.

[20] (JD) Formerly Bonin and Volcano Islands.

[21] (T8) Valid prefix January 1, 1994 or after. (KC6 prior to this date.)

[22] (KP5, KP4) Only contacts made March 1, 1979, and after, count for this entity.

[23] (OK-OL, OM) Only contacts made January 1, 1993, and after, count for this entity.

[24] (P2) Only contacts made September 16, 1975, and after, count for this entity.

[25] (P4) Only contacts made January 1, 1986, and after, count for this entity.

Zone Notes can be found with Prefix Cross References.

[26] (P5) Only contacts made May 14, 1995, and after count for this entity.

[27] (SØ) Contacts with Rio de Oro (Spanish Sahara), EA9, also count for this entity.

[28] (T2) Only contacts made January 1, 1976, and after, count for this entity.

[29] (E7) New prefix for Bosnia-Herzegovina effective November 17, 2007. Contacts are valid for this entity effective October 15, 1991.

[30] (TL) Only contacts made August 13, 1960, and after, count for this entity.

[31] (TN) Only contacts made August 15, 1960, and after, count for this entity.

[32] (TR) Only contacts made August 17, 1960, and after, count for this entity.

[33] (TT) Only contacts made August 11, 1960, and after, count for this entity.

[34] (TU) Only contacts made August 7, 1960, and after, count for this entity.

[35] (TY) Only contacts made August 1, 1960, and after, count for this entity.

[36] (TZ) Only contacts made June 20, 1960, and after, count for this entity.

[37] (V4, VP2) For DXCC credit for contacts made May 31, 1958 and before, see page 97, June 1958 *QST*.

[38] (V6) Includes Yap Islands January 1, 1981, and after.

[39] (XT) Only contacts made August 5, 1960, and after, count for this entity.

[40] (YB) Only contacts made May 1, 1963, and after, count for this entity.

[41] (Z3) Only contacts made September 8, 1991, and after, count for this entity.

[42] (ZC4) Only contacts made August 16, 1960, and after, count for this entity.

[43] (E4) Only contacts made February 1, 1999 and after, count for this entity.

[44] (4W) Only contacts made March 1, 2000, and after, count for this entity.

[45] (FK/C) Only contacts made March 23, 2000, and after, count for this entity.

[46] (VP6) Only contacts made November 16, 2001, and after, count for this entity.

[47] (4O) Only contacts made June 28, 2006, and after, count for this entity.

[48] (KH8) Only contacts made July 22, 2006, and after, count for this entity.

[49] (FJ) Only contacts made December 14, 2007, and after, count for this entity.

[50] (PJ2) Only contacts made October 10, 2010, and after, count for this entity.

[51] (PJ4) Only contacts made October 10, 2010, and after, count for this entity.

[52] (PJ5, 6) Only contacts made October 10, 2010, and after, count for this entity.

[53] (PJ7) Only contacts made October 10, 2010, and after, count for this entity.

▲Also 3Y, 8J1, ATØ, DPØ, FT8Y, LU, OR4, R1AN, VKØ, VP8, ZL5, ZS1, ZXØ, etc. QSL via entity under whose auspices the particular station is operating. The availability of a third-party traffic agreement and a QSL Bureau applies to the entity under whose auspices the particular station is operating.

DELETED ENTITIES

Credit for any of these entities can be given if the date of contact in question agrees with the date(s) shown in the corresponding footnote.

Prefix	Entity	Continent	ZONE ITU	ZONE CQ	MIXED	PHONE	CW	RTTY	SAT	160	80	40	30	20	17	15	12	10	6
2	Blenheim Reef	AF	41	39															
3	Geyser Reef	AF	53	39															
4	Abu Ail Is.	AS	39	21															
1M[1, 5]	Minerva Reef	OC	62	32															
4W[6]	Yemen Arab Rep.	AS	39	21															
7J1[7]	Okino Tori-shima	AS	45	27															
8Z4[8]	Saudi Arabia/Iraq Neut. Zone	AS	39	21															
8Z5, 9K3[9]	Kuwait/Saudi Arabia Neut. Zone	AS	39	21															
9S4[10]	Saar	EU	28	14															
9U5[11]	Ruanda-Urundi	AF	52	36															
AC3[1, 12]	Sikkim	AS	41	22															
AC4[1, 13]	Tibet	AS	41	23															
C9[14]	Manchuria	AS	33	24															
CN2[15]	Tangier	AF	37	33															
CR8[16]	Damao, Diu	AS	41	22															
CR8[16]	Goa	AS	41	22															
CR8, CR10[17]	Portuguese Timor	OC	54	28															
DA-DM[18]	Germany	EU	28	14															
DM, Y2-9[19]	German Dem. Rep.	EU	28	14															
EA9[20]	Ifni	AF	37	33															
FF[21]	French West Africa	AF	46	35															
FH, FB8[22]	Comoros	AF	53	39															
FI8[23]	French Indo-China	AS	49	26															
FN8[24]	French India	AS	41	22															
FQ8[25]	Fr. Equatorial Africa	AF	47,52	36															
HK0[26]	Bajo Nuevo	NA	11	08															
HK0,KP3,KS4[26]	Serrana Bank & Roncador Cay	NA	11	07															
I1[27]	Trieste	EU	28	15															
I5[28]	Italian Somaliland	AF	48	37															
JZ0[29]	Netherlands N. Guinea	OC	51	28															
KR6,8,JR6,KA6[30]	Okinawa (Ryukyu Is.)	AS	45	25															
KS4[31]	Swan Is.	NA	11	07															
KZ5[32]	Canal Zone	NA	11	07															
OK-OM[33]	Czechoslovakia	EU	28	15															
P2, VK9[34]	Papua Territory	OC	51	28															
P2, VK9[34]	Terr. New Guinea	OC	51	28															
PJ[35]	Bonaire, Curacao	SA	11	09															
PJ[35]	St. Maarten, Saba, St. Eustatius	NA	11	08															
PK1-3[36]	Java	OC	54	28															
PK4[36]	Sumatra	OC	54	28															
PK5[36]	Netherlands Borneo	OC	54	28															
PK6[36]	Celebe & Molucca Is.	OC	54	28															
ST0[37]	Southern Sudan	AF	47, 48	34															

Prefix	Entity	Continent	ITU	CQ	MIXED	PHONE	CW	RTTY	SAT	160	80	40	30	20	17	15	12	10	6
UN1[38]	Karelo-Finnish Rep.	EU	19	16															
VO[39]	Newfoundland, Labrador	NA	09	02,05															
VQ1, 5H1[40]	Zanzibar	AF	53	37															
VQ6[41]	British Somaliland	AF	48	37															
VQ9[42]	Aldabra	AF	53	39															
VQ9[42]	Desroches	AF	53	39															
VQ9[42]	Farquhar	AF	53	39															
VS2, 9M2[43]	Malaya	AS	54	28															
VS4[43]	Sarawak	OC	54	28															
VS9A, P, S[44]	People's Dem. Rep. of Yemen	AS	39	21															
VS9H[45]	Kuria Muria I.	AS	39	21															
VS9K[46]	Kamaran Is.	AS	39	21															
ZC5[43]	British North Borneo	OC	54	28															
ZC6, 4X1[47]	Palestine	AS	39	20															
ZD4[48]	Gold Coast, Togoland	AF	46	35															
ZS9[50]	Walvis Bay	AF	57	38															
ZSØ, 1[49]	Penguin Is.	AF	57	38															

NOTES:

[1] Unofficial prefix.

[2] (Blenheim Reef) Only contacts made from May 4, 1967, to June 30, 1975, count for this entity. Contacts made July 1, 1975, and after, count as Chagos (VQ9).

[3] (Geyser Reef) Only contacts made from May 4, 1967, to February 28, 1978, count for this entity.

[4] (Abu Ail Is.) Only contacts made March 30, 1991, and before, count for this entity.

[5] (1M) Only contacts made from July 15, 1972, and before, count for this entity. Contacts made July 16, 1972, and after, count as Tonga (A3).

[6] (4W) Only contacts made May 21, 1990, and before, count for this entity.

[7] (7J1) Only contacts made May 30, 1976, to November 30, 1980, count for this entity. Contacts made December 1, 1980, and after, count as Ogasawara (JD1).

[8] (8Z4) Only contacts made December 25, 1981, and before, count for this entity.

[9] (8Z5, 9K3) Only contacts made December 14, 1969, and before, count for this entity.

[10] (9S4) Only contacts made March 31, 1957, and before, count for this entity.

[11] (9U5) Only contacts made from July 1, 1960, to June 30, 1962, count for this entity. Contacts made July 1, 1962, and after, count as Burundi (9U) or Rwanda (9X).

[12] (AC3) Only contacts made April 30, 1975, and before, count for this entity. Contacts made May 1, 1975, and after, count as India (VU).

[13] (AC4) Only contacts made May 30, 1974, and before, count for this entity. Contacts made May 31, 1974 and after, count as China (BY).

[14] (C9) Only contacts made September 15, 1963, and before, count for this entity. Contacts made September 16, 1963, and after, count as China (BY).

[15] (CN2) Only contacts made June 30, 1960, and before, count for this entity. Contacts made July 1, 1960, and after, count as Morocco (CN).

[16] (CR8) Only contacts made December 31, 1961, and before, count for this entity.

[17] (CR8, CR10) Only contacts made September 14, 1976, and before, count for this entity.

[18] (DA-DM) Only contacts made September 16, 1973, and before, count for this entity. Contacts made September 17, 1973, and after, count as either FRG (DA-DL) or GDR (Y2-Y9).

[19] (DM, Y2-Y9) Only contacts made from September 17, 1973 and October 2, 1990 count for this entity. On October 3, 1990 the GDR became part of the FRG.

[20] (EA9) Only contacts made May 13, 1969, and before, count for this entity.

[21] (FF) Only contacts made August 6, 1960, and before, count for this entity.

[22] (FH, FB8) Only contacts made July 5, 1975, and before, count for this entity. Contacts made July 6, 1975, and after, count as Comoros (D6) or Mayotte (FH).

[23] (FI8) Only contacts made December 20, 1950, and before, count for this entity.

[24] (FN8) Only contacts made October 31, 1954, and before count for this entity.

[25] (FQ8) Only contacts made August 16, 1960, and before, will count for this entity.

[26] (HKØ, KP3, KS4) Only contacts made September 16, 1981, and before, count for this entity. Contacts made September 17, 1981, and after, count as San Andres (HKØ).

[27] (I1) Only contacts made March 31, 1957, and before, count for this entity. Contacts made April 1, 1957, and after, count as Italy (I).

[28] (I5) Only contacts made June 30, 1960, and before, count for this entity.

[29] (JZØ) Only contacts made April 30, 1963, and before, count for this entity.

[30] (KR6, 8, JR6, KA6) Only contacts made May 14, 1972, and before, count for this entity. Contacts made May 15, 1972, and after, count as Japan (JA).

[31] (KS4) Only contacts made August 31, 1972, and before, count for this entity. Contacts made September 1, 1972, and after, count as Honduras (HR).

[32] (KZ5) Only contacts made September 30, 1979, and before, count for this entity.

[33] (OK-OM) Only contacts made December 31, 1992, and before, count for this entity.

[34] (P2, VK9) Only contacts made September 15, 1975, and before, count for this entity. Contacts made September 16, 1975, and after, count as Papua New Guinea (P2).

[35] (PJ) Only contacts made October 9, 2010, and before, count for this entity.

[36] (PK1-6) Only contacts made April 30, 1963, and before, count for this entity. Contacts made May 1, 1963, and after, count as Indonesia.

[37] (STØ) Only contacts made between May 7, 1972 and December 31, 1994, count for this entity.

[38] (UN1) Only contacts made June 30, 1960, and before, count for this entity. Contacts made July 1, 1960, and after, count as European RSFSR (UA).

[39] (VO) Only contacts made March 31, 1949, and before, count for this entity. Contacts made April 1, 1949, and after, count as Canada (VE).

[40] (VQ1, 5H1) Only contacts made May 31, 1974, and before, count for this entity. Contacts made June 1, 1974, and after, count as Tanzania (5H).

[41] (VQ6) Only contacts made June 30, 1960, and before, count for this entity.

[42] (VQ9) Only contacts made June 28, 1976, and before, count for this entity. Contacts made June 29, 1976, and after, count as Seychelles (S7).

[43] (VS2, VS4, ZC5, 9M2) Only contacts made September 15, 1963, and before, count for this entity. Contacts made September 16, 1963, and after, count as West Malaysia (9M2) or East Malaysia (9M6, 8).

[44] (VS9A, P, S) Only contacts made May 21, 1990, and before, count for this entity.

[45] (VS9H) Only contacts made November 29, 1967, and before, count for this entity.

[46] (VS9K) Only contacts made on March 10, 1982, and before, count for this entity.

[47] (ZC6, 4X1) Only contacts made June 30, 1968, and before, count for this entity. Contacts made July 1, 1968, and after, count as Israel (4X).

[48] (ZD4) Only contacts made March 5, 1957, and before, count for this entity.

[49] (ZSØ, 1) Only contacts made February 28, 1994, and before, count for this entity.

[50] (ZS9) Only contacts made from September 1, 1977, to February 28, 1994, count for this entity.

A8 = EL
AC (before 1972) = A5
AH = KH
AL7 = KL7
AM-AO = EA
AT-AW = VU
AX = VK
AY-AZ = LU
CF-CK = VE
CL = CO
CQ-CS = CT
CR3 (before 1974) = J5
CR4 (before 1976) = D4
CR5 (before 1976) = S9
CR6 (before 1976) = D2
CR7 (before 1976) = C9
CR9 (before 1985) = XX9
CT2 (before 1986) = CU
CXØ = CE9/VP8
CY-CZ = VE
CYØ (before 1985) = CY9
D7 = HL
DM-DT (before 1980) = Y2-9
DS-DT = HL
E2 = HS
EAØ (before 1969) = 3C
EK, EM-EO, ER-ES, EU-EZ = U
ER (after 1992) = UO
EU (after 1991) = UC
FA-FF (after 1983) =F
FA (before 1963) = 7X
FB8 (before 1961) = 5R
FB8 (before 1985) = FT
FC (before 1985) = TK
FD8 (before 1961) = 5V
FE8 (before 1961) =TJ
FL (before 1978) = J2
FU8 (before 1982) = YJ
GB = G
GC (before 1977) = GJ or GU
H2 = 5B
H3 = HP
H5 (Bophutatswana) = ZS
H7 = YN
HE = HB
HM (before 1982) = HL

HT = YN
HU = YS
HW-HY = F
J4 = SV
KA1 = JD1
KA2AA-KA9ZZ = JA
KB6 (before 1979) = KH1
KC4 (Navassa) = KP1
KC6 (before 1990) = V6
KC6 (before 1998) = T8
KG6 (before 1979) = KH2
KG6I (before 1970) = JD1
KG6R, S, T (before 1979) = KHØ
KH7 (before 1996) = KH7K
KJ6 (before 1979) = KH3
KM6 (before 1979) = KH4
KP4 (Desecheo) = KP5
KP6 (before 1979) = KH5
KS6 (before 1979) = KH8
KV4 (before 1979) = KP2
KW6 (before 1979) = KH9
KX6 (before 1990) = V7
L2-9 = LU
M = G
M1 (before 1984) = T7
MP4B (before 1972) = A9
MP4M (before 1972) = A4
MP4Q (before 1972) = A7
MP4T, D (before 1972) = A6
NH = KH
NL7 = KL7
NP = KP
OQ (before 1961) = 9Q
P3 = 5B
P4 (before 1986) = PJ
PX (before 1970) = C3
RA, RN = UA
RB-RR = UB-UR
RS = U
RT = UB
RU-RX = U
S4 (Ciskei) = 0ZS
S8 (Transkei) = ZS
T4 = CO
T4 (Venda) = ZS
T9 = E7
TH, TM, TO-TQ, TV-TX = F
UB (before 1994) = UZ
UC (before 1991) = EU

UD (before 1994) = 4J
UF (before 1994) = 4L
UG (before 1994) = EK
UH (before 1993) = EZ
UI (before 1994) = UJ
UJ (before 1993) = EY
UL (before 1994) = UN
UM (before 1993) = EX
UO (before 1994) = ER
UP (before 1991) = LY
UQ (before 1992) = YL
UR (before 1991) = ES
V9 (Venda) = ZS
VA-VG = VE
VH-VN = VK
VK9 (Nauru) = C2
VP1 (before 1982) = V3
VP2A (before 1982) = V2
VP2D (before 1979) = J7
VP2G (before 1975) = J3
VP2K (before 1984) = V4 or VP2E
VP2L (before 1980) = J6
VP2S (before 1980) = J8
VP3 (before 1967) = 8R
VP4 (before 1963) = 9Y
VP5 (Jamaica) = 6Y
VP6 (before 1967) = 8P
VP7 (before 1974) = C6
VQ2 (before 1965) = 9J
VQ3 (before 1962) = 5H
VQ4 (before 1964) = 5Z
VQ5 (before 1963) = 5X
VQ8 (before 1969) = 3B
VQ8 (Chagos) = VQ9
VQ9 (Seychelles) = S7
VR1 (before 1980) = T3
VR2 (before 1971) = 3D2
VR2 (after 1991) = VS6
VR3 (before 1980) = T32
VR4 (before 1979) = H4
VR5 (before 1971) = A3
VR6 (before 1998) = VP6
VR8 (before 1979) = T2
VS1 (before 1966) = 9V
VS5 (before 1985) = V8
VS6 (before 1997) = VR
VS7 (before 1949) = 4S
VS9M = 8Q

VS9O (before 1961) = A4
VX-VY = CYØ/VE
WH = KH
WL7 = KL7
WP = KP
XJ-XO = VE
XP = OX
XQ-XR = CE
XV = 3W
XX7 (before 1976) = C9
YU2 (before 1992) = 9A
YU3 (before1992) = S5
YU4 (before 1992) = T9
YU5 (before 1992) = Z3
ZB1 (before 1965) = 9H
ZD1 (before 1962) = 9L
ZD2 (before 1961) = 5N
ZD3 (before 1966) = C5
ZD5 (before 1969) = 3DA
ZD6 (before 1965) = 7Q
ZE (before 1981) = Z2-9
ZK1 (after June 2006) = E5
ZK9 (1983) = ZK2
ZM6 (before 1963) = 5W
ZM7 (before 1984) = ZK3
ZS3 (before 1991) = V5
ZS7 (before 1969) = 3D6
ZS8 (before 1967) = 7P
ZS9 (before 1967) = A2
ZV-ZZ = PY
2D = GD
2E = G
2I = GI
2J = GJ
2M = GM
2U = GU
2W = GW
3B-3C (before 1968) = VE
3D6 (before 1988) = 3DA
3G = CE
3Z = SP
4A-4C = XE
4D-4I = DU
4J-4L = U
4J (after 1991) = EK
4J1F (before 1994) = R1MV
4K (before 1994) = UA
4K1 (before 1994) = CE9/KC4
4K2 (before 1994) = R1FJ

4K3 (before 1994) = UA
4K4 (before 1994) = UAØ
4L (after 1991) = UF
4M = YV
4N-4O = YU
4T = OA
4U1VIC = OE
4V = HH
5J-5K = HK
5L-5M = EL
6C = YK
6D-6J = XE
6K-6N=HL
6O = T5
6T-6U = ST
7A-7I = YB
7G (before 1967) = 3X
7J-7N = JA
7JI = JA1 or JD1
7S = SM
7Z = HZ
8A-8I = YB
8J-8N = JA
8O = A2
8S = SM
9A (before 1984) = T7
9B-9D = EP
9E-9F = ET

CONTINENT
AF = AFRICA
AN = ANTARCTICA
AS = ASIA
EU = EUROPE
NA = NORTH AMERICA
OC = OCEANIA
SA = SOUTH AMERICA

ZONE NOTES
(A) 33, 42, 43, 44
(B) 67, 69-74
(C) 12, 13, 29, 30, 32, 38, 39
(D) 12, 13, 15
(E) 19, 20, 29, 30
(F) 20-26, 30-35, 75
(G) 16, 17, 18, 19, 23
(H) 2, 3, 4, 9, 75
(I) 55, 58, 59

ALLOCATION OF INTERNATIONAL CALL SIGN SERIES ▬▬▬▬▬▬▬

Call Sign Series	Allocated to
AAA-ALZ	United States of America
AMA-AOZ	Spain
APA-ASZ	Pakistan
ATA-AWZ	India
AXA-AXZ	Australia
AYA-AZZ	Argentina
A2A-A2Z	Botswana
A3A-A3Z	Tonga
A4A-A4Z	Oman
A5A-A5Z	Bhutan
A6A-A6Z	United Arab Emirates
A7A-A7Z	Qatar
A8A-A8Z	Liberia
A9A-A9Z	Bahrain
BAA-BZZ	China (People's Republic of)
CAA-CEZ	Chile
CFA-CKZ	Canada
CLA-CMZ	Cuba
CNA-CNZ	Morocco
COA-COZ	Cuba
CPA-CPZ	Bolivia
CQA-CUZ	Portugal
CVA-CXZ	Uruguay
CYA-CZZ	Canada
C2A-C2Z	Nauru
C3A-C3Z	Andorra
C4A-C4Z	Cyprus
C5A-C5Z	Gambia
C6A-C6Z	Bahamas
C7A-C7Z	World Meteorological Organization
C8A-C9Z	Mozambique
DAA-DRZ	Germany (Federal Rep of)
DSA-DTZ	Korea (Rep of)
DUA-DZZ	Philippines
D2A-D3Z	Angola
D4A-D4Z	Cape Verde
D5A-D5Z	Liberia
D6A-D6Z	Comoros
D7A-D9Z	Korea (Rep of)
EAA-EHZ	Spain
EIA-EJZ	Ireland
EKA-EKZ	Armenia
ELA-ELZ	Liberia
EMA-EOZ	Ukraine
EPA-EQZ	Iran (Islamic Rep of)
ERA-ERZ	Moldova
ESA-ESZ	Estonia
ETA-ETZ	Ethiopia
EUA-EWZ	Belarus
EXA-EXZ	Kyrgyz Republic
EYA-EYZ	Tajikistan
EZA-EZZ	Turkmenistan
E2A-E2Z	Thailand
E3A-E3Z	Eritrea
E4A-E4Z	Palestinian Authority
E5A-E5Z	New Zealand - Cook Islands
FAA-FZZ	France
GAA-GZZ	United Kingdom of Great Britain and Northern Ireland
HAA-HAZ	Hungary
HBA-HBZ	Switzerland
HCA-HDZ	Ecuador
HEA-HEZ	Switzerland
HFA-HFZ	Poland
HGA-HGZ	Hungary
HHA-HHZ	Haiti
HIA-HIZ	Dominican Republic
HJA-HKZ	Colombia
HLA-HLZ	Korea (Rep of)
HMA-HMZ	Korea (Dem People's Rep of)
HNA-HNZ	Iraq
HOA-HPZ	Panama
HQA-HRZ	Honduras
HSA-HSZ	Thailand
HTA-HTZ	Nicaragua
HUA-HUZ	El Salvador

Call Sign Series	Allocated to
HVA-HVZ	Vatican City State
HWA-HYZ	France
HZA-HZZ	Saudi Arabia
H2A-H2Z	Cyprus
H3A-H3Z	Panama
H4A-H4Z	Solomon Islands
H6A-H7Z	Nicaragua
H8A-H9Z	Panama
IAA-IZZ	Italy
JAA-JSZ	Japan
JTA-JVZ	Mongolia
JWA-JXZ	Norway
JYA-JYZ	Jordan
JZA-JZZ	Indonesia
J2A-J2Z	Djibouti
J3A-J3Z	Grenada
J4A-J4Z	Greece
J5A-J5Z	Guinea-Bissau
J6A-J6Z	Saint Lucia
J7A-J7Z	Dominica
J8A-J8Z	St. Vincent and the Grenadines
KAA-KZZ	United States of America
LAA-LNZ	Norway
LOA-LWZ	Argentina
LXA-LXZ	Luxembourg
LYA-LYZ	Lithuania
LZA-LZZ	Bulgaria
L2A-L9Z	Argentina
MAA-MZZ	United Kingdom of Great Britain and Northern Ireland
NAA-NZZ	United States of America
OAA-OCZ	Peru
ODA-ODZ	Lebanon
OEA-OEZ	Austria
OFA-OJZ	Finland
OKA-OLZ	Czech Republic
OMA-OMZ	Slovak Republic
ONA-OTZ	Belgium
OUA-OZZ	Denmark
PAA-PIZ	Netherlands
PJA-PJZ	Netherlands Antilles
PKA-POZ	Indonesia
PPA-PYZ	Brazil
PZA-PZZ	Suriname
P2A-P2Z	Papua New Guinea
P3A-P3Z	Cyprus
P4A-P4Z	Aruba
P5A-P9Z	Korea (Dem People's Rep of)
RAA-RZZ	Russian Federation
SAA-SMZ	Sweden
SNA-SRZ	Poland
• SSA-SSM	Egypt (Arab Rep of)
• SSN-STZ	Sudan
SUA-SUZ	Egypt (Arab Rep of)
SVA-SZZ	Greece
S2A-S3Z	Bangladesh
S5A-S5Z	Slovenia
S6A-S6Z	Singapore
S7A-S7Z	Seychelles
S8A-S8Z	South Africa (Rep of)
S9A-S9Z	Sao Tome and Principe
TAA-TCZ	Turkey
TDA-TDZ	Guatemala
TEA-TEZ	Costa Rica
TFA-TFZ	Iceland
TGA-TGZ	Guatemala
THA-THZ	France
TIA-TIZ	Costa Rica
TJA-TJZ	Cameroon
TKA-TKZ	France
TLA-TLZ	Central African Rep
TMA-TMZ	France
TNA-TNZ	Congo (Rep of the)
TOA-TQZ	France
TRA-TRZ	Gabon
TSA-TSZ	Tunisia
TTA-TTZ	Chad

Call Sign Series	Allocated to	Call Sign Series	Allocated to
TUA-TUZ	Cote d'Ivoire	3XA-3XZ	Guinea
TVA-TXZ	France	3YA-3YZ	Norway
TYA-TYZ	Benin	3ZA-3ZZ	Poland
TZA-TZZ	Mali	4AA-4CZ	Mexico
T2A-T2Z	Tuvalu	4DA-4IZ	Philippines
T3A-T3Z	Kiribati	4JA-4KZ	Azerbaijani
T4A-T4Z	Cuba	4LA-4LZ	Georgia
T5A-T5Z	Somalia	4MA-4MZ	Venezuela
T6A-T6Z	Afghanistan	4OA-4OZ	Montenegro (Republic of)
T7A-T7Z	San Marino	4PA-4SZ	Sri Lanka
T8A-T8Z	Palau	4TA-4TZ	Peru
T9A-T9Z	Bosnia and Herzegovina	4UA-4UZ	United Nations
UAA-UIZ	Russian Federation	4VA-4VZ	Haiti
UJA-UMZ	Uzbekistan	4WA-4WZ	Timor-Leste
UNA-UQZ	Kazakhstan	4XA-4XZ	Israel
URA-UZZ	Ukraine	4YA-4YZ	International Civil Aviation Organization
VAA-VGZ	Canada	4ZA-4ZZ	Israel
VHA-VNZ	Australia	5AA-5AZ	Libya
VOA-VOZ	Canada	5BA-5BZ	Cyprus
VPA-VSZ	United Kingdom of Great Britain and Northern Ireland	5CA-5GZ	Morocco
VRA-VRZ	China (People's Republic of) - Hong Kong	5HA-5IZ	Tanzania
VSA-VSZ	United Kingdom of Great Britain and Northern Ireland	5JA-5KZ	Colombia
VTA-VWZ	India	5LA-5MZ	Liberia
VXA-VYZ	Canada	5NA-5OZ	Nigeria
VZA-VZZ	Australia	5PA-5QZ	Denmark
V2A-V2Z	Antigua and Barbuda	5RA-5SZ	Madagascar
V3A-V3Z	Belize	5TA-5TZ	Mauritania
V4A-V4Z	Saint Kitts and Nevis	5UA-5UZ	Niger
V5A-V5Z	Namibia	5VA-5VZ	Togolese Rep
V6A-V6Z	Micronesia (Federated States of)	5WA-5WZ	Samoa
V7A-V7Z	Marshall Islands	5XA-5XZ	Uganda
V8A-V8Z	Brunei Darussalam	5YA-5ZZ	Kenya
WAA-WZZ	United States of America	6AA-6BZ	Egypt
XAA-XIZ	Mexico	6CA-6CZ	Syria
XJA-XOZ	Canada	6DA-6JZ	Mexico
XPA-XPZ	Denmark	6KA-6NZ	Korea (Rep of)
XQA-XRZ	Chile	6OA-6OZ	Somalia
XSA-XSZ	China (People's Republic of)	6PA-6SZ	Pakistan
XTA-XTZ	Burkina Faso	6TA-6UZ	Sudan
XUA-XUZ	Cambodia (Kingdom of)	6VA-6WZ	Senegal
XVA-XVZ	Viet Nam	6XA-6XZ	Madagascar
XWA-XWZ	Laos (People's Dem Rep)	6YA-6YZ	Jamaica
XXA-XXZ	China (People's Republic of) - Macao	6ZA-6ZZ	Liberia
XYA-XZZ	Myanmar	7AA-7IZ	Indonesia
YAA-YAZ	Afghanistan	7JA-7NZ	Japan
YBA-YHZ	Indonesia	7OA-7OZ	Yemen
YIA-YIZ	Iraq	7PA-7PZ	Lesotho
YJA-YJZ	Vanuatu	7QA-7QZ	Malawi
YKA-YKZ	Syrian Arab Rep	7RA-7RZ	Algeria
YLA-YLZ	Latvia	7SA-7SZ	Sweden
YMA-YMZ	Turkey	7TA-7YZ	Algeria
YNA-YNZ	Nicaragua	7ZA-7ZZ	Saudi Arabia
YOA-YRZ	Romania	8AA-8IZ	Indonesia
YSA-YSZ	El Salvador	8JA-8NZ	Japan
YTA-YUZ	Serbia (Republic of)	8OA-8OZ	Botswana
YVA-YYZ	Venezuela	8PA-8PZ	Barbados
Y2A-Y9Z	Germany (Federal Rep of)	8QA-8QZ	Maldives
ZAA-ZAZ	Albania	8RA-8RZ	Guyana
ZBA-ZJZ	United Kingdom of Great Britain and Northern Ireland	8SA-8SZ	Sweden
ZKA-ZMZ	New Zealand	8TA-8YZ	India
ZNA-ZOZ	United Kingdom of Great Britain and Northern Ireland	8ZA-8ZZ	Saudi Arabia
ZPA-ZPZ	Paraguay	9AA-9AZ	Croatia
ZQA-ZQZ	United Kingdom of Great Britain and Northern Ireland	9BA-9DZ	Iran
ZRA-ZUZ	South Africa (Rep of)	9EA-9FZ	Ethiopia
ZVA-ZZZ	Brazil	9GA-9GZ	Ghana
Z2A-Z2Z	Zimbabwe	9HA-9HZ	Malta
Z3A-Z3Z	Former Yugoslav Republic of Macedonia	9IA-9JZ	Zambia
2AA-2ZZ	United Kindom of Great Britain and Northern Ireland	9KA-9KZ	Kuwait
3AA-3AZ	Monaco	9LA-9LZ	Sierra Leone
3BA-3BZ	Mauritius	9MA-9MZ	Malaysia
3CA-3CZ	Equatorial Guinea	9NA-9NZ	Nepal
3DA-3DM	Swaziland	9OA-9TZ	Congo (Dem Rep of)
3DN-3DZ	Fiji	9UA-9UZ	Burundi
3EA-3FZ	Panama	9VA-9VZ	Singapore
3GA-3GZ	Chile	9WA-9WZ	Malaysia
3HA-3UZ	China (People's Republic of)	9XA-9XZ	Rwanda
3VA-3VZ	Tunisia	9YZ-9ZZ	Trinidad and Tobago
3WA-3WZ	Viet Nam		

Morse Code Character Set[1]

A	didah	• —
B	dahdididit	— •••
C	dahdidahdit	— • — •
D	dahdidit	— ••
E	dit	•
F	dididahdit	•• — •
G	dahdahdit	— — •
H	didididit	••••
I	didit	••
J	didahdahdah	• — — —
K	dahdidah	— • —
L	didahdidit	• — ••
M	dahdah	— —
N	dahdit	— •
O	dahdahdah	— — —
P	didahdahdit	• — — •
Q	dahdahdidah	— — • —
R	didahdit	• — •
S	dididit	•••
T	dah	—
U	dididah	•• —
V	didididah	••• —
W	didahdah	• — —
X	dahdididah	— •• —
Y	dahdidahdah	— • — —
Z	dahdahdidit	— — ••

1	didahdahdahdah	• — — — —
2	dididahdahdah	•• — — —
3	didididahdah	••• — —
4	dididididah	•••• —
5	didididit	•••••
6	dahdidididit	— ••••
7	dahdahdididit	— — •••
8	dahdahdahdidit	— — — ••
9	dahdahdahdahdit	— — — — •
0	dahdahdahdahdah	— — — — —

At [@]	didahdahdidahdit	• — — • — •	$\overline{AC}$
Period [.]:	didahdidahdidah	• — • — • —	$\overline{AAA}$
Comma [,]:	dahdahdididahdah	— — •• — —	$\overline{MIM}$
Question mark or request for repetition [?]:	dididahdahdidit	•• — — ••	$\overline{IMI}$
Error:	dididididididit	••••••••	$\overline{HH}$
Hyphen or dash [–]:	dahdidididah	— •••• —	$\overline{DU}$
Double dash [=]	dahdididah	— ••• —	$\overline{BT}$
Colon [:]:	dahdahdahdididit	— — — •••	$\overline{OS}$
Semicolon [;]:	dahdidahdidahdit	— • — • — •	$\overline{KR}$
Left parenthesis [(]:	dahdidahdahdit	— • — — •	$\overline{KN}$
Right parenthesis [)]:	dahdidahdahddidah	— • — — • —	$\overline{KK}$
Fraction bar [/]:	dahdididahdit	— •• — •	$\overline{DN}$
Quotation marks ["]:	didahdididahdit	• — •• — •	$\overline{AF}$
Dollar sign [$]:	didididahdidahdit	••• — • —	$\overline{SX}$
Apostrophe [']:	didahdahdahdahdit	• — — — — •	$\overline{WG}$
Paragraph [¶]:	didahdidahdit	• — • — •	$\overline{AL}$
Underline [_]:	dididahdahdidah	•• — — • —	$\overline{IQ}$
Starting signal:	dahdidahdidah	— • — • —	$\overline{KA}$
Wait:	didahdididit	• — •••	$\overline{AS}$
End of message or cross [+]:	didahdidahdit	• — • — •	$\overline{AR}$
Invitation to transmit [K]:	dahdidah	— • —	K
End of work:	dididahdidah	••• — • —	$\overline{SK}$
Understood:	dididahdit	••• — •	$\overline{SN}$

Notes:

1. Not all Morse characters shown are used in FCC code tests. License applicants are responsible for knowing, and may be tested on, the 26 letters, the numerals 0 to 9, the period, the comma, the question mark, $\overline{AR}$, $\overline{SK}$, $\overline{BT}$ and fraction bar [$\overline{DN}$].

2. The following letters are used in certain European languages which use the Latin alphabet:

Ä, Ą	didahdidah	• — • —
Á, Å, À, Â	didahdahdidah	• — — • —
Ç, Ć	dahdidahdidit	— • — ••
É, È, Ę	dididahdidit	•• — ••
È	didahdididah	• — ••—
Ê	dahdididahdit	— •• — •
Ö, Ô, Ó	dahdahdahdit	— — — •
Ñ	dahdahdidahdah	— — • — —
Ü	dididahdah	•• — —
Ź	dahdahdidit	— —••
Z	dahdahdididah	— —•• —
CH, Ş	dahdahdahdah	— — — —

3. Special Esperanto characters:

$\hat{C}$	dahdidahdidit	— • — ••	
$\hat{S}$	didididahdit	••• — •	
$\hat{J}$	didahdahdahdit	• — — — •	
$\hat{H}$	dahdidahdahdit	— • — — •	
$\hat{U}$	dididahdah	•• — —	
$\hat{G}$	dahdahdidahdit	— — • — •	

4. Signals used in other radio services:

Interrogatory	dididahdidah	•• — • —	$\overline{INT}$
Emergency silence	didididahdah	•••• — —	$\overline{HM}$
Executive follows	dididahdidah	•• — •• —	$\overline{IX}$
Break–in signal	dahdahdahdahdah	— — — — —	$\overline{TTTTT}$
Emergency signal	dididahdahdahdididit	••• — — — •••	$\overline{SOS}$
Relay of distress	dahdidididahdididahdidit	— •• — •• — ••	$\overline{DDD}$

Morse Code for Other Languages

Code	Japanese	Korean	Arabic	Hebrew	Russian	Greek
•	he	a		vav	Е,Э E	E epsilon
—	mu	ŏ	ta	tav	Т T	T tau
••	nigori	ya	ya	yod	И I	I iota
•—	i	o	alif	aleph	А A	A alpha
—•	ta	yo	noon	nun	Н N	N nu
——	yo	m	meem	mem	М M	M mu
•••	ra	yŏ	seen	shin	С S	Σ sigma
••—	u		ta	tet	У U	ΟΤ omicron ypsilon
•—•	na	yu	ra	reish	Р R	P rho
•——	ya	p(b)	waw	tzadi	В V	Ω omega
—••	ho		dal	dalet	Д D	Δ delta
—•—	wa	-ng	kaf	chaf	К K	K kappa
——•	ri	s	ghain	gimmel	Г G	Γ gamma
———	re	p'	kha	heh	О O	O omicron
••••	nu	u	ha	chet	Х H	H eta
•••—	ku	r-(l)	dad		Ж J	HT eta ypsilon
••—•	ti	n	fa	feh	Ф F	Φ phi
••——	no				Ю yu	AT alpha ypsilon
•—••	ka	k(g)	lam	lamed	Л L	Λ lambda
•—•—	ro	ch(j)	ain		Я ya	ΑΙ alpha iota
•——•	tu	h	jeem	peh	П P	Π pi
•———	wo	t(d)	ba	ayen	Й Y	ΤΙ ypsilon iota
—•••	ha	k'	sad	bet	Б B	B beta
—••—	ma	ch'	tha	samech	ь,ъ mute	Ξ xi
—•—•	ni	e	za		Ц TS	Θ theta
—•——	ke	t'	dhal	zain	Ы I	T ypsilon
——••	hu	ae	qaf	kof	З Z	Z zeta
——•—	ne		zay		Щ SHCH	Ψ psi
———•	so		sheen		Ч CH	ET epsilon ypsilon
————	ko		he		Ш SH	X khi
••—••	to					
••—•—	mi					
••——•	han-nigori					
•—•••	o					
•—••—	(w)i					
•—•—•	n					
•—•—•	te					
•—•——	(w)e					
•——•—	hyphen					
•———•	se					
—•••—	me					
—••—•	mo					
—•—••	yu					
—•—•—	~ki					
——•••	sa					
——••—	ru					
——•—•	e					
——•——	hi					
———••	si					
———•—	a					
————•	su					
•—•••—			lam-alif			

Spanish Phonetics

America	ah-MAIR-ika
Brasil	brah-SIL
Canada	cana-DAH
Dinamarca	dina-MAR-ka
Espana	es-PAHN-yah
Francia	FRAHN-seeah
Grenada	gre-NAH-dah
Holanda	oh-LONN-dah
Italia	i-TAL-eeah
Japon	hop-OWN
Kilowatio	kilo-WAT-eeoh
Lima	LIMA
Mejico	MEH-heeco
Norvega	nor-WAY-gah
Ontario	on-TAR-eeoh
Portugal	portu-GAL
Quito	KEY-toe
Roma	ROW-mah
Santiago	santee-AH-go
Toronto	tor-ON-toe
Uniforme	oonee-FORM-eh
Victoria	vic-TOR-eeah
Washington, Wisky	washingtone, wisky
Xilofono	see-LOW-phono
Yucatan	yuca-TAN
Zelandia	see-LAND-eeah
W	DOE-bleh-vay

0	cero	SEH-roe
1	uno	OO-no
2	dos	DOS
3	tres	TRAYCE
4	cuatro	KWAT-roe
5	cinco	SINK-oh
6	seis	SAYCE
7	siete	see-AY-teh
8	ocho	OCH-oh
9	nueve	new-AY-veh

—John Mason Jr., EA4AXW

A large selection of phonetic alphabets is at
http://www.cl.cam.ac.uk/users/bck1/menu.html
and
http://www.columbia.edu/~fuat/cuarc/phonetic.html

Morse Abbeviated ("Cut") Numbers

Numeral	Long Number			Abbreviated Number		Equivalent Character
1	didahdahdahdah	•————		didah	•—	A
2	dididahdahdah	••———		dididah	••—	U
3	didididahdah	•••——		didididah	•••—	V
4	didididah	••••—		didididah	••••—	4
5	dididididit	•••••		dididididit	••••• or •	5 or E
6	dahdidididit	—••••		dahdidididit	—••••	6
7	dahdahdididit	——•••		dahdididit	—•••	B
8	dahdahdahdidit	———••		dahdidit	—••	D
9	dahdahdahdahdit	————•		dahdit	—•	N
0	dahdahdahdahdah	—————		dah	—	T

Note: These abbreviated numbers are not legal for use in call signs. They should be used only where there is agreement between operators and when no confusion will result.

DX Operating Code

For W/VE Amateurs

Some DXers have caused considerable confusion and interference in their efforts to work DX stations. The points below, if observed by all W/VE amateurs, will help make DX more enjoyable for all.

1) *Call* DX only after he calls CQ, QRZ? or signs $\overline{SK}$, or voice equivalents thereof. Make your calls short.

2) Do not call a DX station:

a) On the frequency of the station he is calling until you are sure the QSO is over ($\overline{SK}$).

b) Because you hear someone else calling him.

c) When he signs $\overline{KN}$, AR or CL.

d) Exactly on his frequency.

e) After he calls a directional CQ, unless of course you are in the right direction or area.

3) Keep within frequency band limits. Some DX stations can get away with working outside, but you cannot.

4) Observe calling instructions given by DX stations. Example: 15U means "call 15 kHz up from my frequency." 15D means down, etc.

5) Give honest reports. Many DX stations depend on W/VE reports for adjustment of station and equipment.

6) Keep your signal clean. Key clicks, ripple, feedback or splatter gives you a bad reputation and may get you a citation from the FCC.

7) *Listen* and call the station you want. Calling CQ DX is not the best assurance that the rare DX will reply.

8) When there are several W or VE stations waiting, avoid asking DX to "listen for a friend." Also avoid engaging him in a ragchew against his wishes.

For Overseas Amateurs

To all overseas amateur stations:

In their eagerness to work you, many W and VE amateurs resort to practices that cause confusion and QRM. Most of this is good-intentioned but ill-advised; some of it is intentional and selfish. The key to the cessation of unethical DX operating practices is in your hands. We believe that your adoption of certain operating habits will increase your enjoyment of Amateur Radio and that of amateurs on this side who are eager to work you. We recommend your adoption of the following principles:

1) Do not answer calls on your own frequency.

2) Answer calls from W/VE stations only when their signals are of good quality.

3) Refuse to answer calls from other stations when you are already in contact with someone, and do not acknowledge calls from amateurs who indicate they wish to be "next."

4) Give *everybody* a break. When many W/VE amateurs are patiently and quietly waiting to work you, avoid complying with requests to "listen for a friend."

5) Tell listeners where to call you by indicating how many kilohertz up (U) or down (D) from your frequency you are listening.

6) Use the ARRL-recommended ending signals, especially $\overline{KN}$ to indicate to impatient listeners the status of the QSO.

$\overline{KN}$ means "Go ahead (specific station); all others keep out."

7) Let it be known that you avoid working amateurs who are constant violators of these principles.

ARRL Procedural Signals (Prosigns)

In general, the CW prosigns are used on all data modes as well, although word abbreviations may be spelled out. That is, "CLEAR" might be used rather than "CL" on radioteletype. Additional radioteletype conventions appear at the end of the table.

Situation	CW	Voice
check for a clear frequency	QRL?	Is the frequency in use?
seek contact with any station	CQ	CQ
after call to specific named station or to indicate end of message	AR	over, end of message
invite any station to transmit	K	go
invite a specific named station to transmit	KN	go only
invite receiving station to transmit	BK	back to you
all received correctly	R	received
please stand by	AS	wait, stand by
end of contact (sent before call sign)	SK	clear
going off the air	CL	closing station

Additional RTTY prosigns

SK QRZ—Ending contact, but listening on frequency.
SK KN—Ending contact, but listening for one last transmission from the other station.
SK SZ—Signing off and listening on the frequency for any other calls.

Q Signals

These Q signals most often need to be expressed with brevity and clarity in amateur work. (Q abbreviations take the form of questions only when each is sent followed by a question mark.)

QRA   What is the name of your station? The name of your station is _____.

QRG   Will you tell me my exact frequency (or that of _____)? Your exact frequency (or that of _____) is _____ kHz.

QRH   Does my frequency vary? Your frequency varies.

QRI   How is the tone of my transmission? The tone of your transmission is _____ (1. Good; 2. Variable; 3. Bad).

QRJ   Are you receiving me badly? I cannot receive you. Your signals are too weak.

QRK   What is the intelligibility of my signals (or those of _____)? The intelligibility of your signals (or those of _____) is _____ (1. Bad; 2. Poor; 3. Fair; 4. Good; 5. Excellent).

QRL   Are you busy? I am busy (or I am busy with _____). Please do not interfere.

QRM   Is my transmission being interfered with? Your transmission is being interfered with (1. Nil; 2. Slightly; 3. Moderately; 4. Severely; 5. Extremely.)

QRN   Are you troubled by static? I am troubled by static _____ (1-5 as under QRM).

QRO   Shall I increase power? Increase power.

QRP   Shall I decrease power? Decrease power.

QRQ   Shall I send faster? Send faster (_____ WPM).

QRS   Shall I send more slowly? Send more slowly (_____ WPM).

QRT   Shall I stop sending? Stop sending.

QRU   Have you anything for me? I have nothing for you.

QRV   Are you ready? I am ready.

QRW   Shall I inform _____ that you are calling on _____ kHz? Please inform _____ that I am calling on _____ kHz.

QRX   When will you call me again? I will call you again at _____ hours (on _____ kHz).

QRY   What is my turn? Your turn is numbered _____

QRZ   Who is calling me? You are being called by _____ (on _____ kHz).

QSA   What is the strength of my signals (or those of _____)? The strength of your signals (or those of _____) is _____

(1. Scarcely perceptible; 2. Weak; 3. Fairly good; 4. Good; 5. Very good).

QSB   Are my signals fading? Your signals are fading.

QSD   Is my keying defective? Your keying is defective.

QSG   Shall I send _____ messages at a time? Send _____ messages at a time.

QSK   Can you hear me between your signals and if so can I break in on your transmission? I can hear you between my signals; break in on my transmission.

QSL   Can you acknowledge receipt? I am acknowledging receipt.

QSM   Shall I repeat the last message which I sent you, or some previous message? Repeat the last message which you sent me [or message(s) number(s) _____].

QSN   Did you hear me (or _____) on _____ kHz? I did hear you (or _____) on _____ kHz.

QSO   Can you communicate with _____ direct or by relay? I can communicate with _____ direct (or by relay through _____).

QSP   Will you relay to _____? I will relay to _____

QST   General call preceding a message addressed to all amateurs and ARRL members. This is in effect "CQ ARRL."

QSU   Shall I send or reply on this frequency (or on _____ kHz)? Send or reply on this frequency (or _____ kHz).

QSV   Shall I send a series of Vs on this frequency (or on _____ kHz)? Send a series of Vs on this frequency (or on _____ kHz).

QSW   Will you send on this frequency (or on _____ kHz)? I am going to send on this frequency (or on _____ kHz).

QSX   Will you listen to _____ on _____ kHz? I am listening to _____ on _____ kHz.

QSY   Shall I change to transmission on another frequency? Change to transmission on another frequency (or on _____ kHz).

QSZ   Shall I send each word or group more than once? Send each word or group twice (or _____ times).

QTA   Shall I cancel message number _____? Cancel message number _____

QTB   Do you agree with my counting of words? I do not agree

	with your counting of words. I will repeat the first letter or digit of each word or group.	
QTC	How many messages have you to send? I have _____ messages for you (or for _____).	
QTH	What is your location? My location is _____	
QTR	What is the correct time? The correct time is _____	
QTV	Shall I stand guard for you? Stand guard for me.	
QTX	Will you keep your station open for further communication with me? Keep your station open for me.	
QUA	Have you news of _____? I have news of _____.	

ARRL QN Signals

QNA*	Answer in prearranged order.
QNB	Act as relay between _____ and _____.
QNC	All net stations copy. I have a message for all net stations.
QND*	Net is Directed (Controlled by net control station.)
QNE*	Entire net stand by.
QNF	Net is Free (not controlled).
QNG	Take over as net control station
QNH	Your net frequency is High.
QNI	Net stations report in. I am reporting into the net. (Follow with a list of traffic or QRU.)
QNJ	Can you copy me?
QNK*	Transmit messages for _____ to _____.
QNL	Your net frequency is Low.
QNM*	You are QRMing the net. Stand by.
QNN	Net control station is _____. What station has net control?
QNO	Station is leaving the net.
QNP	Unable to copy you. Unable to copy _____.

QNQ*	Move frequency to _____ and wait for _____ to finish handling traffic. Then send him traffic for _____.
QNR*	Answer _____ and Receive traffic.
QNS	Following Stations are in the net.* (follow with list.) Request list of stations in the net.
QNT	I request permission to leave the net for _____ minutes.
QNU*	The net has traffic for *you*. Stand by.
QNV*	Establish contact with _____ on this frequency. If successful, move to _____ and send him traffic for _____.
QNW	How do I route messages for _____?
QNX	You are excused from the net.*
QNY*	Shift to another frequency (or to _____ kHz) to clear traffic with _____.
QNZ	Zero beat your signal with mine.

*For use only by the Net Control Station.

Notes on Use of QN Signals

These QN signals are special ARRL signals for use in amateur CW nets *only*. They are not for use in casual amateur conversation. Other meanings that may be used in other services do not apply. Do not use QN signals on phone nets. *Say it with words.* QN signals need not be followed by a question mark, even though the meaning may be interrogatory.

The RST System

Readability

1—Unreadable.
2—Barely readable, occasional words distinguishable.
3—Readable with considerable difficulty.
4—Readable with practically no difficulty.
5—Perfectly readable.

Signal Strength

1—Faint signals, barely perceptible.
2—Very weak signals.
3—Weak signals.
4—Fair signals.
5—Fairly good signals.
6—Good signals.
7—Moderately strong signals.
8—Strong signals.
9—Extremely strong signals.

Tone

1—Sixty-cycle ac or less, very rough and broad.
2—Very rough ac, very harsh and broad.
3—Rough ac tone, rectified but not filtered.
4—Rough note, some trace of filtering.
5—Filtered rectified ac but strongly ripple-modulated.
6—Filtered tone, definite trace of ripple modulation.
7—Near pure tone, trace of ripple modulation.
8—Near perfect tone, slight trace of modulation.
9—Perfect tone, no trace of ripple of modulation of any kind.

If the signal has the characteristic steadiness of crystal control, add the letter X to the RST report. If there is a chirp, add the letter C. Similarly for a click, add K. (See FCC Regulations §97.307, Emissions Standards.) The above reporting system is used on both CW and voice; leave out the "tone" report on voice.

CW Abbreviations

AA	All after	HI	The telegraphic laugh; high	SKED	Schedule
AB	All before	HR	Here, hear	SRI	Sorry
AB	About	HV	Have	SSB	Single sideband
ADR	Address	HW	How	SVC	Service; prefix to service message
AGN	Again	LID	A poor operator		
ANT	Antenna	MA, MILS	Milliamperes	T	Zero
BCI	Broadcast interference	MSG	Message; prefix to radiogram	TFC	Traffic
BCL	Broadcast listener	N	No	TMW	Tomorrow
BK	Break; break me; break in	NCS	Net control station	TNX-TKS	Thanks
BN	All between; been	ND	Nothing doing	TT	That
BUG	Semi-automatic key	NIL	Nothing; I have nothing for you	TU	Thank you
B4	Before	NM	No more	TVI	Television interference
C	Yes	NR	Number	TX	Transmitter
CFM	Confirm; I confirm	NW	Now; I resume transmission	TXT	Text
CK	Check	OB	Old boy	UR-URS	Your; you're; yours
CL	I am closing my station; call	OC	Old chap	VFO	Variable-frequency oscillator
CLD-CLG	Called; calling	OM	Old man	VY	Very
CQ	Calling any station	OP-OPR	Operator	WA	Word after
CUD	Could	OT	Old timer; old top	WB	Word before
CUL	See you later	PBL	Preamble	WD-WDS	Word; words
CW	Continuous wave (i.e., radio-telegraph)	PSE	Please	WKD-WKG	Worked; working
		PWR	Power	WL	Well; will
DE	From	PX	Press	WUD	Would
DLD-DLVD	Delivered	R	Received as transmitted; are	WX	Weather
DR	Dear	RCD	Received	XCVR	Transceiver
DX	Distance, foreign countries	RCVR (RX)	Receiver	XMTR (TX)	Transmitter
ES	And, &	REF	Refer to; referring to; reference	XTAL	Crystal
FB	Fine business, excellent	RFI	Radio Frequency Interference	XYL (YF)	Wife
FM	Frequency modulation	RIG	Station equipment	YL	Young lady
GA	Go ahead (or resume sending)	RPT	Repeat; I repeat; report	73	Best regards
GB	Good-by	RTTY	Radioteletype	88	Love and Kisses
GBA	Give better address	RX	Receiver		
GE	Good evening	SASE	Self-addressed, stamped envelope		
GG	Going				
GM	Good morning	SED	Said		
GN	Good night	SIG	Signature; signal		
GND	Ground	SINE	Operator's personal initials or nickname		
GUD	Good				

Although abbreviations help to cut down unnecessary transmission, make it a rule not to abbreviate unnecessarily when working an operator of unknown experience.

ITU Recommended Phonetics

A — Alfa (**AL** FAH)
B — Bravo (**BRAH** VOH)
C — Charlie (**CHAR** LEE OR **SHAR** LEE)
D — Delta (**DELL** TAH)
E — Echo (**ECK** OH)
F — Foxtrot (**FOKS** TROT)
G — Golf (**GOLF**)
H — Hotel (HOH **TELL**)
I — India (**IN** DEE AH)
J — Juliet (**JEW** LEE ETT)
K — Kilo (**KEY** LOH)
L — Lima (**LEE** MAH)
M — Mike (**MIKE**)
N — November (NO **VEM** BER)
O — Oscar (**OSS** CAH)
P — Papa (PAH **PAH**)

Q — Quebec (KEH **BECK**)
R — Romeo (**ROW** ME OH)
S — Sierra (SEE *AIR* RAH)
T — Tango (**TANG** GO)
U — Uniform (**YOU** NEE FORM or **OO** NEE FORM)
V — Victor (**VIK** TAH)
W — Whiskey (**WISS** KEY)
X — X-Ray (**ECKS** RAY)
Y — Yankee (**YANG** KEY)
Z — Zulu (**ZOO** LOO)

Note: The **Boldfaced** syllables are emphasized. The pronunciations shown in the table were designed for speakers from all international languages. The pronunciations given for "Oscar" and "Victor" may seem awkward to English-speaking people in the U.S.

ARRL NUMBERED RADIOGRAMS

Group One—For Possible "Relief Emergency" Use

ONE	Everyone safe here. Please don't worry.
TWO	Coming home as soon as possible.
THREE	Am in _____ hospital. Receiving excellent care and recovering fine.
FOUR	Only slight property damage here. Do not be concerned about disaster reports.
FIVE	Am moving to new location. Send no further mail or communication. Will inform you of new address when relocated.
SIX	Will contact you as soon as possible.
SEVEN	Please reply by Amateur Radio through the amateur delivering this message. This is a free public service.
EIGHT	Need additional _____ mobile or portable equipment for immediate emergency use.
NINE	Additional _____ radio operators needed to assist with emergency at this location.
TEN	Please contact _____. Advise to standby and provide further emergency information, instructions or assistance.
ELEVEN	Establish Amateur Radio emergency communications with _____ on _____ MHz.
TWELVE	Anxious to hear from you. No word in some time. Please contact me as soon as possible.
THIRTEEN	Medical emergency situation exits here.
FOURTEEN	Situation here becoming critical. Losses and damage from _____ increasing.
FIFTEEN	Please advise your condition and what help is needed.
SIXTEEN	Property damage very severe in this area.
SEVENTEEN	REACT communications services also available. Establish REACT communication with _____ on channel _____.
EIGHTEEN	Please contact me as soon as possible at _____.
NINETEEN	Request health and welfare report on _____. (State name, address and telephone number.)
TWENTY	Temporarily stranded. Will need some assistance. Please contact me at _____.
TWENTY ONE	Search and Rescue assistance is needed by local authorities here. Advise availability.
TWENTY TWO	Need accurate information on the extent and type of conditions now existing at your location. Please furnish this information and reply without delay.
TWENTY THREE	Report at once the accessibility and best way to reach your location.
TWENTY FOUR	Evacuation of residents from this area urgently needed. Advise plans for help.
TWENTY FIVE	Furnish as soon as possible the weather conditions at your location.
TWENTY SIX	Help and care for evacuation of sick and injured from this location needed at once.

Emergency/priority messages originating from official sources must carry the signature of the originating official.

Group Two—Routine Messages

FORTY SIX	Greetings on your birthday and best wishes for many more to come.
FORTY SEVEN	Reference your message number _____ to _____ delivered on _____ at _____ UTC.
FIFTY	Greetings by Amateur Radio.
FIFTY ONE	Greetings by Amateur Radio. This message is sent as a free public service by ham radio operators at _____. Am having a wonderful time.
FIFTY TWO	Really enjoyed being with you. Looking forward to getting together again.
FIFTY THREE	Received your _____. It's appreciated; many thanks.
FIFTY FOUR	Many thanks for your good wishes.
FIFTY FIVE	Good news is always welcome. Very delighted to hear about yours.
FIFTY SIX	Congratulations on your _____, a most worthy and deserved achievement.
FIFTY SEVEN	Wish we could be together.
FIFTY EIGHT	Have a wonderful time. Let us know when you return.
FIFTY NINE	Congratulations on the new arrival. Hope mother and child are well.
*SIXTY	Wishing you the best of everything on _____.
SIXTY ONE	Wishing you a very Merry Christmas and a Happy New Year.
*SIXTY TWO	Greetings and best wishes to you for a pleasant _____ holiday season.
SIXTY THREE	Victory or defeat, our best wishes are with you. Hope you win.
SIXTY FOUR	Arrived safely at _____.
SIXTY FIVE	Arriving _____ on _____. Please arrange to meet me there.
SIXTY SIX	DX QSLs are on hand for you at the _____ QSL Bureau. Send _____ self addressed envelopes.
SIXTY SEVEN	Your message number _____ undeliverable because of _____. Please advise.
SIXTY EIGHT	Sorry to hear you are ill. Best wishes for a speedy recovery.
SIXTY NINE	Welcome to the _____. We are glad to have you with us and hope you will enjoy the fun and fellowship of the organization.

*Can be used for all holidays.

Note: ARL numbers should be spelled out at all times.

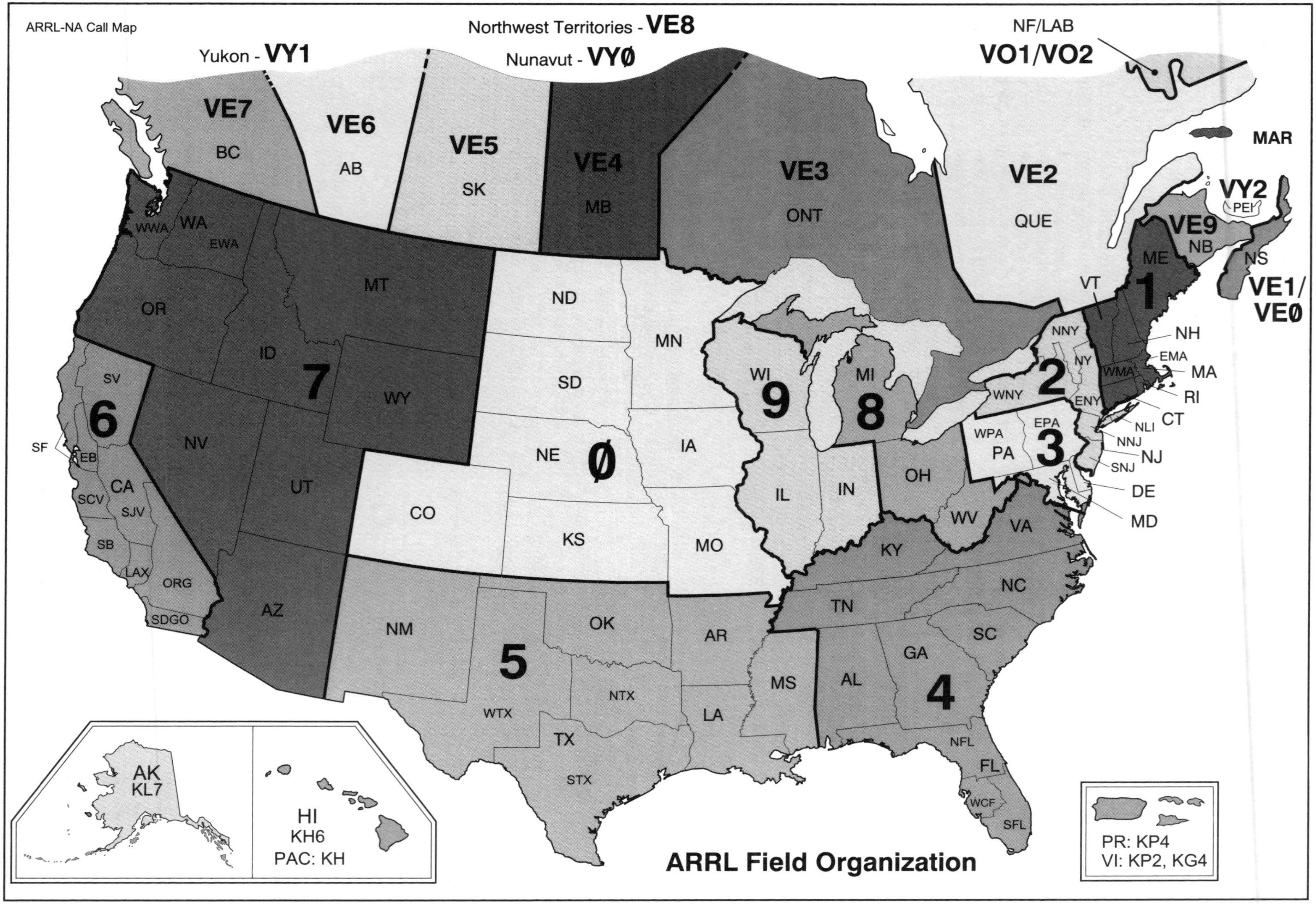

ARRL-NA Call Map
Northwest Territories - VE8
Yukon - VY1
Nunavut - VYØ
NF/LAB
VO1/VO2
VE7
BC
VE6
AB
VE5
SK
VE4
MB
VE3
ONT
VE2
QUE
MAR
VY2
PEI
VE9
NB
NS
VE1/
VEØ
WWA
WA
EWA
OR
ID
MT
WY
7
SV
6
SF
EB
CA
SCV
SJV
SB
LAX
ORG
SDGO
NV
UT
AZ
ND
SD
NE
Ø
KS
CO
MN
IA
MO
WI
9
IL
IN
MI
8
OH
NNY
NY
2
WNY
ENY
WPA
PA
EPA
3
VT
ME
1
NH
EMA
MA
WMA
RI
CT
NLI
NNJ
NJ
SNJ
DE
MD
WV
VA
KY
NC
TN
SC
GA
AL
4
NFL
FL
WCF
SFL
NM
5
OK
AR
MS
LA
NTX
WTX
TX
STX
AK
KL7
HI
KH6
PAC: KH
PR: KP4
VI: KP2, KG4
ARRL Field Organization

A map showing US states, Canadian provinces and ARRL/RAC Sections.

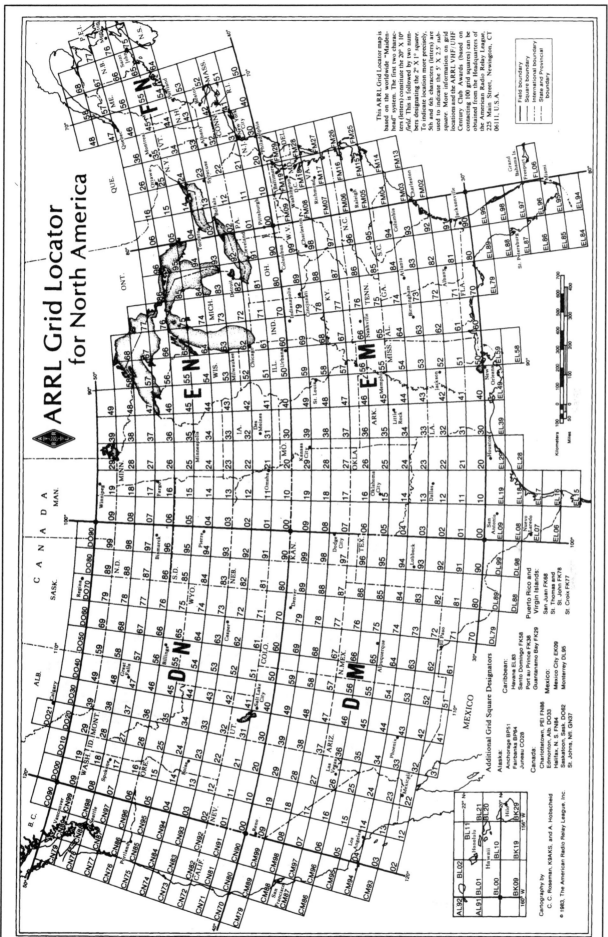

ARRL Grid Locator Map for North America. This map and the World Grid Locator Map are available from ARRL.

CALIFORNIA COUNTIES/ARRL SECTION
HAM OUTLINE MAP #27

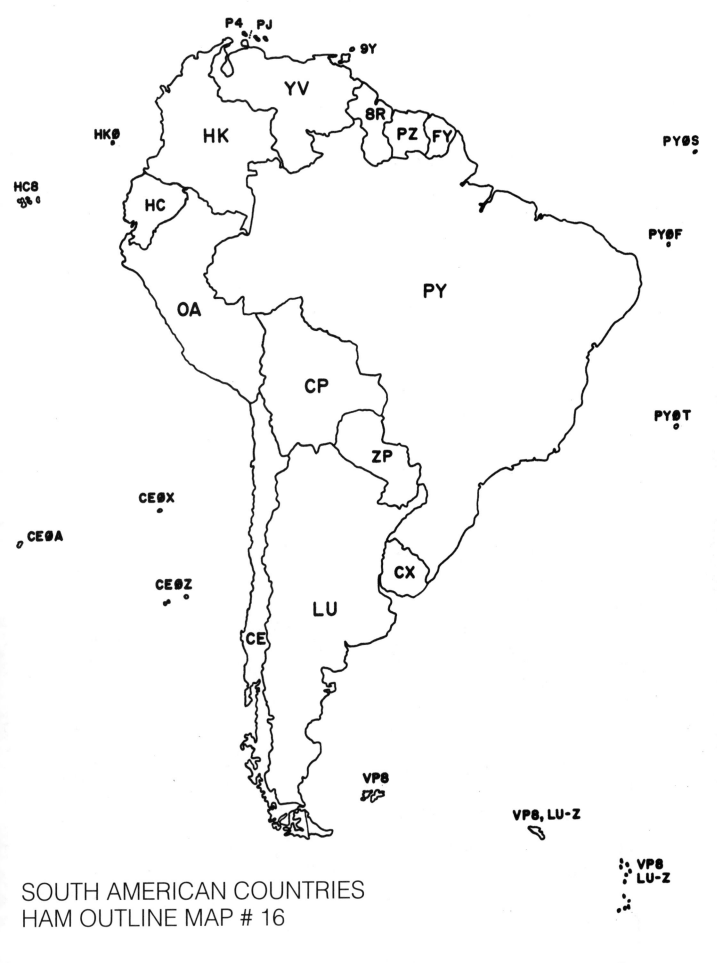

P4 PJ

9Y

YV

HKØ

HK

8R

PZ FY

PYØS

HC8

HC

PYØF

OA

PY

CP

PYØT

ZP

CEØX

CEØA

CX

CEØZ

LU

CE

VP8

VP8, LU-Z

VP8
LU-Z

SOUTH AMERICAN COUNTRIES
HAM OUTLINE MAP # 16

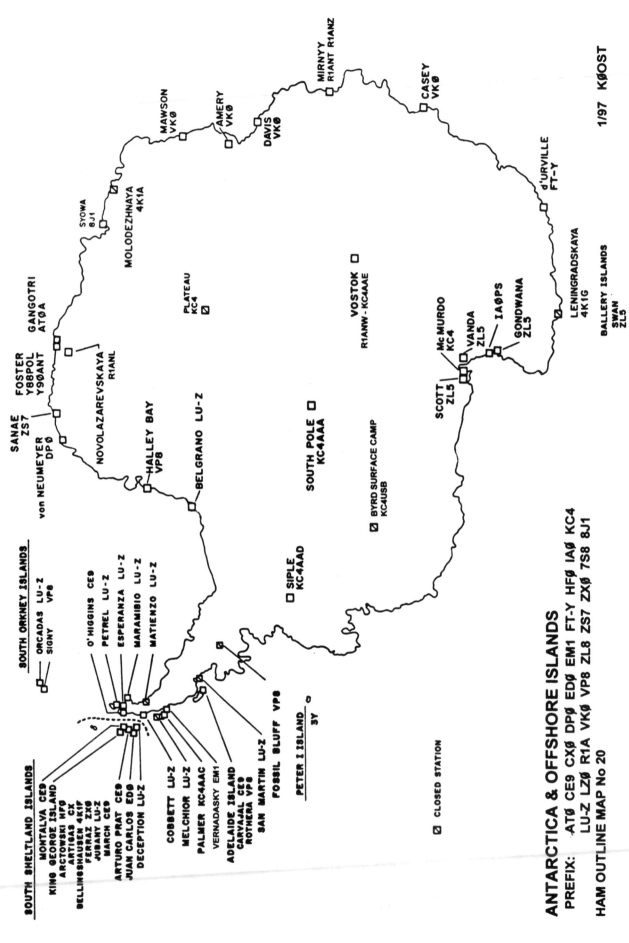

ANTARCTICA & OFFSHORE ISLANDS

PREFIX: ATØ CE9 CXØ DPØ EDØ EM1 FT-Y HFØ IAØ KC4 LU-Z LZØ R1A VKØ VP8 ZL8 ZS7 ZXØ 7S8 8J1

HAM OUTLINE MAP No 20

1/97 KØOST

⌧ CLOSED STATION

SOUTH ORKNEY ISLANDS
- ORCADAS LU-Z
- SIGNY VP8

SOUTH SHETLAND ISLANDS
- MONTALVA CE9
- KING GEORGE ISLAND
- ARCTOWSKI HFØ
- ARTIGAS CX
- BELLINGSHAUSEN 4K1F
- FERRAZ ZXØ
- JUBANY LU-Z
- MARCH CE9
- ARTURO PRAT CE9
- JUAN CARLOS EDØ
- DECEPTION LU-Z

- O'HIGGINS CE9
- PETREL LU-Z
- ESPERANZA LU-Z
- MARAMBIO LU-Z
- MATIENZO LU-Z

- COBBETT LU-Z
- MELCHIOR LU-Z
- PALMER KC4AAC
- VERNADASKY EM1

ADELAIDE ISLAND
- CARVAJAL CE9
- ROTHERA VP8
- SAN MARTIN LU-Z

- FOSSIL BLUFF VP8

PETER ISLAND 3Y

- SANAE ZS7
- FOSTER Y88POL Y9ØANT
- GANGOTRI ATØA
- von NEUMEYER DPØ
- NOVOLAZAREVSKAYA R1ANL
- HALLEY BAY VP8
- BELGRANO LU-Z
- SYOWA 8J1
- MOLODEZHNAYA 4K1A
- PLATEAU KC4
- SIPLE KC4AAD
- SOUTH POLE KC4AAA
- BYRD SURFACE CAMP KC4USB
- VOSTOK ☐
- R1ANW - KC4AAE
- MAWSON VKØ
- AMERY VKØ
- DAVIS VKØ
- MIRNYY R1ANT R1ANZ
- CASEY VKØ
- d'URVILLE FT-Y
- LENINGRADSKAYA 4K1G
- BALLERY ISLANDS
- SWAN ZL5
- McMURDO KC4
- SCOTT ZL5
- VANDA ZL5
- IAØPS
- GONDWANA ZL5

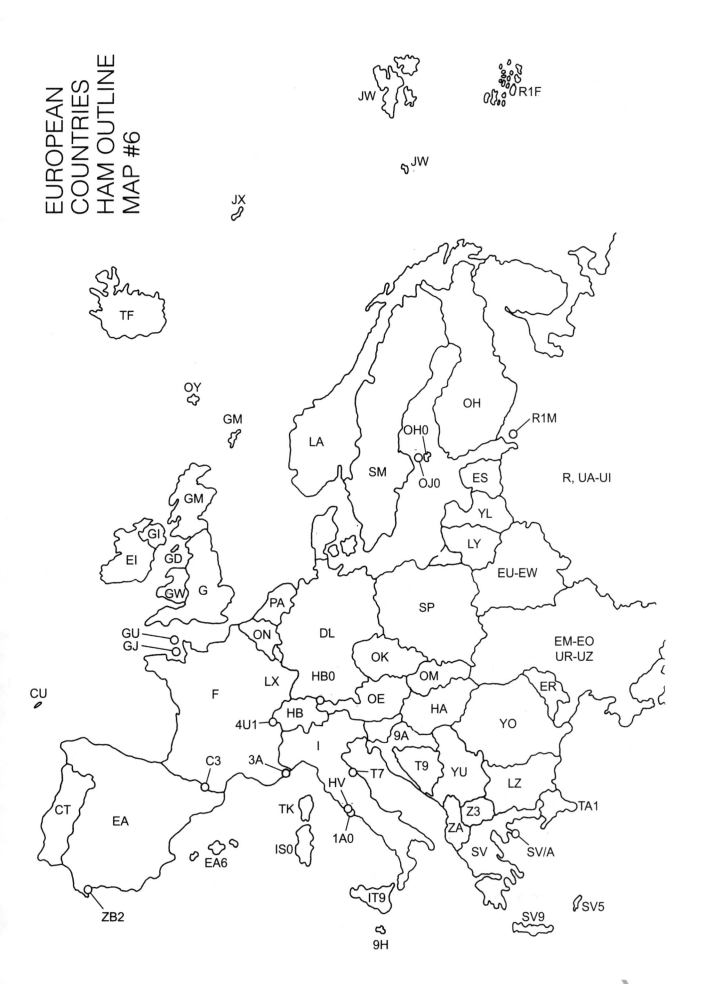

EUROPEAN
COUNTRIES
HAM OUTLINE
MAP #6

JW

R1F

JW

JX

TF

OY

GM

LA

OH

OH0

R1M

SM

OJ0

ES

R, UA-UI

GM

YL

GI

LY

EI

GD

EU-EW

GW

G

SP

PA

ON

DL

EM-EO
UR-UZ

GU

OK

GJ

OM

ER

CU

LX

HB0

OE

HA

YO

F

HB

4U1

9A

I

T7

T9

YU

LZ

C3

3A

HV

TA1

CT

TK

Z3

EA

ZA

1A0

SV/A

ISO

SV

EA6

ZB2

IT9

SV9

SV5

9H

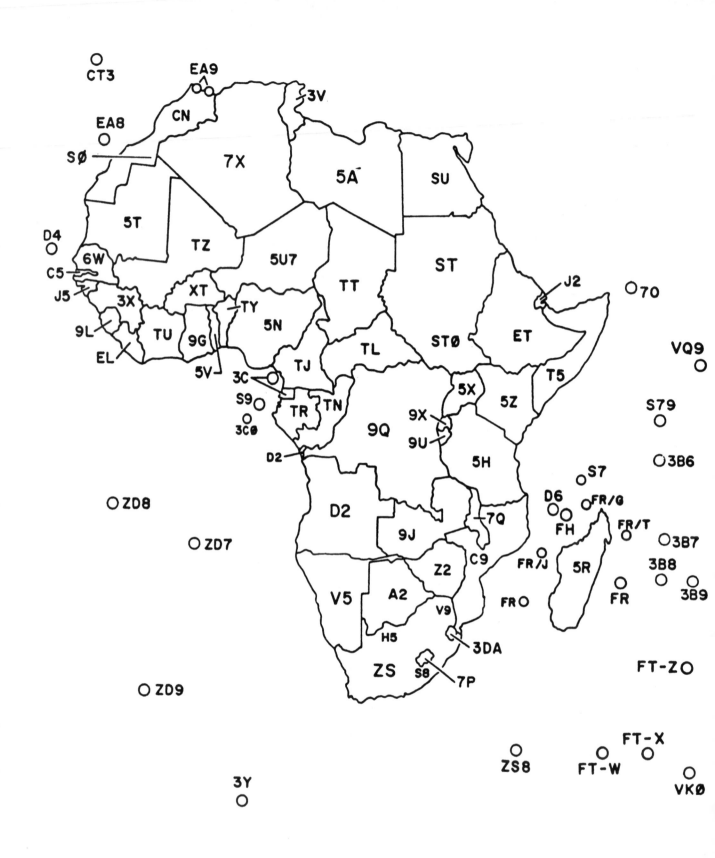

AFRICAN COUNTRIES
HAM OUTLINE MAP No 22

1/97 KØOST

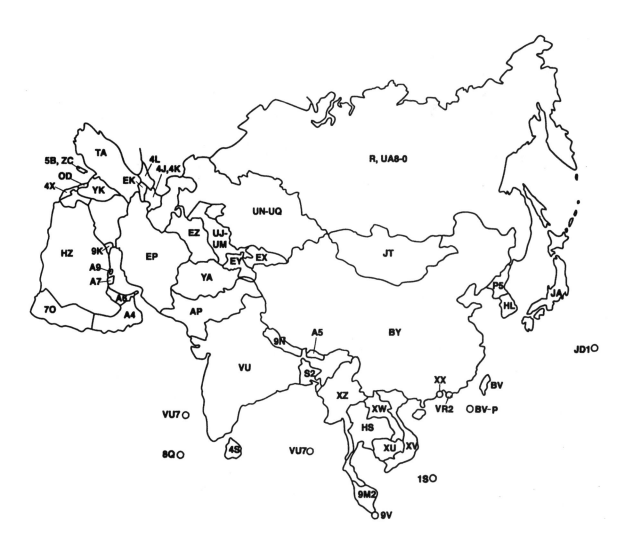

**ASIAN COUNTRIES
HAM OUTLINE MAP No 1**

3/00   KØOST

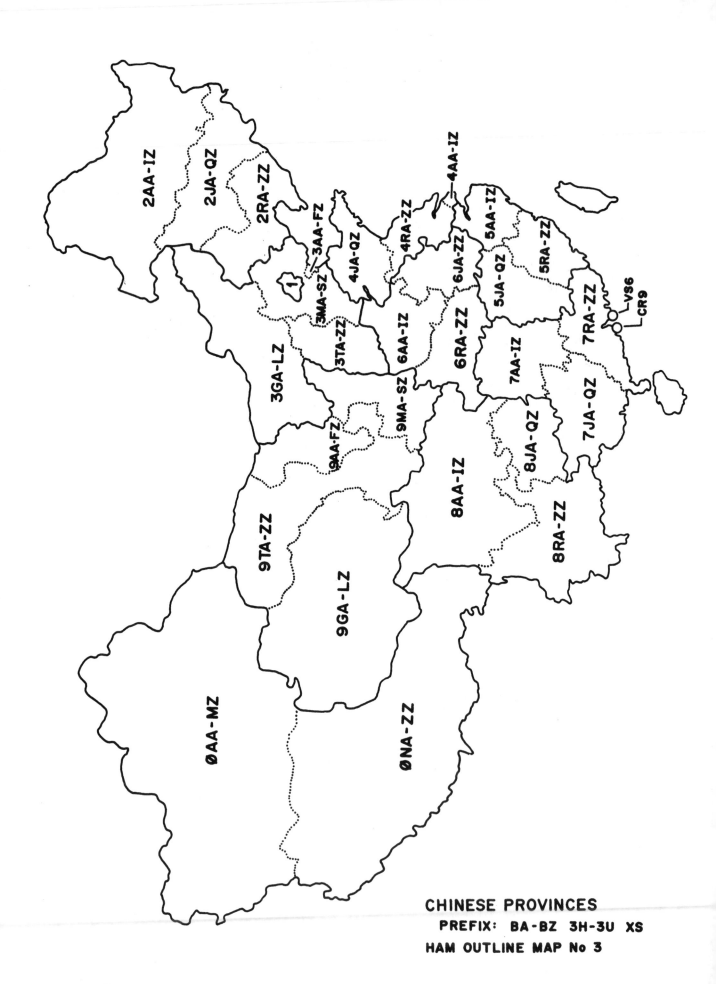

CHINESE PROVINCES
PREFIX: BA-BZ 3H-3U XS
HAM OUTLINE MAP No 3

ARRL Field Organization

The United States is divided into 15 ARRL Divisions. The ARRL full members in each of these divisions elect a director and a vice director to represent them on the League's Board of Directors. The Board determines the policies of the League, which are carried out by the Headquarters staff. A director's function is principally policymaking at the highest level, but the Board of Directors is all-powerful in the conduct of League affairs.

The 15 divisions are further broken down into 71 sections, and the ARRL full members in each section elect a Section Manager (SM). The SM is the senior elected ARRL official in the section, and in cooperation with the director, fosters and encourages all ARRL activities within the section. A breakdown of sections within each division (and counties within each splitstate section) follows:

ATLANTIC DIVISION: *Delaware, Eastern Pennsylvania* (Adams, Berks, Bradford, Bucks, Carbon, Chester, Columbia, Cumberland, Dauphin, Delaware, Juniata, Lackawanna, Lancaster, Lebanon, Lehigh, Luzerne, Lycoming, Monroe, Montgomery, Montour, Northhampton, Northumberland, Perry, Philadelphia, Pike, Schuylkill, Snyder, Sullivan, Susquehanna, Tioga, Union, Wayne, Wyoming, York); *Northern New York* (Clinton, Essex, Franklin, Fulton, Hamilton, Jefferson, Lewis, Montgomery, Schoharie, St. Lawrence); *Maryland -D.C.*; *Southern New Jersey* (Atlantic, Burlington, Camden, Cape May, Cumberland, Gloucester, Mercer, Ocean, Salem); *Western New York* (Allegany, Broome, Cattaraugus, Cayuga, Chautauqua, Chemung, Chenango, Cortland, Delaware, Erie, Genesee, Herkimer, Livingston, Madison, Monroe, Niagara, Oneida, Onondaga, Ontario, Orleans, Oswego, Otsego, Schuyler, Seneca, Steuben, Tioga, Tompkins, Wayne, Wyoming, Yates); *Western Pennsylvania* (those counties not listed under Eastern Pennsylvania).

CENTRAL DIVISION: *Illinois; Indiana; Wisconsin.*

DAKOTA DIVISION: *Minnesota; North Dakota; South Dakota.*

DELTA DIVISION: *Arkansas; Louisiana; Mississippi, Tennessee*

GREAT LAKES DIVISION; *Kentucky, Michigan; Ohio.*

HUDSON DIVISION: Eastern New York (Albany, Columbia, Dutchess, Greene, Orange, Putnam, Rensselaer, Rockland, Saratoga, Schenectady, Sullivan, Ulster, Warren, Washington, Westchester); *N.Y.C.-L.I.* (Bronx, Kings, Nassau, New York, Queens, Staten Island, Suffolk); *Northern New Jersey* (Bergen, Essex, Hudson, Hunterdon, Middlesex, Monmouth, Morris, Passaic, Somerset, Sussex, Union, Warren).

MIDWEST DIVISION: *Iowa; Kansas, Missouri, Nebraska.*

NEW ENGLAND DIVISION: *Connecticut, Maine, Eastern Massachusetts* (Barnstable, Bristol, Dukes, Essex, Middlesex, Nantucket, Norfolk, Plymouth, Suffolk); *New Hampshire; Rhode Island, Vermont, Western Massachusetts* (those counties not listed under Eastern Massachusetts).

NORTHWESTERN DIVISION: *Alaska; Idaho; Montana; Oregon; Eastern Washington* (Adams, Asotin, Benton, Chelan, Columbia, Douglas, Ferry, Franklin, Garfield, Grant, Kittitas, Klickitat, Lincoln, Okangogan, Pend Oreille, Spokane, Stevens, Walla, Walla, Whitman, Yakima); *Western Washington* (Challam, Clark Cowlitz, Grays Harbor Island, Jefferson, King, Kitsap, Lewis, Mason, Pacific, Pierce, San Juan, Skagit, Skamania, Snohomish, Thurston, Wahkiakum, Whatcom).

PACIFIC DIVISION: *East Bay* (Alameda, Contra Costa, Napa, Solano); *Nevada; Pacific* (Hawaii and U.S. possessions in the Pacific); *Sacramento Valley* (Alpine, Amador, Butte, Colusa, El Dorado, Glenn, Lassen, Modoc, Nevada, Placer, Plumas, Sacramento, Shasta, Sierra, Siskiyou, Sutter, Tehama, Trinity, Yolo, Yuba); *San Francisco*, (Del Norte, Humboldt, Lake, Marin, Mendocino, San Francisco, Sonoma); *San Joaquin Valley* (Calaveras, Fresno, Kern, Kings, Madera, Mariposa, Merced,

ARRL-Divisions

Mono, San Joaquin, Stanislaus, Tulare, Tuolumne); *Santa Clara Valley* (Monterey, San Benito, San Mateo, Santa Clara, Santa Cruz).

ROANOKE DIVISION: *North Carolina, South Carolina; Virginia; West Virginia.*

ROCKY MOUNTAIN DIVISION: *Colorado; Utah; New Mexico, Wyoming.*

SOUTHEASTERN DIVISION: *Alabama; Georgia; Northern Florida* (Alachua, Baker, Bay, Bradford, Calhoun, Citrus, Clay, Columbia, Dixie, Duval, Escambia, Flagler, Franklin, Gadsden, Gilchrist, Gulf, Hamilton, Hernando, Holmes, Jackson, Jefferson, Lafayette, Lake, Leon, Levy, Liberty, Madison, Marion, Nassau, Okaloosa, Orange, Pasco, Putnam, Santa Rosa, Seminole, St. Johns, Sumter, Suwanee, Taylor, Union, Volusia, Wakulla, Walton, Washington); *Southern Florida* (Brevard, Broward, Collier, Dade, Glades, Hendry, Indian River, Lee, Martin, Monroe, Okeechobee, Osceola, Palm Beach and St. Lucie); *Puerto Rico; U.S. Virgin Islands; West Central Florida* (Charlotte, DeSoto, Hardee, Highlands, Hillsborough, Manatee, Pinellas, Polk and Sarasota).

SOUTHWESTERN DIVISION: *Arizona; Los Angeles; Orange* (Inyo, Orange, Riverside, San Bernardino); *San Diego* (Imperial, San Diego); *Santa Barbara* (San Luis Obispo, Santa Barbara, Ventura).

WEST GULF DIVISION: *North Texas* (Anderson, Archer, Baylor, Bell, Bosque, Bowie, Brown, Camp, Cass, Cherokee, Clay, Collin, Comanche, Cooke, Coryell, Dallas, Delta, Denton, Eastland, Ellis, Erath, Falls, Fannin, Franklin, Freestone, Grayson, Gregg, Hamilton, Harrison, Henderson, Hill, Hopkins, Hunt, Jack, Johnson, Kaufman, Lamar, Lampasas, Limestone, McLennan, Marion, Mills, Montague, Morris, Nacogdoches, Navarro, Palo Pinto, Panola, Parker, Rains, Red River, Rockwall, Rusk, Shelby, Smith, Somervell, Stephens, Tarrant, Throckmorton, Titus, Upshur, Van Zandt, Wichita, Wilbarger, Wise, Wood, Young); *Oklahoma; South Texas* (Angelina, Aransas, Atacosa, Austin, Bandera, Bastrop, Bee, Bexar, Blanco, Brazoria, Brazos, Brooks, Burleson, Burnet, Caldwell, Calhoun, Cameron, Chambers, Colorado, Comal, Concho, DeWitt, Dimmitt, Duval, Edwards, Fayette, Fort Bend, Frio, Galveston, Gillespie, Goliad, Gonzales, Grimes, Guadalupe, Hardin, Harris, Hays, Hidalgo, Houston, Jackson, Jasper, Jefferson, Jim Hogg, Jim Wells, Karnes, Kendall, Kenedy, Kerr, Kimble, Kinney, Kleberg, LaSalle, Lavaca, Lee, Leon, Liberty, Live Oak, Llano, Madison, Mason, Matagorda, Maverick, McCulloch, McMullen, Medina, Menard, Milam, Montgomery, Newton, Nueces, Orange, Polk, Real, Refugio, Robertson, Sabine, San Augustine, San Jacinto, San Patricio, San Saba, Starr, Travis, Trinity, Tyle, Uvalde, Val Verde, Victoria, Walker, Waller, Washington, Webb, Wharton, Willacy, Williamson, Wilson, Zapata, Zavala); *West Texas* (Andrews, Armstrong, Bailey, Bordon, Brewster, Briscoe, Callahan, Carson, Castro, Childress, Cochran, Coke, Coleman, Collingsworth, Cottle, Crane, Crockett, Crosby, Culberson, Dallam, Dawson, Deaf Smith, Dickens, Donley, Ector, El Paso, Fischer, Floyd, Foard, Gaines, Garza, Glasscock, Gray, Hale, Hall, Hansford, Hardeman, Hartley, Haskell, Hemphill, Hockley, Howard Hudspeth, Hutchinson, Irion, Jeff Davis, Jones, Kent, King, Knox, Lamb, Lipscomb, Loving, Lubbock, Lynn, Martin, Midland, Mitchell, Moore, Motley, Nolan, Ochiltree, Oldham, Parmer, Pecos, Potter, Presidio, Randall, Reagan, Reeves, Roberts, Runnels, Schleicher, Scurry, Shackelford, Sherman, Sterling, Stonewall, Sutton, Swisher, Taylor, Terrell, Terry, Tom Green, Upton, Ward, Wheeler, Winkler, Yoakum).

RAC RADIO AMATEURS OF CANADA-CANADA; *Alberta; British Columbia; Manitoba; Maritime* (Nova Scotia, New Brunswick, Prince Edward Island); *Newfoundland/ Labrador, Ontario; Quebec; Saskatchewan.*

SECTION MANAGER

The Section Manager is accountable for carrying out the duties of the office in accordance with ARRL policies established by the Board of Directors and shall act in the best interests of Amateur Radio. In discharging these responsibilities, the Section Manager:

a) Recruits, appoints, and supervises section-level staff to administer the Field Organization's principal areas of responsibility in the section. These areas are emergency communications, message traffic relay, technical activity/problem solving, volunteer monitoring, government relations, public relations in the general community, information services for amateurs, and cooperation with affiliated clubs.

b) Appoints qualified ARRL members in the section to other volunteer positions in support of Field Organization objectives, and may authorize section-level staff to make such appointments.

c) Keeps well informed concerning matters of ARRL policy so as to administer the Field Organization in accordance with current policy and so as to provide correct information in response to members' inquiries.

d) Supervises the activities of the section-level staff, monitors the performance of the Field Organization volunteers, and provides guidance as necessary to ensure that appointees act in the best interests of Amateur Radio and in accordance with ARRL policies.

e) Maintains liaison with the Division Director; makes periodic reports to the Director regarding the status of Section activities; receives from the Director information and guidance pertaining to matters of mutual concern and interest; serves on the Division Cabinet and renders advice as requested by the Director.

f) Conducts correspondence and other communications with ARRL members and affiliated clubs in the Section; makes personal visits to clubs, hamfests, and conventions; responds to members' questions and concerns or refers them to an appropriate person or office in the League organization; maintains liaison with representative frequency coordinator(s) having jurisdiction in the Section.

g) Writes, or supervises preparation of, a monthly "Section News;" uses electronic communications, such as the Internet, to distribute information about Section activities and to encourage member participation in the Field Organization.

h) Each new Section Manager shall be required to participate in a Section Manager orientation training session that is conducted by ARRL Headquarters.

i) Promotes recruitment of new amateurs and new ARRL members; encourages attitudes and actions which welcome new radio amateurs and integrate them into League and club activities.

ARRL LEADERSHIP APPOINTMENTS

Field Organization leadership appointments are available to qualified ARRL full members in each section. Functions of these leadership officials are described below.

Recruitment of new hams and League members is an integral part of the job of every League appointee. Appointees should take advantage of every opportunity to recruit a new ham or member to foster growth of Field Organization programs, and our abilities to serve the public.

Assistant Section Manager

The ASM is an ARRL section-level official appointed by the Section Manager. An ASM may be appointed if the Section Manager believes such an appointment is desirable to meet the goals of the ARRL Field Organization in that section. Thus, the ASM is appointed at the complete discretion of the Section Manager, and serves at the pleasure of the Section Manager.

1) The ASM may serve as a general assistant to the Section Manager or as a specialist. That is, the ASM may assist the Section Manager with general leadership matters as the Section Manager's understudy, or the ASM may be assigned to handle a

specific important function that does not fail within the scope of the duties of the Section Manager's other assistants.

2) At the Section Manager's discretion, the ASM may be designated as the recommended successor to the incumbent Section Manager, in case the Section Manager resigns or is otherwise unable to finish the term of office.

3) The ASM should be familiar with the "Guidelines for the ARRL Section Manager," which contains the fundamentals of general section management.

4) The ASM must be an ARRL Full Member, holding at least a Novice class license.

Section Emergency Coordinator

The SEC is the assistant to the SM for emergency preparedness. The SEC is appointed by the SM to take care of all matters pertaining to emergency communications and the Amateur Radio Emergency Service (ARES) on a section wide basis. The SEC post is one of top importance in the section and the individual appointed to it should devote all possible energy and effort to this one challenging organizational program for Amateur Radio. There is only one SEC appointed in each section of the ARRL Field Organization.

SEC qualifications and functions:

1) Encourage all groups of community amateurs to establish a local emergency organization.

2) Advise the SM on all section emergency policy and planning, including the development of a section emergency communications plan.

3) Cooperate and coordinate with the Section Traffic Manager so that emergency nets and traffic nets in the section present a united public service front, particularly in the proper routing of Welfare traffic in emergency situations. Cooperation and coordination should also be maintained with other section leadership officials as appropriate, particularly with the State Government Liaison and Public Information Coordinator.

4) Recommend candidates for Emergency Coordinator and District Emergency Coordinator appointments (and cancellations) to the Section Manager and determine areas of jurisdiction of each amateur so appointed. At the SM's discretion, the SEC may be directly in charge of making (and canceling) such appointments. In the same way, the SEC can handle the Official Emergency Station appointments.

5) Promote ARES membership drives, meetings, activities, tests, procedures, etc., at the section level.

6) Collect and consolidate Emergency Coordinator (or District Emergency Coordinator) monthly reports and submit monthly progress summaries to the SM and ARRL Headquarters. This includes the timely reporting of emergency and public safety communications rendered in the section for inclusion in *QST*.

7) Maintain contact with other communication services and serve as liaison at the section level with all agencies served in the public interest, particularly in connection with state and local government, civil preparedness, Federal Emergency Management Agency, Red Cross, Salvation Army, the National Weather Service, and so on. Such contact is maintained in cooperation with the State Government Liaison.

8) Section Emergency Coordinators are encouraged to earn certification in Levels 1, 2, and 3 of the ARRL Emergency Communications Course.

Requirements: Full ARRL membership; Technician class license or higher.

Section Traffic Manager

The STM is appointed by the Section Manager to supervise traffic handling organization at the section level — that is, to coordinate all traffic efforts within the section, regardless of mode or National Traffic System affiliation, so that routings within the section and connections with other networks and digital traffic nodes will result in orderly and efficient traffic flow. The STM

should be a person at home and familiar with traffic handling on all modes, must have at least a Technician class license, and should possess the willingness and ability to devote equal consideration and time to all section traffic matters. The STM must be a Full ARRL Member.

The duties of the STM include the following:

1) Establish, administer, and promote a traffic handling program at the section level, based on, but not restricted to, National Traffic System networks.

2) Develop and implement one or more effective training programs within the section that address the needs of both traditional and digital modes of traffic handling. Insure that Net Managers place particular emphasis on the needs of amateurs new to formal network traffic handling, as well as those who receive, send, and deliver formal traffic on a "casual" basis, via RTTY, AMTOR, and Packet based message storage and bulletin board systems.

3) Cooperate and coordinate with the Section Emergency Coordinator so that traffic nets and emergency nets in the section present a unified public service front.

4) Recommend candidates for Net Managers and Official Relay Station appointments to the SM. Issue appointments/cancellations and appropriate certificates. At the SM's discretion, the STM may directly make or cancel NM and ORS appointments.

5) Insure that all traffic nets within the section are properly and adequately staffed, with appropriate direction to Net Managers, as required, which results in coverage of all Net Control and liaison functions. Assign liaison coverage adequate to insure that all digital bulletin boards and message storage systems within the section are polled on a daily basis, to prevent misaddressed, lingering, or duplicated radiogram-formatted message traffic.

6) Maintain familiarity with proper traffic handling and directed net procedures applicable to all normally-used modes within the section.

7) Collect and prepare accurate monthly net reports and submit them to ARRL Headquarters, either directly or via the Section Manager, but in any case on or prior to the established deadlines.

8) Section Traffic Managers are encouraged to earn certification in Levels 1, 2, and 3 of the ARRL Emergency Communications Course.

Affiliated Club Coordinator

The ACC is the primary contact and resource person for each Amateur Radio club in the section, specializing in motivating, providing assistance and coordinating joint activities of radio clubs. The ACC is appointed by, and reports to, the Section Manager. Duties and qualifications of the ACC include:

1) Get to know the Amateur Radio clubs' members and officers person to person in his section. Learn their needs, strengths and interests and work with them to make clubs effective resources in their communities and more enjoyable for their members.

2) Encourage affiliated clubs in the section to become more active and, if the club is already healthy and effective, to apply as a Special Service Club (SSC).

3) Supply interested clubs with SSC application forms.

4) Assist clubs in completing SSC application forms.

5) Help clubs establish workable programs to use as SSCs.

6) Approve SSC application forms and pass them to the SM.

7) Work with other section leadership officials (Section Emergency Coordinator, Public Information Coordinator, Technical Coordinator, State Government Liaison, etc.) to insure that clubs are involved in the mainstream of ARRL Field Organization activities.

8) Encourage new clubs to become ARRL affiliated.

9) Ensure that annual reports (updates officers, liaison mailing addresses etc.) are forthcoming from all affiliated clubs.

10) Full ARRL membership is a requirement.

Official Observer Coordinator

The OOC is an ARRL section-level leadership official, appointed by the Section Manager, for two related purposes: to supervise the maintenance monitoring work of the section Official Observers, and to coordinate special Amateur Auxiliary efforts with Headquarters and the SM.

The Official Observer program has operated for more than a half century. In this time, OO appointees have assisted thousands of amateurs whose signals, or operating procedures, were not in compliance with the FCC regulations. The function of the OO is to listen for amateurs who might otherwise come to the attention of the FCC and to advise them by mail of the irregularity observed. The OO program is, in essence, for the benefit of amateurs who want to be helped. OOs must meet high standards of expertise and experience. It is the job of the OO Coordinator to recruit, supervise and direct the efforts of OOs in the section, and to report their activity monthly to the Section Manager, and Headquarters.

With the inception of the Amateur Auxiliary to the FCC, the role of the OOC is greater today than ever before. A key liaison in the Auxiliary, the OOC assists OOs in evidence gathering and conveys evidentiary materials to Headquarters for handling with the FCC.

Full operational details of the Amateur Auxiliary program are contained in the Training Manual.

Requirements: General Class or higher class with a minimum of four years experience as Technician or higher; Full ARRL membership, and certification in the Amateur Auxiliary.

The OOC appointee shall have been an Official Observer for a minimum of two (2) years before starting the appointment, and shall maintain active OO status while holding the OOC appointment

Public Information Coordinator

The ARRL Public Information Coordinator (PIC) is a section-level official appointed by and reports to the Section Manager (SM) as the section's expert on public information and public relations matters. The PIC is responsible for organizing, training, guiding and coordinating the activities of the Public Information Officers (PIOs) within the section.

The Public Information Coordinator must be a Full member of the ARRL and, preferably, have professional public relations or journalism experience or a significantly related background in dealing with the public media.

The purpose of public relations goes beyond column inches and minutes of air time. Those are means to an end — generally, telling a specific story about hams, ham radio or ham-related activities for a specific purpose. Goals may range from recruiting potential hams for a licensing course to improving public awareness of amateurs' service to the community. Likewise, success is measured not in column inches or air time, but in how well that story gets across and how effectively it generates the desired results.

For this reason, public relations are not conducted in a vacuum. Even the best PR is wasted without effective follow-up. To do this best, PR activities must be well-timed and well-coordinated within the amateur community, so that clubs, Elmers, instructors and so on are prepared to deal with the interest the PR generates. Effective PICs will convey this goal-oriented perspective and attitude to their PIOs and help them coordinate public relations efforts with others in their sections.

Recruitment of new hams and League members is an integral part of the job of every League appointee. Appointees should take advantage of every opportunity to recruit a new ham or member to foster growth of Field Organization programs, and our abilities to serve the public.

Specific Duties of the Public Information Coordinator:

1) Advises the Section Manager on building and maintaining a positive public image for Amateur Radio in the section; keeps the SM informed of all significant events which would benefit from the SM's personal involvement and reports regularly to the SM on activities.

2) Counsels the SM in dealing with the media and with government officials, particularly when representing the ARRL and/or Amateur Radio in a public forum.

3) Maintains contact with other section level League officials, particularly the Section Manager and others such as the State Government Liaison, Section Emergency Coordinator, Affiliated Club Coordinator and Bulletin Manager on matters appropriate for their attention and to otherwise help to assure and promote a coordinated and cohesive ARRL Field Organization.

4) Works closely with the section Affiliated Club Coordinator and ARRL-affiliated clubs in the section to recruit and train a team of Public Information Officers (PIOs). With the approval of the Section Manager, makes PIO appointments within the section.

5) Works with the SM and other PICs in the division to develop regional training programs for PIOs and club publicity chairpersons.

6) Coordinates public relations efforts for events and activities which may involve more than one section, and provides input on matters before the League's Public Relations Committee for discussion or action.

7) Establishes and coordinates a section-wide Speakers Bureau to provide knowledgeable and effective speakers who are available to address community groups about Amateur Radio, and works with PIOs to promote interest among those groups.

8) Helps local PIOs to recognize and publicize newsworthy stories in their areas. Monitors news releases sent out by the PIOs for stories of broader interest and offers constructive comments for possible improvement. Helps local PIOs in learning to deal with, and attempting to minimize, any negative publicity about Amateur Radio or to correct negative stories incorrectly ascribed to Amateur Radio operators.

9) Working with the PIOs, develops and maintains a comprehensive list of media outlets and contacts in the section for use in section-wide or nationwide mailings.

10) Helps local PIOs prepare emergency response PR kits containing general information on Amateur Radio and on local clubs, which may be distributed in advance to local Emergency Coordinators and District Emergency Coordinators for use in dealing with the media during emergencies.

11) Works with PIOs, SM and ARRL staff to identify and publicize League-related stories of local or regional interest, including election or appointment of ARRL leadership officials, scholarship winners/award winners, QST articles by local authors or local achievements noted or featured in QST.

12) Familiarizes self with ARRL Public Service Announcements (PSAs), brochures and audiovisual materials; assists PIOs in arranging air time for PSAs; helps PIOs and speakers choose and secure appropriate brochures and audiovisual materials for events or presentations.

13) At the request of the Section Manager or Division Director, may assist with preparation of a section or division newsletter.

14) Encourages, organizes and conducts public information/public relations sessions at ARRL hamfests and conventions.

15) Works with PIOs to encourage activities that place Amateur Radio in the public eye, including demonstrations, Field Day activities, etc. and assures that sponsoring organizations are prepared to follow-up on interest generated by these activities.

State Government Liaison

The State Government Liaison (SGL) is an Amateur Radio

operator who is cognizant of state legislative and regulatory proposals in the normal course of events and who can monitor and respond appropriately to those proposals having the potential to affect Amateur Radio. This is an active, responsive mission, not merely a passive, "stand by the sidelines and watch" function.

The SGL collects and promulgates information on state legislation and regulation affecting Amateur Radio and works closely with Clubs and the Section Manager(s) in assuring that the laws work to the mutual benefit of society and the Amateur Radio Service. The importance of working closely with clubs (the critically-important local representatives of Amateur Radio), and ARRL Section Managers, cannot be overemphasized. Keep in close contact with your clubs and SMs!

The SGL guides, encourages and supports individual radio amateurs and clubs in representing the interests of the Amateur Radio Service at all levels, including the federal level, when needed and coordinated with the ARRL Headquarters. The active SGL also cooperates closely with other section-level officials, particularly the Section Emergency Coordinator and the Public Information Coordinator.

The SGL must be an ARRL Full member. The SGL reports directly to the Section Manager regularly and also keeps ARRL Headquarters informed of all appropriate activities and developments involving the interface of Amateur Radio and government legislative or regulatory matters, particularly those with policy implications. Ideally, the SGL will have access to, or a relationship with, the bill room at the state capitol in order to examine legislation as it is introduced. It is also helpful for the SGL to monitor the dockets of relevant state agencies such as the department of environmental protection, which might promulgate regulations affecting Amateur Radio. In addition, the SGL will monitor the news for stories of regulatory or legislative initiatives.

When monitoring and responding to state issues, SGLs should watch for key words that could affect Amateur Radio. Antennas (dish, microwave, PCS, cellular, towers, structures, satellite, television, lighting), Mobile radio, radio receivers, radio interference, television interference, scanners, license plates, cable television, ham radio, headphones in automobiles, lightning protection, antenna radiation, biological effects of radio signals are a few of the examples of what to look for.

In those states where there is more than one section, the Section Managers whose territories do not encompass the state capital may simply defer to the Liaison appointed by their counterpart in the section where the state capital is located. In this case, the Liaison is expected to communicate equally with all Section Managers (and Section Emergency Coordinators and other section-level League officials). In sections where there is more than one government entity (i.e., Maryland-DC and Pacific) there may be a Liaison appointed for each entity.

The job of heading off potentially undesirable state government actions is critically important to the Amateur Radio community! Be active and responsive, and above all, work closely with your clubs, Section Managers, and ARRL Headquarters.

Technical Coordinator

The ARRL Technical Coordinator (TC) is a section-level official appointed by the Section Manager to coordinate all technical activities within the section. The Technical Coordinator must be an ARRL Full member holding a Novice class (or higher) amateur license. The Technical Coordinator reports to the Section Manager and is expected to maintain contact with other section-level appointees as appropriate to insure a unified ARRL Field Organization within the section. The duties of the Technical Coordinator are as follows:

1) Supervise and coordinate the work of the section's Technical Specialists (TSs).

2) Encourage amateurs in the section to share their technical achievements with others through the pages of *QST*, and at club meetings, hamfests and conventions.

3) Promote technical advances and experimentation at vhf/uhf and with specialized modes, and work closely with enthusiasts in these fields within the section.

4) Serve as an advisor to radio clubs that sponsor training programs for obtaining amateur licenses or upgraded licenses in cooperation with the ARRL Affiliated Club Coordinator.

5) In times of emergency or disaster, function as the coordinator for establishing an array of equipment for communications use and be available to supply technical expertise to government and relief agencies to set up emergency communications networks, in cooperation with the ARRL Section Emergency Coordinator.

6) Refer amateurs in the section who need technical advice to local TSs.

7) Encourage clubs to develop, and TSs to serve on, RFI and TVI committees in the section for the purpose of rendering technical assistance as needed.

8) Be available to assist local technical program committees in arranging suitable programs for ARRL hamfests and conventions.

9) Convey the views of section amateurs and TSs about the technical contents of *QST* and ARRL books to ARRL HQ. Suggestions for improvements should also be called to the attention of the ARRL HQ technical staff.

10) Work with the appointed ARRL TAs (technical advisors) when called upon.

11) Be available to give technical talks at club meetings, hamfests and conventions in the section.

District Emergency Coordinator

The ARRL District Emergency Coordinator is appointed by the SEC to supervise the efforts of local Emergency Coordinators in the defined district. The DEC's duties involve the following:

1) Coordinate the training, organization and emergency participation of Emergency Coordinators in your district of jurisdiction.

2) Make local decisions in the absence of the SEC or through coordination with the SEC, concerning the allotment of available amateurs and equipment during an emergency.

3) Coordinate the interrelationship between local emergency plans and between communications networks within your area of jurisdiction.

4) Act as backup for local areas without an Emergency Coordinator and assist in maintaining contact with governmental and other agencies within your area of jurisdiction.

5) Provide direction in the routing and handling of emergency communications of either a formal or tactical nature, with specific emphasis being placed on Welfare traffic.

6) Recommend EC appointments to the SEC.

7) Coordinate the reporting and documenting of ARES activities in your district of jurisdiction.

8) Act as a model emergency communicator as evidenced by dedication to purpose, reliability and understanding of emergency communications.

9) Be fully conversant in National Traffic System routing and procedures as well as have a thorough understanding of the locale and role of all vital governmental and volunteer agencies that could be involved in an emergency.

10) District Emergency Coordinators are encouraged to earn certification in Levels 1 and 2 of the ARRL Emergency Communications Course.

Requirements: Technician or higher class; Full ARRL membership.

Emergency Coordinator

The ARRL Emergency Coordinator is a key team player in ARES on the local emergency scene. Working with the Section Emergency Coordinator, the DEC and Official Emergency Stations, the EC prepares for, and engages in management of communications needs in disasters. EC duties include:

1) Promote and enhance the activities of the Amateur Radio Emergency Service (ARES) for the benefit of the public as a voluntary, non-commercial communications service.

2) Manage and coordinate the training, organization and emergency participation of interested amateurs working in support of the communities, agencies or functions designated by the Section Emergency Coordinator/Section Manager.

3) Establish viable working relationships with federal, state, county, city governmental and private agencies in the ARES jurisdictional area which need the services of ARES in emergencies. Determine what agencies are active in your area, evaluate each of their needs, and which ones you are capable of meeting, and then prioritize these agencies and needs. Discuss your planning with your Section Emergency Coordinator and then with your counterparts in each of the agencies. Ensure they are all aware of your ARES group's capabilities, and perhaps more importantly, your limitations.

4) Develop detailed local operational plans with "served" agency officials in your jurisdiction that set forth precisely what each of your expectations are during a disaster operation. Work jointly to establish protocols for mutual trust and respect. All matters involving recruitment and utilization of ARES volunteers are directed by you, in response to the needs assessed by the agency officials. Technical issues involving message format, security of message transmission, Disaster Welfare Inquiry policies, and others, should be reviewed and expounded upon in your detailed local operations plans.

5) Establish local communications networks run on a regular basis and periodically test those networks by conducting realistic drills.

6) Establish an emergency traffic plan, with Welfare Traffic inclusive, utilizing the National Traffic System as one active component for traffic handling. Establish an operational liaison with local and section nets, particularly for handling Welfare traffic in an emergency situation.

7) In times of disaster, evaluate the communications needs of the jurisdiction and respond quickly to those needs. The EC will assume authority and responsibility for emergency response and performance by ARES personnel under his jurisdiction.

8) Work with other non-ARES amateur provider-groups to establish mutual respect and understanding, and a coordination mechanism for the good of the public and Amateur Radio. The goal is to foster an efficient and effective Amateur Radio response overall.

9) Work for growth in your ARES program, making it a stronger, more valuable resource and hence able to meet more of the agencies' local needs. There are thousands of new Technicians coming into the amateur service that would make ideal additions to your AIRES roster. A stronger ARES means a better ability to serve your communities in times of need and a greater sense of pride for Amateur Radio by both amateurs and the public.

10) Report regularly to the SEC, as required.

11) Emergency Coordinators are encouraged to earn certification in Level 1 of the ARRL Emergency Communications Course.

Requirements: Technician or higher class license; Full ARRL membership

Net Manager

For coordinating and supervising traffic handling activities in the section, the SM may appoint one or more Net Managers, usually on recommendation of the Section Traffic Manager. The number of NMs appointed may depend on a section's geographical size, the number of nets operating in the section, or other factors having to do with the way the section is organized. In some cases, there may be only one net manager in charge of the one section net, or one NM for the phone net, one for the

CW net. In larger or more traffic-active sections there may be several, including NMs for the VHF net or nets, for the RTTY net, or NTS local nets or packet nodes not controlled by ECs. All ARRL NMs should work under the STM in a coordinated section traffic plan.

Some nets cover more than one section but operate in NTS at the section level. In this case, the Net Manager is selected by agreement among the STMs concerned and the NM appointment conferred on him by his resident SM. Some NMs are system operators of, or sysop recommended operators active on, participating NTS packet boards.

NMs may conduct any testing of candidates for ORS appointment that they consider necessary before making appointment recommendations to the STM. Net Managers also have the function of requiring that all traffic handled through an NTS net or node be in proper ARRL form.

Recruitment of new hams and League members is an integral part of the job of every League appointee. Appointees should take advantage of every opportunity to recruit a new ham or member to foster growth of Field Organization programs, and our abilities to serve the public.

Requirements: Novice class license or higher; Full ARRL membership.

ARRL STATION APPOINTMENTS

Field Organization station and individual appointments are available to qualified ARRL full members in each section. The detailed qualifications are given below.

Recruitment of new hams and League members is an integral part of the job of every League appointee. Appointees should take advantage of every opportunity to recruit a new ham or member to foster growth of Field Organization programs, and our abilities to serve the public.

Official Relay Station

This is a traffic-handling appointment that is open to all classes of license. This appointment applies equally to all modes and all parts of the spectrum. It is for traffic-handlers, regardless of mode employed or part of the spectrum used.

The potential value of the skilled operator with traffic know-how to his country and community is enhanced by his ability and the readiness of his station to function in the community interest in case of emergency. Traffic awareness and experience are often the signs by which mature amateurs may be distinguished.

Traditionally, there have been considerable differences between procedures for traffic handling by CW, phone, RTTY, ASCII, packet and other modes. Appointment requirements for ORS do not deal with these, but with factors equally applicable to all modes. The appointed ORS may confine activities to one mode or one part of the spectrum if he wishes. There is no versatility requirement, although versatility does indeed make it possible for anyone to perform a more complete public service. There is, however, the expectation that the ORS will set the example in traffic handling however it is done. To the extent that he is deficient in performing traffic functions by any mode, to that extent he does not meet the qualifications for the appointment. Here are the basic requirements:

1) Full ARRL membership and Novice Class license or higher.

2) Code and/or voice transmission capability.

3) Transmissions, by whatever mode, must be of the highest quality, both technically and operationally. For example, CW signals must be pure, chirpless, clickless, code sending must be well spaced and properly formed. Voice transmission must be of proper modulation percentage or deviation, precisely enunciated with minimum distortion.

4) All ORS are expected to follow standard ARRL operating practices (message form, ending signals, abbreviations or prowords, etc.).

5) Regular participation in traffic activities, either independent or ARRL-sponsored. The latter is encouraged, but not required.

6) Handle all record communications speedily and reliably and set the example in efficient operating procedures. All traffic is relayed or delivered promptly after receipt.

Report monthly to the STM, including a breakdown of traffic handled during the past calendar month.

Official Emergency Station

Amateur operators may be appointed as an Official Emergency Station (OES) by their Section Emergency Coordinator (SEC) or Section Manager (SM) at the recommendation of the EC, or DEC (if no EC) holding jurisdiction. The OES appointee must be an ARRL member and set high standards of emergency preparedness and operating. The OES appointee makes a deeper commitment to the ARES program in terms of functionality than does the rank-and-file ARES registrant.

The requirements and qualifications for the position include the following: Full ARRL membership; experience as an ARES registrant; regular participation in the local ARES organization including drills and tests; participation in emergency nets and actual emergency situations; regular reporting of activities.

The OES appointee is appointed to carry out specific functions and assignments designated by the appropriate EC or DEC. The OES appointee and the presiding EC or DEC, at the time of the OES appointment, will mutually develop a detailed, operational function/assignment and commitment for the new appointee. Together, they will develop a responsibility plan for the individual OES appointee that makes the best use of the individual's skills and abilities. During drills and actual emergency situations, the OES appointee will be expected to implement his/her function with professionalism and minimal supervision.

Functions assigned may include, but are not limited to, the following major areas of responsibility:

Operations — Responsible for specific, pre-determined operational assignments during drills or actual emergency situations. Examples include: Net Control Station or Net Liaison for a specific ARES net; Manage operation of a specified ARES VHF or HF digital BBS or MBO, or point-to-point link; Operate station at a specified emergency management office, Red Cross shelter or other served agency operations point.

Administration — Responsible for specific, pre-determined administrative tasks as assigned in the initial appointment commitment by the presiding ARES official. Examples include: Recruitment of ARES members; liaison with Public Information Officer to coordinate public information for the media; ARES registration data base management; victim/refugee data base management; equipment inventory; training; reporting; and post-event analysis.

Liaison — Responsible for specific, pre-determined liaison responsibilities as assigned by the presiding EC or DEC. Examples include: Maintaining contact with assigned served agencies; Maintaining liaison with specified NTS nets; Maintaining liaison with ARES officials in adjacent jurisdictions; Liaison with mutual assistance or "jump" teams.

Logistics — Responsible for specific, pre-determined logistical functions as assigned. Examples include: Transportation; Supplies management and procurement (food, fuel, water, etc.); Equipment maintenance and procurement—radios, computers, generators, batteries, antennas.

Management Assistant — Responsible for serving as an assistant manager to the EC, DEC or SEC based on specific functional assignments or geographic areas of jurisdiction.

Consulting — Responsible for consulting to ARES officials in specific area of expertise.

OES appointees may be assigned to pre-disaster, post-disaster, and recovery functions. These functions must be specified in the OES's appointment commitment plan.

The OES appointee is expected to participate in planning meetings, and post-event evaluations. Following each drill or actual event, the EC/DEC and the OES appointee should review and update the OES assignment as required. The OES appointee must keep a detailed log of events during drills and actual events in his/her sphere of responsibility to facilitate this review.

Continuation of the appointment is at the discretion of the appointing official, based upon the OES appointee's fulfillment of the tasks he/she has agreed to perform.

Official Emergency Stations are encouraged to earn certification in Level 1 of the ARRL Emergency Communications Course.

Public Information Officer

ARRL Public Information Officers (PIOs) are appointed by their Section Manager and report to their ARRL section Public Information Coordinator (PIC). The Section Manager may, at their discretion, delegate this appointment power to the section PIC. PIOs are generally recommended by an affiliated club for appointment consideration and must be full ARRL members. Training for PIOs should be provided regularly on a sectional or regional basis by the PIC and/or other qualified people.

Good "grass roots" public relations activities involve regular and frequent publicizing of amateur activities through local news media plus community activities; school programs; presentations to service clubs and community organizations; exhibits and demonstrations; and other efforts which create a positive public image for Amateur Radio.

The purpose of public relations goes beyond column inches and minutes of air time. Those are means to an end — generally, telling a specific story about hams, ham radio or ham-related activities for a specific purpose. Goals may range from recruiting potential hams for a licensing course to improving public awareness of amateurs' service to the community. Likewise, success is measured not in column inches or air time, but in how well that story gets across and how effectively it generates the desired results.

For this reason, public relations are not conducted in a vacuum. Even the best PR is wasted without effective follow-up. To do this best, PR activities must be well-timed and well-coordinated within the amateur community, so that clubs, Elmers, instructors and so on are prepared to deal with the interest the PR generates.

Recruitment of new hams and League members is an integral part of the job of every League appointee. Appointees should take advantage of every opportunity to recruit a new ham or member to foster growth of Field Organization programs, and our abilities to serve the public.

Specific Duties of the Public Information Officer:

1) Establishes and maintains a list of media contacts in the local area; strives to establish and maintain personal contacts with appropriate representatives of those media (e.g., editors, news directors, science reporters, etc.).

2) Becomes a contact for the local media and assures that editors/reporters who need information about Amateur Radio know where to find it.

3) Works with Local Government Liaisons to establish personal contacts with local government officials where possible and explain to them, briefly and non-technically, about Amateur Radio and how it can help their communities.

4) Keeps informed of activities by local hams and identifies and publicizes those that are newsworthy or carry human interest appeal. (This is usually done through news releases or suggestions for interviews or feature stories).

5) Attempts to deal with and minimize any negative publicity about Amateur Radio and to correct any negative stories which are incorrectly ascribed to Amateur Radio operators.

6) Generates advance publicity through the local media of scheduled activities of interest to the general public, including

licensing classes, hamfests, club meetings, Field Day operations, etc.

7) Works with the section PIC to identify and publicize League-related stories of local news interest, including election and appointment of local hams to leadership positions, *QST* articles by local authors or local achievements noted or featured in *QST*.

8) Maintains contact with other League officials in the local area, particularly the Emergency Coordinator and/or District Emergency Coordinator. With the PIC, helps prepare an emergency response PR kit, including general brochures on Amateur Radio and specific information about local clubs. Distributes them to ECs and DECs before an emergency occurs. During emergencies, these kits should be made available to reporters at the scene or at a command post. The PIO should help summarize Amateur Radio activity in an ongoing situation, and follow up any significant emergency communications activities with prompt reporting to the media of the extent and nature of Amateur Radio involvement.

9) Assists the section PIC in recruiting hams for the section's Speakers Bureau; promotes interest among community and service organizations in finding out more about Amateur Radio through the bureau and relays requests to the PIC.

10) Helps individual hams and radio clubs to develop and promote good ideas for community projects and special events to display Amateur Radio to the public in a positive light.

11) Attends regional training sessions sponsored by section PICs.

12) Becomes familiar with ARRL Public Service Announcements (PSAs), brochures and audiovisual materials; contacts local radio and TV stations to arrange airing of Amateur Radio PSAs; secures appropriate brochures and audiovisual materials for use in conjunction with planned activities.

13) Keeps the section PIC fully informed on activities and places PIC on news release mailing list.

Official Observer

The Official Observer program has been sponsored by the League for more than 50 years to help amateurs help each other. Official Observer appointees have assisted thousands of amateurs to maintain their transmitting equipment and operating procedures in compliance with the regulations. The object of the OO program is to notify amateurs by mail of operating/technical irregularities before they come to the attention of the FCC.

The OO is also the backbone of the Amateur Auxiliary to the FCC. OOs are certified in the Auxiliary by passing a mandatory written examination.

The OO performs his function by listening rather than transmitting, keeping an ear out for such things as frequency instability, harmonics, hum, key clicks, broad signals, distorted audio, over deviation, out-of-band operation, etc. The OO completes his task once the notification card is sent.

In hard-core rules violations cases, OOs refer problems to higher echelons of the Amateur Auxiliary, and may be requested to gather evidence for possible FCC enforcement actions. Requirements follow:

1) Must take and pass examination to be certified as a member of the Amateur Auxiliary, an FCC requirement, based on study of the ARRL's *Amateur Auxiliary Training Manual.*

2) Must be an ARRL Full Member and have been a licensee of Technician Class or higher for at least four years.

3) Must report to the OO Coordinator regularly on FSD-23.

4) Maintain regular activity in sending out advisory notices as needed.

The OO program is one of the most important functions of the League. A sincere dedication to helping our brother and sister amateurs is required for appointment. Recruitment of new hams and League members is an integral part of the job of every League appointee. Appointees should take advantage of every opportunity to recruit a new ham or member to foster growth of Field Organization programs, and our abilities to serve the public.

Technical Specialist

For a section team to be effective in one of the most important arenas in Amateur Radio, technology, there must be a cadre of qualified, competent Technical Specialists (TSs). "Advancement of the radio art" is a profound obligation we incur under the rules of the FCC. TSs help meet this obligation.

Appointment by the SM, or TC under delegated authority from the SM, the TS supports the TC in two main areas of responsibility: Radio Frequency Interference, and Technical Information. TSs can specialize in certain specific technical areas, or can be generalists. Here is a list of specific job duties:

1) Serve as a technical advisor to local hams and clubs. Correspond by telephone and letter on tech topics. Refer correspondents to other sources if specific topic is outside TS's knowledge.

2) Serve as advisor in radio frequency interference issues. RFI can drive a wedge in neighbor and city relations. It will be the TS with a cool head who will resolve problems. Local hams will come to you for guidance in dealing with interference problems.

3) Speak at local clubs on popular tech topics. Let local clubs know you're available and willing.

4) Represent ARRL at technical symposiums in industry; serve on CATV advisory committees; advise municipal governments on technical matters.

5) Work with other ARRL officials and appointees when called upon for technical advice, especially in emergency communications situations where technical prowess can mean the difference in getting a communications system up and running, the difference between life and death.

6) Handle other miscellaneous technically-related tasks assigned by the Technical Coordinator.

Technical Specialists must hold Novice or higher class license; ARRL membership required.

Local Government Liaison

The Local Government Liaison (LGL) is primarily responsible for monitoring proposals and actions by local government bodies and officials which may affect Amateur Radio; for working with the local PIO to alert section leadership officials and area amateurs to any such proposals or actions, and for coordinating local responses. In addition, the LGL serves as a primary contact for amateurs encountering problems dealing with local government agencies, for those who want to avoid problems and for local officials who wish to work with amateurs or simply learn more about Amateur Radio. The most effective LGL will be able to monitor local government dockets consistently, muster local, organized support quickly when necessary, and be well known in the local amateur community as the point man for local government problems. The LGL must be a Full Member of the ARRL. LGLs are appointed by and report to the Section Manager, or State Government Liaison (acting under delegated authority from the SM).

Specific Responsibilities:

1) Monitor proposals and actions of town/city councils, zoning boards, zoning appeals boards, and any other legislative or regulatory agencies or officials below the state level whose actions can directly or indirectly affect Amateur Radio.

2) Attend meetings of those bodies when possible, to become familiar with their policies, procedures and members. Assist local amateurs in their dealings with local boards and agencies.

3) Be available to educate elected and appointed officials, formally and informally, about the value of Amateur Radio to their community.

4) Work with the PIO or PIC to inform local amateurs, the SGL

and the SM of any proposals of actions which may affect Amateur Radio, and report regularly on progress or lack thereof.

5) Work with the PIO to organize the necessary local response to any significant proposals or actions, either negative or positive, and coordinate that response.

6) Refer amateurs seeking ARRL Volunteer Counsels to HQ.

7) Register on mailing list for Planning Commission meeting agendas.

8) Work with the PIO and local clubs to build and/or maintain good relations between Amateur Radio and local officials. (for example, invite the mayor to a club dinner or council members to Field Day.)

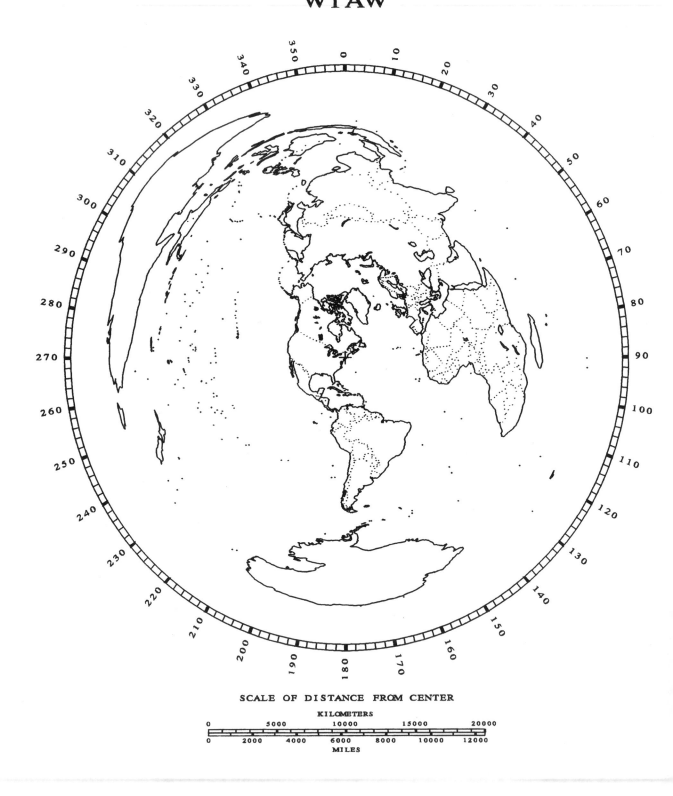

K5ZI AZIMUTHAL EQUIDISTANT MAP CENTERED ON

W1AW

SCALE OF DISTANCE FROM CENTER

KILOMETERS

K5ZI AZIMUTHAL EQUIDISTANT MAP CENTERED ON
Eastern USA

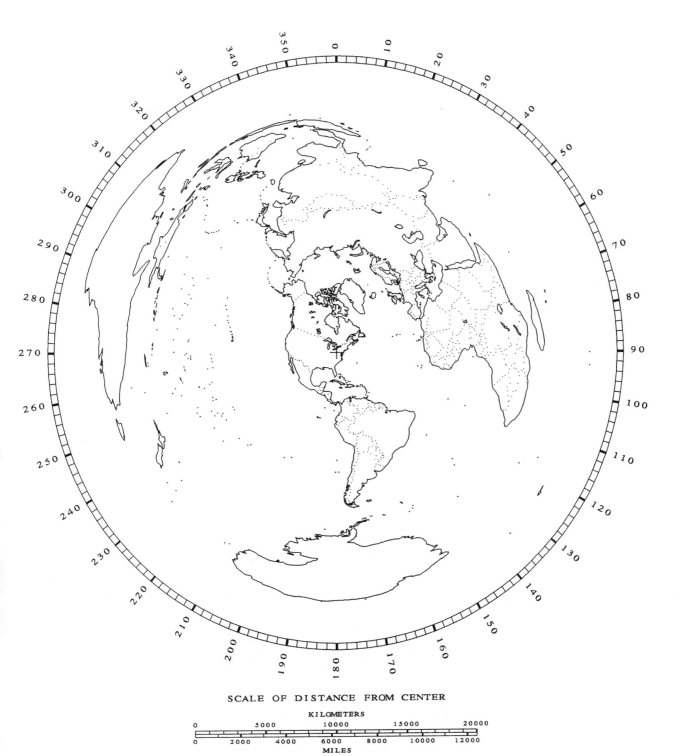

SCALE OF DISTANCE FROM CENTER

KILOMETERS

| 0 | 5000 | 10000 | 15000 | 20000 |

MILES

| 0 | 2000 | 4000 | 6000 | 8000 | 10000 | 12000 |

K5ZI AZIMUTHAL EQUIDISTANT MAP CENTERED ON
Central USA

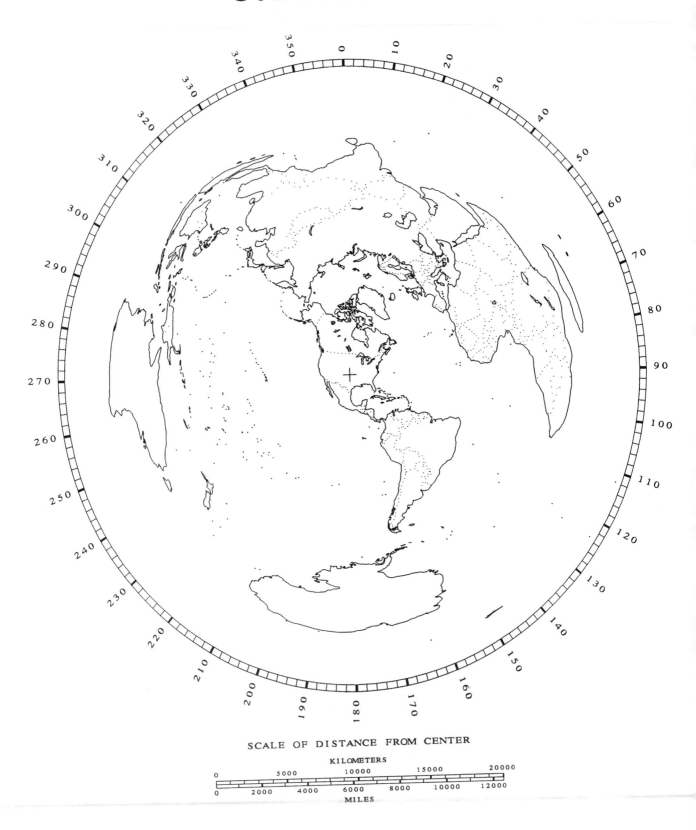

SCALE OF DISTANCE FROM CENTER

KILOMETERS

| 0 | 5000 | 10000 | 15000 | 20000 |

| 0 | 2000 | 4000 | 6000 | 8000 | 10000 | 12000 |

MILES

K5ZI AZIMUTHAL EQUIDISTANT MAP CENTERED ON
Western USA

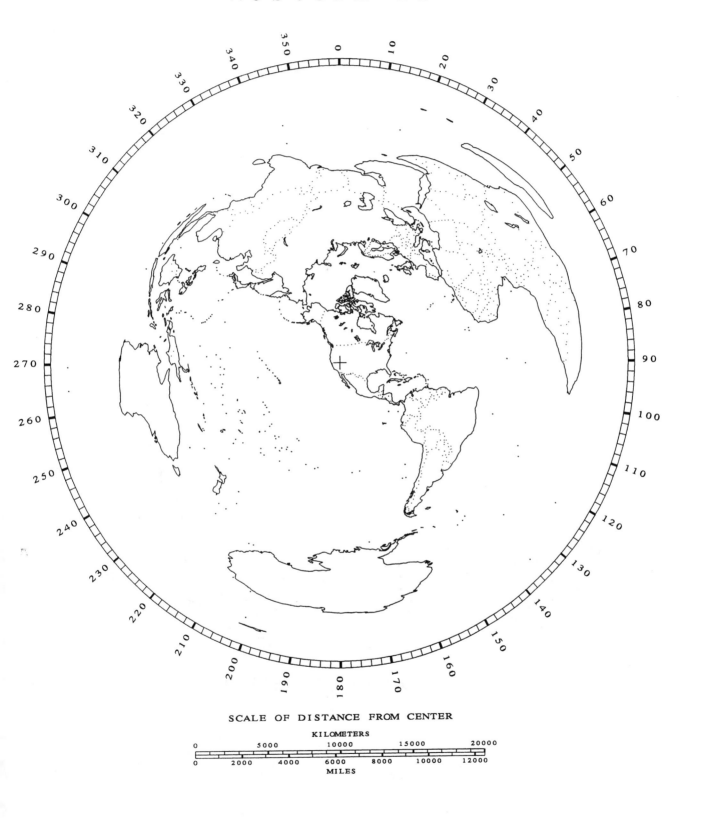

SCALE OF DISTANCE FROM CENTER

KILOMETERS

0   5000   10000   15000   20000

0   2000   4000   6000   8000   10000   12000

MILES

K5ZI AZIMUTHAL EQUIDISTANT MAP CENTERED ON
Alaska

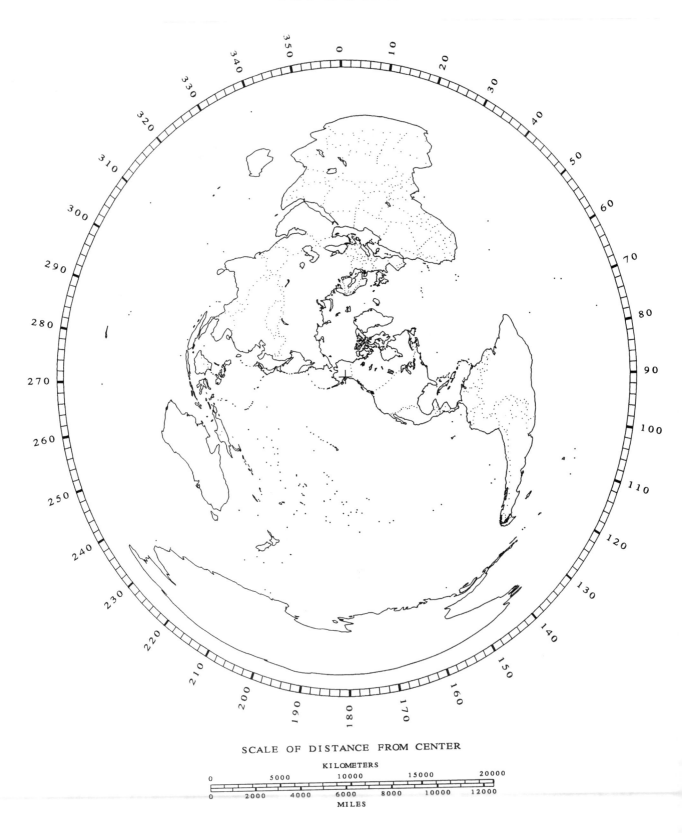

SCALE OF DISTANCE FROM CENTER

KILOMETERS

0   5000   10000   15000   20000

0   2000   4000   6000   8000   10000   12000

MILES

K5ZI AZIMUTHAL EQUIDISTANT MAP CENTERED ON
Hawaii

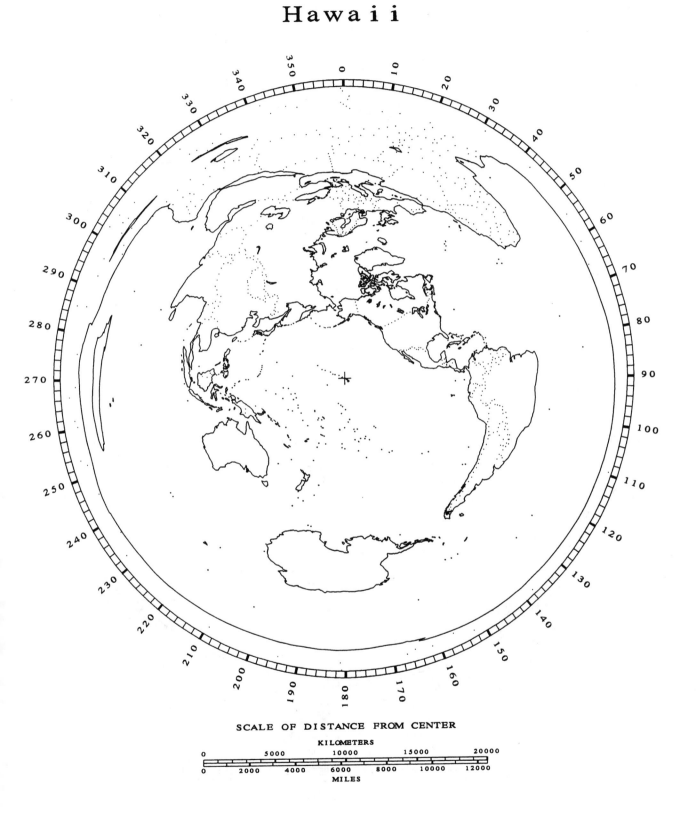

SCALE OF DISTANCE FROM CENTER

KILOMETERS

0   5000   10000   15000   20000

0   2000   4000   6000   8000   10000   12000

MILES

Caribbean

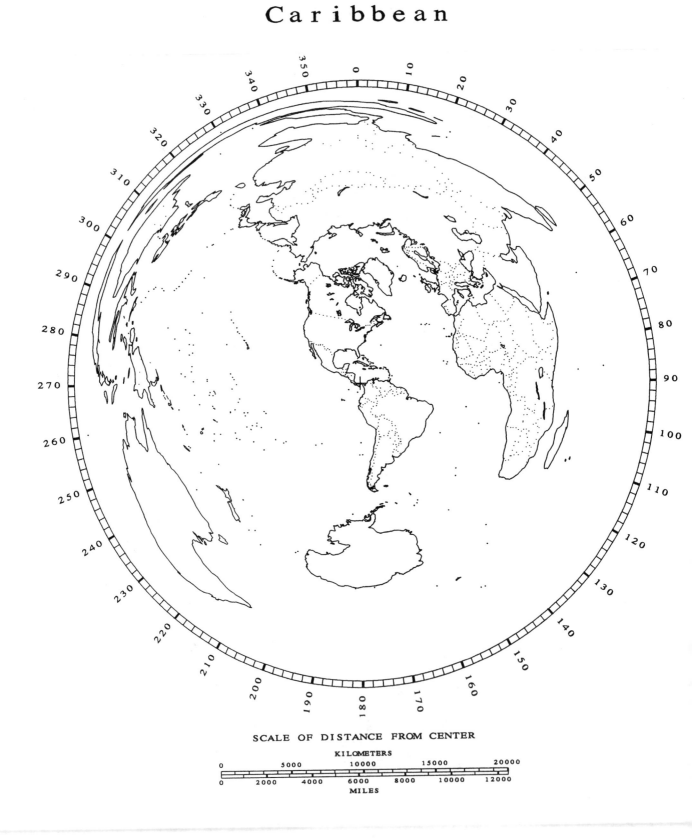

SCALE OF DISTANCE FROM CENTER

Eastern South America

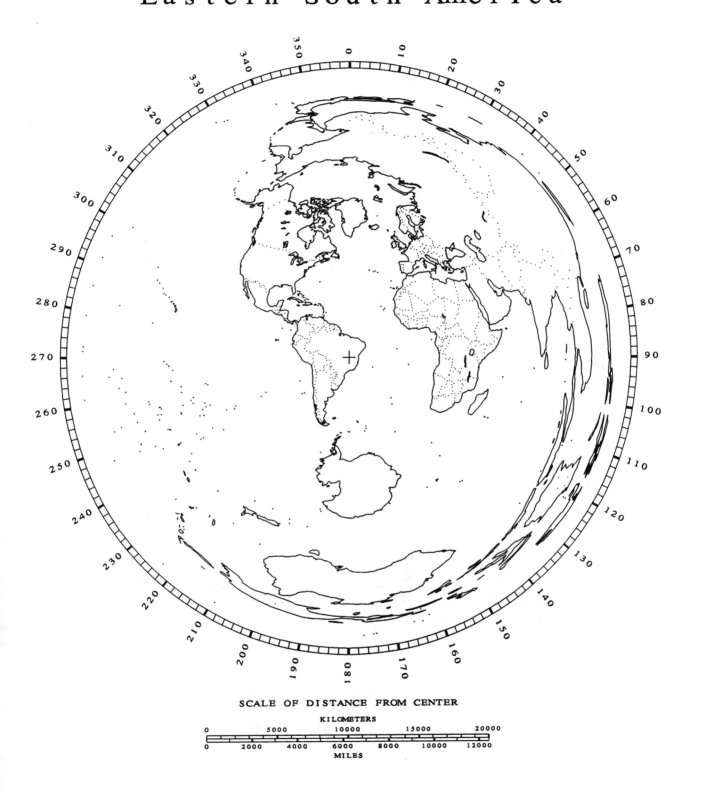

SCALE OF DISTANCE FROM CENTER

KILOMETERS

0   5000   10000   15000   20000

0   2000   4000   6000   8000   10000   12000

MILES

Southern South America

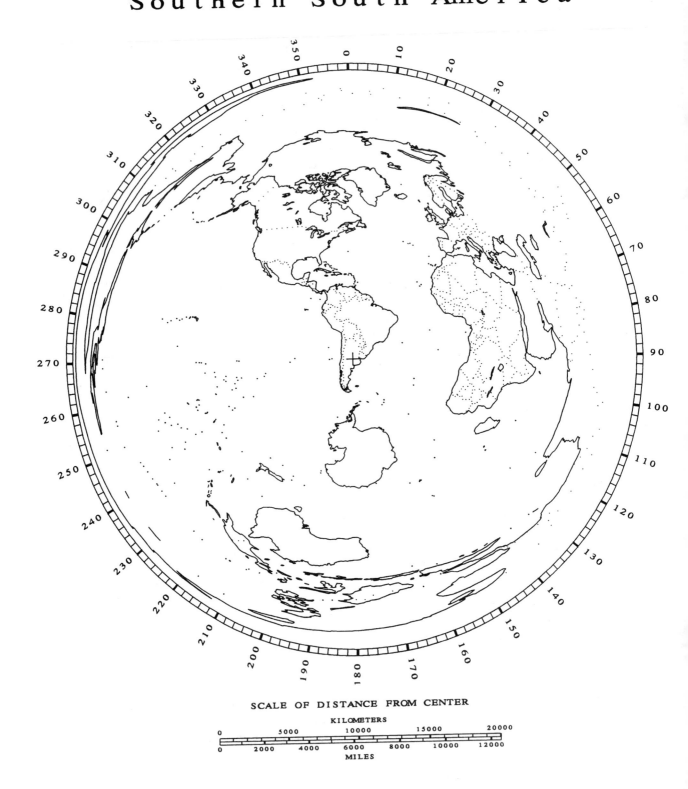

SCALE OF DISTANCE FROM CENTER

K5ZI AZIMUTHAL EQUIDISTANT MAP CENTERED ON

Antarctica

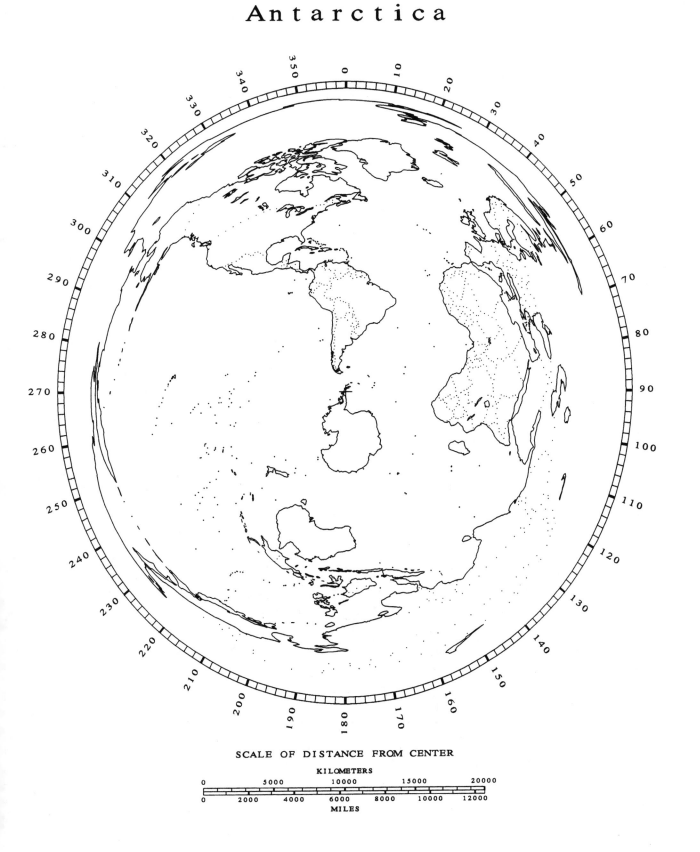

SCALE OF DISTANCE FROM CENTER

KILOMETERS

MILES

K5ZI AZIMUTHAL EQUIDISTANT MAP CENTERED ON
Western Europe

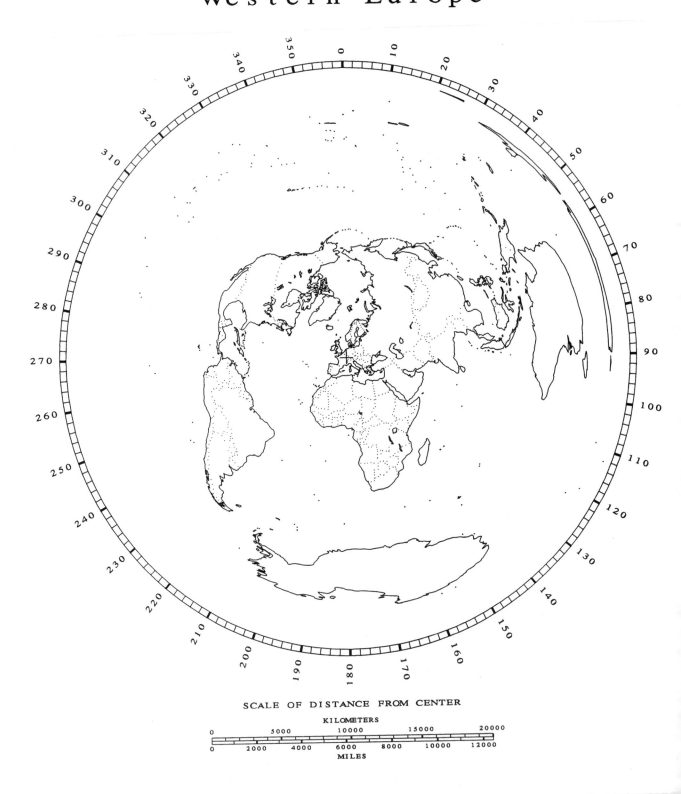

SCALE OF DISTANCE FROM CENTER

K5ZI AZIMUTHAL EQUIDISTANT MAP CENTERED ON
Eastern Europe

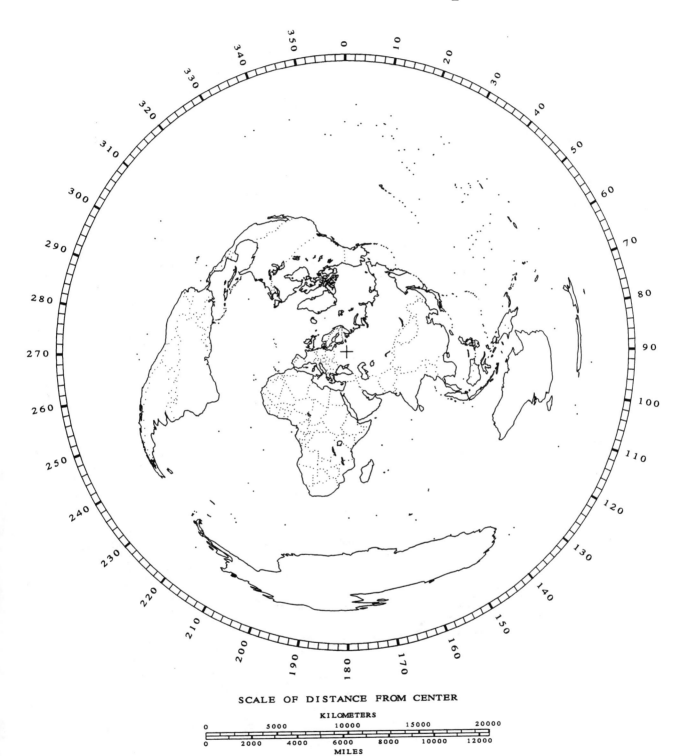

SCALE OF DISTANCE FROM CENTER

KILOMETERS

0   5000   10000   15000   20000

0   2000   4000   6000   8000   10000   12000

MILES

K5ZI AZIMUTHAL EQUIDISTANT MAP CENTERED ON
West Africa

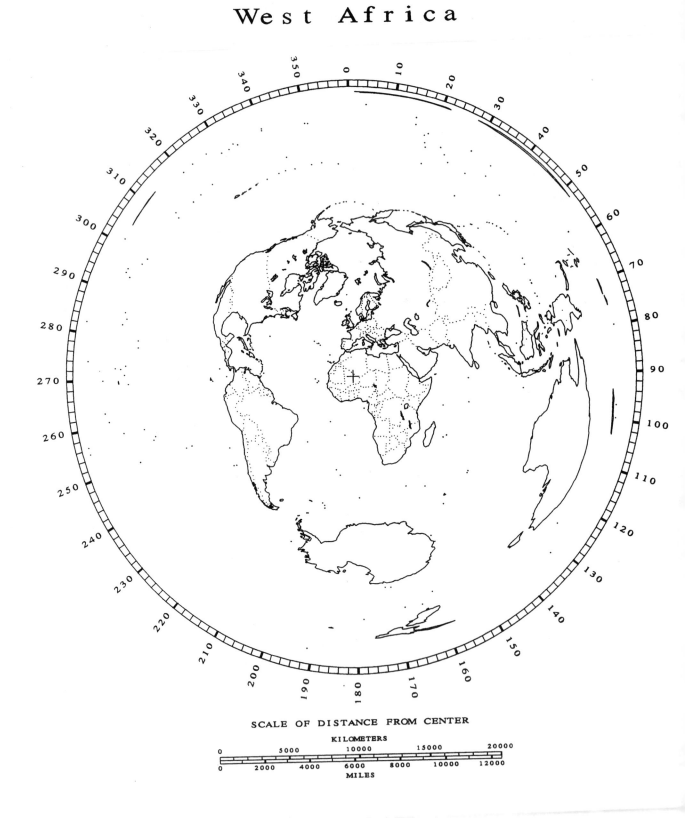

SCALE OF DISTANCE FROM CENTER

KILOMETERS

| 0 | 5000 | 10000 | 15000 | 20000 |

| 0 | 2000 | 4000 | 6000 | 8000 | 10000 | 12000 |

MILES

K5ZI AZIMUTHAL EQUIDISTANT MAP CENTERED ON
East Africa

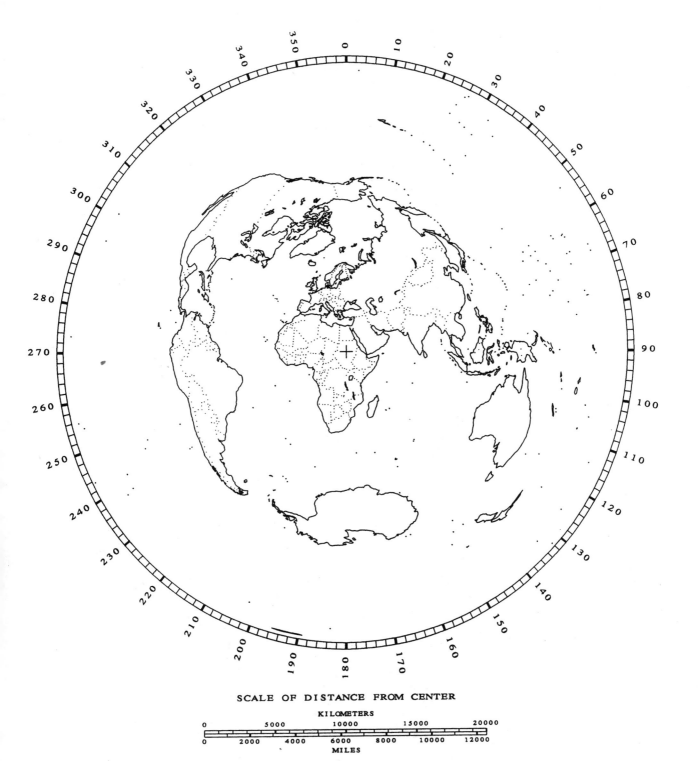

SCALE OF DISTANCE FROM CENTER

KILOMETERS

| 0 | 5000 | 10000 | 15000 | 20000 |

| 0 | 2000 | 4000 | 6000 | 8000 | 10000 | 12000 |

MILES

K5ZI AZIMUTHAL EQUIDISTANT MAP CENTERED ON
Southern Africa

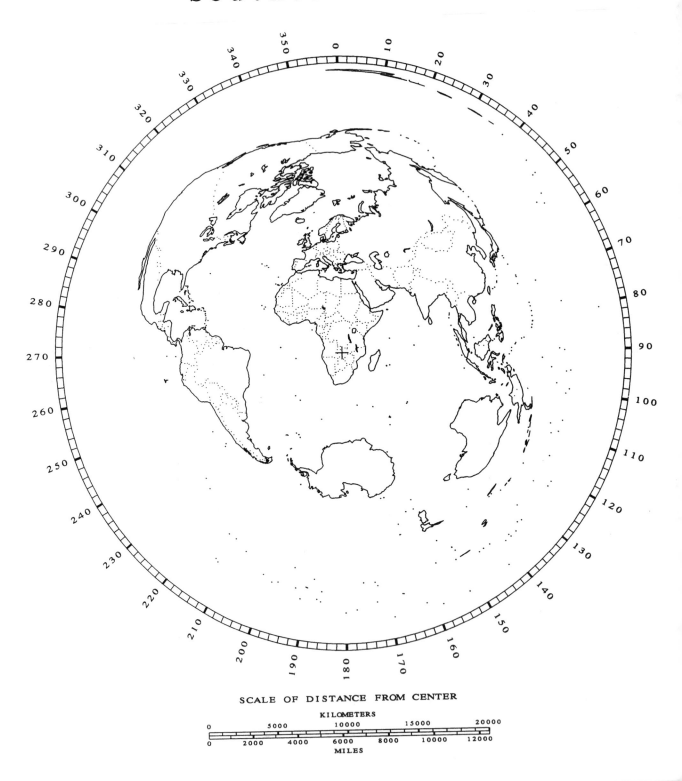

SCALE OF DISTANCE FROM CENTER

KILOMETERS

0		5000		10000		15000		20000
0	2000	4000		6000	8000	10000		12000

MILES

K5ZI AZIMUTHAL EQUIDISTANT MAP CENTERED ON
Near East

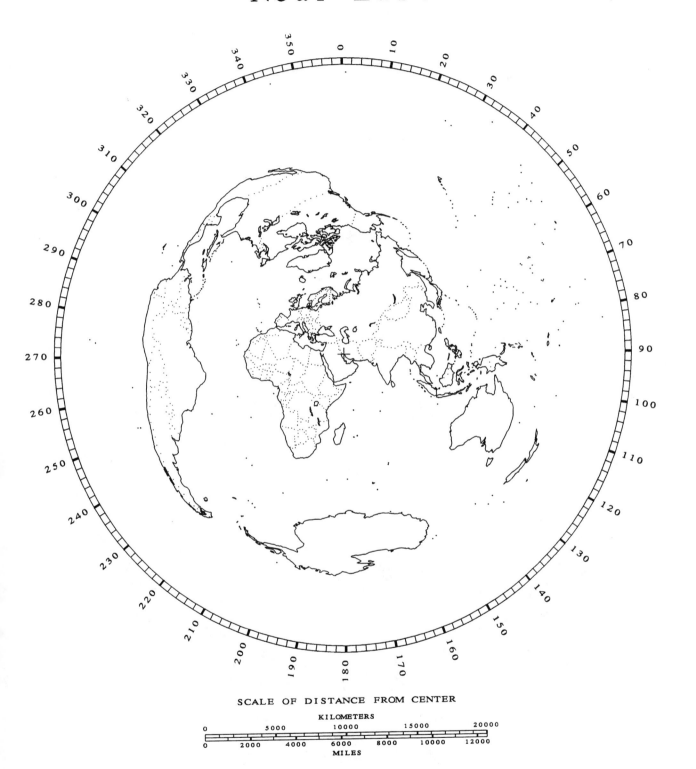

SCALE OF DISTANCE FROM CENTER

KILOMETERS

0   5000   10000   15000   20000

0   2000   4000   6000   8000   10000   12000

MILES

K5ZI AZIMUTHAL EQUIDISTANT MAP CENTERED ON
Southern Asia

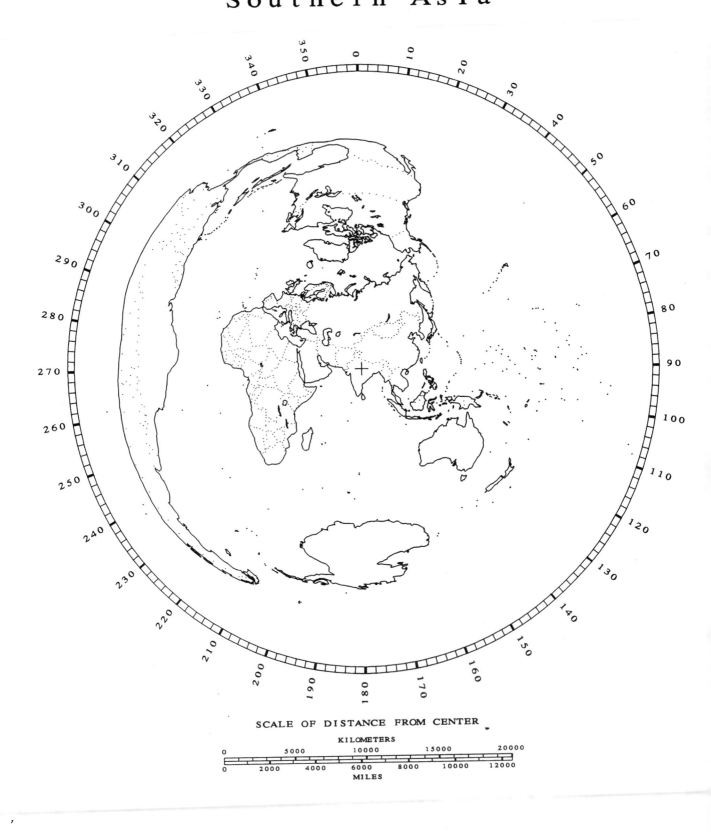

SCALE OF DISTANCE FROM CENTER

KILOMETERS

| 0 | 5000 | 10000 | 15000 | 20000 |

| 0 | 2000 | 4000 | 6000 | 8000 | 10000 | 12000 |

MILES

K5ZI AZIMUTHAL EQUIDISTANT MAP CENTERED ON
Southeast Asia

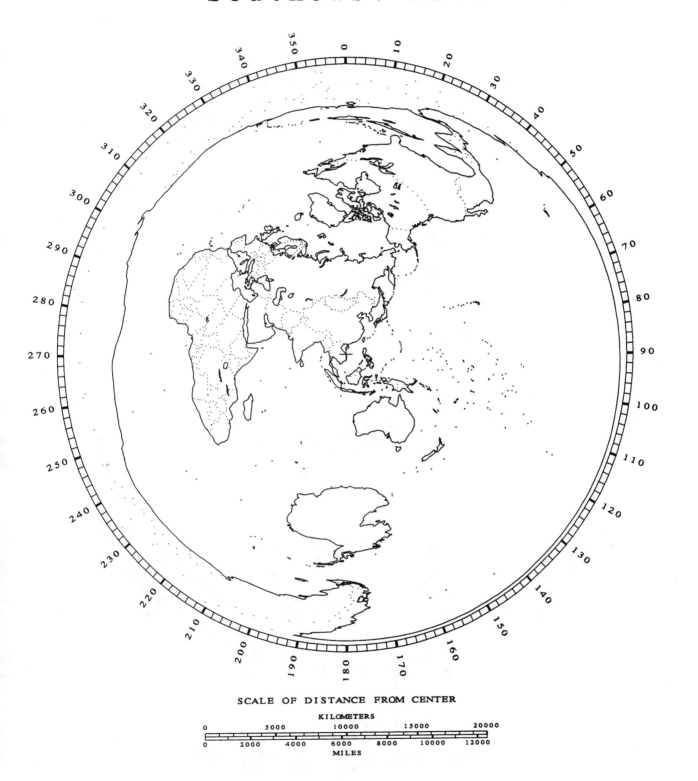

SCALE OF DISTANCE FROM CENTER

KILOMETERS

| 0 | 5000 | 10000 | 15000 | 20000 |

| 0 | 2000 | 4000 | 6000 | 8000 | 10000 | 12000 |

MILES

K5ZI AZIMUTHAL EQUIDISTANT MAP CENTERED ON
Far East

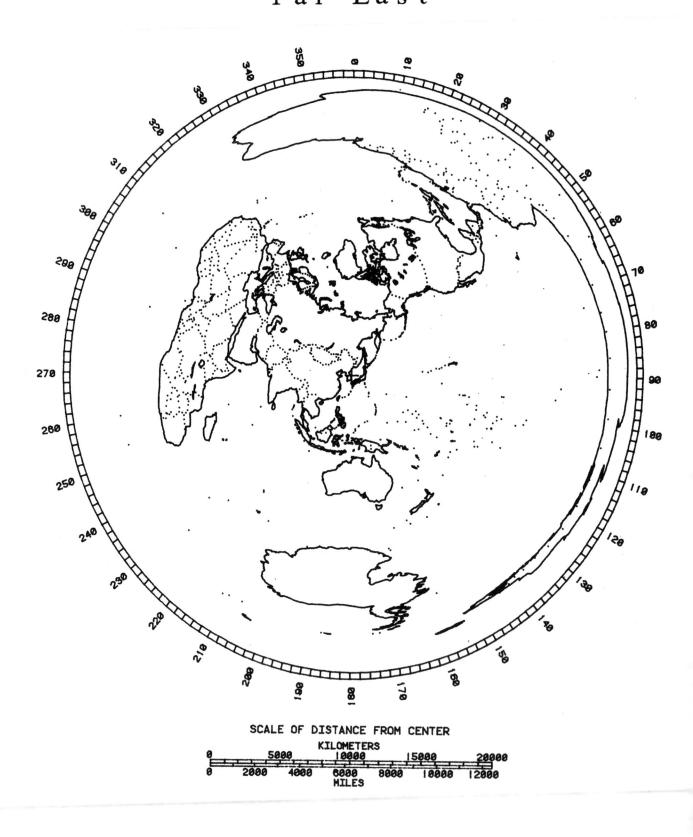

SCALE OF DISTANCE FROM CENTER
KILOMETERS

K5ZI AZIMUTHAL EQUIDISTANT MAP CENTERED ON
Australia

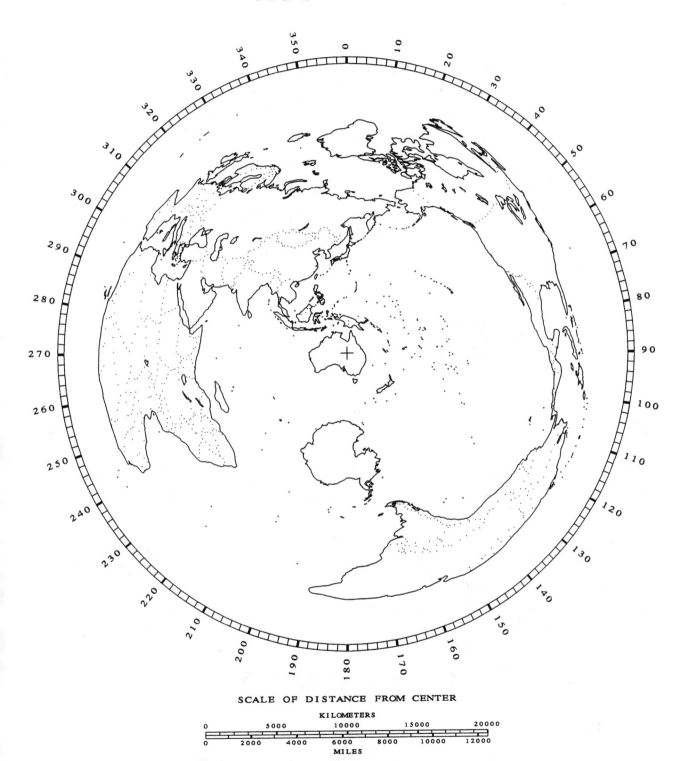

SCALE OF DISTANCE FROM CENTER

KILOMETERS

MILES

K5ZI AZIMUTHAL EQUIDISTANT MAP CENTERED ON
South Pacific

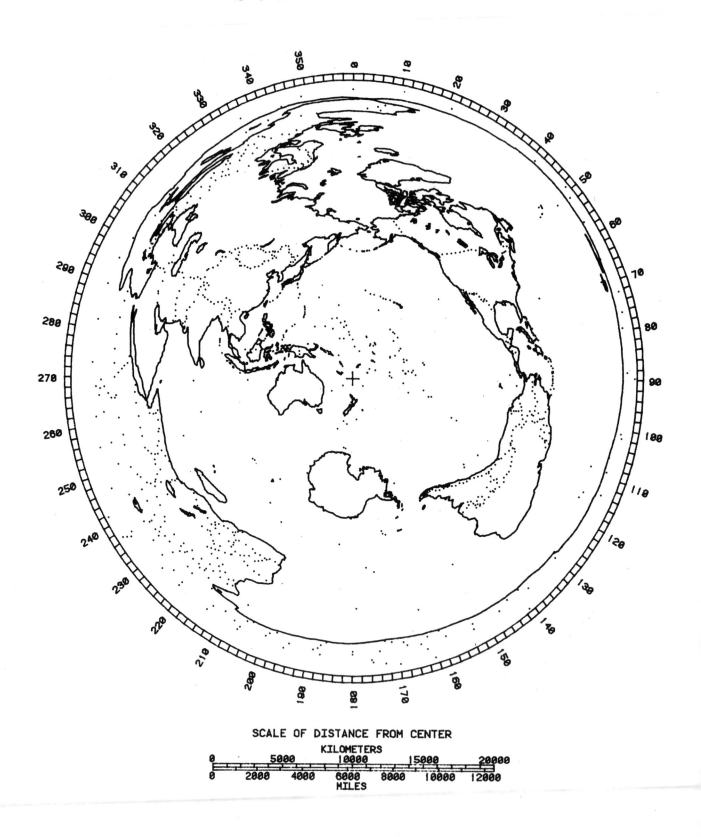

SCALE OF DISTANCE FROM CENTER
KILOMETERS

MILES

Index

5 Band DX Century Club (5BDXCC) 12-6
5 Band Worked All States (5BWAS) 12-3
5 Band Worked All Zones (5BWAZ) 12-8

A

A-1 Operator Club 12-4
Abbreviations, CW 13-26
Activities (in Amateur Radio, overview) 1-3ff
Activity nights.. 3-2
Amateur Extra Certificate 12-4
Amateur Radio Emergency Service (ARES) 4-12
    ARESMAT (mutual aid) 4-26
Amateur television (ATV) 9-1ff
    Antennas 9-9
    Digital 9-12
    Equipment 9-5
    Feed lines 9-10
    History 9-3
    Modulation types 9-4
    P-level reporting system.................................... 9-5
    Projects 9-11
    Repeaters... 9-12
American Red Cross 4-15
AMSAT 10-3
Antennas 1-13ff
    Amateur television (ATV) 9-9
    Contest.. 7-24
    DXing (basic).. 6-2
    High band... 7-25
    Low band.. 7-27
    PRB-11.. 11-5
    Simple HF dipole... 1-14
    Table of HF dipole lengths.................................. 1-16
    Troubleshooting.. 1-16
    VHF/UHF ground plane....................................... 1-14
APCO 4-16
    APCO-25.. 2-19
APRS (Automatic Packet/Position Reporting System) ... 2-25
ARRL
    Amateur Radio Emergency Service (ARES)............. 4-12
    Contest Log E-Mail Addresses............................. 7-19
    DX Century Club (DXCC) Rules 13-2
    Field Day 7-7
    Field Organization 13-37
    Field Organization appointments 4-13
    Field Organization map...................................... 13-28
    Grid locator map... 13-29
    Help for new hams 1-7
    Incoming QSL Service Bureau System................... 6-22
    Leadership Appointments 13-38
    Logbook of the World 12-10
    Numbered Radiograms 13-27
    Operating awards.. 12-2ff
    Outgoing QSL Service 6-21
    Procedural signals (prosigns).............................. 13-24
    QN signals for CW nets....................................... 5-3
    Radiogram.. 5-5
    Station Appointments 13-42

ARRL DXCC Handbook 6-3
Association of Public Safety Communications Officials
    International (APCO) 4-16
Aurora... 3-7, 3-12
Authorized transmissions... 11-10
Autopatch 2-7
Auxiliary operation 11-13
Awards.. 12-1ff
    5 Band DX Century Club (5BDXCC)....................... 12-6
    5 Band Worked All States (5BWAS)....................... 12-3
    5 Band Worked All Zones (5BWAZ) 12-8
    A-1 Operator Club 12-4
    Amateur Extra Certificate 12-4
    CQ DX Awards Program 6-12, 12-8
    DX 6-11
    DX Century Club (DXCC) 6-12, 12-5
    DXCC Challenge.. 12-6
    IOTA 6-12
    Islands on the Air (IOTA) 12-7
    Logbook of the World 12-10
    QRP DXCC 12-6
    US Islands.. 6-12
    USA County Award 12-9
    VHF/UHF... 3-20
    VHF/UHF Century Club (VUCC)............... 3-20, 6-12, 12-4
    Worked All Continents (WAC) 6-11, 12-3
    Worked All States (WAS) 6-11, 12-2
    Worked All Zones (WAZ)..................................... 12-7
Az/el rotator 10-5

B

Band plans.. 2-8, 2-9, 11-8
    VHF/UHF.. 2-8
Bands
    Overview 1-24
    Propagation summary... 6-13
    Rules summary.. 11-16
    US Amateur Radio 1-22
Beacons... 1-21, 6-15
Broadcasting... 11-11

C

Cabrillo 7-19
Call signs
    International prefix list 13-19
    Structure 11-5
    Vanity 11-5
CEPT... 11-9
Check (message) 5-7
CITEL 11-9
Citizen Corps 4-15
Clubs 1-7
    Contest.. 7-17
    Repeater 2-7
Code of Federal Regulations (CFR) 11-2
Coded squelch.. 2-14
Contest (Contesting).. 7-1ff

Antennas 7-27
Basic procedures 7-6
Basics 7-4
Computers and software 7-10
DX 6-10, 6-12
Ergonomics 7-29
Ethics 7-18
Exchange 7-4
Glossary 7-32
HF digital 8-5
History 7-2
Intermediate operating 7-9
Log checking 7-22
Log submission 7-19
Making a QSO 7-6
Multi-operator 7-31
Overview 1-5
Personal preparation 7-30
RTTY 7-20
Rules 7-5
Scoring 7-5
Search and pounce 7-7
Single Operator Assisted (SOA) 7-14
Software, RTTY 8-5
Spotting networks 7-12
Strategy 7-13, 7-16
Two-radio 7-25
VHF/UHF 3-15
Control operator 11-9
County hunting 12-9
Courses
    ARRL Emergency Communications 4-3
    FEMA Emergency Communications 4-4
CQ DX Awards Program 12-8
Crossband repeat 2-18
CTCSS 2-14
    Tone frequencies 2-14
CW
    Abbreviations 13-26
    Contest QSOs 7-6
    DXing with 6-3
    Morse Abbreviated ("Cut") Numbers 13-22
    Morse code character set 13-21
    Morse Code for Other Languages 13-22
    Operating procedures 1-28
    Traffic handling 5-3

D
D-STAR 2-19
Digital modes 1-6, 8-1ff
    Amateur television (ATV) 9-12
    AMBE 8-9
    AOR 8-9
    APCO-25 2-19
    APRS 2-25
    D-STAR 2-19
    D-STAR data 2-28
    Hellschreiber 8-7
    HF 8-1
    MFSK16 8-6
    Packet radio 2-21
    PACSAT satellites 10-6
    PACTOR 8-7
    PropNET 2-27
    PSK31 8-6
    RTTY 8-4
    Sound cards 2-23, 8-3

VHF/UHF data 2-21
Voice 2-18, 8-9
WinDRM 8-10
Winlink 2000 .... 2-28, 8-8
WSJT 3-11
Dipole antenna 1-14
Direction finding, radio 2-13
Disaster communications 4-18
Distress, stations in 4-27
District Emergency Coordinator (DEC) 4-13
Doppler shift 10-4
DX (DXing) 6-1ff
    Basic equipment 6-1
    Basic operating 6-3
    Contests 6-10, 6-12
    History 6-26
    Intermediate 6-8
    Operating Code 13-23
    Operating procedures 1-30
    Overview 1-4
    Pileups 6-9
    Resources 6-27
    Spotting networks 6-7
DX Century Club (DXCC) 6-12, 12-5
    Entities list 13-7
    Rules 13-2
DXCC Challenge 12-6
DXpeditions 6-10, 6-16
    Documentation 6-18
    Going on 6-18
    Micro-Lite Penguins 6-17
    Techniques for working 6-17

E
EchoLink 2-17
Emergency communications 4-1ff
    ARES 4-12
    ARRL appointments 4-13
    Emergency Operations Center (EOC) 4-7
    Getting started 4-3
    Incident Command System (ICS) 4-10
    Message handling 4-7
    Message traffic 4-11
    National Incident Management System (NIMS) 4-10
    Net operator training 4-6
    Personal checklist 4-14
    Plans and procedures 4-2
    Radio Amateur Civil Emergency Service (RACES) ... 4-14
    Repeater operation during 2-11
    Rules 11-17
    Served agencies 4-15
    Simulated Emergency Test 4-5
    Training 4-3
    Training exercises 4-5
Emergency Coordinator (EC) 4-13
Emergency Operations Center (EOC) 4-7
Emission standards 11-17
eQSO 2-17
Equipment
    Accessories 1-11, 7-27
    Amateur television (ATV) 9-5
    Contest 7-24
    Digital modes 8-2
    DXing (basic) 6-1
    Filters 7-28
    HF 1-9
    HF mobile 1-19

Mobile stations 1-18
Packet radio 2-22
Receiver performance 6-4
Satellite 10-5
Selecting 1-8
SSTV 9-15
Two-radio contesting 7-25
VHF/UHF 1-9, 1-18, 6-3
Vintage 1-12
Ethics, contesting 7-18

F

Facsimile (FAX) 9-16
FCC rules 11-1ff
    Part 97 11-3
    Subpart A, General Provisions 11-4
    Subpart B, Station Operation Standards 11-7
    Subpart C, Special Operations 11-13
    Subpart D, Technical Standards 11-15
    Subpart E, Providing Emergency Communications ... 11-17
    Subpart F, Qualifying Examination Systems 11-19
FEMA 4-15
Field Day 7-7
FM operation 2-1ff
Frequency (Frequencies)
    Considerate Operator's Frequency Guide 1-23
    Coordination 2-11
    US Amateur Bands 1-22
    VHF/UHF/EHF Calling 1-23

G

Getting started 1-7
Gray line propagation 6-16
Grid locators 3-3
Guest operating 1-31

H

Handling Instructions (message) 5-8
Hellschreiber 8-7
HF
    Digital modes 8-1
    Propagation summary 6-13
    Repeaters 2-11
Hilltopping 3-14
Hospital Disaster Support Communications
    System (HDSCS) 4-25

I

Identification, station 11-12
Image communications 9-1ff
    ATV 9-1
    Facsimile 9-16
    SSTV 9-13
Incident Command System (ICS) 4-10
Inter-American Telecommunication Commission
    (CITEL) 11-2
Interference 11-9
    DX operating 6-6
    Repeater 2-13
International Telecommunication Union (ITU) 11-2
IRLP (Internet Radio Linking Project) 2-17
Islands on the Air (IOTA) 6-12, 12-7

J

Jammers 6-6

L

License (Licensing)
    Amateur Radio Station and Operator 11-4
    CEPT 11-9
    Classes 11-15
    Exam rules 11-19
    IARP 11-9
    Renewal 11-4
    Updates 11-4
Linear transponders 10-1
Linked repeaters 2-15
Linking
    Internet 2-17
Links, control 11-13
LiTZ operation 2-12
Logbook of the World 6-19, 12-10
Logging
    Cabrillo format 7-19
    Contest checking 7-22
    Contest software 7-10
    Requirements 1-31
    Software, DXing 6-2
Long path propagation 6-16

M

Major Disaster Emergency Coordinator (MDEC) 4-20
Maps
    2-meter channel spacing 2-10
    African countries 13-34
    Antarctica 13-32
    ARRL Divisions 13-37
    ARRL Field Organization 13-28
    Asian countries 13-35
    Azimuthal Equidistant 13-46ff
    California counties 13-30
    Chinese provinces 13-36
    European countries 13-33
    Grid locators 13-29
    South American countries 13-31
Message forwarding system rules 11-14
Meteor
    Scatter 3-9
    Showers 3-10
MFSK16 8-6
Micro-Lite Penguins DXpedition 6-17
Military Affiliate Radio System (MARS) 5-10
Mobile stations 1-16
Moonbounce (EME) 3-7, 3-15
Morse code
    Abbreviated ("Cut") Numbers 13-22
    Character Set (Table) 13-21
    Other Languages (Table) 13-22
Multi-operator contesting 7-31

N

National Incident Management System (NIMS) 4-10
National Traffic System (NTS) 4-15, 5-13
National Volunteer Organizations Active in Disaster
    (NVOAD) 4-16
National Weather Service 4-16
Net 3-19
    Control Station (NCS) 5-11
    Emergency communications 4-6
    Repeater 2-12
    Traffic handling 5-2

O

Official Emergency Station (OES) 4-13
Operating procedures
    CW 1-28
    DX contacts 1-30
    Phone 1-26
OSCAR 51 10-3
OSCAR 52 10-5

P

Packet radio 2-21
PACTOR 8-7
Phone
    Contest QSOs 7-6
    ITU Recommended Phonetics 13-26
    Operating procedures 1-26
    Spanish Phonetics 13-22
    Traffic handling 5-4
Phonetics 13-26
Pileups (DX) 6-9
Portable operation 3-14, 3-16
PRB-1 (antenna regulations) 11-5
Prefix (international list) 13-19
Procedural Signals (Prosigns) 13-24
Prohibited communications 11-10
Propagation 3-4
    Aurora 3-7
    Beacons 1-21, 6-15
    By band 1-24
    Ducting 3-5
    Gray line 6-16
    Long path 6-16
    Moonbounce (EME) 3-7, 3-14
    Scatter 3-6
    Sporadic E 3-6
    Summary, HF bands 6-13
    VHF/UHF 3-4, 3-13
PropNET (Propagation Network) 2-27
PSK31 8-6
Public service 1-5, 4-1ff
Public Service Honor Roll (PSHR) 5-15

Q

Q Signals 13-24
QRP DXCC 12-6
QSL cards 6-19
QSLing 1-33, 6-19
    Electronic QSLing 6-19
    Incoming bureau system 6-22
    Logbook of the World 6-19, 12-10
    Paper cards 6-19
    QSL service, outgoing 6-20
    Sending and receiving paper cards 6-19

R

Radio Amateur Civil Emergency Service (RACES) 4-14
Radio direction finding 2-13
Radiogram 5-5
Receiver characteristics 6-4
Reciprocal operating 11-9
Red Cross 4-15
Remote operation 11-13
Repeaters 2-2
    Amateur television (ATV) 9-12
    Autopatch 2-7
    Crossband 2-18
    Emergency communications 2-11
    Glossary 2-4
    Hardware 2-3
    HF 2-11
    Interference 2-13
    Linked 2-15
    Nets 2-12
    Operating techniques 2-5
    Rules 11-14
    Timers 2-12
    VHF/UHF 2-2
RST System 13-25
RTTY (radioteletype) 8-4
    Contesting 7-20
Rules and regulations 2-16, 11-1ff

S

Safety
    Antenna 1-13
    Emergency communications 4-22
    Mobile stations 1-16
Salvation Army Team Emergency Radio Network
    (SATERN) 4-18
Satellites 10-1ff
    FM repeater 10-3
    Modes 10-6
    Operating techniques 10-5
    OSCAR 52 10-4
    PACSATS 10-6
    SSB/CW 10-4
    Tracking 10-2
Scatter propagation 3-6
Search and pounce 7-7
Search and rescue 4-25
Section Emergency Coordinator (SEC) 4-13
Served agencies 4-15, 4-17
Simplex 2-8
Simplex frequencies 2-8
Simulated Emergency Test (SET) 4-5
Single Operator Assisted (SOA) 7-14
SKYWARN 4-16
Slow-scan television (SSTV) 9-13
Software
    Contest 7-10
    Digital modes 8-3
    Satellite 10-3, 10-7
    SSTV 9-15
Sound cards 8-2, 9-15
Space communications 1-4
Spanish Phonetics (Table) 13-22
Spectrum sharing 11-8
Sporadic E 3-6, 3-12
Spotting networks 6-7, 7-12
Squelch
    Digital coded (DCS) 2-15
    Tone coded (CTCSS) 2-14
Standards
    Emission 11-17
    External RF power amplifiers 11-17
Station
    Ergonomics 7-29
    Log 1-31
    Mobile 1-16
    Setup at home 1-13
Subparts, Part 97 11-3

T

Tables
Allocation of International Call Sign Series 13-19
Amateur Operator Licenses 11-4
Amateur Spectrum by ITU Region 11-15
Antenna Lengths in Feet 1-16
ARES Personal Checklist... 4-14
ARRL Contest Log E-Mail Addresses 7-19
ARRL Numbered Radiograms 13-27
ARRL Operating Awards 1-5
ARRL Procedural Signals (Prosigns) 13-24
ARRL QN Signals for CW Net Use 5-3
Common VHF/UHF Activity Nights............................. 3-2
Considerate Operator's Frequency Guide......... 1-23, 11-8
Consistently Active Amateur Satellites..................... 10-2
CTCSS Tone Frequencies.. 2-14
CW Abbreviations.................................... 1-29, 13-26
Digital Contests 8-5
FCC Allocated Prefixes for Areas Outside
      Continental US 11-5
Handling Instructions.. 5-8
ITU Recommended Phonetics 13-26
Meteor Showers 3-10
Morse Abbreviated ("Cut") Numbers 13-22
Morse Code Character Set 13-21
Morse Code for Other Languages........................... 13-22
National Traffic System Routing Guide...................... 5-14
North American VHF/UHF Calling Frequencies 3-2
North American VHF/UHF/EHF Calling
      Frequencies 1-23
Phonetic Alphabet.. 1-26
Popular HF Digital Frequencies................................. 8-4
Q Signals... 1-27, 13-24
RST System 1-26, 13-25
Satellite Modes Demystified.................................... 10-6
Simplex Frequencies.. 2-8
Spanish Phonetics 13-22
SSTV Formats.. 9-14
Third-Party Traffic Agreements.............................. 11-12
US Amateur Radio Bands 1-22
VHF/UHF Activity Nights 1-23
Third party communications 11-11
Time, Universal Coordinated (UTC) 1-32
Traffic handling 5-1ff
Book messages.. 5-11
Message check 5-7
Message delivery 5-9
Message form 5-5
Net Control Station (NCS)... 5-11
Nets 5-2
On CW 5-3
Phone.. 5-4
Public events 5-12
Tropospheric ducting 3-5

U

Universal Coordinated Time (UTC) 1-32
US Call Districts (map) 11-6
US Islands program 6-12
USA County Award... 12-9
UTC Explained 1-32

V

Vanity call signs 11-5
VHF/UHF
Activity nights 3-2
Antenna, ground plane... 1-14
Awards 3-20
Band plans 2-8
Calling frequencies.. 1-23, 3-2
Channel spacing, FM 2-9
Contests 3-15, 7-23
Digital data modes 2-21
Equipment 1-9, 1-18
FM operation 2-1ff
Grid locators.. 3-3
Hilltopping 3-14
Meteor scatter 3-9
Nets 3-19
Packet radio 2-21
Portable operation 3-14, 3-16
Propagation... 3-4
Repeaters... 2-2
Simplex 2-8
SSB/CW operation 3-1ff
Troubleshooting.. 3-20
VHF/UHF Century Club (VUCC) 6-12, 12-4
Voice, Digital.. 2-18, 8-9
VoIP (Voice over Internet Protocol)
EchoLink 2-17
IRLP 2-17
Rules.. 2-16
Volunteer Examiner (VE) 11-19

W

Weather
Nets 4-21
Spotting.. 4-19
Wilderness protocol 2-12
WinDRM 8-10
Winlink 2000 .... 2-28, 8-8
WIRES-II... 2-17
Worked All Continents (WAC)........................... 6-11, 12-3
Worked All States (WAS)..................................... 6-11
Worked All Zones (WAZ) 12-7
World Radio Conference (WRC) 11-2
WSJT.. 3-11

Notes

Notes

Notes

Notes

Notes

Notes

Notes